Jacob and the Night of Faith

"*Perichoresis* is one of the most ancient descriptions of the divine life, and its popularity has exploded in recent theology. Yet this is the first high-quality, systematic treatment of the 'divine dance' that I have seen in decades. Gregory Gorsuch has chosen the right authors and topics to both explain and draw the reader in to the magic of this concept. After understanding *perichoresis*, you will never do theology in quite the same way again."

—PHILIP CLAYTON, author of *Adventures in the Spirit*

"This is first a brilliant and exquisitely detailed exploration of intellectual developments across the disciplines as related to Christian visions of *perichoresis*. Yet, in setting these developments in dialogue with theological perspectives, Gregory Gorsuch also opens new and challenging vistas of possibility—both in theology and beyond. This is essential reading for anyone concerned with moving beyond the metaphysics of self-contained entities."

—KENNETH J. GERGEN, senior research professor of psychology, Swarthmore College

"Taking the plunge of love into freely evolving relationships with our fellow beings and with our ultimate Sponsor prompts a rethinking of reality, meaning, truth, divinity, person, relationship, community, time, eternity, and faith. Gregory Gorsuch fearlessly follows the 'logic of spirit' in exploring this conceptual landscape and refining the arguments of Christian theology accordingly."

—STEVEN G. SMITH, professor emeritus of philosophy and religious studies, Millsaps College

"Conversations in *first theology* have been mostly percolating under the radar the last two decades even as theologies of the Third Article have gained momentum. The *analogia spiritus* proposed here brings these together in a compelling way via a robust theology of *perichoresis* that also serves to orient us toward a fully perichoretic theology. Gorsuch invites us all to reconsider how our beliefs and practices—among so many other binarily formulated theological concepts—are both distinct and yet mutually informative and transformative when the Spirit has the first word!"

—AMOS YONG, professor of theology and mission, Fuller Theological Seminary

Seldom have I read a dissertation as sophisticated in its conceptual analysis as well as creative in its probing and original contribution to contemporary theological issues.

—RAY S. ANDERSON, Fuller Seminary

Most striking was [Gorsuch's] ability to join theology into conversation with other intellectual disciplines in a way that allowed for mutual illumination, without permitting any one side to dominate the interaction. The thesis brought together an impressive array of non-theological disciplines, in order to explore their potential resonance with theology around his central theme of modes of relationality. He showed an astonishing ability to empathise with and 'inhabit' the logical and conceptual world of each and an impressive maturity in avoiding simplistic reductions of each to some common language.

—ALISTAIR MCFADYEN, University of Leeds

His capacity for rigorous reflection has appeared in a number of philosophical and theological papers . . . where he shows considerable flair for well-informed original thought. His eventual writing and research will inevitably be well-informed and potentially ground breaking for theology and the several cultures which it addresses.

—JAMES E. LODER, Princeton Theological Seminary

Greg's dissertation was without doubt the most creative thesis I have supervised—and the most challenging. It is an essay in pneumatology that treats the way in which the Holy Spirit interacts with the human spirit . . . Yet it is also an essay in postmodernity, the relation of theology to human developmental psychology, and the relation of time to eternity. Essentially, it's an attempt to bring some of Kierkegaard's insights into the nature of authentic faith to bear on contemporary theology. . . . He has an infectious enthusiasm for the connections he sees between thinkers, and even between disciplines. He is especially interested in the convergence between quantum physics, psychotherapy, and theology, having as they do the common theme of "relationality."

—KEVIN J. VANHOOZER, University of Edinburgh
(currently at Trinity Evangelical Divinity School)

Jacob and the Night of Faith

Analogia Spiritus

GREGORY SCOTT GORSUCH

☙PICKWICK *Publications* · Eugene, Oregon

JACOB AND THE NIGHT OF FAITH
Analogia Spiritus

Copyright © 2024 Gregory Scott Gorsuch. All rights reserved. Except for brief quotations in critical publications or reviews, no part of this book may be reproduced in any manner without prior written permission from the publisher. Write: Permissions, Wipf and Stock Publishers, 199 W. 8th Ave., Suite 3, Eugene, OR 97401.

Pickwick Publications
An Imprint of Wipf and Stock Publishers
199 W. 8th Ave., Suite 3
Eugene, OR 97401

www.wipfandstock.com

PAPERBACK ISBN: 978-1-6667-7473-3
HARDCOVER ISBN: 978-1-6667-7474-0
EBOOK ISBN: 978-1-6667-7475-7

Cataloguing-in-Publication data:

Names: Gorsuch, Gregory Scott, author.

Title: Jacob and the night of faith : analogia spiritus / Gregory Scott Gorsuch.

Description: Eugene, OR : Pickwick Publications, 2024 | Includes bibliographical references and indexes.

Identifiers: ISBN 978-1-6667-7473-3 (paperback) | ISBN 978-1-6667-7474-0 (hardcover) | ISBN 978-1-6667-7475-7 (ebook)

Subjects: LCSH: Holy Spirit. | Trinity. | Kierkegaard, Søren, 1813–1855. | Theology. | Theology, Doctrinal.

Classification: BT121.3 .G67 2024 (paperback) | BT121.3 .G67 (ebook)

03/21/24

Scripture taken from the New King James Version®. Copyright © 1982 by Thomas Nelson. Used by permission. All rights reserved.

To the one with whom
I dance into glory
altogether separate
Cheryl

For certain, you have to be lost to find a place that can't be found, elseways everyone would know where it was.

—Captain Hector Barbosa

Contents

	Prologue: Jacob: The Knight of Faith by Vestigio Trinitas	ix
	Preface	xxi
	Acknowledgments	xxv
	Abbreviations of Reference Works	xxvii
1	Introduction	1
2	Meaning as *Perichoresis*: Theological Method and Knowledge as the Shape of Desire	54
3	Human Spirit	145
3A	*Perichoresis* in Persons: Human Emotions and Bicameral Synthesis	149
3B	*Perichoresis* in Dialogical Relations: Alistair McFadyen's Christian Social Theory of Personhood	176
3C	*Perichoresis* as Persons: Loder, Piaget, and Kierkegaard	196
4	*Perichoresis* in the Trinity: Moltmann and the Spirit of God	245
5A	*Perichoresis* of Time and Eternity: *Analogia Spiritus* in "Immanence" and "Transcendence"	268
5B	Quantum Dynamics: Relationship (Consciousness) Constitutes Reality	343
6	The Perichoretic Redemptive Relation of Christ to the World: The Complementarity of Church and Culture	368
7	Conclusion: *Perichoresis* All in All	383
	Bibliography	393
	Name Index	409
	Subject Index	415
	Scripture Index	419

Prologue

Jacob: The ~~K~~night of Faith

by Vestigio Trinitas

The absolutely different or wholly Other cannot be translated into any language. To the contrary, this altarity inflicts an incurable wound upon language. Always open, this wound lies between the lines it (impossibly) both supports and undercuts. This loss of language can never be re-covered.... [This is] the difference that infinitely defers the eschatological movement of reappropriation. Offering no promise of arrival, this Other calls: "Come."

MARK C. TAYLOR[1]

And he took one of the stones of that place and put it at his head, and he lay down in that place to sleep. Then he dreamed, and behold, a ladder was set up on the earth, and its top reached to heaven; and there the angels of God were ascending and descending on it.... Then Jacob awoke from his sleep and said, "Surely the Lord is in this place, and *I did not know it.*... This is none other than the house of God, and *this is the gate of heaven!*... And this stone which I have set as a pillar shall be God's house."

GEN 28:11–12, 16–17, 22 (EMPHASIS ADDED)

---

1. Taylor, *Altarity*, 344.

Then Jacob was left alone; and a Man wrestled with him until the breaking of day.... And He said, "Let me go, for the day breaks." But he said, "I will not let You go unless You bless me!" So He said to him, "What is your name?" And he said, "Jacob." And He said, "Your name shall no longer be called Jacob, but Israel; for you have struggled with God and with men, *and have prevailed*."... And Jacob called the name of the place Peniel: "For I have seen God face to face, and my life is preserved."

GEN 32:24, 26–28 (EMPHASIS ADDED)

"But who do you say I am?" And Simon Peter answered, "You are the Christ, the Son of the living God." Jesus said to him, "Blessed are you, Simon Bar-Jonah, for flesh and blood has not revealed this to you, but My Father who is in heaven. I also say to you that you are Peter, and on this rock I will build My church, and the gates of Hades shall not prevail against it. And I will give you the keys of the kingdom of heaven, whatever *you* bind on earth will be bound in heaven."

MATT 16:15–19 (EMPHASIS ADDED)

INVITED TO THE DANCE: DE-LIBERATION *WITHIN* THE ETERNAL *MOMENT*

Faith is like sleep. We don't do it, will ourselves to sleep; we relax all effort, let go, and give ourselves to it. Then, in its time, unannounced, it "comes," and we fall to rest.

The System began disintegrating the day the Writer reminded us that an "out-law," Abraham, heard the ineffable in a command that lay beyond all known ethical and rational thinking, something within the voice ostensibly contrary to any re-membrance (re-petition) of the original promise. "Abraham keeps silent, . . . he *cannot* speak,"[2] he "isolates himself as higher than the universal,"[3] then, unthinkably, he acts. "The singularity of the believer constitutes a remainder that *cannot* be comprehended by reason and *cannot* be assimilated by morality."[4] Abraham, for Søren Kierkegaard, was the father of faith, in another voice, the ultimate "knight of faith."

---

2. Kierkegaard, *FT*, 122.
3. Kierkegaard, *FT*, 65.
4. Taylor, *Altarity*, 345.

Kierkegaard's less Christian friends, Johannes de Silentio and Frater Taciturnus, together with Mark C. Taylor, surmise through the deconstruction of the word that word cannot re-member or retrieve its original spokeness (meaning). And so, for Taylor, atheology supplants theology, and the *totally* other God emerges again, "offering no promise of arrival." The Other can only *call*: "come." So, Abraham hearing an ineffable remains silent and acts. He floats over seventy thousand fathoms, an infinite qualitative difference (IQD) between God and humanity. The friends "paradoxically" redress the distance in a God-man—a philosophical (rational) rendering under modern metaphysics still dripping with Hellenistic derivatives. Their work portends the death of transcendence.

Karl Barth, spying this infinite difference, employs it (IQD) in denouncing the well-worked immanence of modern liberal theology. Allying Kierkegaard's friend's Abraham, he creates what many detractors call a theology of revelational positivism, forwarding again a transcendent impositional God that once again tames the freedom and self-determination of humanity. God speaks and acts from beyond, a gift, a Word in and for us. Settled. Even natural revelation receives a hearty "Nein" from the young Barth—nothing of God reflects within the natural.

But, is this totally other God of the "God-man" the whole story of Kierkegaard? Kierkegaard *indirectly* ornaments everything he edits with signs, modes, and dynamics that suggest the necessary corollary of an *incarnational imperative of mutuality* (IIM) that is necessary for *a filial* relationship with God. If such relations are filial, something of God must become human, and something of humanity must become divine. Because of the risen Christ (not "God-man") we face a hard reality—we are not God and fall into brokenness of spirit. This is the condition to become fully spirit (differentiated) in relation to the Absolute (Spirit)—thus the possibility of relating "absolutely with the Absolute"[5]—*analogia spiritus*. Kierkegaard everywhere leaves *indirect* traces that indeed humanity, all humanity, is somehow a synthesis of time *and eternity*, the finite *and the infinite*! In indirection, the Editor always tasks us with completing the meaning. Kierkegaard's true IQD is not between former metaphysical (and anthropological) renderings of God and humanity. The Incarnation of Jesus Christ, an actual historical person and Incarnation, not simply the idea of a God-man, forever transforms this divide. His IQD abhorrence remains with Hegel's *material* synthesis of the temporal and Eternal, the finite and the infinite, not between God and humanity. The perichoretic nature of human relations infects everything that

---

5. Kierkegaard, *CUP*, 347

Kierkegaard edits and writes. It seems Kierkegaard installs an inseparable corollary to his friend's IQD, his IIM, indirectly and in plain sight.

As Barth counters with *Church Dogmatics*, he soon surmises Kierkegaard's anthropological and pneumatological implications of this Incarnation and Resurrection—Kierkegaard's "Ingen (*nein!*)" to Barth. It turns out Kierkegaard's insistence that an independent human spirit somehow interacts directly with God's Spirit, absolute relating to Absolute, was a little too aggressive for Barth's context. It reveals an *interaction* between divine and human spirit that Barth considered too difficult to parse in his time.[6] Much more complex, Kierkegaard is a pneumatologist and anthropologist of Christology; Barth, sensing as much, put Kierkegaard back on the shelf. But, the focus of Kierkegaard's friends upon "infinite resignation" leaves the true night of faith buried within the text. The continuing rise of immanence (Hegel and on into poststructuralism, marching lockstep with materialism) and, to some degree, the overbearing priority of unilateral transcendence (Barth) ultimately renders faith (and the text) frozen, still, fragmented, unfinished, anomalous, desperate, and eventually robotic. Did such a critique ever leave the house of reason or escape the seduction of universals? I think not. Refusing to die, it only explores *the waste land* of this world and leaves us in infinite resignation with an irrevocable loss of attainment in this lifetime.

On the other hand, Barth offers a Word that does indeed come to us, albeit impositionally in unilateral relations (no hope of earthly filial relations). Either way, the former forecloses on transcendence and the other on natural revelation and the transforming of humanity from degree to degree. Either way, reason, empiricism, or the human spirit cannot express or reflect the divine. They are qualitatively different, separated by an infinitely deep canyon between subject and Subject. The light of this world cannot illuminate God or the transcendent.

In one respect, however, they are correct; we cannot find God in the light of this world. And so, the death of reason and transcendence leaves us under the totalitarian rule of immanence, which threatens to destroy whatever trust remains among us—leaving nothing between us but the "will to

---

6. In "Schleiermacher," 278, Barth tells us: "What I have already intimated here and there to good friends, would be the possibility of a theology of the third article, in other words, a theology predominantly and decisively of the Holy Spirit. Everything which needs to be said, considered and believed about God the Father and God the Son in an understanding of the first and second articles might be shown and illuminated in its foundations through God the Holy Spirit." He thought it was "still too difficult to distinguish between God's Spirit and man's spirit."

power." "The horror of it all." But Kierkegaard insists that to encounter the Absolute is entrance into darkness—the ultimate *horror religiosus*.[7]

> Man has a natural dread of walking in the dark—what wonder then that he has a dread of the absolute, of which it is true that no night and "no deepest gloom is half so dark" as this gloom and this night, where all relative ends (the common milestones and sign-posts), where all relative considerations (the lanterns which are normally a help to us), where even the tenderest and sincerest feelings of devotion—are quenched . . . for otherwise it is not unconditionally the absolute.[8]

For some, transcendence is too dark; for others it is too divinely distant. With Abraham, they must remain silent. However, Abraham is not the final preeminent actor! Even Kierkegaard leaves buried the real treasure within the Text, right in front of our eyes beneath a flashing neon arrow no less—albeit buried in darkness. He leaves buried for our indirect discovery a more profound treasure just beyond the first—a faith more scandalous than the first—the true seat of passion, of filial encounter. Venture a little further, and the transaction screams of much more than listening and doing what you are told. How can we argue that "the absolute different or wholly Other cannot be translated into any language" or even that "this altarity inflicts an *incurable* wound upon language"[9] when hundreds in Jerusalem that thunderous day witnessed its coming, its translation into all languages—*ad extra* filling in and cementing the traces, no less within each person's unique mother tongue, altogether separate! Indeed, Kierkegaard had his hands on the monster. His friends didn't read far enough into the Text, into the absolute darkness, unwilling to face the true qualitative difference—the void—*the birth of oneself becoming spirit*. Who would have thought the ticket to transcendence was death, facing the Absolute, allowing oneself to become the sacrifice (Isaac). Isaac must remain preeminently important for one thing, the willingness to die, for letting himself go into the *moment* (naked without reason). He could have easily resisted his aged father. He could have held tight to a fabricated alterity, denied transcendence, and stumbled about in immanence.

With the death of transcendence came a "flatulent knowledge" that was as insubstantial as their clothing [not "held fast"] falling away upon

---

7. Taylor suggests: "The transgression of transcendence creates a sense of horror—a horror that is not simply repulsive but is at the same time attractive." Taylor, *Altarity*, 364.

8. Bretall, *Kierkegaard Anthology*, 426.

9. Taylor, *Altarity*, 344, emphasis added.

every movement. They still look for movement, any movement, in all sorts of slits, cracks, and cubbyholes. No one can dance in a rational *or* poststructural world; I mean, really dance (*choreia*), everywhere, all around (*peri*), in Time. For them, the whole of reality—the making of reality—lay still, beyond them.[10]

Abraham hears the ineffable call to risk what he had for more. In infinite resignation, he heard the Voice beyond, the penultimate modicum of faith. Silentio demands it was the greatest act of faith—Abraham—in the full light of day doing the unthinkable. And here Silentio and friends stop reading—the descending ladder of God was enough for them. But Kierkegaard claims that time and eternity, finitude and infinity, can come together *within* the world (faith), within existential consciousness (the "sudden" between, the spirit that is relationship itself). Leaving the Hellenistic world of subject-subject, he insists that this *"beyond in the midst of our life"*[11] is alive between us—subject-relationship-subject—a Power within our relationships filling our words with shared meaning, albeit beyond the visible light of day (reason).[12] And now, for a moment, we must part company with his friends and read a little further.

> Abraham hears the ineffable in God's command; it transforms him, and he does it.
> God sees the ineffable in Jacob's *passion* struggling against God; it transforms God,
> and God does it, delightfully.

Even Poststructuralism misses the indirection of Kierkegaard, as they remain behind perseverating upon the penultimate action of faith in Abraham. No one knows what to do with Jacob (save the esoteric twisting of the hidden)! Jacob *decisively* expresses *all* his desire, longing, choice, freedom, and self-determination through his impassioned struggle with God—*in the darkness* of *analogia spiritus*! Jacob's ladder descends and, in becoming spirit, also *ascends* with every other passionate spirit throughout Time—wrestling *within* the Eternal night just before the wounded Word rises anew into the daylight of each new cosmic interaction. A gift, to be sure.

---

10. Eliot, *Four Quartets*: "I said to my soul, be still and wait without hope, for hope would be hope for the wrong thing; wait without love, for love would be love of the wrong thing; there is yet faith, but the faith and the love are all in the waiting. Wait without thought, for you are not ready for thought: So the darkness shall be the light, and the stillness the dancing."

11. Bonhoeffer, *Letters and Papers from Prison*, 367.

12. Kierkegaard tells us, "Worldly wisdom thinks that love is a relationship between man and man. Christianity teaches that love is a *relationship* between: man-God-man, that is, God *is* the middle term." *WL*, 113 (emphases added).

The penultimate aspect of faith in Abraham prepares us for the ultimate aspect of faith in Jacob; together, they enter into the fullness of time. Even more scandalous than Abraham, who does the unthinkable, Jacob's passion expresses his own ineffable and impassioned desires against God, and prevails—God does it! Abraham heard and did the will of God. But Jacob, somehow *perceiving more* and wanting more, wrestles in defiance within the co-conditioning Eternal *moment* ("beyond" and prior to the light) as the impassioned desires of his heart, a prodigal coming home, transforms God within God's Eternity. Together with Peter's identification from within this same darkness, they excite God (Christ) more than any other moments in history! *Filial relations* and *relational theosis* obtain—a being emerges capable of knowing God as God.

Jacob becomes the first recognized true co-creator, the greatest co-creator in history! And no one seems to see the flashing neon sign of name and nation. Abraham ultimately acquiesces to God, but Jacob, *in passion*, does not: he insists upon receiving the blessing that his spirit senses is his to desire—*for even in his fighting God, he is fully given to God*. No one seems to acknowledge the true miracle of creation in the darkness before every gestalt of human consciousness—that lightning strike of the Eternal making all life possible. History knows no nation of Moses, Abraham, or David, only Israel. Besides Abraham and Sarah's slight name change, God only completely changes two other names in all the scriptures: Jacob (deceiver) to Israel (struggles with God), and Simon (listen) to Peter (rock). Could the cartographers have been any more explicit in establishing the preeminence of what is happening in Jacob and Peter? They signal the "mystery which has been hidden from ages and from generations" (Col 1:26), this deep mystery hidden within the Jacobian darkness, beyond all flesh and blood, just before (each) new dawn?

Along with Peter, Jacob experiences firsthand the rock (the place) of divine-human contact, where heaven and earth come together, simultaneously.[13] With every daybreak comes the Word (creation)—the relative relating to the relative—always a wound within the resurrecting; yet heaven and earth come together in each preceding night of the *analogia spiritus*—a *mutual co-conditioning* of spirit to Spirit . . . *if* one is willing to enter the cruciform (Isaac). Within the dark night of the Eternal—absolute relates to Absolute *before* each resurrecting dawn. Each cosmic encounter heralds the potential site of divine-human *holistic* interaction where our words become re-spoken in the gifting of the Word, synchronizing billions of spirits into

---

13. Only through polyrhythmic wrestling can two migrating (rubato) heartbeats come together, simultaneously.

syncopating unity prior to the coming of the word—a potentially ever-present *moment* that incorporates human self-determination within a differentiated unity. This is the rock, the site upon which the people of God in two (developmental st)ages emerge, with Jacob and Peter. Here billions of infinities (spirits) dance unseen in analogical relation with God's Eternity (Spirit)—each spirit appropriately and synchronously dancing in Time to the eschatological music of *perichoresis* (love).[14]

The one Absolute Spirit of the System (Hegel) is not found in Jacob or the true nation of Israel; instead, we find the harmonizing dance of billions of spirits back and forth, in and out of time, dancing altogether separate. It can only happen in darkness, not totally beyond, but hidden within the flesh, a rupture and blood no less real than a rock. It is the only place one could hope to find it, on earth, through darkness, struggling and suffering with the One in his Time. It is here the Writer's friends stumble forward in the darkness, failing to recognize that Jacob wrestled the One and knew not his name, a name refused and unable to be given in the asking. Though Jacob may have stood before flesh and blood, he knew from no flesh and blood and by no light of day that God had come into the world—a *moment* of *theosis*. It was then he knew that somehow, someway, the ladder *also* ascends unto the Eternal, and so he boldly climbs, wrestles, wins, and perceives the face of God.[15] Prayer for Jacob was not just listening, learning, and accepting the will of God; it was human de-liberation of spirit-to-Spirit antecedent to and therefore inclusive within the Eternal—*affecting* the very providence of God in Time.[16]

---

14. Bonhoeffer, *Sanctorum Communio*, 48: "*The person ever and again arises and passes away in time.* The person does not exist timelessly; a person is not static, but dynamic. . . . The person is re-created again and again in the perpetual flux of life. Subjective spirit becomes eternally significant only in relation to the absolute spirit."

15. Still imprisoned by his obsession with noumena and phenomena, the last gasp of modernity (not postmodernity), Derrida argues: "It goes without saying that [the *a* of différance] cannot be exposed. . . . Now if différance is (and I also cross out the "is") what makes possible the presentation of the being-present, it is never presented as such. . . . The trace . . . Always differing and deferring . . . erases itself in presenting itself (*Margins*, 5–6, 17)." He believes with Moses and the Apostle John that neither différance or God can be seen or encountered in the present, "for no man shall see me and live" (Exod 33:20; John 1:18). But Jacob picks up his cross and, like Isaac willing to die, dies from his presence and enters *analogia spiritus*, and beyond all "presence" in the midst of life enters Christ's Time, wrestles him, and "sees" (perceives) the face of God, and lives. In Jacob we find the true postmodern. But Derrida and Taylor relegate *analogia spiritus*, God, and différance totally beyond us, leaving Jacob's *perceiving* buried.

16. Lossky, *Image*, 97–98: "The descent (κατάβασις) of the divine person of Christ makes human persons capable of an ascent (ἀνάβασις) in the Holy Spirit."

In Jacob's victory emerges a new ontology, a relational metaphysics. Barth's *analogia relationis* (a timorous attempt at Kierkegaardian metaphysics) only found half the ladder, and half a ladder does not end the Cartesian efforts of modernity in which all things similar mutually relate (*analogia entis*). Nor does it end the play of those who refuse *being*, for the no-*being* of poststructuralism still wanders upon the playground of *being*, deliriously and cryptically bearing universals in their vacant transgressions (only in the land of *being* does no-*being* find meaning). But, far from the approved criteria of either, the faithful transgressions of Jacob in the night expose a *universal dynamic of relationality* through which all things different mutually and meaningfully relate (*analogia spiritus*, the engine of *perichoresis*). As the quantum enigma in our new science sings the siren songs of the Writer once again, we no longer dance in a world out there (of being). We dance when two or more gather together with Christ (knowingly or not), worlds created in the dancing, with all the dancers, billions of dancers. These are the worlds in which *persons* dance collectively, worlds that pulse with movement, emerge, expand, disappear, and have no bounds but the syncopating lead of the risen One who orchestrates all movement in love. These are worlds of *mutual co-conditioning* in which Abraham moves with God, *and* Jacob, moving mountains into the Aegean Sea, prevails over (and with) God; worlds in which what Peter decides in perichoretic faith (*actus directus/fides directa*) becomes Christ's reflexive will (*actus reflectus*).

From the trauma of God, the wound through which earth leaves its seed and heaven proffers the child, comes the sustaining gift. (Maybe Levinas, Kierkegaard, and Taylor are right, God is female, or something of God.) In the going and coming of ladders, the wrestling God of Jacob can only happen in the night—where absolute wrestles with Absolute before Time. Such gods that walk the Emmaus road must ultimately disappear in the light if they are to be truly known, filially, as God, in Time.[17] Though the wounds of the Eternal are visible, the Eternal is not; a blind spot to be sure, defying material or 'natural' synthesis—the Divine *must* leave before daybreak or more than wound the wrestler destroy. For here is the site of the infinite qualitative difference. But Jacob becomes spirit and wrestles *in the night* where spirits *move together*. A risen Christ comes to Jacob in the *analogia spiritus*, a holistic knowing, a co-conditioning *moment*, antecedent and beyond all image, word, and the relative. If they wrestle into the day, the wrestler becomes god; that would mean pantheism and the annihilation of identity. If you want shared Absolute Spirit, talk to a pantheist or the Borgs of the twenty-fourth century; Jacob won't know what you're talking about.

---

17. Cf. with Phillip and the Ethiopian Eunuch (Acts 8:28–40).

For he saw the face of God as God in the night and survived what modernity and poststructuralism deny.

In simultaneity shared meaning obtains—but always with respect to the relative meaning-frame of each participant, altogether separate. Without the analogous relations of absolute to Absolute (spirit to spirit) there is no shared meaning among true difference. We are relative creatures of difference moving and floating *within* relationships, not upon an Aegean Sea of being. For every assemblage of traces amid altarity must suffer crucifixion again and again to rise in mutuality—in cruciform movement with Christ. But there are no deaths among robots or Borgs.

Traces (words) alone lead us into solipsism. Poststructuralists make mountains of molehills with the evanescence of traces as they escape all divine contingency, themselves gods in the making. But Jacob was about Word *and Spirit*. The word must be wounded for *analogia spiritus* to enable mutuality. Though words are the house of being, they form upon an antecedent breath, a breath (spirit) without and before being.[18] Spirit is asymmetrically complementary to word.

Therefore, this "stumbling stone and rock of offense"[19] is no more a geographical location than apostolic succession or even solely Jesus Christ himself! Neither are they the Keys of Peter. Within various development stages and through a darker glass they may have been provisional rocks, but the rock has always been that Power endemic within relationship itself, that Power of which the Writer speaks that moves within the interstices of our dialogical dance. This is the "mystery among the Gentiles," a tripartite perichoretic heartbeat sustaining all creation simply because God Incarnationally loves the world. It is the unseen blind spot of the Eternal *moment* before each relational gestalt (word) that lies beneath the rational. If in *purity of heart* all that we are ventures in, our spirit and all such spirits come into dynamic analogical relation with the fullness of the Eternal Spirit from which the risen One constitutes all relationships, synchronizing billions of freedoms, desires, and disappointments into a swirling unity of synchronizing gestalts, a unity of difference (Pentecost), a unity of love. This is the Power that sustains the freedom and self-determination necessary for the emergence of a being that might *itself* know God as God. This Eternal recurrence

---

18. Marion, *God without Being*.

19. "They did not seek it by *faith*, but as it were, by the works of the law [reason, or not-reason]. For they stumbled at the stumbling *stone*. As it is written: 'Behold, I lay in Zion a stumbling *stone* and *rock* of offense, and whoever *believes* on Him will not be put to shame'" (Rom 9:32–33, emphasis added). These are those unwilling to *live in* transformation from one degree to another (2 Cor 3:18).

comes to each *open* spirit until all hearts beat together decisively.[20] It happens only under the covers of night, beyond sight, in a flash so dense no light can escape. If Abraham is scandalous, Jacob is mad—an even greater *horror religiosus*! Within such a scandal the Writer's categories expand; his Religiousness A and B transform, but the spirit of the Writer still remains.

Upon this rock the Text transforms again and again. The rightness of each new reading rides upon *epistemic dispositions* (the *how*—the crucifixion). Each new meaning (*what*) and its rightness (*how*) explode from the darkness appropriately infecting each new response, each new generation. From this rock leaps all creation, creativity, human freedom in co-conditioning transtemporal relations *within* divine providence, and the evolutionary emergence of relational *theosis* (the driver of human origins). The rock is *perichoresis*—the great eucharistic dance in which the *nature* of God (*perichoresis*), in due course, synchronizes all in all.

Mark C. Taylor is *Erring* when he employs the modern conception of the eschatological. "This loss of language can never be re-covered. . . . [This is] the difference that infinitely defers the eschatological movement of reappropriation. Offering no promise of arrival, this Other calls: 'Come'." Like all poststructuralists, he believes we cannot completely share meaning with another; we simply harvest the traces into our own eisegetical movements, passing like ships in the night. Calling across the water between us, we never obtain. Taylor's theological rendering of the eschatological is teaming with metaphysical residuals that echo Pannenberg's completions, the historical totality (all Hegelian derivatives). Any such manifestation of totality within any contextualization will always fall short—"infinitely defer[ring] such eschatological 'completions.'" Taylor never gets past the friend's "God-man" or modern anthropology. Like most philosophers, Kierkegaard's anthropology is beyond them.

The Editor demands, "do not confuse them [his friends] with me!" "The eternal essential truth is not behind him but in front of him *through its being in existence or having existed so that if the individual does not existentially and in existence lay hold of the truth, he will never lay hold of it.*"[21] In other words, whether on earth or in the eschaton, Christ and the Spirit will always mediate and orchestrate the dance—perichoretically. With many nations diversity will forever explode in unprecedented difference. In resurrecting, we know like him, not in some final eschatonic stage of completeness, but in living transformation, in *perichoresis*! The eschatological

---

20. *Open* spirits pick up their cross and are willing to die to their existing knowledge, convictions, and life, and then passionately enter into the fuller emerging paradigms of truth, justice, and love that they sense are there (Matt 10:37–39; Luke 14:26, 27, 33).

21. Kierkegaard, *CUP*, 187, emphasis added.

moment is *always* a differentiated unity, never uniformity or completion. When we fully venture into our relations, *analogia spiritus* recontextualizes our relativities in analogical relation to the fullness of Christ's Time. Truth and meaning are shared in every complete *moment* in history or the eschaton. Such moments transform our "sin" in any age—a eucharistic *moment* of consubstantiation, if you will, causing other madmen to cry, "Sin boldly."

Within the perichoretic dance, I see Luther and Calvin dancing together, paradox and transformation (differing dynamics within *perichoresis*), spirit antecedent with word, twirling together around and around, in and out of Time. Within *being*, they never arrive. But Kierkegaard and his friends are never just about being. They come in the *analogia spiritus* through the *moments* that create movement, dancing.

If it sounds as if all metaphysics is being thrown to the wind, it is! The breath upon which words form *is* evident, universally evident. We feel it; we see it move the in leaves of our collective movements. And so, we must explore the wind upon which no light can shine. Does the wind not fascinate us all, this quantum substratum within the ether that bears the seeds of reason and morals *within* each *moment*? This invisible dance of spirits that makes all life and movement possible within *the waste land* must become philosophical grist, scientific criterion, and once again, first philosophy in theology. If we passionately listen,[22] we can hear the "delicate whispering" (1 Kgs 19:12) of the winds moving through the leaves, as absolutes wrestle beneath the dancing play of relatives. "Those who hear not the music, think the dancers mad."[23]

Faith indeed comes to us like sleep in the night, a gift. When we let go and allow our entire self into the venture of living transformation, we become spirit and enter the *analogia spiritus*—the antecedent co-conditioning *moment* of absolute (spirit) relating to Absolute (Spirit). Only then in the twinkling of an eye can we enter our rest as Christ turns to us, a gift in hand, and co-conditionally says, "*Your* faith has set you free."

---

22. Or, as Steven Smith, a doctor of spirit as first philosophy, might contend, even if we do not passionately listen. Smith, *Concept of the Spiritual*.

23. The quote remains anonymous, though some credit Friedrich Nietzsche with its basic idea in *Thus Spoke Zarathustra*.

Preface

THE INVISIBLE WIND AND SPIRIT: OF LEAPS AND FIRST FLIGHTS

There is still no clear and compelling theory of explanation for morphological transference in genetic theory. What Darwin was *privileged* to initiate still struggles to take flight; even Neo-Darwinians, epigenetics, and all the King's men have yet to put Humpty-Dumpty back together again (even after 2.7 billion dollars spent on the Human Genome Project). The forest is difficult to see among the trees of Materialism. Most amusingly, the King's men and the general academy of evolutionary theorists continue to formally castigate all theories entailing epigenetic activity outside the stricture of materialism (e.g., morphic resonance, water memory, non-local action, human quantum entanglement within dynamics of Hilbert Space, etc.). Abominations are any notions that the collective spirit of a species' history, which is no less determinately real than the present, might holistically condition the existing spirit of an organism. Eyes flame when suppositions of a ghost in the machine slips over the moat and under the doors of their academic siege. They can assimilate no such ghosts without the fortress falling and exposing their nakedness. Power is power. Yes, the gifts of Enlightenment correct the innocence of unfettered darkness and superstitions of the Middle Ages; there is no going back. Yet, the Enlightenment nightmare continues forward with intentional innocence or denial. Agendas are agendas.

John Hands, in his comprehensive survey on human evolution, *Cosmosapiens*, graciously warns that the "absence of evidence is not evidence of absence. [Most scientists] of the eighteenth century would have dismissed as preposterous the idea that there existed a cosmic field that accounted for electrical magnetic phenomena (science currently considers that the electromagnetic field is infinite in range)."[1] If it were not for the original speculations of James Clerk Maxwell and Michael Faraday, what Lord Kelvin claimed to his death (1905) were machinations of mysticism (more right than he knew), a unified theory of electricity, magnetism, and light would never have emerged out of the Newtonian prison of eighteenth and nineteenth-century science. Maxwell and Faraday were devout Christians, to a degree mystics, both experiencing the field-like phenomenon of God's Spirit interacting with their own spirit. Are we not surprised such men would discover such things?

> Pure science is divinely inspired. It is a godsend, a blessing from the spirit, a sacred mandate, an act of divine providence. It is a heavenly gift to the people. It does not belong to the corrupt merchants, money lenders and Pharisees, who have turned the temple of science into a den of thieves.[2]

And so it is with our study of the wind. Though materially imperceptible, the supervening nature of spirit, like the wind, affects the observable and measurable. As a nestling perched upon the nest edge, fueled only by parental example, genetic traces, *and* an ineffable voice calling it beyond: it leaps, giving itself to the winds. And still, whole schools of theology disavow the notion of spirit from the theological landscape (πνεῦμα: the holistic presence and operating mechanism of an organism)—a holistic differentiated living totality of an organism that is supervenient over body *and mind* (νοῦς: the relative and temporal aspects within the operating principal of an organism). Entire linguistic systems have collapsed these two concepts, mind and spirit, (portmanteau), into *geist, esprit, geest*, etc. Danish, on the other hand, might have contributed to the Writer's differentiated sense of the absolute (πνεῦμα/ånd, νοῦς/sind). If they cannot drag such categories, heuristics, and dynamics of spirit into the light of their exclusive certainty and control, they eliminate them altogether from language and theory as innocent tropes of a naïve past. Science has always been about engaging *all* reality and what constitutes reality.

Charles Taylor warns us that the Enlightenment has given to us with one hand and stolen from us with the other. Is πνεῦμα a relic from the past, or does it represent something within human and divine relations, heaven forbid, something real and tangible that might be necessary for a fuller understanding of the divine-human relationship and anthropology? Might

---

1. Hands, *Cosmosapiens*, 198.
2. Attributed to Anthon St. Maarten.

spirit be as real as the non-local action of quantum theory that exceeds the speed of light or Kierkegaard's "sudden" *moment* within the interstices of dialogical Time? This thesis contends that further expansion of our understanding of the divine-human relationship hinges upon not only recovering the historical use of πνεῦμα but further expanding our knowledge of the logic of spirit as well. We have many new conceptual tools and lenses unavailable to former explorations through which to explore and understand the nature of spirit. In this respect, our pilgrimage will be intensely interdisciplinary as we allow various disciplines of thought to condition each other in order to bring greater clarity and insight to our understanding of spirit.

On a personal note: my exploration into the dynamics of *perichoresis* did not begin with the Church Fathers, through whom the concept first emerges in its primitive articulation. It began before I even knew of the concept. During my initial theological development, in concert with readings in postmodern sensitive communication theory, developmental theory, literary critical theory, social theory, postmodern philosophy, and my initial undergraduate major of physics, I began developing my own personal metaphysics reflecting a "tripartite, dual aspect, monism" (comical I admit). It was popping up everywhere I looked. Soon, I stumbled upon the theological dynamic of *perichoresis* and realized I was already unknowingly part of a theological thread that spans millennia. Most prominent within this tapestry was Søren Kierkegaard, to whom I had always been drawn, irresistibly. Immediately after learning of *perichoresis,* I learned of her younger sister *analogia spiritus*, even more beautiful than the first, even closer to what I was seeking—the *coup de grâce*. I would spend a lifetime saturating myself in their cosmic omnipresence, exploring them and applying them theologically and ecclesiastically to know better and understand that Presence that first touched me alone in a room during the atheism of my early college years, a Presence that, days afterwards, exploded in my readings of the New Testament as the face of that Presence manifested as Christ. Though I struggle mightily with the bastard children of Christianity—Christendom, democratic liberalism, and modern science—they remain mistresses all, in whom by grace I see the glory of God to this day.

What is at stake within this study is a perichoretic Christian metaphysics that provides the fundamental landscape for addressing issues of profound consequence in theology: (1) redressing the modern death or isolation of transcendence with a new understanding of *relational dynamics* through which free, temporal, and self-determining human beings might mutually relate with an Eternal God of providence, (2) laying the framework for a viable Christian *pluralistic hypothesis* in an increasingly pluralistic world, and (3) providing a *theological anthropology* for an enhanced narrative of Christian redemption that better addresses our understanding of human spirit, *human origins*, and *theodicy*

—Gregory Scott Gorsuch, March 2023

Acknowledgments

This text grew from the fertile soil of the University of Edinburgh under a PhD mentor who gave me the freedom to travel uncharted paths attempting to express a novel postmodern shift within theological metaphysics. I am deeply grateful to Kevin Vanhoozer for taking on this project and struggling through years of my often dyslexic, unreadable essays. I am equally thankful for the external examiner of the thesis, Alistair McFadyen, who thought it exemplary, in serious need of professional editing, and publication. It took a little longer than expected due to my varied life interests and unending discoveries of the divine in every discipline of thought I wandered. At some point, one needs to stop and just write.

What sits before you now is only a kernel of what it was then. It is not a new thesis, but expanded, updated, and far more lucid than the original thesis. The many years between its birth and maturity have hopefully made a challenging work more accessible to critical readers as they travel through disparate disciplines at complex, often dense, levels of engagement. In proffering a Christian metaphysics of *perichoresis* and a new reading of the Scriptures, I consolingly request of the reader much patience, deliberate (unhurried) reading, and a willingness to explore new continents of thinking and imagining.

My gratitude goes out to those who encouraged me through my aversion to academics and my academic pathologies, while pushing me to develop these ideas at greater levels of inquiry: Robert Weber, Ray Anderson, Donald Hagner, James Loder, Colin Gunton, et al. I thank those conversational partners, too many to mention, who kept me company through the winters of my theological discontent; you know who you are. And special thanks to Alan Beasley, Ryan and Steve Provonsha, and Bruce Taylor for their editorial and proofing help. Appreciation must also be given to the publishing crew at Wipf and Stock for holding my hand through the process.

I absolve all the above of any errors within the text due to an insecure theologian endlessly messing with what always seems to him unfinished.

Finally, I offer my warmest regards and gratefulness to my cherished partner in the Dance of Life, Cheryl, and our two daughters for braving the travel to faraway lands in which to birth and pen these ideas.

Abbreviations of Reference Works

Kierkegaard, Søren

CA   *The Concept of Dread*. Translated by Walter Lowrie. Princeton: Princeton University Press, 1957.

CD   *Christian Discourses*. Translated by Walter Lowrie. New York: Oxford University Press, 1940.

CUP *Concluding Unscientific Postscript*. Translated by David F. Swenson and Walter Lowrie. Princeton: Princeton University Press, 1968.

ED   *Edifying Discourses*. Translated by David F. Swenson. Minneapolis: Augsburg, 1943.

EO1 *Either/Or*. Vol. 1. Translated by David F. et al. Princeton: Princeton University Press, 1944.

EO2 *Either/Or*. Vol. 2. Translated by Walter Lowrie. London: Oxford University Press, 1944.

FT   *Fear and Trembling*. Translated by Walter Lowrie. Princeton: Princeton University Press, 1941.

JK   *The Journals of Kierkegaard*. Edited and translated by Alexander Dru. New York: Harper and Row, 1939.

JPH *Journals and Papers*. Edited and translated by Howard V. Hong et al. 7 vols. Bloomington: Indiana University Press, 1967–68.

PF   *Philosophical Fragments*. Translated by David F. Swenson, revised Howard V. Hong. Princeton: Princeton University Press, 1962.

PFH   *Philosophical Fragments*, Translated by Howard V. Hong et al. 7 vols. Princeton: Princeton University Press, 1985–.

PH   *Purity of Heart Is to Will One Thing.* Translated by Douglas V. Steere. New York: Harper, 1956.

SUD   *Sickness unto Death.* Translated by Walter Lowrie. Princeton: Princeton University Press, 1941.

TC   *Training in Christianity.* Translated by Walter Lowrie. Princeton: Princeton University Press, 1960.

WL   *Works of Love.* Translated by Howard V. Hong and Edna H. Hong. New York: Harper and Row, 1962.

Moltmann, Jürgen

CG   *The Crucified God.* Translated by R. A. Wilson and John Bowden. New York: Harper and Row, 1974.

COG   *The Coming of God: Christian Eschatology.* Translated by M. Kohl. Minneapolis: Fortress, 1996.

CPS   *The Church in the Power of the Spirit.* New York: Harper and Row, 1977.

GC   *God in Creation: An Ecological Doctrine of Creation.* Translated by M. Kohl. London: SCM, 1985.

SL   *The Spirit of Life: A Universal Affirmation.* Translated by M. Kohl. London: SCM, 1992.

TKG   *The Trinity and the Kingdom of God.* Translated by M. Kohl. London: SCM, 1981.

Others

CD   Barth, Karl, *Church Dogmatics.* Edited and translated by T. F. Torrance and G. W. Bromiley. Edinburgh: T. & T. Clark, 1936–69.

CP   McFadyen, Alistair, I. *The Call to Personhood.* Cambridge: Cambridge University Press, 1990.

KM   Loder, James E., and W. Jim Neidhardt. *The Knight's Move: The Relational Logic of the Spirit in Theology and Science.* Colorado Springs, CO: Helmers and Howard, 1992.

ABBREVIATIONS OF REFERENCE WORKS

LS Loder, James E. *The Logic of the Spirit: Human Development in Theological Perspective.* San Francisco: Jossey-Bass, 1998.

TM Loder, James E. *The Transforming Moment: Understanding Convictional Experiences.* London: Harper and Row, 1981.

1

Introduction

[I pray] that they may all be one, *as* You, Father, are in Me, and I in You; *so that* they also may be one in Us.

JOHN 17:21 (emphasis added)

The transformation into the divine image will become ever more profound, and the image of Christ in us will continue to increase in clarity. This is a progression in us from one level of understanding to another and from one degree of clarity to another, toward an ever-increasing perfection in the form of likeness to the image of the Son of God . . . 'And all of us, who with unveiled faces let the glory of the Lord be reflect in us, are thereby transformed into his image from glory to glory.'

DIETRICH BONHOEFFER[1]

THE THEOLOGICAL SHIFT

We are irrevocably within a philosophical and theological reformation, a cycle to be sure; as Peter Hodgson expresses it,[2] an enlarging helix spiral slowly developing (expanding) through time. Existing social and ecclesial

---

1. Bonhoeffer, *Discipleship*, 286.
2. Hodgson, *God in History*, 241; cf. Hart, *Imagination*, 60–68.

structures continue to expand, integrate, and deepen within themselves. With Bonhoeffer, are we to look for an expansion of theological meaning into a religionless-secular expression of Christianity, for the transformation or translation of the inexpressible mysteries within Christianity (*arkandisziplin*) into public language, looking for God in "the beyond in the midst of our lives"?[3] Will the immense knowledge currently emerging integrate and enrich our traditional theological structures, possibly expand them into an even greater understanding of God, Christ, and the life of Christian faith? In many respects, the gap between the church and culture continues to narrow, liberal or conservative. The underlying structures of atonement continue to mature, thereby revealing more meaningful structures of social theory, communication theory, the anatomy of relationships, and our understanding of love.

We must address the longings and disappointments within each culture in new ways and subsume them into richer praxes and relational paradigms within the church. The success of such efforts will be confirmed as new and greater meaning emerges within the Scriptures, especially when meaning comes to previously meaningless or significantly problematic passages. Society, the church, and the academy must address the desperate cries for greater coherence and meaning. For example, one noted social psychologist suggests we "reduce the tendency to place moral judgment on the other (or the self). We are, instead, invited to spread the concern to the network of relations from which issues of conflict or wrong-doing arise."[4] He is not erasing the ethical culpability of the individual but wisely expanding the ethical spectrum. Though intensely personal and responsible, every personal decision also emerges within a complexity of interpenetrating relations and social choreographies.

The former "stability" of science is likewise in current upheaval. The Newtonian worldview no longer adequately reflects reality as we know it. Philosophy and theology must continue integrating the emerging evidence from Quantum, Relativity, and Chaos/thermodynamic theories, which are not going away. These theories are no longer merely speculative. Whether we like it or not, time bends, and in some way both reality and consciousness inextricably connect.[5] Like earlier epochs (e.g., the Copernican revolu-

---

3. Bonhoeffer, *Discipleship*, 280–82.
4. Gergen, "Social Theory," 11.
5. For example, the Delayed Choice Quantum Eraser experiment compellingly suggests that matter and reality are dependent on consciousness. Causality now transcends our typical linear cause and effect notions of interactions. Experiments reveal either retrocausality or, to be explored later, transtemporal co-conditioning reciprocity (a holistic interaction through a bending of time). The scientific community is reluctant

tion), we must allow these new phenomena and insights to transform our worldview and theology to appropriately communicate within our world the constantly expanding truths of the Scriptures and the Christian faith.

Relational Ontology

Nancey Murphy argues that theological progress in understanding God's action in the world must evolve and that we revise our current metaphysical notions of causation and matter.[6] In this regard, significant changes in metaphysics are necessary and suggest the need for a *relational* ontology. Colin Gunton distinguishes between two senses of the relational. The first idealizing sense has to do with things being "known only in terms of their relation to us, or rather as they appear to us; the second, realist sense, is that according to which things have their (objective) being in relation." The first contains nuances of relativism; the latter and focus of this thesis leads to an understanding of relativity that maintains the difference of all things within a universal dynamic of relationality—a theory of differentiated unity. *Mutuality is not through similarity of being, but through a universal relationality that mediates difference.* Gunton argues that in "the latter understanding, there is an ontology of relationality: things are constituted by their relation to other things."[7] Much like our expanding and evolving understanding of atonement theory throughout history, this thesis seeks to expand the ancient theological concepts of relationality and *perichoresis* from their original precursive meanings by bringing them into dialogue with paralleling dynamics currently emerging in various disciplines of thought and interdisciplinary theology.

When considering an infinite eternal God and finite temporal humanity, relational dynamics and divine-human mutuality take shape in four primary ways within contemporary Christian theology. In *Classical thought* (e.g., Thomas Aquinas), God is assumed to be outside time, affects history in time, but is not temporally affected in any eternal way we can completely understand. *Process theology* has posited God within time to establish greater temporal mutuality. Here God does not know the future before it

---

to provide theories concerning these phenomena because that would require relinquishing the pervasive materialist worldview within the academy. Nevertheless, many are beginning to acknowledge the necessity of at least a cosmic consciousness (e.g., designated mass-media science spokesman Michio Kaku now openly acknowledges the necessity of a "collective consciousness").

6. Murphy, "Divine Action," 326, 338.
7. Gunton, *One, Three, Many*, 194n18.

happens, which does present a more agreeable God to human temporality. However, this strains the deeper more paradoxical elements of faith, God's preeminent promises, and our personal and dialogical relation to a personal God. More recently, Barth, Pannenberg, Moltmann, Gunton, and James Loder, present a *trinitarian* God that relates in Time but proleptically from the future in an expanding, more complex understanding of time and mutuality. Ultimately, these theologies employ relational dynamics of differentiated unity in which persons participate analogically in the Eternal light of the Logos and in *moments* that contain the fullness of time. Theories of spontaneous, self-organizing processes within developmental and thermodynamic science reinforce such theological development. Loder suggests such dynamics considered within trinitarian theology and from the point of the resurrection create a "*prefiguring* of the 'new creation,' . . . giving rise to new order [that] could be seen as a wrinkle in time, a leap into the future, bringing the future into the present ahead of time."[8] This still leaves us with an imposing Eternal God and an Abrahamic faith—a heavy christological imposition that ultimately limits any true sense of human self-determination and freedom.

In great sympathy with these latter theorists, this thesis attempts to expand their theological intuitions by proposing a more nuanced understanding of human self-determination and freedom. Their theologies do not obviate the impositional God of Classical thinking clearly enough. Neither do they explain how human action within some form of self-determination authentically and filially relates with an Eternally constituted God, the undeniable claim of the Scriptures. This thesis suggests that God from the future affects human temporal existence, yet unlike these previous theorists, it considers the possibility that temporal humans constituting within the dynamics of faith are potentially drawn into a Jacobian *co-conditioning* relationship with the Eternal dimensions of a creating God. Human beings can participate in God's Eternal preeminent act of creation through various dynamics within their dialogical activity. Therefore, coupling our current developments in trinitarian thought with an expanding understanding of theological anthropology (a *living* metaphysics of movement) creates the possibility of a fourth consideration, *perichoretic theology*. In this manner, the notion of prolepsis broadens into a *holistic* mutual co-conditioning interaction between the human spirit and the dynamic singularity of God's Eternal Spirit *antecedent* to each (and every) moment of creation. An appropriate relational disposition allows and draws humanity into such antecedent dynamics. As such, God remains an asymmetrical influence

---

8. Loder and Neidhardt, *KM*, 215, emphasis added.

while humanity and creation remain contingent yet still potentially self-determined *within* acts of true Jacobian faith (passion). Such a theological course, however, struggles for further development and adequate expression from beneath the weight of existing Classical and Reformed heuristics. We need new ways of understanding the dynamics active in the transforming process of *theosis*, the bold claims of the early church fathers—the divinization of some aspect of humanity.[9] Though the linguistic limitations of the church fathers led them to such bold, possibly indulgent, anthropological over-statements, this thesis attempts to redress their considerations by presenting *theosis* as the divine trinitarian relationality of *perichoresis* reflectively emerging within human *relations*. Just as physics has undergone periodic re-paradigming (e.g., expanding its language and explanatory capacity in the wake of irrefutable quantum data), so must every other discipline of thought, notwithstanding theology.

This thesis proposes a relational ontology that relativizes our notions of reality, causality, and simultaneity through constituting human persons and sociology *within* the emerging third term of the relationship. This phenomenon is contingent upon God's unique relationship with humanity. Through this relationship (by definition), the dynamic of *perichoresis* to some degree analogically *reflects* within human interactions (replete with various distortions—sin). Such a dynamic replaces the idea of a universal frame of reference in which all things similar mutually relate (*analogia entis*) with a universal dynamic of relationality through which all things different mutually and meaningfully relate (*analogia spiritus*)—*perichoresis*. Such a thesis eventually addresses the standing critique of poststructuralism.

Investigating new paradigmatic soundings intensifies the difficulty of this study. In significant paradigm shifts, the meaning and use of our former language transform; no-thing stays the same. In this respect, this thesis will attempt to liberate, develop, and expand our understanding of the Christian Scriptures and tradition from the former historically limited Hellenistic philosophical and linguistic structuring that captively frames them.

---

9. Athanasius: "He became man that we might be made God" (*On the Incarnation* 54.3, in Underhill, *Mysticism*, 419). Augustine: "I heard . . . thy voice from on high crying unto me, 'I am the Food of the full grown: grow, and then thou shalt feed on Me. Nor shalt thou change Me into thy substance as thou changest the food of thy flesh, but thou shalt be changed into Mine'" (*Confessions* 7.10, in Underhill, *Mysticism*, 419). Maximus the Confessor: "By nature man remains wholly human in soul and body, but by grace he becomes wholly God both in his soul and in his body" (Moltmann, *SL*, 94). Basil of Caesarea: "The souls inhabited by the Spirit . . . themselves are rendered wholly spiritual [and] from this source comes . . . the power to become divine" (*De Spiritus Sancto*, in Bettenson, *Later Fathers*, 71).

The "Will to Power": Is There Nothing Good That Dwells within Our Flesh? Reconsideration: Is There Nothing Good That Dwells within Our Relations?

The predominate creed of the humanities and biological sciences today, whether modern or postmodern, maintains that biological survival remains the fundamental force in the hierarchy of needs within humanity. From Thomas Huxley's Darwin and Nietzsche to Wittgenstein and French Poststructuralism, the claim remains the same, the defining force in nature and human existence is the will to power. Power ensures survival.[10] In this respect, the church has not gone untouched. Commensurate themes vitiate theological structures leading to over-simplistic doctrines of a totally other God and total depravity of humanity. Nothing of personhood or culture remains significant for experiencing the sacred. Indirectly, the pervasive influence and agenda of "the will to power," "scientism," and the materialist worldview of Modernity help shape the meaning of the church's claim that "nothing good dwells within our flesh."[11] Christ's prayer and its message (John 17:21; cf. 1 Cor 15; 2 Cor 3:18) maintain that some level of goodness is transforming humanity over time. The *closed structuring* of the singular individual or society sustains no goodness; however, a degree of goodness actively dwells within the Power that enables and constitutes all relations to the Other (themself, others, or God).

We are only now just beginning to "remember" that which was always too "simple," too "familiar," that which is still most "powerful."[12] Like water to a fish, which sees not the water because it has never known existence outside of it, the ancient Greeks had yet to develop a word for today's understanding of relationship![13] Therefore, any concept of relationship playing an

---

10. Though Nietzsche's non-metaphysical phenomenological phrase is more pervasive in its implications, self-preservation is by far its most common "consequence." Cf. Copleston, *History*, 7:408.

11. "Flesh" is not the body, neither does it represent the whole person. Within this thesis, the "flesh" is understood as the *enclosed person*, what Kierkegaard calls a negative unity. However, because of that Power constituting all *open* relations with the Other, either as a relationship unto itself (personhood) or within social relations, therein resides the possibility of goodness both within us and between us.

12. Allusion here made to Wittgenstein, *Philosophical Investigations*, 50e.

13. For example, typical of the New Testament, when the author of Matthew in 19:10 attempts to express the generic concept of relationship and the relatedness of one person to another, "εἰ οὕτως ἐστὶν ἡ αἰτία τοῦ ἀνθρώπου μετὰ τῆς γυναικός, . . ." ("If the cause of the man with his wife . . ."), he is reduced to employing the Greek concepts of cause and effect (αἰτία, cause). The concept of relationship as we currently use it—as something uniquely created *between* us that is distinct from the persons participating—had yet to emerge with an explicit signifier, something which one could use in theory

articulated role in theological or philosophical development two thousand years ago was significantly handicapped compared to today. If indeed we live and move and have our being within a relational ontology, the ancient Greeks and biblical writers would have struggled to express and articulate it. Therefore, when appropriate, our later developing and progressive linguistic capacities aid in expanding the original author's intended meaning.[14] A primary theme of this thesis is to reveal such linguistic limitations within the language and forms of life expressed within the Scriptures and expose their unavoidable shortcomings due to such limiting metaphysical structuring that alternatively come to life within a relational ontology.

If the Spirit emanates as the love and relationship between the Father and the Son (Augustine), mediating the interanimation of the two, while sustaining their personhood and difference (subject-relationship-subject), then we obviate the Hellenistic linguistic limitations within a subject-subject ontology that create the need for concepts like "indwelling," or "I in you," and "you in me." Such linguistic structuring immediately creates a mountain of theological anomalies and paradoxes. Only after centuries of theological struggle does any clear sense of the Spirit emerge as the third term or as mediating the relationship between the Father and Son. Therefore, if the dynamic of *perichoresis*, which some were using to refer to the relationship within the immanent Trinity, was potentially, analogically, and reflectively emerging within human beings and human socialization, then it might help in restructuring how we understand and express all relationality (i.e., we need a metaphysical adjustment).

For example, "the Spirit is *within* you" might be better understood as the transforming action in human beings by the *relationship between* their spirit and the Spirit of God (*analogia spiritus*). The often scientific concept of "*indwelling* the nature of the other" results from a mediating *mutual co-conditioning relationship between* persons, the world, or God. In each case, the relationship emerges as a living third term *between* and *surrounding* two or more that then transparently mediates a mutual co-conditioning while intensifying each person's individuality. Such a relational ontology would radically alter our thinking and provide a more coherent and fruitful understanding of the Scriptures, theology, and our integration of faith within the whole of life.

---

development. The Greek concept of *koinonia* generally meant a sharing of something and was differently oriented than "φίλος, where the bond is that of relationship or love" (Hauck, "κοινός," in *TDNT* 3:797). The Hebrews had a limited equivalent in "covenant."

14. N.b., the ancient Greeks also had no word or developed concept for our use of *synchronize, process, reality, transcendence, immanence*, and many other vital concepts employed within our current theological lexicons.

We have only recently come to understand more fully that only relationships constitute human beings. Can we then consider that something reflective within human relations exists as a good and positive force that is intrinsic to being fully human?[15] *Personhood* as relational is more than "flesh" and generally constitutes in some degree of open and active relations with the Power that constitutes it. Even though our conscience reflects an active force of goodness within us and our relations, we might theorize that it is possible to completely resist this presence within our relations. Tragically much of the church's current notion of sin and its corresponding meaning of life in Christ is again falling into cultural obsolescence simply because the church is failing to mature in its understanding of sin, relational dynamics, and the person-in-relation. Church and culture inextricably entwine, and the church's lack of development has eroded Christ's redemptive complementarity between church and culture.

The Phenomenon of Suicide

Can we continue to imply that the single foundational force within human life is the (neo)Darwinian, Freudian, and Heideggerian "struggle against death," or biological annihilation? Is it merely the struggle to ensure the most efficient course for progeny? Is this the ground that motivates and sustains human flourishing?[16] Furthermore, is Richard Dawkins right? "We are only physical survival machines—robot vehicles blindly programmed to preserve the selfish molecules known as genes."[17] Or, alternatively, does another more fundamental force within us create fear of death and the "survival machine?" Might the primal goal of human beings be the notion of peace and unity through egalitarian compromise, fleeing all conflict, pain, and violence in the world? Admittedly, persons often sacrifice their social or biological life to achieve social peace and tranquility (e.g., sacrificing oneself in war to end war or leaving a conflictual relationship). However, this also is not fundamental.[18]

Indeed, the struggle for self-distinction from the world is an undeniable force in life (biological survival being only one aspect). But, is that

---

15. Cf. Zimmermann, *Humanism*.

16. Kierkegaard's "dread," "despair," and "death," though inclusive of physical death, did not ultimately refer to physical death but rather relational death. The bulk of European existentialism that grew from Kierkegaard's thought failed to acknowledge the centrality of his theological and relational meaning.

17. Dawkins, *Selfish Gene*, v. Furthermore, he claims that his "central message has become textbook orthodoxy" (viii).

18. Cf. Volf, *Exclusion and Embrace*, an excellent treatment of this theme.

all there is?[19] In his 1997 Gifford Lectures, Holmes Rolston III argues that "genes are favored if and only if they 'make a contribution' or have a part, a 'share' in the integrated coping capacities of the whole organism."[20] Rolston effectively presents a much more satisfying notion of gene activity than Dawkins's singular "selfish" gene agenda. For Rolston, the gene is driven by an immanent force *both* inward toward self-distinction and outward in co-operative integration. This reflects a foundational reality and metaphysical force constituting the drive for power in humanity as a *desire to relate* perichoretically—ultimately, to relate as genuinely and intimately as possible with the Other while experiencing the intensification of personhood.[21] This latter possibility reveals itself to be the probable rationale when we consider the act of suicide. The phenomenon of suicide itself seemingly negates the metaphysics of survival. Why would one kill oneself *if* the simple continuation of biological life is the most fundamental force within human existence? Also, many acts of suicide happen within states of peace and unity.

What motivates suicide is the experience of relational purposelessness—the real or perceived loss of existing or potential meaningful relationships.[22] Every suicide, in one way or another, bears witness to the death of intimacy or imagined loss of its possibility. Stories of broken relationships, isolation, or *loneliness* color each case. Developmentalist James Loder tells us, "Harry Stack Sullivan, noted psychoanalyst, said he could bring patients to relive almost any experience from anxiety to violent trauma, but he could not bring them to relive loneliness. . . . [Loneliness] is the closest we can come to experiencing our own death. Loneliness is proximate to death."[23] Even if loneliness is simply a genetic response to the loss of a relationship in which to procreate, it still makes no sense that a person would then end life and all future possibilities of procreation if indeed the *fundamental* drive was survival and procreation.[24] In other words, loneliness (the loss of

19. Philip Hefner tells us: "We distrust the term *survival* if it refers simply to the biological perpetuation of life, because we suspect that if that is what nature is up to, it is not enough for us" (*Human Factor*, 74).

20. Rolston, *Genes*, 72.

21. This is evident even if, with Lévinas, we posit that our responsibility to the other takes asymmetrical priority over that of God.

22. Even the ideological sacrifice we associate with war, terrorist activities, or protecting loved ones result from a foundational desire for protecting authentic relationship and bonding.

23. Loder, *TM*, 81.

24. Ending one's life due to the loss of all meaningful relations or apparent hope of relations is reasonable when considering authentic relationship itself as the foundational desire of human beings. Ending one's biological life remains an irrational response if the foundational desire in human beings is biological life itself.

authentic relations) and the existentialist sense of nothingness is far more threatening to human life than biological annihilation or social conflict. Even the internal drive for peace and unity or egalitarian compromise that flees from *all* struggles, disruption, and violence fails to traverse the suffering, pain, and conflict necessary to maintain *meaningful* interaction in a world of difference.

When former foundational notions of human existence, such as "significance,"[25] are reinterpreted according to this more primordial relational desire, they are deepened and enriched. Respectively, the "will to power" reinterprets as *relational* insurance or currency. In other words, the attainment of "significance" and "power" merely represent currencies we think insure and secure that which is most fundamental—*authentic relationship*, intimacy, love, and perichoretic relations. This does not negate the reality of "will to power" or "significance." It simply necessitates their practical expansion and redefining in relation to an even more fundamental dynamic within human existence. The essential question then becomes, what is meant by *authentic* or perichoretic relations?

The Logic or Shape of Authentic Relationship

How are we to understand, identify, and substantiate authentic from inauthentic relationships? What is *perichoresis*, this seemingly inexplicable expression of love and relationship reflectively emanating from a trinitarian God? Are there analogies in human relations and the world that reflect *perichoresis*? Each subsequent chapter will compare the theological concept of *perichoresis* with parallel postmodern dynamics emerging in various disciplines of thought that reveal surprisingly parallel dynamics. These dynamics currently emerging within the humanities and sciences both parallel what we know of *perichoresis* and ultimately offer new potential heuristics for expanding our growing theological knowledge of *perichoresis*. Though our understanding is provisional and always expanding, the life and witness of Christ and the Spirit of God, as well as Christ's admonition that humanity imitate his relationship with the Father, necessitates our continuing inquiry and growth in this matter. Finally, because *perichoresis* is a pneumatological issue, we must explore one of the most obscure and ubiquitous concepts in any language—spirit (πνεῦμα) and the logic of spirit, which, it turns out, has everything to do with the notion of authenticity and inauthenticity within relationality.

---

25. Cf. Sullivan, *Interpersonal Theory of Psychiatry*; Rogers, *Client Centered Therapy*.

If accurately understood, such a dynamic should begin to reveal insights into many of the Modern paradoxes. Imre Lakatos once playfully suggested, "all our scientific beliefs are, always have been, and always will be false."[26] Every new discovery, so it seems, only reflects an eternal truth. Over time anomalies immediately begin to weigh in, which when heavy enough motivate the search for yet fuller expressions of reality. So, where is the truth? In a seemingly contrary sense, Ludwig Wittgenstein broadly taught us that *all* human actions are truth and have meaning; all metaphysical construals, though inflated, nevertheless emerge from these actions. Similarly, Heidegger suggests, "untruth must derive from the essence of truth. Only because truth and untruth are not, *in essence*, indifferent to one another can a true proposition contrast so sharply with its correspondingly untrue proposition."[27] Circumspectly, we can all sense the propriety of these statements despite their joint affirmation and paradoxical nature. Our world constantly changes, all of it, and yet somehow, we long for and find a provisional level of continuity within it. In this respect, the shape of authentic relationship will have everything to do with our concept of spirit. This is especially true if we consider spirit as relationship itself and ontologically primary to word, the house of being.

Spirit as First Philosophy and Theological Prolegomena: Smith and Dabney

The embattled issue of theological prolegomena is still largely deliberated within the residuals of Hellenistic metaphysics—*analogia entis*, subject-subject relations, and the asymmetrical priority of substance (and Word). Theologically, however, T. F. Torrance insists "we must operate with an *open* epistemology in which we allow the way of our knowing to be clarified and modified *pari passu* with advance in deeper and fuller knowledge of the object and that we will be unable to set forth an account of that way of knowing in advance."[28] Theologically this inverts our typical methodological considerations. Therefore, to know God in Christ necessitates a radical epistemological openness, a relational disposition through which our *entire* spirit must become vulnerably open. If D. Lyle Dabney is correct, and the word is constructed upon a *preceding* breath (spirit), then

---

26. Cited by MacIntyre, "Epistemological Crises," 73.
27. Heidegger, *Existence and Being*, 310.
28. Torrance, *Theological Science*, 10.

> We must insist against Barth that it is the *Spirit* of God and not simply the *Word* of God that is properly basic to Christian theology, then against Schleiermacher we must maintain that it is the Spirit *of* God and not *human* spirituality that is the proper subject matter for an appropriate prolegomenon to theology.... The Spirit of God is not human spirit aspiring to the divine, but neither is it the subjectivity of God making an object of the human.... Rather than *sub*jective or *ob*jective, the Spirit is better conceived as *trans*jective; that is to say, that by which we as individuals are transcended, engaged, oriented beyond ourselves, and related to God and neighbor from the very beginning.[29]

Dabney's consideration suggests that any notion of metaphysical grounding for faith and theology would better rest in a trinitarian coupling of Christ *and* the Spirit, acknowledging the asymmetrical priority of God's Spirit.

In an extended philosophical essay on spirit as first philosophy, Steven G. Smith argues that "seeing" and "emotion" are not actions of a human agent but a mode of existence.[30] In considering the difference between *pneuma* and *psyche*, and discounting the pejorative understanding of intentional existence "as *standing* or as *seeing*," Smith argues for the necessity of motion, in motion, e-motion as the primordial forms of existence. Rather than the circular reasoning of uprooting or alienating oneself to go forth into the place of another, or demanding as much from the other, which he recognizes as positions of stasis (and I would argue are the results of antiquated Hellenistic ontological derivatives), he suggests "it is both sufficient and necessary to parallel my motion with the motion of others, in relationship."[31] Smith argues that any worthy ontological soundings must necessarily include motion.

> The spiritual constraint coming before the constraint of intelligibility as such has already demanded motion of us.... The otherness of the others opens up space between me and them; their claim on me sets me in motion in that space.

In other words, spirit is a precursor within our "practical sort of seeing,... [and] emotion" before intelligibility. From this antecedent movement with the other,

> We thus arrive at a conception of the spiritual, bringing all phenomenological and logical considerations into this rising.

---

29. Dabney, "Otherwise," 160–61.
30. Smith, *Concept of the Spiritual*, 105.
31. Smith, *Concept of the Spiritual*, 104.

> Aiming and riding are what *further* we are doing when we do things, on account of which . . . intentional concepts are applied to our physical behavior; rising to the others is the *first* "further."[32]

Smith also acknowledges the necessity of determination. "The life of an intentional being will consist of some mixture of determining and being-determined."[33] He then suggests various dynamics of "codetermining" in which the determining of all participants within a relationship need not conflict and can emerge in syncopated relatedness. In this respect, Smith considers reason "as a tool of intension and . . . exists in an interintentional context" that emerges in a constraining and formulating way between relational participants. In consideration of *perichoresis*, this reflects the willingness to open to the other as that necessary cross to bear that leads to the emergence of co-*reason*ableness, objective knowledge, truth, and synchronicity that only emerges from the primordial *between* of relationship, which is spirit.

Smith affirms Lévinas's promise that the Infinite offers "an unquestionable relationship with exteriority," but, unlike Hegel, it is an *open* "unknowable" that necessitates "justice instead of a truth."[34] It is an adventure, like the Patriarch Abraham (and one could add, Jacob and the entire list of faithful in Hebrews 11), that never intends on returning home like the perennially homeward bound adventures of Ulysses and the Hellenic way. Yet, in vulnerability, Abraham "keeps going outward." It "must prevent its affirmations from becoming an imprisoning, other-reducing dogmatism."[35]

> The philosophy of the spiritual is groundless because the others to whom it is offered are no ground to have or stand on. . . . The naïve assumption that in reasoning one refers to "the things themselves," . . . is lost to it. The referential, descriptive and correspondential dimension of reasoning is not done away with . . . but it is enfolded by the dimension in which intention meets intention. The sense in which intention itself, both yours and mine, is enfolded by the natural and social factuality of our real intentions, [i.e.] "What shall we make of it?"[36]

---

32. Smith, *Concept of the Spiritual*, 105.
33. Smith, *Concept of the Spiritual*, 106.
34. Smith, *Concept of the Spiritual*, 138.
35. Smith, *Concept of the Spiritual*, 152.
36. Smith, *Concept of the Spiritual*, 152.

The spirit between becomes for Smith the site of a dynamic admixture from which the shape of the relationship must emerge.

> It superordinates itself in the scheme of meaning and will not allow itself to be belied by the constraint of reality; . . . its freedom from reality is not the first thing about it, but the second, entailed by the first thing, which is the superordination of spiritual to nonspiritual existence in the event of living with others.[37]

Therefore, this primordial place of superordination and "common indwelling"[38] is the transparent "unobservable gesture"[39] upon which all relationships, consciousness, and knowing emerge. For Steven G. Smith, this is precisely the concept of spirit, which inevitably must become first philosophy.

Accordingly, Dabney concludes that "the question of Spirit is prior to that of the Word."[40] So,

> What would be the result if we took Smith's illuminating observation that "word," or "speech" or "language" is not properly basic but rather assume an even more fundamental relational reality, "spirit," . . . what kind of . . . "first theology" would result if the "Wholly Other" who is revealed alone through the Word was seen to be, in fact, not that which is ultimately basic, but as itself assuming an even more fundamental reality, a relational reality, the Holy Spirit? What would it look like if we began a theology with a prolegomenon giving an account of "interpersonal relationship in the Spirit" instead of "identity in the continuity of God-consciousness" or "otherness in the discontinuity of the Word"? Initially it can be said that such a first theology would have *pneumatology* . . . as its theme and a theology of *continuity in creation and re-creation through the discontinuity of sin and death as its end*. . . . How is it that the Word of God can be the Word of the Wholly Other and not just our own word "spoken in a loud voice"? The answer is to be found in the Spirit of God in whom we are "Otherwise engaged" from the first, in that we are established and maintained in relationship with the One who is truly Other, the Wholly other with whom we are not identical and yet with whom we are always related.[41]

---

37. Smith, *Concept of the Spiritual*, 154.
38. Smith, *Concept of the Spiritual*, 233.
39. Smith, *Concept of the Spiritual*, 153.
40. Dabney, "Otherwise," 163.
41. Dabney, "Otherwise," 158–61.

INTRODUCTION

The power of spirit as first philosophy and an ontology of relationality explode with meaning beneath the text.

Spirit as First Philosophy and Relational Ontology—Expanding the Text

As promised, this thesis will provide meaning to scriptural passages that formerly have had little or no meaning within our current theological structures. As a precursor to forthcoming expositions within this study, let us briefly look at how spirit as first philosophy and a relational ontology eventually bring greater clarity, coherence, and power to the text.

If indeed the spirit (breath) asymmetrically precedes and is the medium upon which the word constitutes, then we can begin to understand why Christ emphatically prioritizes our interaction with the Spirit before himself. "Anyone who speaks a word against the Son of Man, it will be forgiven him; but whoever speaks against ["blasphemes," or I might add resists] the Holy Spirit, it will not be forgiven him, either in this age or in the age to come" (Matt 12:32). As we will see later, only within a perichoretic theology does this passage take on any coherent meaning with the rest of the Scriptures. This passage alone is entirely incoherent with the rest of Scripture *if* spirit is not first philosophy. This does not lessen the atoning necessity of Christ's Incarnation, crucifixion, and resurrection but sublimates the knowledge of Christ and the knowing event to our antecedent interaction of openness to the Spirit of God and Christ (i.e., an entire trinitarian encounter).

Likewise, for all the New Testament language concerning the various factors for redemption, few orient from the perspective of Christ speaking from the eschaton. Two of these passages in Matthew show Christ's acknowledgment of a *fundamental* contingency for redemption. In both Matt 7:21–23 ("And then I will declare to them, 'I never knew you;' depart from Me") and Matt 25:31–46 ("inasmuch as you did not do it to one of the least of these, you did not do it to Me"), Jesus reduces all belief, following, hearing, loving, and acknowledgment of him to whether he is first *authentically known* and engaged. In other words, all belief, following, hearing, loving, and acknowledgment of Jesus as the Christ is only meaningful according to *how* he is known and related to. Authentic relationship as wholeness, in passion—as spirit—is primordial and necessary to all else. Again, we will discuss these passages and the human necessity of becoming spirit (for *analogia spiritus*) more in-depth later. Nevertheless, this emphasizes the essential association of spirit and relationship as first principles for theology.

Kierkegaard's Concept of Spirit

Though this thesis is deeply indebted to Kierkegaard, it begins with but then expands and extrapolates his thinking considering various scientific and social scientific findings since his time. Therefore, much of this thesis emerges putting Kierkegaard in co-conditioning dialogue with the various interdisciplinary findings within this study. We will further develop his already complex relational dynamics into expanding theories of how time and eternity perichoretically juxtapose and potentially co-condition each other. Though he never used the word *perichoresis*, his understanding of how God interacts with and transforms human beings deepens our understanding of *perichoresis*.

Søren Kierkegaard, as much as any before him, sought to understand the enigmatic nature of spirit within human existence. Most important, he insists upon the distinction of human spirit in analogical relation to the divine spirit. He did this by uniquely positing human being as a synthesis between time and eternity, the finite and the infinite. We first need to differentiate between the idea of *pneuma* and *psyche* in Kierkegaard and how this might give rise to new heuristics. Most continental philosophy does little to distinguish these concepts (evident in linguistic restrictions), but for this thesis and Kierkegaard, there is a significant difference.

> By virtue of the relationship *subsisting between* the eternal truth and the existing individual, the paradox came into being. . . . How does the paradox come into being? By putting the eternal essential truth into *juxtaposition* with existence. . . . [If] the subject is prevented by sin from taking himself back into the eternal, now he need not trouble himself about this; for now the eternal essential truth is not behind him but in front of him, through its being in existence or having existed so that if the individual does not existentially and in existence lay hold of the truth, he will never lay hold of it.[42]

The often-unnoticed uniqueness in this coupling is the creation of the third term, the "subsisting between" of the relationship itself, which creates the potential for human spirit or self as a relationship—the dynamic tensive (not a material) synthesis as consciousness. For Kierkegaard, it has everything to do with correctly understanding the concept of spirit and the dynamics of relationship, which for him are the same.

---

42. Kierkegaard, *CUP*, 187, emphasis added. Though Kierkegaard wanted his works cited according to his pseudonyms, when that pseudonym states what would be agreeable to Kierkegaard himself at some level of thinking, I will at times refer them directly to Kierkegaard for the sake of brevity.

INTRODUCTION

In Hegelian parody, the Writer-Pneumatologist says, "Man is spirit. But what is spirit? Spirit is the self. But what is the self? The *self is a relation* which relates itself to its own self."[43] As merely a relational synthesis of the temporal and the eternal, the individual is not yet a self. "In the relation between two, the relation is the third term as a negative unity, and the two relate themselves to the relation, and in the relation to the relation; such a relation is that between soul and body, when man is regarded as soul."[44] At this point, the soul is still weighed down and locked into the finite, at best, what Kierkegaard calls a "small infinity." Kierkegaard here presents us with the confluence of, in one manner of thinking, sensory datum within the temporal aspect of human experience (the relative) in contrast to the human experiencing kairos time that is an effect of being in relation to the eternal (a dynamic absolute). In itself, this confluence as soul is still not self or spirit. This new relationship between the two remains "nothing more than the brutes" until relationship to something outside itself constitutes it.[45]

> If on the contrary, the relation relates itself to its own self, the relation is then the positive third term, and this is the self. Such a relation . . . must either have constituted itself or have been constituted by another. . . . But this relation (the third term) is in turn *a relation relating itself to that which constituted the whole relation*. . . . The self cannot of itself attain and remain in equilibrium and rest by itself, but only by relating itself to that Power which constituted the whole relation. . . . [By] relating itself to its own self and by *willing to be itself* the self is grounded transparently in the Power which posited it.[46]

Here we begin to see the emergence of Kierkegaard's tripartite structure of relationality. The new relation becomes a *positive* third term only to the degree it is "willing to be itself" in relation to another or self, and this is accomplished by "the self [being] grounded transparently in the Power which

43. Kierkegaard, *SUD*, 146–47, emphasis added. Even with his Hegelian proclivities, Pannenberg anthropologically reflects Kierkegaard's notion of spirit, presenting it as a naturalistic "exocentric centeredness" outside oneself (*PFH*, 96–104).

44. Kierkegaard, *SUD*, 146.

45. When Anti-Climacus (Kierkegaard) tells us that "such a derived, constituted, relation is the human self, a relation which relates itself to its own self, and in relating itself to its own self relates itself to another" (*SUD*, 146), C. Stephen Evans argues that his use of "another" in this case means others. Hence, from this point on in *SUD*, human beings must be considered inherently relational and grist for social theory (Evans, "Unconscious," 82–83). Cf. also Bonhoeffer: "Only in interaction with one another is the spirit of human beings ever revealed; this is the essence of spirit, to be oneself through being in the other" (Bonhoeffer, *Sanctorum Communio*, 73).

46. Kierkegaard, *SUD*, 146, emphasis added.

posited it."⁴⁷ For Kierkegaard, only when the *whole* person ("willing to be itself"—non-bifurcated) grounds itself transparently in that Power which posits itself—the relationship—does it become spirit.⁴⁸ When it becomes spirit, it relates absolutely (holistically) to the Absolute.⁴⁹ Moreover, this dynamic self-folded in on itself produces the "I/self" or "I/me" living synthesis in motion (e-motion). Therefore, the constituting of the self happens within a tripartite dynamic structure by relating to the Other.⁵⁰ Only through relating as spirit to that Power that posits the relationship does the person analogically constitute in relation to the Eternal and the infinite, thereby in freedom with limitless possibilities. Evans argues that this "Power" is the divine action of God as Person in relation to the individual through Christ, which constitutes the individual as person.⁵¹ In a more inclusive structuring, this thesis will argue that the Power is not specifically (with Evans or Loder) "through Christ," but rather a dynamic reflective within and between us by God's trinitarian relationship to humanity's tripartite aspects respectively. This entails the presence of Christ, the Spirit, and the Father beyond them relating directly with those respective aspects within humanity. Within the development of this thesis, humanity's divine contingency is simply the product of being uniquely *related* to by the divine. By

---

47. Kierkegaard, *SUD*, 147. The noun "Power" by Climacus or Kierkegaard is typically understood as indirect reference to Christ. Within this thesis, however, I wish to argue that Kierkegaard knew that this constituting force within relations was potentially far more complex than simply attributing this action to Christ alone, but rather a complementarity of action between Christ and the Spirit.

48. Loder, *KM*, 250.

49. Kierkegaard, *CUP*, 347.

50. The term "Other" will here refer to both God and the wholeness or spirit of other persons. The obvious allusion to Emmanuel Lévinas is intentional. The quality of our receptiveness (gaze) into "what cannot become a content, which [our] thought would embrace" establishes the significance of the Other; "it is uncontainable, it leads [us] beyond" (Lévinas, *Ethics*, 86). "The face is signification, and signification without context, . . . the meaning of something [in the usual sense] is in its relation to another thing. Here, to the contrary, the face is meaning all by itself" (86). This *prima facia* seems contrary to a relational hermeneutic and constitution of social person. However, Lévinas is simply describing this essential human factor that is identifiable in Loder and Kierkegaard's relational logic of human spirit as perichoretic (a relationship unto itself, or the "Christ within us"); see Loder, *KM*; Kierkegaard, *SUD*. The unitive ground of the emerging third term (the relationship itself), which both mediates and constitutes the self and the other in relationship and is infinitely capable, is perichoretically reflective within God's trinitarian relationship to humanity in Christ. Though Lévinas would refuse the ideas of Trinity, *perichoresis*, and Christ, this infinite mediational factor within the relational structures of all human beings is that same quality or dynamic Lévinas observes within the face as the Other.

51. Evans, "Unconscious," 83.

nature of Christ's Incarnation (and the dialogical structuring of incarnation, crucifixion, and resurrection), all cosmic relations subsist in reflecting this divine dynamic of *perichoresis* at some level. These dynamics contingently reflecting within cosmic relations transcend the focal consciousness of their trinitarian source by nature (and definition) of their holistic and perichoretic properties. Because God's relatedness to the cosmos is personal (i.e., God experiencing the world through Christ), humanity's relatedness takes on a personal (filial) nature within its relatedness to the extent humanity gives itself fully to be affected by genuine relations with the Other (i.e., passionately).

Human existence is a *kinetic* constitution of the temporal and eternal. For Kierkegaard, the Eternal has dialogically come into time in the midst of the relationship between us (through spirit); truth is a potentiality that emerges between us relative to each specific relational occurrence (Religiousness A). Therefore, any abstracting of knowledge (speculation) into time-less inflated truths outside the *kinetic* constitution of the existing occurrence is, always has been, and will be technically empty. Truth is never a template one applies over reality, rather something that emerges uniquely within the integrity of each relational moment (dialogical cycle). Within these cycles, as Kierkegaard argues, the degree a person ventures everything is the degree they become full person-in-relation and constitute in the truth. Heidegger here speaks of an always-necessary freedom of truth as "*a relationship of open resolve* and not one locked up within itself."[52] In this respect, when the *whole* self becomes transparently grounded by the constituting Power within the relationship, its knowledge becomes analogous to the eternal truth. As we shall see later, these enigmatic poles (time and eternity) within the paradox reflect two poles or cycles of dialogical interaction, two aspects of life that dynamically (never materially or universally) synthesize within existence (in motion).

This holistic notion of person as spirit will often present a reoccurring difficulty for many readers. From this point forward, spirit will *never* mean something divisible from any aspect of the person (the soul or the body), unlike the common Platonist's (dualistic) renderings of an embodied spirit. Without a body, there is no human spirit, and the body is to be considered part of human spirit. When spirit is given to create life (or more to the point, perichoretically reflects within the creature and materiality), it represents a complementarity under the supervenient operating center of the creature, of which consciousness is only a part. The soul, as such, is not yet spirit. The soul and the body are drawn up into personal spirit when in relationship to

---

52. Heidegger, *Existence and Being*, 314.

Jacob and the Night of Faith

the Other (producing the "I"-in-relation to self or others). Within it resides the soul, the body, the relative, and the whirlwind of the absolute (its whole-centeredness) that is human spirit. The social dimension of human spirit is commensurate with Bonhoeffer's insistence that "human spirit in its entirety is woven into sociality and rests on the basic-relation of I and You."[53]

However, the holistic aspect of the "I" as an absolute relating to the absolute of the Other is beyond image. Though it includes (reflects) the entire person, this transparent spiritual encounter is antecedent to its cognitive reflexive response as self or "I"-in-relational-movement-to (or with)-another. In a strange sense, the first aspect of encounter with another is transparent—a seemingly invisible being encountering the invisible being of another (or as Marion might suggest, "saturation"). Image immediately follows. Though this transparent "being" is generally understood as the Kantian noumena (the world-in-itself, out there), a relational ontology initiates from the relationship (spirit) first, not "being." In one sense, spirit as relationship bridges the ontological divide of noumena and phenomena (a Hellenistic construct) by perichoretically *creating* (mediating) reality *within* all relations, respectively. In effect, *perichoresis* creates a personal or relational backdoor into the noumena, or more radically to the point, there is no noumena or phenomena, it is created (and re-created) again and again within each *moment* of "I"-in-relation-to-another. This is not idealism, and there is no realism—a world "out there." This is a world sustained through Christ within a perichoretic ontology because "God so loved the world." It is a world so connected to consciousness that the "ideal" and the "real" simply become false dichotomies in a much richer and more complex set of contingencies. They are antiquated props of a necessary stage along the way of redemption (1 Cor 15:20–49; 2 Cor 3:18). When the wind of God blew across the cosmos, and God breathed upon all life and filially into humanity, the wormhole of dominion—co-creation—set creation on an inverted trajectory of design as Christ, and with him all that was becoming genuinely human, became spirit. Each becoming spirit according to its own kind.

Antecedent to reflexive response within human beings, *analogia spiritus* analogically relates (trans-lates) the "noumena" of the Other and the self holistically within each participant. Optimally, a holistic shared meaning then rises through each person's unique meaning-frame so that *the uniqueness of each person* experiences the same shared meaning. In fully redeemed humanity there is no remainder. When appropriate, the meaning-frame of each open participant may undergo a transformation that enriches themself and/or the Other without loss of identity. In this respect, authentic relations

---

53. Bonhoeffer, *Sanctorum Communio*, 73.

become a matter of justice and grace rather than Hellenistic correspondence and representation of what is "out there."

Therefore, "what is spirit?" "The individual becomes infinite [spirit] only by virtue of making the absolute venture,"[54] by "venturing everything"[55] fully into relationship; and to that degree, one will "perceive analogies in the realm of the spirit."[56] For Kierkegaard, to venture everything means to relate absolutely to that which is Absolute (spirit to Spirit), and therefore, genuine selfhood requires the always incomplete but maturing process of becoming conscious of God. Even though God constitutes human being a relation (in God's likeness), God releases human beings in freedom,[57] and therefore, as Evans suggests:

> The problem comes into being when the adult lacks a God-relationship and thus gives to the relations with other human selves (and with what is less than human) a priority and ultimacy such relations do not deserve. I am not here talking merely about a case of "arrested development," a case in which an individual does not discover God and fails to grow, but the case in which the individual chooses not to grow by suppressing the knowledge of God.[58]

It is not the conceptual level of the knowledge of God that is of specific concern here, but the *disposition* of openness the individual exhibits toward the possible acquisition of such knowledge might it be true. Such a disposition characterizes Kierkegaard's notion of venturing all.

Therefore, for Kierkegaard, spirit is irreducibly the self-constituted-*as-whole-self* in relation to the Other, just as the analogy of spirits is self-constituting-*as-whole-self* while in holistic relation to the Other-constituting-as-*whole-self*. This holistic interaction happens prereflexively in undifferentiated interaction asymmetrically prior to yet inclusive of all relevant relative aspects within the integration before our reflexive response. This is the Jacobian night, the analogical co-conditioning interaction between Eternity and the person as spirit within the Kierkegaardian *moment*.

---

54. Kierkegaard, *CUP*, 379.
55. Kierkegaard, *CUP*, 382.
56. Kierkegaard, *CUP*, 379.
57. Kierkegaard, *SUD*, 149.
58. Evans, "Unconscious," 84. Cf. also, Bonhoeffer: "For Christian philosophy the human person originates only in relation to the divine; the divine person transcends the human person, who both resists and is overwhelmed by the divine" (*Sanctorum Communio*, 49).

This sudden dynamic *moment* conditions the relative aspects that emerge uniquely within reflexive consciousness.

Therefore, spirit is the dynamic totality of the self-in-relation, and spirit is the dynamic social totality that emerges from all open relationships. To be explained in detail later: relational responses in which any relevant aspects of oneself are personally closed-off from being affected or transformed by genuine relations from the Other, fragments the individual and to that degree inhibits them from becoming spirit absolutely (e.g., hiding parts of the self to self, various forms of denial, and unwillingness to open to truth or reality). As Kierkegaard states in one of his titles, *Purity of Heart is to Will One Thing*. By this, he means, (1) a person "must in truth will the good, ... be willing to do all for it [and] ... willing to suffer all for it," as well as (2) "live as an 'individual.' ... For he who is not himself a unity is never really anything wholly and decisively."[59] This is authentic relation, auth-entic (self-being). *Authentic relation happens when two or more relate with their whole being.* Until we better understand and develop the notion of spirit—the holistic dynamic of perichoretic relationality—we will be hard pressed to emerge from the historically alternating swings between Parmenides's whole (Plato) and Heraclitus's parts (Aristotle), which typify our Western (Greek) heritage. Note that perichoretic dynamics are active for Johannes Climacus and Anti-Climacus. In the former (Johannes, Religiousness A), a person experiences *analogia spiritus* as a prereflexive "blind-spot" within relational dialectics before constituting in time and relationship. For the latter (Anti, Religiousness B), *perichoresis* becomes a living dynamic through which optimally the person constitutes personally in Christ's Time, moving together transparently with Christ as the Eternal begins to flow within his Time.

Perichoresis

Up to this point, the relational concept of *perichoresis* has been announced, teased, and vaguely articulated. To the uninitiated, it is a mystery, largely still unclear. For many theologians familiar with the term, its use here is already falling beyond its orthodox use. Proffering *perichoresis* as an ontological replacement for millennia of Greek dialectics seems over-ambitious, makes no sense, and academically insane. I make no claim otherwise. Such an ontological shift and exploration in today's established theological landscape will make no sense. The meaning-frame of both Paul and Jesus were heavily framed within a Hebraic ontology and linguistic structuring, secondarily Hellenistic. Therefore, the meaning of various scriptural passages

---

59. Kierkegaard, *PH*, 122, 184.

is often diminished, forced, and meaningless within a Hellenistic meaning-frame. Nevertheless, what Jesus and Paul were attempting to communicate transcends both Hellenistic or Hebraic ontologies and forecasts a new and expanding understanding of the world, relationships, humanity, and God.

Humanity is only in its awakening stages of becoming fully Christ-like. The dynamics of *perichoresis* and *analogia spiritus* are steadily coming into their potential ontological significance. It is challenging to proffer an ontological dynamic of which we experience so little because of its distortion within humanity and the relatively diminished level of faith currently struggling for expression within the church. If suggesting that the church experiences little faith, and that we are just beginning to scratch the surface of love's fullness offends the reader, then let the offense stand. Kierkegaard's critique of Christendom stands to this day. Few (in the affluent and entitled West) are willing to engage the suffering, shame, and void necessary to attain the level of faith witnessed by the heroes of the Scriptures, me included. Look not for *perichoresis* or *analogia spiritus* to necessarily make sense of your world at large; look for it in the interstices of life's most meaningful and passionate moments, in the mysteries and wonder we occasionally experience in special moments with each other, the world, or God. It is a relatively unnoticeable dynamic slowly manifesting itself within the interstices of cosmic relations, steadily transforming the world.[60] And so it is we must

---

60. This is because: (1) *perichoresis* is distorted, and (2) as Wittgenstein suggests, we are swimming in it. Like water to a fish, or air to humanity, we are too close to it, and like all ontological dynamics, it become transparent.

Bonhoeffer refuses to theologically deny these passages that highlight the continuing earthly transformations that disappear before his Reformed theological associates: (the epigraph warrants restating) "The transformation in the divine image will become *ever more profound*, and the image of Christ in us will *continue to increase in clarity*. This is a progression in us from one level of understanding to another and from one degree of clarity to another, toward an ever-increasing perfection in the form of likeness to the image of the Son of God" (Bonhoeffer, *Discipleship*, 286, emphasis added).

In the church's accepted and often encouraged theological and spiritual stasis, we must ask, what is it that Paul said is transforming within ourselves? The world is evolving and transforming. "Now the Lord is the Spirit; and where the Spirit of the Lord is, there is liberty. But we all, with unveiled face, beholding as in a mirror the glory of the Lord, are being transformed into the same image *from one degree to another*, just as by the Spirit of the Lord" (2 Cor 3:17-18, emphasis added). What is transforming throughout history? "But now Christ is risen from the dead and has become the first fruits of those who have fallen asleep.... For he must reign till He has put all enemies under His feet. The last enemy that will be destroyed [along with "all rule and all authority and power"] is death.... that God may be all in all" (1 Cor 15:20-28). This speaks undeniably about the history of the world! "But this Man, after He had offered one sacrifice for sins forever, sat down at the right hand of God, from that time *waiting* till His enemies are made His footstool. For by one offering He has perfected forever those who are *being* sanctified" (Heb 10:12-14). Note well the active (not past tense)

explore the moments of wonder within our lives. This is the Jacobian ladder to God, the rock upon which true community must grow.

For the Cappadocians and John Damascene, *perichoresis* meant "mutual interpenetration or eternal circulation of divine life" amongst the persons of the Trinity.[61] It was John Damascene "who first used *perichoresis* as a technical term in trinitarian theology," and placed it "on a level with the unity of the divine nature as the ground of divine unity."[62] Etymologically the term contains *peri*, meaning "around" and "at all points," and *choreo* meaning "to proceed," "to make room," and even "to dance." Similarly, concerning the Latin use (*circumincessio*), Loder presents what, for this thesis, will be a provisional preliminary understanding of this dynamic: "that among the persons there is mutual interpenetration at all points *without loss of identity*. Individuality and mutuality are simultaneously affirmed, and the members of the Trinity can change places without changing their identity."[63] The original understanding of *perichoresis* emphasizes a spiritual activity of interpenetration and indwelling. This thesis redefines the notion of shared "indwelling," equally emphasizing the intensifying of each participant's individuality. The common understanding of "indwelling" leads to an over-simplified construct that limits our understanding of *perichoresis*. Alternatively, Loder, Gunton, and Kierkegaard consider *perichoresis* an irreducible dynamic that the first two refer to as interpenetration, but what this thesis will refer to as a holistic mutual co-conditioning of shared meaning and synchronized action *mediated through the third term of the relationship*. Therefore, this thesis will explore many more potential characteristics of *perichoresis* than the initial and preliminary use and understanding of the church fathers or recent scholarship. They simply lacked the language, developed concepts, forms of life, and heuristics available today. The relational dynamics of *perichoresis* are not something we simply attribute to God's Spirit alone. If indeed, we are exploring the possibility of *perichoresis* as the very nature of the godhead and, therefore an ontological dynamic that ultimately sustains all creation, and if God's Spirit, as St. Augustine conjectures, is the love and relationship shared between the Father and the Son, then we need to consider that this ontological structuring might ultimately and analogically reflect throughout the persons of the Trinity and from there

---

predicates. As stated in the chapter's epigraph, the final goal is that humanity would relate with each other *as* Christ relates to the Father, *in order that* humankind might relate with them (John 17:21). This is the *historical unfolding* of what the church fathers referred to as *theosis*, what this thesis further clarifies as "relational *theosis*."

61. Badcock, *Light*, 240.
62. Badcock, *Light*, 240–41.
63. Loder, *KM*, 23.

into all creation accordingly. The Spirit mediating the relationship between the Father and the Son would necessarily then become person (each according to their respective character), no less than the other two due to the transforming effect through its relationship to the others. In this respect, as Loder argues, "the unity of the Trinity *is* the relationality, and the relationality *is* the unity."[64] Therefore, we cannot define *perichoresis* as the sole action of the Spirit, one person of the Trinity, but is itself an ontological dynamic characterizing the relationship and personhood throughout, that which can indeed be called the *nature* of God. As such, we can consider the technical term *perichoresis* is love.

This is where Hegel errs. Unlike Kierkegaard, his thinking was circumscribed by antiquated linguistic limitations and undeveloped categories (chapter 5A). Human spirit became a borrowed extension of God's Spirit, which eventually led to a pantheism and ultimately to social constructs of inseparable collectives. With Loder, Gunton, and Kierkegaard, *perichoresis* maintains the autonomy of personhood (human and divine) while facilitating shared meaning and co-conditioning relations. Therefore, within human beings, self emerges as a relationship unto itself, and then again by relation to the Other becomes spirit and attains full personhood. This is the image of God—the image *reflecting* within humanity because God uniquely relates to them (John 17:21; 2 Cor 3:18); therefore, preeminent within such a dynamic is a creating mutuality (oneness) while sustaining disparate beings (e.g., male and female; Gen 1:27).

The irreducible dynamic of *perichoresis* as a relational ontology is nonsense within the Cartesian meaning-frame. If it begins to make sense within the Cartesian paradigm, then this thesis is failing to communicate the true nature of *perichoresis*. *Perichoresis* creates alternative notions of causation compared to Hellenistic (and Modern) ontologies, expanding the idea of causation to nonlocal and transtemporal interactions. Ultimately, Loder suggests, perichoretic dynamics are inherent to some degree in all cosmic relations and reflectively become the ontological dynamics creating and sustaining all creation. Moreover, Jürgen Moltmann, in two pivotal works, explores the temporal and spatial qualities within the divine nature of *perichoresis*.[65] Colin Gunton has noted:

---

64. Loder, *KM*, 23.

65. Moltmann, *TKG* and *GC*. The temporal perichoretic dynamic within the Trinity is by far the most challenging application of *perichoresis* to grasp. Failure to do so is the single most crucial factor in understanding Moltmann's theology, as well as transforming our concept of causality (correcting Newtonian linear concepts of time and container concepts of space). We will explore these alternative notions of causality in a later chapter on the *perichoresis* of time and eternity and the quantum enigma. This

> Because it has long been taught that to be human is to to [sic] be created in the image of God, the idea that human beings should in some way be perichoretic beings is not a difficult one to envisage. The sad truth is, however, that the notion has rarely been taken seriously, . . . the individualist teaches that we are what we are in separation from our neighbour, the collectivist that we are so involved with others in society that we lose particularity.[66]

Furthermore, Moltmann suggests that "*perichoresis* is not just something existing between like and like in the divine Trinity: it also exists between the unlike natures of God and human beings."[67] Herein lies the difficulty in understanding *perichoresis* more fully. If one drags the concept back into a Greek metaphysical orientation or even Reformed thought, it will not make total theological or anthropological sense. The irreducible dynamic and existential tension to which Gunton points in *perichoresis* is an entirely new and expanding metaphysical paradigm with altogether different notions of relationality. For this reason, theologians like Randall Otto and Kevin Vanhoozer struggle to understand the complete nature of *perichoresis*.[68] Such

---

will offer new ways of understanding the role and effect of the Eternal within divine and human experience.

66. Gunton, *One, Three, Many*, 168–69.

67. Moltmann, "World," 39.

68. We see this in Vanhoozer's critique of *perichoresis*: "To suggest that God is in perichoretic relationship with the world is to imply that the world is in some sense constitutive of the divine identity" (*Remythologizing*, 151). Here he is responding to the alternative claims of Clayton's panentheistic proclivities and has pulled the concept of identity back into its meaning-frame within classical relational dynamics, and the typical understanding of *perichoresis* in its unifying dynamics without the later development and emphasis of the intensification of personhood—a differentiated unity. *Perichoresis* emphatically *maintains* and keeps distinct the identity and personhood of each relating member, divine as divine, and human as human, each distinct unto itself. Vanhoozer concludes, "This approach views God as entering into perichoretic relation with the world by virtue of creating it (i.e., making space inside himself for it)" (157). However, in the most developed understanding of *perichoresis*, there is no "indwelling" or being "inside" another. "Indwelling" was the closest concept within a classical linguistic framework of subject-subject relationality through which one could provisionally communicate a limited understanding and application of *perichoresis*. In Vanhoozer's deconstructive or inverted citation of Clayton, he argues against the simultaneous deliberation (co-conditioning) of divine and human will within *perichoresis*: "One shares in the 'mind of Christ' by imitating his example. . . . This is a moral rather than a mystical or covenantal union: to be 'in Christ' . . . means to subordinate one's own will to the will of the divine" (156). At this point, both Vanhoozer and Clayton fail to understand *perichoresis* within its fuller metaphysical sounding, and neither understand the immense importance of Jacob regarding faith and the divine-human interaction of *analogia spiritus*. The experience of faith in Jacob reveals, no, it boldly announces, the anatomy of *perichoresis* and *analogia spiritus*. In company with most

misconceptions are understandable within paradigm shifts; it is difficult for many to maintain these metaphysical distinctions and new logic without pulling us back into Hellenistic renderings. Even proponents of *perichoresis* find it challenging to maintain these distinctions throughout our theological articulations. No doubt, this thesis will struggle with this same difficulty. After all, it is an *emerging* concept.

Significantly, Gunton's challenge has become the primary anthropological goal of the study—that humans are what they "are in perichoretic reciprocity."[69] In this respect, this thesis advances an anthropological theology, which argues that *much of the traditional polemics in theology, specifically the concept of God, result from underdeveloped anthropological considerations*. A renewed look at the constitutive nature of human persons as perichoretic, informed by various developments within contemporary thought, provides alternative structures for understanding the divine-human interaction. As stated earlier, it lays the foundations for solving age-old theological problems like divine providence, human freedom, and theodicy. It also enables us to consider the feasibility and logic of a God who does not know the future before it happens, as well as humans in time able to contextually portend the future (prophecy) and proleptically and *ontologically* experience in some way the *reality* of events yet unfulfilled—faith (Heb 11:1).

Some of Kierkegaard's friends, specifically Johannes Climacus, point to an infinite qualitative difference (IQD) between God and humanity, which is "paradoxically" brought together in the God-man—a philosophical rendering in accordance with Hellenistic metaphysics. Alternatively, Kierkegaard, indirectly ornaments everything he edits (writes) with signs and dynamics suggesting the corollary of an incarnational imperative of mutuality (IIM). Meaning, if there is to be filial relations, something of God must become human, and something of humanity must become divine. As we have just considered, because of Christ, humanity is given the potential to become fully spirit (differentiated) by that Power that creates all relations, which provides human persons with the possibility of relating "absolutely with the Absolute"—*analogia spiritus*. The Editor always tasks us with completing the meaning. Kierkegaard's true IQD is not between Hellenized renderings of God and humanity, the Incarnation of Jesus Christ forever transforms this divide. His abhorrence remains with Hegel's material synthesis of the

---

theologians, they miss the primary meaning of Jacob and the night of faith. Therefore, in theological denial, Jacob remains a skeleton in their closet.

69. Gunton, *One, Three, Many*, 170. Gunton argues that "there is no true freedom which does not also allow for the fact that we are passive as well as active in relation to others and the world," and that human beings are a perichoretic synthesis of both "dimensions": the social (active) and the individual (passive).

temporal and Eternal, the finite and the infinite (the subject of chapter 5A). The perichoretic nature of human relations vitiates everything Kierkegaard edits.

Perichoresis is always tripartite in nature, as suggested by James Loder's use of Kierkegaard. For Kierkegaard, says Loder, "mutuality becomes a positive third term, not obliterating but intensifying the polarities"; furthermore, "the reality of mutuality becomes self-conscious, or aware of itself as such." Similarly, Bonhoeffer tells us:

> Two wills encountering one another form a structure. A third person joining them sees not just one person connected to the other; rather, the will of the structure, as a third factor, resists the newcomer with a resistance not identical with the wills of the two individuals. Sometimes this is even more powerful than that of either individual—or than the sum of all the individuals, if this is at all conceivable. Precisely this structure is objective spirit.[70]

For Bonhoeffer, "objective spirit" is the emergent social structure of community, a tangible shape of a social relationality bathing language with living meaning, as if it was an emergent living entity itself.

This idea leads to Kierkegaard's insistence on human participation in the divine ground, and what this thesis characterizes as mutual co-conditioning. Therefore, though perichoretic dynamics are only completely realized within the godhead, it reflects structurally at every level of human existence, though usually distorted by sin (more on sin later). Thus, optimally, perichoretic relations create the same correlative meaning in each (open) participant through the mediating *third term* of the emergent relationship. It holistically conditions mutual meaning within the unique meaning-frame of each participant in order to attain *mutuality in difference*. One might think of the emerging spirit or Spirit as the translator, or better yet, the creator of meaning between various meaning-frames. This often necessitates that one or more of the participants undergo degrees of transformation within their meaning-frame. However, no participants transform beyond their ability to maintain a contiguous identity. That is why our transformations happen from one degree to another (2 Cor 3:18) rather than all at once.

In *perichoresis*, the whole of the relationship by which the participants co-constitute becomes greater than the sum of its constituent parts. This vital concept must not be confused with theories like Joseph Bracken's social elevation of the metaphysical reality of community over the sum

---

70. Bonhoeffer, *Sanctorum Communio*, 98.

of its constituent persons.[71] Because it takes place by virtue of that Power (trinitarian action) that dynamically constitutes it, more can emerge (be created) than what is technically within the parts or the sum of the existing parts.[72] Though it is reflective of the source of the relationship and the fullness each person experiences from it, it never coerces the spirits of the participants. On the contrary, Gunton tells us that *perichoresis* "particularizes the *hypostases*" of the constituent parts of the relationship, sustaining "their own distinct and particular existence, *by virtue of and not in face of their relationality* to the other."[73] It facilitates the appropriate interanimation of meaning while, for the most part, conterminously sustaining the distinctive personality and meaning-frame of each person. However, if persons openly and passionately engage the Other, their knowing and meaning-frame may expand or transform by virtue of the third term of the relationship. The unfolding of creation happens *within* relationship itself, and from the *moment between* each dialogical cycling comes possibility and freedom in the form of new creation.[74]

The perichoretic dynamic as a human function within language is apparent in Philip Hefner's recent linguistic and hermeneutical defense of employing terms of one genre within another. He contends:

> It is widely acknowledged that when terms do cross boundaries, meanings are transferred from the first area of usage to the new one.... What is not so readily acknowledged, it seems, is that when a term crosses boundaries new meanings are contributed from the second realm. It is the *interaction* of all the meanings that the term can encompass that provides insight.... The term is given a new

---

71. Bracken, *Triune*, 7. This is a process notion that ultimately employs the Hegelian dynamic of Absolute Spirit (shared spirit).

72. Cf. Bonhoeffer, "*The person is willed by God, in concrete vitality, wholeness, and uniqueness as an ultimate unity. Social relations must be understood, then, as purely interpersonal and building on the uniqueness and separateness of persons. The person cannot be overcome by apersonal spirit; no 'unity' can negate the plurality of persons. The social basic category is the I-You relation. The You of the other person is the divine You. Thus the way to the other person's You is the same as the way to the divine You, either through acknowledgment or rejection. The individual becomes a person ever and again through the other, in the moment.* The other person presents us with the same challenge to our knowing as does God" (*Sanctorum Communio*, 55-56).

73. Gunton, *One, Three, Many*, 190, 194.

74. Bonhoeffer: "*The person ever and again arises and passes away in time....* the person is re-created again and again in the perpetual flux of life" (*Sanctorum Communio*, 48).

currency and usefulness that is identical with none of the [previous] specific usages, even though it encompasses all of them.[75]

This hermeneutical and transformative phenomenon, the dynamic that empowers metaphor, transparently occurs within the Jacobian night and empowers perichoretic relations. Not only in such interdisciplinary correlations does new meaning greater than that of any of the previous meanings emerge, but this dynamic instantly transforms and enriches the original meaning of the term in the original, affecting genre! Furthermore, we should note that the *interrelatedness* of the contributing genres is likewise enhanced by each genre's new and specific enhancement. As the web of interrelations grows, our immediate and holistic experience deepens (intensifies).[76] As we increasingly correlate various linguistic elements through ongoing relational interaction, greater *intimacy* and *fullness of life* perichoretically/evolutionally emerge. Again, one of the goals of this study is to illustrate and locate this irreducible dynamic within human relations and consciousness.

Within this thesis, the dynamic of *perichoresis* is synonymous with the Christian understanding of *agape*, and informs our understanding of love. Jean-Luc Marion in *God without Being* argues that love is the fundamental nature of God, as well as human meaning. Not only does *perichoresis* concentrically relate with love, it is the primordial site of all desire and longing. This short introduction should provide the reader with a preliminary understanding of *perichoresis* and its proposed development within this thesis. The concept of *perichoresis* will steadily expand and deepen as we explore various interdisciplinary reflections of *perichoresis*.

---

75. Hefner, "Sociobiology," 123–24, emphasis added. He supplies an example in the term *evolution*: "it appears in four phrases: 'cosmic evolution,' 'biological evolution,' 'evolution of the individual from conception to death,' and 'cultural evolution'" (124). "It is clear that the processes, as well as their mechanisms, are not the same in these four domains. Insight occurs at the point when we ask how the four uses of the term *evolution* are related and whether there is some important sense in which they constitute one wholistic process. What happens in that moment of insight is that a new valorization of the term *evolution* takes place. . . . There is no reason why the lower meanings should suppress the higher. Rather, the various meanings are conjoined" (124), and each specific use becomes perichoretically enriched.

76. Referring to the last note: there is little doubt that the original meaning of "evolution" within its original nineteenth-century biological use pales in comparison to the fullness of its biological use today.

Integration of Disciplines

This study will attempt to maintain a working conceptual integration of various forms of thought and disciplines. As mentioned, integrative efforts working toward and within an alternative metaphysical paradigm necessitate the stretching and ultimately the transformation of existing language.[77] Therefore, every attempt will be made to employ concepts like *perichoresis*, differentiated unity, and *analogia spiritus* appropriately and sensitively throughout the spectrum of disciplines. The goal of such an effort is to expand the understanding of current dynamics within these various disciplines and, more to point, apply any new heuristics for exploring new meaning within these theological terms and concepts. Nevertheless, within my existing knowledge of these disciplines, I try to transition the reader as effectively as possible within the limited space given. In this respect, I beg the reader's patience and indulgence in dragging them relentlessly through the depths of multiple disciplines, which inevitably lie outside the critical view of any person, including this author. The purpose of such interdisciplinary engagement is to reveal *perichoresis* as an emerging metaphysical dynamic that permeates and inevitably mediates all cosmic interactions. Again, this thesis was not born by looking at the world through a theologically perichoretic lens but from first seeing similar ontological dynamics emerging within disparate disciplines of research and *then* learning about the similarly structured theological term and dynamic of *perichoresis*.

Analogia Spiritus: The Invisible Dance of Spirits

> The Spirit Himself bears witness with our spirit, . . . [making] intercession for us with groanings which cannot be uttered. (Rom 8:16, 26)

How do we account for historical and personal continuity when it is becoming increasingly clear that the structure of transformation within the

---

77. Cf. Hefner, "Sociobiology," 123–24; Ricoeur, *Symbolism*, 347–57. Hefner, in response to criticisms about his unhealthy "terminological hygiene . . . using terms or referring to concepts with meanings other than those under which they are commonly understood in ordinary parlance," argues: "Unfortunately, it is impossible to abide by [these] injunctions, and in some ways even foolish to attempt to. Words and concepts are always stretching themselves beyond what common parlance understands, and they are always crossing boundaries from one domain to another—even to areas in which they are said not to belong. . . . When words assume symbolic and mythic status, seeking to relate concrete empirical data to large and primal realities, they defy the efforts of most linguistic sanitary engineers" (123).

human organism and society is holistic? Unlike the concept of change, transformation necessitates a change of the whole structure in which nothing stays the same,[78] which begs the question, what then facilitates and mediates transformation, especially in human beings with some level of self-determination? This brings us to the essential concept within this thesis, *analogia spiritus*.

Our knowledge of the Holy Spirit, *Creator Spiritus*, and even the generic notion of spirit are notably the most diverse and unsettled concepts in theological discourse. Until this necessary dimension of theology begins to take a more coherent and eminent placement within our theories of reality and understanding of relationship, theology will continue to flounder (especially in a pluralistic age). This study follows in the wake of the twentieth century's surmounting literature that critically engages the idea of spirit. Because of the unique nature of spirit, it is not only highly conceivable but probable that such overlapping interdisciplinary investigations will ultimately guide us to groundbreaking insights and clues to a more coherent understanding of spirit. Moreover, greater theological and scriptural coherence will ultimately confirm the success of these insights.

Spirit, within this study (divine or human), will refer to the central organizing principal (and principle) of person, community, or society of which consciousness is only the top of the iceberg. Spirit *opens* and *organizes* the constituting process of the whole of that psychic and bodily organism, and likewise within all social and relational interactions.[79] With God, the Spirit that emanates from (as) the relationship between the Father and Son becomes the dynamic *process* of awareness and holistic presence through which God *wholly* constitutes within God's trinitarian relation and with creation. Similarly, human beings constitute as person-in-relation to the Other through an analogically similar *process* of awareness and holistic presence.

Recent developments in quantum physics also indicate the necessity of a relational ontology that undergirds all cosmic reality. Recent experiments[80] suggest that consciousness, which emerges from relationship, constitutes quantum reality out of quantum wave function potentiality. So, it seems, whether it be divine, human, or cosmic consciousness, reality is

---

78. Cf. Aristotle's *Politics*, 1.1260B, "The virtue of a part must be determined by looking at the virtue of a whole."

79. For example, in a trinitarian/perichoretic manner, Christ, more than likely, defines the notion of body reflected throughout the godhead, respective to the character of each person of the Trinity, even though the notion of body in the Spirit and the Father remains speculative. Cf. Gunton, *One, Three, Many*, for a slightly different approach to the particularizing function of spirit.

80. See, e.g., the Delayed Choice Quantum Eraser experiment.

contingent upon relation to some form of consciousness. This scientific evidence suggests that antecedent holistic dynamics within quantum reality display similar characteristics that parallel the phenomena of *analogia spiritus* within *perichoresis*. Both contain *transtemporal dynamics*, while non-quantum theories in physics and non-perichoretic ontologies in theology are at a loss to explain or integrate the emerging data within their respective fields. We will explore this further in a section on quantum dynamics and *perichoresis*.

Similarly, as we have noted, Steven Smith's work advocates spirit as first philosophy and gives spirit asymmetrical priority over word in all interactions.[81] Iain McGilchrist's comprehensive survey on hemispherical dynamics in neurology also points to the holistic activity of the right hemisphere as the mechanism of first contact between persons and the outside world before that of the "word" orienting left hemisphere.[82] More on these later.

The notion of *analogia spiritus* within this thesis refers to *the process that constitutes whole persons in analogical relation to the whole of the Other*. Again, the whole person as spirit is not the soul or the mind but includes these and the body. It is a unifying process and state of becoming which cannot be reduced to or materially limited to the reflexive or cognitive response but lies antecedent, around, and beyond these components. Inclusive of these components of self, the "I" emerges in relationship. Descriptively, in divine-human relations, *analogia spiritus* happens in the prereflexive transparent Jacobian *moment* within dialogical interchange, an infinite *moment* (of openness), for example, processing the interaction between the whole presence of God and that of the individual just before response (closure, cognition, gestalt). There are fundamental distinctions between this constituting dynamic in the divine and the human. Human processing fundamentally constitutes in an eternalized temporal relatedness, while God (the Father) constitutes within the Trinity and, therefore, in a temporalized Eternal relatedness.

Because God's personhood constitutes in perfect perichoretic relationship with the Eternal (regardless of person), when God's *whole* being analogically relates to the *whole* being of human persons, the antecedent co-conditioning of *analogia spiritus* (Absolute relating to absolute) happen before image and therefore condition image response. The forthcoming chapters on emotions and the bicameral brain will locate this dynamic anthropologically. This precognitive dynamic potentially informs and constitutes human spirit in analogical relation to the Eternal. In its potentiality it

81. Smith, *Concept of the Spiritual*.
82. McGilchrist, *Master*, Part One.

Jacob and the Night of Faith

ultimately provides the mutual co-conditioning of God's Eternality within the processing of human gestalt into cognition. Within *analogia spiritus* (the Kierkegaardian *moment*)—the gaze of awareness just before gestalt— all that we are and desire potentially affect the creative *moment* within each interaction. To the degree we are fully open to the Other, the relationship is drawn into relation with this trinitarian action of God (in Christ). Through this sustaining trinitarian activity of creation, all such *moments* within the history of humanity become affectively present to all other *moments* holistically through the Spirit, in *analogia spiritus*. They then constitute into each respective gestalt in Time by Christ through whom "all things hold together" and "are created" (Col 1:16–17). The creating action is not principally our own; however, as shown in the story and actions of Jacob, the process of *analogia spiritus* effectively draws the person's existential concerns, longings, and desires into analogical co-conditioning with the Eternal deliberation of God antecedent to (i.e., before the sun rises) God's act of creation and our gestalt into time. All this processing and eventual gestalt happen transparently within a Kierkegaardian *moment*, in the blink of an eye. Moltmann argues:

> Because God's creative activity has no analogy, it is also unimaginable. The divine act of creation is never described in differentiated terms. Nor is it dissected into a number of different processes. It is unified and unique. This means among other things that time is excluded from the act of creation, for time always requires duration, and creation takes place *suddenly*, as it were—in a *moment*.[83]

The spirit of redeemed humanity, in prereflexive analogical relation to this divine action (passion), becomes a co-conditioning participant forwarding its own passionate longings and faith desires affecting the divine act of creation, as illustrated in the story of Jacob's passionate encounters in the night. Only in this manner and to this degree do human beings become co-creators.

Again, because *analogia spiritus* is a holistic experience, humans likewise experience it in an undifferentiated manner—during the *gaze* of awareness (openness). It is most noticeable within and specifically at the end of our prereflexive gaze just before we transition to understanding (gestalt). Within healthy interaction, both speaker *and* listener amazingly experience this same unitive *moment* (and shared meaning) at the same time from both sides of constantly rotating dialogical cycles. It arises whenever two or more people intend each other in open co-awareness; this instantly creates a

---

83. Moltmann, *GC*, 73, emphasis added.

unifying relational *field*, no less independently alive than themselves, upon which all participants within the interaction create and share meaning. This medium of shared relationship is the emergent third term of the spirit between them. That Power that constitutes all relationships transparently mediates the relationship, within which each participant perichoretically has its indirect but no less real influence and self-determination. The nature of all human relations analogically reflects some degree of the perichoretic nature of its creator, and it is this *nature* within the particularity and character of each person and relationship that influences God's creating activity (1 Pet 1:2–4). Here, we experience *de-liberation*, a process by which our existential concerns are holistically set before new possibilities as we liberate from our frozen position in time and kinetically flow in co-conditioning movement and choice *with* God's creative action. "Where the Spirit of the Lord is, there is liberty" (2 Cor 3:17), and upon this ground lies the subsequent possibility of transformation (re-creation) within authentic relations. The degree of transformation is relative to the degree relations are genuine, better yet, to the degree we are *willing* to engage the possibility of genuine relations. As lived experience or allegory, Jacob's nights of faith reveal the awakening of humanity into the *de-liberating* co-conditioning darkness of God's Eternal activity through *analogia spiritus*, wherein faith emerges, holistically affecting the divine deliberation of God's gift—the descending *and* ascending ladder of faith. This understanding of faith can only emerge in relation to a trinitarian God relating to tripartite humanity; it is foreign to the stasis of Greek or Hegelian gods.

This is the ontological dynamic reflected within the entire cosmos simply because a trinitarian God relates with and loves the world. In this way, spirit emerges and dissipates with the beginning and cessation of every interaction. We might expect in some way that the *nature* of any creator would eventually and reflectively permeate all that it creates. As such, any being like human beings emerging within that creation and given freedom to remove themselves from, deny, or in some way resist engaging through that *nature* would then experience turmoil, dread, and alienation (sin) upon such resistance. We would assume not even God can entirely remove Godself from God's *nature*. But if God is uniquely creating humanity with the capacity to know God as God (relational *theosis*), it would necessitate the freedom to resist such relations. Therefore, in one sense, we might consider that God never did create Hell. Hell results from the capacity given to human beings to create their own world with the freedom to resist relationship with God. It could be the singular creation of humanity *not* co-created with the divine. Welcome to our world, or at least a large part of it.

The concept of *analogia spiritus* will expand throughout the thesis. Nevertheless, a vital understanding of this (immanent) sustaining action of *Spiritus Creator* within creation is essential to fully understand the action of the Holy Spirit at the personal and triune level. To this end, we will investigate the complexity of God's action as Spirit in the work of Jürgen Moltmann.

Moltmann's Notion of Trinity and Spirit

Moltmann's Trinity is a perichoretic differentiated unity and emphasizes the need to further understand God's Spirit and the Spirit's *multidimensional* and enigmatic activity that the Scriptures clearly express.[84] Given such diversity of manifestations, we must enter any such study of God's Spirit and various actions and manifestations with open and creative thinking.

> The *presence* of the divine Spirit in creation must be further differentiated, theologically; for we have to distinguish between his cosmic, his reconciling and his redeeming indwelling. The way the Spirit in his indwelling *acts* will have to be differentiated in each given case according to the mode of his self-manifestation as subject, as energy, or as potentiality. The *efficacy* of the Spirit can then be differentiated into his creating, his preserving, his renewing and his consummating activity.[85]

None of these are technically the same but represent manifestations of God's Spirit accordingly. The typical understanding of Cosmic Spirit is the spirit that energizes life itself, that life source that "returns to God upon death."[86]

---

84. He enumerates the activities and manifestations of the Spirit of God in multiple ways: the divine energy of life, cosmic Spirit, God's presence, God's Shekinah, Messianic expectations, the Spirit of Christ, *Spiritus Creator*, and the person of the Holy Spirit within the Trinity, among others.

85. Moltmann, GC, 12.

86. Moltmann, SL, 41. Cf. Moltmann's consideration: "Theologically this Spirit must be called the Spirit of God and the presence of God in the creature he has made. But according to biblical usage, this is not the Holy Spirit. The Holy Spirit is the name given to the Spirit of redemption and sanctification . . . the Spirit of Christ . . . who allows Christ . . . to become Gestalt—in believers" (GC, 263). A more comprehensive utilization of *perichoresis* and de-Hellenizing residuals within Moltmann's thought would obviate his need to place the Spirit of God "in" the creature he has made. Just as Christ's Time temporalizes the Father's Eternality (a Moltmann consideration, i.e., each aspect of each Person affecting the Other by sheer relationship to the Other), so we need to consider that the spirit of human beings emerges as its own human spirit by shear perichoretic relationship to God. The spirit of the human being then analogically experiences the holistic Presence of God in *analogia spiritus* within the primordial dynamics of relationship. This emergence of spirit within human beings is a reflective

INTRODUCTION

Spiritus Creator can be thought of as the Spirit of God transparently creating and sustaining life and all cosmic relations simply by God relating to creation (in Christ)—no other action needed by God than sheer relationship itself. The Holy Spirit refers to the Spirit as God's transcendent personal action and presence to human awareness. This diversity of activity results from both God's internal perichoretic activity within the Trinity, and the various forms or modes of self-manifestation within specific divine action related to each spacetime event or occurrence. I suggest Moltmann's prudent recognition of the complexity of the Bible's expression of God's Spirit implores us to develop greater articulation in this regard, which affects our consideration of the Spirit's role in trinitarian, personal, and cosmic relatedness. In this respect, we must begin to acknowledge spirit as active in a diversity of ways within every interaction. Any serious theory of *perichoresis* as a relational ontology that creates and facilitates all reality must consider that the generic presence of spirit is primordially and transparently active (and at times emergent *ex nihilo*) within *every* cosmic interaction, most notably in personal relations. In this respect, the emergence of spirit within all cosmic interactions, notwithstanding the various manifestations of God's Spirit, will be innumerable, each according to the nature and character of the relationship, participants, and all relevant matters.

Within the divine-human interaction, for example, there is the spirit of the person, the objective spirit of the community, the emerging spirit of each relationship, and the Spirit of God all functioning at some affective co-conditioning level within *analogia spiritus* depending upon the nature of the interaction. A perichoretic ontology necessitates the presence and/or emergence of spirit (the relationship) at every level within the interaction. Everything from the quantum wave function, to matter, to biological cells, to human beings, and God, in some way constitutes in a multiplicity of spirits within each interaction. In this respect, the activity of God's Spirit, human spirit, and all cosmic aspects of spirit are to some degree active within all human interactions.

A forthcoming chapter on the Trinity will elaborate further on the much maligned and shallow understanding of Moltmann's understanding of each person of the Trinity and their transformative effects on each other's personhood. Finally, it should be noted: that to speak anything about God (which is theology) is always provisional, risky, and ultimately wrong from any Hellenistic or rational perspective. Therefore, further explorations into

---

dynamic by virtue of God's relatedness to humanity in Christ (katoptrizómenoi, "beholding as in a mirror"; 2 Cor 3:18). God's Spirit within the world and in humanity creates the ontological engine of transformation, the emergence of life, and eventually the primordial desire to relate perichoretically.

the Trinity must continue despite the prohibitions against such explorations by the theological police, who themselves satisfyingly maintain theologies rife with theological and scriptural incoherence.[87]

Person in Dialogical Constitution: Prereflexion/Reflexion in Social Relations

For a fuller understanding of perichoretic relationality, we will compare a theory of perichoretic social dynamics with the social theory of Alistair McFadyen, specifically, the dialogical bipolarity he identifies within communicative action. All human communicative acts necessitate dialogical modulations of prereflexion (awareness, openness) and reflexion (response, closure). These polar distinctions represent dialogical cycles *within* the unitive perichoretic structure that is relationship itself.[88] Likewise, speaking of love (eros) as a participatory relation, Moltmann tells us that

> lovers are counterpart and presence for one another. . . . Counterpart and presence alternate in the rhythm of life, and must do so; for pure presence is imperceptible. In order to know one another, the lovers need not only union but detachment; not merely desire but also the setting-free; not solely the going out of the self but the withdrawal of the self too; not community alone, but also personhood."[89]

Many contemporary streams of theological anthropology (e.g., process theology) have begun to re-situate the heart of the divine-human point-of-contact at more complex levels within personal and social structuring. Most are active at preconscious prereflexive levels of human experience. Within this thesis, all knowledge and understanding constitute within and emerge from such dynamics. From birth onward, we are irresistibly drawn into a pulsating reflexivity constituting *person*-in-relation, then back to subsequent prereflexive opening of awareness into the matrix from which we emerge.[90] Ultimately all desire, even the desire to end one's life, issues in some way from this *fundamental desire to perichoretically connect with*

---

87. Gorsuch, "*Perichoresis* and Projection."

88. Similarly, Wolfhart Pannenberg understands human nature as a tension between "centeredness" and "openness." Yet, because of his Hegelian proclivities, his notion of human experience and relationality ultimately fall short of Kierkegaardian structuring (Pannenberg, *Anthropology*).

89. Moltmann, *SL*, 262.

90. Cf. McFadyen, *CP*, 122: "[Personal identity or] individuality cannot be constituted by total openness but by total or partial closure."

others, the world, and God in increasingly meaningful ways. Suicide results from a substantial lack of attainment. Human desires emerge from a host of relational factors and contingencies that converge in front of, within, and behind the conscious focal meaning and intentional locus of human beings as they organize and constitute as person-in-relation.[91] McFadyen notes: "Individual spirit is the organisational energy through which both oneself and the boundary between oneself and others are structured. Individual spirit organises the form and content of communication by regulating openness and closure."[92] Like Kierkegaard, McFadyen believes humans constitute as persons *within* their respective relations to the world; relation to God begins in *becoming* spirit. For McFadyen:

> It is individual spirit which is initially transformed in redemption by being placed in the context of relation with God. Such transformation effects a newly organised identity which shows itself in a new patterning of relations around the person.[93]

In a more developed statement, he emphasizes the "passive" and free characteristics of God's analogical effect upon the human spirit (i.e., *analogia spiritus*):

> God's communication creates the ontological possibility of freedom-in-response which includes the passive moment involved in understanding. The power of the Holy Spirit through which the transformation of faith occurs is not coercive in an heteronomous sense, but imploring, beguiling and perhaps even compulsive—but it is so internally: i.e. it appeals to, transforms, but does not destroy the identity and rationality structure of the person.... It does not take the form of logical, rational propositions but, *paradigmatically*, the crucifixion of the incarnate which, in appealing to human understanding, actually *transforms* the understanding contained in human predicates.[94]

We do well to note the "paradigmatic" and "transformative" nature of God's Spirit's influences on the configuring process of human spirit and its

---

91. The term "relational contingencies" includes *every* relevant factor that comes to bear upon the person within a given event occurrence (memory, relational patterns, other participants, responsibilities, the immanent or transcendent presence of God, etc.). It also includes the suppression of contingencies into "nonaffective zones" due to individual posturing and relational disposition, e.g., the memory (shame) of one's action toward another or another's action toward oneself.

92. McFadyen, *CP*, 116; cf. Gunton, *One, Three, Many*.

93. McFadyen, *CP*, 116.

94. McFadyen, *CP*, 299n1, emphasis added.

cruciform call to relax the boundaries of self in vulnerability and openly enter the space of the relationship (the Other). The Spirit does not inject information or facts (from *facere*, to make) *per se* into the individual. Instead, the human spirit conditions in its self-organizing and configuring process antecedent to its constituent response (e.g., its linguistic structuring). This influence is not coercive or counteractive, merely transparently and transformatively mediational in attempting to expand each participant's meaning-frame (world) into a unique analogical sharing of meaning—effectively creating and translating meaning between participants.

Again, this prereflexive moment is that *moment* of intentful awareness, listening, and de-liberation that comes before conscious response. Philosophically, we describe this process and *moment* of transition as hypothetico-deductive thought—the emergence of theory or hypothesis where the relation between theory and observation is not strictly deducible. Again, this patterned dialogical dynamic of *perichoresis* reflects in all human relations simply because a trinitarian God actively relates to human beings (creating what Kierkegaard calls the "condition").

Perichoresis in Persons: Emotions and the Tricameral Brain

We are constantly in an emotive state and the primary functions of emotions are unifying, processing, and holistic in nature. They represent our most complete and holistic response to the world. In this chapter we also will look at what I will argue is the tricameral brain and how it also reflects perichoretic dynamics. Neurological studies are now revealing that very little brain activity is conscious, certainly less than five percent, probably less than one percent. Not only is most thought unconscious, most of our *processing* (de-liberation) in thought is also an unconscious and emotive activity. Therefore, most of our decisions and deliberations dynamically happen prereflexive to consciousness, and nearly instantaneously. These are dynamics in which a person's choices, desires, and proclivities are interactively processing in relation to the world around us asymmetrically prior to our conscious response. Such activities reflect the perichoretic dynamics of Kierkegaard's concept of the "sudden," a *moment* in which the eternal and temporal, the absolute and the relative *dynamically* interact within our relations, creating consciousness. In conclusion, these studies forward undeniable evidence that these neurological and emotive processes are most likely the result of human spirit and unquestionably reflect perichoretic dynamics.

INTRODUCTION

Person *as Perichoresis*: Self Becomes Spirit When It Fully Relates to Itself in Reflective Coinherence with the Ground that Posits Self

In chapter 3, we will consider relational dynamics within theological anthropology, drawing from various interdisciplinary interests, most notably human developmental psychology. Again, the principal aim of this section will be to isolate aspects within human development and relational dynamics that analogically parallel with God's Eternal trinitarian and perichoretic activity.

Our study in developmental psychology investigates the transformational and developmental nature of human existence and the emergence of intelligence. Individuals like Jean Piaget and theologian/developmental psychologist James Loder are particularly noteworthy because of their theories on the holistic nature of human relations and transformation. Both these writers argue for the rational necessity of the "nonrational" by revealing irreducible dynamics within human nature. Moreover, they believe these dynamics constitute reason itself. As such, all human knowledge is by nature inherently relational.

In this chapter, we will investigate human participation in the divine ground that constitutes it by considering the transformational dynamics in the work of Piaget, James Loder, and Kierkegaard. Loder argues that patterned relationship has its basis in mutual coinherence and is ultimately contingent upon sacred dynamics.

> Opposites are coinherent in and through this relatedness, and the relatedness is coinherent with itself. Furthermore, it is evident that the self cannot be itself without its centered grounding beyond itself, but it must be a participant in that ground such that its life is preserved and its integrity as spirit is sustained by that ground. Thus, the ground also participates in the self in such a way that both ground and self are sustained as such from the standpoint of the self. In other words, there is a coinherence of the whole patterned activity of the self in and with its ground, and of the ground in and with the self. In essence, *the self is spirit when the pattern governing it is perichoretic.*[95]

He equates this coinherence with the Pauline dynamic of "Christ in us" (Gal 2:20), a mutuality that manifests itself clearly within the dialogical dynamic evident within the trinitarian notion of God and human relations. It also maintains Kierkegaard's insistence that the temporal and eternal poles,

---

95. Loder, *KM*, 292.

of which persons are a synthesis, never materially synthesize,[96] therefore, necessitating within spacetime the dialogical pulsation of opening prereflexive awareness (infinite/eternal) and constituting reflexive closure (finite/temporal).

The eternal and the temporal defy reduction into material synthesis and are maintained only within existential relations (and consciousness); neither are they substantive or universally meaningful outside the existing contingencies of each unique relational *moment*. As relational continencies change, so will shared meaning and truth accordingly. As components, they form an existential unified whole only within that interpretive moment, which is always in constant flux (optimally transforming). According to Loder and Kierkegaard, "*transition itself becomes the very matrix of existence*," rather than the stasis of Hegelian "synthesis." Again, value emerges into time in-tensionally coinherent with the holistic activity of *analogia spiritus* within and antecedent to reflexion. In this way, all relative aspects within our conscious reflections become endowed with irreducible *meaningfulness* to the degree we *wholly* relate as spirit with that Power that constitutes all relations.[97] Identifying this irreducible dynamic active within humanity and all cosmic relations should no doubt deepen our understanding of God's activity in the world and specifically with humanity.

Thermodynamics and Quantum Theory

Consonant with the idea of perichoretic relations and a relational ontology, Prigogine and Stengers insist that:

> Today physics has discovered the need to assert both the distinction and interdependence between units and relations. It now recognizes that, for an interaction to be real, the "nature" of the related things must derive from these relations, while at the same time the relations must derive from the "nature" of the things.[98]

Furthermore,

---

96. Kierkegaard, *CUP*, 169–224, 346–85.

97. Loder, *KM*, 304; Kierkegaard, *CUP*, 376–85: "For there is only one thing to say: venture everything!" (382). "And after the individual has made the venture he is no longer the same individual" (379). For that which is not relative is "*definable solely in terms of the mode of acquisition*" (382).

98. Prigogine and Stengers, *Order Out of Chaos*, 95.

> "Creation of structures" *may* occur with specific non-linear kinetic laws of far-from-equilibrium conditions. The energy and matter exchanged by the system from the outside world is then really transformed into structure.[99]

Recent developments within the scientific inquiry into the nature and characteristics of change in dynamic systems—thermodynamics—present unique claims and new insights into relational dynamics. The growing conviction is that structure somehow emerges *both* within time and in relation to teleological influences (i.e., influences from dynamic systems *en totum*, including that system's future). Though this study cannot engage this subject in critical detail, such theories warrant appropriate mention. These same dynamics will appear within quantum theory as wave function potentiality emerging into structure when engaged within open systems and relationships (e.g., in consciousness).

Time and Eternity: Theology, Philosophy, and Postmodern Physics

A. S. Eddington insists that "any attempt to bridge the domains of experience belonging to the spiritual and physical sides of our nature, *time occupies the key position.*"[100] This thesis investigates the relation of time and eternity within the divine-human relationship. Such considerations have only recently begun to assimilate the new heuristics emerging from postmodern science—relativity theory and quantum thought. Theologians, in line with Kant, have generally rejected conceiving of creation as beginning at some starting point within an "eternal" timeline.[101] More recently, in Post-Kantian thought, Karl Barth attempted to express a notion of Eternality that recovers human time within a particular christological modality as "pure duration."[102] The "beginning" is never just a distant past starting point but that which cyclically becomes fulfilled within the covenant event of the Christ relation. This differs from the concept of creator *causa prima* or the modern deistic notion of creation as a closed system.

---

99. Prigogine, "Unity," 2.

100. Eddington, *Nature*, 91, emphasis added. Prigogine and Stengers, *Order Out of Chaos*, 96, tells us that "only an opening, a widening of science can end the dichotomy between science and philosophy. This widening of science is possible only if we revise our conception of time."

101. Kant, *Critique of Pure Reason*, 306.

102. Karl Barth, *CD* II/1, develops a Boethius-like position of eternity as "pure duration" (*reine Dauer*).

In contradistinction to Barth's self-admitted over-reactive insistence on the *complete* otherliness of God,[103] this project argues that human existence can mutually constitute in analogical relation to a transcendent God in God's eternality. "The death of God . . . is the death of separated transcendence," writes Paul Ricoeur, "we must shed an idea of the divine as wholly other to reach the idea of the divine as spirit immanent in the community."[104] Therefore, the subject of time and eternity and humans constituting in relation to the Eternal in time is one of the critical goals of this study. In this respect, every chapter relies upon this penultimate chapter: The *perichoresis* of time and Eternity. To *the degree human beings relate in full, open, and holistic relation to themselves, others, and God, they potentially emerge in co-conditioning relation to the Eternal; and thereby constitute as a participant affected by and affecting God's Eternal act of creation* (a gift to be sure).

Because of this Kierkegaardian-like *moment*, T. F. Torrance tells us, "the primary theological point to get clear, however, is the ontologically and temporally indivisible nature of the one epiphany or advent of the incarnate Son of God in whom all men and all ages are held together, without any detraction from real differences between different experiences or times."[105] Again, within this thesis, *this dynamic is not to be thought of as creating a universal frame of reference in which all things as similar can be mutually related* (analogia entis). Instead, it is a universal dynamic of relationality through which all things different can mutually relate (analogia spiritus within perichoresis)—*a transtemporal phenomenon*.

Søren Kierkegaard: Social Theorist/Pneumatologist

Though this thesis is not specifically about Kierkegaard, I must acknowledge from the beginning that his thought, more than any other, lights its path. Though he exposes the impotence within the Christendom of his world (and ours), by acknowledging faith as a personal experiencing of God (and thereby the necessity of suffering), it is likely his Reformed enculturation inhibited its fuller expression. Though many consider his driving thesis as largely christological and also anthropological, his unique and radical contribution to theology and metaphysics was pneumatological.[106] Throughout

---

103. Barth, *Humanity of God*, 44–53.
104. Ricoeur, "Fatherhood," 493.
105. Torrance, *Transformation*, 343.
106. H. Berkhof thinks, "Kierkegaard's aim was not to emphasize anthropology but pneumatology in theology, and therefore, like Barth, he considered the renewing Spirit

this study, his views will be a catalyst for exposing the unique insights of many contemporary thinkers.

As was indicated in our earlier consideration of Kierkegaard, I wish to emphasize the misnomer that Kierkegaard's thinking was rigidly individualistic. In *Kierkegaard in Post/Modernity*, Matuštík and Westphal tell us Kierkegaard's

> individualism turns out to be the flip side of a thoroughly relational conception of the self, and is beginning to be seen as having interesting ramifications for social theory and practice. *Almost all of the chapters in this volume can be read as contributions to the ongoing task of critical social theory.*[107]

For Kierkegaard, the internal relationship (dynamic) that creates the self also happens in (perichoretic) tension with the social relations (dynamic). *They cannot be separated.*[108]

Therefore, Kierkegaard's (Anti-Climacus's) notion of personhood necessitates a relatedness to God and the dialogical character that this necessitates and maintains within human sociology.

> The self is the conscious synthesis of infinitude and finitude, which relates itself to itself, whose task is to become itself, a task which can be performed only by means of a relationship to God.... Accordingly, the development consists in moving away from oneself infinitely by the process of infinitizing oneself, and in returning to oneself infinitely by the process of finitizing. If on the contrary the self does not become itself, it is in despair, whether it knows it or not.[109]

---

as the true answer to the anthropocentric endeavors of the culture of the time" (*Two Hundred Years*, 79).

107. Matuštík, Introduction to *Kierkegaard in Post/Modernity*, ix. In reference to Habermas and other contributors to the volume, the editors maintain a "critical social theory in the narrower sense, signifying conversations in which the work of Habermas plays a central role. But in the wider sense of the term, it also includes the feminist discourses addressed in several chapters and a variety of other ways in which Kierkegaard in dialogue turns out to be a social philosopher" (ix).

108. Similarly, Bonhoeffer tells us, "God does not desire a history of individual human beings, but the history of the human community. However, God does not want a community that absorbs the individual into itself, but a community of human beings. In God's eyes, community and individual exists in the same moment and rest in one another. *The collective unit and the individual unit have the same structure* in God's eyes. On these basic-relations rest the concepts of the religious community and the church" (*Sanctorum Communio*, 80, emphasis added).

109. Kierkegaard, *SUD*, 162–63.

Again, Bonhoeffer similarly insists,

> *The person ever and again arises and passes away in time.* The person does not exist timelessly; a person is not static, but dynamic.... [T]he person is re-created again and again in the perpetual flux of life. Subjective spirit becomes eternally significant only in relation to the absolute spirit.[110]

The "infinitizing" of oneself out into relations is the dialogical and modal dynamic of *analogia spiritus*—the holistic inter-action of the *whole* of self to the *whole* of the Other. In this respect, Kierkegaard's notion of using indirect knowledge is an effort to thrust the listener more effectively into this prereflexive non-differentiated aspect of interaction within communication—an attempt to encourage the other to become spirit. To the degree the person ventures all, they become self, make the decision, and move with passion (truth).

INTERDISCIPLINARY CONCERNS

Calvin begins his *Institutes* immediately acknowledging the integrative and holistic nature of theology:

> All our wisdom, if it really deserves the name of wisdom and is true and reliable, really comprehends two things: the knowledge of God and our knowledge of ourselves. These two are connected in many ways, and so it is not so easy to say which of them comes first and then itself affects the other.[111]

Similarly, this theological investigation into relational dynamics will draw upon work in various theological interdisciplinary studies: the philosophy of science (method), hermeneutics, social theory, human development, thermodynamics/quantum theory, and most notably, the study of time (Special Theory of Relativity) and the quantum enigma. Again, this thesis explores similar perichoretic dynamics emerging in these disciplines that then provide further insights toward an alternative hermeneutical key to a postmodern ontology of *perichoresis*. These dynamics are emerging within these disciplines in an effort to circumvent the limitations of modern

---

110. Bonhoeffer, *Sanctorum Communio*, 48.

111. Calvin, *Institutes* I.1.1. Though his point is beneficial, his dependence on classical notions of causality (causation as only temporal and unidirectional) is worth noting. Instead, a perichoretic ontology dimensionalizes causality, adding a prereflexive, holistic, instantaneous, and transformational mutual co-conditioning effect each upon the other.

Cartesian dualism. Such similarity in dynamics is not by accident and if they do indeed bare ontological significance, they *should* be evident in some way or another under every rock we lift. As noted, these interdisciplinary studies can have a co-condition effect on each other. Therefore, though often highly analytical, the force of this study is ultimately comprehensive in nature. Exploring new concepts of metaphysics can be intensely challenging because they require us to think differently, relax our former way of thinking, and play with new forms of understanding. If successful, existing dichotomies like immanence and transcendence may begin to fade into false dichotomies or transform in meaning.

To help the reader from dragging novel perichoretic notions back into Classical logic and Hellenistic derivatives, we will engage a significant number of Scriptures that are currently enigmatic or meaningless within these theological paradigms still employing such metaphysics. For example, as briefly noted earlier, New Testament scholars still do not know what to do with Matt 12:32 (and many associated passages). Here, Jesus asymmetrically prioritizes our relationship to the Spirit of God over that of himself for redemption. This passage and many more New Testament passages are either meaningless, forced, or enigmatically impotent within today's accepted theologies and ontological paradigms. These passages explode with new and fuller meaning within a perichoretic theology and ontology; they do so without loss of meaning and coherence with the balance of the Scriptures. Instead, they deepen the meaning and theological coherence within the entirety of the text. A perichoretic ontology becomes an ascendant research program if it provides: (1) greater scriptural meaning and coherence, (2) resolutions to existing theological anomalies, and most importantly, (3) eventually deepens the faith experience of the church. We will explore this in detail in the next chapter on method and meaning. The final chapters will show how a more developed concept of *perichoresis* can provide better theological orientation for addressing the issues of divine providence and human freedom, theodicy, and the paradoxical relationship of Christ within the complementarity of church and culture.

Interdisciplinary Theology

The certainty of our knowledge results from the quality and depth of interconnections within all our relations and beliefs. In this respect, separating the epistemological issues from the experiential content they attempt to describe is ultimately impossible. To the extent we separate and consider knowledge separate from the whole wealth of experience and conviction, knowledge becomes a closed system of thought and eventually a multiplicity of abstractions. Therefore, in holistic perichoretic dynamics every sphere of life and discourse is eventually integral to theological discourse. Such holistic and existential matters lead Murphy to suggest that "language cannot be static; extension of language into new areas is necessary if it is to be able to express growth in knowledge."[112] Though interdisciplinary studies begin with indefinite analogical interpenetration, constant use and skill within such interactions eventually develop new language and relations within our linguistic structuring. Such relationships eventually proffer novel facts and greater explanatory ability, providing more profound meaning and greater fullness of life. Murphy tells us,

> Even though Christian theology must begin with the Christian tradition (its revelation and the phenomena of the Christian religion), it must proceed to confirmation vis-à-vis reality external to the tradition—that is to contemporary sorts of data—if it is to fulfill its role as a science of God.[113]

Miroslav Volf also argues that all cultural networks of truth, knowledge, and relationships induce effects of power. Though the discussion of power, for the most part, is absent from theology, it figures prominently within the Scriptures.

> The crucified Christ is not a Messiah without power; he is a Messiah with a new kind of power—the power of "what is weak" that puts to shame "the strong," the power of "the things that are not" that reduce to "nothing the things that are" (1 Cor 1:28). Theological reflection . . . must be embodied in the community of the cross *whose particular kind of weakness is a new kind of power inserted into the network of the powers of the world.* . . . It sustains the truth, not so much by providing plausibility structures as by providing a space within networks of power in which the truth about Christ . . . can be lived out.[114]

Because Christians inextricably inhabit a host of multilingual pluralities of culture, differing social structures, and disciplines of thought, "our theologies need to be nonsystemic, contextual and flexible"[115] in order to enter

---

112. Murphy, "Acceptability Criteria," 283.

113. Murphy, *Theology*, 87. Also William Stoeger thinks: "The two languages of science and religion/theology, though different, are not isolated from or out of contact with one another. They continue to be in dynamic interaction in our common cultural and academic fields" ("Describing," 112).

114. Volf, "Theology," 109–10.

115. Volf, "Theology," 110.

co-conditioning relations within such pluralities. Theology's transformative effect upon their "plausible words of wisdom" and their potential transformative effect upon theology must be assessed "with a demonstration of the Spirit and of power" (1 Cor 2:5). As Volf points out, the New Testament says nothing about inhabiting a Christian "cultural-linguistic system" or "texts"; "the "word of Christ" is supposed to *"dwell in them richly,"* not they in the word of Christ (Col 3:16)."[116] Because all linguistic pluralities are ultimately contingent upon the action of a triune God, the *power of truth* within each event occurrence will become evident as *greater fullness of life* (to be developed further in the next chapter). *Only* in the antecedent disposition of open epistemic humility, which offers our weakness into the weakness of Christ, is the power of a theology of the cross fully experienced. Only through this disposition do we come into co-conditioning relationship with God's Eternal dynamics.

If this is the case, theology's interaction and coherence with other disciplines of thought are not only possible but *necessary*. In an agreeable but slightly different perspective, Pannenberg expresses his approach to anthropology:

> The aim is to lay theological claim to the human phenomena described in the anthropological disciplines. To this end, the secular description is accepted as simply a provisional version of the objective reality, a version that needs to be expanded and deepened by showing that the anthropological datum itself contains a further and theologically relevant dimension.[117]

Our goal is to locate a "theologically relevant dimension" or *dynamics* within human developmental processes and the creation of intelligence, and then apply them toward further theological insights. However, as Thiemann rightly cautions:

> The employment of borrowed concepts cannot be equivocal, i.e., a concept cannot be used in a wholly different way in the Christian frame. Thus on certain occasions . . . the theologian

---

116. Volf, "Theology," 104, emphasis added.

117. Pannenberg, *Anthropology*, 19. Cf. Moltmann, *CG*, 292: "What is needed . . . is a *psychological hermeneutics* of the word of the cross, the spirit of freedom and the history of God. Psychological hermeneutics is an interpretation and not a reduction. . . . None of the 'substance' of faith is lost in a psychological hermeneutics of faith. Rather, it gains a new dimension of its incarnation and enters the utter this-worldliness of life as it is lived and obstructed." Cf. also Ricoeur, *Freud and Philosophy*.

might need to show the analogical connections between Christian and non-Christian uses of particular concepts or beliefs.[118]

When we integrate various disciplines within the theological program, the goal is a conceptual integration that enhances both. Nevertheless, as Thiemann rightfully concludes, theology has "no rationale independent of the first-order language of faith"[119] (although he arguably fails to maintain these distinctions methodologically). We will address this questionable Postliberal separation of language into first and second order distinctions in the next chapter. Point being, for example, we must consider that Paul's description of love is nuanced by a host of contextual psychological and relational factors that condition his choice of terminology in communicating to each specific community and relational context and therefore his descriptions, *prima facie*, remain contextual not universal.[120] Similarly, current developmental and clinical psychology have begun to deepen our understanding of love and authentic relationships, which can enrich such historical expressions.[121] Progressively, therefore, as we adapt psychological discourse to theological discourse, such attributes will eventually become theological. Philip Clayton argues that "if the need to argue in a reasonable manner is accepted as essential to theology, it should be acknowledged as intrinsic to theology; it should be granted a place in theology's self-understanding."[122]

Interdisciplinary Method

Because of Loder's research on the logic of spirit, his thoughts concerning interdisciplinary method are worth emphasizing. Loder corroborates Pannenberg's attempt to locate and express the irreducible religious thematic in human beings and the sciences in response to the cited Pannenberg passage.

---

118. Thiemann, *Revelation*, 75.

119. Thiemann, *Revelation*, 75.

120. For example, Paul's description of love in 1 Cor 13 should not be considered universally conclusive. It merely expresses the meaning of love within Paul's specific cultural, linguistic, and social development *at that time* with the Corinthians. It is the kerygmatic beginning of our understanding of love, and not an exhaustive or final description.

121. This is evident in the theological literature over the last century that incorporates psychological hermeneutics and the insights of Kierkegaard, Freud, Jung, and others, e.g., Moltmann's *CG* and Pannenberg's *Anthropology*. One wonders if Barth's overreaction might have been averted with reading more interdisciplinary literature. Bonhoeffer wonders if experiencing other Christian cultures might have helped Barth's theology. See Zimmermann, *Humanism*.

122. Clayton, *Explanation*, 13.

He also appreciates Pannenberg's commitment to the co-conditioning relationship and hermeneutical duality of interpreting theological claims through the human sciences (bottom-up) and the human sciences through theology (top-down). Loder, however, departs from Pannenberg in that he gives asymmetrical priority to revealed theology over natural theology in a way that leans heavily upon the christological convictions of Karl Barth in that the "material supplies the method."[123] For Loder:

> Faith is not fundamentally a developmental phenomenon. If faith is a human response to God's grace, it must be rooted in God and be grounded deeper in psychic bedrock than the developing ego's foundation in a favorable balance of trust over mistrust, all of which is primarily dependent on interaction with a human environment.[124]

Loder is critical of Pannenberg's "balance" and also his indivisibility between God's Spirit and human spirit,[125] which he believes ultimately loses theology into the humanities, falling prey to Hegel's Absolute Spirit. Loder maintains the distinction through the analogy of spirit and the inherent dynamics of *perichoresis*: "the human spirit is to humanity what the Holy Spirit is to God (1 Cor 2:10)."[126] This may appear as a christological imperialism, although Loder believes he is simply supplying

> a christological answer to the question other interdisciplinary methodologies fail to address. . . . [These] positions tacitly introduce a third theme by which theology and nontheological disciplines are held together and interrelated. Obviously, in

---

123. Loder, *LS*, 30. He also thinks: "The natural order is not the context in which to understand God, but the natural order itself must be understood in the context of what God has revealed. By this theological paradigm shift, the sciences of the natural order, including the human sciences, must undergo a transformation by which they enter an indissoluble, contingent relation to revealed theology, functioning as subsciences of its inner intelligibility and as an essential part of the empirical and theoretical claims of its interpretation of God's action in the world" (32–33).

124. Loder, *LS*, 31. Also, "Dynamically, this approach brings theology and the human sciences into a transformational interaction: where human science understandings (or their equivalents) negate the Divine reality, this negation is negated and these understandings are reappropriated in terms of cognate theological concepts; where theological concepts negate the legitimacy of human science insights as elements in the transformational interaction, this negation must also be negated. However, the direction of the transformational dynamic, manifesting its inherent spiritual quality, is always to establish a bi-polar asymmetrical relational unity between the human science understanding and its more comprehensive theological cognate" (Loder, "Normativity," 359–60).

125. Loder's consideration of Pannenberg (Loder and Neidhardt, *KM*).

126. Loder, *LS*, 35.

these approaches, the ruling principle and consequent outcome are neither theology nor human science, but precisely the *tertium quid*.[127]

Therefore, all human sciences must become subsciences through what he calls a "Christomorphic approach through transformation" in which they reappropriate for the "concretization, illumination, or application of theological categories as they come to bear on human experience." And though this thesis replaces Loder's christological *tertium quid* with Kierkegaard's "Power" (the Spirit and Christ),

> It is the relationality, the dynamism of the exchange between these fields of inquiry, that is the reality to be prized. In human science, this is to stress the critical and constructive development of the human spirit. As it joins with the Creator Spirit, there is a bipolar witness to the redemption and consummation of creation in Jesus Christ. Taken together, human spirit and Creator Spirit constitute the relational wholeness of Jesus Christ present to us and effective for us in the immediacy of experience."[128]

Relational dynamics are indeed the primary focus of this thesis, and Loder's concerns reflect the basic method of its inquiry. Nevertheless, because of this christological (more explicitly, perichoretic) dynamic, we must adjust our understanding of a "totally other" God. Every interdisciplinary theological interaction can be analogically reflective and profitable given proper development and humility. Just as boldly, Moltmann suggests:

> All relationships which are analogous to God reflect the primal, reciprocal indwelling and mutual interpenetration of the trinitarian *perichoresis*. . . . All living things—each in its own specific way—live in one another and with one another, from one another and for one another.[129]

Though Moltmann's panentheistic and Hellenistic nuances force him into "indwelling" language, a fuller understanding of perichoretic dynamics as stated earlier maintains the essential difference and autonomy, thus satisfying Moltmann's original relational intuitions.

---

127. Loder, *LS*, 37. *Tertium quid*—a third thing that is indefinite and undefined but is related to two definite or known things.
128. Loder, *LS*, 41.
129. Moltmann, *GC*, 17.

Concluding this preliminary comment on methodology, we should briefly consider why we do theology. In full agreement with Moltmann, theology is:

> A voyage without the certainty of a return, a path into the unknown with many surprises and not without disappointments. . . . [It is about] curiosity. . . . I have never done theology in the form of a defense of ancient doctrines or ecclesiastical dogmas. It has always been a journey of exploration. Consequently my way of thinking is experimental—an adventure of ideas—and my style of communication is to suggest. . . . So I write without any built-in safeguards, recklessly as some people think. My own propositions are intended to be a challenge to other people to think for themselves, . . . belonging just as much to the world as to God. . . . There are theological systems which are not only designed to be non-contradictory in themselves, but aim to remain undisputed from outside too. They are like fortresses which cannot be taken, but which no one can break out of either, and which are therefore starved out. For me theology is not church dogmatics, and not a doctrine of faith. It is *imagination for the kingdom of God* in the world, and for the world in God's kingdom.[130]

In the next chapter, we will investigate the character of meaning by contrasting meaning development within two antithetical research programs. Attempting to integrate the positive insights of both, we will then consider meaning itself as a perichoretic dynamic. Such explorations into the construction of meaning may prove beneficial for theological method.

---

130. Moltmann, *GC*, xiv.

2

Meaning as *Perichoresis*
Theological Method and Knowledge as the Shape of Desire

He is before all things, and in Him all things hold together.[1]

Col 1:17

It is to the prodigals—to those who exhaust all their strength in pursuing what seems to them good and who, after their strength has failed, go on impotently desiring—that the memory of their Father's house comes back. If the son had lived economically he would never have thought of returning.

Simone Weil, Notebooks

EPISTEMOLOGICAL HOLISM VS. RELATIONAL HOLISM: RESTRUCTURING REALITY

Aristotle said, "all men by nature desire to know." In this chapter we will consider the possibility of an even more fundamental notion upon which knowledge emerges and is sustained—"*all humans by nature desire to relate.*" Essential to my overall thesis is that persons constitute through a

---

1. Also Heb 1:3: "He is the radiance of His glory and the image of His reality, upholding all things by the word of His power" (my translation).

perichoretic desire to relate. Knowledge is only one product of this fundamental human drive.

The epistemological indulgence within our modern heritage raises concerns about the creation of meaning within human social interaction. We are quickly losing the innocence of basing our knowledge and understanding *entirely* on self-evident non-inferentials that directly correspond with concept-independent reality.[2] The increasing awareness that reason's effectiveness emerges only *within* paradigms of traditions mandates that we better understand how such holistic dynamics are active within intertraditional and interdisciplinary dialogue. The evidence that holistic dynamics are alive within such dialogues is already evident in the ability of past interdisciplinary and intertraditional interactions to provoke new questions and progressive theories within each other, respectively. Moreover, such activity creates developmental contexts in which existing forms of life evolve into more efficient explanations and fuller experiences.

For the Cartesian mind subjectivity is central. Through the body, the mind receives sensory and linguistic information that refers to pre-developed meaning within the mind. Here, meaning is the exclusive property of the mind, and language becomes the sole vehicle for re-presenting it. Descartes, however, continued to doubt not the certainty of ideas but their veridicality to what they represent. In his reducing the philosophical project, the idea, consciousness, and the self became the indubitable perspective. From this one safe loft of certainty evolved a detached perspective, which then developed into the explicit category of the objective. Observing became the act of categorizing, and knowledge as such, *episteme* (theoretical knowledge), was used to *reference* reality. This began to cut the individual from its holistic totality and knowledge from its complete source of meaning and perception. The infatuation and overindulgence with re-presentation began to diminish the fullness and uniqueness of immediate relations.

---

2. This is a modified understanding of foundationalism originating from Ronald Thiemann, *Revelation*, 158n20. I add the emphasis and proviso "entirely" in emphasizing a foundationalist's certainty grounding in direct unmediated correspondence to concept-independent reality. This thesis, contra Thiemann, will argue that there are social dynamics within the constituting process of our relations that provide the possibility of non-inferential and compelling *forces* within our knowledge and beliefs. Though these dynamics are not reducible to being or the common understanding of knowledge, they are irreducibly active and contingent within human relations. Hence, these living forces remain a "non-inferential" factor for all human knowledge. Though this thesis agrees with Thiemann that provisionality is an inherent quality in all human knowledge, provisionality does not necessarily eliminate its potential diachronic continuity or authority.

In response to Cartesian-inspired subjectivism, emerging postmodern ventures look to breach the growing isolation of the subject. These are many and diverse, but their common goal is acknowledging and understanding holism within the knowing and communicative act. In this section, we shall investigate several developing postmodern theories or programs that have been or might be beneficial for theological discourse and method. We will begin by introducing various theories within the philosophy of science through an evaluation of epistemological holism developed in Nancey Murphy's implementation of Lakatos for theological method. Then we will consider the relational holism in the communicative action of social constructivists Kenneth Gergen, John Shotter, and others, who draw from M. Bakhtin and Wittgenstein, for paralleling perichoretic dynamics. We will conclude the chapter with an inquest into knowledge as the shape of desire and suggest further considerations for theological method.

The Longing for Security in Foundational Theological Beliefs

In *The Eclipse of Biblical Narrative*, Hans Frei reveals the modern tendency to establish hermeneutical *foundations*, such as the history behind the text or the existential orientation within religious awareness. These foundations became the certainty beneath the text. However, some non-foundational alternatives, such as stressing the importance of narrative, suggest that the texts holistically speak for themselves, not privileging any one criterion or locus of meaning. Though this thesis acknowledges the importance of narrative, the affective quality of narrative is of preeminent concern—the holistic dynamics that create meaning within human interaction. Conventionally understood, holism resists the notion that meaning emerges from any one source or loci. Therefore, we will consider that meaning emerges from the interpenetration of various conceptual, experiential, and social fields into irreducible forms of meaning and interaction.

Two Recent Holistic Theories from Philosophy of Science: Kuhn and Lakatos

There are a variety of discussions and theories proposing postmodern holistic alternatives within the philosophy of science. Two such contrasting theories are the implementation of Kuhn or Lakatos for theological method. Thomas Kuhn emphasizes holistic dynamics within his concept of *paradigm* and the deeply integrative nature of knowledge.³ Developed social constructions guide and arrange a tradition's entire structure of thought and interaction. This theory calls for revolutionary gestalt-like changes when a tradition's explanatory and functional ability become laden with anomalies and falls into incoherence. Here, all beliefs and knowledge take shape and emerge from a matrix of co-conditioning relations that make up and support that paradigm. The perennial issues here are that paradigm shifts re-color every aspect of knowledge and, to the modern eye, threaten diachronic continuity suggesting a degree of relativism. Kuhn does address his critic's claim of relativism, but he never engages in any serious discussion on *how* new paradigms emerge and emerge with the power to diminish former anomalies.⁴ Kuhn simply states that "discovery commences with the awareness of anomaly, in other words with the recognition that nature has somehow violated the paradigm-induced expectations that govern normal science,"⁵ and that "anomaly appears only against the background provided by the paradigm."⁶ Lakatos, on the other hand, has also been employed for theology use.

EPISTEMOLOGICAL HOLISM: LAKATOS, NANCEY MURPHY,⁷ AND THE EPISTEMIC WEB   "TO KNOW"

Three contrasting theories by Nancey Murphy, Philip Clayton, and Philip Hefner adapt Imre Lakatos's theory in philosophy of science for theological research method.⁸ Murphy describes epistemological holism as a constellation of beliefs. Each belief gains its rational persuasion by appealing to other beliefs in such a way as to induce, step-by-step, that belief into the constellation.⁹ No beliefs, therefore, are traceable to one foundational belief; instead, their convictive structures within the web of beliefs are due to their specific location and degree of interrelatedness they enjoy within the whole. She appeals heavily to W. V. O. Quine and Alasdair MacIntyre,

---

3. Kuhn, *Revolutions*.
4. The perennial issue of Plato's *Meno*.
5. Kuhn, *Revolutions*, 52–53.
6. Kuhn, *Revolutions*, 65.
7. In addressing Murphy, my former professor with whose work I am familiar, I am addressing the entire postliberal school and associating theological methodologies.
8. Lakatos's most influential works in philosophy of science are "Falsification and the Methodology of Scientific Research Programmes," and "History of Science and Its Rational Reconstructions."
9. Murphy, *Beyond*, 88–89, 94–98.

and, curiously, to Wittgenstein. Though her theory raises many questions, it presents a revealing point of entry into the postmodern research program and notions of methodological criteria.

"Explanatory Function" and "Wider Human Experience" as Co-constituting Elements within the Construction of Meaning

If all knowledge is theory dependent, then additional ad hoc theory can always resolve emerging anomalies between theory (as concept) and phenomena (as experience). This then presents the problem of discerning between ad hoc and legitimately progressive theory development. For Lakatos, the internal and public assessment of whether a conceptual system adequately engages its community in the broadest experience of reality is how well its conceptual system allows for further prediction, discovery, and extension of its explanatory capacity. In other words, as Philip Hefner says, it comes down to whether the tradition succeeds in "extending the explanatory function of the community's faith into the realm of wider human experience."[10] The program becomes degenerative when theoretical changes or ad hoc additions only patch up the incoherence but do not lead to new empirical knowledge. There are reciprocating dynamics at work here. Increasing explanatory capacity in life allegedly enhances and valuatively deepens human experience. Likewise, the wider the experience of life, the greater the ground for explanatory capacities and expanding understanding. Each, in turn, instantiates, enhances, and draws forth the other in the ongoing developmental cycle of increasing human meaning and depth of relations.

Simply put, the primary logic of Lakatos's program is that researchers make auxiliary hypotheses for critical dimensions of the program as public as possible for testability. These auxiliary hypotheses then complement an often-indiscernible fundamental core belief within the program (the "hard core") that might be universally and publicly unverifiable. The criterion for adequacy is the *progress* or disintegration of a tradition, discipline of thought, or research program. The pivotal question, however, becomes: what is progress? *How* do we assess the criterion of growth in an ever-changing and transforming program? Novel data? What is novel? Moreover, on a more positive note, *why* does progress happen (ultimately a theological question)?[11]

---

10. Hefner, *Human Factor*, 261.

11. My concern is the notion of progress and the conventional preoccupation with philosophy's emphasis on negative heuristics. These heuristics reveal disintegration ("epistemological crisis") in theories in contrast to the positive forces which motivate

For Lakatos, according to Murphy, the auxiliary hypotheses are those falsifiable beliefs and understandings drawn from the hard core. Likewise, they give the program its distinctive significance. The authority of the hard core, the general theory assumed through tradition, exhibits no direct inferential foundations that are strictly empirical. Based upon Lakatos's assumption that differing disciplinary discourses are incommensurable (all aspects of knowledge being theory dependent), he argues that the progressive system producing novel facts will continue to enlarge its number of facts; a degenerating program will stagnate.[12] Progress emerges from a program's positive heuristics and only indirectly from negative heuristics. The latter is a plan or methodological rule avoiding falsification of the hard core. The former is a set of suggestions or internal aspect fueling and creating progress by developing and strengthening the potentially "refutable" auxiliary hypotheses.

Murphy offers an example of a progressive theological program in Pannenberg with its hard core—the God of Jesus Christ is the all-determining reality. On the other hand, Hefner offers the example of the tripartite structure of Freud's program (id, ego, and superego) as a deteriorating program.[13] This is evident in the declining influence of his program among current psychiatric researchers. However, he suggests Darwin's original program of evolution through variation, survival, and selection is still a stimulating influence on biological research. Even though it is currently experiencing considerable revision, in Lakatosian terms, it can still be considered progressive and viable.

---

theory progress. Karl Popper, therefore, supplants the positivist verification theory with a criterion of falsifiability. Convinced (with Hume) that inductive generalization could not explain the emergence of theory, Popper argues that theory was a creative and hypothetical construction of human making (Popper, *Logic*, 458). Therefore, we gain epistemological veracity by the negative process of attempting to falsify the theory through experimental methods. Those theories open to such falsifiability then acquire greater empirical status. The point is, such a program assesses epistemological development *primarily* using negative heuristics—its ability to withstand debilitating incoherence and anomaly.

Likewise, MacIntyre's assessment of a tradition's status became the tradition's ability to resist "epistemological crisis." As various epistemological conflicts arise between competing traditions or as a tradition might "lapse into incoherence" from mounting anomalies, they either disintegrate or progress. MacIntyre assesses progress by "an argumentative retelling of that narrative." In other words, "it enable [sic] us to understand its predecessors [*and competitors*] in a newly intelligible way," explaining how and why they came to believe the way they did, and how and why the new development is superior. MacIntyre, "Epistemological Crises," 62–63. This criterion is valuable, but still leaves unanswered *why* progress happens—ultimately a theological issue.

12. Lakatos, "Falsification," 34.
13. Hefner, *Human Factor*, 25.

Nancey Murphy's Theological Implementation of Lakatosian Criteria and Methodology

Murphy's Conceptual Pragmatism and Postmodern Theology

Nancey Murphy designates a minimal doctrine of God as the hard core of the theological venture: trinitarian nature, God's holiness, and Jesus as God's revelation. Her auxiliary hypotheses are the church's doctrines: theories concerning Christ, the church, God, and so on. The data for theology is Scripture, tradition/history, and religious and community experience. The auxiliary hypotheses should be the "consequences"[14] of the hard core, and the data are the "consequences" of the auxiliaries. "The core theory is confirmed by the data that it (indirectly) explains."[15] This conceptual circularity is always evident, but the criterion that adjudicates differing programs and core theories is their respective internal progress.

Murphy's notion of a postmodern theology entails: (1) a holistic epistemology over a foundational epistemology, (2) a philosophy of language emphasizing language as action and meaning as use over referential and representational notions of language, and (3) a renewed importance and irreducibility of the community.[16] The language games of a community precede individual development, and therefore, the development of knowledge and practices are tradition dependent. Likewise, community consensus becomes a primary criterion in developing knowledge and practice. In this respect, she suggests Hegel's "antifoundationalism and nonreductive sense of community"[17] gain currency and provide resources for postmodern theology. She suggests that "doctrines of revelation no longer serve as the foundation upon which systematic theology rests . . . but are instead included in the theoretical structure to explain communities' assorted ways of 'taking Scripture as authority.'"[18] All three of these basic revisions are laudable in what they seek to produce within theology; however, her execution warrants further critical assessment.

Murphy has also drawn upon the new models of language theory in Wittgenstein and Austin to emphasize the non-referential dynamic in language. Speech-act theory and a performative notion of language replace the understanding that language communicates symbols, which refer to meaning in the speaker's mind, that then re-associate with meanings in the

---

14. Murphy, *Theology*, 186.
15. Murphy, *Theology*, 186.
16. Murphy, *Theology*, 201.
17. Murphy, *Theology*, 201n42.
18. Murphy, *Theology*, 209.

listener's mind. Though this is an attempt to escape the Cartesian construction of meaning, many using these theories have simply re-instituted the mechanisms of modernity at other levels within the community's structuring, installing a disguised rationalism and empiricism into a larger community corpus. This subsumes a holistic hard core of Christianity back again into, effectively, another discipline.[19] Though Murphy states, "there is no sharp dividing line between method and content,"[20] her description of the hard core in the theological project as second-order theological belief or hypotheses as distinct from the community's actual faith experience is problematic. In this respect, we must consider how close her method and content really are. Similarly, an immediate concern arises when one confronts her stated typology of understanding knowledge as either "outside-in" or "inside-out,"[21] which relates to her assimilation of Thiemann's bifurcation of first-order faith experience, emphasizing social praxis, and second-order theological language, emphasizing conceptual coherence. Such a bifurcation of meaning itself questions these theologians's true break from the modern philosophical and anthropological paradigm.

Symbol (Concept) + Experience = Meaning: Holism

This type of epistemological holism tends to privilege a specific notion of *episteme* and the cognitive aspect of meaning by setting it apart as a language game in itself. By positing any separation between faith practice and theological language, such thinking has already distanced itself from a true holism, which recognizes the difficulties and impropriety of isolating knowledge from its full context. Reacting to positivism and existentialism, Eugene Gendlin suggests they can be "advanced, not by changing either, but by adding a missing systematic piece between them. This piece has, of course, a broader significance than just their need for it: it is *the relationship between symbolizing and preconceptual experiencing*. In this relationship meaning is formed."[22] Philip Hefner broadens the equation by using *concept*

---

19. Cf. Donald Bloesch's critique of Ronald Thiemann. Bloesch, *Word and Spirit*, 3.

20. Murphy, *Theology*, 183.

21. Murphy, "Acceptability Criteria," 275–76. She assumes these categories from her former teacher Wallace Matson in which all philosophical approaches are broken down into two categories "outside-in," representing an Aristotelian trajectory, and "inside-out," the Platonic. I believe her oversight in failing to consider the efforts of Heidegger to transcend and broaden these Greek (Socratic) categories by considering the pre-Socratics reveals her perennial appeal to antiquated neo-Kantian dualistic structures. This issue will become more critical as we progress.

22. Gendlin, *Experiencing*, xxvii, emphasis added.

to correspond to Gendlin's term *symbol*: concept + experience = meaning.[23] In this respect, any truly holistic theory of human knowledge and meaning must take seriously both the conceptual aspect of human existence (*episteme*) and the nature of experience with its complexity of forces and contingencies that bear upon the making of meaning. H. G. Gadamer notes that the concept of experience is poorly articulated in philosophy (notwithstanding theological attempts).[24] Therefore, any plausible holistic theory of knowledge must always attempt to explain and factor experience within the equation of human understanding and meaning.

Since Descartes, Jürgen Moltmann notes, we began interpreting the notion of human understanding as emerging from the subject-object relationship as if the entire structure of the human subject and experience were invariant.[25] Therefore, objectivity was verifiable through *repeatability*. The identification of the true self (subjectivity) became the totality of consciousness which elevated the notion of reason and will above those of the senses and various tacit aspects of human experience.

> We acquire most of our experiences neither through our consciousness, nor through our reason, nor as the result of any deliberate intention. . . . It therefore seems too narrow and too "ego-centric" to relate experience merely to "the life of the consciousness" and "the activity of the reason," and to exclude whatever does not belong to these contexts.[26]

Furthermore, the complex process of experiences that are active during the construction and formation of knowledge is so subtle it would be impossible to identify or explain them thoroughly.

> In the elemental experiences of life, love and death we are touched by perceptions of a sensory kind which overpower us to such a degree that we are not master of them. They mould us, and become our companions. There are events in the past which never become "past," but are continually present to us. We repress them, we work on them, we puzzle over them and interpret them, for we have to live with them.[27]

There is no transcendental subjectivity providing humanity with a fixed objective perspective separate from an infinitely complex, ever-changing

23. Hefner, "God and Chaos," 469.
24. Gadamer, *Truth and Method*, 310–11.
25. Moltmann, *Spirit*, 18–29.
26. Moltmann, *Spirit*, 20.
27. Moltmann, *Spirit*, 20.

relationship to our world. As creatures, we constitute within our cosmic relations with others, and "we experience ourselves in the experience of other people."[28] Therefore experience is never an immediate awareness; instead, it is mediated.[29] Human beings are not in complete control of what they experience; in fact, they must eventually relax control to enter the domain of the relation to experience Other. If concept *and experience* produce *meaning*, the complexity and difficulty in establishing hermeneutical principles and theological method go without saying. This intensifies the need for a more inclusive and articulate understanding of holism within theological method and criteria.

The Example of St. Teresa vs. St. Catherine in the Theological Criterion of Religious Experience

Murphy designates the use of religious experience as theological criteria warranted by a faith community's collective discernment and tradition development. Because of its apparent holistic nature, this criterion deserves significant focus. Later we will parallel the experience of the numinal with that holistic dynamic and Power that create all social relations.[30]

In an example of how Murphy would apply Lakatosian method for discerning theologically viable religious experience, she contrasts the spiritual experiences of St. Teresa of Avila and St. Catherine of Siena.[31] She declines the experience of Teresa because Teresa verifies her experience as self-authenticating,[32] while accepting Catherine's experiences because Catherine can verify them through "*observable* changes in the recipient's life." The observable changes, says Murphy, correspond to a "network of other

---

28. Moltmann, *Spirit*, 24.

29. These are predominant themes in both Barth's concept of *imago Dei* and Ricoeur's *Oneself as Another*.

30. Numinal experience is the sustaining aspect within religious experience (and in one respect all experiences) that creates and sustains the meaningful conviction of a spiritual (holistic) presence, truth, concept, or relatedness. Within this thesis, the numinal aspect of experience results within the prereflexive experience of *analogia spiritus*, in which all participants analogically and *holistically* constitute as persons-in-relation to the divine.

31. Murphy, "What?," 113.

32. "This union is above all earthly joys, above all delights, above all consolations, and still more than that. . . . God so places himself in the interior of the soul that when it returns to itself it can in no way doubt that it was in God and God was in it. This truth remains with it so firmly that even though years go by without God's granting that favour again, the soul can neither forget nor doubt that it was in God and God was in it" (Teresa, *Collected Works*, 339).

experiences and phenomena."[33] Validating Teresa's experience through its sheer internal power and resolve is potentially too psychologically and empirically indeterminate for Murphy. However, in Catherine's experience the production of "gladness," "hunger for virtue," "humility," and "charity" are observable verifications of God's presence in religious experience.

In principle, this reasoning is satisfactory. However, is it all that simple? In other words, how might Murphy, who is a radical pacifist, construe the "gladness" and "charity" in Christ's relation to the Pharisees, money changers, and the inter-cultural and familial disintegration he forecasts on his account (Luke 12:49–53)? Is Christ's perennial impatience and vocal disgust for the disciples's lack of progress in faith charitable? Are Paul's relations with John, Mark, or the apostles at Antioch laced with humility and hunger for virtue? I believe they may be. However, assuming such criteria as "objective" or "observable" is not as straightforward as Murphy thinks. Though self-deception is always a potential factor, emerging psychological insights into our relationships continue to expose many new and ulterior motives in what was traditionally understood as charity. Self-deceptive controlling, acts of dominance, self-motivating acquiescence in codependency, or genuine self-givenness often vitiate apparent charity. According to Murphy's understanding of empirical, I suggest it is impossible to empirically discern these acts with any certainty or universal consensus, even within one's personal religious community. The first step of how a therapist senses what type of behavior lies *within* charitable behavior is through hypothetico-deductive reasoning (intuition); secondary reflections then test it deductively in reverse. As any therapist will concur, peaceful behavior and non-conflictual coexistence as an observable criterion in contrast to conflictual relations are never conclusive data of charitable, right, felicitous, or authentic interpersonal relations. Even with an established discernment process within a specific faith community, applying the empirical method is much more dynamic and complex than Murphy expresses.

Murphy's Evidential Nature of Fruit in Theological Criteria

Utilizing the "evidential" fruit of the Spirit that Paul offers as observable *behavior*, repeatable for the empirical manner that she employs, is philosophically naïve. Without further acknowledging, identifying, and personally experiencing the full wealth of experience *within each specific event occasion*, the notion of observable becomes abstract and impotent. Acknowledgment of such criteria for theological considerations necessitates a

33. Murphy, "What?," 113.

MEANING AS PERICHORESIS

subjective and communal intersubjective experience that transcends Murphy's notion of observability. This is not to claim such criteria (sanctified behaviors) are not, in principle, empirical (verifiable); in the holistic sense, they in principle are.[34] My concern is that Murphy's desire for a criterion of *episteme* (scientific knowledge) instantly dissociates from the broader, more holistic process of *phronesis* (wisdom).[35] What she attempts in the above methodological example is insufficient for establishing religious experience as theological data. Murphy assumes such observable intracommunal criteria are always diachronically coterminous; this would remove the observable criterion outside the transformative developmental dynamics within the tradition that produces its progress. With this bifurcation of language, she also rips the epistemic from the process of *phronesis*.

Is there not, however, a christological factor within the Christian criteria of religious experience? For example, because of the unique nature of Jesus' claim (*his* unique relationship with the Father), when Jesus says, "I am the way, the truth and the life," this "living utterance of the Living Word, cannot be severed from the Living Presence whence it is spoken."[36] Murphy weakens her concept of holism by differentiating and prioritizing her notion of the public ("observable") from the religious experience itself as a first step second-order theological move. Only secondarily is this verifiable account of the experience set before the tribunal of community consensus, which then engages the numinal discerning "yea/nay" of the community.[37] The theological consideration of religious experience must entail irreducibly the theologian's (and community's) openness to and, to some degree, engagement with the numinal aspect through which such experiences and propositions express their full meaning.

The fruit that the Christ relationship produces is non-reducible to any structural notion of *episteme*. Paul wrote his epistles within specific communal contexts and relationships, whose meaning will be particular to those event occurrences. Only through *phronesis* is historical unity (diachronic continuity) in Paul's writing given a unified meaning *relative to each new reading*. *Phronesis* is empirical in a more complex sense; only when earlier complex sets of relations holistically and analogically associate with later sets of relations can *phronesis* attain. Because each relational occurrence is different and Christ's full character existentially and uniquely incarnates

---

34. Gadamer, *Truth and Method*, 283–89.

35. As used here, phronesis is the quality of experiencing knowledge and judgment in a holistic, intuitive manner within the uniqueness of each relational occurrence.

36. Gangadean, "Universal Grammar," 4.

37. Murphy, *Theology*, ch. 5.

within each event accordingly, notwithstanding each stage of development within the church, the criterion of fruit must ultimately remain in experiential and developmental flux. This is not to suggest that one period's criterion of fruit replaces the next but simply allows for the expanding and appropriate reconfiguring of our understanding and experience of it.

The establishment of theological criteria is by nature no less contingent, whether personally subjective or communal. Clayton claims that the "nature of the social phenomenon necessitates that explanations make reference to the semantic synthesizing function of the individual self, as well as to the interplay between individual worlds and shared social worlds."[38] Though the individual is developmentally dependent and sustained within community, the communitive level of discernment and explanations are no more *objective* than the personal level; they are simply more comprehensive. Piaget and others claim the *dynamics* of personal reflection and social dialogue are indistinguishable to the point that neither can be shown to precede the other developmentally.[39] There is no principal difference in their basic dynamic structuring. The origins and development of self (reflection) and community (dialogue) are mutually distinct yet interconnected events.

Therefore, it is methodologically naïve to set apart specific observable data as distinctly different in their performative dynamics than the convictive nature of the subjective. Neither do the convictive forces (veridical or spurious) subjectively active within the individual entirely circumvent or escape the social. In other words, self-inducement is just as present within the lives of whole cultures (cultural-inducement). Richard Swinburne once said in a BBC interview that the holocaust was not the product of one madman deceiving an entire culture but a communitive development proceeding from thousands of communitive decisions made over a hundred years leading up to it that institute cultural-inducement.[40]

In this respect, Jesus explicitly and socially gave his disciples all the data needed to identify who He was within their context. He insists, however, that their final recognition of himself emerges *personally, subjectively*, and reflectively in an *indirect* manner resulting from their complete openness to that Power that constitutes all relationships, which does not obviate one's social contingencies. In other words, only through the prereflexive play of *analogia spiritus* are we able to acknowledge Christ's divinity authentically. One can experience such knowledge in community but not fully equate it

---

38. Murphy, *Theology*, 99.

39. Piaget, *Six Psychological Studies*, 40. Likewise, the work of Vygotsky, Bakhtin, and others argue that internal reflections indeed are internalized discourse.

40. Such "cultural inducements" are well established in the work of Hannah Arendt, Jacques Ellul, and more recently by Mattias Desmet in *The Psychology of Totalitarianism*.

MEANING AS PERICHORESIS

with community. Though socially conditioned and transmitted, Christ insists we ultimately identity and know him in a hypothetico-deductive manner (through no "flesh," Matt 16:17). No inductive or deductive source of socialized empirical verification could provide the proper configuration to the whole puzzle (Kierkegaard). Likewise, according to John and Paul, this activity of the Holy Spirit does not obviate the social contingencies of personal and social relations (1 Cor 2; 1 John 2). Recognition, *as such*, becomes the establishing rock of Christianity and takes asymmetrical priority over any simple or verifiable defining of fruits. The two cannot be severed; praxis is of extreme importance, but the separation of such fruits from firsthand experience and appropriate recontextualizations leads to an infinite regressive defining of that fruit that becomes problematic, rendering the fruit impotent. In this respect, the *what* and *how* of Christ's identity becomes mysteriously synonymous.[41] Murphy does not implement this aspect of believing, experiencing or doing theology emphatically enough. For her, the Spirit's activity in theology primarily lies within the process of community verification *of* objectifiable criteria. In contrast, the theologian's holistic or faith experience *within* theological reflection is necessary for producing the appropriate theological/faith meaning during such thinking or discourse. With Kuhn and Wittgenstein, Lindbeck thinks,

> The norms of reasonableness are too rich and subtle to be adequately specified in any general theory of reason or knowledge. . . . Thus reasonableness in religion and theology, as in other domains, has something of that aesthetic character, that quality of unformalizable skill.[42]

Lindbeck is extremely aware of the depth, integration, and complexity of theological knowledge. However, in this regard, much of Murphy's relational logic (reasoning) becomes too linear and needs to dimensionalize into a fuller holism, as does her notion of religious experience as theological criteria.

---

41. Murphy acknowledges that her Lakatosian program takes account of the Plantinga "presupposition" and the Barth/T. F. Torrance demand that the nature of the object determines the proper method of inquiry (Torrance, *Theological Science*, 10). However, she fails to realize the radical epistemological dynamics ("inversion" or divine contingency) that these individuals require of human inquiry in the knowing event and knowledge of an *Eternal* God.

42. Lindbeck, *Nature of Doctrine*, 130.

Critical Investigation of Murphy

Lakatos, says Murphy, argues that degenerating programs can sometimes be "sleepers" and, over time, may emerge as progressive programs.[43] Feyerabend, however, rightly argues that such an open contingency without time restraints fatally damages the Lakatosian notion of progress.[44] In this respect, Murphy's Lakatosian program will be reconsidered within a more comprehensive theological-anthropological paradigm to address Feyerabend's concern.

Let us look at four primary areas of inquiry into Murphy's method: (1) her selective use of Wittgenstein and language as predominately non-referential, (2) the empirical notions of observability, belief, and *episteme*, (3) the criterion of progress and the potential unseen universal component, and (4) the potential lack of intellectual virtue and *phronesis* she employs within her conceptual holism (person and relationships as good, rather than act as good). All four of these result from bifurcating the experiential and the cognitive/conceptual in her effort to produce empirical criteria of *episteme*. Polanyi, whose categories this thesis will implement, similarly presents a separation between the focal and tacit awareness within knowledge and meaning construction, yet he never fails to maintain their unitary tension and the irreducibility of their complementarity in the construction of meaning. Ultimately, I believe Murphy fails to engage the arduous journey of expanding the historical notions of the empirical.

(1) Theology, Language as Non-referential, and the Incarnational Aspect of Meaning

In a critique of Nicholas Wolterstorff, Tim Ward questions Wolterstorff's understanding and use of Searle, Austin, and Wittgenstein's notion of speech-act and language games. "Speech-act theorists do indeed distinguish between locution and illocution, but they do so in order to describe *different aspects of the same speech-act*, and not, as Wolterstorff does, in order to set up two entirely different kinds of act."[45] I believe Murphy has executed a similar move in her use and understanding of Wittgenstein to argue the

---

43. Murphy, "Divine Action," 102; also Cf. Hefner, *Human Factor*, 25.

44. Feyerabend, "Consolations." Also, van Huyssteen tells us, "because theological programs have been shown not to function at all like scientific research programs in Murphy's model, Lakatos's criterion of relative empirical progress could hardly be used to adjudicate between competing theological theories or schools" (*Essays*, 86).

45. Ward, "Making Meaningful," 3.

predominance of language use as non-referential. First, she calls for a non-referential emphasis in language theory to escape the abuses of Modernity; then, she divides first-level faith practice and second-level theological language concerning that practice. Is this an appropriate implementation of Wittgensteinian understanding of language practice?

For Murphy, the force of Paul's message in Scripture comes through the "just enough" observable evidence to believe reasonably in the testimony.[46] Again, her focus here is the observability of the evidence within the second-level language game of theology. And again, she separates the language of theology from the holistic mediational *aspect* of the faith experience. Fergus Kerr tells us that Wittgenstein is not suggesting we do not grasp the object of assertions, which is the referential aspect of language, but "[denies] that one is able to get hold of anything independently of one's being initiated into certain common practices."[47] Murphy fails to consider the personal and corporate *perceivability* and condition of the Holy Spirit and spiritual dynamics *within* theological discourse. In this respect, one wonders how associative her method and content really are when considering the theological descriptions of and speech-acts of Teresa of Avila, Abraham, or Jacob.

Philip Clayton tells us that, among other things, "the nature of assertions is to refer to extralinguistic states of affairs."[48] Any thought to the contrary significantly removes the notion of ontological reference and materially alters the entire theological program, most notably, the idea of the hard core. This bifurcation of language reduces the content of the hard core to mere *episteme* and eliminates any true holism. Such notions of holism recognize the complexity of belief structure but fail to draw the full wealth of human convictional forces at play in theological method and discourse. Such forces integral within theological knowledge and experience are, among other things, emotions, intellectual and relational dispositions and virtues, vocational security and insecurity, and the experience of the numinal. Each aspect is essential and usually subconscious in developing and sustaining theological knowledge. "It seems strange," says Clayton, "for theologians to rush in to reduce their own discipline to another."[49] In other words, Clayton's theological methodology rightly keeps "the question of [theology's] objective truth *within the theological endeavor itself*."[50] Theological method must insist that the "Living Word" and the full wealth of

---

46. Murphy, "Textual Relativism," 262–63.
47. Kerr, *Theology after Wittgenstein*, 102–4.
48. Clayton, *Explanation*, 172.
49. Clayton, *Explanation*, 172.
50. Clayton, *Explanation*, 172.

predications and communicative faith practices that gave rise to Christian theology remain inseparably within the act of Christian theology. Unfortunately, Murphy inappropriately drags her understanding of non-referential language, taken from her first acquired discipline of philosophy of science, without appropriate adjustment into theological method.

Wittgenstein's Holism: The Unity of Language, Reason, and Experience

Though Wittgenstein would object to reducing Christianity, human life, or metaphysics into one arrogant unitary theory or base them upon any foundational claim, he, as much as any other, shows us that knowledge and reason irreducibly exist as communitive interaction (meaning as use or action).[51] Language as use implies that we use it for something, and therefore this theory concentrically equates with the idea that all knowledge is relational. Though Wittgenstein's work may only be of limited theological value, his transcending the modern concept of the subject is incisive. That Murphy has critically adopted him for use in theological method makes him an even more suitable dialogue partner for this current discussion.

I have argued that the designation of criteria for intrasystematic or second-level use based upon rational or empirically defined standards risks underdetermining various unconsidered supporting aspects of grammar (actions) that contribute to communications. For Wittgenstein, these fundamental developments within our relations and practices become the unseen "familiar" foundations upon which various language games and rational thought constitute. Concerning the intrasystematic notion of truth and reason, Fergus Kerr notes that Wittgenstein believes

> the meanings that establish the house of reason are not inside our individual minds. They are out in the open, constituting the space, wherever two or three gather to exchange gifts or threats or stories and songs. . . . The claim of reason is so exorbitant in our metaphysically inflated self-understanding that it is hard for us to acknowledge what is obvious: the phenomena, including the language games that give rise to the possibility of rational thought in the first place.[52]

All rational and intrasystematic truths are merely relational meanings that constitute *within* transactions. They are contingent upon various developed

---

51. Wittgenstein, *Blue and Brown*, 4.
52. Kerr, *Theology after Wittgenstein*, 118.

skills (language games). Many of these skills are "hidden" phenomena within the interaction. Wittgenstein further notes that

> the aspects of things that are most important for us are hidden because of their simplicity and familiarity. (One is unable to notice something—because it is always before one's eyes.) The real foundations of his inquiry do not strike a man at all. Unless that fact has at some time struck him.—And this means: we fail to be struck by what, once seen, is most striking and most powerful.[53]

Concerning such "hidden" "foundations" (of reason) of which Wittgenstein wrote, Kerr points to a "*natural* order that pervades and sustains our culture," a relatedness to the world which underlies all human perception, cognitive construction, knowledge and interest.[54] For him, any concept of reason (causal relatedness) as separable from the whole of active human relatedness to the world is the illusion of the idealist, who is

> for Wittgenstein, the man who has to have a reason for accepting the existence even of his own hands. All that we do and say has to rest upon some assumption or hypothesis, some view or belief, or more generally, some web of beliefs. Our relation to the world, on this account, is essentially cognitive. What is primary and foundational, according to Wittgenstein, is, however, neither ideas nor beliefs nor any other class of mental events, but human beings in *a multiplicity of transactions* with one another.[55]

Therefore, if Wittgenstein and Kerr are correct, then the intrasystematic order of adequacy and meaning becomes incomplete and distorted when we cognitively differentiate it in any way from the full dynamic of the interaction. The temptation by some postliberals to bifurcate first- and second-order language games within various forms of discourse comes from the failure to realize the holistic unity of the conceptual and experiential within meaning and imposes an inappropriate certainty and control upon one's own continuity of relations. The temptation to devise two *levels* within meaning (discourse and experience) occurs when that which is most fundamental, most powerful, and most important disappears within the interaction.

That which is most powerful within discourse lies within the unseen tacit presence of the interaction. Like water to a fish, though oblivious to the existence of water, it never ceases to experience the force and presence

---

53. Wittgenstein, *Philosophical Investigations*, 50e.
54. Kerr, *Theology after Wittgenstein*, 118.
55. Kerr, *Theology after Wittgenstein*, 119, emphasis added.

of this basic phenomenon.[56] We cannot separate these phenomena within the irreducibility of meaning and relationship. Our expressions and actions with one another are actively developing complexities of shared synthesized experiences that socially organize into whole acts of meaningful interactions. Such countless elements and complexities lie inherent within all communications. It would be tragic to segregate various aspects of language (e.g., "explanatory," "rational," "empirical," or "observable") from the faith practice it attempts to explain for technical theological use. All language contains all sorts of unseen phenomena. In this respect, faith experience, which inhabits our theological expressions, must remain an inherent *re-occurring* experience within all authentic theological interactions, rational or otherwise. Nothing lies outside the transaction itself; we never share a "belief," we share or communicate a *believing*. In a Kierkegaardian manner, *one does not refer to God as much as the whole transaction communicating one's own believing in God then refers to God.*[57]

Wittgenstein and Rational Criteria

The pertinent Wittgensteinian principle for this discussion is not to assume that the *unseen phenomena* are any less real or ultimately less verifiable than what we consider empirical within the personal or social constructions of reason. Furthermore, we must acknowledge the complexity of every transaction in its struggle for unitive alignment and understanding amid the unique unseen phenomena of each person's language development. Though they are unseen, there are many "living" forces implicit and tacit within the existing transaction. Therefore, we must resist the temptation that we are methodologically able to designate explicit, rational constructions or intrasystematic notions of criteria away from marginalized aspects of the *phenomena*.[58]

---

56. As the old philosopher's saying goes: "I don't know who discovered water, but I'm certain it wasn't a fish."

57. For example, in *CUP*, Climacus and Kierkegaard sharply emphasize the *how* of belief over the *what* of belief, i.e., it is not the word that refers but the entire action of one's believing that refers.

58. Similarly, the Marxist critique is also relevant: "One of the most difficult tasks confronting philosophers is to descend from the world of thought to the actual world. . . . The philosophers have only to dissolve their language into the ordinary language, from which it is abstracted, in order to recognize it as the distorted language of the actual world, and to realize that neither thoughts nor language in themselves form a realm of their own, that they are only *manifestations* of actual life" (Marx and Engels, *Collected Works*, 5:446–47).

The deep structure of theological knowledge appears when we consider the early theological positions and later reversals of many academically successful theologians (e.g., pre-1914 Karl Barth, early John Hick, or Eta Linnemann). The radical and sometimes almost instant theological reversals driven by non-"theological" criteria powerfully suggest that these theologians's earlier theological structures contained peripheral unseen non-"theological" forces within those early theological convictions.[59] More fundamental aspects within the theologically unseen sociological and interpersonal world motivate such radical shifts. Wittgenstein might suggest that the full content of Barth's earlier theology may have appeared similar to his mentors, but time eventually exposed differing unseen aspects between them. This is why Barth's reaction was immediate; he could not rationalize the political actions of his former theological mentors with his personal theological understanding and experience, despite their original resemblances. If he was experiencing the exact same language game in his theological thinking as his mentors, his reaction would not have been so immediate and violent. Strictly speaking, there is no unifying *absolute* language game within the living faith or paradigm of a particular community; there are living communities with multiple individuals who have different histories and experiences from which no overarching episteme or observables can be extracted from its existential fullness for the use of assessing community continuity with certainty. Each theologian remains in differentiated unity, slightly or significantly different than the others. The unseen "foundations" or core forces within their beliefs become apparent through time and further development, if at all.

Whether any religious considerations are commensurate with Wittgenstein's notion of the natural phenomena of relations is irrelevant; the structure of Wittgenstein's thinking is that the more "important" and more "powerful" phenomena within *relations* are tacit, even unconscious, and therefore recessively implicit within our reasoning. Wittgenstein, for example, generally considers the greater pretension of reason and moral absolutes as the hidden phenomena of the will to power.[60] These radical theological shifts reveal that their earlier ratiocination and internal coherence were methodologically incomplete and subsequently subverted by

---

59. If specific extra-theological data (e.g., German theologians supporting the war policy of Wilhelm II) create a violent shift in one's theological position, then that former position was never merely theological. Barth's theological convictions had never changed, but when he heard about his former mentors's political position, he knew something was seriously wrong with their theology and immediately began expanding his own. Barth, *Humanity of God*, 14.

60. Kerr, *Theology after Wittgenstein*, 60, 118–19.

Jacob and the Night of Faith

non-"theological" *phenomena*. Ultimately, every experience or discipline of thought affects theological inquiry.

This is consonant with Ricoeur's conviction that more lies within the actor or discipline's language and action than the focal intention of the author. Clayton informs us, "Ricoeur denies that ascertaining what the actors meant by their actions is all we aim for in trying to understand them." The intended meaning is not the entirety of what we engage. "Explanations in social science [and theology] need not be tied to the self-understandings of the agents involved."[61] In this respect, we can never exclusively constitute meaning solely by or within ourselves or the author, but by and within the immediate interaction. More is always in the text than what the author *initially and focally* intends. The author's original meaning immediately dies the moment after writing to resurrect and incarnate within each new reading, each new relational horizon. Because of the infinite algorithms of contingencies in each new reading, new meaning constantly arises in acts of *phronesis* even if the original (and evolving) intent drifts from the initial focal awareness of the author. However, each new felicitous resurrection of meaning never analogically conflicts with the infinite possibilities of other felicitous readings. A reader from outside the immediate community might later learn things from the text that explicitly eluded the original author, yet those things were implicitly tacit (latent, recessive, pregnant, or a potential) within the author's awareness and therefore focally emerge from the tacit within new relational horizons.[62] Moreover, in this respect, Barth correctly

---

61. Clayton, *Explanations*, 72.

62. For example (please allow the playfulness): A classic written by an old fish was read centuries later by flying fish who had since developed focal awareness and knowledge of water (because they discovered air—*différance*—and thus water). The flyers, nevertheless, still learned much about water from the old one's writings simply because the logic of water played an obvious though implicit role in the author's experience and narrative. Though the author had no focal knowledge of water, nor was it properly within the *sensus literalis* of his text, it was, nevertheless, within his tacit and practical experience that backgrounds his focal awareness and narrative. If, however, we object by claiming that the tacit is indeed implicit within the *sensus literalis* and that we, the flyers, have a felicitous connection with that *sensus literalis* (*compositus*), then what are we to say of the future fuller interpretations of the "walkers" in relation to the flyer's meaning? What is the literal sense—the authorial intention—when a thousand various cultures in one age of humanity might exegete the Scriptures with a thousand slightly different "literal" meanings, all of them potentially suitable, all of them potentially implicit within the original communicational occurrence, and none ultimately conflicting? All writings immediately fall into a trans-jective horizon, and all readers must enter that same movement. In this sense, if all of what was "literally" contained within the authorial intent of the Scriptures were written down one by one, I suppose that even the world itself could not contain the books that would be written. Cf. also Marion, *God without Being*, 156. This in no way negates the possibility of errant reading or

states that every significant theological author of the past is alive within the current conversation.⁶³ Each new developing relationship (communitive reading) draws out more of what was formerly tacit beneath the author's intended (focal) meaning. In this respect, authors and texts may experience revolving episodes of honor and villainization throughout history.

THE UNSEEN UNIVERSAL: THE BIFURCATION OF HUMAN MEANING LEADS TO THE LOSS OF THE UNIVERSAL DYNAMIC WITHIN HUMAN EXPERIENCE AND THEOLOGICAL CRITERIA

According to Kerr, Wittgenstein thinks it is illusory to establish *truth by rational causal connections* and interconnecting rational beliefs within a networking web. Meaning is the irreducible quality of the whole transaction with one another. In this manner, intrasystematic truth claims must appropriately articulate and factor the precedence of meaning itself. All grammar, whether seen or unseen, is performative and ultimately indivisible within the utterance.

Regardless of our conclusions concerning Wittgenstein's theological usefulness, his insistence upon acknowledging simple *phenomena* underneath the "metaphysical" determinations is critical. Therefore, we must strive to identify and include as much as possible of this unseen grammar within the theological explanatory equation and theological interaction. Moreover, we must never establish such phenomena as conclusive sets of criteria. Instead, all criteria must remain open-ended, constantly opening again and again for plural, equitable, and revising employment within each interaction. In this respect, Murphy's concerns for the *appropriate* necessity and function of the explanatory and rational capacity (per Wittgenstein) fails to acknowledge the attempts within this thesis to legitimate Wittgenstein's insistence upon *difference*.⁶⁴ In *The One, the Three, and the Many*, Colin Gunton similarly emphasizes the necessity of difference. He effectively reveals this differentiating dynamic in the logic of spirit and the role of spirit in relational dynamics.

---

interpretation or that the author is without intent, merely that we must recognize "the task is infinite." Cf. Schleiermacher, *Hermeneutics*, 246n12.

63. Barth, *Protestant Theology*.

64. Wittgenstein reported to his friend Maurice O'Conner Drury that he considered using as a motto for *Investigations* what he remembered as a quotation from King Lear—"I'll teach you differences" (Fann, *Ludwig Wittgenstein*, 69). In the end, he used the motto from Nestroy. Kerr suggests this was probably due to the eventuality that the quote was "misremembered" from *King Lear*, and he was forced to abandon it (from private conversation with Fergus Kerr, 1998).

Returning to the unitary (yet dipolar) structure of meaning, all intrasystematic adequacy or reasoning as such ultimately falls into intrasystematic paradox (Quine's notion of antinomical paradox)[65] which is never, in itself, coherent or reasonable. Furthermore, with J. Wentzel van Huyssteen, I believe Murphy's positive heuristic of public *observability* and notion of the "criterion of empirical progress,"[66] *as she defines it*, reveals a cryptic foundationalism of a late modern character despite her noted intentions otherwise.[67] Thiemann is guilty as well, but not necessarily Lindbeck. Ultimately, Lindbeck is consonant with the corresponding views of Wittgenstein and John Milbank. The natural sciences are not as critically affected by the more complex personal and relational issues of theology and humanities.[68] However, these less complex methodological features within the natural sciences become the most prominent and fundamental features within Murphy's theological implementation of the Lakatosian method. Van Huyssteen also cautions whether or not such an implementation can "adequately cope with the broader and more complex problem of meaning as highlighted by the social sciences."[69] On the other hand, Clayton's insightful consideration of Lakatosian method for theological use "mandates the employment in the human sciences [and eventually theology] of methods not applicable in natural science."[70] This does not necessitate an evacuation of a Lakatosian scheme but a more comprehensive and appropriate understanding of *how* we must implement it theologically.

For Lindbeck, a genuinely holistic criterion exists for adjudication between differing cultural-linguistic systems of similar competence through the broad criterion of "performance." He acknowledges that factors in transcommunal performances between various cultural-linguistic systems are somehow comparable. This recognizes that some universal or teleological force active within and upon human experience creates or provides a performative criterion. By splitting the wholeness within method and privileging the intrasystematic dialectic (reason, *episteme*), Murphy and Thiemann forfeit the one conclusive indicator we have—desire and the fullness of life (developed below). Though Lindbeck refrains from specifying any *modus significandi* or *universalia*, he emphatically acknowledges a universal

---

65. Jackson, "Kierkegaard's Metatheology."
66. Murphy, *Theology*, 204.
67. Cf. Huyssteen, *Essays*, 88.
68. Clayton, *Explanations*.
69. Huyssteen, *Essays*, 87.
70. Clayton, *Explanations*, 73. In his Gifford Lectures (*Religions*), Ian Barbour similarly agrees with Clayton.

(non-relativism) component active *within* human interactions.⁷¹ What these theologians attempt to gain by parsing language into first and second order has some limited value; however, without consideration given to the holistic dimensions of *analogia spiritus* and the logic of its activity within theological discourse leaves their methodology and project incomplete.

Later in the chapter, I will argue that language's referential and non-referential designations become false dichotomies when understood within the relational paradigm of meaning as *perichoresis*. Nevertheless, the loss of referential language altogether, or the overemphasis of it in reaction to Modernity, ultimately hastens the loss of the self.

(2) The Inadequacy of Separating Concept and Experience within Theological Methodology: Observability, Episteme, and the Compromise of Holism

Ronald Thiemann distinguishes between the first-order discourse of faith experience and practice, and second-order theological discourse concerning that experience. George Lindbeck speaks of the intrasystematic and ontological truth *aspects* of statements. Nancey Murphy draws upon Thiemann's distinctions, contending that they are functionally different in their theological use, as do Thiemann and Lindbeck. Though they attempt to hold some connection of second-order discourse with first-order faith practice, they maintain the distinction, nonetheless. This conflicts with, for example, the direction of Moltmann's theological method,⁷² which seeks a more ambitious holism to transcend these distinctions. In response to Murphy's brand of epistemological holism, van Huyssteen says she "lacks a well-developed theory of experience."⁷³

Murphy argues that transcendental or correspondent notions of truth must give way to coherentist methodologies of "intrasystematic" adequacy

---

71. This is because Lindbeck, *Nature of Doctrine*, 134, recognizes and identifies "the ultimate test in this as in other areas is performance." He refuses to bifurcate completely or functionally the "intrasystematic" and "ontological" aspects of truth statements for methodological purposes (64). Nevertheless, he alludes to a universal dynamic within the criterion of "performance."

72. Refer to the earlier discussion of Moltmann's critique.

73. Huyssteen, *Essays*, 84. For Murphy's response to van Huyssteen see, "Critical Realism" and "Limits." In the latter article, she accuses him of being only a partial postmodernist and, therefore, unable to understand postmodernity in its essence (335). More importantly, her reasons why she is not a foundationalist and bears no universal criterion of rationality are ultimately unsatisfying considering van Huyssteen's later cited critiques. As far as I know, she has never responded to the charge that she "lacks a well-developed theory of experience."

or second-order language whose primary criteria is internal coherence. Kierkegaard, Nietzsche, Heidegger, and Derrida, each in their own way, effectively argue that internal coherence ultimately in itself is illusory. Kierkegaard, for example, argues that the truth of any religious knowledge is always objectively paradoxical (ultimately non-coherent). Truth and meaning are to be associated first with the "mode" and felicitous nature of the relationship itself that constitutes the individual. As Kierkegaard notes,

> *The objective accent falls on WHAT is said, the subjective accent on HOW it is said.* This distinction . . . receives definite expression in the principle that what is in itself true may in the mouth of such and such a person become untrue (181). . . . But the eternal essential truth is by no means in itself a paradox; but it becomes paradoxical by virtue of its relationship to an existing individual (183).[74]

In this respect,

> Truth in its very being is not the duplication of being in terms of thought. . . . For knowing the truth is something which follows as a matter of course from being the truth [and] . . . it becomes untruth when knowing the truth is separated from being the truth.[75]

The relationship in which the individual and participants are of one mind[76] constitutes the relationship in the greatest truth and meaning.[77] Such an understanding suggests that truth is a quality of the relationship itself, which incorporates but is not reducible to the factors of coherence, reason, communitive consensus, progress, or nature of experience.

Kierkegaard's insights do not entirely set aside the project of modernity, which echoes quite resoundingly in the thinking of Murphy and

---

74. Kierkegaard, *CUP*, 178.
75. Kierkegaard, *TC*, 201.
76. Cf. Kierkegaard, *Purity of Heart*.
77. "When the question of the truth is raised subjectively, reflection is directed subjectively to the nature of the individual's relationship; if only the mode of this relationship is in the truth, the individual is in the truth even if he should happen to be thus related to what is not true," (*CUP*, 178) i.e., contrary to the notion that "truth is understanding [and] knowledge, . . . in primitive Christianity all expressions were constructed with a view to truth as a form of being" (*TC*, 202). This mode of openness (infinite resignation) to the Other constitutes authentic existential relations. Because humans focally know only in part in existence, truth is never the object's re-presentation but the degree of authentic relations the person has with the Other, even if that knowledge is not as conceptually complete as others. Our knowledge of Christ, e.g., is always invariant, always more than our *conceptual* understanding of him.

Thiemann, it simply requires its completion or proper institution within a fuller and more adequate paradigm of meaning construction. Human meaning ultimately finds no suitable resting place in the subject of late modernity, nor the complete incommensurability of language games or inter-system dialogue of most postmodern theories. The bifurcation of the theological event from its source of origination and continuity (faith experience) to a language game whose adequacy we assess through internal coherence is simply a cryptic fallback into the rationalism of Modernity—yet another desperate grasp for Hegelian control and certainty. Kierkegaard's thesis dismantles the reified System, and those unable to understand his critique (or that of Poststructuralism) are left to reassemble the fallen blocks of Modernity (Rationalism and the "will to power"). The internal coherence of the intrasystematic (closed) system soon becomes irrational (internally incoherent) before the nonrational forces within all traditions and the play of deconstructionists who use each system's *own* internal logic to mock it. Nevertheless, the aspect of internal coherence is useful and necessary within any methodology as a valuable criterion of conceptual adequacy *within* true holism. As a conceptually isolated criterion, it too becomes naked and impotent.

Conceptual coherence cannot be a theological factor outside its existential integration with experience into meaning. In other words, *holism cannot be merely conceptual or just coherent; it must be the whole of the person in existence (relationship)*. Coherence within *phronesis*, on the other hand, incorporates many of those holistic aspects of existence as well as the conceptual. A truly pragmatic research program should emerge from the whole of experience, and the whole of human experience contains the common ground of what it is to experience as human. (In later chapters, we will consider developmentalist attempts to isolate some of those universal structures and dynamics fundamental to being human.) Mere conceptual progress and novel fact (*facere*) cannot judge adequacy (though these are undoubtedly helpful and necessary). The conceptual and the experiential *together* create a holistic performative meaning—and with it, a level of *fullness of life*. This irreducible value of meaning reflects the quality and level of the relationship and its content. Forthcoming is an explanation of this criterion as the degree of *perichoresis* experienced within relationships. It seems to be the intent of Murphy, Lindbeck, and other postliberals to incorporate these more holistic qualities within theory development and assessment, but, for myself, they fail to complete their project compellingly.

Murphy's hard core and overall program, however, entails a treatment of theory as interrelated beliefs that emphasize *episteme* (scientific or theoretical knowledge) and *techne* (skillful knowledge) in relative exclusion to what Gadamer refers to as *phronesis*—knowledge that guides practical human activity. In other words, *phronesis* as *an insight* into what is right in each situation or action.[78] Ironically, Murphy, a conceptual pragmatist,[79] only minimally attains any degree of *phronesis* (practical knowledge in application) because of her functional distinction between the conceptual and experiential and her failure to forward an adequate theory of experience. She, in effect, subordinates experience to knowledge (*episteme*/*techne*) within theological discourse. This critique of her is also consonant with Paul Feyerabend's (et al.) criticism that Lakatos and many current philosophy of science trends remain within a rationalist tradition that alienates it from the whole of practical life.[80]

Holism compromised

Is there not something in the community's faith experience that interpenetrates all conceptual theory in a manner that defies distillation into mere conceptualization? As argued, associating belief in general as *episteme* and *techne* is problematic. Contra Moltmann, Murphy's epistemological holism fails to maintain that all knowledge be inextricably and existentially rooted in faith experience and application. In a similar critique of Murphy, van Huyssteen stipulates that

> a holistic epistemology implies more than communal discernment and communal consensus for contemporary theological reflection: it also demands a broader intersubjective coherence that goes beyond the parameters of the experience and reflection of the believing community. . . . The very distinction between "hard core beliefs" and others that can be regarded as auxiliary hypotheses within an attempt at a holistic postmodern theology invariably raises the spectre of a Plantinganian, weak form of foundationalism.[81]

Because of the nature of theological knowledge (knowledge of a God who is the all-determining reality), the theological hard core must be more than a belief. In theology, the hard core necessitates *experiencing* immanent-transcendent analogical dynamics, both given and gift, natural and

---

78. Gadamer, *Truth and Method*, 278–89. A discussion of *phronesis* is forthcoming. (Many thanks to Kevin Vanhoozer, my mentor for this thesis, for steering me toward the concept of *phronesis*.)

79. Murphy, "Limits," 351.

80. Feyerabend, *Against Method*; Kulka, "Problems"; Suppe, *Structure*, 659–70.

81. Huyssteen, *Essays*, 233.

revealed, that come to bear upon the individual in existential relation to a disclosing God. If our theological discourse is meaningful, this aspect of the divine-human relation must be actively inclusive within such discourse and reflection. Therefore, within the Lakatosian research program, we cannot segregate functionally or technically the *theological* core from sustaining aspects of experience within the communitive faith experience, which must travel with and remain present within all theological interaction.

The problem of Murphy's functional bifurcation results partly from her superimposition of the Quinian web of beliefs (with its outer circle of experience, intermittent content of networking beliefs, and an inner core of consecrated beliefs) upon the Lakatosian model. This effectively divorces the full wealth of experience from the Lakatosian hard core of the research project. Instead, she argues that a theological hard core should be a "judgment" concerning what "Christianity is basically all about."[82] Are judgments of this nature ever mere conceptualizations, theories, or knowledge without the creative re-constituting convictive force about which the judgment is being made? I think not. *God must be experientially active within the theological exercise.*

Again, Murphy's conviction that knowledge develops either "outside-in" or "inside-out" should warrant our caution, especially in theological discourse.[83] In Murphy's use of Quine's notion of outer experience and inward *a priori* established core beliefs that are untouchables, she provides two options alone, of which she privileges the Aristotelian outside-in. Therefore, the belt of auxiliary hypotheses and outer beliefs, which are closer to experience, protect the inner core beliefs, while the core beliefs are not directly verifiable by any form of experience. In agreement with van Huyssteen, I believe this emphasis on beliefs alone within the hard core of a *theological* research program is equivalent to foundationalism (which is not strictly the case in the natural sciences). However, within this thesis's holistic dipolar aspect of understanding human meaning (concept + experience), I wish to argue with Kierkegaard that knowledge develops and constitutes *both* "outside-in" and "inside-out" concurrently.[84] In this respect, Murphy and most postliberal theologies employ a false dichotomy or, more accurately, continue antiquated metaphysical structuring.

82. Murphy, *Beyond*, 103.

83. This is tragically equivalent to Linda Zagzebski's (*Virtues of the Mind*) characterizing the primary controversy of epistemological studies as divided between the internalist and the externalist theories of knowledge.

84. We shall later discuss the consonant Kierkegaardian categories that humans are a synthesis of both time and eternity, the finite and the infinite, and how this affects the creation of meaning.

Jacob and the Night of Faith

If spirit is that holistic configurative activity of both divine and human existence, through which every relationship constitutes, then Murphy's shallow implementation of the Lakatosian program is theologically problematic. Theological knowledge of the hard core and all associating theories must constantly and existentially reconstitute within the active immanent-transcendent interaction between human spirit and divine Spirit.[85] As the *whole* of the individual (spirit) encounters the *whole* of God (Spirit), or person or thing for that matter, the existing sensory, cultural, and linguistic structures within the individual (the inappropriately understood "inside") *together* with the immediate sensory data flowing in from outside the person (the "outside") enter into the instantaneous configuring (co-conditioning) process of *analogia spiritus*. There is no "inside-out" or "outside-in" causal direction of experience; the interaction is holistic and, *therefore, a unified co-conditioning moment contingent upon the constituting Power of the relation*ship. For Kierkegaard, this latter dimension of holistic relating potentially takes place *in relation* to the Eternal, and with it echoes the call of Christ to bear our cross, a personal willingness to relax all that we are or know within the knowing event, which is an ethical action. As we shall see in chapter 5A, there are ways to theorize how the Eternal and relative co-condition each other; and how the Eternal can reciprocatively affect our process of conceptualization, existential experience, and meaning (history).

William Stoeger contends that the "extraordinary and pervasive *relationship* of creatures with the divine, in which we ourselves participate, occurs at the very core of our beings and is hidden from our eyes."[86] He speaks of the *analogia spiritus* active within the Jacobian night and rightfully insists that, in some way, we participate in divine-human co-conditioning. The hard core of a research program must contain a more holistic experiential contingency than that which a pragmatic conceptual theory (structured *episteme* and *techne*) or reliabilist theory can produce. Therefore, *analogia spiritus* and the experiencing of the numinal not only happens from "inside-out" but correlationally configures data from the "outside-in" into personal and social meaning of a revelatory nature (gift); and this is active only to the degree persons fully open in relations to all relevant aspects of world, self, and God (authentic relations).

---

85. Knowledge of God, not unlike our knowledge in the natural sciences, necessitates the configurative, existential, and transformative action of the Other (molecule, persons, or God) in self-disclosure.

86. Stoeger, "Describing," 128, emphasis added.

3) The Criterion of Progress and the Unseen Teleological Component

For Murphy and Lakatos, internal progress ultimately becomes the criterion for adjudicating *between* intercommunal systems of thought. Using Alasdair MacIntyre, Murphy argues that a tradition's integrity and authority are exclusively internal within the tradition socially.[87] This moves the authority from the individual to the community, shifting the authority from the subjective to the intersubjective. But unfortunately, this does little in developing a method for *positively* comparing and associating claims between differing traditions, notwithstanding its relative inability to explain how intrasystematic progress happens.[88] MacIntyre, in his Gifford lectures,[89] argues that seemingly incommensurate traditions are comparable in their respective abilities to transcend internal epistemological crises. In other words, each tradition bears the possibility through time that an internal crisis will render its explanatory power impotent. This, however, is a negative account of human epistemic development (assessment by default), reflecting entropy and the second law of thermodynamics. In other words, whose respective epistemic structures (a closed system) can survive the debilitating character of the world's development (an open system) the longest? Such theories ultimately fail to supply adequate *positive heuristic* of why the world continues to produce irreducible emergent properties and developmental progression to higher states of organization (in epistemic or pragmatic structures).

The problem of theorizing any such positive heuristic in the absence of "self-evident non-inferentials" upon which to establish knowledge arises because Murphy and MacIntyre infer *all aspects* of knowledge and understanding are theory dependent. Basing our knowledge and understanding upon *completely* self-evident non-inferentials, which directly correspond to concept-independent reality, is indeed dubious. On the other hand, theorizing that *every aspect and dynamic* that constitute human understanding and meaning is relative or inferential is just as dubious. Knowledge, understanding, and meaning may indeed bear contextually relative elements, but because they constitute from within living interactions, how participants couple them within potential universal or teleological dynamics is a concern of Kierkegaard.

---

87. Murphy, "Divine Action," 104.

88. Murphy utilizes MacIntyre's thesis that between disparate and incommensurable traditions, "one party *can* emerge as undoubtedly rationally superior.... A tradition fails on its own terms when a solution to an epistemological crisis cannot be found ... that measures up to the tradition's own internal standards of rationality" (*Beyond*, 106).

89. MacIntyre, *Three Rival Versions*.

Teleology and Fruitfulness

One of the Lakatosian terms for progress is fruitfulness, which generally means the coherent extension of an explanatory capacity into a fuller experience of the world. If progress is inherently a criterion for the viability of all traditions, are we not implying an unseen universal dynamic and teleological criterion active *within* our notion of fruitfulness? This must be a universal dynamic within holistic human relations that inevitably gives rise to meaning itself.

Within the cultural-linguistic hermeneutical approach, Lindbeck recognizes no immediate intelligible rationale by which *inter*systematic dialogue can effectively happen. Yet, as just noted, there is an implicit methodological acknowledgment of universal dynamics within his understanding of holistic human existence. Similarly, as a conceptual pragmatist, Murphy (in association with Thiemann and MacIntyre) argues "we can still make transcommunal judgments about the relative epistemic worth of competing explanations,"[90] based upon their respective "progress."

As stated, this is a wholly agreeable criterion for adjudicating between disparate communities, but she, like Lindbeck, refrains from naming *universalia*. Yet, unlike Lindbeck, she proffers a methodological program of *epistemological rationality* by which she believes we can evaluatively contrast "transcommunal judgments." Such a program cryptically relies on universal teleological forces or elements in human existence, which ultimately adjudicate and establish such judgments: "somehow I know *my progress* is greater than yours." In this respect, the epistemic incommensurability must obviously be an aspect of an even greater commensurable reality (relation) and likewise only has meaning, any meaning, in direct relation to that reality. This suggests an analogy of wholes active as a denominator within any such adjudicating procedures, whether or not one fails to acknowledge or understand such dynamics.

It is not yet clear within such a method how we can justify comparisons between one system's internal fruitfulness with that of another. Might not Murphy's notion of successful epistemological development be another system's notion of failure? *Why is explanatory proliferation desirable* over the simple sustaining of wonder (Wittgenstein's "rain dance") or the child's innocent and perennial wonder that seems to dissipate with the attainment of each new explanation? Any attempt to answer why human flourishing must seek explanatory progress infers indubitable first principles, characterizes human existence as a whole, and therefore immediately plants the seeds of

---

90. Murphy, "Limits," 356.

a metaphysic. Mere epistemic rational proliferation alone could signify industry, technocratic advancement, and will to power rather than a longing for truth. Murphy holds to the incommensurability of intrasystematic systems but, with MacIntyre, argues for transcommunal assessment through progress. Yet, how can she implement the criterion of progress within cultural and religious spheres? Here Murphy's program struggles with internal incoherence. The methodological bifurcation of the intrasystematic from the ontological aspect of human existence leaves her with no criteria to make the adjudicating leap between the various transcommunal notions of progress, yet she makes it anyway. Even if we reduce progress to a tradition's survival, we have designated a universal (ontological) factor—survival.

Despite the temporality of genocidal political force upon traditions, we must admit that most traditions willingly die, refuse to resurrect, or steadily evolve into existing alternative traditions because of their living interaction with other traditions. In other words, there is always the presence of an adjudicating *universalia within our interactions*, intra- or intercommunal. One tradition dies (never to resurrect) *always* because a contrasting tradition provides greater *fullness of life*—a criterion that includes all of Murphy's factors and more. Nevertheless, her method, once again, indirectly begins to reflect the character of Modernity as she transcommunally imposes her intrasystematic notion of progress.

How do we rationally arrive at the meaning of "charity," "gladness," "hunger for virtue," and "humility?" Ultimately, these criteria reflect the same potential insights and pathologies from either individual reflection or communitive interaction. What Murphy first criticizes as unstable within the self-evidencing dynamic of individuals has, in effect, merely become what we know to be the instability of the community-evidencing dynamic of the community (e.g., mob-rule). The non-inferentials of the individual simply succumb to the non-inferentials of the community. Rather than the individual, the community now decides what to prejudice as observable. The phenomena of Nazi Germany, one of the more intelligent communities in the world, should effectively caution the value of such theorizing.

In the end, to have any notion of progress and fruitfulness, which my thesis heartily supports, necessitates acknowledging ontological or teleological dynamics active within the whole of human existence, even if we only experience them holistically, beyond image. In Hefner (as well as Pannenberg), the concept of the empirical is more inclusive and holistic. Hefner disagrees with

> those who deny that universal statements concerning human beings are possible. So-called postmodern perspectives, including

relativistic or cultural-linguistic hermeneutic approaches to local communities, refuse to engage in discussion of cross-cultural, universal ideas. To this objection, I argue that the denial of universals is itself an example of a careless universal statement.[91]

Conversely, Murphy critically asks if

> a universal human experience that serves as the ground of theology does not (necessarily or generally) involve the empirical claim that there is an experience phenomenologically the same in all cultures and traditions, . . . [then] how can one know with the requisite foundational certainty that there is such a universal grounding beneath the varied manifestations or religious sensibilities?[92]

Whether one like David Tracy, Paul Ricoeur, or Hefner would be satisfied with the question as stated is a moot point. She answers her own question of how we can "know with the requisite foundational certainty that there is such a grounding" by suggesting her own notion of *progress*. With Lakatos and Lindbeck, she believes that progress and performance ultimately factor in some way as criteria for adjudicating cultural evolution and *inter*communal issues. Furthermore, "fruitfulness" is a criterion with an internal teleological component, even if that component is mysteriously open-ended. Whether assessing negative or positive functions or criteria, it still implies the existence of a universal component or dynamic active within their assessment. The identification and naming are irrelevant, the presence of such a component seems irrefutable.

(4) Lack of Epistemic Humility and Intellectual Virtue

Any discursive methodology that institutes (1) a specifically epistemological holism, (2) the incommensurability of various communicative discourses, and (3) the intercommunal criterion of internal progress, yet refrains from theorizing why a program's progress can be comparable to that of another, has in no uncertain terms fallen into epistemic arrogance and sectarianism.[93] Such methodological structuring refuses to consider

---

91. Hefner, *Human Factor*, 58.

92. Murphy, "Divine Action," 52.

93. Thiselton tells us, "If each competing group, class, ethnic tradition, gender, guild, or party produces its own *internal* criteria of supposed rationality in order to serve its own power-interests, rational debate collapses *not only into mere rhetoric*, but soon also into *accusation, blame, corporate self-righteousness and conflict*" (*Interpreting God*, 134). I choose the word "arrogance" because it implies a willful disposition that most often becomes a subconscious sediment within our epistemic posturing; I

the possibility of authentic transformative relations between disparate traditions and denies the historical success of such transformative relations exposing their wholesale epistemological entrenchment.[94] This entrenchment is visible in the reluctance of such methodologically framed traditions to enter the struggle of transcommunal relations and expand their own epistemic horizons. For example, even in agnostic Tom Holland's history of Christianity (*Dominion*), he gives no quarter to the past abuses and evils of Christendom, yet repeatedly reveals the effects of Christianity in transforming other cultures and religions, creating the emergence of (atheistic) democratic liberalism, and a more developed understanding of divine-human encounter verses other religious traditions (e.g., contrasting various religion's scriptural hermeneutics).[95] He argues this accomplishment is not through Christianity's explanatory power, internal coherence, formal missionary efforts, etc., but simply through its interacting presence alongside societies and other religions. For Holland, it happens through the greater fullness of life Christianity exhibits in its underlying commitment to and often rare emulation of Christ's weakness and *openness* to the world, which he contrasts against the driving supposition of strength in every other political or religious system. Whether in agreement with Holland or not, his willingness to engage an alien system of thought and identify such positive dynamics within it is academically responsible, virtuous, honest, and open. In this respect, many postliberal methodologies fail to account seriously enough for the personal factor of relational closedness—the unwillingness to seek or account for common ground and the Habermasian call to cross-border engagement. The suppression of such interaction is ultimately the primary cause of sustained disagreement and "incommensurability" within theological and interdisciplinary dialogue rather than the incommensurability of language games.

Scripture warns us that the quality of our relationship with God is equivalent to the quality of our relationship with others.[96] Until the warnings of Kierkegaard, the development of Enlightenment epistemic virtue

---

likewise suggest that this is a quality of relations none completely escapes, but some build as fortresses of safety to elude suffering and potential shame.

94. Given that humanity has only been able to communicate and travel in mass over the last few centuries, the necessity for cross-cultural dialogue, assessment, and tolerance has only recently begun to emerge in earnest. Such dialogue will necessarily be disruptive and, at times, adversarial.

95. Arguing differently, Vattimo, *After Christianity*, presents the same conclusions.

96. See 1 John; cf. also Bonhoeffer, *Sanctorum Communio*, 73: "'Man's whole spirituality becomes evident only along with others: the essence of spirit is that the self is through being in the other.'"

was minimal. Only recently has the character of the theologian's epistemic posture *and openness* to the Other become a vital methodological concern. On the other hand, such willingness in no way obligates blind subservience to the other, nor does it mandate interaction (Rom 14). It does, however, target our refusal to be *fully* open to those *relationships* we choose to engage that are reciprocatively open. The growing amount of literature concerned with this issue in epistemological and methodological discussions corroborates this charge.[97] Linda Zagzebski and others effectively argue that in virtue theory, "the primary object of evaluation is persons rather than acts."

> Justified beliefs are like right acts. Intellectual virtue, on the other hand, is a quality of persons which I believe cannot be reduced to a disposition to have justified beliefs any more than moral virtue can be reduced to a disposition to perform right acts. . . . knowledge is true belief arising from acts of intellectual virtue.[98]

If we agree that the constituting dynamic of persons happens within relationships, Zagzebski's general position is laudable. Though we cannot reduce the virtuous quality in a person to "a disposition" to have "justified belief" or "perform right acts," *we can align virtue with the disposition or willingness to [wholly] venture ourselves into authentic relationships*. In this respect, our beliefs and actions become theologically meaningful to the degree of openness within each participant. The primary point is that intellectual virtue must become an explicit methodological factor, especially in theology.

Inappropriate relational forces affecting theological research are many: overdetermined unwillingness by another to disclose self, malicious attempts to control or instrumentalize knowledge for ulterior motives, e.g., the refusal to relax one's position to faithfully hear another's position at the risk of being wrong, etc. Moltmann insists authentic relationships necessitate a degree of "risk" and even "suffering." Our relations are authentic when we are willing to venture our current state of knowledge (upon the cross), even if that results in the demise of our current status and pride.

Murphy, Holism, and Supervenience: Theological Adjustment

The subject of holism emerges in various forms of discourse. For example, philosophy institutes the concept of supervenience to express the top-down causality and the transfer of information between seemingly disparate levels

---

97. Zagzebski, *Virtues*; Montmarquet, *Epistemic Virtue*, to name a few.

98. Zagzebski, "*Phronesis*," 207. Cf. McIntyre's internal nonfoundational notion of practice or act as the subject of virtue (*After Virtue*, 187).

of interacting dynamic systems.[99] For example, a supervenient relationship exists between the mind and body, with the mind supervenient over the body. Murphy uses supervenience to express a fuller holism than merely asserting epistemological holism. For her, it means "that whole systems and their parts mutually condition one another."[100] This admirably but only partially reflects the dynamics within *perichoresis*. As a philosopher of science and philosophical theologian, Murphy uses supervenience to expand her causal structuring.

She states that higher level organizations are supervenient over lower level systems and that only the logic within the higher level(s) can fully explain the lower level logic of an activity. There is a "surplus of meaning in the higher-level terms, relating to context, to larger causal systems, that cannot be captured by means of the lower-level language."[101] In this respect, she begins to clear space for the development of theological integration into the various natural and human sciences that echo the earlier stated methodological insistence of Loder and other theologians that theology takes supervenient asymmetrical priority over other disciplines in interdisciplinary dialogue.

I wish to emphasize, in addition to Murphy, that perichoretically the logic of *the higher level must be implicitly active and experientially resident within the lower level logic and activity* (as in the case between humanity and God). For example, I could imagine most fish have no explicit or focal awareness of water, yet they experience water and its play within the internal logic (action) of their relations. Therefore, the logic of spirit ("water") is a higher level order of knowledge and experience that is superveniently present in some way within the lower level logic of humanity's personal and relational thought and action. Murphy herself theorizes[102] that personal consciousness and action (human or divine) are probable factors and contingencies that superveniently affect the physical through quantum level indeterminacy. In this same respect, the higher level of mental consciousness in human nature is supervenient to the lower level "biological" functions of bodily action. In other words, even the logic *within* the lower level systems displays an unexplained indeterminacy and an incompleteness (which in the reductionist discourse of physics includes quantum dynamics). It is the conviction of Murphy and others that this indeterminacy plays a vital role

---

99. Antony Flew says supervenient characteristics are "properties or qualities that depend on some other property or quality" (*Dictionary of Philosophy*, 345).

100. Murphy, "Divine Action," 144.

101. Murphy, "Divine Action," 144.

102. Murphy, "Divine Action," 340.

in the causal nexus of the higher level *within* the lower. As T. F. Torrance alludes, the closed logic of any lower level system is either incomplete or indeterminate and ultimately incoherent within its formal logic.[103] And, though the higher system and logic always have asymmetrical influence, any closed inquiry within a lower system and logic will reveal indeterminate points within itself that refer to the higher system logic implicitly resident *within* its own lower structuralizing. Therefore, a complete methodological discussion in theology must seek to understand how God's higher level relational logic integrates into the lower level logic of faith and theology proper.

If God relates with humanity, then we might expect human existence, relationships, and knowledge might in some way reflect God's higher and supervening logic. In our search for useful theological criteria, this thesis explores how the higher level logic of a trinitarian God potentially reflects within the lower level logic of humanity.[104] Therefore, in theology we must experience what creates the possibility of the whole that is greater than the sum of the parts. In other words, humans must reflectively experience as spirit in analogical relation to God's experience as Spirit. Furthermore, the logic of spirit must somehow be inherent within all structures of knowledge and human experience while unifying, organizing, and differentiating.

This temporarily ends our assessment of Murphy's theological method, to which we will later return, which now brings us to the more radical trajectory of the social constructivist theory of human experience. In transition, I would like to reassert that, as humans, we desire to relate authentically with the Other. Yet, as sinners, unwilling to enter the suffering, shame, relational vulnerability, and conflict needed for authentic relations, we develop relational patterns that largely entomb such relations into passionless existence. This eventually taints the doxastic structure of all our knowledge, which has ultimately led many developmentalist into social relativism.

SOCIAL CONSTRUCTIVIST THEORY—THE DESIRE TO RELATE

Recently, social constructivists and communication theorists have begun to dislodge the emergence of meaning from solely within the Cartesian psyche and relocate its dependence on dynamics that are both within the relationship and form the relationship. As insights grow, we are becoming more aware that knowledge and meaning take shape *within* the metaphysical

---

103. Torrance, *Resurrection*, 179–93.

104. Cf. Huyssteen, *Essays*, 89; Lucas, "Temporality of God," 240, in which the latter argues that love is an acceptable principle in equating nature and God's activity.

dynamics of the relationship itself.[105] I briefly wish to introduce and use this developing literature[106] that posits relationship as the matrix of reality to present an essential aspect of the perichoretic dynamic. These developments offer alternative scholarly trajectories in relational theories, which reflect the same dynamics in *perichoresis* and perichoretic relations.

Developmentalist Kenneth Gergen believes this new literature, which he feels continues the spirit of Wittgenstein, increasingly places the "locus of meaning within the process of relations itself. That is, individual subjectivity is abandoned as the primary site upon which meaning originates and understanding emerges; attention moves from the within to the between."[107] Though he expresses that this literature genre presents no comprehensive account of how this is to be understood, it is becoming increasingly apparent that "the enormously rich language we have for depicting inner states is itself not a product of such *mental* states but of relational coordination. The language does not thus 'depict,' so much as it constructs what we take to be the character of subjectivity."[108] He goes on to say:

> Each new form of "saying" is simultaneously a new form of relating, and with potentially different consequences. . . . Relying on the work of Vygotsky and Bakhtin, many developmentalists have begun to reconceptualize thought as internal language. On this account, cognitive processes are not the possessions of single individuals so much as their relationships speaking through them. . . . We may conceptualize emotions as elements within relational scenarios, actions that gain their intelligibility and necessity from patterns of interchange. Here it is possible to view anger or depression not as a personal event, but as a constituent of a particular relational dance.[109]

Meaning in one's speech emerges only within the supplemental action of the other. It, therefore, does not constitute within the lone mind or utterance (or text), nor does it technically lie within the speech-act (Searle, Austin); the hermeneutical dynamic and the making of meaning emerge

---

105. Gergen thinks: "If we can grant the preeminence of relationship in fostering human intelligibility, we are positioned to reconsider the foundational assumptions within the humanist tradition." This attempts "to reconceptualize these concepts in terms of a relational ontology" ("Social Theory," 8).

106. For example, Gergen, *Realities and Relationships*; Shotter, *Conversational Realities*; Bakhtin, *Toward a Philosophy*; Bakhtin, *Dialogical Imagination*; Bruner, *Acts of Meaning*; Potter and Wetherell, *Discourse*; Wertsch, *Vygotsky*; Billig, *Arguing and Thinking*.

107. Gergen, "Relationships," 4.

108. Gergen, "Relationships," 6.

109. Gergen, "Relationships," 7.

from within the third term or unity of the emerging relationship. Citing research on the evolving structure and focus of women's magazine articles from the 1950s to the 1980s, Gergen notes a significant change from "taking care of either the relational partner or the self" to a new vision "found in which 'the relationship' is created as an object for the readers."[110] Toward the end of this section, we will parallel these social constructivist theories with Kierkegaard's theological insistence that the self constitutes as a relationship to itself or the Other.

The individual alone can never "mean" anything. Without the necessary supplemental action of another-in-response the act becomes nonsense. This entails two distinct living worlds coming into dialogical contact. "At this moment," says John Shotter,

> when a speaker in one world turns from addressing those in another and invites their creative bridging of the gap thus created in their responsive rejoinders, a new world is created between them, with influences from the unique worlds of both participants, and from their shared cultural worlds, at work in it. . . . The special unity or wholeness that emerges when two or more different worlds, or different "freedoms" (Steiner, 1989) meet, exists only in the fleeting moment of their meeting. It is in their sustained focus on, and the special way in which they 'poetically' articulate the details of what occurs in fleeting interactive or dialogical moments—without the need to step out of such moments as if to observe and to describe them from a distance—that is so special in their nontheoretical approach.[111]

Unlike Cartesian subjectivism, where meaning localizes only within the subjective consciousness, the point of convergence and meaning takes place from within the emergent world of the immediate relationship. It is as if a new creation or mediational background emerges when two or more persons begin to relate or intend one another.

For Shotter, this displays specific characteristics. The first is that "we cannot not be responsive to each other."[112] The force within us to relate is greater than we can resist. Therefore, when addressed, we must consider even our effort to ignore as an active response *in* relationship. In normal relations, the listener always assumes an active and dynamic "responsive attitude" toward the speaker. Bakhtin tells us the listener "adopts this

---

110. Gergen, "Technology," 12.

111. Shotter, "Life," 75, emphasis added. John Shotter is a communicational theorist.

112. Shotter, "Life," 76.

responsive attitude for the entire duration of the process of listening and understanding."[113] On the other side,

> [the speaker] does not expect passive understanding that, so to speak, only duplicates his or her own idea in someone else's mind (as in Saussure's model of linguistic communication . . .). Rather, the speaker talks with an expectation of a response, agreement, sympathy, objection, execution, and so forth.[114]

This suggests more of a *relational-responsive* communicative dynamic than the *representational-referential* Cartesian understanding. In this respect, we find it offensive if the listener's "response attitude" is not spontaneously open to authentically constituting in relation to our speech. "Here," Bakhtin suggests, "in a component of non-rational impulsiveness—not only tolerated but actually demanded—we find an important way in which the interactional order differs from other kinds of social order."[115] The speaker expects an open "response attitude," which does not predetermine or overdetermine the meaning. In this respect, as Kierkegaard calls for the listener's "infinite resignation" toward the Other, Bakhtin considers that the human speaker "demands" it from his listener.

Shotter tells us such spontaneous openness in response is "very different from either naturally *caused* activity, or from actions done by individuals for a *reason*. It is activity, so to speak, *distributed* between us; it is *joint action* in the sense that it is action we do as a group, as a collective, as a 'we' or an 'us.'"[116] Though "response attitude" takes place within a particular social background that is culturally structured, the communicative action still warrants open and spontaneous awareness from the participants. Such a demand emerges from within the immediacy of the relationship. "The performed act," says Bakhtin,

> concentrates, correlates, and resolves within a unitary and unique and, this time, final context both the sense and the fact, the universal and the individual, the real and the ideal, for everything enters into the composition of its answerable motivation. The performed act constitutes a going out once and for all from within the possibility as such into what is once-occurrent.[117]

---

113. Bakhtin, *Speech Genres*, 68.
114. Bakhtin, *Speech Genres*, 69, 91.
115. Bakhtin, *Speech Genres*, 115.
116. Shotter, "Life," 77.
117. Bakhtin, "Toward a Philosophy," 29.

Therefore, though the listener's "response attitude" must be open and spontaneous, the response will be specific, personal, and chosen. It is *the* response, at *that* moment, *to all* things relevant.

Shotter characterizes the *dialogical structure* of this complex active confluence as having a "dynamic, continually changing, oscillating, pulsating character, such that its structure at any one moment is very different from its structure at another."[118] Bakhtin describes a dialogical structure constituting a "plurality of unmerged consciousnesses."[119] Shotter further describes this dialogical dynamic (not necessarily just linguistic) as a pulsation between unity and plurality within the relationship.

> It is only in each unique interactive moment, as one individual ceases to address him- or herself to the others and becomes him- or herself an addressee, that a unity is formed. In each uncertain once-occurrent event of Being, in which we encounter others radically different and distinct from ourselves, they call out from us responses which we are incapable of calling out from ourselves. But it is in these moments also, that we are joined with them and present to each other as the distinct individuals we are.[120]

If I begin to read aloud a portion of an essay I have been working on to a friend, I never cease to be amazed at how poorly it reads in their presence despite the countless hours I might have spent alone on it beforehand. Though just as potentially pathological, direct interpersonal relationship constitutes us more intensely and responsibly than when we are only in relation to our internal *social audience*. We are caught up into an activity bigger than the sum of each. Something is happening both inside us and between us.[121] "Even if I know a given person thoroughly," says Bakhtin, "and I also know myself, I still have to grasp the truth of our interrelationship, the truth of the unitary and unique event that links us and in which we are participants."[122] These descriptions reflect many of the dynamic characteristics of perichoretic relations and indicate the necessary shift in our understanding of how meaning constitutes and transforms in relations. This affects our understanding of both knowledge and methodology.

---

118. Shotter, "Life," 78.//
119. Bakhtin, *Problems*, 9.//
120. Shotter, "Life," 78.//
121. This transcends Heidegger's "attunement" (*Gestimmtheit*) or "mood" (*Stimmung*) (*Being and Time*, 311).//
122. Bakhtin, "Toward a Philosophy," 17–18.

Personal Reflection and Knowledge as Relationship

These theoreticians have suggested, like Piaget before them, that whether soliloquy of personal reflection or active social relations, the immediacy of relationship constitutes all human consciousness. Volosinov tells us:

> Each person's inner world and thought has its stabilized social audience that comprises the environment in which reasons, motives, values, and so on are fashioned. . . . Orientation of the word toward the addressee has an extremely high significance. In point of fact, word is a two-sided act. It is determined equally by whose word it is and for whom it is meant. . . . Each and every word expresses the "one" in relation to the "other."[123]

In this way, our responsive reason, desire, motive, memory, and even personal reflection are never entirely our own. Instead, it is a complex momentary juxtaposing of influences from many directions, past, present and future (as desire, expectation, and possibility), constituting and conditioning our experience and the relationship according to our unique organizing character. This personal style and manner of constituting present us uniquely to the other as the person we are. Likewise, language, experience, and even knowledge are relationships. They are never the sole property of the individual (even in reflection). Instead, they become the shapes and forms of the immediate relationship, never completely re-presenting the past, nor demanding universal or *literal* expectation of its present meaning or the future even in the analogical continuity of the promise.

Convinced of needed change, these social constructivists suggest we radically reconfigure metaphysics toward a relational ontology by which human existence constitutes not within the self but relationship. In this respect, the relational dynamic itself, in some way, becomes the primordial essence.

Methodological Considerations

Such radical maneuvers, however, have grievous consequences for our consideration of method. "Traditionally," Shotter suggests,

> we have always been concerned with patterns and order, with what is stable and repeatable, with what can be calculated and measured, with understanding things by finding the hidden laws or principles determining their nature. We are quite unused to

---

123. Volosinov, *Marxism*, 86.

the idea that the events of importance to us in our investigations, are unique, novel, unmeasurable events, not repetitions.[124]

If the certainty of re-presentation, as postmoderns view it, has begun to erode, how can we assess a relationship's continuity, equity, and morality? Let's briefly look at two possibilities within this movement.

"Relational Sublime"

Gergen questions the effectiveness of a "continuous renegotiation of meaning" that dialectically transpires in most narrative accounts bouncing back and forth between individuals or communities. He is also concerned with the limited range of discourses such activity can include. Finally, the functionality of these communicative theories amid ever-changing relational structuring is troublesome.[125] Therefore, he suggests we begin to reconsider an ancient concept, which he resurrects as the "relational sublime." We must move "beyond narrative as the center of our interest to the relational matrix from which narrative understandings emerge."[126] We can envision this condition as "pure relatedness." Similar to an ocean,

> All the individual waves are given form by each other, and we must recognize with awe the potential of a singular movement of the entirety. . . . We cannot articulate the character of the sublime, for our languages are themselves only local manifestations of the whole.[127]

Gergen seeks to "resuscitate" and "re-signify" this Western idea of the "relational sublime" from eighteen centuries ago. He begins this resurrection by summoning forth the first-century ideas of Greek critic Dionysus Longinus that acknowledge a source in the "great writings" that brings "power and irresistible might to bear" in the written word, a power that he traces to nature's blessing for the "inward greatness of the soul." He traces its presence in history through Edmund Burke, Kant, Wordsworth, Coleridge, and Schiller to Emerson. They acknowledge something beyond our words that give them their force, "something beyond reason which causes reason to

---

124. Shotter, "Life," 84.

125. These concerns echo the concerns of Piaget and Loder in accommodating the transformational matrix that operates between morphological restructuring, which narrative accounts generally overlook (treated more fully in an upcoming chapter).

126. Gergen, "Relationships," 10.

127. Gergen, "Relationships," 10.

leap up." Though it is beyond articulation, it can be appreciated. It is the "primordial processes of relationship—the pulsing coordination."

> It is not the "inward greatness of the soul," . . . but the process of relatedness which enable such passages to carry us with them. Likewise the source of "awe," "inspiration," or "terror" is not to be found in nature (with Wordsworth), or in the person (with Emerson), but within unfathomable processes of relatedness which make meaning possible. The capacity to give life to words, and thus to transform culture, is not usefully traced to internal resources, but to relatedness—which serves as the source of all articulation, and which simultaneously remains beyond its reach.[128]

Gergen points to a relational ontology, offering the "relational sublime" as its qualitative criterion for relational adequacy, contrast, and progress. This relational dynamic is the source of all human existence. It inhabits every relationship to the degree the relationship constitutes in association with the dynamic nature of that force that creates it. When Aristotle says, "all men by nature desire to know," he acknowledges such a sublime within the act of knowing itself. The relational sublime is not only what ultimately establishes the structure of relational adequacy, but the sense of rightness and the source of goodness and virtue we experience within its logic.

"Social Poetics"

Shotter similarly suggests a form of "social poetics." Utilizing Bakhtin and George Steiner, he presents a dynamic in human interactions, a movement beyond the collective sums that takes up the moment or event and presents it in its own time, in a new way. Speaking of the artistic or poetic moment "happening to us," Steiner observes:

> That which comes to call on us—that idiom, we saw, connotes visitation and summons—will very often do so unbidden. Even when there is a readiness, as in the concert hall, in the museum, in the moment of chosen reading, the true entrance into us will not occur by an act of will. . . . But each and everyone of us, however bounded our sensibility, will have known such unbidden, unexpected entrances by irrevocable guests.[129]

---

128. Gergen, "Technology," 11.
129. Steiner, *Real Presences*, 179–80.

Social poetics, which supports all discourse and dialogical activity, "strikes" and "arrests" us from pre-patterned response to engage us responsively with the freedom and uniqueness of the other, which is necessary for the authentic "meeting between freedoms."[130] It is a process by which we are first "arrested" within the moment of our openness as we enter into an active tension with the Other, giving rise to a mutual co-configuring toward "*creative understanding*."[131] No knowledge, ordering, nuance, or historical event rendering remains the same when they are analogically "called up" for immediate service; our method, says Shotter, must never lead "to a final, fixed account of what something 'really' means." Reflecting the earlier discussion of Wittgenstein, Bakhtin insists:

> At any moment in the development of the dialogue there are immense, boundless masses of forgotten contextual meanings, but at certain moments . . . they are recalled and invigorated in renewed form (in a new context). Nothing is absolutely dead: every meaning will have its homecoming festival.[132]

Therefore, social poetics, which are to some degree inherent in all human relatedness, creates its own logic that is holistically (whole as an event) synchronous with its relational environment. It is essential, however, to note that social poetics takes place in the transitional moments of dialogical interactions. Bakhtin continues:

> When I experience an object actually, I thereby carry out something in relation to it; the object enters into relation with that which is to-be-achieved, grows in it—within my relationship to that object. Pure givenness cannot be experienced actually. Insofar as I am actually experiencing an object, even if I do so by thinking of it, it becomes a changing moment in the ongoing event of my experiencing (thinking) it, i.e., it assumes the

---

130. Steiner, *Real Presences*, 152.

131. Steiner tells us: "*Creative understanding* does not renounce itself, its own place in time, its own culture; and it forgets nothing. . . . In the realm of culture, outsideness is a most powerful factor in understanding. It is only in the eyes of *another* culture that foreign culture reveals itself fully and profoundly. . . . A meaning only reveals its depths once it has encountered and come into contact with another, foreign meaning: they engage in a kind of dialogue, which surmounts the closeness and one-sidedness of these particular meanings, these cultures. We raise new questions for a foreign culture, ones that it did not raise itself; we seek answers to our questions to it; and the foreign culture responds to us by revealing to us its new aspects and new semantic depths" (Steiner, *Real Presences*, 7).

132. Bakhtin, *Speech Genres*, 170.

character of something-yet-to-be-achieved. Or, to be exact, it is given to me within a certain event-unity.[133]

Within such "event-unity," all relevant structures, knowledge, memory, and so forth *resurrect* and *incarnate* into "a certain, living, concrete, and palpable (intuitable) once-occurrent whole—an event."[134] In concert, Shotter indirectly presents us with two basic aspects of and criteria for genuine relationship, which parallel the broader categories of prereflexive awareness and reflexive conceptualization. How we open in awareness to the world establishes how we will experience life. From within the forming relational engagement, we "articulate our language entwined activities more clearly to ourselves, so that we can come, not to a theoretical, but to a more elaborate and refined practical grasp of how to make sense of them,"[135] which may or may not provide theory or greater explanatory capacity. Most important, it is an existential practical configuring of all the relevant relational elements while relaxing the imposition of pre-established theory upon the experience.

Bakhtin's Silent and Irreducible Structure of Relationship: Methodological Implications

These social constructivists emphasize the need for ongoing relational openness and place a premium on increasing the frequency and diversity of interactions. They suggest a universal relational dynamic beyond articulation that creates a mutual collating of all things relevant into relational event-unities in movement. It supports all our knowledge, and the relational sublime and social poetics assess its value, not reason. Such dynamics allow us to live, change, and responsively encounter the freedom of the Other within structure rather than structure oppressing the encounter (i.e., allowing the possible to emerge in co-conditioning relation to known theory rather than being oppressed by it). It is the door through which all novelty and invention come. However, this literature comes dangerously close to losing the subject altogether within the collective. However, if one listens carefully to certain intonations within this literature, a specific and redeemable dialogical pattern emerges.

This literature begins to present us with not only the relational sublime but also the shape of genuine relationships. In a description of Dostoevsky's writing, Bakhtin adventitiously provides us with his structure to

133. Bakhtin, "Toward a Philosophy," 32.
134. Bakhtin, "Toward a Philosophy," 32.
135. Bakhtin, "Toward a Philosophy," 15.

social reality, "*a plurality of consciousnesses, with equal rights and each with its own world*, combine but are not merged in the unity of the event."[136] A fundamental shape of relationality becomes apparent in which multiple consciousnesses mutually share in the co-conditioning of meaning without losing personal identity. The ground upon which consciousnesses "combine" but do not "merge" remains back-ground within Bakhtin and the others, but their description parallels that which continues to struggle for fuller expression in the Christian relational dynamic of *perichoresis*. We are immersed within this social dynamic and emerge, constitute, and transform within the intersubjectivity of the communicative act without losing personhood into a sea of Single consciousness.

For Gergen, the "world" of the relationship and its configurative dynamics must analogically and mutually relate to what he refers to as the "sacred."[137] Continuity throughout human epistemological development *can only be supported through relational dynamics at holistic levels of existence both between and within* persons.

PERICHORESIS

We have briefly considered two radically different approaches to the formation of meaning and even though they are significantly different projects, each speak to the emergence and integrity of meaning. Murphy presents an epistemological holism that emphasizes the importance of community consensus and internal epistemological coherence. She offers an epistemological understanding of progress as a criterion of program adequacy. She believes in the incommensurability between diverse communities and esteems the value of empirical falsifiability, epistemological crisis, and the importance of tradition in theological methodology. All these play a role in creating convictional *beliefs*. However, the incommensurable nature of cross-tradition discourse inhibits the community's willingness to engage fully and authentically with foreign communities. Such positions ultimately assume sectarian postures within a pluralistic world. Murphy's theorizing, however, lacks any substantial theory elaborating on the hypothetico-deductive experience from which novelty and invention emerge. When asked the origin of hypothetico-deductive moments, she answers, "We don't know."[138] When pressed on the possibility of a holistic relationship between human and divine spirit, or any notion of the logic of spirit, she generally retreats to the working criteria of

---

136. Bakhtin, *Problems*, 6.
137. Gergen, "Relationships," 10.
138. Personal conversation with Nancey Murphy, 1992.

modern philosophy. It is baffling to see a theological methodology unwilling to offer any holistic criterion resulting from spirit or logic of spirit other than what presence might be active in community consensus. Yet, atheists like John Shotter and former agnostic Kenneth Gergen have been compelled to proffer holistic theories and criteria of "social poetics" and the "sacred" that cross intertraditional dialogical borders.[139]

Social constructivists acknowledge the illusive certainty of epistemologically heavy methodologies, the necessity of epistemic humility, and sensitivity to truly holistic criteria like the relational sublime and social poetics, which result from holistic dynamics within the relational event. Because meaning forever reconstitutes anew from the uniqueness of each new occurrence, such methodologies encourage the complete venture of self for re-constitution from out of *authentic* relations. However, the downside is that forced relativity within epistemic structuring often sacrifices conviction for epistemological ambivalence or cloaks hidden convictional agendas. Epistemic distinctiveness and the transcendent character of the *individual*-in-relation can be lost among many of these theorists, as well as many of the fruitful additions of Modernity.

Perichoresis as a relational paradigm incorporates the *positive* thrust of both these approaches, including passionately held convictional *beliefs* and the *holistic dynamics of relationship* that transform such beliefs. In this respect, the social constructivist's late twentieth-century trajectory echoes and proliferates the sixth-century concept of *perichoresis* and the theological attempt to understand the internal relationship of the Christian Trinity. This structurally Kierkegaardian dynamic and method engenders *full conviction* in one's existing epistemic *structuring and beliefs* while paradoxically supporting transformational possibilities within *genuine relations*.[140]

The Dialogical Characteristic—Pulsation (Openness and Closure)—of Perichoretic Relations

Again, *the perichoretic dynamic enables the polarities of a relationship to remain distinct entities while each constitutes respectively from within the*

---

139. During his process of discovery and implementing the criterion of the "relational sublime," Kenneth Gergen states that he became a theist in 1998. He concluded that something of a divine nature necessarily mediates social relations. Personal discussion with Gergen, 2001.

140. This represents one of the primary themes of *Concluding Unscientific Postscripts* (specifically in 518–19) and represents the epistemic posture of *"a relationship of open resolve* and not one locked up within itself," as suggested by Heidegger, *Being and Time*, 314.

Jacob and the Night of Faith

emerging mutuality of the relational unity. The relationship as the once-occurring event becomes the positive third term intensifying the polarities of the participants while facilitating a mutual co-conditioning exchange. Within human relations, the parts, or aspects, consist of all the relevant relative elements that each person brings into the relationship (focal and tacit), including all relevant details within the existing life context. That *Power* that creates relationship provides the possibility of the greater that emerges, which facilitates, for example, the configurative source of metaphor, simile, etc., from which we respectively construct meaning through the play of various worlds within this irreducible differentiated unity. Though similar to social constructivist dynamics, *perichoresis* goes one step further within the irreducibility of its dynamics; it maintains the continuity of identity of the self (the "I") and the integrity of the relationship throughout all changes and transformations. As we shall see in forthcoming chapters, this is impossible without persons themselves analogically participating in the transparent ground of this transitional matrix. In other words, *perichoresis* facilitates persons becoming whole persons (spirit) and maintaining self in counter-distinction to the world and, if I might be so bold, providing the power to create worlds within themselves, and yet in analogical reciprocity to the same wholeness of the Other *and* that Source that creates and mediates all interactions. Each individual constitutes relative to the existing possibilities within the relationship. However, the relationship itself actively constitutes the individual's existential concerns, desires, and longings within the transformational mix, embedding each person eschatologically in time to the degree that each ventures everything into the relational occurrence.

Shotter suggests a similar understanding of a "new world"—the relationship—which is "created between" the "worlds" of the relatants and the "special unity or wholeness" which emerges when any two meet.[141] In this respect, he alludes to a tripartite structure in relationships. Yet, most social constructivists understand this third aspect of the relationship as completely encompassing the participants within itself (Hegel). Therefore, I wish to emphasize a Kierkegaardian-like irreducible perichoretic dynamic in which *the* mediating third term of the relationship Gracefully creates the medium through which whole spirits (persons) analogically and dynamically constitute in relation to other whole spirits (to the degree persons become spirit). Because of the nature of this Power, exhibiting these same dynamics within its personhood(s) and constitution, it does not draw humanity or creation into itself but relates to them as such, perichoretically. In this respect, the "special unity or wholeness" that Shotter expresses, which seems closer to

---

141. Shotter, "Life," 75.

Hegel's Absolute Spirit, is adjusted to a tripartite perichoretic paradigm entailing *analogia spiritus*. This allows for a more nuanced ethical variable within the individual's willingness to relate wholly to the Other (or not).

The dynamics of *perichoresis* are apparent in the dialogical cycles of human existence. One aspect is the mode of prereflexive awareness in which the person opens to and enters *relations*. The other aspect is the reflexive response of *self*-in-relation from out of the consecrating dynamics of *analogia spiritus*. This dialogical dynamic facilitates reciprocating pulses of openness and closure within dialogical relations. The prereflexive process of awareness (*analogia spiritus*) is when the person seeks to scan, apprehend, and synchronize the swirling composite of intentions, elements, and nature within the interaction toward eventual reflexion and understanding. This is the bed-rock of Jacob upon which all filial divine-human relations emerge; here are the ladders of coming and going within the Jacobian night, the deliberation of wills, desires, and longings that wrestle simultaneously within the Eternal just before its flash into existence; this is the unseen black hole, looked past, denied by those who must have control, the black hole from which no light can escape, the *analogia spiritus* upon which no light can shine. This is equivalent to Bakhtin's moment which

> concentrates, correlates, and resolves within a unitary and unique and, this time, final context both the sense and the fact, the universal and the individual, the real and the ideal, for everything enters into the composition of its answerable motivation.[142]

Within this temporally passive yet eternally active configurative *moment* (process) of *pre*reflexion, individuality gives (donates) itself to the relationship to become wholly related, integrated, surprised, and transformed by the Other. This is the infinite, eternal mode of human being of which Kierkegaard speaks. Heidegger tells us:

> The whole behaviour of historical man, . . . whether understood or not, is tuned and by this attunement [*Gestimmtheit*] raised up to the plane of what-is-in-totality. The manifest character of what-is-in-totality is not identical with the sum of known actualities. . . . Man's behaviour is attuned to the manifest character of what-is-in-totality. But this "in-totality" appears, in the field of vision of our daily calculations and activities, as something incalculable and incomprehensible. It cannot be understood in terms of what manifestly "is," whether this be part of nature or of history. Although itself ceaselessly determining all things, this "in-totality" nevertheless remains something indeterminate

---

142. Bakhtin, "Toward a Philosophy," 29.

and indeterminable, and is thus generally confused with what is readiest at hand and most easily thought of. At the same time this determining factor is not just *nothing*: it is a concealment of what-is-in-totality. Precisely because "letting be" always, in each case, lets each thing be in its proper relationship and thus reveals it, it immediately conceals what-is in totality.[143]

Heidegger beautifully alludes to the logic of spirit, the perichoretic dynamic, and its gracious constituting of persons in *their* "proper relationship," and within their respective meaning-frames. The "attunement" is the analogical synchronizing of relations between the person's "what-is-in-totality," that which is "not identical with the sum," and "the manifest character of what-is-in-totality." Moreover, the "what-is-in-totality" stands tacit beneath all our focal knowledge (Polanyi).

Though the infinite and finite, the temporal and the Eternal, cannot materially synthesize, they can perichoretically and dialogically synthesize within existential consciousness, mediated by the momentary synthesis *outside*, *between*, and *within* themselves, participating in this creative activity of the Trinity. Mediated by the third term, each person analogically shares in the dynamic mutual reciprocity and the interpenetration and interanimation of meaning.[144]

In deference to Gergen and others who tend to sacrifice the subject into a collective holism (a dualism or monism in contrast to an irreducible differentiated unity), the perichoretic *moment* instantiates the person as *individual*-in-relation. *Through* social interaction, persons attain something *greater* than the existing collective sum, which produces creative possibilities (in contrast to determinate possibilities). It creates the prophetic, the novel—that which stands apart from the existing world, from all that was. It supports the state of becoming and mutual co-conditioning. How does this *greater* come from the emerging properties within open and free interaction? Infinite resignation into the relationship brings the possibility of emergence (*creatio ex nihilo*)—antecedently affecting God's creative activity in the *analogia spiritus*, the co-conditioning encounter with the Other before the creation of time. *From within* the communicative discourse of physics, Einstein identifies cosmic properties that could not have logically come from the sum total of existing physics. Yet, these properties come into existence *through* his attempts to express them in community and ultimately from the

---

143. Heidegger, *Being and Time*, 311–12.

144. These characteristics of "indwelling" within *perichoresis*, with slight alteration, are repurposed from Gunton, *One, Three, Many*, 163, and parallel Loder's "logic of spirit" that we will investigate shortly.

"stabilized social audience" of his reflective soliloquies. This compels us to consider with Kierkegaard that human beings are a relationship unto themselves from which, somehow, someway, solitary prophets continue to arise among the ashes of entrenched traditions to produce greater explanatory and pragmatic progress.[145] From the Christian understanding of Christ's claim of being the Word, that in which all things consist (are held together), Jean-Luc Marion tells us "in him coincide—or rather *commune*—the sign, the locutor, and the referent.... And hence the Word, the Said, finally says nothing; he lets people speak, he lets people talk, 'Jesus gave him no answer' (John 19:19 = Luke 23:9)."[146] From the Power and dynamic that posits self as a relationship unto itself, instantiating the *person*-in-relation, individuals transcend but do not lose their social construction or personhood.

In this respect, Kierkegaard's enigmatic structuring allows the individual to exist both fully open to authentic relations and alternatively engenders full closure—the choice, the leap—within each relational occurrence. These dialogical modalities, however, force us to consider the mediating dynamic of the relationship itself as the transitional matrix, the moment of transition cyclically from awareness to conceptualization, from conceptualization back to awareness. Theologically, the Irenaean two hands of God—the Spirit and Jesus Christ—and the nature of the divine reflecting within humanity mediate all dialogical moments, most notably transition moments.[147] When we open from constituted-being (reflexion) into awareness, the Spirit of God engages and influences (*analogia spiritus*, prereflexive co-conditioning); when we constitute person-in-relation from awareness into being, we reflexively constitute christologically (brought-back-together, Col 1:17). To the extent we are willing to venture ourselves fully within authentic relationship (Mark 8:35; 10:15, 29–30; i.e., "pick up our cross daily") our mode of relating becomes compatible with that cruciform Power. To the degree we experience *perichoresis*, we become co-creators. Because of sin, our unwillingness to venture all, we minimally experience *perichoresis* (Religiousness A equivalent); when we fully venture all into relation with the Other (moments of full redemption), *perichoresis*

---

145. Wallace, "Revitalization Movements," describe this force and sequence within cultural evolution: (1) a person has a vision, (2) communication of revelation, (3) win over converts, (4) cultural transformation, (5) re-shaping of all society, and (6) revitalization is attained. Such transformations do not happen until one individual enters a culture's existing struggles and anomalies with sufficient personal penetration and intensity to then emerge with a redemptive gestalt and strategy.

146. Marion, *God without Being*, 140, emphasis added.

147. This basic Irenaean trajectory within the dynamic of *perichoresis* is found in Gunton, *One, Three, Many*; Gunton, *Trinitarian Theology*; Gunton, *Triune Creator*.

becomes a radical quality of existential living (Religiousness B equivalent—rare and episodic). Only in venturing ourselves wholly into our relations ("in the midst of two or more") and then act decisively (Peter and the keys of heaven, Matt 16:18–19) does progress, novelty and truth emerge from the "once-occurrent event" of co-creation.[148] In this respect, truth is right relationship, and only from within each existential moment can one stand in truth. *Only in infinite resignation can one truly act decisively.* Only then do the appropriate doxastic structures emerge from each moment to the next (alas, we rarely venture all, sin). As such, relationship constitutes all knowledge. And truth is a quality we attain in venturing all. When we venture all, passion and authority enter our knowledge and action, and the incursion of the relational sublime allows us to decisively say, "here I stand."

Does this obviate entirely the incommensurability that seemingly exists between various communities of thought and faith (language games)? Yes and no. Yes, perfect *perichoresis* (love) transgresses "incommensurabilities," but to do so, according to Kierkegaard, we must be *willing* to venture all. Furthermore, there must be complete openness in dialogue, which has two hurdles to clear. First, dialogue takes time. However, we will soon reconsider the biblical event of Pentecost as a proleptic portending of instantaneous perichoretic translation of meaning into infinitely diverse meaning-frames resulting from fully redeemed/evolved human interactions.[149] This should caution all insistence that various language games are ultimately incommensurable. Second, we all enter our interaction with untouchable beliefs, closely guarding our decaying manna from day to day instead of offering it into the Jacobian night before each new day. This relational disposition of closeness is what Kierkegaard refers to as sin, and all are culpable. One might imagine, as our cultures, disciplines of thought, and religions continue to mix through our exponentially growing capacity of modern travel, communications, and interpenetrating economies that our largely unconscious fears of the Other might slowly dissipate into more trusting dispositions of relationships and, therefore, the possibility of greater depths of perichoretic (commensurable) relations. (Or, to the contrary, one might imagine the opposite effect beneath the crushing force of social engineering for agendas of control. Alas, the world will take its course accordingly.) Nevertheless, beneath the epistemic incommensurability of

---

148. Matt 11:23–26: ὃς ἂν εἴπῃ . . . καὶ μὴ διακριθῇ ἐν τῇ καρδίᾳ αὐτοῦ ἀλλὰ πιστεύῃ ὅτι ὃ λαλεῖ γίνεται, ἔσται αὐτῷ (whoever says . . . and does not doubt in his heart, but believes that what he says is going to happen, it shall be granted him).

149. Until then, dialogical time is necessary, but grace is nothing more than time in which to evolve, redeem, i.e., drawing further into trusting that Power that constitutes all relations in love.

disparate communities lays the possibility of a commensurable spirit of openness and grace, each remaining open to the other in sacred recognition and transforming sensitivity in respect of difference.

Miroslav Volf would here caution our attention to the necessity of identity and the variable states of development within relations of plurality.[150] A person or community never transforms into full Christlikeness in a single transformation, but from one degree to another (2 Cor 3:18). Why? To maintain some coterminous sense of identity. Therefore, dialogical relations must continue in love amid difference (Rom 14:1—15:6). Grace covers difference, the diversity in our transitioning developmental stages, while maintaining our evolving identities.

Perichoretic dynamics suggest a methodological development that broadly includes *both* research project's methodological considerations and one in which firmly held beliefs are possible. At the same time, *perichoresis* creates the freedom for change and transformation within expanding contexts due to ongoing and proliferating interactions. We will now consider possible methodological structuring in relation to perichoretic dynamics and then discuss aspects of *perichoresis* as functional criteria for determining the integrity of religious experience.

A THEOLOGICAL METHOD OF COMPLEMENTARITY: (A) THE REFLEXIVE CRITERIA (INTERNAL COHERENCE, EXPLANATORY POWER, ETC.) AND (B) THE PREREFLEXIVE CRITERION OF *FULLNESS OF LIFE*

Meaning and Value: Fullness of Life

Concept and experience arise together in human relations to produce *meaning*. Methodologically, meaning is reducible to neither cognition (christomorphic) or experience (*analogia spiritus*) alone; its relational adequacy—quality and value—is holistic and thus strides the complementarity of humanity's (Christ's) paradoxical synthesis of the finite and the infinite, time and eternity, within dialogical cycling (human participation in the creative activity of the Trinity). This valuative and irreducible criterion of meaning and relational quality becomes *fullness of life*, which is instantly transcommunitive in nature.[151] As a criterion, fullness of life is a perichoretic synthesis of the semantic/conceptual articulation *and* the depth of

---

150. Volf, *Exclusion and Embrace*.

151. Transcommunitive signifies that which holistically communicates, evaluates, and adjudicates between various communities, traditions, and cultures.

experiencing. As such, it presents itself as the final theological criterion which emerges holistically from the dialogical synthesis of these two floating[152] *variables*—the conceptual and experiential.

Higher Levels of Meaning through Increased Explanatory Function and Wider Experiences of the World

Again, the level of meaning is the perichoretic product of (1) the degree of diversity and integration of the explanatory and semantic capacities (conceptual development, focal), (2) the depth and quality of experience (awareness or presence, tacit), and (3) the degree to which the person's and/or community's relational dynamic transparently reflects *perichoresis*—that Power which constitutes all relationships. These aspects of personal existence cyclically and dialogically synthesize person-in-relation. Generally, persons and societies with greater explanatory capacities are *capable* of greater meaning within their interactions, but not necessarily. This is noticeable in both cultural evolution and biological strata. For example, the level of intimacy and fullness of life that primitive cultures experience during filial or sexual relations or in experiencing beauty and awe is less than what is possible within more evolved societies with greater explanatory capacities.[153]

---

152. "Floating" signifies variability and indeterminacy in emphasizing not their provisional but their personal, contextual, developmental, and relative structuring and nature. The term should hauntingly remind the reader of Kierkegaard's insistence that humans constitute in time, therefore always in contextual flux. *CUP*, 180–89.

153. Fullness of life is not merely a product of a person's capacity to become spirit—wholly constitute in relation to that Power. That is only a portion of the equation. Primitive societies are not lacking in their capacity to experience significant amounts of awe and mystery, "Eternity in their hearts," or to become spirit, wholly constitute. The degree of conceptual articulation and explanatory capacity (linguistic development) provides the potential for a broader scope of experience that provides greater perichoretic interanimation of that awe and beauty within our natural understanding and experience. In a telling novel by naturalist and explorer Peter Matthiessen of ineffective missionary efforts into South America, *At Play in the Fields of the Lord*, he effectively reveals how both individuals within an advanced culture, e.g., twentieth-century American Christian fundamentalism, can effectively reduce its potential for fullness of life through systematic closure to various depths of experience, and conversely how primitive cultures are unable to attain the higher levels of fullness of life possible in more advanced civilizations. He presents the primitive's sexual activity as an experience they enjoy slightly above that of mastication. As they went into the bushes for such activity, others stood by and watched. The Eternal weight of their actions and the perichoretic reflection of their purview and development within the finite still lie partially within their Garden's innocence. This does not delimit the passion they potentially experience within such activity, but it limits the culture's *potential* for fullness of life and greater states of meaning.

On the experiential side, Kierkegaard presents a decisive point in his contrasting of two men praying. One prays within a more informed meaning-frame, another within a more limited one. However, because the latter prays with the "passion of the infinite" ("venturing all"), he more wholly constitutes and with greater awareness and experiential depth (presence), and therefore, despite his limiting meaning-frame, his prayer is more meaning*ful*.[154] Likewise, the New Testament writers went to great lengths to reveal an authority (ἐξουσία) in Jesus' call to the disciples that transcends the rational and existing social response norms of the community. A simple "follow me" highlights the instantaneous meaning*fulness* and quality of the relationship from Jesus' sheer presence *within* the relationship with little accommodating conceptual conditioning (Mark 2:14). Nevertheless, meaning and fullness of life do not emerge from sheer presence or passion but the synthesis and product of all these dialogical dipolar aspects in relation to that constituting Power. Nevertheless, the holistic prereflexive aspect of the experience and *how* we enter our relationships take *asymmetrical priority* over the cognitive reflexive (relative) factors.[155]

Both these dialogical components of interactions resemble the primary nature in Kierkegaard's Religiousness A and B, respectively. Religiousness B transformatively incorporates the stages before it (aesthetic, ethical, and Religiousness A) within itself. The immanent contingencies of Religiousness A are not rendered meaningless within Religiousness B; instead, the immanent transforms, rising to new levels of meaning when drawn into perichoretic relation with Religiousness B.

---

154. Existential meaning (passion) as the quality of a relationship is the great demand of Kierkegaard. He illustrates this in his well-known contrast of two prayers. One is from a "Christian" who goes up to the house of the true God with a true conception of that God and then prays with a closed spirit (truncating his awareness into the full possibilities or contingencies). The quality of his relationship is quite low, which empties the superior conceptual articulation of its fuller meaning. The other is one who lives in an idolatrous community and prays with the entire passion of the infinite, and even though he sets his eyes upon the image of an idol, Climacus (as well as Kierkegaard) concludes: he "prays in truth to God though he worships an idol: the other prays falsely to the true God, and hence worships in fact an idol." The obvious difference is the integrity and quality of the relationship itself—the *how* of the interaction. Though the higher conceptual and experiential development enhances the *potential* quality of the interaction, the ultimate meaningfulness of the relationship is asymmetrically dependent upon the relational disposition of each participant. Kant's distinction of fact/value is ultimately unable to articulate what these Kierkegaardian distinctions bring to life. This will become more explicit in our sections on human development. *CUP*, 179.

155. Cf. current neurological and psychology studies, e.g., Damasio, *Descartes' Error*; McGilchrist, *Master*.

Because immediate experience is an aspect of this indivisible product, meaning is never experienced the same way twice. This presents us with two modes of criteria for methodological consideration. We can critically attain *contextual* criteria by (1) verifying systems of explanatory capacity through their ability to produce wider experiences of life, and reciprocally (2) verifying wider frames of experience through their ability to stimulate more diverse explanatory functions—progress. Similar to Lakatos, we can only effectively use such criteria intrasystematically.[156] To accomplish this adequately for theological criteria, Murphy's "observable" stricture of criteria ("empirical") must expand to *perceivable*. By removing the visual metaphor prominent within the natural sciences and broadening our purview within the human sciences and theology, we can more fully consider the conceptual and holistically experiential criteria evident and necessary within these disciplines. These dialectical criteria stand only within the contextual moment of occurrence, and their full doxastic character depends on more holistic levels of experiencing.[157]

---

156. Hefner, *Human Factor*, 261.

157. We might contrast this discussion (and thesis) with a paralleling discussion between Fr. Henri Bouillard and Barth (T. F. Torrance), in which Bouillard "agrees with Barth that we cannot know God except through God, on the foundation of Biblical revelation and through faith, but insists that we must add that it is *we* who know God. While the objective foundation of faith resides in divine revelation, 'the subjective foundation of its possibility resides necessarily in us; otherwise, it would not be our certainty. The possibility of the natural knowledge of God is the transcendental condition of the knowledge of faith'" (Torrance, *Transformation*, 301, emphasis added). Because the nature and logic of *perichoresis* do not attain ontological status in the divine-human relational theologies of Barth, Torrance, or Bouillard (Bouillard being the closest), the concept of co-conditioning (*analogia spiritus*) remains foreign. Barth and Torrance cannot justify Bouillard's necessity that the "subjective foundation" be the sole property of humanity. If one allows that the nature of God (*perichoresis*) potentially and analogically reflects within human sociology and personhood because of its unique perichoretic relationship to God in Christ, then faith's foundation rises within both simultaneously and independently by definition of *perichoresis* itself.

Torrance, however, believes such "abstractions" are useless in presenting God if they "detach the structure of natural theology from any ground in the being of God as he really is." Myopically centering on the "being" of God, Torrance and Barth are unable or unwilling to institute the full logic of *perichoresis* and its quality of irreducibly maintaining the respective "being" of each participant (respective "immanences") while allowing them to reflectively co-condition each other ontologically in perichoretic dynamics. Of course, in perichoretic relations (God's nature, not being), there is always the "detachment from being," even within the Trinity! However, *perichoresis*, by definition, obviates that "detachment." I wonder if Barth truly understood that each of Kierkegaard's stages transforms when subsumed into the next and its theological implications. In other words, the dynamics of Religiousness A don't disappear in Religiousness B; they remain yet transform. We will revisit this discussion in chapter 5A.

This fundamental dynamic within our interactions is the ground and product of meaning. Like Gergen's "relational sublime," the criterion fullness of life emerges irreducibly as a quality of meaning. It foundationally locates not in beliefs or knowledge, but as the tensive unity within relationship (person or social), and therefore transcends all "incommensurability." As Gergen contends, the locus of meaning fundamentally lies "within the process of interaction itself."[158] Again, this criterion does not abrogate but instantiates and incorporates the categories of dialectics.

An example of the asymmetrical priority of the holistic aspect of our knowledge, beliefs, and experience over the cognitive/rational appears in the faith of Paul. Wolterstorff comments:

> Paul seems to have come to believe in the resurrection at the same time that he came to have faith in Jesus; he did not go out first to conduct elaborate historical investigations. One gets the impression that Paul would have believed in the resurrection even if all the historical evidence were against it.[159]

There was a quality within Paul's numinal (holistic) experience, a configurative force *within* his epistemic structuring that supersedes, reconfigures, and even subverts his previous understanding of Christ. Something instantly happens in that once-occurrent experience that *paradigmatically reconfigures all* his knowledge, convictions, and behavior. As Torrance insists, theological knowledge necessitates an open, flexible epistemology.[160] This

---

158. Gergen, "Relationships," 4.

159. Wolterstorff, "Faith," 27.

160. "It is scientifically false to begin with epistemology. On the other hand, it must be admitted that we operate with an inchoate epistemology as soon as we begin to engage in theological inquiry, that is with a tacit understanding of how we know God, although it can yield a proper epistemology only as we advance in the knowledge of God and submit our actual knowing to criticism and control in accordance with the nature of the object of our knowledge. This means that all the way through theological inquiry we must operate with an *open* epistemology in which we allow the way of our knowing to be clarified and modified *pari passu* with advance in deeper and fuller knowledge of the object, and that we will be unable to set forth an account of that way of knowing in advance but only by looking back from what has been established as knowledge" (Torrance, *Theological Science*, 10).

requires epistemic posturing that constantly submits its entire structuring in *metanoia* (repentance) into the holistic reconstitution within genuine relations. Such relational posturing trustingly prioritizes the transformative asymmetrical complementarity of *analogia spiritus* configuratively active within our empirical (experiential) verification and historical continuity.

St. Teresa and St. Catherine: Phronesis *over* Episteme/Techne

Is it not conceivable, for example, that Teresa's book, *The Interior Castle*, has had a greater sanctifying influence and widespread impact upon more readers over the centuries than Catherine's *Divine Dialogues* (both "fruitfully" and theologically)?[161] Moreover, is it not conceivable despite Catherine's supposed balance between the inner and outer life (noted by Murphy), that Teresa's *The Interior Castle* has gone on to affect more transformative changes in readers than Catherine's writings that supposedly have a more "observable" and verifiable character? Such writings, like Teresa's, by simply presenting their personal narrative, relational disposition, and subsequent experience of God, can often encourage that same openness and dispositional ground within readers, allowing God to engage the soul more deeply. These are theologically notable criteria. These experiences indeed are sociologically *perceivable* in *phronesis*. Likewise, the assessment of such experiences must eventually transcend the perceptive operators used in theory development within the natural sciences ("observability") due to the character of what is being studied. This is not to say there are no appropriate empirical markers, merely that some criteria will be perceivable more holistically and pragmatically. In this respect, an outlying question might become: Do Teresa's writings bear more of the fruit that Murphy is so keen to assess within its readers than those of Catherine's? These are measurable criteria. Or, again, are they?

What is it that inevitably informs us that "charitable" actions are charitable rather than a selfish escape from conflictual relationships (e.g., co-dependency/enmeshment)? Again, much of what yesterday's Christian communities categorized as "charitable," today's contemporary psychology and socio-culture evolution expose as destructive behavior. Such criteria (charity) must operate at the level of *phronesis* that transcends the typical structures of *episteme*. Simple behavior as repeatable action is never normative diachronically. Like religious experience, it will produce fruit that sustains historical continuity, albeit through *phronesis*.[162] The "observ-

---

161. I am quite certain many more copies of this classic are sold than St. Catherine's.
162. For Kierkegaard continuity, "a conclusion of causes," is experienced holistically.

able" behavior is only one aspect of verification of religious experience; as "evidence" of *the whole*, it is inconclusive. The continuity of each spontaneous and novel response in contrast to former "observable" social patterns is *perceivable* only in the context of action as *phronesis*. Implementing "observables" without *phronesis* imposes a teleological finality outside existence; what Paul would consider "bringing Christ down from above" (Rom 10:6). Therefore, the primary and stronger aspect of verification is the text's ability to pass on analogically *the whole* of the former context-specific meaning and experience holistically to the new context-specific relationship. We will only perceive the conceptual, explanatory, and "observable" continuity within their traditional coordinates after the leap and subsequent transformation (analogy). However, these latter criteria as episteme are secondary, and because of the necessity for *phronesis*, they too require of the assessor an appropriate "leap" beyond reason ("empiricism"). Otherwise, are we to believe that St. Catherine's 1300s conceptual understanding of love is the same as, for example, Elisabeth Moltmann-Wendel's today?[163]

Such criteria, therefore, as Murphy has narrowly defined, are, in principle, inconclusive for theology according to what Lakatos designates as a positive heuristic—a program that holistically considers all relevant data within the complex rationale of that community's structures of meaning. By implementing Hume's categories for theology, Murphy has incorporated the empiricism of modernity (via W. V. O. Quine) as her positive heuristic, installing the un-"empirical" logic of Christianity (community discernment) as her negative heuristic (which protects the hard core "belief"). The alternative necessitates the hard work of broadening the methodological intent of Lakatos into a truer holism for theological explanation that entails the full wealth of knowledge, experience, and meaning exhibited and required within theology. As Jürgen Moltmann insists, we must cease the modern practice of bifurcating knowledge, feeling, and experience.[164] If the

---

Faith is that constituting tacit dimension of knowledge and experience upon which all 'observables' or reason float. Therefore, in the temporal movements of 'observables' or reason, "continuity is lacking, or at any rate it has continuity only in reverse, that is, at the beginning it does not manifest itself as continuity" (*JPH*, 3:399–400).

163. I refer to her paper "Does Nothing Good Dwell in My Flesh?" because I believe it exhibits a maturity, quality, and insight not found in St. Catherine yet consonant within St. Teresa. Might it be that relational disposition, a reader's holistically engagement of the text, and the potential experience of the ineffable play a significant role as criteria for validating religious experience? Religious experience is a complex consideration far beyond "observables."

164. "Reason has to be woven into the fabric of the feelings, and consciousness has to be assimilated into the experiences of the body" (Moltmann, *SL*, 173; cf. Jaggar, "Love"; Zagzebski, *Virtues*).

above consideration of St. Teresa is accurate, her experience and writings assume the possibility of communitively perceiving the invisible (the numinal), and she linguistically provides the structure of the faith experience for those who want to make this move but do not know how. That which her writings communicate (her existing narrative, relational disposition, and experience) is indeed socially transmittable and ultimately socially verifiable, however, only because it is perceivable through *phronesis*. Such criterion, however, will forever remain outside Hume's, and it seems Murphy's, categorical (philosophical) distinctions of what is empirically verifiable.

Again, this is not to negate the empirical notion in theological methodology that Murphy and Hefner seek to appropriate but merely attempts to dimensionalize the concept and caution against its degeneration into less than holistic use within theology. Though the notion of the empirical (that which is "repeatable" and "falsifiable") contains both conceptual and experiential elements, it cannot be reduced to either, nor are they "repeatable" outside the phronetic dynamic of *perichoresis* for analytical assessment in theology.

Kierkegaard points to a relational dynamic by which we might theoretically attain existential certainty. However, this perichoretic synthesis that Kierkegaard develops necessitates the proper human pathos in relation to the existential truth.[165] From childhood, our open disposition—our willingness to engage ourselves fully within the process of awareness, to believe and acknowledge *all things* (1 Cor 13)—soon denigrates into suppressive mechanisms resisting potential threats from others. We inappropriately utilize these relational mechanisms as constant vigilantes against the necessary openness required for authentic relationships. These vows of closure become relational styles that ultimately denigrate our relationships with others and affect our relationship with God. Within harsh social environments, these patterned responses become quite immediate and unconscious. They quickly find their home amid various social contracts and relational choreographies. However, within the matrix of each relational moment lies the latent capacity to leap outside those patterned responses as *moments* of Grace shock us with freedom and a purview of the beauty, truth, and presence within every new event-unity that we could not otherwise perceive. It is sometimes a conscious choice (leap), however, most often, the choice is made unconsciously as our passion for greater fullness of life silently wrestles against these unseen mechanisms of fear of the Jacobian night. Either way, when our longing for more finally swells into a significant level of passion, the willingness to venture all breaks forth, and we enter into new levels of perichoretic relations and potential transformation.

---

165. Kierkegaard, *CUP*, 516–19.

MEANING AS PERICHORESIS

A lack of *willingness* to constitute in infinite resignation distorts *analogia spiritus* and limits the "energy," "earnestness," and "pathos,"[166] by which we constitute as whole persons-in-relations in relation to that constituting Power. Only to the degree we enter *analogia spiritus* do we appropriate *phronesis*. Until we seriously draw this admittedly Pandora's box into our theological methodology, we forfeit important and valuable criteria in critical theological research.

Let us consider two integral relational conditions that create and embody truth-conducive relationships. The first comes from recent scientific insights within thermodynamics that suggest fluctuations (dynamics) within open systems create irreversible processes of higher organization.[167] We might consider desire or longing as the fundamental source motivating such perichoretic relations (fluctuations). As such, longings themselves might qualify as possible criteria revealing the quality of perichoretic relations. Secondly, because "knowledge is a state whose value is holistic"[168] the doxastic structure of all knowledge warrants that epistemic humility is given ample integration into method. Doing theology, or any discipline, is an ethical act. Both these conditions are imperative for the holistic perception of fullness of life within meaning (and knowledge). Furthermore, only by this terminal and constantly expanding criterion of fullness of life do we encounter a degree of certainty and faith within our beliefs, knowledge, and relations. Such certainty only comes to us holistically within an *open system*—the analogical relation of the *whole person* to the *whole of the Spirit and the Eternal*. Are we willing with Isaac to sacrifice? Though this criterion is affective transcommunally, meaning itself reflects some level of this unobservable interaction in each event-unity (Heb 4:12).

From a broadened Lakatosian trajectory, it appears theological criteria for "progress" must entail not only some aspect of conceptual and pragmatic explanatory extension and coherence (reason) but also the additional widening of human experience, which together (the focal and the tacit aspect of experience) provide a holistic criterion within meaning—greater fullness of life. For example, this project provides new meaning to scriptural passages, some of which have previously had little or no coherent meaning within the totality of the Scriptures. These, in turn, will provide even greater coherence to the text and existing theological understanding. Eventually, this should deepen the Christian faith experience within the community. Each, in sequence, validates the value of the other. For the most part, the adjudication

---

166. Kierkegaard's terms.
167. For example, Prigogine and Stengers, *Order Out of Chaos*.
168. Zagzebski, *Virtues*, 316.

of episteme is through greater explanatory power, textual coherence, and theological coherence. On the other hand, fullness of life becomes evident holistically within the individual and faith community. Both sets of criteria, the focal and the tacit, the finite and the infinite, the conceptual and the experiential, form an existential complementarity that produces meaning itself—our methodology must be broad enough to perceive all that is active within meaning.

The Perichoretic Logic of a Universal Criterion of Fullness of Life

The theological project and its criteria will always undergo conceptual and experiential change as it develops throughout history. Our understanding of God, tradition, and the Scriptures undergoes constant expansion. Moltmann thinks,

> In history, the messianic becoming-human of the human being remains incomplete and uncompletable. It is only the eschatological annihilation of death, the redemption of the body on a new earth and under a new heaven, which will consummate the "becoming" process of human beings, thereby fulfilling their creaturely destiny.[169]

The problem is not that some new verifying criteria might emerge other than charity or the traditional criteria of religious experience. Ossification of a criterion's meaning or "observability" would be tragic.[170]

Though beneficial, we cannot prescribe charity by a set of diachronically "observable" behaviors. Charity, or love, refers to the quality of authentic relationality (*perichoresis*), and the conceptual and experiential rendering of these relational states are still evolving. It is no different for theological knowledge and doctrine. As we learn and experience more about the world and our relations to each other and God, new properties will continue to emerge that will further enrich its meaning. Though charity is always charity within the larger changing Christian context (diachronically), its meaning and use as a criterion are likewise constantly in social and

---

169. Moltmann, *GC*, 227. Because of an open history, Moltmann refers to Dilthey's assumption that "human being is not fixed by nature." Cf. Landmann, *Philosophische*, 251.

170. Inappropriate ossification of criteria is presently evident in many forms of religious fundamentalism that insist upon anachronistically defining, e.g., love as a set of social behaviors rather than allowing our growing knowledge of human relations to enrich its meaning and perceivability.

conceptual development.[171] Though we can never suggest a complete and final "observable" understanding of love, we can always analogically *perceive* its diachronic continuity within each unique context. This same dynamic applies to our concept of spirit throughout the history of the church.

This is not relativism but relativity of difference, nor does it necessitate diachronic discontinuity within relational activity or transitions. The perichoretic dynamic within relationality gracefully supports the individual appropriately and transformatively throughout its history. Participation within the relationship will be genuine to the degree human participation interanimates and attunes (*abgestimmt*)[172] its mode of relationality to the nature of the constituting dynamics within the interaction. Therefore, every relational choreography, style, or objective spirit that develops in families and cultures that reflect the greatest degree of *perichoresis* and having the greatest degree of fullness of life (the best explanatory capacity together with the most profound experience of life) will stand in contrast to others that do not. Individuals silently experience this ultimate criterion holistically at play within intercommunal interactions motivating social mobility and migration between and within cultures, religious denominations, and traditions. Developing conceptual forms that flourish maintain perichoretic continuity in persons, relationships, and cultures through their christomorphic transformations throughout history.

Both Barth and Moltmann express a perichoretic-like social constitution of self from which meaning uniquely emerges. Moltmann suggests:

> Social experience stands in the same correlation to experience of God as experience of the self. . . . The person who knows God, knows himself. The person who knows himself, knows God. This applies to one's neighbour equally [e.g., see Mt 25:31f]. . . . In experiencing the affection of others we experience God. In being loved we sense the nearness of God, in hate we feel God's remoteness.[173]

Moltmann here deepens Calvin's earlier cited consideration. Though theology is a distinctive discourse dependent upon God and his Word, it is not easy within theological knowledge "to say which of them comes first

---

171. McFadyen tells us such designations "take contingent form. They are a part of God's history with God's People and do not destroy the past but transform its interpretation and therefore the way in which it is present" (*CP*, 56), which he rightfully places in direct contrast to Bultmann's "dehistoricisation" (n27).

172. Heidegger, *Being and Time*, 311.

173. Moltmann, *SL*, 220.

and then itself affects the other,"[174] divine, personal, or social knowledge. Therefore, our theological development is partially verifiable by its ability to produce *fullness of life* within communitive transactions. Furthermore, a greater understanding of authentic (perichoretic) relations, specifically the character of *both* the dialogical cycles of openness and closure would provide theological and ethical benefit.

The Possibility of a Hybrid Hard Core Theory from Theology and Social Psychology

We might expect that the data and patterns within the observations of human developmental and social psychology, specifically those that pertain to transformative dynamics, would be capable of eventually integrating into the theological paradigm. A hybrid theological program integrating social psychology would eventually verify itself through its ability to deepen human meaning and fullness of life. Furthermore, such a program would become evident by deepening the explanatory function and increasing the experience of the world and relationships within the respective mother disciplines.

In this respect, Philip Hefner argues that the teleonomic development (purpose and meaning) of human existence emerges within natural processes and that "nature is the medium through which the world, including human beings, receives knowledge, *as well as grace*."[175] Therefore, there are no "religious concepts of human meaning and purpose [that] derive from otherworldly sources of revelation rather than from within nature itself."[176] This strongly unitive understanding bases itself on an enhanced understanding of divine-human mutuality; yet, if understood correctly, it does not negate the immanent, transcendent, Eternal, and preeminent activity of a differentiated personal God who speaks to humanity. However, this unique and mysterious relationship between "nature" and Christ is an essential methodological factor. In this respect, all nature *constitutes* (Col 1:17) within the relational logic of spirit-to-Spirit (Eternal). Moltmann similarly stipulates:

> As far as the dimension of theology is concerned . . . we can discover transcendence in every experience, not merely in experience of the self. For this, the term immanent transcendence

---

174. Calvin, *Institutes*, I.1.1.
175. Hefner, *Human Factor*, 57, emphasis added.
176. Hefner, *Human Factor*, 58.

> offers itself. Every experience that happens to us or that we have, can possess a transcendent, inward side, The experience of God's Spirit is . . . also a constitutive element in the experience of the "Thou," in the experience of sociality, and in the experience of nature. . . . If experiences of God embrace experiences of life, then—seen in reverse—experiences of life can also embrace experiences of God . . . . To experience God in all things presupposes that there is a transcendence which is immanent in things and which can be inductively discovered. It is the infinite in the finite, the eternal in the temporal, and the enduring in the transitory. . . . If we can call what for us is nature, "God's creation," we have already invoked its immanent transcendence.[177]

In this respect, theology is potentially integrative of every experience and every discipline of thought. Likewise, every experience and discipline of thought reveals elements of grace. We must begin to expand our understanding of experiencing God and the natural within a more unified expression of relational dynamics than what former theological languages could explicitly express.

Therefore, with Hefner, I wish to affirm the empirical and pragmatic nature of the theological program. However, concerning the "natural" and the "evidential," *"we must learn how to discern the dimension of ultimacy in nature's processes and how to conceptualize them."*[178] By ultimacy, Hefner refers to "the meaning of God" and "the dimension of the holy in human existence."[179] Furthermore, he insists that we be "concerned with the way things are in the profoundest dimension, that of ultimacy."[180] Hefner considers the human experience of the ultimate as immanently active and inherent (supervenient) within the natural processes. Hence, failure to understand (and experience) this phenomenon within the natural processes will necessarily eschew our understanding and explanation of the whole and the parts. In this respect, this study justifies and qualifies its use of developmental and social psychology and, in a more limited fashion, postmodern theoretical physics into a hybrid theological program.

---

177. Moltmann, *SL*, 34–36. This also was a growing concern of Bonhoeffer, culminating in his prison letters.
178. Hefner, *Human Factor*, 74.
179. Hefner, *Human Factor*, 32.
180. Hefner, *Human Factor*, 33.

JACOB AND THE NIGHT OF FAITH

REFLECTIONS ON KNOWLEDGE AS THE SHAPE OF DESIRE

In this section, we shall consider the thesis that all human desires or longings *primordially* emerge from God's sustaining relation to humanity and that the foundation of all human desire and longings is to relate perichoretically (John 17:11, 21). If so, all life, relations, memory, knowledge, and meaning emerge as textured longings and desires through one's unique socio-historic sedimentation (paralleling the left-brain hemispheric activity *conditioning the* right hemispheric activity of apprehension).[181] This formation of mental and spirit activity between the whole and relative aspects of consciousness is perichoretic. In this respect, knowledge is shaped relationship; moreover, knowledge is the shaping of our desire, much like words taking shape upon our breath. Our socio-historic sedimentation and developing ego texture all animation, movement, and relations, optimally as whole spirit reflecting that Power. Ego emerges and develops because that is the shape of *perichoresis*—a *differentiated* unity. With the development of ego comes, by definition, the ability to relate perichoretically (in full reflection of and in relation to that Power). When the ego fails to take shape in relation to or reflect that Power, the texturing of desire, actions, thoughts, and knowledge become distorted regarding that Power.

The perichoretic dynamic within life stimulates ever-greater differentiation (objectification) with corresponding re-integration into the whole of our meaning-frame (our tacit awareness). If the primordial state of desire is that life force within humanity and the animating force within all knowledge and meaning, then we might consider that which is most fundamental and most desirable is *to* relate in synchronicity with that Power that creates all relations. In this respect, relationships attain their fullest expression when they become transparently complementary to that activity of the Trinity. Either way, by grace all things are created and held together, whether by one's own distorted reflecting nature, or in synchronicity with Christ in his Time.

Relational Triangulation and Its Perichoretic Redemption

In the Gospel of John, Jesus asks the Father to create within his followers the ability to relate with each other as They relate. Christ was broadening and transforming worship, all religious activities, and life into more intimate communitive interactions with each other and God. This began the migration from the endless proliferation of law into one holistic dynamic

---

181. The next chapter will investigate how bicameral brain activity reflects perichoretic dynamics.

of love by replacing the third term of the law and covenant with *perichoresis*. *Perichoresis* was a living relationship between us and the Other, one with infinite possibilities and the potential for right relationship, truth, and beauty from within the immediacy of each unique interaction. The provisional aids of law, social codes, principalities, and powers are the grace that buys the time and space necessary for transforming the intrinsic desires and longings of the heart freely through attraction (not punishment) into synchronicity (1 Cor 15:20–28) with Christlikeness from one degree to another (2 Cor 3:18). As ugly and difficult as that might be historically, they are provisionally sanctioned to provide the space and time for free human movement into synchronicity with God's all in all.[182] This process necessitates a relational de-triangulation that shifts the directing impetus and constituting dynamics of relationships from external sources to that of our own heart—our spirit in direct perichoretic relations with the Holy Spirit (*analogia spiritus*). It is a historical process of sanctification transforming competing and distorted desires into singleness of mind. This transforms disciplined behavior (motivated by reasons outside the intrinsic concerns of the relationship) into impassioned action relevant to and appropriate for each unique interaction.[183] For example, my wife prefers that my desire to be with her and enjoyment of her not come from a desire to honor God or the laws of God; instead, she would rather it come from *my* deep attraction to her and a love that *I* feel intrinsically for her (even though God's love for me frees me to fully open to her in my love).

This is what it means that Christ "must reign till He has put all enemies under his feet?" Amid the chaos of conflicting desires and distortions within persons and cultures, the echo of *perichoresis* within all interactions constantly draws all persons and cultures into ever-greater differentiation and corresponding re-integration. The telemetry of ethics is systematically transforming from laws, rules, and exterior authorities into the internal and

---

182. This explains the enigmatic "purpose" of Christ in Rev 17:12–18, in which the rulers of the world (the ten horns), (1) "are of one mind," giving their power and authority to the beast, (2) "make war with the Lamb," yet (3) "God has put it into their hearts to fulfill His purpose, to be of one mind, and to give their kingdom to the beast, until the words of God are fulfilled." In other words, in Christ creating the space and time for human freedom to work out its demonic distortions and, degree by degree, release into faith, Christ comes not to bring peace, but allows (sanctions) the fire and sword necessary for humanity to know God as God (Matt 10:34–39). Echoing Bouillard, if it is to be *our* knowing it must be *our desire*, and ultimately *our choice*, albeit it perichoretically, least we be slaves rather than friends.

183. This is the apparent trajectory of Jesus' statement in Matt 5:17—6:34; the law is not fulfilled until we intrinsically and fully desire what the law portends (right relationship).

intrinsic desires of the heart (Heb 10:16). With each transformation of *analogia spiritus* and re-integration (expansion of the whole), the doxastic structure within relations increases. In human development, the increasing categories of life, which emerges through ongoing interactions, increase the complexity of our tacit background, supporting more nuanced social interactions. Reciprocally, this augments the experiential and holistic penetration of our focal awareness, creating more intimate, profound, and meaningful relations. In short, the perichoretic depth of our potential relations increases, and as our relations become more perichoretic in nature, we experience higher levels of consciousness and greater fullness of life. The willingness to venture all before the Other (responding to the call to bear our cross) draws us into true freedom, a freedom that coordinates the co-conditioning creativity of the Trinity and persons who relate as they relate.[184]

The Criterion of Desire

How could desire be a foundational dynamic of human existence worth employing as a primary criterion for theological research? Moltmann tells us that "love is a desire" and that God is the most desirable.[185] Milbank points to the primary goodness of all desire in its infinite longing. This thesis claims that it is the fundamental human drive to relate as God relates (perichoretically) and that *all* desire, even distorted desire, traces back to that initial reflective emergence within the soul. It is the gift and curse of Christ's prayer for all humanity.

If all desire is emergent upon such an infinite, good and holy desire, how can we consider the desire to rape and murder as emerging from the good? Developmentalists and social theorists have just begun to unravel the multitude of historical decisions, transactions, and relational choreographies that misshape and twist this foundational desire from what originates within the reflection of goodness. H. Richard Niebuhr says, "This is Calvin's basic assumption, that the evil within culture was simply perverted good."[186]

---

184. The creative act is never within the solitary act of humanity. Only God creates. Nevertheless, the chapter on the *perichoresis* of Time and Eternity explains how Eternity has come into perichoretic relation to Time through Christ within our relationships. The act of creation occurs constantly within a perichoretic temporal-eternal feedback loop that the Trinity supports. God creates through Christ and through him all those who act in faith share co-dominion in God's creating. This holistic *moment* of co-conditioning faith (knowing of Christ) is the mystery of the "Christ in you" (Col 1:24–27) that lies possible in each dialogical moment.

185. Moltmann, *SL*, 248.

186. Niebuhr, *Christ and Culture*, 195–97.

Various suppressive mechanisms self-encode into our sedimentation and "response attitude" toward the Other and distort the primordial call to whole personhood (becoming spirit), which inhibits full entrance into the third term of the relationship. For example, why do tyrants and murderers kill? Why would they distort that very thing they supposedly desire? They do it because they believe it will ensure or deepen relationships elsewhere, or they resist authenticity because it exposes the illusion of authenticity in their current relationships, or from deep anger for not attaining what they sense is possible. Does the tyrant kill for power? If so, it is because he believes it to be social collateral (power attracts). Does he do it in anger? This results from the loss or absence of meaningful relationships or their perceived impossibility ("I am beyond the possibility of being loved"). All motives are prereflexively constructed and reducible to this one original desire that is the foundational Power within all prereflexive awareness—the haunting irrepressible desire to connect with the Other meaningfully.[187] The personal and cultural sedimentation, which shapes desire through the selective and active twisting of this primordial desire, is the site of the ethical, not desire itself. Therefore, desire in its primordial state within the constituting drive of each relational occurrence is the deconstructing and reconstructional force of all personal, interpersonal, and cultural development. This fundamental force within relational dynamics must direct our developmental trajectory and evolving method. All desire is, at some point, the irresistible pull of perichoretic relations.[188]

A person in well-intended relations becomes aware of relationally destructive behavior only because of this one preeminent infinite and primordial desire, or as the Writer would insist, by allowing the nature of that Power that constitutes all relations to reflect within us. This is a conditioning force within individual and social relations that emerges strictly from within the relationship's dynamic, distorted as it may be. Knowledge is a set of connecting relations. Therefore, the integrity of knowledge is established

---

187. Similarly, on the subject of bonding, committed relationships, and the Covenant of God, Ray Anderson tells us: "The very concept of betrayal requires that there be something to betray. And in betrayal, love is both source and object. We betray when we feel that our own love is betrayed by the failure of others. . . . The sin of betrayal is already contextualized by the greater fact of the relationship. Betrayal is the negative evidence that the relationship is real. For without the reality of the relation, betrayal is not possible. The positive evidence of the relation continues to exist as an actuality bound up in the personhood of the one betrayed" (*Judas*, 36, 81).

188. Again, this parallels Heidegger's insight that "untruth must derive from the essence of truth. Only because truth and untruth are not in essence indifferent to one another, can a true proposition contrast so sharply with its correspondingly untrue proposition" (*Being and Time*, 310).

by what is ultimately most desirable and satisfying. The infinite, more fundamental longings will eventually expose shortened desires through its perennial call to more genuine relations or, in the case of science, more felicitous interactions. Only after being exposed, in retrospection, do we observe or identify the faulty structures of a shortened or twisted desire, passion, exchange, or knowledge. In this respect, desire must similarly convict, seduce, guide, and transform within our theological programs.

Desire and Relations in Lakatos

Like language, research programs develop and establish themselves by their functional adaptability, increasing knowledge, and proliferation of explanatory capacity. The primal operator driving such communitive interaction and eventual development is a desire—the "analogy of the infinite," or love (*perichoresis*), which constantly draws the individual into ever-increasing relational intimacy and meaning. Lévinas tells us that

> the relation to the Infinite is not a knowledge, but a Desire. . . . Desire cannot be satisfied; that Desire in some way nourishes itself on its own hungers and is augmented by its satisfaction; that Desire is like a thought which thinks more than it thinks, or more than what it thinks. It is a paradoxical structure, without doubt, but one which is no more so than this presence of the Infinite in a finite act.[189]

The primordial nature of desire demands that "we cannot not be responsive to each other."[190] It defies the stolid existence of non-interaction and status quo.[191] Even the passive gaze of the contemplative actively relates to that which is beyond and yet within the conceptual. Desire in human nature is equivalent to the proleptic teleological force beneath all thermodynamic fluctuations that keep the system active and order emerging out of chaos in open systems (the force at play within complementarity of mass/gravity/fusion and wave/energy/diffusion). Desire in humans for perichoretic relations is the same force that fuels the criterion of progress in Lakatosian methodology. Irreducibly implicit within this criterion is

189. Lévinas, *Ethics*, 92.
190. Shotter, "Life," 76.

191. Non-relation, non-activity, is meaninglessness. "Man finds nothing so intolerable as to be in a state of absolute rest, without exercising any passions, being unemployed, having no diversion, and living without any effort. It is then that he thinks he faces emptiness, loneliness, a sense of inadequacy, feeling dependent, helpless, and living a meaningless life" (Pascal, *Mind on Fire*, 73.

the reciprocating dialogical desire for both the depth and wonder of experience and the explanatory force of the conceptual, each reciprocally (perichoretically) stimulating the other, each alive within their respective side of the dialogical cycle.

This desire, which stimulates the progress within Lakatosian theory, is an attempt to make explicit what is, for example, already implicit within MacIntyre's thesis. By implicit, I mean the active dynamic within his theory that is not explicitly acknowledged. Why does an intracommunal epistemic crisis arise within a tradition? It is either: (1) because that tradition (a) begins to pragmatically experience the world in a manner beyond its linguistic and explanatory capability, or (b) somehow perceives that a contrasting tradition enjoys a greater explanatory capacity and greater meaning in life, or (2) from an "immanent" internal source within the human condition (a relationship unto itself), they become dissatisfied with the existing state of existence and, like Jacob, simply long for more. In each possible scenario, the valuative operator of desire is active within the dynamic of relationship and contrast. Humans are constantly drawn into increasing interconnections while paradoxically experiencing continuity and change.[192] The "immanent" impress is evident within what Marion refers to as boredom:

> Boredom becomes disinterested in everything, . . . withdraws from every interest that would make it enter among beings. It disengages itself from them, leaves its place among them empty. . . . Boredom withdraws from being and from its stakes . . . for the Being that speaks in it no longer manages "to make itself interesting."[193]

Similarly, Michael Gelven sees this same balancing dynamic within our experience of disgust. Whether in our deepest "scarlet debauchery" or our most harmoniously fulfilling moments, there is always more. Even after our experiences of ecstasy, there follows the inevitable cry of disgust: the spirit is willing, but the flesh is weak. Gelven concludes, "perhaps spirit begins right there, with disgust."[194]

Gunton points to this analogy of the infinite, which is active within our awareness, in Coleridge's notion of idea: "the profundity and dynamic inexhaustibility of the ideas, for they give rise, as the mind interacts with reality, to possibilities for ever deeper involvement in the truth of things."[195]

---

192. Ricoeur, *Oneself*.
193. Marion, *God without Being*, 118.
194. Gelven, *Spirit*, 5.
195. Gunton, *One, Three, Many*, 144. This "metaphysical" notion of ideas concerning "reality" and "things," though "inexhaustible," is contrary to the non-metaphysical

Coleridge's notion of the idea expresses the irreducible experience in the tension of dynamic meaning. Within every idea, there is always more.

These joint forces press from within and without the individual (or tradition), motivating the gaze and interest beyond. Whether negative or positive, both sets of forces, "immanent" or "transcendent," are at play, inducing this complementarity within desire and perichoretic relations. This positive dynamic that pulls progress forward and ultimately adjudicates value between disparate competing traditions must emerge immanently from within and yet transcendently from outside the totality of the relationship that is self or tradition. The human quest is simply a search for meaning, that which is irreducible.

Therefore, the desire to relate as the fundamental constitutive force within human nature is the driver within Lakatos's notion of progress for research programs. The pervasiveness of this force and desire begins to signal an identifiable dynamic within theological discourse, which may eventually be empirically helpful (falsifiable/public). If indeed such a desire is foundationally fundamental, and our knowledge, understanding, and identification of such authenticity within relations are increasing (e.g., in the emergence of psychology), then the quality of our knowledge in every way will improve in all sectors. Furthermore, if these same patterns and understanding of relations are commensurate with the notions of Christian faith and practice, it should eventually deepen theological understanding and our experience of the Christian faith. Finally, because this same possibility is open to all religions and traditions, it can condition our methods and provide hope toward a peaceful confluence, drawing us collectively to more profound and informed meaningful experiences within the world, ourselves, and the sacred.

The Universal Criterion of Desire and Its Fulfillment

Lindbeck follows Austin in arguing for the criterion of performance, while Murphy and Hefner, following Lakatos, discuss progress (novel facts) and

---

formations of Wittgenstein and Milbank, yet it attempts to express, contra Wittgenstein, that explanation never destroys wonder but endlessly incites it and opens ground for even broader wonder. For Gunton, Coleridge, Hefner, Moltmann, etc., eschatological ultimacy exists both within (immanent) and perichoretically "parallel" to the natural reality of things (transcendent). For this, Moltmann employs the term "immanent transcendence." For Wittgenstein, the destruction of wonder through explanation, which is not to be confused with the "believe" and "know" of Kierkegaard's Postscripts, *CUP*, 189, seems to result from his assumption that all desire for explanatory grip and reason is largely maniacal, the result of the will to power.

fruitfulness, respectively. Both these are helpful, yet the process of progress and performance among the traditions takes place at the deepest level of human meaning, far beyond the static immediacy of categories in harmony, form, and the semblance of internal cohesion. The safety, consistency, and coherence of epistemic structuring must give way to broader notions of performatives and *phronesis*[196] in which valuative assessment emerges holistically within the relational context itself. Again, "the norms of reasonableness are too rich and subtle to be specified adequately in any general theory of reason or knowledge,"[197] therefore, the "ultimate test" is whether new ideas are "conceptually powerful and practically useful" within relationships,[198] or simply put, provide greater understanding and satisfaction within our interactions.

Such relational criterion corresponds to the irreversibility of novel emergent properties and higher organization that emerge in open systems. This means that within open systems of natural relations, higher states of organization increasingly and irreversibly emerge out of chaotic and chance fluctuations that cancel entropy.[199] Entropy and distortion immediately set in with the institution of any closed system, spatially or temporally (e.g., reified conceptualization). Similarly, when relationships are pre- or over-determined by pre-fixed rational structures and beliefs that are not open to attunement or transformation, the relationship or cultural system will begin to diminish in satisfaction (disgust). The system eventually suffers intransigent anomalies rather than transformative development.

In this respect, all knowledge existentially emerges as shapes of sociocultural response to desire. Though these communicative connections generally emerge in socially recognizable patterns, they always begin with an inherent desire to relate (awareness) and form into meaningful social structures we call knowledge (gestalts). It happens in the twinkling of an eye. All knowledge dynamically remains a differentiated unity in perichoretic tension birthed of desire.

The degree and quality of differentiation and unity one experiences within the perichoretic cycles produces the irreducible quality of fullness of life—that which most satisfies the primordial human desire to relate perichoretically, thus yielding the greatest meaning in life. Ultimately, fullness of life is the criterion by which one assesses "progress" and distinguishes

---

196. Cf. Poteat's use of Austin, in *Polanyian Meditations*, 123.

197. Lindbeck, *Doctrines*, 130.

198. Lindbeck, *Doctrines*, 134.

199. Cf. Peacocke, "God's Interaction"; Peacocke, "Chance and Law"; Peacocke, "Disguised Friend."

"performance." Our idea of re-presentation and repetition in method must mature accordingly. John Milbank believes: "'The way' is not theoretically known but must be constituted through judgment in the repeated construction and recognition of examples, which cannot be literally copied if they are to be genuinely 'repeated.'"[200] "Desire shapes truth beyond the imminent implications of any logical order, so rendering the Christian logos a continuous product, as well as a process of 'art.'"[201] Therefore, any consideration of the coherent and empirical ("repeatable") quality of knowledge sought within theological discourse (closed system criterion) must factor in the holistic and performative criterion of fullness of life (open system criteria). In other words, methodologically, a theological understanding within its well-suited contextual home should provide the optimum fullness of life in contrast to known alternatives.

In this respect, I take my preliminary comprehensive and theological cue for criteria from Wittgenstein (and Gunton). In the broadest but most important sense possible, we perceive, construct, and experience simply what interests us, and any holistic or performative status within our experiences is a product of each respective interaction.[202] I cite the following statement by Milbank at length as a trinitarian explanation of this dynamic of knowledge as the shape of desire:

> The human mind does not "correspond" to reality, but arises within a process which gives rise to "effects of meaning." It is a particularly intense network of such effects. Our bodily energies and drives (for Augustine . . . which images the power of the divine Father) are made "present" and articulate (so alone constituted and sustained) through the happening of linguistic "meaning," which is also the event of a "truth" which cannot "correspond." For Augustine this second moment is the cultural training of the artist's ingenium; it is also that active memory by which we constantly learn through repeating our individual and collective biographies. Knowledge "surfaces" as the process of learning, which is true if divinely "illumined"—it is not a knowledge of an object outside that process (God being this process, in its infinite plenitude). . . . The mind is only illumined by the divine Logos, if also our "preceding" energies, and our "emergent" desires, correspond to the Father and the Spirit, respectively. We know what we want to know, and although all desiring is an "informed" desiring, desire shapes truth beyond

---

200. Milbank, "Postmodern," 235.
201. Milbank, "Postmodern," 234.
202. Cf. the Hegelian notion of praxis developed in Hodgson, *God in History*.

> the imminent implications of any logical order, so rendering the Christian logos a continuous product as well as a process of "art." Moreover, if all that "is" is good and true, then no positive reality can be false as a "mistake," or as "non-correspondence," but only false as deficient presence, embodying the short-fall of an inadequate desire. Now desire, not Greek "knowledge," mediates to us reality.... All desire is good so long as it is a restless desire (a more-desiring desire) which is moved by infinite lack, the pull of the "goal."[203]

In other words, the final universal criterion of "fruitfulness" between various research programs, theological or otherwise, will inevitably be, in the broad and natural sense, what is most desirable—that which, in the end, is most wholly and relationally satisfying. This does not dismiss reason but expresses what empowers it and upon which it floats. For Milbank, the correspondence of truth is never a re-presentation of reality (a strictly sociocultural training) but a dynamic primordial correlation that happens within the existential construction of meaning. A "novel fact" and a progressive program will inevitably be those expanding ideas, traditions, knowledge, insights, and "rationales" that are most relationally satisfying. This broad criterion of holistic satisfaction—*fullness of life*—does not negate but includes the qualities of coherence, synthesis, balance, reference, reason, and learned action. However, it is never something we impose upon relations but qualities that emerge again and again from within them. The very nature of what constitutes all relations—which is "always already" within the relationship—affects and reveals the relational adequacy (truth) even though it is socially constructed. Our failure to perceive and experience this fullness within our interactions is a matter of socialized and personalized structures of suppression. Milbank calls it a "deficient presence, embodying the shortfall of an inadequate desire." In this respect, desire is never wrong, merely inadequate, shortened, and therefore distorted. Moral turpitude is simply a question of suppressing presence within our interactions and thus suppressing transcendent desire.[204]

203. Milbank, "Postmodern," 234.

204. Because our shortened structures cannot define perfect relatedness (full "presence"), might efforts to break from and expand those structures toward greater fullness of life be considered sin? Does each "degree" of "transformation" into his likeness (2 Cor 3:18) entail an element of arbitrary action taking leave of existing socially approved structures? Within each relational context and stage of development, by virtue of *analogia spiritus*, we can perceive some degree of the extra beyond. If in ethical confidence (ignorance or innocence), we venture all, it is not sin. Herein lies sin: when we shorten our presence within the relationship by suppressing or denying any relevant aspect of reality and refuse to enter with complete openness into the third term

In the spirit of Kierkegaard, Marion argues that even our image and knowledge of "Gxd" always falls short becoming an idol short of its referent. Milbank similarly suggests that "knowledge," as the sole property of the subject, fails to be appropriate methodological currency. Instead, it is the extent to which one opens to the ground of desire, perichoretically and dynamically co-inherent within the immediate occurrence. It is a desire or longing that refuses to stop at the visible *eidolon* (*eido, video*), a dynamic that not only reflects the quality of the *analogia spiritus* but iconically (*eikon, eoika*) brings the participants and all relevant elements into perichoretic interaction.

Desire, therefore, not only opens but announces the ground of interaction. Only through selective inattention (conscious or subconscious, focal or embedded) do we suppress the immanent transcendent call to relationship where all knowledge constitutes existentially. Such relational dispositions and postures restrict entrance with Jacob into the fullness of *analogia spiritus*. Not only does the relationship itself provide the truth of knowledge—it is the truth. Always unique, it cannot be wrong, but it can be suppressed, shortened, or distorted.

For Heidegger, Dasein does not construct or develop the true, it uncovers it.[205] It is a gift of the relationship itself, not hiding to be uncovered but created amid two or more coming together. Because we constitute as spirit—a relationship unto ourselves—personal and cultural forms ("moods") of relating condition and often suppress the truth, diminishing the immanent transcendent (relational) ground within our knowledge and longings.

Therefore, within open relations, the most meaningful forms of life in a community, tradition, or culture, in contrast to others, have the greatest fullness of life. For example, in 1993, while attending the University of Riverside, I experienced many of the young Japanese students wanting to remain in the country after graduation. Upon returning it was difficult for them to re-assimilate fully back into traditional Japanese culture. This phenomenon alarmed the Japanese establishment, which instituted various measures to isolate their students from American culture and force re-culturalization (suppression). A reverse migration among Americans or Westerners to Japan at that time was virtually nonexistent. Similarly, American Christian Fundamentalism experiences the same phenomenon when

---

of the relationship. It is a refusal to become spirit, wherein the appropriate freedom and redemptive context will draw persons or traditions into each respective degree of transformation. The general understanding of sin, in this regard, must transform. It was inevitable that the old covenant biblical use of sin was to meet its revolutionary overthrow in the life of Christ and the later war cry to "Sin boldly" (Luther).

205. Heidegger, *Being and Time*, 261.

its youth attend secular universities. This in no way confirms the value of *every aspect* within each meaning-frame over that of another. Still, both incidences suggest the possibility that despite the contrasting complexity of developing values, one collectively provides greater fullness of life than the other. In the least, something within the attracting culture satisfies a desire that the original culture lacks. Ultimately, each will effectively transform the other to a greater or lesser degree accordingly. A research program that effectively institutes the *universalia* of the desire for authentic relationship (love) as a fundamental criterion supplementing the criteria of dialectics, begins to employ a positive heuristic and holistic criteria for progress. Such developing criteria help to explain various social migrations and provide trans-cultural criterion.

The integrity of our reasoning, beliefs, and knowledge is ultimately reducible to this one fundamental claim. The web of our knowledge and linguistic meaning does not ultimately correspond to anything other than the "'preceding' energies" and "'emergent' desires" which dialogically emanate from within the "multiplicity of transactions with one another," which, for Milbank, constitute in relation to the Trinity.

REFLECTIONS ON EPISTEMIC HUMILITY AND *ANALOGIA SPIRITUS*: GADAMER, ARISTOTLE, AND *PHRONESIS*

In *Truth and Method*, Hans-Georg Gadamer uses Aristotle to argue that the hermeneutical problem entails a unified process of understanding, interpretation, and application. If these aspects are ultimately inseparable in their emergence, and if *application* is uniquely contingent upon the specific context and relational occurrence, then all transactions "must be understood at every moment, in every particular situation, in a new and different way. Understanding here is always application[206] . . . [and] is, then, a particular case of the application of something universal to a particular situation."[207] Unlike the Aristotelian notion of *episteme* (theoretical knowledge), he introduces *phronesis* as an aspect of knowledge that "does not seek to establish what exists,"[208] but seeks to *relate responsibly* with that which is ever-changing. *Phronesis* is a moral knowledge that characterizes the appropriateness of

---

206. Gadamer, *Truth and Method*, 275.
207. Gadamer, *Truth and Method*, 278.
208. Gadamer, *Truth and Method*, 280.

attunement. It is a self-knowledge that must come from within "oneself."[209] Unlike *episteme* and *techne*, *phronesis* emerges and dies with each unique occurrence. "Aristotle says in general that *phronesis* is concerned with the means to an end (*ta pros to telos*) and not with the *telos* itself."[210] In this sense, Kierkegaard's notion of *inwardness* discussed earlier is consonant with Aristotle. By proffering the whole self through one's "inner infinity," the individual opens toward and considers *all* elements and contingencies relevant within the interaction. In seeking "the whole inwardness of his personality, his nature is purified and he himself brought into immediate relation to the external Power whose omnipresence interpenetrates the whole of existence."[211] Kierkegaard insists this "immediacy" is how "something universal" applies itself within "a particular situation."

Gadamer presents the hermeneutical task, even the "empirical" one, as much more multifaceted than Modernist presuppose. Even empirical knowledge is not outside the dynamic of *phronesis*. Gadamer argues that even Aristotle "does not regard a system of laws as true law, in an absolute sense, but considers the concept of equity as a necessary adjunct to law."[212] In this respect, all knowledge is personal and relational, therefore, ethically contingent upon the individual's openness to the Other—an ethical prerequisite for understanding and relationship.

Phronesis, according to Aristotle, is contingent upon, first, the notion of *sunesis*, which entails a "concern, not about myself, but about the other person,"[213] in other words, for *phronesis* to occur one must submit oneself to the *possibility* of revision in relation to the Other. Secondly, in a commitment to what is right, while acknowledging all relevant contingencies, one must seek to *unite* with the other in *mutual interest* in a special reciprocating bond of openness to think *together*. In this respect, Aristotle's notion of *phronesis* reflects specific dynamics of *perichoresis*. Aristotle's consideration of *phronesis* relaxes self-concern for concern about the other; however, within perichoretic relations the self-constitutes *not in total givenness to the other* but in total givenness to the emergent third term—the relationship itself. This creates the qualitative leap necessary for an active horizon of mutuality. Aristotle's "concern, not about oneself, but about the other person," is here adjusted into a *concern about the entire relationship, self and Other*.[214] It is

---

209. Gadamer, *Truth and Method*, 282.
210. Gadamer, *Truth and Method*, 525n225.
211. Kierkegaard, *EO2*, 141.
212. Gadamer, *Truth and Method*, 284.
213. Gadamer, *Truth and Method*, 288.
214. When Christ calls us to die to self, he is not calling us to resign ourselves

worth noting, again, that Aristotle did not have the conceptual luxury of the *relationship* as a created third term between participants. This relational contingency incorporates concern for others and the self *within* an immediate, transparent context of possibility and ethics (mediation of Christ and the Spirit). This better reflects Gadamer's concern for "*mutual* interest" and thinking through the issue together.[215]

To the extent we meet these relational conditions, *phronesis* becomes an active quality of our knowledge, maintaining an *open system* of active development and relations (*sunesis*, humility). Such a *disposition* (acknowledged dependence upon the Other, i.e., ongoing epistemological repentance) brings about the possibility of true empirical knowledge (continuity) together with the inherent forces active within the interaction that create the necessary ethical and teleological attunement for proper doxastic structuring. First, however, we must consider that these aspects of knowledge are inclusive in any notion of empirical knowledge and capable of social discernment, even in categories seemingly allusive as religious experience. Where some emphasize epistemological rationale and "empirical" behavior (*episteme* or *techne*) as criteria for authentic numinal experiences to guard against psychological "self-inducement," we must go further and emphasize the necessity of *phronesis*. Are there ways of exposing, for example, self-induced counterfeits and overdetermination within the process of *phronesis* by assessing the quality of the perichoretic dynamics within it? Most certainly.

Epistemic Humility: Non-inferentials in Relation Rather Than Reaction

Constant change characterizes the history of theological progress, cycling between stable periods of developing internal coherence and community consensus on the one hand. Then comes the disruptive mounting of

---

entirely to the will of or for the good of the Other. Such an act dehumanizes us, and our desires become an extension of the Other's desires, ultimately dissatisfying. Instead, Christ calls us to give ourselves and others up to him (Mark 10:29–30) in whom all things are "held-together" in love and righteousness (Col 1:17), by him who existentially creates and synchronizes all relations, i.e., by our engaging and honoring the sacredness amid the Relationship.

215. For example, though we live in evolving societies requiring seasons of developmental stability (stages), we should not, in principle, remain open to overdetermination or abuse by another; allowing such overdetermination reveals a closedness to the forces within the relationship revealing the true character of that behavior. Moreover, once known, allowing such behavior to continue unacknowledged is destructive to *all* within the relationship, holding all to a life less satisfying.

anomalies and the emergence of expanding paradigm shifts on the other (Kuhn). Evolution and redemption constantly mandate change. Historically, growth and transformation happen between generational cycles. One generation dies off as the next is freer to institute new changes. Because of modern communications and the mounting accumulation of knowledge, the velocity of change (social evolution) accelerates this process to within generations. Therefore, the methodological implementation of epistemic humility is becoming urgent in a pluralistic world. Theologically we need to learn to die more often; we need to venture into the uncharted territories of our relational dispositions and *how* we hold our beliefs, previously only mildly thought integral to theological discourse. Yes, there will always be those who are incapable of change or who refuse (Rom 14:14–23, and our earlier example of Lord Kelvin); nevertheless, we need to institute accountability mechanisms exposing reactive rather than relational discourse.

Various authoritative networks, conscious and unconscious, establish programs of knowledge and beliefs within each tradition. Many beliefs bear a non-inferential (transcendent) character within those convictions. Non-inferential forces and aspects within our convictions are numerous; (1) implicit actions and meaning that have yet to emerge within linguistic or conscious categories (e.g., "relationship" within ancient Greece and the dynamics of enmeshment within psychology that expand our understanding of love), (2) relational configurations holistically active within our praxis that are far too complex for cognitive or focal articulation, (3) aspects and dynamics so basic and primary they have become tacit within our thinking, (4) relational patterns of suppression that develop into subconscious styles of relating, and (5) numinal influences, to name a few.[216] All these "unseen" motivations create pockets of seemingly "non-inferential" aspects within our convictions. The *reactive* happens when some of these motivations unconsciously inhibit open and genuine interactions, imbuing theological assertions with clouded meanings and obstructive intransigence. It is naïve to think that suppressed anger, envy, or ambition does not negatively condition the doxastic meaning of theological assertions. "Unseen" living histories and "non-inferential" elements transform the simplest and clearest theological expressions, propositions, or narratives. None of us go untouched.

In this respect, rational dialectic *reaction* must shift into an inclusive response of *open relatedness*. With epistemic humility, we need to go beyond acknowledging difference and prize difference in the variety of

---

216. Many of these combine to create Paul's "authorities and powers" that mediate cultural, social, and personal relations (1 Cor 15:24).

contextualizations. The notion of *perichoresis* is again preeminent in which we allow the *fullness* of each individual, program, or concept to freely enter the forming mutuality of the relationship. None of this is possible without the willingness to be transformed within genuine relations while at the same time standing for what we believe, especially resisting intransigence and closure in the other (reactivity). The alternating dialogical cycles (modalities) within perichoretic relations here become essential. These require complete openness to the Other and alternatively decisive closure within our dialogical cycling. We must distinguish epistemic humility from the open tolerance or mandated relativism of various Poststructural perspectives. Maintaining and holding certain core beliefs may be necessary against competing programs and elements that bear lesser fullness of life. At the same time, some may need to maintain existing beliefs due to certain developmental (in)capacities and contextual contingencies against programs with greater fullness of life (Rom 14:14). Nevertheless, social evolution and the process of redemption are not entirely dissimilar. John M. Templeton suggests

> Religion will grow not in union but through freedom and competition. Originality and discovery derive from variety, not uniformity.... If our concepts are divine truths, then they will not suffer in competition with other concepts.... By spirited and loving competition, the truth will be purified and strengthened. Progress comes from competition and this is what churches need most.... The true religions should welcome competition because then they are put to the test, and if they are true, they will survive. Only an inferior religion needs to prevent competition, lest its inferiority should be exposed. Tolerance is a divine virtue but can become a vehicle for apathy. Millions of people are thoroughly tolerant toward diverse religions; but rarely do such people go down in history as creators or benefactors or leaders of any religion. The use of tolerance is mainly to keep us humble so that we may listen with an open heart and an inquiring mind.... More than tolerance, we need competition.[217]

The emerging mutuality of the positive third term—the relationship—does not obliterate but intensifies the fullness of each participant. This give-and-take choreography within the dance necessitates both epistemic humility and decisiveness on the part of all.

This presents two methodological considerations. First, all knowledge must remain open to revision (growth) and potential transformation in a

217. Templeton, *Humble Approach*, 85–86.

posture of *epistemic humility* (Rom 14:14—15:6).[218] There must be an ongoing resolve to develop method and criteria that disclose as much as possible the conscious and subconscious forces active within theological research, most notably religious experience. Finally, Zagzebski argues that we cannot separate theology and theologians as people. Therefore, theology must integrate the corroborative findings in the human sciences (e.g., psychology, sociology, and political action) that produce better theologians (persons) exposing hidden "non-theological" affections and motives within theology.

Theology necessitates some degree of experiencing grace and the numinal factor of God's influences within our interactions. To maintain such influences, Jean-Luc Marion suggests three things: suffering, willingness to transcend the restfulness of epistemic certainty, and living within a theological place always beyond our immediate grasp.

> As the teacher becomes a theologian by aiming in the text at the referent, he must have an anticipated understanding of the referent, for lack of which he will not be able to spot its effects of meaning in the text. There are many exegetes or theologians who commit massive misinterpretations of texts, . . . not for want of knowledge, but out of ignorance of what is in question, of the thing itself. . . . He who claims to go beyond the text as far as the Word must therefore know whereof he speaks: to know, by experience, charity, in short, "to have learned from what he suffered" (Heb. 5:8) like Christ . . . here is the qualification, extrascientific but essential, that makes the theologian: the referent is not taught, since it is encountered by mystical union.[219]

The distinction is doing theo*logy* as a closed system or *theo*logy as an open system (program). The latter provides the genuine transactions necessary to dimensionalize and maintain (iconically illuminate) our theological knowledge, *while* maintaining full conviction in one's beliefs (all things considered in each moment), which continuously expand and transform throughout history (Bonhoeffer). Therefore, true (doxastic) theological progress comes only to the extent that theologians fully *understand* (*sunesis*) and *experience*

---

218. In other words, Christians, for example, are not entirely and genuinely engaging the Hindu unless they are, in principle, *willing* to have their current narrative and epistemic structuring transformed or even somehow subsumed into the Hindu paradigm within authentic interaction. Even though one may currently hold their existing beliefs with an infinity of passion, hypothetically, no one can completely anticipate the future and know all things. We come to genuine faith in God, the pinnacle and height of all knowledge (and as we should know all things), with a child's confidence.

219. Marion, *God without Being*, 155.

(*phronesis*) all relevant aspects necessary within their discipline according to the relational logic of *perichoresis*. Marion thinks:

> Theological thought undoubtedly never experienced in such an imperative way the duty of formulating its own radically theological logic (which especially does not mean "dialectical theology," etc.); undoubtedly its responsibility never appeared as great with respect to all thought in expectation of a "new beginning"; but theological thought undoubtedly never stole away with so much fear from its theological task.[220]

Our *theo*logic, when clearly perceived, speaks for itself. As long as there is need within our crippled attempts to differentiate between *theo*logy and theo*logy*, there is value in falsifying as much theo*logy* as possible through its own internal incoherence and lack of fullness of life while appropriately engaging interdisciplinary conditioning. There will be no attempt to supply such methodological specifics with this limited overview, but methodological issues of this nature must further develop.[221]

The Prereflexive Between—*analogia spiritus*

Within all relationships (social or personal reflection) emerge new worlds between. Each new interaction creates a dynamic differentiated unity. Intensions attune within the dynamic forming matrix, and with initial communications, a spirit of mutual intention emerges, a "mood" (Heidegger), as relational dispositions uniquely shape the form and integrity of the transaction. It immediately affects the organizing process, the identity of the participants, and the character of immanent transcendence within the relationship. These holistic communiqués immediately interpenetrate and subsume into the creating flux of the relationship, which optimally reflects the shape of that Power that creates it. Only upon this creative ground that lies beyond us, between us, yet paradoxically within us, do words become meaningful.

---

220. Marion, *God without Being*, 182.

221. The accumulating insights of psychology continue to expose the various mechanisms and motivations that vitiate our relations. As this information grows and becomes part of theological discourse, I suspect theological discourse can only benefit. Nevertheless, our implementation must be appropriate and critical. As a colleague suggests, "clinical psychology, because of the great stature it enjoys in society, and because of the power it wields over the (mental) health of bodies, will always write from a privileged vantage point that at the very least operates subconsciously to project an agenda of power and dominance (the 'Kevorkian' effect)" (Personal conversation with Rick Berchiolli).

This prereflexive dialogical dynamic presents much more than just a deepening relation of two associating worlds through natural codes, symbols, concepts, and behaviors that referentially de-code and interpret within each participant's mind. This reflects only the tip of the iceberg of what transpires within interpretive dynamics. Our dialogical cycling is much more complex, always initiating with the prereflexive entrance of two or more in composite response awareness. Only upon this initiating ontological foundation of relation do symbols re-assume their social meaning unique for that moment. This grows into intensely complex acts of communication, constantly communicating more than the focal intentions. This dynamic forming matrix of the third term perichoretically (holistically) informs the semiotic configurations emerging from it respectively into each participant.

The event of Pentecost exposes this special dynamic within the communicative act revealing its holistic and mediational nature. Words were spoken and understood through a medium and dynamic of holistic analogical communication. During Pentecost, the Spirit and Christ did not implant the words and meaning of the speaker into the listener. Instead, in a proleptic portending of fully evolved (redeemed) humanity, each open listener was momentarily gifted with the full capacity of the mediating dynamics active within perichoretic relations. Within the prereflexive moments of their listening, they enter the emergent world of the mediating relationship in which the speaker's meaning co-conditionally creates meaning respectively within each person's unique meaning-frame and communicative capacity. How many times while lecturing in class does a particular student walk in late, and we immediately sense a change in how we shape and deliver our thoughts. In this transformative dynamic, the Spirit alone is not transferring or translating information, rather, spirits are active in a much more complex and wonderful way. As the Apostle's intention and thoughts begin to take shape, his thoughts configuratively begin to take shape from within the forming matrix of the unique event-occurrence while being co-conditioned by all those present. Within the third term of the relationship through *analogia spiritus*, the Spirit of God and the spirit of each person (disposed toward open and authentic relations) proleptically experience a fullness of perichoretic communications. Fully participating in the creational life of the Trinity, each participant receives the speaker's meaning in their own (the listener's) mother tongue and meaning-frame. This corresponds to the differentiated unity unique to *perichoresis*, in which all participants share the same meaning relative to each one's unique meaning-frame *while* maintaining their identity and intensifying personhood.

However, the special event of Pentecost remains just that, a proleptic phenomenon of guidance—a portending heuristic image of *analogia spiritus*. This announcement of the Spirit's "It is finished" and special "imputation" of fully redeemed communion circumvents, for that moment, the personal and social redemptive process through which humanity progressively develops complete trust in God's faithfulness. It also defines the role of the Spirit in human interaction, a contingency into which humanity, dare I say, must evolve (a process of redemption). It is a process and contingency in which humans must be radically free to choose, or should I say, be so disposed.[222] Such a disposition in *our* unveiling our shame is necessary for the Spirit to affect its continual transformational process within us. We must remember that some heard and understood the Apostles, and others, hearing nonsense, thought them intoxicated. As we will consider in our forthcoming chapter on human development, transformational interaction necessitates our willingness to enter what Loder calls the "void" (Isaac's infinite resignation). The arduous and lengthy process of social evolution/redemption through ongoing interaction in utter freedom is necessary for humanity to reflect *perichoresis* inevitably and completely within themselves, "sharers [κοίνωνοί] of the divine nature" (2 Pet 1:4).

This is the logic of spirit (analogical holism) through which symbol, word, or story are necessary for communication and yet impotent without the asymmetrical priority of the prereflexive dynamic of *analogia spiritus* creating and mediating whole ideas analogically between persons—the coming, together, simultaneously.[223] Meaning creates according to the existing socialization capacities or that which is creatable (transformable, developable) within each person. Though the Other conditions the openness of person, symbol, or speech, each transform (understand, mean) within their personal or socialized capacities. Upon this eucharistic dynamic of *analogia spiritus*, all semiotic openness existentially attunes from within the dynamic mediating matrix of the third term and yet relatively (perichoretically) within each participant. The degree of communicational integrity each person experiences will correspond to the degree of epistemic humility and semiotic openness for structural conditioning by the Other within each participant—a relational disposition. When Christ tells the "many"

---

222. This exposes our current syntactical limitations resulting from antiquated ontological development and, therefore, its current difficulty in communicating relational dynamics like *holistic co-conditioning* and transtemporal causation. Disposition is a chosen state within human beings, or is it? I can choose to act, but can "I" dispose myself? Yes and no. It leaves me in the struggle of Rom 5–7; nevertheless, our current linguistic development leaves me (us) handicapped.

223. Again, this reflects what agnostic communication theorists and non-Christian developmentalist like Shotter and Gergen are discovering—a dynamic within human communications that mediates meaning and in development transformational stage transitions.

who lived their life in his name, "I never knew you," we have to consider that their relational disposition throughout their religious and socialized lives were locked in closure and rigid protectionism (Matt 5:23; 25:45). Any effective criteria for the assessment of relational integrity begins with holistic experiencing of relational satisfaction or "sublime." From this marker, all knowable equations of relational legitimacy or illegitimacy emerge.

Perichoretically meaning emerges in "dynamic mutual reciprocity, interpenetration and interanimation" with the Other.[224] Something new emerges in each interaction and person that was not previously in either. In this way, says Milbank, the

> existing harmonies, existing "extensions" of time and space, constantly give rise to new "intentions," to movements of the Spirit to further creative expression, new temporal unraveling of creation *ex nihilo*, in which human beings most consciously participate.[225]

The emergence of new properties is evident in the human imagination, an example of perichoretic participation in reflection.[226] The self constitutes as a relationship unto itself (by virtue of the Trinity's relationship to humanity, the "Christ in us") while simultaneously in relation to the world.

Humility as Complete Entrance into Relational Mediation

Relational openness and the iconic gaze ensure the integrity of knowledge. Closedness compromises all knowledge, not to be confused with closure or making a stand.[227] Many developmental and social theorists today continue to work with relational paradigms that struggle to balance the relational aperture between individuals in a pluralistic world. Within the subject-object or I-thou paradigm, a person can never open entirely to the other without endangering self to the freedom of the other. Yet, how can we even consider genuine connection and relationality without acknowledging, in some way,

---

224. Gunton, *One, Three, Many*, 163. Again, this thesis restitutes the dynamics of "interpenetration and interanimation" within the third term of the relationship. Persons do not interpenetrate each other. This distinction is vitally important, and its necessity will become clearer as the thesis develops.

225. Milbank, "Postmodern," 236.

226. This dynamic becomes noticeable, for example, when listening to a piece of music while viewing a picture, film, or picturesque view out our window. To the degree we release ourselves toward the fullness of their unique one-time event-occurrence, each will begin to draw properties out of the other that would not have been otherwise.

227. Cf. Zagzebski, "*Phronesis*," 209.

its necessity? The Poststructuralist's critique exposes the hopelessness of Greek dialectics in this regard. Nevertheless, the apparent semiotic relativism of Poststructuralism ultimately creates suspicion, and with suspicion, inevitably fear then violence.[228]

Addressing this issue, Kierkegaard's relational structuring points to a perichoretic relational dynamic that provides the freedom to offer the whole self into the relationship and, thereby, authenticity (self/spirit). So it seems, he requires it. We cannot presume or determine the authenticity of the interaction from outside each unique relational occurrence. In this regard, the character and nature of that Power are of critical importance. Such a presence, influence, and dynamic within transactions universally provide the ethical character and influencing structure for each relative interaction.[229] This does not cast developed knowledge, social codes, and established judgments to the wind of nihilistic relativism but necessitates that participants open themselves and their semiotic structuring to the appropriate transformative forces mediating such interactions. Transformation announces itself and transpires only when compelling factors reveal themselves within the relationship. Without openness, one never perceives such announcements. And only to the extent we venture ourselves, can we stand in authority.

This "call" from within the relations, says Heidegger, "comes from me and yet from beyond me and over me."[230] An ontology of *perichoresis* means that the mediational source universally active within all interactions is also independently reflective within ourselves to the degree of vulnerability we enter the relationship. From the Christian point of view, it is our experience and conviction of God's love in Christ that provides the context and freedom to venture all. Such an ontology asymmetrically prioritizes the personal transformational dynamic over the stages of individual or cultural growth within the complementarity of transition-stage development (further established in our next chapter).

Because we always communicate more than we focally intend, which include the unique distortions, shortened desires, and closures that condition the "literal" meaning and the doxastic structure of our knowledge and communication, epistemic humility is a necessity. Such unseen actors within our expressions potentially contain diverse meanings in which seemingly

---

228. Cf. Thiselton, *Interpreting*, 135.

229. To the extent the self fully consolidates in singleness of mind and its "inner infinity," which always includes the person's full social and cosmic contingencies, the self will constitute appropriately in "immediate relation to the external Power whose omnipresence interpenetrates the whole of existence" and "posits self." Kierkegaard, *EO2*, 141; *SUD*, 146–47. Cf. Matt 18:16, 20; Luke 12:11–12.

230. Heidegger, *Being and Time*, 320.

equivalent religious and theological expressions eventually reveal themselves to be quite different (e.g., Barth in contrast to his theological mentors before WWI, and Bonhoeffer in contrast to the German Lutheran church before WWII). Every relevant aspect in our personal meaning-frame perichoretically conditions all our knowledge and beliefs.

Theological method, therefore, must eventually implement a broader (more complex) concept of falsification and holistic forms of awareness (emotional and numinal inclusive). In their terms "performance" and "progress," Lindbeck and Lakatos implicitly suggest that a tradition's development is a complex set of factors that we can only assess over time. If we can isolate what inhibits human transformation and identify and expose unwillingness to enter open theological interactions, e.g., epistemic pride or ideological intransigence, it could only benefit our theological programs.

CONCLUSION

The primary purpose of this chapter was not so much to consider current trends in theological method or hermeneutics but to use them to investigate the primordial structure of meaning itself. The positive insights of two divergent research programs were compared to perichoretic dynamics that associate with Kierkegaard's understanding of relational dynamics. The dynamics of *perichoresis* will become clearer as the thesis progresses and we note their emergence within other disciplines. The goal is that each new insight will condition and expand the theological concept of *perichoresis* and *analogia spiritus*, bringing more coherence and meaning to themselves and the Scriptures.

The most acknowledged characteristic of *perichoresis* is never more apparent than in the emergence of meaning and its multi-dimensional and constituting nature. One of the most famous alleged quotes of Albert Einstein was that "The most incomprehensible thing about the world is that it is comprehensible. . . . [T]he fact that it is comprehensible is a miracle." Meaning defies reduction into any distinct loci and constitutes within a relational dynamic through which seemingly infinite fields prereflexively interpenetrate and reveal themselves intelligently within human consciousness. There is never meaning in the text, nor in the reader or in culture, but only within the immediate integrating fields of relations where two or more come together. In each relational occurrence, something emerges—a creation that has never been before. We now know scientifically, for example, that time is a sociological construct and reality is far more complex and dimensional than we generally imagine. Likewise, meaning does not exist

MEANING AS PERICHORESIS

out there in the world or on the shelf. Meaning incarnates itself anew *within the world of each transaction*.

Continuity becomes the product of linguistic and cultural training in which our past, present, and future (imagined) understanding dynamically interanimate through our analogical relationship to that mediating Power. Einstein also purportedly said, "Human beings, vegetables, or cosmic dust, we all dance to a mysterious tune intoned in the distance by an invisible player." Such an "invisible player" and Power sustains human beings as a differentiated unity. All rationality occurs within evolving, floating paradigms, meaningful only within its paradigm of birth. And yet, even our paradigms eventually submit to the confluencing dance of commensurability between themselves. The numerator of continuity (reason) forever rides upon the tacit denominator of a whole to a song that creates the dance (analogy) of wholes, where meaning resurrects, incarnating again and again after every crucifixion.

The world is becoming increasingly comprehensible because Jesus requested that we might relate, as the Father relates to him, so that we also might relate with them. Here, humanity and reason dynamically move within its well-suited dialogical home.[231] We are creatures and can never move within an Eternal frame of reference. We must be satisfied to live provisionally but boldly within each moment (picking the apple but never ingesting it to be our own). The gift of every new gestalt alone (manna) nourishes and sustains our life together in the *moment*. The apple is much more juicy and tempting, but as Kierkegaard advises, there is indeed objective and Eternal truth, but humanity constitutes in time, so (like manna) we must relinquish the power of our perceived continuity and reason found in each relational occurrence to reconstitute in each new light of day.[232] Christ knew, allowing Jacob to drag him (the truth) from the night into the light of a new day, would have destroyed both truth and Jacob.

From within the stirring waters of awareness, our concerns and response take shape in the form of word, action, and belief, which when respoken, create new worlds, worlds unknown before the speaking. With sublimity, they fall into a world with a new unspeakableness as both speaker and listener learn from the speaking. As Marion so vividly recounts:

> Thus speaking our words, the Word re-doubles his incarnation, or rather accomplishes it absolutely, since language constitutes us more carnally than our flesh. Such an incarnation in our

---

231. How rationality grounds itself within our social development; cf. McFadyen, *CP*.
232. Matt 10:38–39; Mark 10:29–30.

words can be undertaken only by the Word, who comes to us before our words.[233]

We enter all relations through some degree of *analogia spiritus*, a holistic interaction through which Christ and the Spirit mediate our de-liberation of social and collective intent. Therein, our words fill with new meaning, for he came to make all things new, each existential *moment*. Our sacrifice into the relationship does not obliterate the self but intensifies it by meaningfully incarnating us eucharistically with Christ into the world.

The continuity, certainty, and timelessness of the text is mediated, yet co-conditioned. The perichoretic cycling of incarnation, crucifixion, and resurrection, eternally inform its expanding history as each unique and developing reader co-conditions its always new and active meaningfulness. Nevertheless, the text in itself remains meaningless, dust upon the shelf, echoing Kierkegaard's insistence that a human being outside active relationship "is not yet a self."[234] For all the socialized order, coherence, and acceptability in the life of the dispassionate psychologist in the novel *Equus*, he eventually concedes to his depraved client: "That boy has known a passion more ferocious than I have felt in any second of my life. . . . [H]e stands in the dark for an hour, sucking the sweat off his God's hairy cheek! . . . [I]n the morning, I put away my books on the cultural shelf."[235] What do we do with such infinite desire from which true knowing takes shape? What establishes its truth anew, each moment?

---

233. Marion, *God without Being*, 141.
234. Kierkegaard, *TC*, 146.
235. Shaffer, *Equus*, 82–83.

3

Human Spirit

Life is measured by the number of things you are alive to.

MALTBIE B. BABCOCK

INTRODUCTION

James Loder understands the Holy Spirit as the third person of the Trinity who proceeds from the Father and the Son—the Spirit "is the relationship between them."[1] Furthermore,

> for human nature, to partake in this Spirit is to participate in the inner life of God. Thus, statements of dialectical unity (e.g. one person, two natures; three persons, one essence; *creatio ex nihilo* of the natural order as simultaneously contingent and independent; human nature as both dead yet alive; God fully present yet coming; human relationships as mutual creation of each other in mutual coinherence) only genuinely illuminate creation, human existence, and the Divine nature if they are

---

1. Loder and Neidhardt, *KM*, 21. For Loder, the relational understanding of the constituting dynamic of the Trinity owes much to the *De Trinitate* of Augustine (354–430). However, Athanasius, Epiphanius, and the Cappadocian fathers, notably Gregory of Nazianzus, present a clearer picture of the relational dynamic inherent within the Trinity.

understood from within the inner life of God; that is, by God's Spirit according to God's self-knowledge.[2]

This does not, for Loder, transgress Augustine's prohibition of the *vestigium trinitatis*, although it is consonant with Alasdair Heron's call to revision the Holy Spirit as relational,[3] and Thomas Torrance's prohibition of reducing the Holy Spirit to ecclesiology or mere socialization of collective human spirit.[4]

This section investigates the possibility of human existence participating in the inner life of the Trinity and where and how this might happen in human experience. If a God, who constitutes Eternally, mutually relates to humanity in spacetime, we might suspect, as Gunton suggests, that human spirit is dynamically analogical to God's own relational dynamics and, therefore, perichoretic in nature. This section will investigate the perichoretic dynamic of human spirit: First, human emotions as self in relationship to itself; second, Alastair McFadyen's Christian theory of person constituting in dialogical relation with others; and third, developmentalist James Loder's use of Jean Piaget and Kierkegaard arguing that human beings are created in the dynamic process and image of *perichoresis*. These investigations will provide an understanding of human experience that analogically associate with the internal activity of the Trinity.

IMPORTANCE OF HUMAN AWARENESS AS THE FUNCTION OF HUMAN SPIRIT

Awareness and cognitive response represent two complementary modes within dialogical action. Awareness is the state of openness intending the Other, which is prereflexive, therefore, partly preconscious. This is the anthropological site where the Eternal activity of the Trinity interacts with persons during this *process* of human awareness (the Kierkegaardian *moment* transitioning a person from awareness to cognitive gestalt). Functionally, this makes possible Philip Hefner's hypothesis that humans are God's co-creators, nature's self-consciousness, and conceptualizers of the ultimate.[5] Human beings constitute (Col 1:17, con-sist, are put together) as persons-in-relation. In this respect, we might think of the *Spiritus Creator* as the active presence of God in Kierkegaard's Religiousness A, immanent encounter, in contrast the Holy Spirit in Religiousness B, personal,

---

2. Loder and Neidhardt, *KM*, 21.
3. Heron, *Holy Spirit*.
4. Torrance, *Reconstruction*, 229–39; Torrance, *Trinitarian Faith*.
5. Hefner, *Human Factor*.

transcendent encounter.[6] The relationship of *Spiritus Creator* to the human spirit (the whole of a person) begins as an active potential—awakening the developmental process that enables the increasing creaturely structuralizing and openness to the world. *Spiritus Creator*, in co-conditioning relation with all open systems, creates ever-widening choreographies of increasing diverse particularization and reciprocatively more integrated and expanding interrelations, which ecologically creates greater fullness of life and meaning within the world. For example, to the degree we open to the Other (love) intensifies, not diminishes, our sense of personhood and individuality. The degree and depth of our perichoretic interrelatedness establishes the degree to which understanding becomes its *own*, diminishing what persons or relationships experience tacitly and unconsciously hide, suppress, triangulate, thus making the relationship more cognitively meaningful.[7] This happens to the degree our structures emerge from a response awareness that faces the entirety of truth and possibility within the interaction—as human spirit; the cyclical process repeating encounters of otherliness, the void, and subsequent transformations expand our personal meaning-frame.[8]

From out of *this process of awareness*, we constitute self-in-relation. This is an essential point in understanding *perichoresis* within human relations. Only to the degree we experience *analogia spiritus* within this *moment* that then flashes into cognitive response are we drawn into relation with God's Spirit (the Eternal) and constitute in co-conditioning gestalt or word with Christ (in truth). The passion within Jacob signals his entrance, the divinely celebrated entrance, into a state of perichoretic analogical

---

6. This refers to the upcoming discussion on the Spirit, where Moltmann suggests that an emphasis upon the Spirit of God as solely the agent of redemption fails to acknowledge the Spirit's activity as the "divine energy of life, which according to the Old Testament ideas interpenetrates all the living" (Moltmann, *SL*, 8). The activity of the Spirit is actively "connected . . . with the body and nature," as well as with "God, faith, the Christian life, the church and prayer." "If we talk in Hebrew about Yahweh's *ruach*, we are saying; God is . . . a force in body and soul, humanity and nature, . . . *ruach* was also the breath of life and the power to live enjoyed by human beings and animals (Eccl 12:7). . . . The *ruach* . . . keeps all things in being and in life. . . . Ps 104:29-30: "When thou takest away their *ruach* they die. When thou sendest forth thy *ruach* they are created; and thou renewest the face of the ground" (*SL*, 40–42).

7. See Matt 25:14–30, the parable of the talents.

8. A three-year-old girl screams in terror whenever a train "violently" speeds past the seaside campground. This continues despite the incessant reassurances of her panicking parents—"it's okay, it won't hurt you." However, only when the parents cease "comforting" the child, allowing the child to suffer the dread alone twice, does the knowledge that "it's truly okay" become her *own*. The triangulation of safety through "the parents" ends in the perichoretic emergence of personal knowledge and adjusted structuring within the child herself.

co-conditioning with an Eternal God. In the following subchapters we will examine *perichoresis* as reflected in human relations in three ways. The first are the emotions and the brain's bicameral hemispheric phenomenon as *perichoresis in* human beings. In the second we will consider the social theory of Alastair McFadyen and *perichoresis between* human beings. Then we will explore the notion of *perichoresis as* human being in the work of James Loder and Søren Kierkegaard.

3A

Perichoresis in Persons
Human Emotions and Bicameral Synthesis

> The spirit of a man is the lamp of the Lord, Searching all the inner depths of his heart.
>
> Prov 20:27

EMOTIONS AS SPIRIT IN PERSONS

If there is agreement upon anything within the contemporary discussion on human emotions, it is that they are complex, and there is no shortage of competing theories to explain them. However, there is agreement that emotions themselves are *dynamic, unified* complexities. *What* emotions contain is of interest to this study, but more so *that* emotions are constitutive and *how*. This chapter will parallel the similarities between human emotions and dynamics within *perichoresis*. After emotions, we will cover paralleling dynamics within the bicameral brain in which emotions play a significant role and point to associating perichoretic dynamics. If the association is suitable, it might help us understand the dynamic of *perichoresis* more fully and present human dynamics that might be instrumental in our communication with and perception of the divine.

The significant quality of emotions is their incredible ability to relationally *collate* a complexity of relational factors and contingencies in an instant of time and conversely, *sustain* certain relational factors across time.

The amalgamation of these various contingencies into a meaningful and appropriate single unified emotive response happens prereflexively (subconsciously), in other words, without cognitive or linear processing within a sequential causal network. For example, if A happens, then response [B-C-D] E. [B, C, D] = subconscious contingencies; E = conscious response. If the response creates fear, the elimination of C may relieve the fear within the response. As emotive response, this reveals the human spirit's instantaneous process and ability to organize and unify self within relationship. In this respect, Ronald De Sousa argues that emotions are inherently rational, even though they may often seem irrational due to the unconscious nature of elements producing that emotion. These dynamics are well-known to any successful therapist.

Alternatively, the emotive activity in human spirit is active at the birth of new meaning. These are situations in which we encounter an unknown that does not immediately integrate into our immediate meaning-frame and history. The excess stimulus defies relational equilibrium while remaining only holistically meaningful through minimal subconscious conditioning. In this case, the emergent emotive function of human spirit always begins with some level of wonder, dread, suppression, denial, etc. These are secondary emotive responses of which the person is not always conscious or focally aware but subconsciously play a substantial but tacit role in meaning-making.

There are many current theories of emotions, but as such, specific theories bear little weight in this study. Though differing theories and paradigms of emotions champion various attributes, most of them agree upon the primary attributes of interest to this study. The earliest understanding of emotions came in response to the primary, more visible emotions (e.g., fear and anger) but is currently evolving into a broader and more circumspect understanding. The antiquated understanding gives way to the belief that emotional states are *always* present and interrelate with every other aspect of human life. Within a motivational/perceptual theory of emotions, Robert Leeper tells us,

> emotions are . . . not just rare events, of intense sorts, as the traditional ideas about emotions portray them as being, but as more or less perpetually active motives and do most of their work at moderate or weak intensities. . . . At such lower levels, emotions do most of their work without the individual's having any notable thought of being motivated, because the emotional

processes tend to be experienced as objectified or projected as perceptions of the situation.[1]

Emotional states are ever present within all human relations and inseparable from and integrally connect to every element of human functioning. Reason, knowledge (epistemology), and morality are but a few functions in which emotions play an essential role.

We should not confuse feelings with emotions; feelings are never abstract; you never feel fear when you are not afraid. Ray Anderson tells us, "Feelings are an essential and accurate expression of self, . . . feelings *are* the self."[2] Emotions, on the other hand, are not always felt.[3] They can be suppressed, such as fear masquerading as tension during a job interview or belief intransigence resulting from the possibility of a lifetime of scholarly work being supplanted. Following are some essential attributes of emotions that interest this study.

1. Emotions are "sometimes *subceived* and sometimes wholly beneath consciousness."[4] Nevertheless, these emotions directly affect the individual's holistic experience.

2. Some emotions reflect typical *physiological responses*, which we may or may not directly feel.[5] However, emotions principally "differ from feelings, sensations, or physiological responses in that they are dispositional rather than episodic."[6] The positivist understanding of emotions is no longer tenable as sole disruptions of rational judgments, conscious thoughts, and observations.

However, the physiological does play an enormous role in emotions and may very well be crucial to their development. Stephan Strasser argues that all knowing and recognition are not a result of the mind (Descartes) but, as Merleau-Ponty has pointed out, of the body-ego (a mind-body). For example, before the subject-object tension takes shape in human development (e.g., in the neonate), a "feeling subject, feels himself by the fact that he feels his *fellow-subject*."[7] This happens through various sensations and tactile stimulation, at which point there is no other fellow-object, only

1. Leeper, "Motivational," 152.
2. Anderson, *Self Care*, 64.
3. Roberts, "What an Emotion Is," 189.
4. Roberts, "What an Emotion Is," 183, emphasis added.
5. See Alston, "Emotive Meaning," 481; Roberts, "What an Emotion Is," 183; Lyons, *Emotion*.
6. Jaggar, "Love and Knowledge," 149, see 146–53.
7. Strasser, "Feeling," 300, emphasis added.

himself—umwelt (surrounding world), which only later develops into a *we*, later yet into an I. The neonate's earliest awareness develops as a "nonobjectifying mode of awareness."[8] From this point on and throughout the development of awareness, Strasser argues all awareness begins with "what was at first *one*—feeling one's own state and feeling the other—[and only then] separates out." The "objectifying and reflecting mode of awareness . . . is but an 'upper layer.' Our original feeling and emotional mode of awareness is indeed hidden by it, but it remains there."[9] Antonio Damasio adds,

> At each moment the state of self is constructed, from the ground up. It is an evanescent reference state, so continuously and consistently *re*constructed that the owner never knows it is being *re*made. . . . But our self, or better even, our metaself, only "learns" about that "now" an instant later. . . . The present is never here. We are hopelessly late for consciousness.[10]

Because of our functional roots in infant body-ego development, human existence is "not at first perceived, thought or sought after; it is primarily lived, through feeling." It is this enigmatic unitive mind-body dynamic that creates and sustains the synthesis of experience and concept, bringing the process of awareness into the constitution of self, which so characterizes and enables the emotive response of human beings.

3. Usually, an emotion is contingent upon the individual *believing* some state of affairs,[11] or it may correspond to a judgment.[12] In this regard, the emotional faculty acts as the instantaneous mechanism collating everything of relevance into a holistic response. In this manner, emotions comprise all relevant conscious knowns and subconscious affecting "unknowns" wrapped up into one holistic response.

4. Similarly, emotions are generally *motivational*; they contain, says Robert C. Roberts, concerned reactions or dispositions to "propositional objects in the sense that what the emotion is about, of, for, at, or to can in principle be specified propositionally."[13]

---

8. Strasser, "Feeling," 305.
9. Strasser, "Feeling," 306.
10. Damasio, *Descartes' Error*, 240.
11. See Roberts, "What an Emotion Is," 183; Alston, "Emotive Meaning," 485.
12. Roberts, "What an Emotion Is," 195.
13. Roberts, "What an Emotion Is," 183; cf. Leeper, "Motivational," 152–55.

5. Similarly, Alston refers to emotions as "*perceptual* evaluation[s] of something."[14] Furthermore, Roberts argues that emotions are "serious concern-based *construals*."[15] Employing the word construals, he rightly acknowledges the personal factor of *theory-laden perception* while assuming that emotions *construct* meaning.

6. Roberts notes, "emotions are not, except incidentally, directly reflexive, whereas feelings of construed condition are always so."[16] Because emotions are construals and holistic dispositions contingent upon existing relational factors (some being subconscious or linguistically vague, as in dread or wonder), they are *prereflexive* motivations and constructions that flow into reflexive responses. In contrast, feelings are immediate reflexive states of sensation, just as *episteme* reflects a "coherent" and socially embedded linguistic structure (both are reflexive). We can better understand emotions as "living" bridges between human awareness (openness) and human reflexion (closure).

7. Emotions share corresponding formal properties and similar "logics" with *desire*. Jenefer Robertson suggests that the cognitive elements in emotions are not dispassionate judgments; they are "a construal or way of thinking *A* as *P*," and a way which is "governed (caused) . . . and also 'colored' by our desires."[17] She concludes that

> although an occurrent emotional state cannot be *defined* as a conception of something determined by desires, a particular occurrent emotional state may be identical with the occurrence of nothing but a thought, provided it has the right historical links with the agent's desires.[18]

In other words, though an emotion may not be the direct result of a desire, the corresponding thought behind the emotion initially develops in relation to a desire. In this respect, all emotions are the result of desires.

Furthermore, in pointing to the wide range of phenomena that characterize contemporary understandings of emotions (from "knee-jerk" responses to highly socialized aesthetic and relational responses), Alison Jaggar views "so-called instinctive, nonintentional feelings as the biological

---

14. Alston, "Emotive Meaning," 481, emphasis added; cf. Leeper, "Motivational," 156; Jaggar, "Love and Knowledge," 154.
15. Roberts, "What an Emotion Is," 184, emphasis added.
16. Roberts, "What an Emotion Is," 190.
17. Robertson, "Emotion," 736.
18. Robertson, "Emotion," 731.

raw material from which full-fledged human emotions develop."[19] Here, we consider the foundation of all emotions to be a socially and genetically structured complexity of basic desires and values, or as this thesis maintains, prereflexively originating from the most basic of desires, *perichoresis*. All desire initially emerges in perichoretic relation to the Other (whether in the presence or thought of the Other—the world, persons, or God), and emotions provide the value structure to our world.[20]

8. Most importantly, there is an overwhelming consensus that emotions are "typically experienced as *unified states of mind*, rather than as sets of components (for example, a belief + a desire + a physiological perturbation + some behavior)."[21] Again, we are back to this concept of something (the emotion) emerging as *greater* than the sum of the parts.[22] In this respect, emotions are similar to gestalt and hypothetico-deductive reasoning. Rather than a static collective or shape of images or beliefs, emotions represent sustained *holistic relational dispositions and construals* that emerge within each transaction—the person's holistic response within existence.[23] Such concerned construals, dispositions, or appraisals are contingent upon one's immediate focus and can often change as quickly (instantly) as changing the focus. For example, experiencing fear when climbing a ladder to paint a three-story window immediately transforms the moment you see your three-year-old daughter in the window trapped by a raging fire. The emotion constitutes from within each unique set of factors and contingencies (both external and internal to the individual). When approaching the ladder, the value of "not harming (or killing) yourself" while painting a house produces fear; in relation to "your daughter's life," it *instantly* transforms into empowering courage.

---

19. Jaggar, "Love and Knowledge," 167n6.

20. Jaggar, "Love and Knowledge," 153: "If we had no emotional responses to the world, it is inconceivable that we should ever come to value one state of affairs more highly than another."

21. Roberts, "What an Emotion Is," 184. For many, emotions "[do] not form a natural class" (Rorty, "Explaining Emotions," 1), are "'whole persons'" (Jaggar, "Love and Knowledge," 153), are "what-is-in-totality" (Heidegger, *Existence and Being*, 334); see also Alston, "Emotive Meaning," 486.

22. Robert Leeper describes the holistic dynamic of emotions as "dynamically organized in the further sense that the total process tends to govern the properties of perceived parts within such larger wholes," which reflects the dynamics of supervenience ("Motivational," 160).

23. Leeper tells us emotions "are *long-sustained perceptions of the more enduring and significant aspects of such situations*" ("Motivational," 156).

Another feature of emotions, says Robertson, is their "resistance to summing."[24] In the case of the stronger emotions, when that which produces them begins to reach a cognitive or rational equilibrium (resolution)—a coherent summing—the emotion dissipates. This brings us full circle to the first attribute—emotions are personal responses of the *whole* self. Emotions always entail the collective focusing of all that the individual is, both conceived and subceived aspects, into holistic focal relation. This reveals the *deliberational* dynamics within emotions, including unconscious factors. These same dynamics can happen unconsciously within intersubjective experiences between persons, in which unconscious factors between both persons successfully deliberate without focally attending to those factors. Is it that difficult to imagine the same thing happening within our relationship (or wrestling) with God—*analogia spiritus?*

These attributes (by no means complete or distinct) reveal the complexity within emotions and their constitutive dynamics. The primary point is that emotions are *holistic collations* of casually related and dynamic factors into a meaningful whole. They are *instant de-liberations* (calculations) of factors *within* us and our relationships without having to calculate them sequentially or consciously. By adding a few new factors into the relational equation, an alternative emotive response may emerge instantly without the individual's being able to give a reason. This is often evident after a counselor uncovers the causal network of relational activity that once exposed begins to release the fear and corresponding destructive behavior.[25] Emotions configure and reconfigure diverse and complex sets of information, beliefs, and desires within human interaction instantaneously and subconsciously, even when some or most of those influences and factors are unconscious. Even more remarkable, these holistic emotive states within one person can instantly affect and transform the holistic state within another. For example, the anger within a person might instantly dissipate when they come into the presence of someone experiencing an extreme sense of peace and tranquility. In these common instances, the infinite wholeness of one person communicates immense amounts of information holistically through sheer

---

24. Robertson, "Emotion," 735.

25. Many of us have witnessed the *immediate* release of anxiety and fear in a friend when, after our noticing particular shameful aspects within their lives (long since become invisible to themselves), we directly or indirectly communicate that despite such "damning" factors, we still enjoy and value their friendship. Such suppression, buried within their personal sedimentation and active in an unconscious relational style or response, is perceivable within that person as an emotion, e.g., fear or insecurity. When the factor of potential rejection concerning the hidden issue disappears, there is an immediate release from the corresponding fear even though that friend may not be conscious of his own prior sub-reasoning (relational equation).

presence, transforming the other without speaking a word or making a gesture. Such activity between individuals brings us closer to understanding the dynamic of *analogia spiritus* within *perichoresis*, in which information and the adjudication of differing constellations of causal networks happen instantly and "invisibly." Such prereflexive dynamics tacitly support, background, and create meaning within consciousness.

Emotions, Epistemology, and Reason

Historically, western philosophical tradition has predominately considered emotions as "potentially or actually subversive of knowledge."[26] Paralleling Moltmann's earlier sentiments on Modernity, Abraham Heschel contends, "the disparagement of emotion was made possible by ascribing to the rational faculty a power of sovereignty over the objects of its comprehension, thought being the active, inert material of comprehension."[27] Similarly, Zagzebski affirms "the treatment of belief as a psychic state independent of non-cognitive states is happily nearing its demise."[28] Regarding reason and emotions, philosopher Ronald De Sousa argues that emotions are inherently rational.[29]

Concerning emotions and epistemology, Heschel goes on to say,

> the act of thinking of an object is in itself an act of being moved by the object. In thinking we do not create an object; we are challenged by it. Thus, thought is part of emotion. We think because we are moved, a fact of which we are not always conscious. Emotion may be defined as *the consciousness of being moved*.[30]

Heschel seeks to affirm the person, not as a point of "inert" focus, but as one who is principally changed by the other, and the emotive response is the evidence of this moving of consciousness. Nevertheless, his formation of this dynamic ultimately needs to expand.

---

26. Jaggar, "Love and Knowledge," 145; she cites notable exceptions as Hume, Nietzsche, Dewey, and James.

27. Heschel, *Prophets*, 2:96. Accordingly, Moltmann suggests "if modern men and women are to be healed, the segregated intellect has to be integrated into receptive and perceptive reason, and reason has to be woven into the fabric of the feelings, and consciousness has to be assimilated into the experiences of the body" (*SL*, 173).

28. Zagzebski, *Virtues*, 51; furthermore, one of her concerns is to "point out some of the numerous ways states of believing are connected with feeling states and states of emotion" (51).

29. De Sousa, *Rationality of Emotion*.

30. Heschel, *Prophets*, 2:96, emphasis added.

Similarly, John Macmurray, in *Reason and Emotion*, believes the emotional life

> is not, as we so often think, subordinate, or subsidiary to the mind. It is the core and essence of human life. The intellect arises out of it, is rooted in it, draws its nourishment and sustenance from it, and is the subordinate partner in the human economy. This is because the intellect is essentially instrumental. Thinking is not living. At its worst it is a substitute for living; at its best a means of living better.... The emotional life is our life, both as awareness of the world and action in the world.[31]

Developmental psychology tells us the intellect begins to perfect its ability to think abstractly around eleven to thirteen years of age. This is the age of reason when objective and subjective categories start to take on greater distinction. In this respect, reason is indeed a subordinate development, and with it comes the propensity to separate the sensations, feelings, and emotions from the "rational" structures in our awareness—the dawning of ideology and the loss of childlikeness. Ray Anderson adds,

> Our emotions, because they are stimulated by feelings and sense perception, provide the primary link with reality external to the self. The intellect is an instrumental factor in rationality through its power of discrimination, reflection, and intentionality.[32]

This affirms Macmurray's notion that human knowledge and experience are a living construct or synthesis of the world and oneself. Likewise, Antonio Damasio thinks that

> the reasoning system evolved as an extension of the automatic emotional system, with emotion playing diverse roles in the reasoning process.... [and] assists with the process of holding in mind the multiple facts that must be considered in order to

---

31. Macmurray, *Reason and Emotion*, 75. When this distortion becomes extreme, Dietrich Bonhoeffer calls it "folly." "Stupidity is a more dangerous enemy of the good than malice.... Against stupidity we are defenseless. Neither protests nor the use of force accomplish anything here; reasons fall on deaf ears; facts that contradict one's prejudgment simply need not be believed.... In all this the stupid person, in contrast to the malicious one, is utterly self-satisfied" (*Prison Letters*, 52). Ray Anderson adds, "When the mind has become captive to the power of an ideology, it becomes blind to the consequences of its actions and insensitive to the pleadings of the emotions" (*Self Care*, 86).

32. Anderson, *Self Care*, 86. Antonio Damasio (paralleling McGilchrist) tells us, "Intriguingly, the representation of extrapersonal space, as well as the processes of emotion, involve a right-hemisphere *dominance*" (*Descartes' Error*, 66, emphasis added).

> reach a decision. . . . Certain aspects of the process of emotion and feeling are indispensable for rationality.[33]

However, the relational dynamic within Macmurray's understanding and most others need to expand. For example, in another description of reason and emotions, Macmurray adds,

> It is not that our feelings have a secondary and subordinate capacity for being rational or irrational. It is that reason is primarily an affair of emotion, and that the rationality of thought is the derivative and secondary one. For if reason is the capacity to act in terms of *the nature of the object*, it is emotion which stands directly behind activity determining its substance and direction, while thought is related to action indirectly and through emotion, determining only its form, and that only partially.[34]

I want to affirm wholeheartedly that emotions ground reason, determining to some degree the form of the thought within the constituting dynamic *interaction* between the subject and the Other—*perichoresis*.[35] However, a problem arises when Macmurray defines reason as "the capacity to behave in terms of the nature of the object, that is to say, to behave objectively. Reason is thus our capacity for objectivity."[36] Yes, reason is part of the capacity for objectification, but how is the psyche perceiving the "nature" of the other? Not through reason. A popular explanation is that consciousness somehow "indwells" the nature of the other. Or, we fall back into Greek metaphysics that gives the rational faculty a power of sovereignty over [or metaphysical insight into] the objects of its comprehension. This type of language tends to continue the shortened subject-object paradigm of modernity (throwing us into the alternatives of mysticism vs. positivism).[37] Such language assumes that somehow *our nature* "behaves" or consciously assimilates the "nature" of the other. How is it that *we* are able, as Polanyi similarly argues, to "indwell" or "inhabit" the framework (nature) of the other and remain ourselves without, in some sense, falling into the other?

---

33. Damasio, *Descartes' Error*, xi, xvii.
34. Macmurray, *Reason and Emotion*, 26.
35. When persons come into relation with another entity, the relational dynamic is perichoretic: *reason* as conceptual, *feelings* as experience, and *emotions* as the *individual*-in-relation.
36. Macmurray, *Reason and Emotion*, 19.
37. These thoughts are likewise echoed by Gunton's acknowledging Macmurray's proximity toward persons as *perichoresis* but alludes to his lacking the proper eschatological contingencies ("Christ in us") within such a perichoretic dynamic. Gunton, *One, Three, Many*, 169n18; cf. also Aves, "Persons in Relation," 133.

Current theological language continues to employ concepts like "indwell," "inhabit," and "become one with," to describe interactive engagement. This descriptive shortfall creates a host of theological and anthropological problems that continue to this day. It also leads to an antiquated and truncated notion of *perichoresis*, notwithstanding emotions. What is missing is the creative third term of the relationship itself that fails to maintain the fuller logic of spirit, which is cosmically pervasive.

Perichoretic Structure of Emotions

For Macmurray, reason constitutes in terms of the nature of the object. In contrast, *perichoresis* constitutes the individual in terms of the mediating formative matrix of the relational unity itself, not by directly "indwelling the nature of the other." Furthermore, only to the extent the participants venture their entire selves into the constituting presence of the relationship does the mediating third term effectively draw them into the knowing process with the other. In this manner, the participants do not constitute in unmediated encounter with the nature of the other. Instead, they constitute by that perichoretic Power within the relationship itself that facilitates and presents (creates) the appropriate mutuality of the participants to each other respectively. This is the "indwelling" from which each human spirit personally and analogically experiences the world and the Other as "[*coming*] from me and yet from beyond me and over me."[38] Again, this prereflexive Jacobian activity occurs antecedent to the reflexive emergence into the light of consciousness. This mediation necessitates a theological contingency, what Gergen refers to as the sacred or what Christians perceive as the "Christ in us"—the divine-human communicational dynamic symbolized as the Rock that enables all dialogical co-conditioning relations between persons and creation.

Emotions emerge from our *givenness* and *response* within the perichoretic tension between the Other and ourselves.

> Sometimes a person may try for several moments, without success, to "see" something in a figure [e.g., the 3-D pictures hidden within the dots], and then suddenly he does see it. It "came," as we say; and in such cases we have clearly that odd mixture of passivity and activity so characteristic of our experience of emotions.[39]

---

38. Heidegger, *Being and Time*, 320, emphasis added.
39. Roberts, "What an Emotion Is," 193.

This odd mixture of passivity and activity can be broken down into three aspects: the intending and releasing of self in open awareness (human *activity*), the emergence of the relationship (human *passivity*, the "indwelling"), and the subsequent reconstituting of the Other respectively within the self-in-relationship (gestalt, reflexion, or act). The latter act of constituting in relation to that Power that constitutes all relationships is gift, a gift from within the Jacobian night that emanates from the interanimation of all relevant contingencies, personal, cosmic, and divine. It undoubtedly arrives in a wounded limp because rare is the moment of true passion in which all is fully ventured (sin). If self approaches infinite resignation, the relationship becomes the will of "I, not I (*analogia spiritus*), but (transparently) Christ." The individual must be sufficiently willing to *perceive* and *act* in the first and latter movements respectively. Because emotions are the unified tension of all relevant forces and elements within the relationship, this synthesis of the many begins to reflect the radically holistic nature of the *analogia spiritus* within perichoretic dynamics.

One psychological theory maintains that emotions are motivational (relational dispositions between existing cognitive social structures and factors). Strasser thinks they are existential and precognitive (feelings as cognitive and perceptual). He argues that fear employs a cognitive perception of specific danger, which he classifies as only a feeling. An infant is furious not because it is hungry but because its existence is menaced, which is dread (an emotion), not fear. Dread, for the toddler, is the feeling of being threatened by the unknown, the strange. For Strasser, emotions are the ongoing processes of objectification through the nonobjectifying mode of awareness, the emerging of objectivity from what is "first *one*." Furthermore, this innate and unique dynamic facilitates and creates new linguistic and relational structures. Though cognitive factors may not motivate certain emotions, the non-cognitive factors giving rise to them are indeed holistically perceivable.

Strasser argues that the three primary emotional tendencies are the innate desire for *pleasure*, the innate need for *security*, and the desire for *power*. As with our earlier inquiry into the motivating forces of suicide, James Loder (with Piaget) would ask, "why"?[40] Why do humans desire and long for anything, let alone pleasure, security, and power? We seek security and power for what? For survival? For Loder, Piaget, and myself, this explanation is incomplete. Developmentally speaking, for Strasser, pleasure is existence as *subject-world* (*umwelt*), wholeness with the world. Why, then, do consciousness and ego perennially constitute as *individual*-in-relation while concurrently desiring existence in unity with the world? Within an

---

40. Loder and Neidhardt, *KM*, 161.

ontology of *perichoresis*, it is irreducibly both. Again, the phenomenon of suicide itself suggests that power and security are not the foundational motivations in life but rather the real or perceived death of meaning-in-relationship, intimacy. If an irreducible perichoretic relational dynamic creates and develops personhood, a picture begins to form that explains the primary concerns of motivational and existential theorists. This irreducible and fundamental desire within human nature constitutes person-in-relation-to-the-Other.[41] Both exist as a complementarity, just as with wave-particle duality. If you want to focus on electron diffraction, you will see its particle-like properties; if you are interested in the photoelectric effect, then wave-like qualities. Loder and Neidhardt tell us,

> The sets of concepts referring to the same phenomenon or object do not necessarily exist on the same conceptual level; their distinctiveness yet interrelatedness together in a unitary whole is then preserved by a *differentiated* relationality maintained by the asymmetric character of the relations constituting the relationship between the two levels.[42]

Similarly, in the contrasting emphasis between Gunton and Milbank, as in current theoretical particle physics—where wave qualities and shifting inter*relations* take slight precedence over particle attributes—the relation itself takes asymmetrical priority over relating entities, just as does value over fact, the Eternal over temporal, and transformation over stages in development.

For example, the experience of wonder or dread is the relational call of something new pushing to emerge from experience into linguistic or focal consciousness. Similarly, within motivational theories, emotions like fear and joy express the state of existing networks of relational factors and whether they need adjustment or change for the individual to remain in relational equilibrium. Again, emotions often disclose relational states otherwise unarticulated within conscious understanding. Overall, emotions are the guardians (the functioning) of a relational ontology *in* persons that innately drive human flourishing by maintaining the desire or "call" to relate perichoretically—irreducibly as person-*in*-relation-*to*-another. Such a dynamic, if only weakly, reflects within human spirit and between it and others. In the midst, *analogia spiritus* plays a vital role. Whether the wonder

---

41. This understanding of perichoretic dynamics and a relational ontology reflective of the Trinity provides a better focus on the complementarity of Gunton's notion of "substantiality" (*One, Three, Many*, 188–95) and Milbank's "shifting relations and generations in time" (*Social Theory*, 426).

42. Loder and Neidhardt, *KM*, 310.

of nature disclosing its infinite depths or the foreboding dread of a schoolgirl as her family disintegrates in divorce, emotions are a *call* to the opening of self to constitute and transform in authentic relations, a *call* (or scream) for the dynamic reconfiguring of one's existing understanding and experience into a more confederated relatedness of particularities (equilibrium).

Therefore, emotions reflect the person's perichoretic state within relations and play a role in expressing the degree of fullness of life we experience. This not only explains the desire for peaceful relations and solidarity but also the desire for personal uniqueness and the dynamic of individual and social flourishing that drives cultural development. It also explains why our emotions in certain situations compel us to seek synergistic relations in both social and personal orientations (priestly unanimity), yet in other situations, they disruptively propel us away from inadequate or unsatisfying uniformity (prophetic disruption). When appropriately construed, boredom and many other emotive responses motivate us toward more profound dynamic relations. We eventually experience boredom—the *loss of meaning* (or perichoretic relations)—even in the most advanced conceptual schemes if they cease to progress toward greater perichoretic intimacy—Eternity in our hearts. This is the perennial and transparent immanent transcendent agitation of *Spiritus Creator* for authentic, undistorted, and most importantly, ever-deepening intimacy within relations. Similarly, "emotional behavior," Strasser notes,

> occurs whenever a subject does not apprehend his situation in an objectifying manner, but immediately, in the light of his existential needs, . . . his desire, his hate, his craving and his dread then take on such proportions that he is overwhelmed by them. The "primordial distance" (*Urdistanz*) which . . . characterizes man as man and enables him to define his attitude towards fellows-subjects, things and situations, completely disappears. And so the objective world built up by the adult loses its meaning for him.[43]

Emotions not only express the cognitively overwhelming and ineffable, but also, according to Iain McGilchrist, they emerge from the same neurological mechanism and holistic capacity that: produces empathy, the experience of consciousness as a whole-in-relation, grounds our experiences, and creates "desire or *longing* towards something, something that lies beyond itself, towards the Other."[44] These are secondary functions that produce our primary emotions—the holistic functioning of the limbic system.

43. Strasser, "Feeling," 302.
44. McGilchrist, *Master*, 171. All knowledge emerges as "informed desiring"

Emotions themselves are not technically moral attributes. For example, experiencing a distorted anger or lust (*desire*) toward another is not the fundamental moral issue. In the following sections, we will identify moral turpitude within the *unwillingness* to become fully aware of *all* the relevant factors creating emotions *that refuse* to transcend the void (double-bind), which lies beyond "any defensive or emergent competencies of the ego."[45] Emotions as virtues rather than distortions have to do with the individual's experience of *phronesis*—a truth-conducive willingness and desire to relate with *all* Reality—which within the human condition necessitates a willingness to suffer in order to experience the greatest degree of reality.

Herein is the answer to Loder's "why"? concerning development. Human spirit and emotions are a holistic *response to the call to unify self in active and genuine relations to the world*—all desire begins here. At these deeper recesses of human consciousness and unifying processes, human spirit encounters God's Spirit in an ongoing reconfigurative process, interactively, analogically, and paradigmatically transforming an entangled web of relations into ever more perichoretic fullness in relation to the Eternal. In this respect, our covenant with that Power invites us from our place in history to play a co-conditioning role within the trinitarian act of Eternal creating. Within this dynamic activity all formation, transformation, and teleological co-conditioning transpires in which the divine orchestrates and cosmically integrates billions of perichoretically active spirits (Gen 9:16–17).

In conclusion, understanding the human emotive response and its function in personal, social, and epistemological matters is imperative for understanding how God ultimately relates with human persons. Theologically this is the eschatological mystery and process of Christ's reconciling all things to himself (Col 1:20) from degree to degree by his Spirit (2 Cor 3:18). Such a dipolar dynamic constituting human relations, with its unique process of creating relations, begins to open room (both space and time) for understanding how human community analogically and mutually relate to those similar dynamics of relatedness within the Eternal unifying dynamic of God. With such an understanding, we can further consider how de-liberation happens analogically and prereflexively between persons and God, drawing humanity into the creative process as *free agents* struggling within the Jacobian night—in an instant! Therefore, the locus

---

(Milbank, "Postmodern," 234), and though "events already take an ideal form, already happen as knowledge, . . . body always is, with and through the incorporeal, as fact always is, with and through value." They instantiate ("in radical dependency") within the immediate experience because of the unique theological "moment of the *passage* of an event from external time into memory" (Milbank, *Social Theory*, 426).

45. Loder, *Transforming Moment*, 178.

of divine-human relation occurs *within* the same dynamics that produce the human emotive process—through the de-liberation of *analogia spiritus*, *ex nihilo*. In this respect, there is no *City of God* paralleling this world to uncover, no hermeneutical program or method that will ensure our relations with God. "It is not a case of the present moving steadily closer to an evolutionary future, but of God opening up the present and drawing it into the future of the kingdom. . . . Its mode of presence cannot therefore be complete or uniform, but determinate, partial and anticipatory."[46] God's Eternal [and] personal relation to the world dialogically emerges within each unique *moment* of history. It is not "finished" before it starts or in some way outside riding above world history; instead, it completes itself within the midst of history. Through the dynamic of trinitarian *perichoresis*, all history potentially participates within the "It is finished" by virtue of the Eternal coming into co-conditioning *relations* with human passion—an emotive interaction.

PERICHORESIS—THE TRICAMERAL BRAIN AND THE BICAMERAL SYNTHESIS OF CONSCIOUSNESS: IAIN McGILCHRIST

Recent research in cognitive neuroscience, as comprehensively compiled in Iain McGilchrist's *The Master and His Emissary*, continues to clarify the asymmetry of the brain and the role of holistic functions within the brain—specifically noting the role of the right hemisphere (RH) as the general location of holistic functioning while accessing the left hemisphere (LH) for sequencing and differentiating functioning. We should not think of the *complete* localization of these two functions into separate hemispheres, merely the predominant function in each hemisphere, respectively. As we have seen with dynamics in other disciplines, this asymmetry and relational tension between the hemispheres also wonderfully reflect the dynamics of *perichoresis* as developed within this thesis. Perichoretic relations, on the other hand, might help to explain certain enigmatic issues within neurological studies. In this respect, one interdisciplinary consideration might be that the bicameral brain is really tricameral, with two halves *and* the corpus callosum with its colony of associates (glands, Thalamus, Hippocampus, etc.) that become, or at least affect, the relations between them.

---

46. Cf. McFadyen, *CP*, 223.

The Perichoretic Nature of Brain Activity between the Right and Left Hemisphere

Perichoretic methodology suggests a cyclical co-conditioning dynamic between our paradigmatic awareness (differentiated knowledge in configuration) and our holistic experiencing of the world. Neurological studies are beginning to reveal these same dynamics active in the bicameral interaction within the brain. Each relational interaction starts with the RH, which, Iain McGilchrist says, "is more in touch with reality, and that it has not just temporal or developmental priority, but ontological supremacy."[47] The RH begins the human experience through a prereflexive holistic experiencing, then immediately the LH (the linguistic hemisphere of categorization and paradigm structuring) processes the experience into language and categories of understanding, which then loops that linguistic categorization to be "grounded by the right hemisphere"[48] resulting in our conscious experience and response to the encounter.

> These two aspects of the world are not symmetrically opposed. They are not equivalent, for example, to the "subjective" and "objective" points of view. . . . The distinction I am trying to make is between, on the one hand, the way in which we experience the world pre-reflectively, before we have had a chance to "view" it at all, or divide it up into bits—a world . . . held in a suspension which embraces each potential "pole," and their togetherness, together. . . . At its simplest, a world where there is "betweenness," and one where there is not. These are not different ways of *thinking about* the world: they are different ways of *being in* the world.[49]

Only after this reintegration into the experiential world does the experience "live." Each new reintegration creates a new dynamic synthesis (betweenness). This reflects the dialogical cycle of perichoretic interaction and relational ontology.

The holistic experiencing always precedes articulation and linguistic categorization. In listening to another, says McGilchrist, we

> listen to what emerges from our language, rather than speak through it. . . . we cannot attain an understanding by *grasping* it for ourselves. It has already to be in us, and the task is to awaken it . . . to bring it into being within us. Similarly we can never

---

47. McGilchrist, *Master*, 195.
48. McGilchrist, *Master*, 195.
49. McGilchrist, *Master*, 31.

> make others understand something unless they already, at some level, understand it. We cannot give them our understanding, only awaken their own, latent, understanding.[50]

The dialogical cycle begins with the enigmatic experiencing of the whole (RH), which is dependent upon existing learned modes of awareness (tacit though constantly evolving), thus apprehending something that immediately triggers a more definitive processing of *what* is being apprehended (LH). This processing is prereflexive. Once identified, it then proffers a provisional idea or identification to the RH in a bi-directional feedback loop between the two modes of experiencing. This produces a final cognitive response (reflexion), establishing a relational tension (existential synthesis) between the two modes of being in the world. Our interactions are a series of cumulative cycles, with each new growth in articulation conditioning a new tacit fullness through which to apprehend the world. Within this tension and play between these modes emerges the potentiality for novelty, learning, and new categories of knowledge. Pragmatically what happens during the moment of apprehension is a cycling feedback loop between the two hemispheres as the subject comes into greater focus.

Within perichoretic communication, holistic encounter takes asymmetrical priority over the descriptive elements to which words secondarily give shape. Meaning is first empathic, then articulated. For Wittgenstein, even the experience of pain is not an innate human response but a socially learned response learned through empathetic interactions. Enigmatically, whole first encounters whole before articulation.

McGilchrist also notes that each hemisphere brings different dynamics of time to the human experience. How they paradoxically function in relationship with each other is vitally important. For example, in considering the nature of music, he argues that

> time itself is (what the left hemisphere would call) paradoxical in nature, and that music does not so much free time from temporality as bring out an aspect that is always present within time, [its intersection with a moment which partakes of eternity]. Similarly it does not so much use the physical to transcend physicality, or use particularity to transcend the particular, as bring out the spirituality latent in what we conceive as physical existence, and uncover the universality that is, as Goethe spent a lifetime trying to express, always latent in the particular.[51]

---

50. McGilchrist, *Master*, 155.

51. McGilchrist, *Master*, 77. He goes on to express that music in every known culture is used to communicate with whatever is beyond, transcendent, "other than" ourselves.

This is a beautiful expression of *perichoresis* and incarnational complementarity (Kierkegaard) in which the temporal and eternal do *not* materially synthesize into a new "thesis." Existential time includes a living tension that produces an intersection with a moment which partakes of eternity. Within Hegelian parlance, time sits within eternity. McGilchrist reconsiders George Steiner's comment that music is time made free of temporality, in other words, moving through a thing to encounter its "roundness, rather than linearity." In the *perichoresis* of time and eternity, time eternalizes (adding "roundness"), and eternity temporalizes (chapter 5). The Kierkegaardian mandate is that these two modalities never become one, other than in living consciousness as a tensive unity within the individual (as a relationship to itself) or social relation; never do time and eternity create a "world out there." Nevertheless, McGilchrist displays an affinity for an incarnational dynamic of complementarity in which we experience a spiritual or holistic dimension of reality (RH attributes) in its irreducible coupling with particularity and time (LH attributes). In a perichoretic rendering, this coupling occurs in the emergence of human spirit that brings together and animates the relationship between the two hemispheres.

Sociologically McGilchrist equates the prereflexive immediate holistic interaction between persons with Merleau-Ponty's reciprocity of communication in which "it is as if the other person's intentions inhabited my body and mine his." The "object of perception . . . is in reality embedded in a context, the nexus of relations among existing things which gives it meaning within the world."[52] Perichoretically, this is the holistic mediation and conditioning of the third term of the relationship mutually co-conditioning the participants within the interaction—*analogia spiritus*.

He also points to Edmund Husserl's idea that an "intersubjectivity" constitutes objective reality—as if we analogically and holistically share our consciousness of embodied existence with others during communication. Two of Husserl's dynamics distinguish themselves within neurological studies. First is the priority of the RH in creating meaning—the holistic and sequential asymmetry of holistic gestalt, even in language dynamics. Husserl links this to the experience of empathy. In our use of words, says McGilchrist, "the world arises from a circular process that circles and searches its origins, more like a picture that comes into focus all at once, than a linear address to a target: by a right-hemisphere process, in other words, rather than a left." Secondly, he argues that empathy grounds our experience of others and *our own experience* in the world.

---

52. McGilchrist, *Master*, 148.

> The direction in which it works appears not to be from within our (separate) selves to within (separate) others, but form shared experience to the development of our own inwardness *and* that of others. We do not need to learn to make the link between our selves and others, because although individual we are not initially separated, but intersubjective in our consciousness.[53]

McGilchrist describes this process of meaning making as circular or spiral-like, active between both the two hemispheres of the brain and between persons. This also indicates the potential presence of a perichoretic dynamic within dialogical interaction—a Power that relates the self to itself within itself while dynamically relating that potential self to the Other (Kierkegaard). Again, the omniscient activity of a mediating dynamic sustaining creation.

Language, in this respect, shapes but does not ground our experience. "Language is necessary neither for categorization, nor for reasoning, nor for concept formation, nor perception: it does not itself bring the landscape of the world in which we live into being." Instead, it "shapes that landscape . . . defining *which* categories or types of entities we see."[54] "Thinking is prior to language," but language provides "fixity" to the world, which can also restrict experience through wrongly giving asymmetrical priority to the conditioning attribution of the LH. At the same time, language is not an abstraction but an extension of life, what in perichoretic dynamics is a de-liberation of meaning within the holistic dynamics of speech (*analogia spiritus*) that adjusts for a unified meaning uniquely understood by each respondent accordingly. As Wittgenstein teaches, to imagine a language means to imagine a form of life—not a virtual *representation* of life, but a *form* of life.[55] A child learns the skill of language in much the same way it learns the skill of life—rules and forms of life acquired through empathic identification with those who are more proficient.

Our relational disposition textures all human interactions and qualitatively affects our ability to apprehend anything. As developed earlier, our disposition toward others and the world has everything to do with what and, more importantly, *how* we perceive and interact. Our disposition toward the Other enhances or inhibits our prereflexive and holistic dynamics within interactions. Neurologically, says McGilchrist,

> The disposition towards the world comes first: any cognitions are subsequent to and consequent on that disposition, which is

---

53. McGilchrist, *Master*, 144–45.
54. McGilchrist, *Master*, 110.
55. Wittgenstein, *Philosophical Investigations*, 8e.

in other words "affect." Affect may too readily be equated with emotion. Emotions are certainly part of affect but are only part of it. Something much broader is implied: a way of . . . relating to the world (or not relating to it), a stance, a disposition, towards the world. . . . [E]motion is very important, and it too is closer to the core of our being than cognition. . . . Several lines of reasoning from the evidence converge to suggest that the essential core of being is subcortical.[56]

The same could be said for all disciplines of thought. If indeed, as McGilchrist suggests, the priority and grounding effect of the RH over the LH is to maintain its proper balance, one would think that a disposition of wonder and infinite resignation necessitates relaxing LH activity to allow the holistic and prereflexive interaction to "master" and most affectively ground the interaction. McGilchrist says, "the main purpose of a large number of [fibers within the corpus callosum] is actually to inhibit—in other words to stop the other hemisphere interfering."[57] Not only must we as persons remain humble within our epistemic structuring, the LH of the brain must also relax its epistemic impositions when the RH is encountering the Other.

McGilchrist's consideration that "the essential core of being is subcortical" presents us with a tricameral brain, not a bicameral brain, in which the non-hemispheric elements of the brain between the hemispheres produces the relationship (the site of mediation) actuating being-with-another. Kierkegaard's notion of infinite resignation, which he believes is necessary for faith, falls squarely into McGilchrist's notion of disposition, which also bears an ethical element. For example, those who do not foreclose on wonder throughout their development and subsequently experience significant moments of transcendence generally approach the world and others with greater openness and new ways of understanding and experiencing life. As philosopher Arne Naess recently said, "Philosophy begins and ends with wondering—profound wondering."[58]

Decisions and the Unconscious

One of the stunning developments in neuroscience, and a discovery that dramatically affects this study, is that *most of our decisions are wholly unconscious, and most of the processing within our conscious decisions is*

---

56. McGilchrist, *Master*, 184–85.
57. McGilchrist, *Master*, 17.
58. Naess, *Life's Philosophy*, 3.

unconscious. McGilchrist, citing the studies of Susan Pockett and Benjamin Libet, denies consciousness any major role in our day-to-day conduct:

> This is only a problem if one imagines that, for me to decide something, I have to have willed it with the conscious part of my mind. Perhaps my unconscious is every bit as much "me." In fact it had better be, because so little of life is conscious at all.[59]

Furthermore, he points to Princeton psychologist Julian Jaynes's seminal work, *The Origin of Consciousness in the Breakdown of the Bicameral Mind*, in which little of what most attribute to consciousness is necessary for the defining elements of human mental life:

> [Jayne] points out that very little brain activity is in fact conscious (current estimates are certainly less than 5 percent, and probably less than 1 percent), and that we take decisions, solve problems, make judgments, discriminate, reason, and so on, without any need for conscious involvement.[60]

This should not be a difficult concept to digest or accept, especially for a Christian theologian when faced with Jesus' expanding of human nature as seen in his Sermon on the Mount, in which he annuls the judgement of outward conscious behavior and legal response pushing culpability into the realm of unconscious wishes, intentions, and choices. Expanding on this, Hans Vailhinger adds,

> The organic function of thought is carried on for the most part *unconsciously*. Should the product finally enter consciousness also, or should consciousness momentarily accompany the processes of logical thought, this light only penetrates to the shallows, and *the actual fundamental processes are carried on in the darkness of the unconscious*. The specifically purposeful operations are chiefly, and in any case at the beginning, wholly instinctive and unconscious, even if they later press forward into the luminous circle of consciousness.[61]

It is essential to note Vailhinger's insistence that "processes" occur largely within the unconscious and emotive activity of the mind. McGilchrist relates these dynamics directly to the process that happens in the interplay between the RH, LH, and corpus callosum before experience rises into consciousness.

---

59. McGilchrist, *Master*, 187.
60. McGilchrist, *Master*, 187.
61. Vailhinger, *Philosophy*, 7, second emphasis mine.

Such mental activity reveals that prereflexive processes of personal deliberation are active before they even come to consciousness, and such activity specifically illuminates the potential nature of Jacob's experience with God and the necessity that such interactions transpire in the darkness of subconscious interaction (preconsciousness) before the light of consciousness. If we can begin to understand the nature of how the separate hemispheres within the bicameral brain interact—how each with their specific and different modalities and perspectives can *mutually interact* (deliberate) almost instantly before the emergence into consciousness—then we might begin to understand how two persons (divine and human) might prereflexively experience a *holistic* dynamic *interaction* before grounding their respective reflexive conscious responses. We explore these social dynamics in the following chapters.

Conclusion

In conclusion, McGilchrist vividly reveals the bicameral (and indirectly the tricameral) nature of the brain's hemispheric modalities of experiencing and interacting with each other and how they relate to the world. Though the research in and evidence from his neurological studies point to many aspects within perichoretic dynamics, he, if for no other reason than the nature of his research, fails to draw their implications to their fullest potential regarding the nature of spirit. He notes that:

> The world that we experience is a product of both hemispheres, clearly, but not in the same way. . . . [T]he left hemisphere depends still on its foundation in something that underwrites it in the right hemisphere (and both of them on something that underwrites them both, *outside the brain*).[62]

Though McGilchrist employs the trajectory of Husserl and Merleau-Ponty, he reconstructs their understanding of intersubjectivity to the idea of "betweenness," which is necessary for genuine communication between persons. And even though he refers to the concept of the eternal in distinction to sequential time, he never develops it for the understanding of dynamics at play between the bicameral interaction of the hemispheres or interpersonal encounters. Instead, after noting that the RH comes to knowledge and understanding instantly through an "aha!," he prioritizes the LH as the true workhorse of communicating knowledge interpersonally.

---

62. McGilchrist, *Master*, 197, emphasis added.

> There is a huge disadvantage for the right hemisphere here. If this knowledge has to be conveyed to someone else, it is in fact essential to be able to offer (apparent) certainties: to be able to repeat the process for the other person, build it up from the bits. . . . By contrast, passing on what the right hemisphere knows requires the other party already to have an understanding of it, which can be awakened in them. . . . [It] is hard for the right hemisphere to be heard at all: what it knows is too complex, hasn't the advantage of having been carved up into pieces that can be neatly strung together, and *it hasn't got a voice anyway*.[63]

McGilchrist here shrinks from noting or developing this engine of "betweenness" as active in its holistic interactive dynamics with that same holistic dynamic in others. In other words, he fails to consider (or speculate due to existing neurological parameters of criteria) the possibility of a prereflexive holistic interaction of each person's right hemisphere with each other before and during each person's LH conditioning, respectively. In perichoretic dynamics, we refer to this as the *analogia spiritus*. Though he forwards hints of such a dynamic within his research, he fails to incorporate them into his understanding of human interaction, thus discounting the prereflexive interactivity between persons and the possibility that the right hemisphere indeed has its own voice, it is simply holistic and, as spirits, interactive in dynamic patterns on a subconscious level. Knowledge is a form of life; each person [uniquely] articulates and knows accordingly as that knowledge ultimately transfers from one person to another through the perichoretic dynamic of *analogia spiritus* (Pentecost). The LH uniquely embeds (textures) the knowledge within each person creating the "house of being" relative for each person. But the living "being" within that house holistically shares and grounds within the RH and respective relations (modality of spirit).

As briefly mentioned, evidence of holistic dynamics operational *between* RH and LH, and *between* interacting persons (as he alludes to in his belief that both are upheld by something "outside the brain") are evident in McGilchrist's query and his eventual surprise in the behavior of the split-brain. Referring to extreme epilepsy patients that have had their two hemispheres surgically separated in the corpus callosum, he notes that:

> Split-brain patients lead remarkably normal lives . . . [and] have not appeared particularly handicapped. Which invites the question, why ever not? . . . Furthermore, . . . even in normal subjects

---

63. McGilchrist, *Master*, 229, emphasis added.

> no connective pathways, even in the corpus callosum, function all the time; and lengthy neurotransmission times across the corpus callosum enforce a degree of interhemispheric independence.[64]

This leaves a materialist-bound neuroscientist with a significant anomaly. Like the discipline of quantum physics, if locked within its materialist strictures, their theories eventually fall morbidly impotent in explaining life and the cosmos. In basing their theories only on the physical and energy phenomena of the bicameral hemispheres, neuroscience has no adequate theory explaining their interaction. The hemispheres obviously interact even though they can find no energy or electromagnetic activity constantly supporting such communicational interplay. As McGilchrist argues,

> the left hemisphere favours analytic, sequential "processing," where the right hemisphere favours parallel "processing" of different streams of "information" simultaneously. . . . The right hemisphere meanwhile tries to take in all the various aspects of what it approaches *at once*.[65]

Note his qualifying use of "processing" and "information" in acknowledging the difficulty and eventual impossibility of accounting for these processes within typical Newtonian structuring where processing takes time. Information represents differentiated items that need processing into a whole, but how does this happen within the strictures of energy limited by "c" (the speed of light)? The neurological discipline, McGilchrist reveals, attempts to explain this seemingly instantaneous holistic process and feedback looping by pointing out that the brain's neurological activity is *not* linear but works with multiple "parallel 'processing.'" Yet, echoing throughout his text, through a plethora of studies and theories, the holistic dynamics of the body and brain, from which greater than the sum of the parts emerge, both materiality and energy seem to ultimately transcends Newtonian architecture. Marie Banich, a leading researcher in hemisphere interaction, notes:

> Interhemispheric interaction is much more than just a mechanism by which one hemisphere "photocopies" experiences and

---

64. McGilchrist, *Master*, 210–11, 494n17, "This position would appear to be supported by a recent review of callosotomy: 'Synchronization and relay of information to inform one hemisphere about the activities of the other hemisphere is a critical function. Another, perhaps more important, function of the corpus callosum is to allow one hemisphere to control and inhibit homologous areas in the other hemisphere, providing a critical pathway for the development of specialized hemispheric functions'" (Devinsky and Laff, "Callosal Lesions," 615).

65. McGilchrist, *Master*, 229, emphasis added.

feeling for its partner. Interhemispheric interaction has important *emergent functions*—functions that cannot be derived from the simple sum of its parts . . . the nature of processing when both hemispheres are involved cannot be predicted from the parts.[66]

Within a relational ontology of *perichoresis*, each bicameral hemisphere's material and energy nature must necessarily communicate through a supervening dynamic that transcends them—the emergence of spirit, which is the whole of the person centrally organizing and incorporating the fullness of the person (body and mind). The spirit (containing mind and body) becomes the emergent third term of the relationship between the hemispheres, forming what Kierkegaard calls the self—a self that is always an existential synthesis between time and eternity, the finite and the infinite, the relative and the absolute (still not the spirit of the whole person). Neuroscience has suggested that most of our decisions, actions, and interactive dynamics are unconscious and manifest within the RH instantaneously. Is it that difficult or offensive to consider that within each living thing, and throughout its evolutionary development, a supervening whole and operating locus emerge through which whole beings holistically interact with the world—a personal spirit that becomes whole spirit as organism (mind and body) or person-in-relation-to-another? If spirit supervenes over and operationally coordinates the material and electrical (finite speed) dynamics into an operating whole, then that spirit would *necessarily* have to transcend the existing considerations and qualities within both materiality and energy, otherwise, it would be impossible to coordinate them. How could various electrical impulses and paralleling processes moving at the speed of light be coordinated by supervening forces that likewise move at the speed of light? From my perspective, that seems irrational. And is it then that difficult to consider that the initial point of contact between living beings, human and divine, entails an emerging prereflexive holistic relation between them that then ontologically mediates and grounds a mutually co-conditioning interaction between them?

The emerging data, theories, and evidence from recent neuroscience provide further evidence for *perichoresis* within and between human interactions. Likewise, the dynamics of *perichoresis* might offer heuristic tools to neuroscience for completing its project. Unfortunately, the growing agendas of the academy over the last fifty years have been to stretch the dead-end of every discipline with "quantum dynamics" in its repulsion of Christianity and its ancient notion of spirit. Yet, as we will consider in an upcoming

66. Banich, "Interaction," 269–70, emphasis added.

chapter on quantum dynamics, the quantum enigma parallels the dynamics of *perichoresis* in reflecting the Christian logic of spirit. Ultimately, all methodologically *isolated* disciplines are crushed under the fatal anomalies that result from their restricting, often agendizing, methodologies and sectarianism because of their aversion to the full wealth of living criteria available.

Iain McGilchrist's monolithic study parallels well with Christian theology and social theory (next chapter). His chosen title, *The Master and His Emissary*, might be more appropriate than first thought. His description of the activity of the left hemisphere analogically equates quite well with humanity as "emissaries" and the "master" as the risen Jesus Christ from within his trinitarian relations creating, sustaining, and adjudicating the longings, disappointments, wishes, and actions of his emissaries—perichoretically—through God's Spirit (John 5:19–30).

3B

Perichoresis in Dialogical Relations
Alistair McFadyen's Christian Social Theory of Personhood

> God does not think, he creates; God does not exist, He is eternal. Man thinks and exists, and existence separates thought and being, holding them apart from one another *in succession*.
>
> SØREN KIERKEGAARD[1]

INTRODUCTION

Various new social and dialogical anthropologies are emerging within Christian theology. Some of these studies that concentrate on human communicational dynamics offer unique perspectives into the human condition. In this section, we will explore the efforts of Alistair McFadyen, who appropriates the philosophical insights of Habermas and others for theology that, in turn, seek to identify ontological and universal dynamics within human existence, most notably in human communication. Both thinkers resolutely maintain theses of rationality and communicative commitment, however, my primary interest in McFadyen is his theory of relationality and its dialogical bipolarity of openness and closure within social and divine-human communication. Basic communication entails openness (awareness) and closure (conceptual constitution of self) within this basic structure. One goal is to investigate the function and process of opening to

---

1. Kierkegaard, *CUP*, 296, emphasis added.

the Other (listening/exploring) as the site of divine-human encounter in communication. Finally, we will focus on McFadyen's understanding of the human dialogical dynamic as contingent upon the Trinity, and specifically its perichoretic nature. From this brief study of McFadyen in discussion with Kierkegaard, I wish to argue that *the dialogical cycle of human existence involves a relational alternation of open awareness as an analogically infinite mode of interaction within the relationship and a reciprocating closure constituting the individual within a finite mode and social context.*[2]

CALL: INDIVIDUALITY AND CONTEXT

In the *Call to Personhood*, McFadyen presents a Christian social theory in which the individual socially constitutes through dialogical communication, arguing that Christ ultimately shapes all undistorted communication through the trinitarian activity of Spirit and Word. This maintains a tension between individualism and collectivism. We understand this dynamic by first considering how Jesus calls his disciples—the "immediate and uncompromising demand to 'leave everything and follow [him].'"[3] Again, this parallels what Kierkegaard refers to as the "infinite resignation" opening to the call. The call is to stand out from their existing context and enter a new meaning-frame that would completely recontextualize them. According to McFadyen, such a call to relations is not denying one's existing relational contexts but rather a call to respond to a new, different, and fuller context. "It is not so much a decontextualising act of self-constitution as a recontextualisation in response to an external address."[4] In such recontextualizations, former identities actively enter into the creative force of the call from Jesus, which has "no presupposition but itself." In the example of Levi, he argues, we are given no antecedent contextual elements suggesting presuppositions; instead, it indicates the call itself creates in the hearer the response it demands.[5] The immediate relation *transforms* the old identity, awakening the disciple to a new future, present, and past upon response.

The call and response free the individual from the enclosure of self. It provides the space and decisive break from our world, creating the possibility of *ex-centric* freedom for authentic relations—the ability for genuine

2. Polanyi similarly describes this cyclical pulsation containing "an oscillation between movements of analysis and integration in which, on balance, integration predominates" (*Knowing*, 130).
3. McFadyen, *CP*, 48.
4. McFadyen, *CP*, 49.
5. McFadyen, *CP*, refers to Vogel, *Body Theology*, ix.

relations to affect or transform us. The call of Jesus is an invitation to a new meaning-frame that is a "new form of communicative subjectivity, a new way of being in relations."[6]

> One's own space-time is de-absolutized in redemption by the co-intention of others with their own equally valid space-time. For ultimate meaning can no longer be found in one's own space-time, which has henceforth to be related to that of others and God; that is, recontextualised and hence relativised.[7]

This does not, however, relativize the historical events of grace that lie within a larger historical communicational context (of which no one contextual understanding of such Truth and meaning is complete). Instead, it places the individual within a mode of interaction and subsequent encounter with God's Spirit and Word in Christ, which determinately relativizes both self and the existing communicational context in relation to God (and subsequently to each other and the Truth).[8]

It is our relation to the Spirit and Christ that draws all undistorted communication into synchronicity with God's trinitarian activity. "This presence of Christ is not an indication of an essence but a movement with others towards Christ between us. . . . Christ is therefore 'in' us as the ground of this self-transcendence, as a centre within us pushing us outwards, and as a centre beyond us pulling us towards God and others."[9] For McFadyen, "Christ between" shapes truth and fidelity within relations between individuals and communities (even those beyond the church).[10]

Therefore, though all communicative contexts may be diversely determined and, as such, unable to immediately agree upon truth, they share an inherent universal dialogical structuring to the degree they are open to the Other. "Once the distortions and limitations of particularity are stripped away" all contexts are technically capable of unity, though not necessarily uniformity.[11] The most crucial factor in communication is not what one knows but *how* one knows. All contexts differ in their capacity for what can be known; therefore, knowledge is always relative to its specific context. Nevertheless, Christ within each unique interactional context, *redeems* the truth and provisionally (existentially) *affirms* its appropriate contextual use

---

6. McFadyen, *CP*, 56.
7. McFadyen, *CP*, 57.
8. This concept of decontextualization is similar to my use of *de-liberation*.
9. McFadyen, *CP*, 60.
10. McFadyen, *CP*, 62.
11. McFadyen, "Truth as Mission," 439, 441.

if the participants are indeed open to the Other (1 Cor 14). Therefore, the limiting scope of a particular context does not limit the potential conviction, which is largely the product of openness to all relevant contingencies. However, a person's *unwillingness* to eventually transcend the "distortions and limitations of particularity" eventually erodes these convictions. For McFadyen, this incarnational dynamic (the *expedient* affirmation and realization of a contextual truth, 1 Cor 6:12) results from a universal christological contingency in all undistorted dialogical communications. Therefore, Christian truth is "not *primarily* propositional," but relational. "It concerns the *proper relationship* between humanity, creation and God."[12] Truth reflects the *genuineness* and response-ability to the call. "When a person is, consciously or otherwise, adopting a hidden agenda, and is therefore not genuinely present in communication, that person's address is distorted because it is not aimed at a true mutuality of understanding."[13] Nevertheless, an appropriate response contains two personal actions, openness ("attending") and closure ("returning") in relationship.

RESPONSE: FROM OPENNESS TO CLOSURE

All undistorted personal response

> requires an *openness* to others and to self-transformation, combined with the *closure* proper to an individually centred identity which is resistant to external overdetermination. This represents a structure of personhood in which both openness and closure are present, *but never total*.[14]

McFadyen recognizes the dialogical necessity of alternating openness for self-transcendence and closure for personal identity. As a purely social dynamic they lie upon a single continuum of interaction which must adjust according to the relational character of the Other and relational appropriateness. One's spirit organizes life-giving energy, relational processes, and

---

12. McFadyen, "Truth as Mission," 447, emphasis added.

13. McFadyen, *CP*, 120. Furthermore, "Making responsible answers to others cannot be a simple, mechanical response to a given stimulus which returns the intention in a way overdetermined by the other. That could hardly be called free or responsible. Yet neither may our responses be completely predetermined by our personal identities or intentions of these others which existed prior to their calls. That could hardly be called a response. *Response must involve attending* and returning to the other as she or he is present in communication. This is a *readiness* to allow the calls of others to transform us in response" (121, emphasis added).

14. McFadyen, *CP*, 121, emphasis added.

projects social consequences into communication. It accomplishes this through a measured openness to the other and optimally establishes its relational posture considering all the relevant factors and contingencies. One's disposition toward God or the possibility of a God (transcendent Reality), conscious or not, affects our relational posturing.

In undistorted communication the Spirit enables "ordered openness in systems," and Christ (Word) "is the form-giver to organised life."[15] One is "alternatingly the object and subject of the process within dialogical communications."[16] In such a process, the futurity which results from the "pull" of God's liberating future and the "push" of past mundane relational sedimentation—the desire for ever greater fullness of life—stimulates an openness toward the transformation of existing personal structures. The "individual spirit organises the form and content of communication by regulating openness and closure," and "it is individual spirit which is initially transformed in redemption by being placed in the enlarged context of relation with God."[17]

DIVINE-HUMAN RELATIONAL ONTOLOGY AND MCFADYEN'S SOCIOLOGICAL PERSPECTIVE

Though he rarely uses the term, McFadyen characterizes the relational dynamic of God and human beings as perichoretic in similar ways to this thesis.[18] But because of my particular focus on the divine-human relationship, I would like to reframe his concerns within a more Kierkegaardian framework. For example, McFadyen primarily concentrates on the dialogical, conversational, and communicational dimensions of interactions. Though McFadyen is synchronous with perichoretic dynamics, his project does little to articulate how divine and human share in the perichoretic process beyond stating Christ in and between us. I would simply like to identify the locus of the divine-human dynamic as co-conditioning and perichoretic within his communication structuring. For example, even though Christ "is not only between but also within the partners to a dialogical relation[19] . . . [therefore] safeguard[ing] the transcendence and individuality of the partners,"[20] he still concludes that one's openness to another must not be to-

15. McFadyen, *CP*, 63.
16. McFadyen, *CP*, 122.
17. McFadyen, *CP*, 116.
18. McFadyen, *CP*, by association; McFayden, "Truth as Mission," 47, directly.
19. McFadyen, *CP*, 59.
20. McFadyen, *CP*, 61.

tal because of possible overdetermining by the other. In purely sociological terms, the individual in our present world must never be completely open or closed to another. Theologically, however, the individual can potentially and safely offer complete openness within the relationship because of Christ's grounding and mediation of all undistorted relationality "not only between but also within the partners to a dialogical relation."[21] Because of common convention, however, McFadyen generally employs the language of interanimation (rather than tripartite dynamics), for example, "Christ *within* ourselves and the other." Within a perichoretic ontology, however, we can expand these dynamics of social interaction using *analogia spiritus* and Christ's constituting action, respectively. This will eventually deepen our understanding of how we maintain individuality while remaining open to appropriate change or transformation. This dialogical orientation of spirit and word facilitates and adjusts our social codes, interactional contexts and reasoning *appropriate to the immediate relationship*. The knowledge of good and evil, and truth (eschatologically), are not ours to project into the relationship. They must emerge anew contextually from within the whole of each unique interaction.[22] Therefore, we should come before another "as one who is not *wholly* determined by the initiating communication."[23]

Theologically, on the other hand, Christ calls us into ongoing recontextualization *only* through himself to others. Even through the distortion of another, Christ negotiates personal transformations and changes in meaning-frames. Though we retain basic relational structuring and historical sedimentation, their meaning and employment can never be ossified. Within the broader *theo*-sociological framework, relational *openness* should optimally be unconstrained. For if "there is no single, non-contextual definition of Christian Truth and . . . truth and meaning are to be found within the particularities of each context,"[24] then the individual must open to the possibility that ever new contexts might transform one's existing meaning-frame.[25] Though the predominance of our relations fall quickly within the specter of normal communitive and social action and codes, *epistemic*

21. McFadyen, *CP*, 59.
22. "Truth does not exist over and above particular location; who Jesus Christ is here and now [e.g.] has to be asked and worked out within the exigencies of the particular situation or context" (McFadyen, "Truth as Mission," 453).
23. McFadyen, *CP*, 119.
24. McFadyen, "Truth as Mission," 452.
25. This does not mean we never stand against the position of individuals or communities who personally and habitually overdetermined others, but "seventy-times-seven" that we openly enter the *call to relations* with them and ideally enter all interactions with an open response attitude.

humility is always necessary. McFadyen tells us that sin is the "absence of genuine communication."

> The basic sin is to lay our search for meaning to rest prematurely; to refer the finite only to itself and idolise it as infinite. "Nurtured in insecurity, sin's motivation is to secure, to anchor human being in a cosmos projected by itself, a creation of its own act of meaning or intentionality." . . . Sin, for an individual, is a distorted way of intending oneself, others and the world in communication which imbues one's limited being, one's personal space and time, with universal meaning.[26]

Therefore "*[in] view of the eschatological and universal nature of the kingdom, openness must be unrestricted.*"[27] For a more purely perichoretic expression of a relational ontology, this social dialogical continuum (open-closed scale) might be expanded within Kierkegaardian categories.

HUMAN SPIRIT AND HOLY SPIRIT

In McFadyen's theory, all undistorted communications base themselves on the universal dynamic of "Christ between us" (spirit and word). With the Spirit and Christ *between* us, full openness and closure are possible within each dialogical cycle. We can think of them as two distinct but interrelating continuums, representing modes of interaction within dialogical dynamics (prereflexive/infinitizing and reflexive/finitizing). Because of this inherent christological dynamic, the human condition is reflectively perichoretic (though distorted).

According to McFadyen's theory, all truth and meaning emerge within a specific and constantly changing context, so our givenness to change and potential transformation is ultimately necessary. This is made possible by the safeguarding "Christ between." Therefore, the call to personhood and genuine relationship necessitates the constant willingness to bear the cross, which always entails risk and the potential death or transformation of something within us. The alternative suppresses, consciously or unconsciously, personal presence due to hidden agendas or motivations.

Closure, on the other hand, is the reconstituting of the individual from their openness. The conceptual gestalt (word/response) reflexively anchors meaning within each moment of the interaction. These two modalities of

---

26. McFadyen, *CP*, 236; cf. Bultmann's notion of faith as openness to the future in *Theology of NT*, 1951–55.

27. McFadyen, *CP*, 248, emphasis added.

relationality cycle continually in alternation.[28] We become response-able (ethically responsive) to *the degree of openness* in which we enter the relationship (not the other) and, a differentiated person to *the degree of closure* based on the decisiveness of personal integration and action resulting from the interaction. The *willingness* to open to the Other reciprocatively affects the quality of closure and intensification of the self. One's initiating openness to the Other and the willingness to constitute as self in distinction to the world (to stand freely as an individual within one's social environment) represents the tandem variables that establishes the degree of fullness of life one experiences. The infinite and finite cycling variables must remain distinct within the relationship and response, but their irreducible synthesis within consciousness creates the christological complementarity of eternity and time. The quality of any relationship (self or social) is only as strong as its openness *and* closure.

Person as Opening in Dialogical Cycle: Person as Spirit Opening to the Parmenidean Absloute

Meaning *en totum* is dependent upon the prereflexive and reflexive aspect of response for each participant. Nevertheless, though all meaning must emerge from out of a prereflexive *moment* of awareness, "meaning is never purely subjective. The 'objectivity' (intersubjective validity) of meaning is present in individuals at a pre-conscious or pre-reflective level."[29] Related to our discussion on emotions and the process of awareness, each situation's incumbent contingencies prereflexively organize with our personal sedimented structures toward an ordered, intentional and conceptual response. For McFadyen, *how* we personally process these dynamics reflects our spirit of relating.

The leap from open awareness to conceptual response presents the paradoxical *moment* between spirit and word, spirit to word—Christ in and between us. To the extent our communication is undistorted and we are *fully present*, we experience a degree of fullness of life. It is here, between the prereflexive process of awareness and resulting constitution, according to McFadyen, that the Holy Spirit analogically and dynamically interacts with the human spirit, creating the ground for freedom and creativity.

---

28. Within the dialogical *kinesis* of relationship, Kierkegaard argues, "the development consists in moving away from oneself infinitely by the process of infinitizing oneself, and in returning to oneself infinitely by the process of finitizing" (*SUD*, 162–63).

29. McFadyen, *CP*, 96.

Because this is a "creative appeal," grace and faith are not subsumed under independent, rational human categories. God's communication creates the ontological possibility of freedom-in-response which includes the passive moment involved in understanding. The power of the Holy Spirit through which the transformation of faith occurs is not coercive in an heteronomous sense, but imploring, beguiling and perhaps even compulsive—but it is so internally: i.e. it appeals to, transforms, but does not destroy the identity and rationality structure of the person. A sign of this is actually the inherent ambiguity (apparently non-compulsive rationality) of God's communication. It does not take the form of logical, rational propositions but, *paradigmatically*, the crucifixion of the incarnate which, in appealing to human understanding, actually *transforms* the understanding contained in human predicates. So God's rule is not despotic because it creatively appeals to human rationality in a way which *allows people to participate through their own rational communication in that rule.*[30]

Here, McFadyen reflects the Jacobian night—a powerful description of *perichoresis* and *analogia spiritus*. This is the "passive" (prereflexive), holistic process of God's Spirit in analogical relation to the human spirit in a pre-"logical-rational" *de-liberational process* leading to gestalt and closure as person-in-relation. In addition to the Reformed emphasis of "descending ladders," McFadyen makes space for the possibility for ascension upon Jacob's ladder as well. This transformational de-liberation not only provides for our personal recontextualization but, as Loder suggests, the ability to "participate in the inner life of God" through our spirit's direct relation to the Holy Spirit (the absolute relating to the Absolute).[31] Again, this is Jacob's rock, the site of mutual co-conditioning that transcends Newtonian categories of time and space. This is the moment of eschatological fullness that not only pulls the future into our experience, but our true prayers, deepest longings, and fears (wrestling) into the Eternal de-liberation of God. A concluding section on human spirit will further consider how our relational disposition becomes closed in personal development, and what initiates the sanctifying process of openness within us. But first, let us first further articulate closure.

---

30. McFadyen, *CP*, 299n1, emphasis added.
31. Loder and Neidhardt, *KM*, 21.

Personhood as Closure: Co-constituting the Heraclitean Relative

The dialogical closure through Christ's call to personhood relativizes the finite contingencies of each situation in relation to the Eternal while Christ, who is also active within perichoretic dynamics, facilitates, adjudicates, and copacedically constitutes these relatives into personhood. Christ and the Spirit through the antecedent *analogia spiritus* facilitates this action that creates the appropriate meaning for each interaction, each happening within their own continuum of activity (perichoretically). One affects the eternal conditioning (the absolute, *analogia spiritus*) and the other the temporal conditioning (the relative, Christ). This same division of dynamics in intrapersonal *perichoresis* within the Trinity is reflected in John 5:19–30. The Spirit and Christ are transparently active in mediating the person's leap from the co-conditioning relations within the Eternal to Christ's conditioning our response (word) within the *moment* that is a hypothetico-deductive experience of *exaiphanes*, the sudden. This closure of standing in differentiation to the world in unique distinction is Christ's (and McFadyen's) call to personhood. This might sound contrary to Christendom's understanding of love, but it corrects it and expands it. Remember Bakhtin's admonition that the speaker "does not expect passive understanding that, so to speak, only duplicates his or her own idea in someone else's mind. . . . Rather, the speaker talks with an expectation of a response, agreement, sympathy, objection, execution, and so forth."[32] The deepest longing of the human heart is to relate as the Trinity relates—full unity (not uniformness) with the Other *while* experiencing the greatest intensification of one's own selfhood and that of the Other.

Broadly speaking, sin is the degree the self constitutes meaning prematurely or shortens desire, overdetermining the relationship rather than allowing appropriate meaning to fully emerge (constitute). Openness excludes nothing, "believes all things," "bears all things," and "rejoices in the truth" (1 Cor 13:6–7). In this respect, sin is both (1) the suppression or bifurcation of our personal and corporate lives, not allowing relevant information into one's personal consideration and constitution, shielding oneself from that transforming Power. Chronic repression or denial embeds within our relational style or cultural choreographies creating universal relational dispositions toward the Other. This preeminently decides good and evil before each encounter and overdetermines the Other assuming the purview of God. (2) Sin is also an unwillingness to fully act upon the truth we encounter in the world. Openness and response go hand-in-hand. Truth

---

32. Bakhtin, *Speech Genres*, 69, 91.

(or personhood) is never to be uncovered; it emerges from within the interaction. Heidegger, for example, was not suggesting the uncovering of truth (ἀλήθεια) as a universal knowledge outside of time (or even transtemporal) but an "uncovering" of the *fullness of the immediate interaction*, the *creation* of which we in large part tend to suppress. Like the Sermon on the Mount, this establishes a certain understanding of sin deep within us all, subconsciously as a disposition active and unavoidable within our development. Both of these are active components of love.

McFadyen acknowledges the universal existence of truth, however, such truth is only available "once the distortions and limitations of particularity are stripped away,"[33] and because "truth and meaning are to be found within the particularities of each context," there may be an indeterminate range of various understandings. Therefore, the truth is to be "worked out within the exigencies of the particular situation or context."[34] In this respect, the personal spirit of being for and intending of others throughout a variety of contexts and relations accomplish true continuity and identity *in* dialogical relations.[35] The form and pattern of the individual's spirit within relations ultimately shape this identity and continuity within personhood.

> So long as one's identity and communication here and now represent a continuity in the intending of oneself and others, then they are organised by and incarnate the same spirit which has structured personal centredness and external orientation in the past and *elsewhere*. It is constancy in one's spirit which determines personal constancy and integrity and which means that one's dependability for others may take a variety of forms.[36]

Though perfect undistorted interaction analogically reflects the relational dynamics of that Power that constitute it, our personal form and pattern of relating also texture and shape those interactions. Continuity of our personhood and relations, as well as truth and meaning, will not be *exact* repetitions or re-presentations of past conceptualizations but obtain in the continuity of spirit that organizes, collates, and creates relational authenticity as well as transformation.[37]

---

33. McFadyen, "Truth as Mission," 438.
34. McFadyen, "Truth as Mission," 452, 453.
35. McFadyen, *CP*, 152.
36. McFadyen, *CP*, 153–54, emphasis added.
37. In the chapter 5A, we will expand McFadyen's "elsewhere" to include one's future as well; i.e., a person's future attainment or near attainment as spirit has a definitive effect upon the organizing spirit and presence of the individual across time (bidirectionally)!

This aligns with Johannes Climacus's (Kierkegaard's) insistence that the "absolute must relate to the absolute ("telos") and the relative to the relative."[38] Paradoxically, through the Spirit and Christ, "existence is a synthesis of the infinite and the finite, and the existing individual is both infinite and finite,"[39] and furthermore, "it is impossible to *become* both at the same time."[40] Person as spirit in its infinite gaze creates the existential dilemma (conflict) that bears the weight of relational authenticity and resultant level of personal conviction. It is the pathos of the infinite gaze into the finiteness of the self. It is the infinitude of the human spirit's radical dependence in analogical relation to the infinite depths of the Spirit of God and subsequent incarnations of God's Word.[41] The degree and character of responsive awareness to the call generates the back*ground*, capacity, and creativity of response in relation to both the created (being) and uncreated (becoming) emergence of constituting in relation to an Eternal God. For Kierkegaard,

> In making a choice it is not so much a question of choosing the right as of the energy, the earnestness, the pathos with which one chooses. Thereby the personality announces its inner infinity, and thereby, in turn, the personality is consolidated. Therefore, even if a man were to choose the wrong, he will nevertheless discover, precisely by reason of the energy by which he chose, that he had chosen the wrong. For the choice being made with the whole inwardness of his personality, his nature is

---

38. For Kierkegaard: "Aesthetic pathos expresses itself in words, and may in its truth indicate that the individual leaves his real self in order to lose himself in the Idea; while existential pathos is present whenever the Idea is brought into relation with the existence of the individual so as to transform it. If in relating itself to the individual's existence the absolute *telos* fails to transform it absolutely, the relationship is not one of existential pathos, but of aesthetic pathos" (*CUP*, 347). "The pathos which adequately corresponds to an eternal happiness consists in the transformation by which everything in the existence of the individual is altered, in and through his mode of existence, so as to bring it into conformity with this highest good" (348).

39. Kierkegaard, *CUP*, 350.

40. Kierkegaard, *CUP*, 376.

41. In Platonic language, Noel O'Donoghue similarly notes: "Sharing then, participation (in the active sense) is, at the source, at once the sharing of infinite sharing, and the giving of an infinite capacity for receiving: *infinites meet in the finite*. The creature is no less infinite than the creator, in the infinity of its radical dependence, its radical nothingness: on this ground rests the infinity of its receptivity: *homo capax Dei*. The mystic makes his own of this negative immensity of openness to the infinite that shares its own being, and in this lived appropriation, experiences the logic of infinity, experiences that finitude reaching to the infinite which is the centre of all creativity as it is the centre of all prayer" (*Heaven in Ordinarie*, 177).

purified and he himself brought into immediate relation to the external Power whose omnipresence interpenetrates the whole of existence.[42]

Therefore, the degree and character of our openness contributes to the character of our closure and ultimately our level of conviction and passion within the interaction, resulting knowledge, or beliefs. To the degree our relational disposition diminishes our spirit from wholly relating with others (suppression), our convictions and fullness of life (passion) diminish.[43] Closure constituting personhood and our degree of fullness of life can only be as substantial as the personal lack of distortion within our relations. However, to the extent a person willingly and fully allows authentic relations, even within distorted choreographies, they become spirit and fully enter the relationship (*perichoresis*—grace). This does not necessitate complete self-disclosure, but that we allow the fullness of each interaction to appropriately affect the fullness of our life in that moment and context— Christ's perennial call to the cross that creates full personhood.

CONTINUITY IN PLURALITY, MCFADYEN AND MACINTYRE: TRUTH-CONDUCIVENESS AND THE *WAY* OF INTENDING THE OTHER IN CONTRAST TO EPISTEMOLOGICAL CONCEPTUAL COHERENCE (A MATTER OF *WHAT* IS PROMISED, JAMES 4–5)

Though the issues of postmodernity concern McFadyen, he is critical of Alistair MacIntyre's use of epistemological or conceptual coherence alone. As we have seen, MacIntyre depends heavily upon the negative and shortened criterion of epistemological coherence *for surviving* "epistemological crisis." This fails to forward any serious positive ontological theory of how we might contrast respective progress within disparate traditions. As previously discussed, the functional separation between the epistemological and the ontological places him in a precarious postmodern dilemma. McFadyen, however, claims that dialogical relations within undistorted communications

---

42. Kierkegaard, *EO2*, 141.

43. In the case of child abuse with its incumbent injunctions of secrecy, McFadyen believes "the information communicated in the abuse cannot be de-energized or dissipated, since it cannot be combined with that which is presently informing the structure of identity (pattern of relating to oneself and others), nor with information from contexts external to the abuse. . . . Who he understands himself to be[,] how he relates to himself, to others and the reality as a whole—all is knocked out of equilibrium" (McFadyen, "Healing," 95–96).

bare ontological force within the universal call of Christ. This call and structuring of *perichoresis* reflecting within all relations, as distorted as it might be, is the contingency missing in MacIntyre's philosophical accounting.[44] One might argue that MacIntyre's criteria is strictly philosophical and therefore unable to theorize theological dynamics. Nevertheless, McFadyen challenges the aptness of functionally reducing a tradition's (or individual's) episteme away from its holistic dynamics. Even Johannes and Anti-Climacus acknowledge an unnamed mediating Power within all interactions.

Philosophy is what one makes it and its criterion what one wishes to critically employ. Communicational theorist and nontheological thinker, John Shotter has found it necessary to institute a criterion of "social poetics" for communicational veridicality; social developmentalist and theist, Kenneth Gergen was dislodged from his agnosticism because of his perceived necessity for something of the "sacred" mediating a relational ontology.[45] On the other hand, MacIntyre chooses to negate such criteria of any kind and therefore falls back into the impotence of Modern agendas and strictures. McFadyen's criterion for ontological fitness ultimately lies not in epistemological coherence but *in* the quality of one's relations. Traditions and their epistemic structuring holistically embody a form and mode of life; there seems to be little disagreement on this. For McFadyen, an objective spirit and rational structuring will emerge within all well intended relations. However, functionally distilling epistemic structures from their holistic non-cognitive states to be carried over *as such* for daily consumption and application is dubious and dysfunctional. Continuity must emerge anew from within every new break of day.

MacIntyre's discussion of epistemic justification, as mentioned earlier, always takes place from a "point of view" of the individual or tradition, or the questionable "perspective outside the traditions." He assumes that all that is epistemically contingent and relevant is wholly contained *within* the "cognitive structure" or the "point of view" or "bird's eye" perspective within the consciousness of the individual or tradition, and he assumes its conscious transferability across time within the tradition. Meaning solely constitutes *in* persons and traditions that are relating rather than persons meaningfully constituting *from within* relations. This is due to his subject-subject ontology rather than subject-relationship-subject. This point may seem trite and unfair, inciting quick retorts that MacIntyre assumes as much within his relational dynamics; however, by implementing an epistemological argument he fails to implement contingencies that McFadyen successfully employs.

44. MacIntyre, "Epistemological Crises."
45. Personal discussion with Gergen, May 3–4, 2001.

Jacob and the Night of Faith

For physicist Michael Ovenden: "There is this complementary, so that the reality we seek lies neither in us nor in the world, but in the *relationships* between us and the world. It is the structure of relationships that is the transcendent thing."[46] Therefore, what calls us *beyond* ourselves cannot be ourselves or the other, but something between. Each call to other through the relationship with its transparent force reflecting *perichoresis* both within and between all things. Just as with personhood, *Spiritus Creator* never grounds the promise in epistemic knowledge for future remembrance or repetition within equations of coherence and continuity. Instead, the promise must always remain the condition of the "way one intends a relation with another." Re-membrance happens only when the absolute (spirit) relates to the Absolute (Spirit) recontextualizing the eternal meaning of the promise within constantly evolving and expanding contexts—*analogia spiritus*.

Therefore, when MacIntyre rightly argues that a tradition's epistemological development must exhibit "some fundamental continuity of the new conceptual and theological structures with the shared beliefs in terms of which the tradition of inquiry had been defined up to this point,"[47] McFadyen would wholeheartedly agree. He would insist, however, that we acknowledge inherent relational dynamics that make diachronic continuity and contrast possible.

Just to be clear, the following recites what is necessary to creates continuity. We can only associate the particulars (episteme) diachronically across each growth stage of a tradition if we analogically consider them each in irreducible relation to their respective synchronic meaning-frames. And yet, each meaning-frame must analogically contrast (both wholes) while we are *within* one of them and not in the other. How? MacIntyre ultimately proffers our undeveloped god-like "bird's eye" perspective. *Analogia spiritus*, however, creates the analogical contrasting of each meaning-frame with that of the other (a gift to be sure). Meaning-frames are the ever-changing denominator of the meaning-making equation in diachronic continuity and contrast. Meanings and *definitions* never remain the same, A_1 to A_2. The former A_1 of X_1 (X representing its entire meaning-frame) finds its continuity with later A_2 of X_2 from the mediation of our spirit with that of *Spiritus Creator*. A constituting dynamic of this nature *must* be outside meaning-frames.[48] In this respect, the "fundamental continuity," is *an irre-*

---

46. Michael Ovenden, cited by Oliver, *Relational Metaphysic*, 5.

47. MacIntyre, "Rationality of Traditions," 212–13.

48. This is consonant with T. F. Torrance's understanding that "Analogies are sets of relations which bear upon each other and point beyond themselves,... beyond the limits of empirical and observational knowledge" (*Convergence*, 230). He then cites James Clerk Maxwell, that "in a scientific point of view the *relation* is the most important thing to

ducible quality and function of the relationship itself, A1 of X1 to A2 of X2, the product of a universal mediating dynamic (Power) that creates relationship. The relations themselves are analogically and holistically related (the *how*), not just the episteme (the *what*). Therefore, if the relationship between A and X is what ultimately bears the weight of A's diachronic continuity, then continuity must be the constitutive function of the relationship itself, the Kierkegaardian *moment* and condition. Such an ontology must rely upon a universal dynamic of relationality holding all things together (a Trinitarian conspiracy).[49] These unacknowledged but identifiable dynamics enable MacIntyre's conceptual continuity, coherence, and judgments of progress despite his philosophical restrictions and acknowledgement otherwise.

In this respect, both MacIntyre (with Murphy, Thiemann, Lindbeck, etc.) employing cryptic unacknowledged criteria of adjudication between what seems to them incommensurable traditions, and French Poststructuralists,[50] for whom no commensurate shared meaning occurs within communications, continue to flounder under the shadow of modern metaphysics that employ a subject-subject understanding of interactions. If no ontological consideration is given to the relationship itself, you necessarily fall back into the shadow of *analogia entis*, in which all things similar mutually relate within an existing universal frame of reference whether one refuses to acknowledge the whole game board or not. Again, relational ontologies that *move* and are living (subject-relationship-subject), like those of Marion, MacFadyen, Loder, Gunton et al., have begun to expose a *universal dynamic of relationality* through which all things different mutually and meaningfully relate (*analogia spiritus-perichoresis*).

---

know" (230), and: "The similarity which constitutes the analogy is not between the phenomena themselves, but between the relations of these phenomena." (240n60).

49. Cf. Kierkegaard, *CUP*, 358: "In the moment of resignation, of deliberation, of choice, the individual is assumed to respect the principle of resignation—but afterwards comes the time for mediation. . . . [But] mediation proves that the individual has never rightly been oriented with respect to the absolute *telos*."

50. French Poststructuralism's modern intellectual indulgence ended the day Derrida conceded to Marion that he could live with a metaphysics that was in *motion* and not static (the pragmatic death, tragically signaled in June 1984 San Francisco). The last gasp of Modernity's struggling existence was realized in its refusal to explore further into the ontological soundings and phenomenon of spirit. N.b., Derrida spent the last decade of his academic life searching the theories of Kierkegaard (from personal conversation with Carl Raschke, 2017), a pneumatologist who was, according to Gadamer, the first to introduce the concept of the *moment*, the *metabole*.

EMPIRICAL VERACITY OF THE OPEN-CLOSED CYCLE OF DIALOGICAL RELATIONS

If all undistorted relations dialogically constitute in complementary relation to the Trinity through the *analogia spiritus* and the creative activity of Christ, then the criterion of progress should not only be possible but *holistically* evidential. MacIntyre concludes we can evidence the meaningful progress and enrichment despite the issues of diachronic discontinuity; however, he fails to effectively explain what constitutes progress, furthermore whose concept of progress. His purpose in *Whose Justice? Which Rationality?* is to refute the relativist claim, but the nature of this "fundamental continuity" remains phantom.

Are those of a primitivist sect encountering modern Western culture irresistibly drawn to it because of its greater epistemological coherence? Do they stop to adjudicate each tradition's internal coherence? Or, as McFadyen argues, the call inseparably encompasses the intellect and the heart, the epistemic and the whole (spirit); despite each tradition's respective and comparable internal coherence (ultimately only a useful abstraction), the immediate call has "no presupposition but itself," the principal criterion is simply greater fullness of life, which includes an ontologically clothed use of coherence.[51] "Everything has its context, and the context always makes a difference.... [However,] individual existence (*ex histēmi*, literally 'standing out'), by definition, involves some form of contrast with and independence from context."[52] Within this complementarity of self and social de-liberation, we must consider that such a criterion of fullness of life is ultimately, yet holistically, evidential.

Atheists/agnostics like Shotter and formerly Gergen fully acknowledge the necessity of it and do not shrink from expanding their purview when necessary. In this respect, McFadyen presents a Christian notion of a universal dynamic within our communications that ultimately present falsifiable claims. He notably provides them in his notion of dialogical openness and closure, which likewise presents ethical claims.[53] MacIntyre limits us to a conceptual factor (a negative criterion within epistemic crisis); McFadyen offers us a dialogical dynamic with positive characteristics incumbent in the whole of universal human existence—meaning*fullness*-in-relation.

---

51. McFadyen, *CP*, 49.

52. McFadyen, *CP*, 48, 280n1.

53. McFadyen, *CP*, chapter 5, dealing with "personal integrity: centredness and orientation on others," and, chapter 6, "ethical resistance: testing the validity of disagreements."

CONCLUSION: MCFADYEN'S SIGNIFICANCE

The significance of McFadyen's social theory for this study is manifold: (1) Acknowledgment of a universal dynamic within all undistorted communications. (2) The alternating dialogical cycling of openness and closure within communications that maintains Kierkegaard's necessary separation of the finite and infinite relational modalities (IQD). (3) The importance of the openness cycle in human-divine interaction. (4) The importance of the closure cycle in obtaining personhood in response to Christ's call. And finally, (5) the necessity of right relationship for truth and the emergence of truth from within each context (re-petition), rather than repeating cognitive impositions upon changing contexts. All of these reflect aspects of *perichoresis*, and some of them mutually extrapolate in relation to perichoretic dynamics. They certainly parallel and help frame many of Kierkegaard's original theories.

To the degree one's spirit is "unrestricted"[54] (undistorted) in relation to the Other, God's Spirit makes its "creative appeal"[55] within this "passive moment involved in understanding."[56] What transpires within this transparent interaction and how it processes through each *moment* into gestalt is central. In the next section on James Loder and Kierkegaard, we will explore further the theological and transformational dynamics active within this passivity. The Jacobian *moment*, however, is the *metabole* (*exaiphanes*), the "suddenly," in which humanity is called into the co-conditioning ascension and descension of analogical relation to the Eternal.

From the perichoretic point of view, openness might be considered one continuum and closure another continuum. One crucial aspect of the prereflexive cycle of openness is that it signals the degree in which we constitute in distinction to it (the world). These distinctions seem paradoxical within antiquated ontologies. For Johannes Climacus (Kierkegaard), it is rationally absurd and ultimately incoherent to consider that the Eternal and time interrelate, furthermore that God becoming human accomplishes this paradoxical relation. And though this Christian notion of the Incarnation is offensive, we reveal our openness or closure in all relations if we prioritize our personal theories and critical demands for understanding against the *possibility* (not the belief) of the offense were it *possible* to understand. In other words, if we decide within our current capacity that the offense is impossible because we currently cannot understand how, then we partially

---

54. McFadyen, *CP*, 248.
55. McFadyen, *CP*, 116.
56. McFadyen, *CP*, 299n1.

close to the fullness of the Other. My concern here is the *willingness* to believe, not the belief itself. The issue of evidence, context, personal history, and existing beliefs are important but those are ultimately issues of the "relative relating to the relative," secondary deliberations. McFadyen starts with that which has no "presupposition," paralleling Kierkegaard's "absolute relating to the Absolute." Concerning the matter of *willingness*, "it is necessary," says Kierkegaard, "to risk everything, to invest absolutely everything in the venture."[57] On the other hand, we may be extremely proficient at entering the other's world and thinking within it, indwelling it (accommodation), yet flee from becoming a self, or taking responsible action within the world (assimilation) and, as McFadyen concludes, "standing out."[58]

To the degree we venture all into the fullness of the relationship (love), we can hold our convictions with an infinite passion (faith) within each response occurrence. For Kierkegaard, Abraham is the perfect "knight of faith"[59] whose encounter with God transforms him and conditions his faith by which he decisively defies the existing reasoning and morality of his world, in faith, through Christ. Jacob, on the other hand, defies the existing reasoning, morality, *and God* of his world and experiences a co-conditioning encounter, in faith, with Christ. Jacob is not only recontextualized by the divine call but recontextualizes God through the transparent activity of Spirit and Christ in which both he and God genuinely affect *each other*. Through perichoretic encounter prior to the light of consciousness, within the dynamic singularity of the Eternal, Jacob deeply affects God the same time God deeply affects him. Upon this rock, *analogia spiritus*, humanity obtains to mutual co-conditioning and finally to filial relations with a trinitarian God. The transforming nature of faith emerges in both Abraham and Jacob (in accommodation and assimilation respectively), but only Jacob's name is completely changed, only Jacob obtains filial status according to God's nature of *perichoresis. His* name alone becomes the name of a nation, not Abraham. Israel, he who wrestles with God, was the first to completely "stand out" from all "authorities and powers" as he and authorities and powers are transformed in a moment of full *co*-conditioning *perichoresis* with God. This has nothing whatsoever to do with the esoteric understanding of Jacob within the mystery religions. Jacob, even in his wrestling with what I believe to be Jesus Christ within the *moment* of *analogia spiritus*, never withdraws his infinite resignation to God with whom he wrestles. He passionately seeks a new relationship with God and pulls a new level of grace

---

57. Kierkegaard, *CUP*, 362.
58. McFadyen, *CP*, 48.
59. Kierkegaard, *FT*, 81–91.

(relations) from the future into the present, as all are called to do, from one degree to another, as we transform into his image through *analogia spiritus* (John 17:21; 2 Cor 3:18). This is why we are secretly drawn to the anti-heroes more than the heroes. Both fight for righteousness, but the anti-heroes expand their arsenal beyond the existing rules and ethical context. They know what exists is provisional and they want more (Epistle of Hebrews). This is why the biblical annals of the faithful are filled with those who lived outside the social and cultic norms (often in "sin"), and when they heard God's word they often contested it. This cannot happen without coming "unrestricted" to the Other (the Eternal) and then seeking to "stand out" in personhood (in time).

In a Christian social theory, McFadyen offers us a universal dynamic active within our communicative structures that creates and defines right relationships reflecting that of the Trinity (love). In the infinite possibilities of relational occurrences and responses, his dialogical structuring offers dynamics that reflect *analogia spiritus*, that allows truth and reason to emerge appropriately within each relational context. In the perichoretic confluencing of all infinite relevant factors: contextual communicative norms and codes, each participant's historic sedimentation and relational dispositions, the constant immanent transcendent call to personhood, the stirring caldron of longings and disappointments, and the wrestling confluence of diverse intentions and wills, not least the will of God, all enter the dance of spirits while in each *moment*, he who defines love, lovingly creates in perfect relation to the Eternal. This is McFadyen's Call to Personhood, the shape of love that provides another iteration of *perichoresis* emerging within the world, one that continues to emerge within an expanding Kingdom, even in its infancy (1 Cor 15:25; Heb 8:13; 10:12–13). It is a call that creates truth from *within* each interactive *moment* for a pluralistic world.

3C

Perichoresis as Persons
Loder, Piaget, and Kierkegaard

> "[Physics] now recognizes that, for an interaction to be real, the 'nature' of the related things must derive from these relations, while at the same time the relations must derive from the 'nature' of the things." That is a statement of created, analogous, *perichoresis*. Everything in the universe is what it is by virtue of its relatedness to everything else.
>
> COLIN GUNTON[1]

INTRODUCTION

The primary goal of this section is to explore the perichoretic understanding of relational dynamics in human development through James Loder, Jean Piaget, and Søren Kierkegaard. Within Loder's developmental theory, transformational dynamics will be of special interest, as well as the importance given to the question of ultimate meaning, especially why and how humans develop. We will then compare human development's essential characteristics with his christology and the theological development of *perichoresis* in trinitarian dynamics. The fundamental questions of how and precisely why human life develops the way it does remain empirically inconclusive. To the extent we can find any correlation between the theoretical relational

---

1. Gunton, *One, Three, Many*, 172. Gunton cites Prigogine and Stengers, *Order Out of Chaos*.

dynamics of the divine and human should further our understanding of divine-human mutuality, which might enrich our understanding of ultimate meaning in human existence. The following is the primary anthropological hypothesis of this section, which will develop as we progress.

> Each stage of human development is conditioned by the previous stage, yet the ultimate meaning within each stage emerges from the quality of the differentiated unity[2] it experiences in relations. In transformational moments, future stages condition the present in a co-conditioning process that happens within a person's prereflexive holistic dynamics within the third term of the relationship. The Power that *co-ordinates*[3] all relations and transforms personal transformational dynamics constitutes all interactions in relation to the Eternal.

How the future conditions the present within the transformational *moment*, reconfiguring our past, present, and future within such kairotic moments happens instantaneously. In such moments persons, as whole spirit (in passion), come into relation with the Eternal through the *analogia spiritus*. Each chapter within this thesis attempts to provide dynamical insights for understanding how time and Eternity enigmatically relate, and reciprocally, a complete understanding of each of these chapters depends upon our understanding our penultimate chapter, the *perichoresis* of time and Eternity. To better understand the effect of the Eternal within human development, we must constantly remember the ever-present two-way nature of Christ and the Spirit within their intratrinitarian temporal and Eternal relations.[4]

---

2. Quality, as such, is the degree of differentiation attained from the *umwelt* in coordination with its relational re-integration. Developmentalist Robert Kegan thinks each new stage of equilibrium accomplishes this through an "evolution of a reduced subject and a greater object for the subject to take, an evolution of lesser subjectivity and greater objectivity, an evolution that is more 'truthful'" (Kegan, *Evolving Self*, 294). The quality, therefore, has to do with the doxastic nature and structure of the reintegration in accordance with that of the whole.

3. "*Co-ordinate*" is not to be understood in the Thomistic manner of paralleling primary and secondary causations so that agency or temporal linear causality (human or divine) precipitate the final effect. Within the theory of *perichoresis, this co-ordinating* and adjudicating process reflects a co-conditioning action within the relationship and its participants. Each passionate entrance into relations (the attainment of spirit) prereflexively proffers their whole self into the transforming matrix that sustains and creates the interaction. The desires and actions emerge within the individual "naturally" and from seemingly nowhere, but they emerge effectively co-ordinated alongside *all* other persons *wholly* relating throughout time. This necessitates a co-ordinating action of the Spirit and Christ in de-liberating all creation.

4. Torrance notes that "Athanasius reminds us that in his incarnation the Son of God had a twofold ministry to fulfil. He was sent both to minister the things of God

RELATIONALITY (NOT REASON) AS THE INTELLIGIBLE ORDER OF REALITY

In *The Knight's Move: The Relational Logic of the Spirit in Theology and Science*, James Loder and Jim Neidhardt[5] contrast the relational logic inherent within human developmental psychology with the development of knowledge in science and theology.[6] They posit a generic concept of spirit in which "spirit refers to *a quality of relationality*, and it is a way to conceptualize the dynamic interactive unity by which two disparate things are held together without loss of their diversity." Spirit, in this generic sense, is a "dynamic interactive unity," an irreducible relationality that forms and maintains relationships between things. However, they wish to distinguish themselves from the many dualisms that vitiate scientific and theological thinking and seek a dynamic relationality that constitutes social relations and personhood as a differentiated unity. They often use the Kierkegaardian/Hegelian contrast to illustrate this distinction.

The study's methodology considers all relationality as analogically reflecting the nature of Jesus Christ. Thus the dynamic relatedness within the christological complementarity of Christ as fully human *and* fully God ultimately defines all expressions of personal, social, and cultural relatedness. To this end, the study attempts to reveal "that a wide diversity of contexts may be illuminated as inherently relational and pointing toward the ultimate relationality revealed in Christ's nature."[7]

Prefacing Theological Statement: Awareness and Gestalt in Theology and Human Intelligence

Loder begins by prefacing the theological point of both Calvin's and Luther's imperative on the Holy Spirit. Calvin states, "Until our minds are intent on

---

to man and to minister the things of man to God" (*Transformation and Convergence*, 344).

5. James Loder was the Mary D. Synnott Professor of the Philosophy of Christian Education at Princeton Theological Seminary (Harvard PhD in Human Developmental Psychology), and Jim Neidhardt, Associate Professor of Physics at the New Jersey Institute of Technology.

6. Due to the primary interest of this thesis, Loder's human developmental and theological thinking, I will usually note the author as only Loder for brevity. Nevertheless, Jim Neidhardt played a significant role in the sections on science.

7. Loder, *TM*, 13. Loder points to the modifications and enrichment of Barth's "natural" theology as developed by T. F. Torrance in *Transformation and Convergence* and *Ground and Grammar*.

the Spirit, Christ is in a manner unemployed because we view him coldly without ourselves and so at a distance from us (*Institutes* III.i.3)."[8] This refers to the "inner witness" of the Spirit, which is necessary for "contemporaneousness" between oneself and Christ as *the Word* to which the Scriptures witness. When divine and human spirits interact, there is "a comprehensive inner consistency, across discontinuous events and times," which relativize disparate events. In other words, in the language of this present thesis, it allows various events to emerge in direct relation to each other, relating across space, time, and between individual minds and cultures. Ultimately, we will consider this relation as dynamically ontological in nature. Loder believes Calvin's returning to the early church fathers broke the medieval synthesis and Greek notions of space and time, thus returning to the notion of the "Spirit of Christ as transcending and traversing the boundaries of space and time."[9]

This notion of spirit eventually provides an understanding of relationality that would later emerge in the human sciences and the theories of, for example, Michael Polanyi, Douglas Hofstadter, and various aspects of Gestalt psychology. The latter focuses on the relationship between figure and ground in which figure-ground reversal (e.g., the familiar duck-rabbit image) is divided by a transitional moment in which you never *see* both interpretation at the same time, and the reversal takes place in a *moment* that Loder calls the "blind spot." He argues that this displays the "mind's inveterate self-relationality"[10] and the phenomenon of relating itself to itself—the ability to intentionally draw a *focal* (conceptual) perspective out of the *whole* of experience (awareness). Unique to human gestalt and self-relationality is the power to *wholly reconstitute*, which necessitates a "blind-spot." This shift

---

8. Loder and Neidhardt, *KM*, 27.

9. Loder and Neidhardt, *KM*, 27. Cf. also Niebuhr, *Christ and Culture*, and the forthcoming chapter 6. Niebuhr notes that for Luther, the Spirit brings Christ and culture into a paradox; for Calvin, the Spirit makes Christ the transformer of culture. Loder focuses on Calvin's distinction of the Spirit as the "transforming and unifying link between Christ and all creation, including the human creation of culture... [that] allows the Son of God in his incarnation to descend from heaven without leaving heaven, and so the unity of Christ is not reduced by any descendants of Hellenic dualism or compromised by any receptacle notions of space" (28). These distinctions between Calvin's transformative and Luther's paradoxical notions of the relationship analogously relate to complementary themes within our earlier methodological discussion: Calvin's transformative perspective focusing upon culture's conceptual transformation from "one degree to another" through its relation to Christ and, in complementarity, Luther's notion of the Spirit's role in maintaining the paradoxical eschatological embeddedness of Christ's Time within chronological time. We will return to this theme in the concluding chapter.

10. Loder, *KM*, 39.

in self-relation (figure-ground reversal) only happens when we holistically throw ourselves into a prereflexive moment that allows for the new gestalt shift. This "leap" is necessary because of the holistic nature of this shift in our awareness. Anything less than a *whole* shift in our capacity to self-reflect or reconstitute would render us unrelatable, albeit analogically, to God's Eternal and infinite nature. For Hofstadter,

> The explanations of "emergent" phenomena in our brains—for instance, ideas, hopes, images, analogies, and finally consciousness and free will—are based on a kind of Strange Loop, an interaction between levels in which the top level reaches back down toward the bottom level and influences it, while at the same time being itself determined by the bottom level. . . . *The self comes into being the moment it has power to reflect itself.*[11]

The moment the mind produces theory in focal response, the self designates itself as form within ground.

This is consonant with Polanyi's understanding of awareness, whereby he describes "personal knowledge" as a bipolar-relational unity in which the focal aspect of consciousness exhibits "marginal control" in its producing insight out of the "tacit dimension."[12] We can roughly equate tacit awareness with the activity of prereflexion within this thesis (as well as right hemispheric activity neurologically). When Polanyi says, "we know more than we can tell," he notes that tacit awareness explicitly inhabits and conditions our focal and conceptual experience and meaning. Ultimately, they are inseparable; we need both to have either. Although Hofstadter attempts to reduce the gestalt within its bipolarity (e.g., as *only* the sum of the sole incumbent properties of the poles), Loder, with Polanyi, maintains the irreducibility of the differentiated-unity in human dynamic. Moreover, they claim that "*relationship*, not either polarity alone, is the vital center of human existence."[13] In this respect, "no conceptual order or linguistic expression, however sophisticated, can grasp the agent of its formulation."[14] The forming matrix of the relational unity becomes a greater whole (experiential) through which individuals co-condition and constitute persons-in-relation. Enlisting John Polkinghorne, Loder thinks "the intelligible order of reality is not in the mind, as Kant thought, or in nature, as Newton thought, but it resides in the relationship between the mind and nature."[15] At this point, Pannenberg's

---

11. Hofstadter, *Gödel*, 709, emphasis added.
12. Polanyi, *Knowing and Being*.
13. Loder, *KM*, 42.
14. Loder, *KM*, 42.
15. Loder, *KM*, 43.

"neo-Hegelian proclivities which tend to equate truth and history, human spirit and Holy Spirit"[16] stand in stark contrast to Tillich and Barth's notion of two-spirit differentiated unity. Loder is emphatic about an irreducible relational (spiritual) dynamic that creates the relationship as a third term, in which the participants "indwell," and which sustains their individuality.[17] This is the basic logic of spirit. Within the relationship emerges *more* than the sum total of constituent individuals and parts; likewise, each person within the relationship becomes more than self. Therefore, Loder affirms a relationality between human spirit and God's Spirit in which "the Spirit Himself bearing witness with our spirit" analogically *expands and kinetically grounds* the human configurative process.[18] This provides the ground and dynamic through which the focal gestalt emerges meaningfully out of one's emerging and dynamic tacit awareness from within the relationship. "It is here that one sees and participates in 'what eye has not seen and ear has not heard,'" as "the self-relational essence of the human spirit and its capacity to draw upon the tacit dimensions of human existence are" analogically drawn into relation with God's trinitarian activity.[19] This dynamic is the heart of Barthian dialectics in which the person constitutes as a contingent differentiated unity.[20]

Loder and Neidhardt, unlike others, do not rely on bipolar models of symmetrical reciprocity. Instead, utilizing "gentle hierarchies," they adopt Polanyi and Niels Bohr's concept of asymmetrical complementarities that

---

16. Loder, *KM*, 305.

17. One of Gunton's primary theses in *One, Three, Many*.

18. Rom 8:16; cf. also 1 Cor 2. Loder also notes that *analogia spiritus* and its quality of relations is the corresponding site of wisdom (*phronesis*).

19. Loder, *KM*, 49, 47.

20. Barth tells us, "The work of the Holy Spirit, however, is to bring and to hold together that which is different and therefore, as it would seem, necessarily and irresistibly disruptive in the relationship of Jesus Christ to His community, namely, the divine working, being, and action on the one side and the human on the other, the creative freedom and act on one side and the creaturely on the other, the eternal reality and possibility on one side and the temporal on the other. His work is to bring and to hold them together, not to identify, intermingle nor confound them, not to change the one into the other nor to merge the one into the other, but to co-ordinate them, to make them parallel, to bring them into harmony and therefore to bind them into a true unity" (*CD* 4/3:761). The point is differentiated unity. Though Barth rightfully acknowledges this work as that of the Spirit, he fails or refuses to articulate the notion of *analogia spiritus* as a prereflexive divine-human interaction in which the desires and contingencies of a person potentially draw into the holistic Kierkegaardian *moment* (the eternal) during human dialogical interaction affectively co-conditioning ("intermingling") human desire with the divine Eternal action of God through God's Spirit (the move of Jacob). Nevertheless, from prereflexion all constitute as differentiated persons in unity.

exhibit *marginal control* in one aspect of the polarity (e.g., "wave" attributes over "particle"). This presents

> a condition in which the bipolar structure's "lower" level is controlled not only by the laws governing its constituent components but also by being subject through its boundary conditions to determination by the laws regulating the "higher" level. In other words, the "lower" level is subject to dual control by the laws applying to its component particulars in themselves and by the specific laws that govern the comprehensive entity, i.e., the "higher" level, formed by them.[21]

This supervenient activity does not necessitate that the higher-level activity swallows up the free or "autonomous" action of lower-level activity. In the penultimate chapter, we will consider how God as love incorporates the unique dynamics and *perichoresis* of time and Eternity into the structure of creation, thereby co-conditionally incorporating all undistorted (genuine) human dialogical activity into God's Eternal de-liberation. This facilitates the free activity of lower-level contingencies that emerge in integrative relation (perichoretically) with that of the higher Eternal and asymmetrically preeminent level of activity within the Trinity. In other words, Jacob literally, not figuratively, wins *against* God's action were it not otherwise contested.

QUANTUM COMPLEMENTARITY AND THE NATURE OF PERICHORESIS

Theoretical physicist Niels Bohr presents an understanding of relationality he refers to as "complementarity" to explain the quantum world. Loder and Neidhardt contrast this notion of "complementarity" with Kierkegaard's parallel understanding of the Absolute Paradox, the Chalcedonian christology, and Polanyi's concept of personal knowledge. Using Bohr's concept of complementarity in contrast with christology, they define various attributes of relationality (reality) that constitute "unity of being."[22] In this respect, *all* reality (*hypostasis*) constitutes as a differentiated unity. Christopher Kaiser draws the following attributes from Bohr's scientific understanding and associates them with christology. I will use these to highlight features of perichoretic relationality essential to this thesis. Nevertheless, though their ideas are valuable, I wish to alter and update them in our later chapter on quantum dynamics.

---

21. Loder, *KM*, 55.

22. They base this upon Christopher Kaiser's (*Logic of Complementarity*) interpretation of Bohr's understanding of complementarity.

(1) Coexhaustiveness and Mutual Exclusiveness

The two modes of a quantum event (wave and particle) are *coexhaustive*. Each account for all known aspects of the event in such a way that describes it *en totum* as wave or particle, yet each is *mutually exclusive*. They are operationally defined in incompatible ways. In christology, Jesus Christ is *coexhaustively* "God" and "human"; yet, in *mutual exclusiveness*, "the two essences, man and God, coexist and coinhere but they do not become confused or mix."[23]

This account, within the triadic notion of perichoretic relations, suggests that each person or entity retains their selfhood while they holistically reconstitute relative to each one's respective character, development, and capacities (i.e., analogically share meaning). Likewise, if all reality constitutes through such a complementarity, we might expect the fundamental desire in life would be to constitute in like manner, as individual-in-relation-to-the-whole (in love or perichoretically).

(2) Common and Conjugate Properties

Each mode contains *common* properties. For example, each has an electrical charge or angular momentum ("spin") and associating *conjugate* properties. For example, the mode of explanation for a particle is spacetime location; for a wave, a momentum-energy vector. Jesus Christ as human and God bears the *common* properties of life and personal quality of existence, yet *conjugate* properties like "a visible particularity and temporality" distinct from an "invisible universality and eternity."

The dynamic of *perichoresis* likewise constitutes an *existential*, not *material*, synthesis creating common and yet conjugate properties within the relationship itself. According to each participant's nature and existing relational configurations, *common* and *conjugate* properties will manifest meaningfully for each within the relationship. In other words, a conjugate attribute of the divine (whole and Eternal) and human (particular and temporal) is evident in human beings as *imago Dei*, and reciprocally the Trinity in the Word become flesh/human. This creates the necessary ontological framework in each for mutual relations and reflects the dialogical distinctions (cycles) previously discussed in the section on McFadyen and Kierkegaard. These distinctions (prereflexive and reflexive, experience and concept, tacit and focal) never dissolve into each other but co-condition each other in the *moment* of transition between the two. This dynamic, for

---

23. Loder, *KM*, 85.

Kierkegaard, ultimately enables authentic interaction in contrast to the ambivalence in mediation within traditional dualistic structures.

(3) Coinherence and Reciprocity

The modes of explanation are *coinherent* and can be described in terms of the other, yet, they do not explicitly contain the properties of the other. We might describe them as the wave being "in" the particle and vice versa. They are *reciprocal* in that they evolve in "alternation" as wave collapses into particle and particle expands back into wave. This christologically creates a *coinherence* of the divine aspects of Logos to the flesh of Jesus, and vice versa. Here the notion of *enanthropesis* (inhominization) of God-the-Word and its reciprocal *theosis* (deification) of the flesh are noted.

Perichoretically, each entity and aspect within the relationship remains distinct yet conditions the Other. Therefore, dynamic activity inherent in God would also be manifest in some way within human existence and vice versa, thus, creating relational (even filial) mutuality. In addition, we might expect progressive harmonization through evolving interaction (redemptive process). Therefore, a relational ontology contains an active inveterate relational dynamic in all relations from which greater and more interrelated order might continue to emerge through time and chaos (fluctuation). Through repeating alternations of coinherence and reciprocity, creation emerges in ever greater freedom, distinction, and particularization, *as well as* increasing synchronicity and harmony, producing ever greater degrees of meaning and intimacy.[24] However, for this fundamental dynamic quality to remain active within creation *itself*, we might consider it necessary that each stage of an organism's development emerges freely and with self-agency through co-conditioning dynamics from out of chaos in order that the emerging organizational locus within creatures maintains its *self* as organism-in-relation-to-the-cosmos. Evolving creation, whether biological,

---

24. In his 1997 Gifford Lectures, Holmes Rolston III revealed gene theory dynamics similar to *perichoresis*. In contrast to the lone fundamental enmity quality of gene relations that Dawkins presents, Rolston presents the sharing nature of genes, aspiring relational integration, and "fit-ness" within the world as the dominant relational nature of genes in tension with their self-preservation tendencies. This fundamental dynamic provides for both gene qualities, entity status, and identity *with* internal motivations toward complex algorithmic interrelations. Rolston provides evidence that genes exhibit drives far greater than just their single or collective drive for physical survival—a complementarity that also moves into ever-developing greater interrelating economies with more pervasive interactive centers of action (eventually consciousnesses), i.e., together toward what I would term greater fullness of life. Thus, the driver of biological evolution is the immanent transcendent force of *perichoresis*.

cultural, or personal, *must contain* an alternation of modes within its developmental nature in order for *itself* to be part of an *interrelated whole*.

(4) Completeness and Equal Necessity

Each mode of explanation is *complete* in itself, not half-particle and half-wave, "nor is it an ambiguous reality."[25] Concurrently, each mode is *equally necessary* for an exhaustive accounting of the whole. "*Completeness* in the complementarity pattern is satisfied by the Chalcedonian statement, "perfect man," "perfect God"; Jesus, is necessarily *both* God *and* human."[26]

Within personal and social *perichoresis*, this necessitates an ongoing instantiating character within each gestalt. Again, the quality of gestalt results from the degree of openness and degree the self enters the prereflexive process of awareness within relations (Kierkegaard's notion of passion and truth).[27] At the same time, each gestalt (conceptualization) is a complete (finite) rendering of reality within the moment, which draws out from the tacit whole (infinite).

(5) Asymmetry and Pointing

Both modes relate *asymmetrically*, providing emergent properties within the quantum event. The higher mode (wave) accounts for the event's stability in a way that the lower mode (particle) cannot. "Thus the modes, existing as they do on separate levels, allow for higher mode explanations of implicit lower-mode phenomena not otherwise accounted for."[28] From the other side of the asymmetrical relationship, "there is a pointing relationship which allows lower-mode explanations to *point* to emergent higher-level accounts." This latter intuitive presence of the higher mode "pointing" within the lower "may almost be said to follow the rule of metaphor."

Loder and Neidhardt note Kaiser as one of the few interpreters of Bohr's notion of complementarity who emphasize the notion of asymmetry and marginal control. It would follow that such an attribute would necessitate an open awareness into the relationship simply because our perception

---

25. Loder, *KM*, 79.
26. Loder, *KM*, 85.
27. Cf. Moltmann, *SL*, 211, "... whenever we are wholly there, undividedly present."
28. Loder, *KM*, 79. Kaiser, *Logic of Complementarity*, 46, specifically sees "different 'levels' of being in matter . . . and Christology, [which account for] an 'emergence' of 'higher' qualities due to the underlying qualitative asymmetry between the two modes of being."

always "points" beyond the conceptually explicit.[29] Therefore, though these attributes are descriptive, the whole of what entails the quantum event is always greater, "hence, causality in the classical sequential sense is denied as a universal principle" and the unity behind complementarity "generalizes the *meaning* of causality."[30]

The *asymmetrical* relation that constitutes Christ accounts for the transcendental qualities within his human nature (the full qualitative engagement of *analogia spiritus*), and the full grounding of his heuristic and relational activity in his life *point* toward his divinity. The lower mode, however, is only meaningful in its direct, nonetheless implicit relation to the higher ground *within it*; in other words, there is no *completely authentic* human nature or relations without an analogous relation to the divine.

Therefore, when a less relationally developed culture or tradition comes into active contact with another more developed than itself (e.g., a Copernican into a Newtonian meaning-frame), it will *not* be able to *fully* experience its meaning or understand its heuristic fullness. If, however, those in the lower meaning-frame are completely open to the more developed group, it may be possible to *sense*, not articulate, the higher system's fullness of life and greater meaning within *their lower implicit* mode of thinking (similar to the phenomenon of Pentecost). Likewise, a person from a higher paradigmatic level of thinking reading an author from a lower-level culture might be able to determine aspects, intentions, and qualities unseen by that author within his lower-level expressions that the author could not articulate. *Analogia spiritus* (the logic of *spirit*) interanimates the complementarity within christology and, to some degree, all undistorted human relationality in which all is effectively ventured.

The truth and rightness of a relationship will come from within it as a living, and existential experience. According to Loder, because relations constitute within an asymmetric complementarity, prioritizing the holistic (spirit) over the particular (word), and prereflexively as spirit-to-spirit, meaning emerges appropriately for each participant through the transparent mediating dynamics of God's Spirit and Christ.[31]

---

29. McGilchrist's (*Master*) research also corroborates these conclusions within the bicameral brain.

30. Loder, *KM*, 80. This observation by Kaiser expresses what goes unseen by Nick Herbert in *Quantum Reality*, who assumes that Bohr's relational reality *determines* the complementarity *within* the immediate context and locality of the event, observer, and measuring device (229), which Bell's theorem now denies. However, because complementarity is asymmetrical, Bell's theorem, which implies non-locality and the interconnectedness of every quantum event *across spacetime*, easily assimilates into Bohr's notion of complementarity.

31. Though physics has been a methodologically bottom-up science historically,

The discriminating factor within this open relatedness is the relationship between human spirit and divine Spirit. As McFadyen and Loder might agree, it is the groundedness of the individual or community's interactional dynamism in Christ that creates the form and identity of the person, but it is the co-inhering trinitarian dynamic of Spirit-to-spirit that creates and dynamically maintains the capacity for open and new forms of communicative order and structuring (2 Cor 3:17–18). Not only does *analogia spiritus* make authentic relations possible between plural developmental relations, it provides the holistic discriminating criteria through which traditions continue to transform in relation to one another.

According to Loder, Bohr's dynamic of complementarity approximates the relational theory of Kierkegaard, in which the nature of synthesis as a complementarity can never be reduced to a Hegelian ontological synthesis in a world "out there." It also redefines the classical sequential sense of causality, which will be the paramount subject in upcoming sections.[32] Before developing this idea further within a perichoretic notion of relationality, we must first investigate Loder's interest in Piaget and human development.

THE HUMAN DEVELOPMENTAL PSYCHOLOGY OF JEAN PIAGET

Introduction

Pannenberg tells us that unless theologians begin to defend the truth about God against the atheistic critique within the discipline of anthropology, their assertions about God and universality will remain ineffective and subjective assurances. Even though we can only know God through God's movement toward humanity, recognizing the truth of God (and reality) always entails an antecedent *willingness* to disrupt our existing plausibility structures. Therefore, anthropology is not ancillary to theology.

> Such has been the sad fate of dialectical theology and in particular the shortfall of Barth. It disdained to take a position on the terrain of anthropology and argue there that the religious thematic is unavoidable. . . . As a result, its very *rejection* of anthropology was a form of *dependence* on anthropological suppositions.[33]

---

new advances in quantum theory reveal that not only is it open at the bottom but asymmetrically top-down over bottom-up (i.e., consciousness in some way or another maintains a supervening relationship over particle activity).

32. Loder, *KM*, 80.
33. Pannenberg, *Anthropology*, 16.

All rational structures develop and sustain themselves within deeply complex and open dynamic interrelations that imbue them with meaning. Though conceptual structures within all disciplines of thought are constantly in flux (even theology), these holistic dynamics ensure interrelated wholeness, continuity, and growth. The complementarity within and between these disciplines is the grist of interdisciplinary theological engagement. Conversely, the rejection of anthropology, the closing of the system, forecloses on an inherent element of theology, the entropy of which, in Barth's case, he would struggle with throughout his theological career.[34]

As a theologian, James Loder takes great interest in developmental psychology and Jean Piaget. Of the modern theorist, Piaget takes the most interest in ontogenetic *and* phylogenetic[35] origins. Pannenberg is similarly attracted to him because he "takes as his starting point the phenomenon [of] . . . the symbiotic vital unity between child and mother (organism and environment)."[36] Both are adamant about the implicit theological theme inherent within this interaction.

Summary of Piaget's Human Developmental Psychology

Developmental psychology is interested in the development and transformation of the structures that produce understanding and intelligence. Piaget's basic model of functional invariants within development entails the *assimilation* of experience into the mind and a reciprocal *accommodation* of the mind to experience. Assimilation refers to appropriating some idea or object of experience into the existing meaning-frame of the person. Accommodation refers to altering the individual's meaning-frame to account for the object or idea. In general experience, both are constantly taking place to create *adaptation*. Until *adaptational equilibrium* occurs, assimilation or accommodation will marginally predominate one over the other. An example of assimilation dominance is play, when accommodation becomes dominant, imitation.[37] With adaptation, *intelligence* increases in its capacity to manage and experience wider ranges of complexity and depths of meaning.

---

34. Pannenberg adds: "As a result, it was defenseless against the suspicion that its faith was something arbitrarily legislated by human beings" (*Anthropology*, 16).

35. Ontogenetic: concerning the development of an individual organism. Phylogenetic: concerning the development of a species or group of related organisms.

36. Loder, *KM*, 346–47.

37. These categories loosely parallel our theological and anthropological categories of spirit (accommodation) and word (assimilation).

Piaget suggests four maturational stages in intelligence development: (1) sensory-motor intelligence; (2) intuitive or preoperational intelligence; (3) concrete operations; (4) and formal operations.[38] These comprise an invariate sequence, each stage requiring the transformation of its basic structures in order to create the next. For Piaget, according to Loder (and Pannenberg), "language is a necessary but insufficient factor in the emergence of the highest stage of intelligence."[39] Mature consciousness is a product of and dependent upon "inverting the subject's initial position with respect to" the "totality."[40] It has been shown[41] that the upper competencies facilitating mature intellectual development necessitate the capacity to "view oneself from outside oneself."[42]

This latter point is pivotal in understanding Piaget's work, which leads us to Piaget's perennial dualities that exist in tension: (1) the duality of stages and transformations, (2) the complementarity of causality and meaning, and (3) complementarity in the drive toward totality.

Duality of Stages and Transformation

In a later reflection on his own research, Piaget recounted:

> What is the relationship between morphisms [stages] and transformation? Which is master? Is it the comparative aspect [morphism] or is it the creative and formative aspect of transformation as I had always thought? And I found that, in the evolution of morphisms, they become increasingly subordinated to transformations. Clearly transformations are master.[43]

Not only are the transformations given marginal control, they indicate that if transformation is the creative and formative modification of one morphism to another, then clearly, "the ground of Piaget's thought is *a dynamic*

---

38. For a summary of these stages, see Loder, *KM*, 150.
39. Loder, *KM*, 151.
40. Piaget, *Six Psychological Studies*, 13.
41. Bruner, *Cognitive Growth*.
42. Piaget's concept of reflection approximates the dynamic of complementarity. "Reflection is nothing other than internal deliberation, that is to say, a discussion which is conducted with oneself just as it might be conducted with real interlocutors or opponents.... Contrariwise, socialized discussion might also be described as externalized reflection. Since all human conduct is both social and individual, this problem, like all analogous questions, comes back to whether the chicken appears before the egg or the egg before the chicken" (Piaget, *Six Psychological Studies*, 40).
43. Bringuer, *Conversations with Piaget*, 6.

state-changing activity which persists throughout the stages."[44] Developmentally, however, if transformations build on the existing structures, we must acknowledge that the original morphic structures intrinsically support the transformational process within themselves and the potential of the forthcoming states. In the initial state lies the transformational dynamic itself. Pannenberg tells us that within Piaget's interactive adaptation process lies the "potential of an innate intelligence, which, however, acquires its structure only as it is developed."

> Piaget calls it a "mistake" to regard "the *a priori* as consisting in structures existing ready-made from the beginning of development." . . . [Instead,] the structures that govern experience must themselves develop. "This *a priori* only appears in the form of essential structures at the end of the evolution of concepts and not at their beginning."[45]

Therefore, a tensive perennial complementarity exists in Piaget in which the emergence of new structures can never embody a final telos or meaning, yet, it is clear, says Loder, "that these structures are, in their advancing complexity, the ultimate achievement and formal terminus of the dynamics of transformation."[46] Loder argues that this *a priori* within each evolving organism from the beginning is that dynamic that constitutes all relationships, a mediating dynamic in which all organisms ultimately reflect within their own developmental dynamics.

Complementarity of Causality and Meaning

A similar tension occurs in the distinctions between causality and meaning (implication). For Piaget, causality does not directly apply to meaningful human consciousness. Instead, consciousness arises from "original" and "specific categories" that selectively ignore and consider various material facts.[47] Piaget believes consciousness develops out of both material causality and the individual's existing meaning-frame, which form a relational complementarity. For example, "consciousness develops directly by implication and meaning, and only indirectly from and in complementarity to

---

44. Loder, *KM*, 152, emphasis added.
45. Pannenberg, *Anthropology*, 348.
46. Loder, *KM*, 154. Piaget notes: "Now as we have come to see more clearly though Gödel but knew long before, the ideal of a structure of all structures is unrealizable" (cited in Loder, *KM*, 147).
47. Fraisse and Piaget, *Experimental Psychology*, ch. 3.

underlying physiological or neurological causes."[48] This produces two types of transformation.

The first is the transformation of the actual stages when a new emerging tacit dimension of meaning ruptures the meaning-frame itself. This is similar to the genitive emergence of new structures in meaning, which provide a wider "stage" (ground) of experience, eventually facilitating an increase in focal articulation and awareness. This type of transformation occurs through *internal theory change* and not directly by material or focal causality (causality which is only apparent within the existing meaning-frames). The second transformational dynamic occurs *within* the existing stage and pertains to the systematic modification of various forms and interrelations within the current stage. This produces greater pragmatic and interrelating efficiencies within one's knowing environment, which at paradigm maturity eventually becomes ground for future paradigm shifts. External causal anomaly produces this type of transformation, which is only intra-paradigmatic in nature. Nevertheless, the primary control of expanding consciousness and developing meaning and intelligence is "the logic of implications *meaning*, not the logic of causality."[49]

These categories parallel our earlier section on meaning, in which concept + experience = meaning. This second aspect of transformation noted above (intra-paradigmatic) produces greater conceptual diversity, which then creates new ground for the further expansion of experience (paradigmatic shift). The first transformational dynamic produces a wider frame of experiencing, which grounds future conceptual expansion and growth. This loosely associates Piaget's complementarity of causality and meaning with the conceptual and experiential modes of human relations. Piaget does not develop his concept of meaning at this point, which simply becomes the irreducible product of these two complementary aspects within human existence, which for this thesis, is the third term of the *relationship itself*. This leads us directly to the third complementarity, which creates totality.

Complementarity in the Drive toward Totality

Both Loder and Pannenberg believe Piaget's most basic but implicit category, which encompasses those already mentioned, is that of *relationship*. Furthermore, Loder believes Piaget "saw the whole context of his theory in terms of an ontology of relationships."[50] Relationship is always the product

48. Loder, *KM*, 155.
49. Loder, *KM*, 155.
50. Loder, *KM*, 156; Pannenberg, *Anthropology*, 347n86.

of a complementarity, which is continually active creating the drive toward totality. "The development of the child is thus a process of differentiation in which the totality must be restored at every stage; the totality thus reappears in a constantly new and enriched form."[51] This begins with various repetitions. The constant "restoration of totality through repetition and assimilation draws the child's attention to itself" (e.g., the sucking reflex).[52] *Totality* functions as both the starting point and goal of behavior and development. Piaget writes:

> The correlative of the idea of totality is, as Høffding has shown, the idea of relationship. Relationship is also a fundamental category in as much as it is immanent in all psychic activity and combines with all other concepts. This is because every totality is a system of relationships just as every relationship is a segment of totality.[53]

We find in Piaget, therefore, the first movement toward what Loder identifies as human spirit and what Pannenberg insistently refers to with religious significance as "ecstatic identification." The broader implication is that the textbook appropriation of Piaget, which places transformation inside a Newtonian container model of the stages, needs to give way to his larger project, in which the stages must situate in a "larger dynamic context."[54] There are a couple of characteristics within this drive toward totality worth noting.

The Reciprocating Dynamic between Totality and Differentiation Is Never Satisfied in Any State of Totality

The common understanding is that Piaget's notion of equilibration is a static balance. On the contrary,

> Equilibration [is] a dynamic cognitive "process," a cycle of cognitive approximations to a state that is never totally satisfied, . . . (1) it entails active compensations to environmental change; (2) it operates to maintain internal coherence; and (3) it represents an ongoing search beyond current cognitive maturity (equilibration is thus a misnomer).[55]

---

51. Pannenberg, *Anthropology*, 347.
52. Pannenberg, *Anthropology*, 347.
53. Piaget, *Origins of Intelligence*, 10.
54. Loder, *KM*, 158.
55. Loder, *KM*, 153.

The process of equilibration is a "genesis" of human behavior and consciousness, *creating the motivation* for states of totality.[56] Furthermore, such transformational fluctuations themselves are capable of creating ontogenetic or spontaneous increases in meaning and emergent organization.[57] "Piaget's work suggests that, through partially disordered encounters with one's cognitive environment, new states of increased intellectual capacity can spontaneously emerge in the human learner *actively interacting* with her or his environment."[58] As we shall see, this dynamic within relationality expands and enriches our understanding of authentic relationships and sin. It becomes the driver within Kierkegaard's claim that all humanity suffers from despair (i.e., until we experience full perichoretic relations with the Other).

This fundamental reciprocating drive within human beings reveals that all human existence emerges in relation to that constituting Power within relationship, which points to and reflectively informs our understanding of *perichoresis*. The drive to interact and the interaction itself is the fundamental drive of human existence. It motivates both individuation and

---

56. A leading interpreter of Piaget, Hans Furth describes Piaget's mature understanding of equilibration as "the self-regulation of human knowing. It regulates the network of cognitive cycles and keeps them in more or less permanent balance (equilibrium). This balance ... is open to the unlimited number of new encounters and perspectives deriving from the interplay of human actions (external and internal). Some of these encounters lead to disturbances of existing balances. In consequence, people experience conflicts or gaps relative to their given systems of knowing. The system which in the first place is responsible for the disturbances then responds in a compensatory manner and overcomes the disturbances to the point of essentially integrating them as part of the system. In doing this, there is a reequilibration, but not simply a return to the old equilibrated system. Rather, the compensation is at the same time the construction of an improved system.... Hence Piaget speaks of an 'increasing' equilibration.... For Piaget, 'structure without function (genesis)' was as incomplete as 'function without structure'" (Furth, *Piaget and Knowledge*, 254).

57. In agreement with Diane McGuiness, Karl Prikram, and Marian Prinazar, Loder suggests that Piaget's equilibration as a continuously changing and self-organizing process might "be analogous to the discovery of Prigogine that in open, nonlinear physical systems processes can be identified that are characterized by temporary stabilities far from thermodynamic equilibrium which depend upon fluxes constrained by initial conditions and the context in which they occur. These temporary stabilities are characterized by global (encompassing the whole system) physical order that spontaneously emerges from nonequilibrium states characterized by global disorder. Before Prigogine's work, nonequilibrium states were considered devoid of any interesting physical information, thermodynamic nonequilibrium was treated as a temporary disturbance of equilibrium rather than a source of new order. But Prigogine's three decades of research established that thermodynamic nonequilibrium can be a source of spontaneous order, or organization spontaneously arising in open systems which exchange energy and matter with their environment" (Loder, *KM*, 159).

58. Loder, *KM*, 159.

harmonic reintegration toward the greatest differentiation in unity possible. Piaget and Pannenberg convincingly reveal the implicit *call* to "totality" inherent within the transformational dynamic. In concert, Colin Gunton argues that within this same transformational dynamic is the *call* for and instantiation of particularization (one's wholeness).[59]

The Pre-cognitive Modality (Awareness) of Piaget's "Totality" (Relationship)

Ernst Schachtel directly supplements Piaget's notion of totality by noting that "acts of focal attention *exclude* the rest of the field (environmental and internal) from that form of consciousness which is designated as focal awareness."[60] Concurrently, Ulric Neisser says this process is pre-cognitive and preattentive when he argues that "preattentive processes *control* . . . immediate bodily motion, or *attention itself*."[61] What we choose to become focally aware of within the vast field of experience (internal and external) is determined prereflexively. Even rationality, as we have already seen, "is 'secondary' in the sense that it works with objects already formed by a 'primary' process. . . . It seems to [Neisser] that *all* directed thinking is an elaboration of this sort, just as *all* visual and auditory perception depends on prior wholistic construction of some kind of unit."[62] The question, then, is how specific attention emerges out of the pre-cognitive totality from within the prereflexive process. At this point, Pannenberg is critical of Piaget's lack of recognizing the religious thematic implicit in his consideration of being drawn to "totality," which he affirms as prereflexive.[63] In another respect,

---

59. Gunton, *One, Three, Many*.
60. Schachtel, *Metamorphosis*, 253.
61. Neisser, *Cognitive Psychology*, 93, emphasis added.
62. Neisser, *Cognitive Psychology*, 302–3.

63. Pannenberg lucidly describes this prereflexive process: "Because subject and object are not yet distinguished within the focus on the whole that is proper to feeling (as distinct from sensation), feeling provides the horizon not only for relating experiences to the whole of the individual's existence but also for grasping impressions as parts of an objective whole which in its turn has its place in the context of the world in its entirety. At this root level, feeling and reason are bound together. Out of it arises the differentiation, occasioned by sense impressions, between feelings, which refer to the self, and reason, which relates to the totality that is the objective world.

In the lived experience these two sides are not yet separated. . . . The concrete grasp of meaning in the lived experience of the meaning of things and events as parts of the wholes which they represent is not to be regarded as a positing of meaning by a subject, because, apart from any other consideration, its origins precede any separation between subjective and objective. Only with the coming of language does the

however, I am sympathetic with Kierkegaard, Loder, and Gunton's position as critical of both Pannenberg and Piaget's lack of religious thematic within the complementary draw to particularization as well, which is an apparent quality of human and trinitarian relational dynamics.[64] For Kierkegaard, the internal force of individuation of human beings is also a religious contingency.[65] Nevertheless, the point is that such forces are active within *analogia spiritus*, the *moment* (movement) between prereflexion and reflexion. However, this can only be the case within the holistic interaction of two separate spirits, which ultimately escapes Pannenberg.

The Hidden Question of Ultimate Meaning

It is well known that Lawrence Kohlberg, a follower of Piaget, established six successive formal stages of moral judgment. Yet, during his work in the 1960s with Harvard students who had scored his highest level six, they surprisingly acknowledged that ethical judgment meant very little to them. Loder points out that they, in effect, "had no answers to the question, *Why be moral?*"[66] Disillusioned about his empirical search for moral reasoning, Kohlberg "recognized the empirical significance of ultimate meaning, and tried to develop a 'stage 7.'" Between then and the time of his tragic suicide in 1987, he failed to answer conclusively, "*Why be moral?*"

Similarly, in Piaget's work on intelligence, we must begin with the question that never explicitly concerns Pannenberg—*why interest?* Piaget remarked, "interest is the proper orientation for every act of mental assimilation."[67] Therefore, where does the *interest* come from that motivates the cognitive act of intelligence from out of the "totality?" Why intelligence? Thus, the unavoidable question in human development remains, why does the neonate even react with interest to the fluctuations within its environment? And, why the reciprocating perennial motivation to adapt within the "totality?" Science has yet to isolate the stimulus for morphological

---

differentiation become definitive, but with an initial focus on a quasi-mythical subjectivity in things, which spontaneously manifest their being through the words that name them. . . . The unity of consciousness arises only in response to the linguistically apprehended identity of things and their order, in which . . . the little word "I" has its point of reference" (*Anthropology*, 518–19).

64. Again, with Pannenberg, this has much to do with his Hegelian proclivities.

65. Kierkegaard, *CUP*, 347–85.

66. Loder, *KM*, 161.

67. Piaget, *Six Psychological Studies*, 34. Schachtel, *Metamorphosis*, 252, also argues that "an autonomous interest in the environment" is fundamental to human being.

development within genetic structuring. We have already noted that biological survival is not the foundation of meaningful life or flourishing.

Concerning the "something" of ultimate meaning that motivates the transformational dynamic, Loder offers Piaget's reference to a "lived out" Spinozism.[68] This paradoxically holds transcendence and immanence together as "modes of an ultimate unity of being." This, however, fails to address the motivating *interest* (force) in human existence that seeks to differentiate, theorize, and constitute itself as a totality in relation to the world and its environmental fluctuations. Loder describes the emergence of meaning and intelligence developmentally:

> Each new stage explicitly embodies the latent structural potential which resided in the previous stage, so the emergence of a higher stage ipso facto becomes the meaning of the previous stages.... If we turn from the stages to the sequence as a whole ... we can see that the meaning of the sequence of intelligence as a whole resides in its enduring, stage-after-stage, tacit aspect, ... the dynamism of transformation by which a relational reality between any two stadial positions is constructed.... Since these patterned dynamics are reenacted in every stage of human development and are the persistent tacit dimension of every new form of intelligence ... as a whole, the ultimate meaning of the four stage sequence must require that *transformation, itself transformed*, become that meaning.[69]

Ultimate meaning cannot come from a metaphysical monism, being, or "unity" but rather from an "inherently relational reality, transforming all proximate transformations in an ultimate transformational relationship between immanence and transcendence,"[70] in other words, a dynamic perichoretic relationality that constantly and alternatively seeks *both* differentiation and unification.

Rather than focus on the question of human existence within the "dichotomous *choice*" and the Modern understanding of the human will, developmentalist Robert Kegan similarly considers the "dialectical *context* which brings the poles into being in the first place."[71] Kegan's Piagetian position presents development as a negotiating dialectical dynamic active within *each* stage of development. It optimally brings the oscillating imbalance of development and construction of new matrices of meaning into an

---

68. Loder, *KM*, 163.
69. Loder, *KM*, 163–64, emphasis added.
70. Loder, *KM*, 164.
71. Kegan, *Evolving Self*, ix.

"interindividual" balance, resulting in a "culture of intimacy" that contains "interdependent self-definition."[72] His dominant theme, which is perichoretic in nature, is *reciprocity*:

> Reciprocity now becomes a matter of at once mutually preserving the other's distinctiveness while interdependently fashioning a bigger context in which these separate identities interpenetrate, by which the separate identities are co-regulated and to which persons invest in affection supervening their separate identities.[73]

In this apt description of the perichoretic dynamic, Kegan describes a dynamic that is evident in all forms of relational evolution, but furthermore presents us with a transformational dynamic definitive of the highest stage of development. *This dynamic which transcends any one stage presents us with what it means to be human.* Rather than the egalitarian alliance which engages the other within the other's current evolutionary position, which tends to ossify the other's protective schemes and thus stultify relational growth, "the *relationship* is wedded most of all to that life motion which the partners do not share so much as *it shares them*."[74] The "life motion," which presents the "bigger context," facilitates transformation in which both the relationship (or All) and the individual reciprocally condition each other continually creating a more integrated intimacy.[75]

Kegan offers a distinctly perichoretic relationality within the evolutionary development of relational intimacy.

> The popular psychological notions of greater differentiation and greater integration as goals are here given a substantive and justifiable meaning. Each new evolutionary truce further differentiates the self from its embeddedness in the world, guaranteeing, in a qualitatively new way, the world's distinct integrity, and thereby creating a more integrated relationship to the world. Each new truce accomplishes this by the evolution of a reduced subject and a greater object for the subject to take, an evolution of lesser subjectivity and greater objectivity, an evolution that is more "truthful"[76]

---

72. Kegan, *Evolving Self*, 118.
73. Kegan, *Evolving Self*, 253–54.
74. Kegan, *Evolving Self*, 254, emphasis added. Cf. also the earlier section on social constructivism.
75. Kegan, *Evolving Self*, 294.
76. Kegan, *Evolving Self*, 295.

For Kegan, this is a fundamental process of humanity. This "life motion," or "transformation, itself transformed" (*analogia spiritus*) is what produces the perichoretic dynamic in all relations in which "*transition itself becomes the very matrix of existence.*"[77] Human as spirit repeatedly seeks individualization and reincorporation-as-individual-in-relation. This perennial force motivating and creating human relations drives culture to ever-greater levels of interaction, intimacy, and holistically, fullness of life.

The ontological nature of human spirit (relationship) emerges in analogical relation to the "open system" of God's Spirit which effectively draws the "infinity" of the individual (in itself a closed system) into the possibility of an interactive reality that includes an interactive matrix permeating the entirety of spacetime, and thus enabling co-ordination with God's similar (infinite) activity and will. Such a dynamic equivalent in Piaget and explicit in Kierkegaard and Loder will allow us to incorporate later the complementarity of time and Eternity into human existence that could not otherwise be possible or imaginable. Such a complementarity, it is hoped, will begin to reveal a developmental process in which a teleological process itself is not merely active in the beginning, but because of the unique dynamic of the Spirit and Christ such a process makes it possible for both this dynamic and subsequent stages to actually *be* the meaning within antecedent stages. Moreover, within such a complementarity of time and Eternity in Christ, history authentically affects God's trinitarian relations (Eternity). For Kierkegaard and Loder, this meaning takes complete hold only within the heuristic "absurdity" of God-Man.

PERSON AS *PERICHORESIS*: LODER AND KIERKEGAARD ON CHRIST, TIME, AND TRANSFORMATION

Introduction

Within this section, we have thus far concentrated upon the predominately immanent aspects of God's action within human relations, the penultimate dynamics active within the Christian experience, which represent Kierkegaard's "Religiousness A." Only upon encountering the christological event and knowledge of Christ, does Kierkegaard believe humanity experiences the fullness of existence possible within divine-human relations. When this occurs, the relationship itself embeds with Christ in his Time and creation history. This is the possibility of moving and thinking in relation to Christ and his paralleling deliberation within the Trinity. This embeddedness can

---

77. Loder, *KM*, 304.

transcend a person's focal understanding (Matt 7:21-23; 25:31-46). Likewise, for Kierkegaard and McFadyen, this personal knowledge of Christ and the relational dynamics it facilitates give ultimate meaning to human life *in every dimension*. Thus far, it has only been argued that ultimate meaning must lie within the integrative and transforming dynamics that facilitate human development. Its importance was to underscore these relational dynamics as universally human. This presents the framework for understanding the complementarities of time and Eternity, immanence transcendence as basic to human existence.

Human Beings as the Dynamic Unity between Time and Eternity

In the previous chapter, we noted the dialogical cycles of openness and closure in the communicational dynamics of McFadyen in parallel with the Kierkegaardian categories of the prereflexive infinite and reflexive finite in human existence. These cycling modes of relationality cannot become a material sum but, for Loder, become "the Now" as the critical unifying locus between the Parmenidean *whole* and Heraclitean *differentiation*. It is a transtemporal *moment* that unifies the grammar of sequential time into meaningful existential wholes (kairological time). It is the moment of insight, the *"aha!"* breaking forth into consciousness with convincing force after a creative gestation process. In science, such brooding gestations can last for many years. Loder is here consonant with the earlier equation of human meaning as the tensive dynamic (unity) of concept and experience: "experience and knowledge are always in a differentiated, bipolar, reciprocal relationship which is, for pedagogical purposes, asymmetrical in the direction of the emphasis being made; but ultimately, it favors experience."[78]

In a conference on "Immanence and Transcendence" at Boston University, Gadamer described the Parmenidean notion of *"sudden blow"* or *metabole* which embodies change in everyday life:

> This blow-like occurrence, opens a new dimension of time, which is called in the later terminology of the New Testament "eschatological" time. . . . Paul says, "you should not keep on waiting for the return of the Savior. He will come without your calculating expectations, like the thief in the night" [cf. 1 Thess 5:2]. Indeed, the same problem regarding the moment of the Second Coming of the Savior, the eschatological moment, is in the Gospel of John, where it is interpreted as the moment in which the believer *accepts* the message. It seems to me that

78. Loder, KM, 237.

we have a pre-shaping of all this in the dialectic of time and of movement in the Platonic view. Strangely enough, I cannot find any trace of this whole theory of the sudden, of the *exaiphanes*, through the whole history of ideas until Kierkegaard.[79]

Exaiphanes is a New Testament word—"suddenly"—used to describe the transfiguration, annunciation, the coming of the Spirit at Pentecost, and Paul's conversion. Gadamer says, "Tillich, Heidegger, Bultmann, and others conceive of "the moment" as *decisive*, but it is in Kierkegaard that its Judeo-Christian understanding converges explicitly with the Platonic-Parmenidean dialectic."[80] For Kierkegaard, the movement of transcendence into time (e.g., the Incarnation) must abandon any conceptual notion of absolute rest, and must instead, says Loder, "adopt *a kinetic mode of reason*":

> In [Kierkegaard's] language, in "a moment" one must make "the leap of faith," which is just as surely an act of thought as it is an act of choice for radical change in one's *whole* being. Yet thought and being must never be collapsed either way, for in the tension between them is the velocity and vitality of existence, "the spirit." Thus, his kinetic claim regarding authentic existence: "Man [person] is spirit."[81]

Part of the logic of spirit is temporal transcendence, not just spatial or conceptual. For Kierkegaard, reason is always a retrospective logic. For logico-mathematical constructs to work, they must freeze the flow of time. Einstein, in this respect, sought, without success, to formulate a mathematics that could embody time within its formulations ("kinematics"). If we view this from the perspective of Greek and Modern metaphysics, it seems to contradict Einstein's complementary belief in a dipolar aspect of timelessness (Spinozian metaphysical idealism) and his own belief that time was ultimately an illusion. Though certain understandings of timelessness *prima facie* seem consonant with the apparent conclusions of his Special Theory of Relativity, this must balance with Einstein's conviction that the conceptual alone was barren if separated from its *dynamic* unity and fullness of temporal experience. Loder believes this complementarity within Einstein's thinking can only occur within the Kierkegaardian kinetic mode of human existence as "spirit" in analogical relation to "the Spirit of Christ."[82] Accord-

---

79. Gadamer, cited in Lawrence, *Beginning*, 7–8.

80. Loder, *KM*, 185.

81. Loder, *KM*, 185–86, emphasis added. Loder's choice of words, "has been made," might better be expressed within this thesis, "being made."

82. Loder, *KM*, 185–89.

ing to T. F. Torrance, this allows "the movement of the eternal in time, . . . a way of thinking by abandoning a point of absolute rest and moving kinetically along with the truth in order to understand it."[83] For example, "in the *Cur Deus Homo* Anselm insists that we must not treat Jesus Christ like a fixed principle, or a logical cypher, from which to extend formal logical connections and thus to build up a system of necessary truth."[84]

In this respect, truth is always a paradox for Kierkegaard; reason is *only* "continuity in reverse."[85] Loder suggests, "this analogy [*analogia spiritus*] would take us into the apocalyptic understanding of time, because to fully participate in the light of the logos would be to see everything that has been made *all at once*—in a moment that contains the fullness of time."[86] The "leap" is the transitional *moment* and *the human* condition necessary for the dynamic (existential) synthesis and transition from the "infinite" prereflexive awareness through the correlational matrix of Christ's constituting dynamic (the relationship) into reflexive constitution. This is a time-embedding move (into consciousness) for Kierkegaard that unifies past, present, and future together, throwing the individual (within the relationship) more deeply into existence than otherwise. "Spirituality is not a leap *out* of time but a leap that releases real time into human existence so the concreteness of the *dunamis* of existence is lived out."[87] We should not contrast the temporal (historical) with a static eternal; instead, history unfolds in direct relation to a *dynamic* Eternal and the possibility of personal relations with God. In our relation to a trinitarian God who facilitates *all* interactions throughout time, we, in effect, come into transtemporal relations with the entire emergence of history in Kierkegaard's *moment*.[88]

---

83. Torrance, *Transformation*, 276–78.

84. Torrance, *Transformation*, 277.

85. Kierkegaard explains: "What I usually express by saying that Christianity consists of paradox, philosophy in mediation, Leibniz expresses by distinguishing between what is above reason and what is against reason. Faith is above reason. By reason he understands, as he says many places, a linking together of truths (enchainement), a conclusion from causes. Faith therefore cannot be proved, demonstrated, comprehended, for the link which makes a linking together possible is missing, and what else does this say than that it is a paradox. This, precisely, is the irregularity in the paradox, continuity is lacking, or at any rate it has continuity only in reverse, that is, at the beginning it does not manifest itself as continuity" (*JPH*, 3:399–400).

86. Loder, *KM*, 186, emphasis added.

87. Loder, *KM*, 198.

88. Cf. Agamben, *Kingdom*, 8. "Messianic time . . . [is] the relation of every moment, every kairos, to the end of time and to eternity. Consequently, what interests Paul is not the final day, the moment at which time ends, but the time that contracts and begins to end. Or, one might say, the time that remains between time and its end."

Prigogine and Time

Loder and Neidhardt provide insight into the dynamic complementarity of time and Eternity by employing Prigogine's thermodynamic theories of how order emerges out of chaos in open dynamic systems. Prigogine suggests a shift in the understanding of how causation transpires in a "more subtle form of reality that involves both time and eternity. . . . Being and Becoming are not to be opposed one to the other: they express two related aspects of reality."[89]

> Broadly speaking, destruction of structures [forms of order] is the situation which occurs in the neighborhood of thermodynamic equilibrium. On the contrary "creation of structures" *may* occur with specific non-linear kinetic laws of far-from-equilibrium conditions. The energy and matter exchanged by the system from the outside world is then really transformed into structure.[90]

This spontaneous self-organizing process, says Loder, could be understood as "reversing the arrow of time if the premise of the movement of time were toward disintegration and increasing entropy." If, however, we view it theologically within trinitarian dynamics and from the point of the resurrection, we could see it as a "*prefiguring* of the 'new creation,' in which giving rise to new order could be seen as a wrinkle in time, a leap into the future, bringing the future into the present ahead of time."[91]

Therefore, how are we to understand the *prefiguring* of creation, the "bringing of the future" into the present, or the experience of seeing "everything *being made all at once*—in a moment that contains the fullness of time?"[92] The problem lies, as most of our issues do, in the Greek and Modern paradigm that incorporate a timeless, absolute point of view or rest inherent within the Platonic distinction of the whole or the eternal. Even for Loder and Neidhardt, the tense of their expressions fights the fullness of their intended meaning. After first looking at Kierkegaard's understanding of how this theological contingency affects the person, we will consider a fuller expression of Loder's and Neidhardt's ideas of time and Eternity. An upcoming chapter on quantum dynamics will explore the potentially ontological nature of such prefiguring.

---

89. Prigogine and Stengers, *Order Out of Chaos*, 310.
90. Prigogine, "Unity of Physical Laws," 2.
91. Loder, *KM*, 215, emphasis added.
92. Loder, *KM*, 186, my paraphrase.

PERSON AS DIPOLAR-ASPECT—PERICHORETIC: LODER AND KIERKEGAARD

For both Loder and Kierkegaard, all life constitutes in relations as a dynamic differentiated unity. Humans not only constitute in perichoretic relation to the world (Process or Spinozian theology), they are first perichoretic beings (a relation unto themselves) who then constitute in perichoretic relation to the world (a trinitarian dynamic). For Kierkegaard, persons constitute *both* individually and socially.

Human Beings as Persons-in-*Perichoresis*

For Loder, *perichoresis* in the Trinity is the mutual "interpenetrating" and "indwelling" of each person without loss of personal identity or corporate mutuality. For Moltmann, all created relationality derives its ultimate meaning from this preeminent relation to this sustaining trinitarian dynamic, which furthermore perichoretically sustains and "indwells" it.[93] Kierkegaard suggests that human beings are, by nature, perichoretic. If the individual is to keep from imploding solely into its own worlds of understanding it generates, or, on the contrary, if it is to keep from fully constituting in relation to its environment, then that Power, which enables it to relate *fully* to itself and others, must sustain it. The key aspects for understanding individual spirit, says Loder, are

> the basic polarization of cognitive modes represented by the bicameral brain; the self-transcendence or agency of initiative by which the "world" is chosen, composed, and believed in; and the transformational dynamics by which that agency works toward the creation and composition of the "world" in which the individual lives.[94]

Furthermore, "only if the self-transcendent agency of the self finds its ground outside and beyond the pattern of self-relatedness can self-relatedness be sustained."[95] In other words, the self-relating pattern of human

---

93. Cf. Moltmann, *GC*, 16, 101.

94. Loder, *KM*, 292.

95. Loder, *KM*, 291. "There are important analogical connections between the impossibility of a closed self-explanatory system as Gödel showed for logic and mathematics and the impossibility of a closed or self-explanatory view of the self-system. The irreducibility of the observer or the creator of the system to the system's own terms is analogous to the irreducibility of the validation of first principles to the logic of their relationship within the system" (n5).

spirit itself must be sustained by a source that allows its own pattern of self-relation to be related back unto itself, thus able to itself be transformed. Such a Power, however, must be grounded transparently. Transparency is related to both the perichoretic nature of moving with Christ and the non-distortion within the person necessary to attain optimal self-relatedness.

As we have already discussed, Kierkegaard is acutely aware of the necessary openness required by the individual to keep this process grounded and centered beyond the individual. Loder identifies this Kierkegaardian pattern as "mutual coinherence," where not only do the participants co-inhere within the relation, but the relation also becomes coinherent with itself. Therefore,

> It is evident that the self cannot be itself without its centered grounding beyond itself, but it must be a participant in that ground such that its life is preserved and its integrity as spirit is sustained by that ground. Thus, the ground also participates in the self in such a way that both ground and self are sustained as such from the standpoint of the self. In other words, there is a co-inherence of the whole patterned activity of the self in and with its ground, and of the ground in and with the self. In essence, *the self is spirit when the pattern governing it is perichoretic.*[96]

Because human nature is spirit (potentially) and analogically reflects the divine nature, (1) it is impossible to fully understand its ontological nature of relationality and subsequent patterning in spacetime categories, but only in analogical relation to the inner life of the Trinity, and (2) we can never reduce the conceptual nature of this patterning to any fixed level of being;[97] it is operative regardless of the discipline of thought or experience, and necessitates a constantly open and developing meaning-frame. For both Loder and Kierkegaard, the human as spirit is ultimately dependent upon the sustaining *hypostatization* of the human spirit in relation to God's Spirit. When Kierkegaard wrote, "the Greeks did not grasp the notion of the spirit in its deepest sense," Loder thinks they not only lost the wholeness of the self "but failed to understand that the human spirit is the subordinate half of an analogy to the Spirit of God."[98]

Kierkegaard also believes spirit grounds in history. Ronald Hall, in *Word and Spirit*, emphasizes the incarnational nature of Kierkegaard's notion of spirit. Because of Christ, spirit is never merely a dipolar *aspect* of the human condition without the complementarity of word or conceptuality; in

---

96. Loder, *KM*, 292.
97. Loder, *KM*, 293.
98. Loder, *KM*, 299.

analogical relation to the Holy Spirit (and thus the Word), it always existentially grounds in spacetime and history. The Greeks had "no world-picture in which spirit could come forth into its full reality,"[99] simply because it lacked the heuristic and conceptual reality of divine Incarnation. With the Incarnation, the Eternal breaks into history, and Word is never without Spirit, nor Spirit without its correlative Word; and yet, never is the couplet ever reduced to a material synthesis. In other words, human life is optimally a living transformational dynamic in existential time that lives within extended sets or stages of orientation that never separate from their existential contingency to this living transformational dynamic. In McGilchrist's terms, the emissary must never rise above or separate from the master.

Therefore, the "Power which posits self" is ultimately, inevitably, and only that power that brings human existence wholly and coherently as person into unified existential relations with the world. Within this condition, human beings: (1) have the capacity to become spirit, relate themselves *fully* to themselves, to experience themselves as whole persons in relation to the world rather than just a behavioral reaction to their environment, (2) maintain a dynamic patterning which is itself potentially open to transformation, and (3) reach their greatest potential when this pattern of relationality includes the heuristics and knowledge of a Christ—Incarnation—that which empowers and frees the *whole* person for full re-constitution and transformational relationship. This latter contingency allows for a personal relationship with a personal God. For Kierkegaard, without the Christian narrative and resultant faith experience of the Incarnation, the individual cannot *wholly* enter perichoretic relations. Only by first *experiencing* the knowledge (personal presence) that a human being lived and claimed to be the positive absurdity of the Absolute Paradox—that God lived as a human person—and thus Eternity has come into time, are we heuristically and relationally (ontologically) able to fully enter the dynamic which calls for the *whole of self* to enter into ongoing transformative relations—love.

In conclusion, the dynamic of *perichoresis* must be a constituting dynamic both *in* persons, creating the individual, and *between* persons, creating relationships. Moreover, the quality of perichoretic relations depends on each participant's capacity, disposition, and willingness for wholeness. In the next chapter, we will analogically compare these same dynamics to those within the godhead, but first, let us briefly reengage the perichoretic constitution of person as social.

---

99. Hall, *Word and Spirit*, 73.

Person as Social in *Perichoresis*

In both Loder and Kierkegaard's thinking, the transformational dynamic is definitive of the highest stage, which is active from the beginning of development to the end. Recalling Piaget's primacy of transformation over stages and Kegan's transformational dynamics being definitive of the whole process, Loder argues that such dynamics are what ultimately create the possibility for mutual and enhancing reciprocity between persons. Because Loder echoes many of the "perichoretic" convictions of McFadyen already considered within the *relational aspects* of his Christian social theory, Loder's understanding of social relations as perichoretic will be abbreviated.

Loder contends the Hegelian understanding of a stage emphasis in dialectics results in pluralistic ambivalence and must give way to Kierkegaard's understanding that

> persons mutually creating each other, in ways that presuppose earlier stages but are no longer dependent upon staging, i.e. "arriving at a higher stage," as an orientation to what it means to be or to become fully human. . . . This triumph of the perichoretic pattern in human development [suggests that] what one experiences at first is so much a part of oneself it cannot be set "out there" and consciously intended. . . . Thus, by the standard pattern of differentiation and reincorporation-as-differentiated, *transition itself becomes the very matrix of existence.* The dynamics of change become the vital center of mutual interaction, not merely the means to higher order stability. . . . [And because] theologically, this means actualization by the presence of the Divine Spirit of the Trinitarian image of God through Jesus Christ as mediating image [within *perichoresis* of self and community] . . . persons can intentionally, as part of who they are because it is integral to how they have developed, provide the other one with the combination of openness and tangible symbolic expression, i.e. the space and the manipulatable symbols thereof, to allow the two (or more) together and separately to repeatedly recompose the world, the "bigger context," such that mutual enhancement can continue. Transitional space mutually provided and symbolically represented means corporate development.[100]

For Kierkegaard, the perichoretic dynamic of person as spirit begins through God's immanent sustaining relation and call to personhood. This internal relation which is an aspect of "Christ in us," allows us to, first, immanently constitute out of the whole of a relationship to the divine. This transparently

---

100. Loder, *KM*, 304–5.

creates the ability for human existence with all its historical sedimentation to constitute as individual in relation to the whole-of-self-in-relation to the world. In this respect, only humanity's transitional and transformational *dynamic* is primordial and immanently fundamental. Everything else is transformable in relationship, including the known or existing transformation structure itself. This transparently provides human existence (fully related) the capacity to *completely* reconstitute and transform (undergo redemption) in its relationships with the world. And, because we can *completely* give ourselves to such ongoing reconstitutive relations, this capacity of relations alone can obtain the unique distinction of *agape*. "The capacity to give love," says Loder, "is directly related to the power of a convicting experience to make developmental time reversible."[101]

Regardless of the existing cultic play and mythic orientations, the degree participants willingly open themselves to being affected by authentic relations establishes the continuity and authenticity of those relations. The conceptual play and orientations are secondary to the degree we experience this universal perichoretic contingency. If truth-conduciveness within relations is consummate, this Power of "the highest stage of relationality" must increasingly reflect and manifest itself within various cultic and mythic play. Greater relational satisfaction and fullness of life become the initial indication of movement toward and into higher transformational dynamics within our relationships.

Therefore, only because persons first perichoretically constitute in relation to that immanently transcendent Power constituting the relationship can they effectively engage authentic social relations. In this way, the *koinonia* community Christ enables negates and affirms the typical anthropological considerations.[102] These processes transform and often co-condition God's Spirit's transcending activity within the community.

> In effect, the idealized reality, toward which Kegan's developmental theory moves, becomes an actual reality only in the cultus of the koinonia (Pannenberg), i.e. only when it is an expression of the cosmic ordering, self-confirming, relationally-constituted reality of the Divine Presence.[103]

---

101. Loder, *TM*, 182. In other words, persons can only free themselves from the adverse developments within their sedimentation, which generally elicit fears of abandonment or absorption, when the whole of themselves can reconstitute within transforming social dynamics.

102. Loder lists some normal socialization processes as determination and defense of territory, initiation rites, rites of intensification, role structures, hierarchical stratification, and legal system.

103. Loder, *KM*, 305.

ATTRIBUTIONS OF PERSONAL *PERICHORESIS*

Loder's understanding of imagination and the intensification of the knowing event leading to discovery is distinctively perichoretic. The imagination's unique characteristics help us understand *perichoresis* in its practical dimension. Kierkegaard tells us:

> Imagination is . . . not one faculty on a par with others, but, if one would so speak, it is the faculty *instar omnium* [for all faculties]. What feeling, knowledge, or will a man has, depends in the last resort upon what imagination he has, that is to say, upon how these things are reflected, i.e. it depends upon imagination. . . . [In] relation to knowledge, imagination is the origin of the categories. . . . Imagination is the possibility of all reflection, and the intensity of this medium is the possibility of the intensity of the self.[104]

Imagination and Language as *Perichoresis*

How can we continuously maintain our beliefs (historically) yet relax their structures for potential growth and developmental transformation? Kierkegaard points to the relational third term and the dynamic that constitutes this relatedness in which *the* transcendent (Eternal) ground and dynamic conditions the person's experiences and interactions. Imagination is the telling function within this dynamic.

"Any assertion of truth," according to Loder, "that does not recognize and accept its primary dependency on some leap of the imagination, some insight, intuition, or vision, is guilty of intellectual dissimulation."[105] Such an error fails to acknowledge *all* knowledge as "personal knowledge" laced with interest specific to the individual and society. Considering Karl Popper, Loder notes that "the logic of induction" is a fallacy, and in deductive reason, "truth is first grasped by an imaginative leap, then demonstrated."[106] Both believe knowledge cannot derive solely from observable data but must be created or invented within the leap of the imagination.[107] "Facts do not determine the theory. Instead, the theory creates the facts, and it is contradiction that creates theory through an act of the imagination."[108] Imagi-

---

104. Kierkegaad, *SUD*, 163–64.
105. Loder, *TM*, 20.
106. Loder, *TM*, 23.
107. See Popper, *Logic*, 458.
108. Loder, *TM*, 23.

nation is the power to generate, shape, and construct a meaningful world in which to live and reconstruct it when that world becomes intractable. Image here is dynamically fundamental for language as metaphor, visual, or ideas. For Kierkegaard, as with Sartre, the image reveals and conceals aspects of the relationship. We always know more than that of which we are focally conscious, and the image conveys a truth more profound than consciousness can grasp.[109] Error develops in consciousness when the person attempts to self-determine the relationship without being willing to constitute within the fullness (the truth) of each unique relationship. This is the phenomenon Loder calls the "eikonic eclipse," the selective (usually defensive) and manipulative limiting of self within the third term of the relations. The relationship itself co-conditions and supports the individual's constructed image. Attempting to describe the dynamic of language and image, poet Ezra Pound tells us,

> All poetic language is the language of exploration. Since the beginning of bad writing, writers have used images as ornaments. The point of Imagism [Pound's approach to poetry] is that it does not use images as ornaments. The image is itself the speech. The image is the word beyond formulated language. . . . The image in not an idea. It is a radiant node or cluster, it is what I can and must perforce call a vortex, from which and through which, and into which ideas are constantly rushing.[110]

The image is a vortex through which countless factors repeatedly come to gestalt, an inner world of constant change. Loder calls the vortex between the cognitive consciousness and the creative unconsciousness the hypnagogic image. The vortex of *the relationship* creates a kinetic "analogy of wholes" through the analogia spiritus upon which all linguistic structuring emerges relative to each participant.

The standard antiquated understanding that words, stimulus, rules, and data systematically compile into meaningful wholes within the person no longer holds—it is much more complex and fascinating. The dynamic of supervenience, for example, suggests that the highest stage and form of order (e.g., human or divine consciousness) has marginal control over lower-level determinations. Therefore, in the *analogia spiritus*, the whole of the

---

109. As we have already seen, empirical evidence is rapidly accumulating within neuropsychology and other related disciplines that reveal this phenomenon. For example, cf. Milner, "Vision without Knowledge," in which he shows evidence that our visual capacity operates on two distinct cordial processes, one facilitating action and the other perception and cognition. Also, McGilchrist, *Master*.

110. Pound, *Caudier Brezeska*, 102, 106.

person, while generating their thoughts, emerges in relation to the whole of the other, even while speaking the words. Their respective meaning and ideas (of imagination) emerge together in a co-conditioning manner through the supporting mediation of the dynamic third term. Out of this prereflexive transparent dynamic and hermeneutical delay, language "suddenly" explodes forth in meaning relative to speaker and listener alike—simultaneously! When this happens, says Loder, "the experience seems to rupture boundaries of imagination while at the same time images rush in to contain it."[111] God's Spirit and *dahbar* (the spoken word), Christ, dynamically mediate and support the participant's communicative act in which all their relevant factors creatively integrate (συνέστηκεν, Col 1:17) and emerge in socially meaningful shapes relative to each person. This forming matrix grounds and sustains itself outside the participants and conditions the flexibility of symbols, details, and in-tensions of the participants; the emerging image (word) communicates an immeasurable and dynamic whole (spirit) capable of an infinite number of interpretations as it analogically traverses the "vortex" into each respective relation and participant. Only a perichoretic emergence of meaning relative to and within each individual can communicate a unified meaning within diverse participants.[112] As we begin to perceive this relational whole, it emerges out of the darkness into the light as an ineffable whole in which images jump forth in personal meaning appropriate to each participant. Loder thinks, for Kierkegaard, all imagery retains a metaphorical or parabolic quality rather than literal. This provides the space necessary for choice, mind, love, and personal identity to constitute uniquely for and within each person.

For Loder, this theory of imagination and relationality within an ontology of *perichoresis* re-frames and eliminates the Modern epistemological dilemma inherent within the Kantian subject-object dichotomy.

> Subjectiv*ism* is the way to solipsism, not the way to truth. But "objectivity" needs to be understood, not as excluding the subject, but as growing out of the mutual indwelling of subject and object. What we call "object" is an emergent synthesis of so-called subjective and objective factors. . . . But where does the

---

111. Loder, *KM*, 250. Walter Lowrie thinks this reflects Saint Paul's experience of being "caught up into Paradise and [hearing] things that . . . no mortal is permitted to repeat" (2 Cor 12:4).

112. Marion, *God without Being*, 156, speaking of scriptural hermeneutics and reflecting perichoretic dynamics, acknowledges a delay in interpretation whereby "a sort of infinite text is composed. . . . It offers, potentially, an infinite reserve of meaning, . . . hence [this] demands an infinity of interpretations, which, each one, leads a fragment of the text back to the Word [relationship], in taking the point of view of the Word."

> theory come from? It comes as contradiction forces the subjective mind of the theoretician to explore tacitly held theories, assumptions and opinions, many of which are as vague or beyond the periphery of consciousness.[113]

A perichoretic relational ontology thrusts human beings into a prereflexive co-conditioning dynamic. Because of the transparency of this perichoretic dynamic, Kantian subject-object distinctions can be theorized, but they miserably fail at explaining the origin and power of human imagination, let alone human existence.

Cognition as conscious focal awareness is humanly conditioned and maintained as an iconic medium within a dynamic personal world that constitutes co-conditionally within the world of each "emerging" relationship. The unconscious, in this regard, is the life of the person and relationship that perceives what is unable (or unwilling) to become fully conscious with adequate meaningful imagery. Within *perichoresis*, we do not indwell the object or nature of the object; instead, that Power ontologically mediates the nature of the object meaningfully to our spirit reflectively within *analogia spiritus*, which then analogically takes shape conceptually within our imagination and flexible meaning-frame.[114]

For example, as I express my ideas, you are rarely conscious of each specific word. You generally and reflexively experience only meaning (ideas and use); your holistic perception (awareness) supervenes within its feedback loop with the lower-structured logic of the symbols employed. The collating of words in relation to meaningful ideas is a prereflexive process (both *personal* and holistic) that does not construct or emerge linearly. Strangely enough, rather than words constructing into meaning, the first movement of communicative dynamic is the creation of a perichoretic relational field. Within this field of encounter, the holistic intentions and transjections of (spirit) and the mounting collection of words, images, and actions instantly co-condition each other until meaning bursts forth. Again, spirit takes asymmetrical priority over word within this co-conditioning process.[115] In this respect, words embody the emergence of meaning; they are the "house of Being" (Heidegger) that hold meaning in time. The in-tension(al) whole of the relationship is created, only secondarily

113. Loder, *KM*, 23–24.

114. This revocates the former restricting concept of "indwelling" from Greek dualism. This historic limitation creates the reason for the historical conflicts and provides the potential resolutions within many theological polemics, e.g., between Reform and Radical Reform notions of divine-human interaction.

115. The reason for my occasional playful plea in academic discussions, "Please, what I mean, not what say" (the frustration of a dyslexic).

constructed, which allows each person to perichoretically and existentially constitute according to their respective in-tension(al) engagement and capacities. The flexibility and morphic capacity of meaningful symbols within persons allows each spirit to requisition, shape, and transform them to best communicate or understand ideas as felicitously as possible between unique personal meaning-frames.

Therefore, the primordial ground of relationship is pneumatological.[116] In the next chapter, we will consider how the Father is not the Father without a Son, and the Spirit proceeds from the Father *of the Son*. In other words, no Word can exist without Spirit, which is not to say the Son (Word) proceeds out of the Spirit. That would be projecting Hellenistic notions of causation upon the perichoretic relationality of God.

Imagination and Experience in Social Relationship: Language as *Perichoresis*

The exemplary narrative, model, and shape of communicational dynamics are radically portrayed in the story of Pentecost (Acts 2) when everyone understood each other despite the diversity in language, intellectual development, and cultural meaning-frames. Meaning is the primary exchange as the words, cultural-linguistic forms, and constructed relational configurations analogically emerge within each person relative to their specific meaning-frame and mother tongue ("they understood in their own language"). I believe that God's pouring forth and announcing the advent of the Holy Spirit during Pentecost was a proleptic portending of fully redeemed humanity—the Spirit's own "It is finished!" expression to the world. As such, in its most perfected state, it may indicate how language truly works.

In this exemplative narrative, we might suspect that persons from a highly developed culture would not be able to completely communicate their thoughts (meaning) to those within a primitive culture, and that which escapes the imagery, the forms of life, and linguistic capacity of the primitive culture would be lost. Yet, because of the character of this communicative transaction, all those entirely open to the speakers within this perichoretic event might intuit much of the extra within the functional structures of their primitive linguistic meaning-frame. Primitive cultures

---

116. Moltmann, *Source of Life*, 24, concludes: "All things are called into being out of God's living breath, and that breath 'holds them together' [Wis 1:7; Isa 34:16] in a community of creation which furthers life. If they cut themselves off from that community, they lose the living Spirit. If they destroy the community, they destroy themselves. *The Spirit of life means especially the connections and cohesions of everything created*" (emphasis added).

might not experience the meaning with the same fullness of life as the others, but it was all there in the relationship to experience either as a manner of praxis (Hodgson) or analogically within their own meaning-frame. On the other hand, an individual with a more developed meaning-frame listening to a primitive speaker would understand the speaker better than the speaker (as Schleiermacher would contend), articulating meaning linguistically that the speaker only intuits contextually within nonlinguistic forms of life. This often occurs in successful teaching or psychotherapy. Within the dynamic world of the relationship between them, the therapist indwells the client's world and aids the client in expanding their horizons, birthing new categories of relational understanding affecting adaptive equilibrium. For example, those who were not entirely open to the speakers heard only the stammering of drunken men (meaningless noise). This is possible only through *analogia spiritus* and the irreducible dynamics of *perichoresis*.

Such complex communicative capacities are evident all around us. For example, my wife and I have distinctly different personalities (ways we express self-identity and intend others), as do our two daughters. Not only do we relate differently to each child to attain optimal communication, but we also each relate differently with each of the girls. We are often amused at how radically different each of us must engage each daughter (especially in correction/punishment) to achieve the same effect on both of them. The specific relationship that forms in each case will uniquely determine the dynamical structuring of truth and adequacy in relation to the entirety of the situation (relativity, the opposite of relativism). Truth is first a matter of *how* before *what* in communication. The matter is far too complex to assess or adjudicate using the sum of the parts; rather, each new relation will form its own existential mutuality. The truth, however, is there, and the commensurability of meaning ultimately lies between, within the relationship, but because of sin (our partial closure to the Other), we fail to enter wholly into the *analogia spiritus* .

Imagination and Experience of the Numinous: The Relation of the Divine and Human

The dynamic of *perichoresis* and *analogia spiritus* also shed light on the mystery and manifestation of the numinous. Kierkegaard records his conversion experience in his journals at 10:30 a.m., May 19, 1838:

> There is an indescribable joy which glows through us as unaccountably as the Apostle's outburst is unexpected: "Rejoice and again I say, Rejoice."—not a joy over this or that, but full of

jubilation, "with hearts and souls and voices"; I rejoice over my joy, of, in, by, at, on, through, with my joy—a heavenly refrain, which cuts short as it were our ordinary song; a joy which cools and refreshes like a breeze, a gust of the tradewind which blows from the Grove of Mamre to the eternal mansions.

As Kierkegaard encounters God, it is significant that he experiences the joy before any imagery becomes conscious. As we have learned, experience comes just before cognition. There is a prereflexive interaction within the forming matrix of all relations in which the creation of what the speaker is about to express takes shape within the prereflexive process of both speaker and listener simultaneously. Here both speaker and listener together release into the holistic process of the mediational event itself, which begins to hint and then signal at cognition before its arrival, a voice calling from the wilderness, announcing and making ready the way of the word/image and the eminent forthcoming of meaning. Within the "transparency" of the co-indwelt third term of the relationship, human spirit(s) and Holy Spirit de-liberate within the moment, a coinherent process of constituting the relationship, where the appropriate imagery takes shape within the person's own meaning-frame. During that moment, that pause, like the pause between one's breathing in and then out, the numinal engages and then flows out into image and response. Loder suggests,

> Although imagery is primarily the property of the human spirit, it is made vulnerable, permeable, and iconically transparent by the Holy Spirit. Although transparency is a primary property of the Holy Spirit, it uses images, making them imageless, so it may be evident that invisible reality exercises marginal control over visible reality.[117]

Within the image is the implicit denial of its ability to convey the full wealth of meaning experienced. Nevertheless, because human spirit, in its wholeness, analogically relates to the fullness of God (Holy Spirit) within the in-tensioned dynamic, the person constitutes in dipolar de-liberation with God's Spirit so that God's Word (and meaning) reflects through the individual's images. In this way, human symbols, inadequate as they may be, can socialize, objectify, and make explicit the analogous meaning of the whole. Jesus, for example, expects the Jews to recognize him as the Messiah and his words as the words of God by virtue of his perfect perichoretic relation to them, despite his radical departure from existing Jewish and rabbinical forms of life. Those who were genuinely open despite their formerly

---

117. Loder, *KM*, 253.

inadequate relational structures would have sensed the compelling numinal force of his actions as an explicit shock of recognition. In the experience of Kierkegaard, Loder describes,

> a swirling vortex of images pour into the pre-conscious arena of [his] search for expression of the ineffable, and many partially adequate images pass and "speak" before the climactic and cumulative image from Genesis gathers up the "chaos" according to a hidden order and the tension is released and the system cools. In this image, Divine initiative and conflicted human existence, a personal history and a biblical story, past and future, are bound up in present time as the concrete visible situation becomes the bearer of an invisible eternal—these are all bisociative connections which tacitly retain their differentiation even in the unifying power of the ecstatic experience.[118]

This explanation makes strikingly obvious what is characteristic in all human relationships, that meaning emerges within a dynamic (bisociative) complementarity of differentiated unity. In one manner of thinking, persons are themselves relationships much like matter taking shape from energy, which attain the provisional status of personhood, and only to that degree within authentic or perichoretic relations or koinonia. Meaning is never "out there" as a currency we pass between us as an Archimedean fact. Merleau-Ponty thinks:

> So long as I keep before me the ideal of an absolute observer, of knowledge in the absence of any viewpoint, I can only see my situation as being a source of error. But once I have acknowledged that through it I am geared to all actions and all knowledge that are meaningful to me, and that it is gradually filled with everything that may be for me, then my contact with the social in the finitude of my situation is revealed to me as the starting point of all truth, including that of science and, since we have some idea of the truth, since we are inside truth and cannot get outside it, all that I can do is define a truth within the situation.[119]

---

118. Loder, *KM*, 253. Cf. Agamben, *Kingdom*, 19: "Just as messianic time is not some other time but, instead, an integral transformation of chronological time, an ultimate experience (an experience of the last things) would entail, first and foremost, experiencing penultimate things differently. In this context eschatology is nothing other than a transformation of the experience of the penultimate. . . . The ultimate reality deactivates, suspends and transforms, the penultimate ones—and yet, it is precisely, and above all, in these penultimate realities that an ultimate reality bears witness and is put to the test."

119. Merleau-Ponty, as cited by Prigogine, *Order Out of Chaos*, 299. Originally from Merleau-Ponty, *Éloge de la Philosophie*, 136–37.

In other words, being inside the Truth, we cannot handle it as currency within our complete control. Even memory is not a meaningful event literally encoded into our brain, but an active relational re-creation.[120] Therefore, what is ineffable within the creation of the relational unity, what we implicitly or holistically experience, becomes explicit only through social adaptation and the existing development and potential transformation of each person's relational configurations. Human spirit analogically reflects those same supervening qualities active in constituting the relationship. "For in Him we live and move and have our being, as also some of your own poets have said, 'For we are also His offspring'" (Acts 17:28). Again, Marion suggests that:

> Incarnate in our words, the Word acquires in them a new unspeakableness, since he can be spoken in them only by the movement of incarnation that is, so to speak, *anterior to the words*, which he speaks and which he lets speak him. Any speech that speaks only from this side of language hence cannot reach the referent.[121]

Meaning emerges within our spirit, optimally, in full relation to the Spirit of Christ, which existentially and transparently incarnates us in meaningful social relations. Words (entities) themselves become constellations of diachronic and synchronic relations, each meaning-fully "delayed" for appropriate reconfiguration within the anterior and in-tension(al) formation of a meaningful whole.[122] As discussed earlier, the continuity of words or forms of life lies in their specific relatedness within the whole. Their diachronic quality comes from their synchronic interrelatedness. This provides the flexibility for reconstitution within differing meaning-frames (e.g., during paradigm shifts). More specifically, this presents a relational theory of "top-down" supervenience, whereby the constituting (transformational)

---

120. For example, Moltmann, *GC*, 115, tells us, "memory does represent a certain re-creation of the past in the present; and expectation does in a sense represent the *new creation* of the future in the present mind" (emphasis added). Cf. also Gunton, *One, Three, Many*, 68.

121. Marion, *God without Being*, 141, emphasis added.

122. Cf. also Braine, *Human Person*, 465–66: "We are never concerned with the understanding of langue as if it were something withstanding in its own right, but only with the understanding of langue as something to be realized in the understanding of parole or speech.... [And yet] we must reiterate that we are not speaking of indeterminacy of meaning or indeterminism as to how speech is to be understood. The openness of a unit of langue to polymorphous use, the flexibility which allows us to use words meaningfully outside the type of context within which they were learnt, the flexibility of which metaphor is only one example, involve that langue-meaning does not by itself determine parole-meaning."

dynamic creating the relationship (meaning) shapes and constitutes all the entities (words) accordingly. Words, as well as propositions, are coterminous with past use, not because they re-present that same meaning from the past (or text) for present meaning construction, but because their similar synchronic placement within former constellations of meaning are analogically adequate for re-creation into new existential constellations appropriate for new and unique interactions.

When the constellation of relations significantly evolves due to increasing or changing complexities, the use of words (meaning) begins to change. When the meaning-frame radically changes, words can sometimes lose continuity with past use altogether. Nevertheless, the transformational dynamic facilitating the emergence of meaning bears marginal control over the use of all relevant words in constructing meaning. As we have seen, this is the same for persons as relations. Accordingly, Kierkegaard's experience of joy before the images within the knowing event shows us the antecedent and preeminent status of *analogia spiritus* over Barth's notion of *analogia relationis*, which focuses more on the eventuality of the word. The antecedent co-conditioning *analogia spiritus*, however, gives us the theological space to reframe Barth's notion of the divine-human point-of-contact, which, as we will see, can dramatically affect our theological understanding of the human will, human as spirit, ethics, and most dramatically, resolve the perennial theological issues of theodicy and the mutuality of divine providence and human freedom.

The Polymorphic Symbols of "Recollection" and the Supervenience of Relating Totalities

In 2 Cor 3:17–18, Paul briefly describes the divine-human relational dynamic:

> Now the Lord is the Spirit; and where the Spirit of the Lord is, there is liberty. But we all, with unveiled face beholding as in a mirror the glory of the Lord, are being transformed into the same image from one degree of glory to another, just as from the Lord, the Spirit.

The word κατοπτρίζομαι ("beholding as in a mirror"), used only once in the New Testament, signifies the beholding of an image that is not an exact recollection or reflection, but one we perceive through a miraculous mirror making visible that which is invisible. It is an iconic viewing. Gerhard Kittel argues Paul is suggesting that it is by the spirit we "see."[123] This parallels the

---

123. Kittel, " κατοπτρίζομαι," *TDNT* 2:696–97.

basic thought in 1 Cor 13:12, where the resulting image through the mirror is dim and partial. Together these passages point to the twofold nature of perceiving the image in the mirror, namely an unveiled perceiving, which does not entirely re-present the image in our explicit cognitive rendering, and the image which to some degree "reflects" this fullness within the interaction. This dynamic is not Platonist but gives us cause to understand why Plato suggests what he does given his limited meaning-frame. Again, we experience a greater whole analogically than we can explicitly articulate.

Furthermore, it seems three basic aspects (or dynamics) of meaning construction condition our perception. The first is pure *analogia spiritus*, which holistically conditions meaning in what appears to be two ways. One is the immediate impression of learned tacit elements that instantly construct and configure (condition) experience, a primarily right hemispheric modality proffering an immediate sense of what is there, a framing of the picture. This generally transcends explicit image and begins before gestalt. The left hemispheric activity then constructs a focal image of the holistic encounter conditioned by the intending dynamics within *analogia spiritus*. The latter is the emissary activity, as noted by McGilchrist, which is ultimately dependent upon the master holistic activity of the right hemisphere or, better yet, the mind. The other aspect of conditioning within the holistic interaction escapes all previously learned tacit or focal traces but leaves us with a sense of something (*analogia spiritus*). These transparent aspects of the encounter generally condition our thought unconsciously, invisibly pushing at us, for example, just before gestalt or discovery.

The inability of the image to convey the fullness of meaning has to do with the incoherent, incomplete, and truncated relational structures available within each person's social development. Nevertheless, "this looking into the divine κατοπτρον mirror has the wonderful result that those who are willing to remove the mask and look are changed into the likeness of what they see (μεταμορφόομαι), i.e., they reflectively share in the δόξα."[124] The "glory" represents the holistic depth of the encounter that informs our images, tacit frameworks, and relational dynamics creating meaningful experience-in-relationship.

Within the holistic analogical conditioning of *analogia spiritus*, there are no attributions of differentiation within the meaning itself. On the contrary, all such attributions are themselves whole new interrelations.[125] Likewise, the differentiated aspects and images that emerge from the

---

124. Kittel, "κατοπτριζόμαι," *TDNT* 2:696.

125. Moltmann, *GC*, 11, tells us "the interrelations of the world cannot be traced back to any components, or universal foundations, . . . in reality relationships are just as primal as the things themselves."

relationship manifest only within each person's respective meaning-frame. Though this occurs within a co-conditioning mutuality and established social codes, meaning *en totum* is created within our spirit, person-in-relation. Nevertheless, the preeminent and emergent relationship itself becomes the supervenient ontological force in which persons correlate in meaningful relation to one another and constitute through the trinitarian dynamic of *perichoresis*.

TIME AND ETERNITY: ESCHATOLOGICAL TIME

The writings of Loder and Kierkegaard express the rich dynamic of *perichoresis* and its dynamic complementarity between time and Eternity, a consideration necessary for any personal notion of divine-human relations. The Kierkegaardian "leap" and moment of synthesis emerges within divine-human relations in which persons participate to some degree in the Eternal light of the Logos, conditioning them in relation to "everything that has been made all at once—in a moment that contains the fullness of time."[126]

> When transformation is no longer merely the dynamic pattern of development working as human spirit within the horizon of adaptation and ego formation but, instead, becomes the pattern of Spiritus Creator, according to which the ego itself and its horizons are radically transformed, then this same pattern prevails, but now on a far more profound scale of being. This is transformation (as in the human spirit) transformed (as by the Holy Spirit).[127]

This constituting action and conditioning of human capacity for transformation through the mediating action within human relations allows such Eternal purviews to condition them holistically. Only this comprehensive relatedness to this massive interactional connection to all kairological time throughout history in our perichoretic relations to Christ endows us the capacity to take "dominion" over creation. All power and dominion are given but only to those willing to bear their cross in relation to the Other. Logically, "all power" and full participation within the Kingdom of Heaven can only disperse as emissaries in existential relations to that mediational matrix that comprehensively interrelates and co-conditions all times, lives, and longings throughout history ("the mind of Christ," 1 Cor 2:11–16).

---

126. Loder, *KM*, 186. Again, within this thesis, Loder's "has been made" might better be understood as "being made."

127. Loder, *KM*, 256.

Without the purview of the risen Christ, we are clueless: the fulfillment of one person's "desire" or "freedom" is quite often another's oppression.[128] Not only does humanity's temporal relation to Christ constitute them in relation to the Eternal, but the Father's Eternal trinitarian relations constitute God temporally in relation to all history.[129] Even the perfect perichoretic relation of the Son to the Father does not technically afford the Son the explicit or focal perception of "everything that has been made all at once." Time and Eternity cannot synthesize in a Hegelian manner, even within the godhead! Nevertheless, when Kierkegaard argues "existence is a synthesis of the infinite and the finite, and the existing individual is both infinite and finite," and furthermore that a person must simultaneously maintain an "absolute relationship to the absolute "telos" and a relative relationship to relative ends,"[130] we might suspect the same constitutional dynamics of *perichoresis* within the divine persons. Therefore, the Son, as human, focally and explicitly constitutes in relation to the world (spacetime) or eschatological new creation (also a spacetime), as well as tacitly conditioned by his perfect pre-reflexive process within the Trinity.[131] Remember, within this thesis, there is no world "out there" in which things relate. Relationships are reality, each technically containing their own spacetime. But because all relationships eventually interrelate, they, to some degree, eventually share a spacetime.[132]

128. Cf. Moltmann, *TC*, 215.

129. Cf. Moltmann, *GC*, 217.

130. Kierkegaard, *CUP*, 347.

131. This transtemporal dynamic of the ascending Christ *ensarkos* will be the subject of the following few chapters and presupposes the work of Torrance, *Resurrection*.

132. It is difficult to imagine a risen Christ constituting temporally and yet omnisciently present throughout all creation (a Newtonian concept). However, it is possible to imagine Christ as the author of all creation when creation is a differentiated unity, and each relationship and consciousness is technically its own spacetime in differentiation. Christ, in this respect, is free to constitute each relation temporally and personally because of its (or their) own spacetime differentiatedness. It seems counterintuitive within our antiquated Newtonian way of thinking, but, as we will see in our penultimate chapter, modern physics eliminates Newtonian cosmology, and the quantum world ultimately suggests a relational cosmology (ontology) contingent in some way upon consciousness. During Christ's physical development on earth, he constitutes within his specific interactions; however, between his resurrection and ascension (according to Barth), he is free to personally constitute in relation to all of history, relative to each historical moment, appropriate to each historical situation. As risen, he can manifest within an infinite amount of spacetime moments because each relational moment has its own differentiated spacetime distinct from every other. Technically there are no scheduling conflicts necessitating Newtonian omniscience. We might think of each created moment, though perichoretically in relation to the entirety of creation, as its own universe and spacetime. Therefore, Christ has been, is, and always will constitute temporally(-in-relation-to-the-Eternal).

The difference between Christ's knowledge during his earthly journey and ours is a matter of intensity and degree of hypostasis within the synthesis of existence (the constant result of complete abandonment into his relationship with the Father) and his purview as God. Our post-resurrected difference will be due to his being first born (raised) and constituting as person in existential relation to all history and the Trinity within its unfolding. As he knows us now, so it seems, we shall know then; but at present, he functions and relates as person in our earthly pilgrimage, enabling us to accomplish what we otherwise could not. Again, this satisfies the incarnational imperative of mutuality; if God is to have filial relations with humanity (as the Scriptures proclaim), something of human beings must become divine, and something of God must become human.

To consider that we experience a far more profound scale of being in relation to Christ may also be misleading for some. A fuller expression of his thinking might be that we experience a far more profound scale of relating within the world, an enhancement of the typical understanding of being and becoming. Even the Father, constituting as person in relation to the Son and the Spirit, does not explicitly know the future before it happens.[133] Within the infinite Eternal, becoming aware of something at any time is to witness it in its happening. The Father becomes aware of everything happening or becoming in a *dynamic* singularity. In effect, the Father's awareness of all things becomes temporalized in his perichoretic relation to the Son. If trinitarian relations entail perfect *perichoresis*, we must assume the Father himself explicitly knows the world only through the Son and the Son's con-sisting metaphysical action in history. This statement cannot be understood using sequential notions of causality in time; the Special Theory of Relativity and Quantum mechanics, however, have now shown us that causality is not bound to our sequential rendering of time. More on this later.[134] Therefore, we might better express human participation within the Eternal light of the Logos as perceiving everything (in history) being made all at once—in a moment that contains the fullness of time. In other words, in the present passive indicative rather than a past tense.[135] Therefore, when

133. Polkinghorne, "Setting the Problem," 9.

134. The point is that Christ (constituting in Time) can say of the Father (constituting Eternally) that "of that day only the Father knows" simply because for the Father, it is always already happening, not happened. As Einstein has shown, there is a position in the universe in which all of history dynamically transpires altogether simultaneously (a dynamic singularity).

135. The indicative mood confirms the reality of an action from the speaker's viewpoint: the subject perceiving in present time the present passive continuous activity. Cf. Agamben, *Kingdom*, 9, 12: "What is at issue is neither the homogenous and infinite line of chronological time (easy to visually represent but empty of all experience) nor the

Loder, with Moltmann and Pannenberg, states that "convictional experiences are to be seen preeminently as a breakthrough from the future,"[136] it means that all such faith experiences emerge in holistic relatedness (in hypostasis) and, through Christ, mutually co-condition each other across spacetime.

The *uni*directional concept of the future proleptically conditioning the present is theologically and biologically limiting and biblically incoherent. It strips the Jacob narrative from its intractable biblical prominence, relegating it to a theological enigma for most theological programs. No one seems to know what to do with Jacob's God-given unparalleled prominence over all others within the Old Covenant. According to Torah, Jacob is the ultimate father of faith, undisputedly. These well-meaning theorists find it difficult to escape the idea of an impositional God and God's preeminent decree as Alpha or, in this case, Omega (Telos), of which we must then come into obedience, as did Abraham. Jacob, on the other hand, passionately struggles with God to retain the blessing that he, by all accounts, speciously attains. However, Jacob's co-conditioning struggle within his relation to God is not disobedience; instead, it shifts obedience to another level of engagement and response. Because of Jacob's passion—his immanent conditioning from *analogia spiritus* throughout his story—he became spirit (in the Kierkegaardian sense) and thereby comes to a depth of relations through which he can condition (affect) God's Eternal action within the Jacobian night *analogia spiritus*. Jacob's dream of the ladder reflects the faith experience of Kierkegaard's Religiousness A, he simply receives it. His later wrestling with God-man, witnessing the face of God (Christ as person) reflects Religiousness B. The earlier experience represents the transparent prereflexive moment of the faith experience that merely breaks into time. In his wrestling encounter he begins to move with Christ in Christ's Time. This represents the mythic status and importance of Jacob—reflecting the "mystery which has been hidden from the ages and from generations, . . . which is Christ in *us* (Col 1:24, 27)." Surely, this is one possible direction toward satisfying Prigogine's call for a "more subtle form of reality that involves both time and eternity."[137] Again, we will explore this theory further in a few chapters.

---

precise and unimaginable instant where it ends. . . . Instead, what is at issue is a time that pulses and moves within chronological time, that transforms chorological time from within. On one hand it is the time that time takes to end."

136. Loder, *KM*, 197.

137. Prigogine, *Order Out of Chaos*, 186.

SUPERVENIENT DYNAMICS IN *PERICHORESIS*

We are now in a better position to expand our notion of supervenience. Earlier, Murphy's use of supervenience was adjusted and enlarged, stressing that supervenient levels of interaction are active at all levels of interaction even though they may not be explicitly evident within lower-level logic. Conversely, the lower-level language has the higher-level logic (and often praxis) within its own unconscious tacit dimensions, even though these higher-level functions are irreducible to the explicit logic of the lower-level activity and understanding (water to the fish versus flying fish). In understanding person as *perichoresis*, the dynamic of human spirit and the notion of *analogia spiritus* provide us with a complementarity in human relationality whereby supervenient qualities of divine relations may or may not be holistically noticeable; nevertheless, they present a potential of holistic reciprocity that facilitates human participation at such levels. Therefore, mutual interaction is possible at a level that interrelates the relational cycles of human existence with those same analogical dynamics within the divine Trinity. This keeps all corresponding "lower-level" consciousness (much of which is relative and focal) from being inconsequential or trivialized. We experience the totality of this interaction only at the spirit (holistic) level. This relocates the ethical response level to the self-structuring posture before such supervening qualities within our relationships, which translates to a relational disposition rather than moralizing our explicit behavior. Jesus suggests this radical adjustment in the Sermon on the Mount.

This in no way diminishes God's personal will and activity within creation but broadens how God works and orchestrates divine will superveniently with it. My wife communicates many things to me, often subconsciously and to some degree unintentionally. In retrospection, I have noticed my subconscious awareness of her subconscious communication and my subconscious response. Such interaction is a direct consequence of *analogia spiritus*. God's supervening (perichoretic) influence and activity at the human level will be affective at many levels of communication and causal interaction, much of this at holistic subconscious levels but no less interactive. Though God speaks, he also influences as we influence: Spirit-to-spirit-to-Spirit. Nevertheless, all such interactions are ultimately coherent and coinherent with God's speaking.

CONCLUSION

In this section, I have attempted to establish the following hypothesis through the work of Loder's developmental psychology, his Kierkegaardian notion of relationality, and its implications for theology:

> Each stage of human development is conditioned by the previous stage, yet the ultimate meaning within each stage emerges from the quality of the differentiated unity it experiences in relations. In transformational moments, future stages condition the present in a co-conditioning process that happens within a person's prereflexive holistic dynamics within the third term of the relationship. The Power that *co-ordinates* all relations and transforms personal transformational dynamics constitutes all interactions in relation to the Eternal.

We are now in a better position to understand how humanity preemptively affects the creating activity of God before the "In the beginning." Just as the unique narrative of Christ opens insights into the anthropological dynamics of relationships, these same relational dynamics provide us with a better understanding of how God relates with us. We have now considered the dynamic of *perichoresis* as meaning (meaning/method as differentiated unity), in persons (emotions), in social communications (McFadyen/Kierkegaard), and as person (Piaget/Loder/Kierkegaard). These insights into the emerging presence of *perichoresis* in the world likewise provide images that inform our understanding of the Master Image of God and how God relates to humanity and the world.

Loder's study in relational dynamics prepares the way for our specific inquiry into the *perichoresis* of time and Eternity and the unity of immanence and transcendence in human existence. However, before investigating this unique Kierkegaardian synthesis between time and Eternity, let us briefly consider the doctrine of the Trinity and, specifically, the multidimensional activity of the Spirit of God.

4

Perichoresis in the Trinity

Moltmann and the Spirit of God

> It is hard to accept the idea that there cannot be an order in the universe because it would offend the free will of God and His omnipotence. So the freedom of God is our condemnation, or at least the condemnation of our pride.... Isn't affirming God's absolute omnipotence and His absolute freedom with regard to His own choices tantamount to demonstrating that God does not exist?
>
> "Adso" (Umberto Eco)[1]

TRINITY AND *PERICHORESIS*

The purpose of this section is to compare various internal and external relational dynamics of the Trinity with corresponding human relational dynamics. This brief consideration of the Trinity and its relational dynamic of *perichoresis* centers on Jürgen Moltmann's work, specifically the relational structures of God's Spirit. We will explore the striking analogical resemblance between the dynamics of the Spirit within this sociology and those corresponding dynamics of human relationality. The goal is to situate the earlier anthropological inquiries theologically.

---

1. Eco, *Name of the Rose*, 492–93.

Though theological structures maintain an asymmetrical methodological influence over our developing anthropological structures, the two form a hermeneutical complementarity that indisputably conditions our understanding of either trinitarian or human relational dynamics.[2] However, within its triune relations, the Spirit of God provides the asymmetrical and analogical force defining *analogia spiritus* that should guide this study (1 Cor 2). Again, Jesus' prayer that we would relate, as he and the Father relate *so that* we might relate with them, exposes the preeminent purpose of Christianity and marks the loci of divine-human mutuality as the dynamic of relationality itself. I read nothing else in the Scriptures that suggests otherwise. The story begins with our inability to do so and God's effort to progressively and inevitably make it so. My primary premise has been that trinitarian sociology grounds the redeeming process of human sociology; therefore, our criterion for assessing such progress should be what best analogically reflects this trinitarian relationality—*perichoresis*.

Furthermore, advances in our knowledge of human relational dynamics should inform our understanding of God's trinitarian dynamics. This study, in many ways, is an anthropological stimulation of theology for their mutual benefit. In the next chapter, we will explore how new advances in our understanding of time within relativity and quantum theory in physics can wonderfully enrich our doctrines of the Trinity, the Spirit, and divine *perichoresis*. For example, it ultimately exposes the theological notions of immanence and transcendence in divine-human relations as specious dichotomies.

Moltmann's read on the Trinity is multifaceted, complex, and often affably unsystematic. Because of its scope, many fail to notice or misconstrue his theological coherence, especially those theologians employing modern evidential strictures in their epistemological configurations of the Trinity, Spirit, and, specifically, *perichoresis*. Many of those critics insist on maintaining ancient historical formulas governing these doctrines while anachronistically assuming these formulations enjoyed the same benefits, categories, and development of today's theology. Though deeply meaningful, Moltmann's theology is experimental, adventurous, and suggestive, leading to his extreme popularity that mystify his critics. Restating these thoughts:

---

2. Though both disciplines contain a theological and a natural dimension in which theological anthropology asymmetrically conditions natural theology, there are times in history when, as Johannes Climacus might suggest, the flourishing humanities must provoke dead religion.

> There are theological systems which are not only designed to be non-contradictory in themselves, but aim to remain undisputed from outside too. They are like fortresses which cannot be taken, but which no one can break out of either.[3]

Moltmann's theology is not about affirming, circumscribing, or ossifying our dogmatic doctrines of faith but *"imagination for the kingdom of God"* that provide ever-increasing diverse images that express our theological knowledge. Therefore, without "built-in safeguards" and in what some regard as reckless, what I perceive as dynamically impressionistic, his theology evokes a rich purview into our faith experience through often scattered but well-placed strokes.[4] His theology's true strength and coherence emerge only within the richness of the theological gestalt (whole) *it creates* within the reader.

Like Loder's analogical synchronicity of relational structures between the divine and human, the knowledge of the Trinity, says Moltmann, is ultimately doxological, and such ideas must "suffer a transformation of meaning."[5] Experiencing God or persons "has to be understood, and can only be understood, in Trinitarian terms."[6] Genuine openness to the other and self-change within relationship necessitates that the subject "enter entirely into his counterpart."[7]

Moltmann's social Trinity is well known and yet rarely fully understood. To most, it seems contradictory. Looking at any ontology through the eyes of another will render countless contradictions. The difficulty during such ontological shifts compounds further with one's failure to stay

---

3. Moltmann, *CG*, xiv.

4. In other words, the realism, whole picture, or meaning within his theology must happen *between* the text and the reader. Impressionistic paintings force the viewer to enter the process of meaning-making, requiring the proper relationship (e.g., three meters back) and active constructive hermeneutical participation through which to communicate the holistic aspects necessary in theological knowledge rather than attempting to reflect reality to the viewer from a universal "realist" point of view.

5. Moltmann, *TKG*, 162.

6. Moltmann, *TKG*, 4.

7. "From time immemorial, experience has been bound up with wonder or with pain. In wonder the subject opens himself for a counterpart and gives himself up to the overwhelming impression. In pain the subject perceives the difference of the other, the contradictions in conflict and the alteration of his own self. In both modes of experience the subject enters entirely into his counterpart" (Moltmann, *TKG*, 4). These categories of ongoing *opening* wonder and *perceiving* difference and re-alteration echo McFadyen's dialogical cycles. Moltmann, however, is less insistent (or consistent) than Loder or Kierkegaard in locating the indwelling within the third term of the relationship rather than the other. In this respect, his language often drags us back into the Modernist's trench of dualism, e.g., "the subject enters into his counterpart."

abreast of the advancements within all disciplines of thought, specifically those of anthropological relevance.

Methodological note: The entirety of Scripture and Christian tradition conclusively reveal a developmental nature even within themselves, both within the Scriptures and the history of faith. In this respect, our understanding of the Trinity will undoubtedly grow, expand, and even transform with the emergence of new and richer relational categories, heuristics, and new insights into both theology and anthropology (Bonhoeffer). This study engages Moltmann's analysis of the Trinity with no intention of seeking the correct historical expressions of the Trinity or even engaging the *filioque* issue in and for itself; the fullest expression of the Trinity lies before us, not behind us. Nevertheless, understanding what the church fathers thought on this matter is essential, and we maintain an appropriate continuity in our growing knowledge. Still, we must remember *there was not even a Greek word for "relationship" or "sycnhronization" during the writing of the New Testament!* In this respect, my purpose in engaging Moltmann on this issue is to explore new potential categories of relationality that might help us to express a fuller understanding of the Trinity than what would have been difficult or impossible to express in the past.

Trinitarian Analogy of Relations

In a terse article on the Trinity and the *filioque*, Moltmann describes the Father as the source of the Son and Spirit; however, the Spirit of God is from the Father and the Son. The Spirit of God always "proceeds *from the Father of the Son*."[8] Citing Boris Bolotov, Moltmann claims:

> The Spirit is the third hypostasis of the Holy Trinity. The Spirit's being presupposes the existence of the Father and the existence of the Son because the Holy Spirit proceeds from the Father and because the Father is the Father of the Son alone. Consequently, as soon as God *proboleus tous pneumatos* is called *Father*, he is thought of as having a Son.

The Spirit presupposes the existence of the Father and Son, and for Moltmann, the Spirit produces the "uniting mutuality and community" of the Trinity.[9] Though the Father constitutes the Trinitarian unity and concentrates around the Son, it is "illuminated through the Spirit." Therefore, corresponding to the wholistic nature of relationship and communication

---

8. Moltmann, "Theological Proposals," 168.
9. Moltmann, *TKG*, 178.

discussed in Loder, God's holistic illuminating knowledge and experience is always "perceived through the Spirit first of all."[10] The relationship as "mutuality and community" results from the agency of the Spirit; however, the idea of relationship also involves the instantiating (*hypostasis*) of individual subjectivity. This individuating dynamic is a fundamental quality of the perichoretic nature of Spirit as well. Nevertheless, the Spirit "issues from . . . the Father's relationship to the Son."[11] Within the mutual indwelling dynamic of *perichoresis*, the "Holy Spirit has its perfect, divine existence (*hypostasis, hyparxis*) from the Father and receives from the Son his relational form (*eidos, prosopon*)."[12] Furthermore, "the 'issuing' of the Spirit from the Father and the 'reception' of his relational perichoretic form from the Father and from the Son are two different processes."[13] Nevertheless, these processes are simultaneous and comprise a relational complementarity and co-conditioning.

Unlike Loder and Kierkegaard, Moltmann, in *The Trinity and the Kingdom of God*, sees the Spirit as a product of the relationship rather than the relationship itself. As we shall see, however, the Spirit becomes more prominent within his later thinking as the principal aspect of the relationship. But, before we address that further, it is important to note a few other trinitarian distinctions.

Trinitarian Relational Attributes

Differentiated Unity

The One God, for Moltmann, is neither a "numerical" or "monadic" One, but a "unity which is differentiated in itself."[14] To understand the concept of differentiated unity, one must transcend the structures of Modern, Platonistic, and even Aristotelian metaphysics.[15] Such immanent and economic trinitarian distinctions within Kantian structuring become problematic. The Persons are not distinguishable from each other in their personal character; "they are just as much united with one another and in one another, since personal character and social character are only two aspects of the

---

10. Moltmann, *TKG*, 178.
11. Moltmann, *TKG*, 184.
12. Moltmann, *TKG*, 186.
13. Moltmann, *TKG*, 188.
14. Moltmann, *TKG*, 137.
15. Moltmann, *TKG*, 150, 158.

same thing."[16] There is no separation of personal character within the perfect sociology of the divine person, yet each person of the Trinity remains distinct in their respective actions concerning the world. This is because God's unity and "at-oneness," its transcendent primal ground, cannot lie in the homogeneity of one divine essence, substance, or identity of one absolute subject.[17] Only a Person as differentiated unity can communicate in relationship, and only a *differentiated* unity can be open to change.[18] The history of God's trinitarian relationship is the eternal *perichoresis* of Father, Son, and Holy Spirit in "their opening of themselves for the reception and unification of the whole creation."[19] This results from a differentiated unity whose perichoretic dynamic ontologically and personally generates from within the uniqueness of their interactions. The history of salvation is the drawing of humanity into God's "eternal triune life with all the fullness of its relationships."

Perichoresis is the "circulatory character of the eternal divine life . . . they live in . . . and dwell in one another to such an extent, that they are one. It is a process of most perfect and intense empathy."[20] Their co-indwelling is *not* intermittent nor after their becoming Persons. In this respect, Word is never Spirit. There is, however, no Word without Spirit or Spirit without Word.[21]

In a more Irenaean trinitarian conceptualization, Gunton similarly describes *perichoresis* as a "dynamic mutual reciprocity, interpenetration and interanimation."[22] Likewise, in creation, "the 'nature' of the related things must derive from these relations, while at the same time the relations must derive from the 'nature' of the things. . . . Everything in the universe is what it is by virtue of its relatedness to everything else."[23] In this respect, Gunton and Moltmann agree that the perichoretic dynamic active in the Trinity generates the ontological quality in *both* the instantiation of individuality *and* mutual relatedness as a complementarity within personal existence, whether in the Godhead or humanity. Furthermore, they approximate the emphasis of Loder and Kierkegaard concerning this

---

16. Moltmann, *TKG*, 150.
17. Moltmann, *TKG*, 150, 157.
18. Moltmann, *TKG*, 150.
19. Moltmann, *TKG*, 157.
20. Moltmann, *TKG*, 174–75.
21. "Word and Spirit, Spirit and Word issue together and simultaneously from the Father, for they mutually condition one another" (Moltmann, *TKG*, 170).
22. Gunton, *One, Three, Many*, 163.
23. Gunton, *One, Three, Many*, 172.

dynamic's irreducibility. This leads to Moltmann's (or Pannenberg's) social Trinity of three subjects and generally provokes critical reactions from Barthian and Modern theologies with their incumbent underdeveloped understandings of human personhood.[24] As we witnessed within certain social constructivists, we have only just begun to realize and integrate this knowledge of the contingency of the subject's social constitution into our theological thinking.

From my perspective, I have no issue with Barth's modified modalistic Trinity illustrating the internal "consciousness" of the one God in God's "subjectivity," in a sense reflecting godself to godself, the Son reflecting the Father via the Spirit. Yet in relations outside the Trinity, one of the persons of the Trinity will manifest according to the character of God's interaction with creation, even though all are perichoretically active within the action.

The Nature of the Persons in the Trinity

Though Moltmann is clear about three persons in the Trinity, he is purposely indeterminate about the nature of Personhood shared between them. Each one's manifestation of Personhood is unique and different from the other. Their "particular individual nature is determined in their relationship to one another."[25]

> The "three Persons" are different, not merely in their relations to one another, but also in respect of their character as Persons, even if the person is to be understood in his relations, and not apart from them. If we wanted to remain specific, we should have to use a different concept in each case when applying the word "person" to the Father, the Son and the Spirit.[26]

Moltmann, unlike Kierkegaard, is reticent to say person *is* relationship; instead, relationship constitutes person. Relations and persons form a complementarity,[27] and are relationally perichoretic.

---

24. One need only consider the aggressiveness of Moltmann and Pannenberg in keeping abreast of concurrent anthropological and psychological developments in relation to Barth to understand one possible aspect creating their respective theological trajectories.

25. Moltmann, *TKG*, 172.

26. Moltmann, *TKG*, 189; cf. Lonergan, *Divinarum*, 236.

27. Moltmann, *TKG*, 186.

The Nature and Character of the Spirit within the Trinity

The Spirit is active in differing ways with the Father, Son, and creation. Moltmann portrays the Spirit as issuing *from the relationship* between the Father and the Son yet emphasizes the Spirit's role in *making space for the relationship*. As for all life, "Life is experienced and lived *in* the Spirit. . . . [I]t is the medium and space for experience."[28] This is a function of the Spirit for the Father and the Son.

> The Holy Spirit allows the Son to shine in the Father and transfigures the Father in the Son. He is the eternal light in which the Father knows the Son and the Son the Father. In the Holy Spirit the eternal divine life arrives at consciousness of itself, therein reflecting its perfect form. . . . Finally, the mutual transfiguration and illumination of the Trinity into the eternal glory of the divine life is bound up with this. This uniting mutuality and community proceeds from *the Holy Spirit*.[29]

Only in the Spirit can the Father and the Son relate with each other. Effectively, the Holy Spirit becomes the essence of the relationship between the two.[30]

Moreover, it only makes sense that if the Spirit interrelates the Father and Son, it must not be lesser, greater, or other than what they are by nature, notwithstanding the attribution of personhood. By logical necessity, if the Father and Son are persons, that which enables the relationship must itself constitute as person. There exist compelling insights into such Trinitarian dynamics that suggest three persons, not two, are needed to create and maintain Personhood.[31]

---

28. Moltmann, *SL*, 157.

29. Moltmann, *TKG*, 176–78.

30. Barth tells us: "The Holy Spirit is the love which is the essence of the relation between these two modes of being of God" (*CD* 1/1:480).

31. Staniloae, "Procession," expanding on Moltmann's concept that the Spirit receives its existence from the Father and his image (εἶδος) from the Son, agrees that the Holy Spirit is a person within the Trinity because of the relationship between the Father and Son, and because of it's intimate and unique relationship to both individually. When the Spirit relates to the Son, thus receiving the image, he must experience the Son while also experiencing the Father to differentiate the Son from the Father and fully know the Son, which entails the Son's knowing of the Father. In analogous reference to human relations, he points out, "no one can exist except in relation with two other persons, and not only in a perpetually closed relationship with one other person" (185). Staniloae asks, how can I live in the fullness of the other's life without knowing the other's other? "I cannot live in the fullness of the life of another—and therefore also in my own—except by also living my relation with his other other, thus making it my own relation. . . . I can say that I know my other in the light of his other other, with whom he is linked. As for me, I must

Moltmann, therefore, is hesitatingly consonant with Loder's use of Kierkegaard—that the Spirit is, to some degree, the relationship becoming a third *hypostasis* (in the case of human or divine relations, a person). Yet when Moltmann says, "it is the nature of the person to give himself *entirely to a counterpart, and to find himself in the other* most of all," he exposes his limitations within his Classical relational dynamics.³² When we consider the Spirit as relationship within an ontology of subject-relationship-subject, Spirit creates the space for the counterparts to experience each other perichoretically.³³ The Spirit now becomes the space of relationship within a perichoretic dynamic which simultaneously affirms not only the individuality of the Father and the Son but, because of the Spirit's unique relations within the Trinity, its own personhood. In this respect, the Spirit facilitates one of the many complementarities that make God a Trinity. God can be encountered or described as a person (God) or as one of the three persons (Father, Son, or Holy Spirit) according to the specific character or modes of relations and relational context, but possibly like quantum dynamics, never any of these manifestations at the same time within their extra-trinitarian relations.

Moltmann's unique and more comprehensive treatment of the Spirit of God hugely benefits this thesis. If the Spirit becomes diversely manifest as the relationship between, for example, the Father and the Son, the Son and creation, the Spirit and humanity (e.g., sustaining human self as a relationship unto itself), etc., then we would expect the Scriptures to name, describe, and present the Spirit's presence, activity, and manifestation in countless ways within its narratives—and, this is indeed what we find within the Scriptures. Therefore, this complex and multi-dimensional dynamic of Spirit in Moltmann's theology is worth noting.

---

see them both differently, not just one of them " (185). Similarly, from the other side, *how am I to keep from dissolving into the other and the other in me if not through experiencing relations outside our specific relationship?* "The third person opens the horizon which can embrace all and frees the relationship between the two from narrowness and from a certain monotony" (185). In this manner, and simultaneous to the begetting of the Son, the Spirit necessarily becomes person so that the relationships become perichoretically complete. As Moltmann concludes, "Only when we are capable of thinking of Persons, relations and changes in the relations *together* does the idea of the Trinity lose its usual static, rigid quality" (*TKG*, 174).

32. Moltmann, *TKG*, 174, emphasis added. Cf. to Moltmann's later writings, e.g., *SL*, in which he begins to approximate the idea of spirit as relationship and becomes aware of the subject-subject limitations.

33. This is in order with Staniloae's suggestion that "the Holy Spirit proceeds from the only Father as He begets the only Son" (Moltmann, *TKG*, 174; cf. Gunton, *One, Three, Many*).

MULTIDIMENSIONAL SPIRIT OF GOD

Moltmann is one of the first major theologians to consider the Spirit and the dynamic of spirit in its multidimensional presence within the Scriptures.[34]

> The *presence* of the divine Spirit in creation must be further differentiated, theologically; for we have to distinguish between his cosmic, his reconciling and his redeeming indwelling. The way the Spirit in his indwelling *acts* will have to be differentiated in each given case according to the mode of his self-manifestation as subject, as energy, or as potentiality. The *efficacy* of the Spirit can then be differentiated into his creating, his preserving, his renewing and his consummating activity.[35]

We can divide these distinctions into three basic categories: cosmic Spirit, *Spiritus Creator*, and Holy Spirit. These distinctions will help reveal the complex dynamic of the Spirit's relations and dimensions of *perichoresis*. For Moltmann, cosmic Spirit is the Spirit that transparently enables and sustains all life and cosmic interrelations.[36] Specifically, within this thesis, spirit also becomes the immanent dynamic within human beings, creating personhood as a relation unto itself. Conversely, the Holy Spirit represents God's transcendent personal action with the world. This is God's internal perichoretic dynamic which presents God as person in relation.

How would Moltmann's categories of the Spirit's manifestations appear when juxtaposed with this thesis's notion of *perichoresis*? Much of the following is from Moltmann; some is my extrapolation of his thinking and categories into various perichoretic categories. The veracity of the identifications and descriptions of the Spirit's manifestations is not my primary concern as much as the concept that the Spirit of God is active in the connectedness of all things, the mediation of all relationships, and the formation, sustenance, organizing principle, and consciousness of all life. Within a truly perichoretic ontology human spirit is not in any way the Spirit of God. It emerges within humanity by sheer perichoretic relation to a trinitarian God and due to being created in a perichoretic world, ontologically—for only such a world could be created by a perichoretic God.

---

34. Some ways Moltmann considers the Spirit of God's activities are the divine energy of life, cosmic Spirit, God's presence, his Shekinah, messianic expectations, the Spirit of Christ, and the Holy Spirit of the Trinity.

35. Moltmann, *GC*, 12.

36. "Theologically this Spirit must be called the Spirit of God and the presence of God in the creature he has made, But according to biblical usage, this is not the Holy Spirit. The Holy Spirit is the name given to the Spirit of redemption and sanctification ... the Spirit of Christ" (Moltmann, *GC*, 263).

Humanity does not "partake" of the divine Spirit but becomes "partakers of the divine nature" (2 Pet 1:4), which is *perichoresis*. Once again, my thesis is that all creation analogically reflects the relational form of the Trinity, not the Classical notions of metaphysics. This is also in keeping with the incarnational imperative of mutuality necessary to maintain a contingent yet free creation.[37] A maturing understanding of a trinitarian ontology necessitates that God's Spirit (as well as the metaphysical presence and activity of Christ) is *both* immanently and transcendently active in all creation.

If indeed we consider all relationships as spirit, then we must start to imagine the almost infinite number of manifestations of spirit within the world. If everything constitutes as word out of spirit, in relationship, and every relationship is spirit, then our notion of spirit must become multidimensional by definition and inherent in all things and interactions, each according to the nature of the entity and interaction. This multidimensional notion of the Spirit of God echoing God's nature throughout the cosmos should reflect the Spirit's multifaceted presence throughout the Scriptures.

Analogia spiritus, in this respect, is the driver of all communicative action within all relationships respective to the character of each interaction. However, they are manifestations of the Spirit appropriate for each relationship manifesting in time (word). This suggests a pneumatological (relational) or, more appropriately, a perichoretic ontology that is alive and active. *The logic within this dynamic is neither reductionistic (Heraclitean) nor holistic (Parmenidean), but a complementarity of both qualities, the dynamics of which only trace back to the fundamental irreducibility of perichoresis reflected within the Trinity.*[38] Such a complementarity between higher and lower forms of relationships always entails complete reciprocity, with the higher structures of relations supervening over the lower forms. The relational dynamic at any level ultimately reflects (issues from) the highest form, the Trinity. Nevertheless, all cosmic relations, even at the chemical or quantum level, reflect these same metaphysical dynamics.

---

37. A perichoretic ontology potentially reflects the very nature of God as a Trinity while obviating Augustine's *vestigium Trinitatis* that he was considering within Greek dialectics. Likewise, the Church fathers struggle with the *vestigium Trinitatis* because of their metaphysical givens and its image of relationality.

38. If the Spirit and Christ are what sustains all relationships. Moltmann suggests that "the human being has really no substance in himself; he is a history. . . . [The Old Testament as narratives] present him in the relationships in which he lives" (*GC*, 257). This reveals the reticence of Moltmann to implement the dynamic of *perichoresis* as an ontological distinction, which by definition creates and maintains human beings as substance-in-relation because of perichoretic relations.

Cosmic Spirit

I will briefly mention two of Moltmann's scriptural readings that motivate his demarcation of cosmic Spirit. He understands the Hebraic concept of Yahweh's *ruach* as the force of life in humanity and nature. Never very far from Yahweh's *dabar*, *ruach* is the sustaining breath of life, "You take away *their ruach*, they die and return to their dust. You send forth *your ruach*, they are created; and you renew the face of the earth" (Ps 104:29–30). Similarly, in death, "the dust will return to the earth as it was, and the *ruach* will return to God who gave it" (Eccl 12:7). In this respect, all that has life and movement has such by the Spirit of God. Paul uses the word spirit for both the Spirit of God and human spirit. For human beings, Moltmann designates spirit as the "psychosomatic totality of the person" and "a 'self' that 'can become an object to himself, a relationship to himself live in his intentionality.'"[39] It also refers to the "self-organization and the self-transcendence of all living things."[40]

Human Spirit

In Moltmann's thinking, the human spirit is cosmic Spirit replete with the dynamic of *perichoresis*, which creates human consciousness and develops into personal identity.[41]

> The Gestalt of the human being, in which body and soul have become united, is a Gestalt formed by the creative Spirit: the human being is a *spirit-Gestalt*. But the Spirit . . . is not merely the creative Spirit: he is at the same time the cosmic Spirit: for body, soul and their Gestalt can only exist in exchange with other living beings in nature and in human society.[42]

Because of this, the perichoretic dynamic is the most fundamental aspect of being human.

> God the Spirit is "the common deity" who binds human beings into higher life with one another and, in this common sphere, makes of them again particular individuals. For though the

---

39. Moltmann, *GC*, 101.
40. Moltmann, *GC*, 16.
41. In the "*imago Trinitatis*," the person emerges from human community "as a *perichoretic* relationship of mutual interpenetration and differentiated unity, . . . [a] Gestalt—the configuration or total pattern—of the lived life . . . formed by the human being and his environment" (*GC*, 259).
42. Moltmann, *GC*, 263.

Spirit in the person is certainly "the common spirit" animating the shared life, he also gives each separate person his own Gestalt and the right to his own unique individuality.[43]

Moltmann argues this is not pantheistic nor panentheistic, but rather Trinitarian.[44] The perichoretic dynamic of relationship allows creation to stand apart from God, and yet "it also simultaneously takes creation into God, though without divinizing it."[45] Here again, Moltmann fights with his linguistic limitations, "taking creation into God." Though I wish to affirm what Moltmann is attempting to facilitate, he does not remain consistent with his application of *perichoresis* in its fullness throughout his theological and anthropological thinking. This is apparent in his resisting the label of panentheism, while his inherited language and Greek relational dynamics make it difficult to express otherwise. These dynamics struggle for consistent expression within a dualistic (subject-subject) rather than tripartite structuring (subject-relationship-subject) of relational dynamics. If he maintains his notion of *perichoresis* and relational dynamics, creation is always "taken into the relationship," not God proper; drawing into the relationship does facilitate, as Loder insists, a "participation in the divine ground" (the relational nature of God, *perichoresis*), precisely what Moltmann is struggling to express).[46]

The perichoretic relation that manifests this multidimensional activity of the Spirit is necessary if human persons are to relate authentically as differentiated beings in unity with God. We witness this struggle in his employment of single quote marks:

> Through the Spirit . . . God himself is 'in us' and we ourselves are 'in God.' . . . We experience the reciprocal *perichoresis* of God and ourselves. . . . It is the communion of reciprocal indwelling. In the Holy Spirit the eternal God participates in our transitory life, and we participate in the eternal life of God. . . . We experience at one and the same time our socialization and our individuation.[47]

In this respect, Moltmann is attempting to transcend his given linguistic strictures. *Something of themselves*—the perichoretic dynamic of human

---

43. Moltmann, *GC*, 267.
44. Moltmann, *GC*, 103.
45. Moltmann, *GC*, 258.
46. N.b. Moltmann was seriously excited by Loder's work. This suggests that Loder expressed things in ways that clarified his own thinking. From personal conversation with Moltmann, 2008.
47. Moltmann, *SL*, 195–96.

spirit—must be mutually concordant and participatory within the relational dynamics of the Trinity.[48] Otherwise, we fall back into the conundrum of Hegel's Absolute Spirit. Because God's Spirit is irreducibly perichoretic, it always differentiates and unifies itself in relation to human spirit. If, indeed, self is a negative relation in and of itself and only a positive relation *in relation* to another (or that Power), we can begin to understand how God and creation "co-indwell" when we qualify the concept within perichoretic dynamics.

Consonant with this thesis's earlier conclusions, Moltmann argues that this dual-spirit perichoretic dynamic between humanity and God is what ultimately creates desire in the heart of humanity for both God[49] and perichoretic relations with the world.[50] In fact, for Moltmann, all desire in creation results from God's relationship to creation.

> The community of love is an *erotic community*: God's loving community with his beloved creation is erotic; the force which differentiates and unites all his creatures is erotic; the rapturous delight of lovers in one another is erotic. . . . "We perceive it as a uniting and intermingling force." The creative Spirit of God is himself Eros.[51]

All longing in the heart of humanity is *its own* developed longing, not that of the Holy Spirit's impregnated into humans. Through openness to the world and immanent relation to *Spiritus Creator*, human spirit, as developed cosmic Spirit, longs to relate perichoretically with the world and the Other. Through openness to God, human spirit comes into analogous relationship with the Holy Spirit, and its desires become shaped accordingly. Taking our cue from Loder's understanding of human imagination, we would suspect that interpreting God's personal action in history would result from the

---

48. "The Holy Spirit reveals the structure of the Spirit of creation, the human spirit, and the Spirit in the whole non-human creation; because it is to this that their experience corresponds" (*GC*, 101).

49. "Love is a desire . . . . God is the most desirable of all" (*SL*, 248). He ends his work on the Trinity with Augustine's decree, "Our hearts are restless until they find rest in thee," and "our hearts are captive until they become free in the glory of the triune God."

50. He here presents the Spirit as indwelling all creation as life, movement, and order. "If the world were completely and wholly godless and forsaken by the Spirit, it would have become nothing (Ps 104:29); it would have ceased to exist" (*SL*, 102). Moreover, because this cosmic Spirit is in, or at least *reflects* within, all things, life emerges. Inevitably, humanity longs for complete and felicitous (perichoretic) relations with all things and God, as all desires (distorted or not) trace back to this fundamental desire.

51. Moltmann, *SL*, 261.

Holy Spirit's analogical action upon the image-making process of human spirit in all ways possible (*analogia spiritus*).[52]

God's Spirit is both transcendent and immanent; its presence forms a complementarity in which the "presence of the infinite in the finite imbues every finite thing, and the community of all finite beings, with self-transcendence."[53] "The transcendence and immanence of the divine Spirit are not mutually contradictory. They are two complementary aspects of its dynamic."[54] One is never without the other. Moltmann points to the "moment lying between the divine Spirit's transcendence and its immanence" and suggests we think of them "triadically" to "grasp the temporal rhythms of life, which *vibrate between transcendence and immanence*"[55] (prereflexion and reflexion).

This dynamic activity of the cosmic Spirit in creation motivates development of life processes to ever-higher relational organization and reflectivity of those dynamics that create it. Ultimately this "creative and life-giving Spirit therefore arrives at consciousness of itself in the human consciousness."[56] According to Moltmann, this is made possible by understanding the cosmos in relation to the Trinity rather than a mechanical model (in which complex systems derive from simple ones). Similar to the notion of supervenience, Moltmann's premise is "the principle that the more complex system explains the simpler one, because it is capable of integrating it; not vice versa."[57] Within this perichoretic dynamic, the Spirit as cosmic Spirit permeates all relationality in nature. We see this in the following:[58] (a) the principle of creativity, creating new possibilities, anticipating new designs (transtemporality); (b) the holistic principle, creating ground for interaction, harmony, and mutual *perichoresis* (relationships), (c) the principle of individuation: instantiating differentiation in all matter and life; providing self-assertion and integration, self-preservation and self-transcendence, (d) the principle of intentionality, openness, and potentiality. This is evident in spirit as anticipation, human as openness to the future,

---

52. Accordingly, to the degree one is *willingly* open and desirous of truth and genuine relations, the Spirit, in whatever form and manifestation (cosmic, *Spiritus Creator*, Holy Spirit, invariably all at once), will without coercive influence, attest and aid in conditioning the most felicitous rendering of truth and appropriate action within each situation.

53. Moltmann, *GC*, 101.

54. Moltmann, *SL*, 227.

55. Moltmann, *SL*, 227, emphasis added.

56. Moltmann, *SL*, 228.

57. Moltmann, *GC*, 100.

58. Moltmann, *GC*, 100.

and the constituting nature of the *project*. Even "the *history* of their lives takes its impress from what they *expect* of life."[59]

These are some essential attributes of spirit in the world contingent upon the dynamic of *perichoresis* (the logic of spirit). These are the relational dynamics through which the providential hand of God can interactively and superveniently accommodate the freedom of passionate humanity. This is a cosmic process that perichoretically objectifies each action and entity, drawing it into increasing self-organization and interrelatedness. Moltmann describes evolutionary and developmental processes as "parts always giving rise to a whole."[60] From atoms to living organisms to human community, across time and in open relatedness, creation itself

> "leaps" from quantity in a particular area into a new quality, . . . with the complexity of the structure, the capacity for communication grows. And with this capacity for communication, the capacity for adaptation and transformation increases in its turn. This, again, widens the range of anticipation [openness].[61]

For Moltmann, creation contains and lies within an immanent-transcendent dynamic that provokes and facilitates the emergence of properties greater than the sum of the former constituent parts. Creation is also a *participatory* system in which the fundamental communication between God and creation transpires at the spirit interaction, yet manifests in word.[62] The spirit of each thing is its highest totality, in the case of persons, the "psychosomatic totality of the person," which entails more than just explicit or focal consciousness. Since relations are primordially spirit-to-spirit, totality-to-totality, *all* of the person optimally comes into relation with God (body, soul, and spirit), not just the "intentional" actions, but the unconscious as well.

> The *testimonium Spiritus Sancti internum* also enables the human being to give himself up to the instinct, the impulse and the guidance of the Holy Spirit: the Spirit is present and at work in the feelings and in the unconscious as well.[63]

---

59. Moltmann, *GC*, 265.
60. Moltmann, *GC*, 203.
61. Moltmann, *GC*, 204. Appropriately, Moltmann employs the infamous Kierkegaardian "leap" to describe the perichoretic emergence of higher order from lesser orders; transformation within the Jacobian third term, the co-conditioning emergence of creation, as life wrestles passionately for greater fullness of life.
62. Moltmann, *GC*, 205.
63. Moltmann, *GC*, 264.

In other words, because of *analogia spiritus*, we constantly communicate more than we can explicitly say, and God communicates more than we can explicitly articulate. In Moltmann, the structure of communication and change is primordially holistic. Therefore the dynamic fullness of relations takes place at this level of interaction, communicating far more than our shortened presence reflects. Here, the word and the temporal potentially fill with Eternal meaning and affect via *analogia spiritus*.

Holy Spirit

In relation to the world, the Holy Spirit is the redemptive and sanctifying action of the *person* of God within creation. For Moltmann, the Holy Spirit represents the action of God as person, the witness of the Father to the divine identity of Jesus Christ as the One through whom God speaks and relates with humanity. When the Holy Spirit comes to humans, God is in personal relationship with the person or community. The Holy Spirit attests to and reveals revelation, just as the cosmic Spirit and *Spiritus Creator* are more pivotal in the general *aspects* of revelation. However, it would be a naïve oversight to isolate any of them within their paralleling and integrating actions within revelation, just as naming any of them in their co-supporting roles as solely responsible for any one type of revelation is ultimately theological agendizing. As generally presented in the past, they represent over-generalized theological distinctions.

Nevertheless, to be inter-personal, the totality of God must relate with the totality (spirit) of human beings. Therefore, for Moltmann, the Holy Spirit and the human spirit must become correlationally dynamic within *perichoresis*. There is ultimately no way within divine-human relations to completely segregate the whole of any one act or communication to one manifestation of God's Spirit. All are commensurately active in concert and with full transcendence and full immanence.

Spiritus Creator

For Moltmann, Christ accomplishes his forward and redeeming relation to the world in his action with Creator Spirit. If cosmic Spirit is the essential *immanent* life source in human beings sustaining life as an individual (creating a relation unto itself), and the Holy Spirit is that *personal transcendent* holistic interaction of God with human spirit within prereflexive awareness, then Creator Spirit is that transforming activity with Christ mediating the moment of transition between our dialogical cycles. To isolate revelation between general and special, divinely non-personal or personal, Religiousness A and B are only helpful in discerning the human response; segregating them as distinct actions from God is ultimately naïve and limiting. Moltmann tells us:

> The transcendence and immanence of the divine Spirit are not mutually contradictory. They are two complementary aspects of its dynamic. The pantheistic interpretation is just as one-sided as the transcendentalist one. Nor does process philosophy's bi-polar interpretation of the life process comprehend the dynamic *moment* lying *between* the divine Spirit's transcendence and its immanence. The orthodox theological distinction between the Spirit's "uncreated" and "created" energies does not take account of its *creative* energies. We understand the dynamic better when we begin to think triadically, so as to *mediate between* the world beyond and this world by way of *the forward movement of process.*[64]

Again, echoing Kierkegaard's insistence that the finite and the infinite existentially synthesize, never materially synthesize, Moltmann argues that even in the perichoretic dynamic, the Spirit facilitates a repeating *rhythmic synthesis* between immanence and transcendence.

"*QUID EST ERGO TEMPUS?*": THE *PERICHORESIS* OF TIME AND ETERNITY

In the *perichoresis* of time and Eternity, "what then is time?" Moltmann interprets human freedom in three ways, freedom in the relationship between subject and object (lordship), between subject and subject (community), and the relationship of the subject to *project* (future). In the latter, a unique dimension of the Spirit enables the transcending of the present toward the future direction. Understanding this unique dynamic in human experience aids our understanding of human freedom in relation to God's Eternal action (freedom). In this way, the present conditions (not determines) the past and is defined "from the future."[65]

Our predominant notions concerning *perichoresis* and gestalt deal primarily with the spatial and visual categories—figure-ground. Moltmann, however, presents the *perichoresis* of time and Eternity, which produces in human experience "a perichoretic understanding of the different modes of

---

64. Moltmann, *SL*, 227, first three emphases mine.
65. Moltmann, *GC*, 123.

time, which interpenetrate one another qualitatively, and cannot simply be quantitatively separated from one another."[66] In this manner, time or times are equivalent to "figure" and Eternity to "ground."

Concept of Eternity

In presenting his idea of time and eternity, Moltmann uses the "time of the feast" (Eliade) to introduce the concept of time as the repetition of eternity. The idea of the reoccurring feast institutes a cyclical structure within the temporal concept in which no event is unique and no past final.

> Everything comes around again. Every moment, everything begins again from the beginning, ... everything really abides.... To experience time like this is not to experience the individuality of events and the irreversibility of their happening. The very opposite is true. This experience of time is the experience of repetition. But the experience of repetition is nothing other than the experience of eternity.[67]

One helpful image is that of circularity by which everything over time is interrelated. The other is repetition. Within this thesis, memory as *perichoresis* is not a neurological recall of a picture or film in the brain but rather a transtemporal ontic leap back into the actual happening of that event; it is a reliving the event from a new context, and therefore we necessarily experience it differently each time we relive it. This is the product of the *perichoresis* of time and eternity. It also reveals the dynamic co-conditioning nature of Eternity and time.

From Augustine, who believes time cannot be a category of eternity, Moltmann then assumes that time is "a definition of created being in its difference from the eternal being of God."[68] Time exists as created time; therefore, God creating the world from eternity can be said to "never '*have created*' at any time, so he has 'never' created."[69] The concern here is to relativize the various tenses of time into a perichoretic unity. There is no past or future in God's eternal act of creating. The past and future are perspectives of human beings in time. In Eternity, God does not create A before B; they emerge in a singular dynamic relation. Time, like space, is simply a product

---

66. Moltmann, *GC*, 125–26.
67. Moltmann, *GC*, 108.
68. Moltmann, *GC*, 113, citing Augustine, "the world is not created *in* time, but *with* time."
69. Moltmann, *GC*, 114.

of relations. For Augustine and Moltmann, the Eternal is not a static set of pictures (relations) on a movie reel in a box,[70] but a swirling transtemporal dynamic of interrelatedness in which the beginning and end emerge in dynamic relation to one another. Everything within its own time(s) in perichoretic relation to God's Eternal dynamic can potentially emerge in relation to everything and every other time. Spacetime is made possible for creation by God's distinctive maintaining of Eternity in Godself.[71] Moltmann here furthers the "temporal symbol for eternity,"[72]—circular movement—by embracing Augustine's God, who transcends historical causal sequence. Humans in relation to God are then "drawn into the circular movement of the divine relationships,"[73] which facilitates the human ability to perichoretically unify its "times" into an existential whole, facilitating the experience and movement of faith, and narrative.

Using Augustine's subjective notion of time—"through memory, sight and expectation, the soul has the ability to unite the times in itself,"[74]—*Moltmann presents various human experiences of time; kairological, historical, messianic, eschatological, and the eternal, which he then argues perichoretically interpenetrate to produce an existential whole greater than the sum of their dynamics.* This occurs in relation to Christ's Time through his perichoretic relation to the Eternal life within the Trinity, which provides "the chance to influence God and to participate in his rule."[75] In this respect, "memory does represent a certain re-creation of the past in the present; and expectation does in a sense represent the new creation of the future in the present mind."[76] Here, Moltmann carefully qualifies the "actualization" of the past and future in the present. In the next chapter, however, we shall investigate the sobering possibility that humanity, in relation to the Trinity, can affect the past and live within the reality (*hypostasis*) of the future from within one's own times. Moltmann says this "implies the participation of

---

70. Cf. an inadequate accounting by William Pollard, which is held by many today: "In the world described by relativity theory life in time is like the slow rolling up of a shade to reveal an already completed picture behind it" (*GC*, 103).

71. Moltmann, *GC*, 114.

72. Moltmann, *SL*, 304.

73. Moltmann, *SL*, 305.

74. Moltmann, *GC*, 115.

75. Moltmann, *TKG*, 221.

76. Moltmann, *GC*, 115; furthermore, "the soul's power of remembrance and hope must in its own way be termed 'creative.' The created mind of man reaches out through time, penetrating past, present and future being; . . . and in this way it partakes of the eternal Creator Spirit and engenders in the soul of human beings a relative eternity, in the sense of a relative simultaneity of past, present and future being" (115).

finite creatures in the infinite existence of God as well as the participation of the eternal God in the creatures' temporal existence."[77] The two never materially synthesize, and we maintain Kierkegaard's "infinite qualitative difference." We can only witness them in the dialogical cycles and history of consciousness, never in the between of Jacob's night of faith, unless one comes into full relations with Christ and then moves with Christ within the Eternal. Nevertheless, because of Christ (Incarnation), time and Eternity come into co-conditioning relatedness so that "God having been made man, humanity might be made unto God" (Athanasius paraphrase).

The linear and cyclical temporal concepts combine within "feedback processes," which ultimately remain open within a *"future as project"* that then "goes beyond *the future as experience*."[78] Here Moltmann refers to Heidegger: "the primary phenomenon of primordial and authentic temporality is the future." Therefore, "traditions and dogmas can be critically relativized, and the hopes which they preserve and the hopes which they suppress can be taken up again;"[79] the absolute claims of traditions are not lost to a skeptical relativism but "lead to a living relationalism in an intricate fabric of interconnections." Shifting paradigms deepen and enrich the appropriate aspects of earlier well-formed claims of traditions. These, furthermore, remain "open" and reconstituting within every living and developing relationship.

"Anticipation" supersedes "extrapolation."

> Extrapolations do not treat the future as an open field of the possible; they see it as a reality already determined by past and present. But this is illusory: it leads to a dangerous blindness to the apocalypse among men and women in the modern system.... Without anticipatory *awareness* we should not discern something that is still in the future at all.[80]

Within the process of awareness, human beings experience the de-liberations from what is and should be (extrapolations). Here, God's prereflexive Eternal in-tensions can prereflexively condition and inform in co-condition relation to our in-tensional self (if whole, passionate) within its anticipatory awareness. Such prereflexive de-liberations break forth in creative moments, eternally establishing us eschatologically and messianically in our

---

77. Moltmann, "Reflections on Chaos," 209.
78. Moltmann, *GC*, 129–30.
79. Moltmann, *GC*, 131.
80. Moltmann, *GC*, 134, emphasis added.

own times.[81] "What human beings are, is not thoroughly determined,"[82] and as Dilthey insists, human nature is not a closed and fixed nature; it is open to the future. Only in complete openness to the Other can we venture into perichoretic relations with the Eternally dynamic Trinity that transform us into his image, from one degree to another.

In conclusion, Moltmann does manage to present a notion of the Trinity and specifically the Spirit, which is consonant with Jacob's ultimate act of faith in *analogia spiritus*, one that places the anticipation, desires, and will of a passionately engaged human being in co-conditioning relation to a risen Christ. Within human de-liberation, Moltmann argues that the Spirit of God offers only its "impulse" and "guidance" in full awareness of the desires and will within each passionate spirit antecedent to each act of creation (the will of Christ), rather than offering the antiquated Reformed predominating "will of God" to be Abrahamically followed.[83] Moltmann exposes Joseph Ratzinger's "notion that in the church people surrender their old 'isolated ego subjectivity' and find themselves in a new, higher 'unity of determining subjects.' . . . [This] over-extension of the head-body image for the church leads to a graduated hierarchy: God-Christ-the body of Christ."[84] In the Spirit, however, is freedom, and within the fellowship of the Spirit,

> Christ is considered to be a "determining subject," the community of Christ can be christologically called a "unity of determining subjects." But in the abundance of the Spirit . . . it is a community in which everyone contributes: . . . it is a non-hierarchical fellowship of equals in the Holy Spirit. . . . The true unity of the church is an image of the perichoretic unity of the Trinity, so it can neither be a collective consciousness which represses the individuality of the persons, nor an individual

---

81. "Because God's creative activity has no analogy, it is also unimaginable. The divine act of creation is never described in differentiated terms. Nor is it dissected into a number of different processes. It is unified and unique. This means among other things that time is excluded from the act of creation, for time always requires duration, and creation takes place *suddenly*, as it were—in a *moment*" (Moltmann, *GC*, 73, emphasis added).

82. Moltmann, *GC*, 229.

83. Moltmann, *GC*, 246.

84. Moltmann, *SL*, 224. Implicating Ratzinger, Moltmann notes, "it is self-evident that this is a way of legitimating the hierarchical constitution of the church." To a lesser degree, could the same not be said for any church doctrine with only a descending "ladder," for any theology prizing only the Abrahamic submittal to a descending God, in which prayer becomes nothing more than listening for the will of God?" (224).

consciousness which neglects what is in common. . . . In this complementarity there is no priority.[85]

Moltmann sees what others miss, avoid, and deny—the flashing neon sign of Jacob. Humanity can be drawn co-conditionally into the Eternal and has its say before the adjudication and providential act of Christ's creating activity. These are the prayers of the heart, forged in passion, in which we risk everything for more. Only the prayer of the older brother listens for God's will, but the passion of the Prodigal opens and enters the heart of the Father and his feast of creation. But "it is hard to accept the idea that there cannot be an order [or human freedom] in the universe because it would offend the free will of God and His omnipotence."[86] Is the freedom of God "our condemnation?" The hardened tablets of such theological ruminations shatter upon the rock of Jacob and Peter—through which the entire redemptive efforts of the Trinity flow into the people of God and all creation. Moltmann breaks open the ineffable "abundance of the Spirit" in all its unfathomable dimensions, most important the perichoretic bending of an eternal faith into time. Jacob discovered the possibility deep within the night, and upon this rock, heaven and earth have conspired ever since.

Nevertheless, the ascending ladder falls to earth if we fail to understand how and where Eternity bends into the human heart. This brings us to our penultimate chapter that attempts to understand the monster upon which the Writer had his hands—the ground where humanity enters into God's personal and Eternal act of creation.

---

85. Moltmann, *SL*, 224.
86. Eco, *Name of the Rose*, 492–93.

5A

Perichoresis of Time and Eternity
Analogia Spiritus in "Immanence" and "Transcendence"

So then, man was said to be a synthesis of soul and body; but he is at the same time *a synthesis of the temporal and the eternal*.

The self is a "relation" between heaven and earth, eternity and time.

The concept around which everything turns in Christianity, the concept which makes all things new, is the fullness of time, is the instant as eternity, and yet this eternity is at once the future and the past.

Just as finitude is the limiting factor in relation to infinitude, so in relation to possibility it is necessity which serves as a check. When the self as a synthesis of finitude and infinitude is once constituted, when already it is κατά δύναμιν [potential], then in order to become it reflects itself in the medium of imagination, and with that the infinite possibility comes into view.

Søren Kierkegaard[1]

Philosophers who maintain that past and future objects are not real existents, or that future events do not have determinate reality, are refuted out of hand by special relativity.

Lawrence Sklar[2]

---

1. *CA*, 76; *ED*, 17, 76; *CA*, 80; *SUD*, 168.
2. Sklar, *Space*, 273; similarly, Putnam, "Time"; Rietdijk, "Rigorous."

INTRODUCTION

Not only do we find perichoretic dynamics analogically active anthropologically, but they also become ontological dynamics resolving many of our persistent theological anomalies. Within each field, the complementarity and *perichoresis* of time and Eternity also factor.[3] For many, it has been a stretch applying the dynamic of *perichoresis* beyond the Trinity into generic relational dynamics, notwithstanding the plausibility of such dynamics active between time and Eternity. Nevertheless, this chapter explores Kierkegaard's thesis that human beings *are* indeed the intersection of time and Eternity. When human beings engage in full passion, Eternity breaks into time. Therefore, understanding the play between time and Eternity is necessary for understanding personhood.[4]

I have attempted thus far to develop notable connections between the dynamics of *perichoresis* and the formation of gestalt while pointing out the predominant understanding of gestalt as spatial and visual.[5] Largely the more subtle and difficult interpolation of temporal dynamics and gestalt has thus far gone undeveloped. For example, T. F. Torrance believes that an individual enters the *parousia* with Christ the moment after death during Christ's ascension, which is concurrent with "the end of time." In this sense, death brings every human instantaneously to the *parousia* simultaneously. "We have to reckon here, however, with something like a 'relativity of simultaneity,'" which rubs against our common sense notions of temporal sequencing.[6] "The primary theological point to get clear, however, is the ontologically and temporally indivisible nature of the one epiphany or advent of the incarnate Son of God in whom all men and all ages are held together, without any detraction from real differences between different individual experiences or times."[7] To explain how everything is relative, not to each other, but to the invariance of light, Einstein uses the concept of

---

3. This chapter will often employ static heuristic tools for conceptually exploring the logic of how the Eternal breaks into the temporal. However, contrary to the static nature of these periodic conceptions they represent the anatomy of what creates and sustains relations in time, in motion. Our relationship to Christ ("Christ within") further alters experience and consciousness, bringing rise to a new kairotic time within our linear experience of time.

4. Similar to Heidegger, personhood constitutes cyclically (rhythmically) within temporality *in relation to the Eternal*.

5. Likewise, it is Kierkegaard's primary contention that we misunderstand time and Eternity "because we *spatialize* a moment, . . . visualizing time instead of thinking it" (*CA*, 77).

6. Torrance, *Transformation*, 342.

7. Torrance, *Transformation*, 343.

"assigning two different but equally real times to the same event." Torrance, however, does

> not wish to argue from relativity theory in physics or cosmology to a solution of the problem we have in Christian theology of understanding temporal experience in Christ when in him the age to come telescopes back into this present age in such a way that in Christ we live simultaneously in two ages or times, the on-going present and the future which comes to meet us.[8]

Though I make no similar pretense that a person can "live simultaneously in two ages or times" (a Newtonian consideration), I do wish to point out perichoretic dynamics and relational heuristics emerging in postmodern science that open the possibility that time can bend around a person so they experience "causal" relatedness between times. This is not only possible but needs to become a vital factor within theology.[9]

This chapter suggests that the *perichoresis* between time and Eternity is a quality of the relationship between God and humanity as new theories in science and philosophy offer creative and alternative heuristics in our understanding of interactive causation. The theological implications will take shape within the discussion of immanence and transcendence by contrasting various aspects of Barth, Hegel, and Kierkegaard.

GOD, TIME, AND SPECIAL THEORY OF RELATIVITY: EXPULSION FROM THE INNOCENCE OF ABSOLUTE TIME AND LINEAR CAUSATION

John Polkinghorne believes "God does not know the future [before it happens]."[10] On the other hand, what are we to make of God's portending the future through prophets *in time* before that future event; or the Christian understanding of faith—the proleptic *experiencing* in some ontological manner the *reality* of future events "having [experienced] them afar off" (Heb 11:1, 13, my paraphrase)? The choice of words chosen by the writer of Hebrews intends an ontological rather than a psychological nature to faith, which nearly all modern translators curiously omit.[11] *My primary thesis*

---

8. Torrance, *Transformation*, 342–43.

9. Cf. Barth's insistence that Christians "do not make or feel or know themselves the contemporaries of Jesus. It is not they who become or are this. It is Jesus who becomes and is their Contemporary" (*CD* 3/2:467 [Again, a Reform consideration]).

10. Polkinghorne, "Setting the Problem," 11.

11. Helmut Köster defines hypostasis as follows: "Faith is now viewed as personal,

is that all these temporal and eternal considerations are necessary mutually for authentic divine-human relations and that a fuller understanding of the dynamic of perichoresis *makes this possible.* Again, according to the incarnational imperative of mutuality, time and sequential reality must somehow condition (affect) God, who relates with humanity as person in *filial* relation. Likewise, the interactive (non-impositional) enabling of prophets and, more specifically, the emergence of *faith* within humanity suggests an aspect of human transcendence of sequential time.[12] The notion is counterintuitive. Like the strange experiences during the dawn of the Copernican age, we live in an age of paradigm-breaking anomalies and emerging insights. The quest is to grasp "a more subtle form of reality involving both time and eternity,"[13] which theologically suggests a rereading of Jacob's formerly inexplicable experiences in the night and how they might reconfigure our understanding of the divine-human interaction. This exploration meaningfully explains these former biblical anomalies within the pre-reflexive

---

subjective conviction. This interpretation has governed Protestant exposition of the passage almost completely.... Yet there can be no question but that this classical Protestant understanding is untenable. The starting-point of exposition must be the ὑπόστασις (reality, essence, or substance) in Hb. 11:1 has to have not only a meaning like that in Greek usage elsewhere but also a sense similar to that it bears in the other Hb. references. It should also be noted that ὑπόστασις here is parallel to ἔλεγχος (proof or verification) and that it occurs in a sentence full of central theological concepts. Now as regards ἔλεγχος it is evident that this does not mean subjective non-doubting nor does it have anything at all to do with conviction; it bears the objective sense of 'demonstration.'... proof of things one cannot see.... If one follows the meaning of ὑπόστασις in Hb. 1:3, then ὑπόστασις ἐλπιζομένων (of things hoped for) bears a similar sense: it is the reality of the goods hoped for, which have by nature a transcendent quality.... In a formulation of incomparable boldness Hb. 11:1 identifies πίστις (faith) with this transcendent reality: Faith is the reality of what is hoped for in exactly the sense in which Jesus is called the χαρακτήρ (representation) of the reality of the transcendent God in 1:3." ("ὑπόστασις" in *TDNT* 8:586-88; English translations of Greek are mine). "It is plain, then, that in Hb. ὑπόστασις always denotes the 'reality' of God which stands contrasted with the corruptible, shadowy, and merely prototypical character of the world but which is paradoxically present in Jesus and is the possession of the community of faith" (587-88).

12. Loder tells us, "In the context of irreversible thermodynamics it is not time per se that is irreversible, but time's determinants.... However, time stripped of its determinants (as can only happen in reflective human consciousness, an inveterately 'open system') *appears* to be reversible in the spontaneous creation of a new order of determinants. Theologically, the experience of the 'reversibility' in faith is a new being in Christ. However... this notion involves 'God's time.' In this context, what *appears* to be reversibility may instead be highly accelerated motion toward the eschatological future in Christ—a wrinkle in time and foretaste of the redemption of all things. This [is a] complex interrelationship between irreversible thermodynamics and Kierkegaard's view of time" (*TM*, 122).

13. Prigogine and Stengers, *Order Out of Chaos*, xxx.

realms of human dialogical cycling as the site of the *mysterium tremendum*, where Eternity conditions time.

This unrelenting paradox has intensified throughout the ages. An inescapable need, however, to theologically accommodate (explain the possibility of) genuine interaction within a pluralistic world and how an Eternal God of providence can filially relate with free and temporal humanity, together with the findings of postmodern physics, has finally broken the back of former metaphysical structures. In the Special Theory of Relativity (STR), as Albert Einstein reveals, "light is always propagated in empty space with a definite velocity c which is independent of the state of motion of the emitting body."[14] Regardless of the relative speed of any two moving frames of reference to a particular light beam, each reference point will always measure its speed at c; in other words, all space and time warp and conform in such a way around the constancy of light (c), or, more bluntly, "for a photon, cruising at the ultimate speed limit, the passage of eternity is but an instant."[15] If this is true, and it has become the common doctrine of physics, and if God precedes the creation of the photon, then our former philosophical affirmation that "only the present (and not the past or future) is determinately real," is no longer tenable as classically understood.

Denying the determinate reality of an event in the future because it does not "exist at the time of the assertion" is as absurd as denying that an object is not real because it is not at the *place* of the assertion. We can no longer separate space and time. The future and past are as determinately real as the present. This, however, does not mandate a determinism, nor does it necessitate a static block universe as once thought in physics. Still, it reveals *a* frame of reference does exist in which past and future events happen simultaneously.[16] Lawrence Sklar tells us that the "philosophers who maintain that past and future objects are not real existents, or that

---

14. Einstein, "Electrodynamics," 891.
15. Zee, *Fearful Symmetry*, 68.
16. As Copleston relates, Boethius similarly and theologically expressed that: "God does not, strictly speaking, 'foresee' anything: God is eternal, eternity being defined in a famous phrase as *interminabilis vitae tota simul et perfecta possessio*, and His knowledge is the knowledge of what is eternally present to Him, of a never-fading instant, not a foreknowledge of things which are future to God. Now, knowledge of a present event does not impose necessity on the event, so that God's knowledge of man's free acts, which from the human viewpoint are future, though from the divine viewpoint they are present, does not make those acts determined and necessary (in the sense of not-free). The eternity of Gods vision, 'which is always present, concurs with the future quality of an action'" (*History*, 2:103).

future events do not have determinate reality, are refuted out of hand by special relativity."[17]

Therefore, we must choose between the traditional theory of temporal relatedness and sequential causality alone or special relativity. "But [we] need not do either, for we can simply accept the consequences, surprising no doubt, but by no means inconsistent or patently absurd, of *relativizing our notions of reality and determinate reality at the same time that we relativize our concepts of simultaneity.*"[18] Just because actions or realities in two different moments in history can causally affect each other (entangle) does not destroy the causal integrity or reality within either frame of reference (synchronic or diachronic). Though we can posit no universal present moment or reference point for something with mass, STR does suggest that all spacetime is relative in relation to the invariance of light. Therefore, if we believe God created light, then STR indicates that there is a specific reference, potentially divine, capable of taking in all history as one unitary *dynamic* singularity. STR and quantum physics suggests such a possibility, if not demand it. Theologically, from this point of reference, we could argue that God (the Father) perceives all of reality as *happening* (not happened) simultaneously.[19]

We will investigate the character of such a "perceiving" in a bit, but first, let us consider the hypothesis that *all reality (past and future) is as determinately real as the present*. The second hypothesis, therefore, is that all reality must, *in some way, be dynamically and singularly real to an Eternal God*. If indeed all history is determinately real (not happen*ed*, but real), it is evident that some aspect of an Eternal God is somehow in singular and simultaneous relation to all history—*trans-temporally*.[20] Therefore, God may not be able to "know" the future before it happens, but because of God's Eternal dimension, God *tacitly* perceives all creation "simultaneously" happening within its *full* interrelatedness and dynamic emergence.

In this regard, the parallel dynamics in Kierkegaard's anthropology are remarkably similar. J. Heywood Thomas tells us Kierkegaard both "attacks

---

17. Sklar, *Space*, 273; similarly, Putnam, "Time"; Rietdijk, "Rigorous."
18. Sklar, *Space*, 275, emphasis added.
19. This is argued by Lucas, *Future*, 220; Stump and Kretzmann, "Eternity," 429–58.
20. I choose to use the term transtemporal over non-temporal. Non-temporal suggests to many a static Platonic non-causal state of eternity, whereas the Eternal within its *perichoresis* with Time is the *fullness* of causal interrelations that include but transcend the historical sequential understanding of cosmic relations. Transtemporality suggests the additional possibility of co-conditioning dynamics that span across time through their active relatedness to the divine and its Eternal frame of reference—the divine side of the *analogia spiritus* vortex.

the view of time which makes the present the only reality" and affirms that "faith is in one important sense a non-historical relation to its object: but it is also a real [ontological] relation. . . . The relation is neither [a purely psychological] memory nor hope but co-presences."[21] Kierkegaard's radical postulate concerning the ontological inseparability of the past, present, and future within authentic human existence became the lone cry in the wilderness, portending the parallel discoveries forthcoming in physics. It was becoming apparent that causality was no respecter of sequential time and that temporality was *in* relatedness and human beings rather than relations and persons in time.[22] Kierkegaard defines Christianity as a relationship to the absolute, and that "in relation to the absolute there is only one tense: the present. . . . And as Christ is the absolute it is easy to see that with respect to Him there is one situation that of contemporaneousness."[23] This suggests a relational ontology in which the Eternal breaks into time, creating a potential causal structuring between the transtemporal, trans-historical, and non-historical dimensions of interactions. Faith is no longer an ideological or psychological projection reconfiguring the real but an ontological dynamic that kinetically emerges within the relationship itself.[24] In both humanity and God, Kierkegaard maintains the possibility of the "condition" in which personhood comes into dynamic relatedness with God's Eternal activity, in other words, transforming cause and effect into mutual conditioning (Abraham). Within this condition, cause and effect release from sole linear temporalization. The *moment* instantly subsumes (transforms) linear causality within a broader holistic co-conditioning of perichoretic relations that span time (Jacob).

Yet, how can the whole be anything other than static? For Moltmann, the perichoretic dynamic of the Trinity differentiating the oneness of God through the begetting of the Son and immediate procession of the Spirit instantly creates a determining transtemporal reality (the Eternal).[25] With

21. Thomas, "Kierkegaard's View of Time," 37, my embellishing clarifications.

22. Time is not a purely subjective emergence, nor is it an ontological universal within a material cosmology. *It is the property of the relationship*, always inclusive of that Power that holds together all things (and relationships). Nevertheless, maintaining these distinctions is important.

23. Kierkegaard, TC, 68; Anti-Climacus reflects the same dynamic of *perichoresis* and *analogia spiritus* that occurred in Jacob's wrestling and Peter's recognition.

24. The "synthesis has only two factors: the temporal and the eternal." Kierkegaard asks, "Where is the third term?" (CA, 76). Unlike Hegel, he argues that it is existential rather than material and contingent upon a Power that can temporally synthesize the contradiction of time and Eternity within consciousness and relations.

25. Cf. Barth: "Not even the pure, eternal being of God as such is non-historical pre-truth, for being triune it is not non-historical but historical even in its eternity" (CD 3/1:66).

the birth, death, and resurrection of Christ, the Relationship became the bearer of Time as a differentiated unity from which all creation "leaps" into existence. All spacetime was created by and relativized in relationship to the Spirit and Christ. At this point, Irenaean-like trinitarian dynamics becomes illustrative.

> God becomes human and constitutes a Trinity: Within this perichoretic Relationship, a) the dynamic transtemporal quality of the Father reconstitutes into an Eternal dynamic relatedness, b) the spacetime differentiation of the begotten Son constitutes within a Trinitarian Temporality with the potential for constituting all cosmic relations, and c) the Spirit emerges as the perichoretic Relationship between the Father and the Son creating the dynamic of *perichoresis*—differentiated unity—and the corresponding dialogical cycles of personal communication between Time and Eternity.

This interpenetrating dynamic of trinitarian *perichoresis*—the very nature of God in Christ and the Spirit—becomes the fundamental and sustaining Power perichoretically establishing creation and facilitating all cosmic relations. As God constitutes godself in divine personal relations, Time is a characteristic *of* personal relationship, the quality of differentiation that sustains personhood, the *medium* between persons-in-relations. J. R. Lucas tells us:

> Time is not a thing that God might or might not create, but a category, a necessary concomitant of the existence of a personal being, . . . It exists because of God: not because of some act of will on His part, but because of His nature. . . . God did not make time, but time stems from God.[26]

In its potential within human beings and sociology; Giorgio Agamben thinks messianic time

> is the time that we ourselves are, the dynamic time where, for the first time, we grasp time, grasp the time that is ours, grasp that we are nothing but that time. On the contrary, it is the only real time, the only time we will ever have. To experience this time implies an integral transformation of ourselves and of our ways of living.[27]

Likewise, not only is time an inherent quality of personhood, but the Eternal nature of God in its perichoretic human form is also a necessary and

---

26. Lucas, *Future*, 213.
27. Agamben, *Kingdom*, 12.

complementary source of personhood.[28] Persons are the *perichoresis* of the finite and the infinite, the temporal and the eternal, and this fundamental structure of personhood and relationship produces the previously established dialogical cycles of personal communication. Let us briefly consider the temporal dynamics of God in the theories of Ian Barbour, Holmes Rolston, and Ted Peters.

Ian Barbour argues that God being immanent at all points, omnisciently knows all events instantly, yet he qualifies the relationship that results from this knowing. "We would have to assume that God influences an event in terms of the pattern of events relevant to its situation and its causal past, which, of course, is uniquely defined for all frames of reference."[29] Putting the contentious issue of "knowing" aside for the moment, I wish to acknowledge the idea that God appropriately manifests Godself in various frames of reference according to its relevant patterns of knowledge. This is not relativism but relativity.

When various traditions experience the same transcendent manifestation of the divine, their respective historical development conditions their cognitive response, notwithstanding potentially transforming those descriptors to a degree. To the degree of openness to the Other (bearing their cross) each person's descriptive response constitutes accordingly. Or, as Agamben would say, "messianic time is . . . a transformation of the experience of the penultimate . . . [that] deactivates, suspends and transforms, the penultimate ones—and yet, it is precisely, and above all, in these penultimate realities that an ultimate reality bears witness."[30] In this respect, tradition and culture perichoretically influence, evolve, and enrich the penultimate, just as the ultimate perichoretically "suspends and transforms" the penultimate through *analogia spiritus*. We might contrast this with the Neo-Kantian pluralistic hypothesis of John Hick that relegates God *an sich* to the noumenal resulting in a plurality of equally veridical historical manifestations (phenomena). Hick ultimately presents a historical relativism, with no ultimate criterion of commensurability between phenomena other than a nondescript sense of incommensurable praxis. A perichoretic theory casts no divide between reality and experience (noumena and phenomena), placing reality as emergent within each relationship, contextually conditioned, and qualitatively dependent on the person's willingness to relate fully with reality. Reality emerges within each relational occurrence employing the appropriate contextual relativities. There is no Kantian noumena "out there" creating phenomena

---

28. See earlier discussions of Loder, Kierkegaard, and Pannenberg.
29. Barbour, *Religion*, 112.
30. Agamben, *Kingdom*, 19.

PERICHORESIS OF TIME AND ETERNITY

in our experience (Newtonian), merely differing relations, contexts, and degrees of openness creating apparent incommensurability between us. The reality ("noumena") is there in our midst (*analogia spiritus*) but manifests within us and our relationships accordingly. Because of this, the commensurable criterion of fullness of life can potentially emerge within contrasting relations, as developed in chapter 2.

Using a panentheistic model, Holmes Rolston sees God as interpenetrating all things and omnipresent in the sense that God materializes and energizes (incarnates) into each spacetime frame of reference. God's revelation is contextually relative yet ultimately consistent with all other relative disclosures and influences according to God's divine nature and will. "If God is anywhere," he writes, "it will be as God 'comes through' in our space-time, relative to our local existence, as God is, so to speak, locally incarnate."[31] Similarly, Ted Peters explains:

> The key is local incarnation—God entering into the created order and taking up residence within a single inertial frame of reference. Through such an incarnation, we find God on both sides of the ledger, eternal and temporal, universal and particular, acting and acted upon.[32]

Though appreciative of Barbour and Rolston, Peters feels their programs fail to resolve many issues because they fail to develop an adequate notion of a trinitarian God. For him, the Eternal Incarnation of God as personal can only come about through a trinitarian God. Furthermore, a trinitarian God can relate within a locally relative manner from the Eternal so that every situation and action God encounters can inform God's response (and influence) in every other historical situation. All these models still beg further clarification and development.

Even though a divine incarnation into local action might begin to suggest how God interrelates all localities, it does not explain how human beings authentically relate with such an all-knowing God in a personal or filial manner. In other words, how do human beings relate in such absoluteness to the Absoluteness of God? If they do not, and we play the creature-creator card to excess, the relationship is not genuinely mutual and filial, and Jacob becomes an overstatement, a theological embarrassment. The history of Christian redemption declares the increasing intimacy into filial proportions, not the antiquated totally-other Gods of Judaism or Islam. In conventional (Abrahamic) theology, humans, bound within the temporal,

31. Rolston, *Genes*, 62.
32. Peters, *God as Trinity*, 159.

can only respond "yea or nay" to God's Word and action. In all situations, God can perceive equitable (ethical) responses to human activity based on an Eternal purview. Still, according to Barth, all human involvement lies posterior to God's becoming aware of the situation and predetermining the appropriate action and response for potential human acceptance. How human freedom genuinely incorporates into God's action (heaven forbid God's personal dialogical response within time) begins and ends with the enigmatic and incessant declaration of "in Christ," and there it ends without further ado. I want to argue that though human will and desires are indeed a consideration within God's preeminent activity for Barth, it is a divine deliberation from which human beings are personally excluded as determining agents (again, Abrahamic in nature). Barth suggests humanity must "acknowledge" God's revealed Word or action (Christ), and in one respect, this is true, but he does not read far enough into the story. He fails to acknowledge the absurdity that there is an antecedent dimension within the relational cycle through which the Absoluteness of God encounters the absoluteness of humanity within the dynamic co-conditioning interaction of *analogia spiritus*. In Barth's faith, the human merely responds after the fact. "Self-determination comes about when God is honored by the creature in harmony with God's predetermination instead of in opposition to it."[33] For Barth, God's "predetermination" issues from God's Eternal nature, but it is unclear how this appropriates any authentic possibility of human being as a self-determining co-creator rather than a cosmic yes-man. Also, where is it that humanity truly affects God or constitutes in genuine mutual reciprocity to God?[34] Where is the God of Jacob, in which humanity struggles with and affects God's preeminent creating, albeit within the swirling dynamics of Eternity?

Therefore, how do we understand later event B informing God's action and influence on earlier event A when A is part of the causality which produces B? It would seem God must know the future before it happens, yet this is not the case. These perennial theological issues begin to unknot when we consider *how* God is person, the nature of gestalt formation, and

---

33. Barth, *CD* II/1:674.

34. This reveals Barth's misappropriation of Kierkegaard's "infinite qualitative difference," which he posits between God and humanity without following through with the broader consequences of Jesus Christ *and the Holy Spirit*. With the knowledge and advent of Christ, Kierkegaard continues to maintain the qualitative difference between time and eternity, so that each *moment* comes into the world respectively within the dialogical consciousness of the Christ and the Spirit *and* potentially in human beings through messianic time in their dialogical alternation between time and Eternity. They are analogically inclusive in both God (a Trinity) and humanity. It is this incompleteness by Barth that inhibits his clean break from Hegelian derivatives.

the notion of person as *perichoresis*. The *perichoresis* of time and eternity exposes the truncated ontology that gives rise to the apparent dichotomies of immanence and transcendence in Western theological use.

IMMANENCE AND TRANSCENDENCE

The theological discussion concerning God's dichotomous categories of God's immanence and transcendence have fallen into intransigence and, for myself (and Moltmann), ambivalence. From my first days as a theological student, I was resistant to and never felt comfortable with the dichotomy; my experience of God's presence suggested otherwise. Most contentious issues within this discussion will find resolution only in a better understanding of time (Eternity) and rethinking causality. We will only unify these persistent categories of God and God's interactive presence in the world into a unified and irreducible complementarity when we reconsider the contemporary anthropological paradigm that resists acknowledging the complementary aspects of the temporal *and eternal* dimensions of humanity. Any theory that emphasizes either aspect of God or God's relation to humanity in exclusion of the other does so because of an insufficient understanding of human existence itself, which inhibits our understanding and experience of full filial divine-human relations. We obscure our concept of God and the divine-human interaction when we fail to *fully* understand human nature, which includes remaining open to the possibility of human nature as expressed in Jesus Christ. To the extent any aspects of human experience correlatively relate to the Eternal dimension of God is pivotal in better understanding these two traditionally Greek concepts.

The contemporary moral crisis in human thinking creates a whirlpool of activity surrounding traditional notions of volition, ethics, and self. As the notion of self further dimensionalizes, human experience and moral action must likewise penetrate deeper into the divine-human interaction, specifically into its holistic interactions. As noted earlier, Gadamer found no evidence of the concept of the metabole, the "sudden blow," the *moment* in history, until Kierkegaard. Therefore, according to Gadamer, it took 1800 years to consider and locate this significant dynamic in the anatomy of human thought and experience of which Christ spoke. Since then, it has unleashed a deluge of philosophical and theological explorations and expansions that continue to this day. Likewise, this thesis drives our explorations ever deeper into our growing knowledge of anthropology, psychology, and sociology. If we are to obviate the reasonable charges of late modernity, we must theoretically expand our understanding of what occurs within the holistic, subconscious, and liminal dimensions of human experience. The necessity of expanding our theological thinking is painfully evident in its failure to account for the scriptural prominence given to Jacob (and the importance given to Peter's recognition of Christ). Until our theologies begin to factor the preeminence of the Jacob narrative theologically (and anthropologically), they will continue to inhibit the faith expression and growth of the church. This anthropological omission is the most damaging factor within most theologies. Nevertheless, as our evolving conceptual capacity and heuristics continue to transform from one degree to another into the image of Christ, our anthropological reclarifications will sharpen with time (Bonhoeffer). What once was obscure is now coming into focus. We can no longer sit theologically stupefied in denial concerning these obvious markers within the text when resolutions to these issues enhance and deepen scriptural coherence at every level. In today's pluralizing world, theology's inability to explain how a transcendent, Eternal, and creating God can filially relate with created temporal humanity, and forward a coherent Christian pluralistic hypothesis, will ultimately render theology impotent.

In some form or another, most contemporary notions of theological anthropology have begun to re-situate human freedom and the divine-human point-of-contact from the immediate focal and reflexive consciousness into the holistic dynamics within human experience and interaction. This includes not only prereflexive aspects but the implications of constituting socially. Ethical action largely transpires within the prereflexive process of awareness antecedent to conscious reflexive response (e.g., the Sermon on the Mount), and we need to develop further our operative and ethical understanding of relational *dispositions* as preeminent over, but not excluding, conscious moral will and disciplined behavior. Our culture and most disciplines of thought largely already know this.

To the extent the person is willing to venture all into the co-conditioning dynamic of the relationship, establishes the prereflexive level of relational openness to that Power which posits self and is the source of all truth and beauty. Kierkegaard argues that the infinite resignation into relationships will eventually convict us of our wrong decisions and guide us into more life-giving ones. An open disposition, or "inner infinity," allows that eternal Power to condition us in truth and continue transformatively expanding our experience of *perichoresis*.[35]

Kierkegaard speaks here of an immanent force within human beings and our relations. When our self-interest closes to the fullness of the relationship (reality), it is not so much the shortened interest that it produces

---

35. Kierkegaard, *EO2*, 141.

that is errant but the selective suppression of various aspects within the relationship—most notably suppressing the interpenetrating Power and source of the good. More problematic is the suppression that creates the malevolent interest that distorts our reflexive desires and actions. The former is systemically primary; the latter is not. Therefore, such categories as reflexive and prereflexive states within dialogical relations will have a tremendous bearing on our understanding of immanence and transcendence as well as ethical action.

"IMMANENCE" AND "TRANSCENDENCE" IN ETHICAL TELEOLOGY

Hegel: Geist as Telos

In a comparative study of freedom in the thought of Hegel and Whitehead, George R. Lucas argues that the Kantian view of "moral teleology is ultimately external to the moral process itself."[36] In other words, the teleological impress within the world process, the aims and purposes by which moral and meaningful intentions come about, are external to the world and world processes themselves. Lucas, however, tells us that Hegel insisted "the pattern or principle of organization of the world-process, be it moral or otherwise, must be 'inner'—in other words, immanent in and in some sense generated by or dependent upon the very processes of development it enables." This process itself contains the entire emergence of all teleological formations. Therefore, a transcendent God independent of the world-process, which is not affected by the world, and yet stands in teleological relation to such world processes, is unacceptable. With this, I am mildly sympathetic; however, for Hegel, God exists within the world-process simply as *Geist*. And *Geist* objectifies the world when individuals experience genuine community. Moreover, *Geist*, or Absolute Spirit, is the immanent means within human experience by which the individual emerges from subjectivism to participate authentically within the world-process, and it is through Absolute Spirit that all entities ultimately relate.

In Hegel and Whitehead, the relationship of the entity to the system in which it configures defines (constitutes) its knowledge of an entity. On a cosmic level this is agreeable. For Hegel, however, the knowledge of the particular *always* implicitly contains the sum of the parts. In many ways, this dynamic resembles the static qualities of the hologram, in which all the individual particles of the holographic picture themselves internally

---

36. Lucas, *Two Views of Freedom*, 113.

contain the entire image (thus allowing the image to appear three-dimensional as one shifts perspective). The relational juxtaposition of the person *within* the whole of the community will define (objectify) that entity accordingly. The question remains, can the individual or specific relationship within this Hegelian matrix ever exceed or transcend the definable sum of the parts within the existing sociocultural configuration and this configuration's own "inner" processes to constitute as a whole self in differentiation to the system? Does the individual ever contain that which is outside Geist, or the person of God? In such a system, Jacob falls into insignificance. To constitute as a *whole person* in complete contrast to the Other and yet also within an interdependent process of interpenetrating relations necessitates the dynamic of *perichoresis* inside dialogical communicational dynamics. Kierkegaard insists as much.

As one notable example of Hegelian thought, Peter Hodgson defines the emergence of freedom as that ability within the system and its entities to expand in ever-developing relational configurations of meaning. This takes place within the relational transfigurative praxis of culture. Within this praxis, *Geist* has its immanent play. Nevertheless, all such activity remains entirely immanent. If all entities are exclusively constitutive of Absolute Spirit, then both world and figurative processes emerge and remain immanent within the whole or the parts. Hegel or Hodgson never connect Geist with a personal, transcendent God independent of the world-process itself.

Hegelianism: Reaction to Classical Theism and Faith

Hegelian themes arose in reaction to concepts of God that personalize a transcendent deity—the Eternal God self-constituting outside the world-process and therefore imposing itself in time upon the world-process. This is a personal God who speaks into history unidirectionally. Revelational words and meanings constitute within the individual or community who must simply choose. From the Hegelian critique, this is unacceptable divine intervention unnaturally imposing itself upon the world and anything but personal. I agree with this critique, but either way, Jacob disappears. In the end, both positions are limited in their traditional expression.

A preponderance of former classical theories, generally Platonic, have left themselves open to being interpreted as presenting an eternal God who, because God is timelessness (outside spacetime), amply supplies the world with timeless truths and telos. As a result, the world becomes an unfolding (or dictation) of salvation history, preeminently predetermined from outside the world-process itself, which seriously diminishes any claim of freedom, genuine agency, and self-determination within the world, or it all rolls into deism. Although neo-orthodoxy has offered alternative theological expressions of God's transcendence concerning time, the primary point is that Hegelian and process theologies arose in reaction to the classical configurations of a timeless God.

Variously, Hegel and Hodgson ultimately de-personalize God and place God entirely in the midst of the world as trans-personal or inter-personal.[37] The immanent theologies, however, leave much unanswered while amputating much of the Scriptures and Christian tradition. For authentic freedom, God and the entire world-process (with persons) must emerge together in their becoming whole. In reaction to what he considers classical theology, Hodgson (Hegel) exchanges the personal predications of God for more fundamental and less personal attributions. Nevertheless, Hodgson struggles to express any coherent concept of God in non-personal predication while constantly falling back into anthropological predication.[38] Ultimately, he fails to consider alternative dual-aspect conceptions of a personal God who then relates with a *dual-aspect* humanity and world trans-historically (holistically) and, therefore, from within the narrative of history as a person. In reacting to undeveloped classical theologies, both Hegel and Hodgson drag the whole notion of God into a temporal and sequential causal structuring of history. Therefore, for Hodgson, no aspect of God in any way experiences a future or teleological formation that could affect persons or events before that future or telos. For the sake of mutuality, and due to inadequate anthropological structuring, God is completely bound within time and history in much the same traditional manner as they conceive human temporal experience. Therefore, God can only constitute (reflexively) within immanence to creation and certainly not in a personal manner to individuals in time. Therefore, the mystery and dynamic of *perichoresis*, an ontological Incarnation bringing the Eternal *existentially* into time, is paradoxical and unrecognizable to them. Ultimately, you lose all transcendence and the biblical understanding of faith.

A PERICHORETIC ANTHROPOLOGICAL ALTERNATIVE

In contrast to classical and Hegelian perspectives, I suggest an alternative view considering a fundamental paradigm shift in anthropology within an expanding ontology. Rather than relating either the immanent or transcendent activities of an Eternal God to temporal humanity, we need to consider

37. Hodgson, *God in History*, 206.
38. Cf. David Pailin's criticism of Hodgson in Pailin, Review of *God in History*, 17.

the possibility that a dipolar humanity constitutes in analogical perichoretic reciprocity to a dipolar God. In such a relationality, as Kierkegaard suggests, the relative aspects of humanity relate with the relative aspects of God (Christ, divine temporal aspect), and the absoluteness of humanity (spirit) relates absolutely with the Absoluteness of God (Spirit, divine eternal aspect). The co-conditioning relationship between the antecedent dynamic of *analogia spiritus* in prereflexion (interacting absolutes that produce the transcendent nature of experience) then conditions the relative aspects of cosmic experience (interacting relativities that produce the immanent nature of experience) producing reflexive consciousness. If undistorted, the person then moves in relation to that Power that creates relations. In a living relation to Jesus Christ, persons move in unison with Christ in his Time (eschatological Time). This roughly equates to Kierkegaard's Religiousness A and B, respectively. Remember, with Kierkegaard, each level transforms the former stages of existence so that the more linear and immanent dynamics of dialogical cycling within Religiousness A are not lost in B; instead, B transforms A as persons and communities begin to move within transformation itself, with divine Time.[39]

Yes, there is an "infinite qualitative difference" between the *Eternity* of God and the *temporality* of humanity, but because the fullness of the divine nature indwelt in Christ, the same also analogically takes residence between Christ and humanity. However, due to the Spirit's and Christ's immanent transcendent relation to humanity, the "infinite qualitative difference" lies not between the personhood of God and humankind *per se* but between the eternal and time. In *perichoresis*, unlike Hegel, the relative and eternal never synthesize but are held existentially in the moving tension of personhood-in-relation that appropriately maintains the infinite qualitative difference within cycling dialogical interaction. Therefore, the paradox is *perichoresis*, the divine nature of love that constitutes Christ, God as Trinity, and increasingly humanity as person and community. All four dialogically and analogically constitute in perichoretic relations. This is why there will forever be a Jacobian dark *moment* within our dialogical cycling in which the "Paradox," the "Condition," that "Power" that constitutes all relations mediates that cycling transition from the eternal ("inner infinity") into time. Optimally, the Eternal co-conditions our eternal, while they dynamically co-condition

---

39. Agamben insightfully exegetes Paul's understanding of Christ's Time as "the ultimate meaning of the messianic vocation is the revocation of every vocation. Just as messianic time transforms chronological time from within, rather than abolishing it, the messianic vocation, thanks to the *hōs mē*, the 'as not,' revokes every vocation, at once voids and transforms every vocation and every condition so as to free them for a new usage" (*Kingdom*, 18).

the Word-co-conditioning-our-word. The Son and Spirit do the same for the Father, as each perichoretically constitute God as person-in-relation to the world. *God still constitutes Eternally in perichoretic relation to time, and humanity still constitutes temporally in perichoretic relation to the Eternal.* We might think of humans as constituting figure-over-ground (focal over tacit), *in* time-over-eternity, and the Father *in* Eternity-over-Time (Spirit and Christ). This alternative thesis attempts to expound many of the qualities within Barth and Moltmann's theologies while expanding their anthropological perspective and notion of human as spirit. We will investigate this subtle twist shortly. First, however, it is necessary to take a brief look at Barth's understanding of time.

Eternity of God as Gestalt, and the Christological *Perichoresis* of Time and Eternity

Karl Barth in *CD* II/1, develops a Boethius-like position of eternity as "pure duration" (*reine Dauer*).[40] "What distinguishes eternity from time" for Barth, says R. H. Roberts, "is that 'origin, movement and goal,' past, present, and future, 'not yet,' 'now,' and 'no more,' rest and movement, potentiality and actuality, and so on, are all held in God's being, his eternity in a pure present."[41] "Eternity," says Barth, "is the essence of God Himself, . . . [and] is not in any way timeless."[42] It is "simultaneous presence." Barth's notion of Eternity is clean of the static qualities endemic to Platonic notions of eternity, and yet this dynamic of Eternity contrasts with "relative time," which he defines as a "one-way sequence and therefore the succession and division of past, present and future, . . . of origin, movement and goal."[43] In Christ, these aspects of relational dynamics perichoretically interpenetrate. In this respect, Barth's notion of time and Eternity resembles a divine *dynamic* gestalt in which "figure" as temporal causal sequence or differentiated "times" (potential "local incarnations") are set in perichoretic complementarity with the "ground" of the Eternal dynamic that is God. This is an intensely personal and christological complementarity for Barth, similar to but not fully commensurate with Kierkegaard's synthesis of time and Eternity.

---

40. Barth, *CD* II/I:608. By "pure duration" is meant divine simultaneity (*Gleichzeitigkeit*) if we understand this as one simultaneous occasion or event with no loss of causal and defining relations, i.e., an event in all its interrelational fullness (transcending sequential causality).

41. Roberts, "Karl Barth's Doctrine of Time," 115.

42. Barth, *CD* III/1:67.

43. Barth, *CD* III/1:67–68.

Within *perichoresis*, human time can synchronize with and constitute in real Time with God's Eternal grounding through Christ and the Spirit. When fully ventured, the prereflexive dynamic of *analogia spiritus* synchronizes the human reflexive gestalt with that of God's Eternal gestalt (*reine Dauer*). This produces the possibility of human kairological existence creating the ontological dynamic of meaningful times and the narrative quality of life, the kinesis of past, present, and future in singleness of duration. God's Eternity likewise takes on a temporal consciousness or "figure" within trinitarian gestalt. Within the christological event, time and Eternity perichoretically transform in their coming into existence as relationship.[44]

Roberts, however, concludes that Barth's christological temporality is incoherent. Barth's prohibition against natural theology simply re-casts the old distinctions of immanence and transcendence into an alternate theological "metaphysics." His unifying structure fails to end the discontinuity between his new construction of reality and that which Roberts contends is still external to it.

> Time, instead of being or substance as such, becomes the medium of relation and disrelation between God and man.... As we have seen, this reality is a single one which brooks no rival or opposition. It either exists and demands submission in the 'acknowledgment' of faith or it cannot exist for those who refuse to grant its totalitarian demands.[45]

I am sympathetic with the general assertion of Roberts, and for all its erudition and perspicuity, my ultimate concern is the extent to which Barth's *Dogmatics* fully institutes Kierkegaard's complementarity of time and Eternity. Roberts, however, in effectively noting Barth's understanding of time as a medium of *relationship*, fails to realize Barth's full logic and his use of the perichoretic dynamic (of which Moltmann is to some extent more appreciative).[46] The christological event, with its irreducible structuring of the time-Eternity complementarity and personal *perichoresis*, is Barth's

---

44. For example, Barth says: "Even the basis of creation in God's eternal decree is not a non-historical pre-truth, for this eternal pre-truth obviously has a historical character in the bosom of eternity." Consequently, "not even the pure eternal being of God as such is non-historical even in its eternity" (*CD* III/1:66).

45. Roberts, "Karl Barth's Doctrine of Time," 144–45.

46. Barth's "Nein" to the *vestigium Trinitatis* responds to nineteenth-century Protestant Liberalism. His later work, *The Humanity of God*, expresses the personal and structural nature of his reaction, thus acknowledging and framing the theological work to be done. Though Moltmann develops in a different direction, both are struggling to express the ultimate structure of relationship in a perichoretic manner.

starting point for us. Time *is* the medium of relationship between humanity and God, and (this) relationship as Christ *is* the ground of space and time.[47]

Barth's desired logic, and certainly Kierkegaard's, provides us with more than "the 'acknowledgment' of faith" (Abrahamic in nature); it also offers filial participation in and personal affectation of the life of God (Jacobian). As stated earlier, a proper understanding of the developing dynamic of *perichoresis* in this thesis obviates Augustine's Neo-Platonic understanding of the Trinity and humanity, and, therefore, his *vestigium Trinitatis*. My goal is to adjust and complement the *perichoresis* of time and Eternity within the godhead of Augustine, Boethius, and finally, Barth with an analogical reciprocating anthropological dynamic of *perichoresis* reflecting in humanity.

"World-Making," Narrative, and Gestalt Faculties within Human Existence

Let us review dynamic human relations to clarify the experiential aspects of gestalt, then analogically relate this to how the *perichoresis* of time and Eternity might be active within both humanity and the godhead. When a dancer conceives and begins her leap within the dance, an entire imaginary movement flashes to mind from the beginning to the end of the proposed leap. This provides the impetus and conditioning for the corresponding series of movements. This process of gestalt formation before gestalt is an instantaneous process and the product of becoming human spirit.

Human spirit formulates all aspects of human existence and possibilities into a "world," narrative, or totality of response to the world; for our dancer, all her abilities, aesthetic desires, environmental factors, and relevant contingencies teleologically configure into an intentful response. Similarly, gestalt is "an automatically perceived pattern or configuration whose component parts are spontaneously organized into a coherent whole"[48] within the prereflexive cycle of the relational process. This definition, drawn from Torrance, explains that, unlike most psychological understandings, this human function includes the "intentional effort in perceiving." In full resignation (passion) human as spirit in prereflexive awareness generates "sudden" gestalt.

This prereflexive formation antecedent to gestalt represents a transtemporal causality, or better yet, *mutual co-conditioning*, within a holistic process of interrelatedness during awareness and de-liberation (Kierkegaard's reflection). This leads to the "sudden" creation of the reflexion into

---

47. Cf. Torrance, *Incarnation*; Torrance, *Resurrection*.
48. Torrance, *Belief in Science*, 137.

conceptual gestalt (transparently through the co-conditioning of the Word). The "pre-" in prereflexive indicates the causal asymmetry of the relationship as a whole upon the person as agent. Francis Watson notes, "the vertical dimension of the divine image is not prior to the horizontal in the sense that the relation of the individual to God is the primary source of his or her personhood, to which a horizontal, human relationality is then added."[49] They occur in simultaneous movement with asymmetrical priority given to spirit over word. In other words, though the "vertical dimension of the divine image" is the efficient cause and source of the relationship, the relationship nevertheless constitutes immediately inclusive of all relevant "horizontal" contingencies. This begins to reveal how the divine-human interaction might unfold together in *mutual co-conditioning* while maintaining Kierkegaard's primary understanding of infinite qualitative difference.

Contrast: Hegel and Process Theology as Temporally Linear

Process theology analogously describes God as the eternal prehensive or primordial consciousness of the world-process, which dialectically conditions the ever-emerging concrescence[50] of history. In this way, divine consciousness and world unfold concurrently. However, this world-process is contingent upon the eternal and divine prehension processing sequentially within an *absolute* notion of time and absolute Spirit. This necessitates a material notion of synthesis within the dialectics; in other words, in each moment a concrescence materially concludes, then re-opens and liberates for the next moment (*aufhebung*). For Hegel or process theology, God cannot know or experience the future in any way other than by extrapolation. This pulls God *completely* into time, similar to the common anthropological understanding of human temporality. Here, divine omniscience means that God (or individuals) can only know the past and what they can potentialize (extrapolate), nothing more. Therefore, only what has and is happening conditions God and God's actions. Nothing future is in retro-causal or conditioning relation to its past. Alternatively, let us reconsider how the temporal and eternal existentially synthesize in human consciousness.

---

49. Watson, *Text*, 115.

50. Whitehead briefly defines "concrescence" as a process in which "prehensions" integrate into physical or mental state.

Causal Dimensions within the Human Temporal Experience

Based on the earlier-mentioned principle of complementarity, Loder concludes, "there is no chronological sequence implied in the actual relationship between the two modes of explanation or between the realities to which they point [wave/particle, eternal/time]. Hence, causality in the classical sequential sense is denied as a universal principle."[51] A preliminary delineation must be made between the sequential causality within temporality in contrast to the potential transtemporal (holistic) mutual conditioning within human experience. The phenomena of holistic transtemporal relatedness between events both transcend and include the phenomena of temporally sequential relatedness. For example, the dancer does not construct a dance move through a linear process from each moment to the next, using inductive logic. By definition, the gestalt process is not sequential in *forming* narrative or movement. Its amalgamation process of creation is purely relational and happens in instantaneous bursts of cognition. That such gestalts (shapes, choreographies) contain sequential movement is because the temporal is one contingency factoring among many within the collating contingencies; neither is the character of the process of gestalt formation linear or temporal; it is instantaneous and transtemporal, coming to us in small movements that we then collate into larger movements.

When considering the dancer's formation logic during the prereflexive process before gestalt, movement 1 was not considered before movement 2, even though m1 comes before m2 within the performed sequence. And though m1 comes before m2 in the sequence, the possibility of m1 within the gestalt was contingent upon the *co-conditioning* contingency m2. In fact, within the formative process toward gestalt (ultimately as final cause), m2 causes m1 as much as m1 does m2. Just as m2 constitutes by its transtemporal relation to m1, so m1 is to m2. Therefore, m1 cannot exist *within the gestalt process* before m2; the dancer's movement comes into her mind in the singular flash of a whole movement, all moments within the movements instantly co-conditioned within the *perichoresis* of time and eternity. Each moment within the movement emerges from a complementarity of sequential contingencies and possibilities and the transtemporal gestalt (telos) in which it was born. This simple but essential activity of human *kinesis* and gestalt reveals two different dynamics within human temporality; gestalt relation (the co-conditioning relation between m1 and m2, regardless of temporal ordering) and linear sequence (m1 unfolds before m2).[52] One is

---

51. Loder, *KM*, 80.

52. Though similar, these are not to be confused with the Greek philosophical categories of actuality and possibility.

transtemporal relatedness (human eternality); the other is linear sequential relatedness (temporal). We experience each within the appropriate dialogical cycles established earlier. Though this distinction may seem obvious and redundant, they provide the appropriate genealogy within human relationality that associate with and potentially facilitate full co-conditioning relations with God's similar trinitarian relational dynamics, even though humanity constitutes in time conditioned by the eternal and God constitutes in the Eternal conditioned by Time.

Reciprocating Temporal Dimensions within the Trinity

Because of the Trinity, God relates both inside time and transtemporally with the world (which includes retro-temporal co-conditioning).[53] The general human prehensive process would involve smaller units of time weaving together into larger units of meaningful kairotic narratives. God as a person (specifically the Father) constitutes Eternally as interactive with all points of history concurrently. Such a prehension would be one divine dynamic singularity instantaneously processing toward an Eternal dynamic gestalt. We might speculate that the Father's gestalt formation would be translucent ground *overlaying* form rather than form within ground.

The person of God likewise constitutes as a differentiated unity. The traditional Judeo-Christian notion of God entails the spoken or begotten contingency of the Logos (*dahbar* and Christ) and constituting Eternally, inclusive of all history. Barth considers the Eternal constituting of God as *both* "simultaneous" or "durational."[54] In this respect, the Eternal process and formation of God's gestalt processes all history *within* its trinitarian deliberation. Such an Eternal prehension of God (specifically the Father) would be determinately real because God constitutes Eternally—*transtemporally*. Christ experiences every moment of history in the focal awareness of his Time while the Spirit frames and conditions his tacit awareness from this "pure duration."

In such a dynamic, God the Father experiences all of history *happening* concurrently. God does not *know* any-thing in history before it happens. Similar to the prereflexive process that leads to the suddenness of human gestalt, so too is the Father's awareness of all history (as Eternal, as Spirit, but in dynamic totality). But, just as in human de-liberation, which takes

---

53. Retro-temporal co-conditioning means occasion A historically happens before occasion B; however, the prereflexive process that constitutes B can potentially condition the prereflexive process constituting A. Cf. Lucas, *Future*, 236.

54. Barth, *CD* III/1:66–70.

place within gestalt formation, so too God relates to all history transtemporally mediating, influencing, and interrelating all creation in co-conditioning relation with all co-creators (Jacobian in nature). If we maintain Kierkegaard's understanding of personhood, the de-liberation process in human beings (spirit) in analogical co-conditioning relation to the infinite deliberation of God in Eternity (Spirit/Father)—*analogia spiritus*—does not materially synthesize with the reflexive conceptualization of humanity, but both human modes then co-condition each other prior to gestalt. That is why *analogia spiritus* is prereflexive, outside time, a leap, resulting in a hypthetico-deductive gestalt.[55]

> The task is to exercise the absolute relationship to the absolute *telos*, striving to reach the maximum of maintaining simultaneously a relationship to the absolute *telos* and to relative ends, not by mediating them, but by making the relationship to the absolute *telos* absolute, and the relationship to the relative ends relative. The relative relationship belongs to the world, *the absolute relationship to the individual himself*; and it is not an easy thing to maintain an absolute relationship to the absolute *telos* and at the same time participate like other men in this and that. . . . *It is the relationship that is decisive*. The task is therefore to exercise myself in the relationship to the absolute *telos* so as always to have it with me, while remaining in the relativities of life."[56]

Just as the dancer in full passion ventures all of herself and every potential relational contingency and factor into the de-liberation of the gestalt formation process, so are all the existent aspects antecedent to each "local

---

55. This is the christological necessity of Kierkegaard and the primary themes of both *Postscripts* and *Training in Christianity*. Christ is both God and human, and we are not God, and neither is the Father human (yet perichoretically humanized in relation to the Son). However, we are all mutually persons because we are differentiated unities perichoretically co-conditioning and dialogically relating within our communities, trinitarian and/or cosmic.

56. Kierkegaard, *CUP*, 364–65, emphases added. Cf. Agamben, *Kingdom*, 26: "Contrary to the contemporary eschatological interpretations, it should not be forgotten that the time of the messiah cannot be, for Paul, a future time. The expression he uses to refer to this time is always *ho nyn kairos*, 'now time.' As he writes in the Second Letter to the Corinthians, '*Idu nyn*, behold, now is the time to gather, behold the day of salvation' (2 Cor 6:2). *Paroika* and *parousia*, the sojourn of the foreigner and the presence of the messiah, have the same structure, expressed in Greek through the preposition *pará*: a presence that distends time, and *already* that is also a *not yet*, a delay that does not put off until later but, instead, a disconnection within the present moment that allows us to grasp time. Living in this time, experiencing this time, is thus not something that the Church can choose, or choose not, to do. It is only in this time that there is a Church at all."

incarnation" drawn into the deliberation process of the trinitarian gestalt through relation to the human Jesus Christ and the Spirit.

What is a mixture of the ideal and the real for the dancer (and Christ) as she performs the leap in time is immediately real for the Father because God constitutes within the dynamic singularity of the Eternal. Faith is the degree one's imaginative gestalt emerges in open co-conditioning relation to God's gestalt in the *analogia spiritus*. To the degree this happens, our imagination transforms into faith, which is the tacit experiencing of the very *reality* of things future through the immediacy of our relation to God—a "presence" unfulfilled in our historical time, *yet no less real*. Faith, if she is passionate, is not the dancer's psychological assurance of completing the movement while halfway through it but her holistically experiencing the ontological reality of the leap and its completion at any time during the movement.[57] Faith is the human analogical participation in the Eternal awareness and constitution of the Trinity.

Therefore, when the predominance of contemporary theological thinking restricts its causal understanding to just the sequential arrow of time, its thinking is antiquated in the light of STR, Bell's Interconnectedness Theory (both evidenced-based and entirely accepted theories in Physics), general causal dynamics in quantum physics, and the Kierkegaardian understanding of relationality. When persons move with christological Time, the causal interactions both supersede and yet incorporate the linear aspects of causality because this Time constitutes in perichoretic relation to the process of divine gestalt. All open human prereflexive moments are instantaneously drawn into co-conditioning relation to God where they de-liberate and potentially transform the person's desires and will in consideration of all other relevant person's longings, desires, and intentions throughout history. In this way, humans experience freedom and self-determination.

---

57. Our knowledge of quantum mechanics also complements this idea scientifically with its concepts of observer or consciousness dependent (created) reality, Bell's interconnectedness theory, and the theory of non-locality. "Non-local interaction links up one location with another without crossing space, without decay, and without delay. A non-local interaction is, in short, *unmediated, unmitigated,* and *immediate*" (Herbert, *Quantum*, 214). Herbert's concern is only with the "phenomenon" as scientifically perceived; therefore, he views the interaction as "unmediated" without giving consideration to how this action occurs. On a practical level, I used to be an accomplished high jumper. On rare occasion, I *knew* the jump was a success a good stride or two from the takeoff point. Other jumpers confess occasionally experiencing this same *absolute knowledge* of clearance moments before liftoff. Without this experience we either clear the bar or not randomly. But we *never* experience a miss after receiving this transcendent experience of ontological knowing. These special experiences of pre-knowledge were rare and random.

Similar to our prolonged gaze into a compilation of various colored dots bursting into a 3-D picture (meaning), God's Eternal gestalt process (Father) dynamically experiences each moment of history (the dots) *unfolding* in complete interrelatedness (form)—suddenly. God's open and *pregnant* Eternity (inclusive of all history) holistically and simultaneously relates to every other *pregnant* moment in history. We experience this pregnancy as potentiality (wave function) or if properly postured, faith. Nevertheless, because of trinitarian *perichoresis, analogia spiritus* transcends yet includes this emerging christological activity (history). Similar to the dynamics of human gestalt, this relational processing of God's Eternal gestalt (activity of the Spirit-to-spirit) facilitates the teleological christological dynamics within the Trinity, co-conditioning the world-process (John 5:16–30).

This teleological dynamic is open in perichoretic complementarity bringing all things to bear upon the openness of each moment and each moment upon all other moments. Therefore it is not impositional or interventional because it is also inside Time and transtemporally informed and conditioned by human desire, choice, and activity. All teleological dynamics are conditioned by (1) the perichoretic nature of reality which relates all things as they develop; (2) the transtemporal co-conditioning (mediating) of all longings, desires, wills, and choices throughout history; (3) the personal will of God, which gracefully orchestrates our determinations (those moving in faith) into copacetic relations through the trinitarian *perichoresis* of Time and Eternity. The difference with human beings is that they are finitely and sequentially contingent in *selfhood*, God is not. The Father transtemporally constitutes as person, and every passionate soul conditions God's creative activity ("predestination"). Again, these instantaneous *moments* before our gestalts are holistic and lie prereflexively invisible within the Jacobian night prior to our constituting into time. However, this transtemporality of trinitarian gestalt—this "simultaneity" of "duration" incorporates the human de-liberational process into its own sequential and conceptual temporality in Christ's Time.[58] This totality of de-liberations (sum of the parts) does not define God's gestalt. The Eternal gestalt of the godhead relates to each point of history, not only as an imaginative divine gestalt, but as a contextually *real* local incarnation that maintains God's personhood and will in relation.

As with the dancer, who allows all single moments within her imaginative gestalt to condition each other individual moment in co-conditioning

58. Furthermore, Barth tells us, "Jesus Christ belongs not only to yesterday, or to-day, or an indefinite future. He belongs to all times simultaneously.... Men do not make or feel or know themselves the contemporaries of Jesus.... It is Jesus who becomes and is their Contemporary" (*CD* III/2:466–67).

relation to the overall gestalt, so it is with God. Because his divine gestalt emanates in *dialogical* relation to the Son it alternatingly conditions and is conditioned by the particulars of history and all the trans-historical gestalt processing moments of humanity.[59] Therefore, all prayer in which one fully and passionately ventures oneself into the Other, even in passionate defiance, deeply affects God. And this is why prayer is largely ineffective; rare are the moments we enter our relations with *passion*.[60]

The Non-sequential Causal Nexus between Divine and Human Gestalt

How can we better articulate transtemporal conditioning if the divine process of gestalt in some way draws each linear historical moment and agency into a teleological co-conditioning from an Eternal dynamic singularity, including God's will? This may still seem paradoxical to many, specifically retroactive conditioning. The traditional logic of time becomes circular and problematic when considering teleological factors that process God's trans-historical purposes (the Eternal) *and* free human agency that authentically affect an Eternal God. However, the problem lies within the question, which mistakenly assumes (contra Kierkegaard) that human experience processes and constitutes *only* within a linear sequential notion of historical temporality. *It* is the same mistake as thinking the ethical lies only within our *conscious* decisions when Jesus in the Sermon on the Mount pushes them deeper into the Jacobian night of prereflexive dispositions and subconscious levels of interaction.

This does not mean that prereflexive hypothetico-deductive processing is illogical or always inductively traceable retrospectively. As our earlier investigations reveal (e.g., in emotions), it simply means the prereflexive process that produces it is largely subconscious, even instantaneous. The imaginative prehension of the dancer's leap within the execution exists in some manner not only before but also *in* and during each moment within the leap. At each moment within the sequence, the entire execution dynamically and tacitly backgrounds, maintains, and provides meaning (direction). In this respect, the human gestalt is imaginatively transtemporal in producing a teleological (kairological) guide, unifying and directing the

---

59. John 5:19–30 reveals the Eternal prereflexive dynamic of divine *perichoresis* as the Son "sees" (holistic) what the Father does, and yet the Son (a human) adjudicates, integrates, and in love synchronizes all thing within the *analogia spiritus* into his Temporal gestalt.

60. These dynamics are entertainingly depicted in the film *Adjustment Bureau*.

existing "now" through time. Herein lies our human faculty through which to analogically relate with God's similar dynamics within the Eternal.[61]

At this point, it is worth considering whether the intermittent moments and particular aspects that shape, form, and condition the gestalt of the dancer are truly differentiated or free in themselves. Within a perichoretic ontology, they *are*, even though they constitute co-conditionally with a transtemporal whole. To the extent we fully venture ourselves, are open to the possibility of greater meaning, and act decisively, our respective contingencies, nature, and context, elevates into a greater divine gestalt of meaning. In one respect, the whole as gestalt is as contingent upon the internal character and nature of the parts, as the parts are the whole. Likewise, the gestalt process of the Father constitutes in perichoretic relation to the Spirit and the Son through whom "all judgement" is left to the Son as the godhead relates with creation. In this manner every passionate gestalt process of humanity correlates, integrates, and appropriately transforms in cosmic synchronization. In this way,

> existing harmonies, existing "extensions" of time and space, constantly give rise to new "intentions," to movements of the Spirit to further creative expression, new temporal unraveling of creation *ex nihilo*, in which human beings most consciously participate.[62]

Phenomena of *Analogia Spiritus* and the *Perichoresis* of Time and Eternity

Having considered that God's dynamic structure of relations is analogically similar to human relations, we can now further articulate how the Eternal breaks into human experience. Human knowledge and information form and communicate at many different levels of experience, some focal (conscious) and some tacit (conscious, subconscious, and unconscious), all no less real and personal than the other. We have come to recognize that the person is not simply a solitary subject, like the monistic conception of God, but a subject-in-relation-to-subject. Likewise, these perichoretic dynamics suggest a communicative patterning and nature to relationality. In considering that the respective cycles or aspects of human relationship are analogically related to God's similar activity and that they might share

---

61. Barth notes: "Time in not eternity. Eternity itself is not timeless. It is the simultaneity and coinherence of past, present and future" (*CD* III/2:526).

62. Milbank, "Postmodern," 236.

information at those respective paralleling cycles, we might consider *that analogia spiritus* supersedes *analogia relationis* in positing with Kierkegaard that the absolute can indeed relate to the Absolute, and the relative to the relative. *Analogia relationis* tends to infer a relating of the Absolute to both the absolute and relative aspects of humanity. This leads to an imperialistic imposition of the Absolute upon the human relative aspects, rather than the human agency of spirit affecting human relatives (albeit while experiencing *analogia spiritus*), thus allowing human agency's openness (or not) and playing a regulative role in the human constituting gestalt (i.e., the possibility of redeeming the human condition). Whatever divine contingencies are within the person's entire purview and context will factor within the perichoretic co-constituting of the fully ventured person. When we focus the nexus of the divine-human interaction upon *analogia spiritus*, we shift the nature of God's cosmic relationships from impositional-interventional (Abrahamic) to influential-interactive (Jacobian) and thus truly filial in nature.

God's Eternal process of gestalt constitutes history through the Son and the Spirit, providing the dynamic ground for human acts of faith and freedom in co-ordination with God's Eternal gestalt through *analogia spiritus*. Therefore, humans are self-determining. For example, in our earlier inquiry, human emotions (spirit) were holistic complexes of various factors and interrelations that we experience at tacit levels of experience. Our decisions are ninety-five percent subconscious, but no less personal. They become the background experience upon which all focal awareness and knowledge frame.

After this highly interactive exchange and reciprocity within the process of de-liberation during our "passive" gaze, we traverse the moment into which our transparent relation to Christ transforms and constitutes us in existence. Reciprocatively, this co-constituting from within the divine relationship itself historicizes God within God's Eternality through Christ. Just as our tacit emotive structures condition our focal engagement within relations, the Father's Eternal dynamic awareness conditions Christ's local incarnational relations. Through *analogia spiritus* we can understand how prophetic experiences and biblical expressions of faith proleptically and analogically emerge in human experience; in other words, how future events might analogically emerge within and condition human experience (not unrelated to Carl Jung's concept of synchronicity).

Ultimately, *within this prereflexive activity between human and divine spirits, the human spirit is analogically (perichoretically) drawn into the eschatological development of telos within the Eternal singularity during* *awareness and de-liberation.*⁶³ This dynamic is not static timelessness but an eschatological rending of the veil, making visible a living transforming *kairos*.⁶⁴ The perichoretic relation to the Eternal creates the *kairos* aspect of relatedness or meaningful period of duration; *chronos* time is the linear relatedness within the *kairotic*. This is also true of the godhead, in which each person of the Trinity experiences in their own way this christological aspect perichoretically. Therefore, time is always the property of the relationship—Christ's creative action within each specific relational occurrence.⁶⁵ Also, we cannot fully equate the Eternal dynamic and activity that transpires during divine awareness directly with the typical notion of kairos time. However, sin (withholding aspects of the self from co-conditioning relations) distorts our movement with Christ in his Time and thrusts us into our socialized objective spirit and the relational choreographies of our community and traditions ("all rule and all authority and power," 1 Cor 15:24; "principalities and powers," Col 2:15).

Time in Perichoretic Relation to the Eternal: Aristotelian Material and Final Causality in Mutual Co-conditioning

Are there ways we might understand and legitimize this currently counter-intuitive possibility of apparent retro-temporal conditioning within human history, in other words, how the fullness of time can affect incident B when B is part of the whole, and specifically part of a linear causal sequence within that whole? More specifically, how can a future event B within a causal sequence condition A, which affects or causes B? Again, the problem arises in projecting our common understanding of time and causality upon the entire godhead and human experience. This does not negate sequential experience but cautions against its totalization and projection into the Eternal (as Hodgson and process theologians are doing).

---

63. In this respect, human flourishing is its own, yet its relation to the Trinity informs and sustains *its* flourishing.

64. One should refrain, at this point, from imposing upon this discussion the distinctions which characterize the German discussion of *"Heilsgeschichte."*

65. Some suggest that cosmic linear chronos is a quality of the physical spacetime "frame associated with the cosmic expansion" of the universe (Craig, "Real Time") or the cosmological existence of background radiation (Drees, "Case"). Although much of this is interesting when considering macro relations, Drees concludes that no such hope for a physical recovery of time is forthcoming (337). In this respect, real time is Christ's Time and, therefore, always the property of the relationship—his creative action within each unique relational moment.

Within a perichoretic understanding, each relationship and interaction is *already* emerging within the dynamic Eternal (gestalt). When a person in time prereflexively opens in awareness, announcing their "inner infinity," it potentially initiates perichoretic relations with that Eternal power through the *analogia spiritus* and into co-conditioning relations with God and all history. For Kierkegaard, when we become spirit we "juxtapose" ourselves absolutely to the Absolute, entering *analogia spiritus* as Christ synchronizes us into copacetic relations. The christological event then locally constitutes us as person-in-relationship within each interaction accordingly.[66] Various degrees of such co-conditioning relations a*re what produce kairological* time within humanity. Therefore, the counterintuitive circularity of A conditioning B that is seemingly retro-conditioning A leads us to the concept of co-conditioning (*perichoresis*).

The specious circularity of time and causation is the logical conclusion if we include each *constituted event* into the sum of the Eternal—the material synthesis of all constitut*ed* events within the Eternal. The mistake adds *constituted event* B materially to the Eternal, which then supposedly affects the previous event that caused it. This understanding, however, imposes linear causality *materially* into the Eternal. Note it is then the *retro*causal effect of B upon the A through the Eternal in a retro-sequence that creates the absurd state of affairs (against Kierkegaard's prohibition otherwise). The Eternal, however, has come into Time, not our time (our de-eternalized time due to sin). Optimally (without sin), all such sequential causal moments first dissolve into a sea of transtemporal perichoretic co-conditioning (causality via *analogia spiritus*) in relation to the dynamic singularity of the Eternal. *Never does the perichoresis of time and Eternity become materially synthesized.* They dynamically gestalt only in Time.

The mistake is dragging constitut*ed* relative events into the absolute Eternal, using a truncated anthropology. B is never conditioned by A materially synthesized with the Eternal. Within a perichoretic anthropology, Bp and Ap (prereflexive *moments* of B and A) co-condition each other in relation to the Eternal through *analogia spiritus* in Christ's Time, a gift that can then emerge in the each event-unity within our time, A and B accordingly.[67]

---

66. Reiterating Kierkegaard: "By virtue of the relationship subsisting *between* the eternal truth and the existing individual, the paradox came into being. . . . [by] putting the eternal essential truth into juxtaposition with existence. . . . [If] the individual does not existentially and in existence lay hold of the truth, he will never lay hold of it" (*CUP*, 187, emphasis added). Kierkegaard's privileging the *how* of truth over the *what* of truth leads to his insistence that the absolute relate directly to the Absolute. "The task is therefore to exercise myself in the relationship to the absolute *telos* so as always to have it with me, while remaining in the relativities of life" (365). Cf. Agamben, *Kingdom*, 18.

67. This is analogically the same relational dynamics we reviewed in the earlier study of human emotions.

Therefore, *the prereflexive process leading to the any event-unity happens in synchronous mutual co-conditioning relation to every other relevant prereflexive process that comes into relation with the Eternal. All prereflexive processes potentially emerge together in causal interrelation or mutual conditioning with the creating transtemporal activity of the Trinity.* This is not a subtle shift in thinking. It is an entire paradigm shift out of the Cartesian box of time and Hegel's error in materially synthesizing time and Eternity. This is the heart of Kierkegaard's insistence on keeping the infinite and finite from material synthesis and relating only "absolutely to the absolute." Because this Power is a person and the nature of persons (perichoretic), there is an anthropic principle *active* within the intelligibility of creation, one in which humanity potentially becomes an active co-creating participant.

This adjusts the Hegelian tendencies of Barbour and Rolston with a trinitarian God who is active *with humanity* (to the degree of its redemptive relationship with Christ *and the Spirit*) on both sides of the ledger, eternal and temporal, universal and particular, acting and being acted upon. Here, God acts in personal action within the relativities of time, and Jacob (with Peter) in their scandalous de-liberation within the prereflexive co-conditioning relation to the Eternal. Here, all human action is self-determined, whether in sin, refusing to enter into co-conditioning relations, or in into co-conditioning relations (love) that affect and often transform God (Christ). However, all judgment is left to Christ and it is Christ alone that creates Time with his purview in relation to the Spirit (and all *analogia spiritus* de-liberations) that is capable of integrating the desires and freedoms of a billion spirits into copacetic and loving unity.

The obtrusive material syntheses of Hegel, in order to obviate the offense of dragging Eternity into Time through Christ and the Spirit, shortened his anthropology. *The comedy of errors begins as soon as he drags the synthesis outside the individual and the existential relationship into the Newtonian box.* Here, the sequential temporality immediately vitiates the Eternal. In Kierkegaard, the human "inner infinity" can holistically relate to the Eternal aspect of a creating God. Such *moments* do not transcend but condition and potentially transform the material, temporal and relative aspects of our experience. "The eternal in speaking about the highest assumes calmly that every man can do it."[68] This potential is always a dynamic possibility within the existential synthesizes that is human being. Kierkegaard insists that "from the God himself everyone receives the condition who by virtue of the condition becomes the disciple, . . . one human being, in so far as he

---

68. Kierkegaard, *WL*, 89.

is a believer, owes nothing to another but everything to the God."[69] *It cannot pass between individuals but must be born from within.* The Eternal is not an immanent quality of the world, but potentially (perichoretically) conditions each spirit personally and all cosmic relations. Even when the Spirit moves in community, it unites within the relationships that are persons and community. Faith emerges in our passionate struggle for full personhood only in the night of Jacob, especially when that struggle challanges God's own always-limited (relative) local manifestation in order to emerge into the next—from one degree of glory to the next. The first impetus of all such redemptive and evolutionary movements must be from within the person if we are to maintain the incarnational imperative of mutuality, and increasingly grow in freedom toward filial relations with God. Kierkegaard defies Hegel's "converting the whole content of faith into the form of a concept,"[70] which consistently fails to explain how faith emerges within the individual. The condition is *analogia spiritus*.

We have considered a logic of how faith emerges in the de-liberational process of human "reflection." Here, the Eternal interaction of all things transpires through the Spirit and Christ. Here, all creation is predetermined from within the mutual co-conditioning dynamic of the Eternal through *analogia spiritus* pulsating throughout the interstices time. Moltmann believes

> this is the special dimension given by the experience of the Spirit. In the Spirit we transcend the present in the direction of God's future . . . This future dimension of freedom has long been overlooked, theologically too, because the freedom of the Christian faith was not understood as being participation in the creative Spirit of God. . . . Freedom means the unhindered participation in the eternal life of the triune God himself, and in its inexhaustible fullness.[71]

When human beings announce their "inner infinity," and the Spirit its Eternal openness, they draw into (pre)reflexive relations with the Trinity through whom all things are (pre)determined. Christ pulls humanity and creation with him into the divine de-liberation of his Spirit, where human beings steadily transform into relating with each other as Christ relates with the Father and Spirit. *The denominator of this holistic co-conditioning de-liberational process, the intersubjective dynamic of dialogical relations, takes asymmetrical precedence over the ensuing co-conditioning numerator of reflexion into personhood*; this is why Kierkegaard insistently prioritized

---

69. Kierkegaard, *PF*, 126–27.
70. Kierkegaard, *FT*, 24.
71. Moltmann, *SL*, 217, 222.

the *how* ("mode," "condition," *analogia spiritus*) of faith and beliefs over the *what*. In the final chapter, we will again review how this dynamic brings meaning to previously indecipherable words of Christ placing asymmetrical redemptive priority on the Spirit over himself.

In this respect, Moltmann's work appropriately corrects Barth's relative neglect of the Spirit in deference to his christological concerns.[72] Nevertheless, as McFadyen adequately argues, personhood by nature necessitates both dialogical "bipolarities" of "call and response,"[73] and they are vitally important for understanding Kierkegaard's *existential* synthesis of the finite and infinite that define personhood—what I call relational *perichoresis*. More is going on within these prereflexive processes than initially assumed.

The traditional impasse between divine providence and human freedom results from former anthropological shortfalls and the unwillingness to factor how the eternal conditions and creates human relations. It happens within each human being (as a relationship unto itself), as each person experiences the dual poles dialogically within themselves and their own internal authoritative conditioning in relation to the Eternal. This reflects Kierkegaard's insistence that "no human being can give an eternal resolution to another or take it from him,"[74] which throws eternal decisiveness and predetermination into the intersubjective (or inter-*trans*jective) *moment* and prereflexive relationship with God. Timothy Jackson tells us,

> Faith, hope, and love, for Kierkegaard, are akin to passive potentials in finite individuals. They may not be intrinsic to human nature as such, but they are obtainable by human nature aided by grace.... Yet even as divine gifts, they must be accepted and built up; faith, hope, and love cannot be necessitated—not even by God. Humans are to assume that the potential for love of God and neighbor is present in all human beings; "true greatness is equally accessible to all" (*FT*, 81).[75]

Human subjectivity, therefore, is thrust into the interactive mutual co-conditioning, de-liberation, and emergence of faith through God's grace. Therefore, the idea of predestination without such consideration, for Kierkegaard, is "a thoroughgoing abortion" that explains nothing.[76]

We can now meaningfully consider the following hypotheses.

---

72. Loder, *KM*, 20n2.
73. McFadyen, *CP*, 121.
74. Kierkegaard, *ED*, 382.
75. Jackson, "Arminian Edification," 241.
76. Kierkegaard, *JK*, 2:56.

- God's relation to humanity in Christ and the Spirit opens up the immanent transcendent possibility through which the human prereflexive experience comes into analogical interaction with God's Eternal dimension—*analogia spiritus*. By drawing the human prereflexive dynamic into perichoretic correlation with the Trinity's preeminent Eternal activity of creation, God establishes humanity in its freedom and mutual relationship to Godself.

- All human relations are contingent upon their transparent relationship to the Trinity, which reflects trinitarian *perichoresis* within, between, and as human spirit(s), enabling the dynamics of the third term within all interactions, creating, communicating, and supporting truth within all relationships relative to the character, development, and meaning-frame of each unique participant respectively. This is not a universal frame of reference in which all things similar mutually relate (*analogia entis*), but rather a universal dynamic of relationality through which all things different might mutually and meaningfully relate (*analogia spiritus* within the ontology of *perichoresis*—metaphysics in motion, a metaphysics still emerging from one degree to another).

THEOLOGICAL IMPLICATIONS OF PERICHORETIC THEOLOGY

As discussed in our earlier chapter on method, many criteria factor in assessing a successful theological program, introspectively and in relation to other research programs. This thesis presents compelling evidence on its behalf in contrast to other programs, most notably in providing greater scriptural coherence and the potential resolution of many theological anomalies. It explains multiple sections of difficult Scriptures, some of which are meaningless, incoherent, or contradictory to most theologies. For example, the title of this thesis facetiously highlights the theological privileging of Abraham's actions and prominence over that of Jacob by most, if not all, existing theological programs; the text clearly presents otherwise. This blatant omission is due to former theological limitations and antiquated heuristics. Nevertheless, it reveals the potency of a perichoretic theology in providing a more meaningful interpretation of the text. The final chapter will offer evidence that reveals entire themes within the Scriptures that previously have gone unnoticed or minimized.

Theologically, perichoretic theology also offers a new logic of spirit begun by Loder and Gunton that begins to assuage many of the perennial conflicts between various theological schools, helping each to maintain and more adequately situate their initial concerns within a more unifying theology (e.g., those theologies that emphasize either divine transcendence or divine immanence over the other in relation to the divine-human point of contact). This next section will briefly reveal how a perichoretic theology unifies *both* these dynamics rather than privileging one aspect of the perichoretic complementarity. Though this thesis is limited in its capacity, it proffers a theological program that is rich with possibility for future theological growth and corrects current deficiencies that are slowly diminishing the church. Hopefully, this section will provide enough evidence to give the reader a sense of its potential and how it begins to address existing theological contradictions that threaten Christianity in its growing challenges from pluralism, scientific advancement, theological incoherence, hidden academic agendas, and the church's fading redemptive potency in the West.

The Goal: Divine-Human Filial Relations—Only through *Analogia Spiritus*

Christ's prayer that humanity might relate with each other as he relates with the Father is the primary theme of redemptive history and the hermeneutical key to the Christian Scriptures. To this goal, human beings transform from one degree to another into his same image through relation to the Spirit of God as they progressively emerge out of chaos and innocence toward becoming person, whole spirit (2 Cor 3:18)—therein analogically reflecting the nature of the Trinity in personhood and community. The Scriptures are quite clear: Christ's coming announces the incarnational imperative of mutuality, calling all humanity into filial relationship with God. Eternity is drawing humanity beyond the beasts or angels into the "*fullness of time*," they are becoming "partakers of the divine nature" (2 Pet 1:4). The infinite qualitative difference is redressed within the ongoing dialogical separation of eternity and time in the prereflexive dynamic of *analogia spiritus* and the reflexive christological response. When we pick up our cross and relate absolutely to the absolute, the relationship emerges from its immanent transcendence within the Jacobian night into vital encounter with a personal God (transcendence) that proffers unprecedented freedom and self-determination within our passion. Upon this rock, we transparently come into relation with the Eternal (the *moment*), and then as a differentiated person, faithfully relate (act, love, stand, fight, or kill) relatively to the relative. Love is not sacrificing to the other but to the relationship and the constituting Power within the relationship, which calls, pulls, and integrates all such relational occurrences into the ultimate universal project of creating beings of a filial nature. All evolution, life, history, social interaction, ethics, and redemption shape and develop according to this goal within the radical freedom and relational dynamics required to create beings of like nature to God. However, the redemptive emergence of such a free being is ugly and monstrous. If one aspect of divine quality in humanity does not emerge within a free, open, and willing process of transformation, then humanity becomes robotic.

Can God release all creation, the human heart, and ethics into the radical space and freedom necessary for self-determining development in relation to that immanent transcendent synchronizing Power that allows and integrates (therefore pre-determines) wars, cosmic horrors, and persons that would kill their own son upon the wishes of such a Power—a Power tasked with synchronizing billions of freedoms within creation? This is grace. The divine nature has many qualities, but among them, freedom and self-determination are paramount, which necessitates that such beings and the creation from which they emerge must emerge *freely* within their passionate choices (acts of faith). By Christ's own admission, he did not come to bring peace, but the possibility of order and goodness rising from the chaos, and ultimately the ability to steadily transform those willing to passionately enter the conflictual ground and suffering (the void) that facilitate all transformations. This is the same monster of the Writer—the *horror religiosus*—only bigger.

Correction of Hegelian-Based Theology (e.g., Process Theology)

The highly rational theologies or their post-structural offspring, in reaction to or synchronous with the Abrahamic monster, fail to escape the truncated ontologies of their birth. Antiquated and undeveloped metaphysics inhibit their perception of anthropological dynamics that reveal *perichoresis* and Jacobian faith. For example, Process theology holds the divine and human together in the co-conditioning dynamic of the divine *Eros* and human *eros*.[77] This thesis affirms many of the prereflexive relational dynamics within John Cobb's Process understanding of human concrescence, and these associating dynamics and the primary goals of Process theology are active within the full logic of *perichoresis*, yet the Eternal still breaks into Time. I offer two potential adjustments to these Hegelian models of relationality.

(1) The divine prehension and Eternal dynamic singularity are transtemporal, not only sequential, providing the possibility for each

---

77. Cf. Cobb, "Natural Causality."

concrescence to analogically constitute in transtemporal relation with God and, thereby, the entire world (even the future). This recaptures the scriptural notions of faith and the eschatological.

(2) The incarnational imperative of mutuality: If there are to be filial relations, something inherent in God must experience as human (Christ), and something inherent in humanity must experience as God (*analogia spiritus*). The theological adjustments that emerge are significant.

Let us review a list of major theological distinctions that these two changes generate in contrast to process thought, Hodgson, and to a lesser degree, many of the panentheistic theologies:

Personal Relationship between God and Humanity

(A) A perichoretic and incarnational logic through which an Eternal God can manifest as person in relation to temporal creation. Likewise, temporal humanity can holistically and analogically relate with the eternality of God.

Co-conditioning Futurity within the Telos of Salvation History

(B) An analogically-relative manifestation of telos and meaning is possible within each *moment* that emerges in eschatological *co-conditioning* integration to all past, present, and future *moments* within history.

Human Condition for Redemption

(C) A human soteriological criterion: (1) relational openness (vulnerability), epistemic humility—venturing the whole of self into the relationship (Abrahamic lesson of openness), and (2) relational closure—becoming person—the willingness to fully constitute in time, as differentiated unity (person) to the world through decisive choice (Jacobian lesson of closure). The action of both Abraham and Jacob contain each dialogical distinctions, and the willingness of Isaac to enter the void of transformation between the two (the cross, death).

Difference Coming Together—Perichoretic Creation of Shared Meaning

(D) The possibility of the eternal conditioning each person and relational occurrence creates the possibility of shared meaning amid different meaning-frames—a unity of difference.

Jacob and the Night of Faith

The Implications for Orthodox Theology

A Viable Pluralistic Hypothesis

(A) Richard Roberts is critical of Barth's exclusivist understanding of christocentric Time and its "totalitarian demands" of a unidirectional divine-to-human relationship, a hallmark distinction of Reformed theology. The redemptive condition in humanity of perichoretic openness (the cross; Abraham/Isaac) and perichoretic closure (the call to differentiated unity; Jacob) obviate these unidirectional dynamics of divine-human relations and satisfy Roberts's concerns. The anthropological quality of *perichoresis* and *analogia spiritus* provide an inclusivism through the Spirit, which dimensionalizes Kierkegaard's natural theology of relationships (Religiousness A), potentially bringing Kierkegaard's pagan who "prays with the *entire passion of the infinite*" into limited redemptive relations, yet maintains the exclusive expression of Christ as the unique historical Incarnation through which all humanity encounters God (knowingly or not: Matt 12:32 + 7:21–23 + 25:31–46, Religiousness B). Johannes Climacus recognizes the redemptive nature of the Spirit active in the world and signals it as more fundamental than the empty christological claims of Christendom, what Barth struggles to express. Throughout his exhaustive *Church Dogmatics*, he necessarily kept Matt 12:32 in theological denial, as most do. Such a reading would have left his entire *Dogmatics* and Christological centrality exposed and found wanting. However, Anti-Climacus recognizes the nuclear dimensions of the Spirit when Christianity includes the passionate personal knowledge of Christ's contemporaneity through the Spirit. Both Anti- and Johannes reveal the active power of redemption within the world: in culture, in religions, in the Christian church, and most of all, within the Kingdom of God. The Spirit of Christ and knowing Christ within either the Kingdom of God (Matt 25:31–46, conscious or unconscious) or the church (Matt 7:21–23, in truth or falsely) is the pinnacle of perichoretic relationality.[78] Again, Kierkegaard never eliminates any of his four stages of faith after attaining the next. Instead, each new stage transforms and integrates the former into itself. Religiousness A falls far short of the redemptive action of Religiousness B; however, upon attainment of Religiousness B, Religiousness A, with its incumbent dynamics, transforms acquiring new and greater functionality and meaning in relation to the supervening qualities of Religiousness B. In this respect, there is an asymmetrical priority of the Spirit

---

78. Agnostic Tom Holland, in *Dominion*, acknowledges these Christian redemptive forces as uniquely (perichoretically) transformational of other cultures and religions through their mere relationship to Christian culture (and often the church).

over that of Christ in redemption. The final chapter will further explain this Scriptural mandate and necessity more fully.

Meaningful Human Freedom and Self-Determination within the World-Process

(B) Loder's Kierkegaardian theological anthropology and concept of perichoretic relations teleologically satisfies George Lucas's insistence that "the pattern or principle of organization of the world-process, be it moral or otherwise, must be immanent in and in some sense generated by or dependent upon the very processes of development it enables."[79] Within this developing understanding of *perichoresis* and *analogia spiritus* (specifically concerning the issue of human freedom and self-determination), immanent dynamics within human beings (human spirit) and all life (spirit of life) come into analogical relation *with* the Spirit of God, not *within* the Spirit of God or as extensions of the Absolute Spirit (Hegel). Because of this, the spirit of each creature analogically reflects the perichoretic dynamics within the *Spiritus Creator* but is free to resist such de-liberation and fall back into its finite social limitations ("rule," "authority," "power," and "principalities").

Truth, Identity, and Continuity within the Relationship—the Miracle of the Moment

(C) Truth and beliefs emerge appropriately in social relations relative to each relational occurrence while maintaining analogical continuity through time. The mediated and mutual co-conditioning *moment* creates shared meaning between persons across time through *the analogia spiritus* and the christological gift that creates personal and shared meaning. *Perichoresis* is necessary to understand truth, grace, time/Eternity, and corroborate Climacus' paradoxical claim in *Postscripts*—that subjectivity is truth, yet history is of decisive importance. The bridging of the infinite qualitative difference can only happen within the dialogical alternation of prereflexion and reflexion within the Jacobian night in order for the absolute truth to meaningfully condition the relative in differentiated unity—bringing Christ's Time into existence—Pentecost. Therefore, truth occurs only in his Time. We can now continue our original teleological discussion before exploring other theological implications of *analogia spiritus*.

---

79. Lucas, *Two Views of Freedom*, 113.

Teleological Forces: Immanent or Transcendent?

Hegel and Hodgson demand that the organizing principle within the world-process be entirely immanent, "immanent in and in some sense generated by or dependent upon the very processes of development it enables." And so it is. As stated earlier, God perichoretically is never outside Time or the world-process (nor is God only in Time). This is, by definition, God as Trinity in *perichoresis*. For cosmic and human self-generation to happen in relation to a personal God, the nature of God and its creation *requires perichoresis* replete with *analogia spiritus*.

The teleological forces are immanent within the emerging world-process because the world and specifically human nature are reflectively perichoretic in relation to a trinitarian God whose nature is perichoretic. If we remain consistent with our idea of a perichoretic ontology, then humanity and the world-process will potentially reflect the nature of the creator in its relation to that creator. Therefore, creation always contains its own perichoretic differentiated unity, and the Trinity within its own personal *perichoresis*. By the very nature of *perichoresis* all creation remains differentiated according to its developmental character and kind. Therefore, *perichoresis*, if fully implemented, makes the *vestigia Trinitatis* a misnomer because the nature of God, *perichoresis* (love), always maintains the difference of character and kind within its unifying dynamics by definition. In the case of human development, it is the finitude of its own immanence that thrusts it into its own infinite longings to which *analogia spiritus* opens human transcendence into ever new stages of transformation. The realm of *analogia spiritus* is the land of Jacob, the place of human freedom and self-determination. All creation emerges within this reflective dynamic of differentiated unity. Therefore, is Prigogine's order emerging out of chaos its *own* order? Yes! Does a process within itself direct, condition, and sustain its emergence? Yes! Does the transformative nature of human beings reflect the nature of the triune creator? Yes! And by this nature its *own* immanence is maintained with transcendence (*analogia spiritus*). Therefore, it is "generated by or dependent upon the very processes of development it enables."

Unlike theologies of total immanence, in perichoretic theology all history dynamically and tacitly affects a personal God within each prereflexive *moment* through the *analogia spiritus*. The immutability of God died on the cross. Therefore, this is not a wholly transcendent God unilaterally intervening from outside the world-process, because the world (and ultimately humanity as co-creator) is "immanently" drawn into the trinitarian "transcendence" and personal relations, while God's "transcendence" is lovingly ventured into the world's "immanent" transcendence (through Christ and the Spirit). *Perichoresis* addresses the most significant distinction between the "immanentalist" and "transcendentalist": *the concept of time and eternity as the space of relationship.* The distinctions of "immanence" and "transcendence" are classical distinctions that emerge within the subject-subject understanding of relationship and the Newtonian understanding of spacetime. This creates havoc with the idea of temporal humanity relating to an Eternal God. In perichoretic relations, humans can constitute in Time that has been Eternalized, and God constitutes in an Eternity that has been temporalized. Because they indwell the third term of the relational unity itself rather than the other through the faculty of their respective spirits (*analogia spiritus*), both poles within persons and the respective character of each person, divine or human, are kept separate and maintained, accordingly. In humanity, this occurs in pulsing cycles of dialogical interaction as it engages the absolute with the absolute (the Spirit) and the relative with the relative (the Word).

When we institute *analogia spiritus* into theological anthropology, we begin to understand how an Eternal God who spans history in one unified prereflexive dynamic singularity can "immanently" relate to humanity within humanity's prereflexion as spirit. Thrusting humanity into such immanent transcendence through *analogia spiritus* allows God to constitute as a co-conditioning "transcendent" person in Christ to a free and self-determining humanity. In a perichoretic ontology, both "immanence" and "transcendence" are possible *if*, as Loder insists, humans willingly participate in that ground of their being that reflects the nature of its trinitarian creator. Humanity is free to do so, or not.

Neither the immanentalist nor transcendentalist succeed in supplying the proper categories sufficient to meet the incarnational imperative of mutuality. Both create numerous questionable and unnecessary ontological distinctions between God and humanity. Each had to emphasize a specific polarity of *perichoresis*, thereby distorting the nature of God and God's relation to the world to produce a provisional, albeit distorted, coherence until the logic of spirit began to come into focus. Again, the problem lies in the deficient anthropological paradigm of both programs that then distort and limit their concept of God in comparison to perichoretic theology.

Jacob and the Night of Faith

THEOLOGICAL IMPLICATIONS OF *ANALOGIA SPIRITUS*

(1) Human Condition for Redemption and the Ethical

Commenting on Iris Murdoch, Colin Gunton discusses the concept of authentic relations and human spirit. While acknowledging the necessary factor of community in constituting the person, he challenges the idea of morality as primarily "will" within socialized relations. He refers to Murdoch's anecdotal rendering of a woman who completely changes her attitude toward her daughter-in-law through mere "moral reflection without change of outward behaviour."[80] Through *imagination*, the person simply attempts to see the other more accurately. The theory is that "there is something prior to willing, a passivity that must precede activity if the activity is to be authentic." Gunton frames this passivity using Murdoch and Simone Weil's understanding of "attention" as

> "a just and loving gaze directed upon an individual reality." It is only as the woman *gives* her full attention to what is *actually there* that possibilities for action become apparent. Or, rather, not *possibilities* at all, for it may well be that moral attention leads to a response in which choice is *precluded*: "If I attend properly I will have no choices and this is the ultimate condition to be aimed at.... This is something of which saints speak and which any artist will readily understand. The idea of a patient, loving regard, directed upon a person, a thing, a situation, presents the will not as unimpeded movement but as something very much more like 'obedience.'" When a situation is understood—and it must be allowed that it may not be—then the right action will be known and, in a sense, imposed. Reality will show us what we ought to do.[81]

We will elaborate upon this provisional use of "obedience" and the concept of "imposition" in a moment, but first, let us focus on Gunton's concern about coming to "reality." His moral argument is that

> freedom is the outcome of true understanding: "not strictly an exercise of the will, but rather the experience of accurate vision which, when this becomes appropriate, occasions action." It is both freedom *from* and freedom *for*: "It is in the capacity to

---

80. Gunton, *Enlightenment*, 74–75.

81. Gunton, *Enlightenment*, 74–75. Gunton is making reference to Murdoch, *Sovereignty*, 34, 40, first emphasis mine.

love, that is to *see*, that the liberation of the soul from fantasy consists."[82]

Gunton thinks the conventional tendency to set the passive and active functions of human experience in opposition must change in favor of a more unitary understanding of freedom and knowledge. This parallels our investigation on emotions and the inseparability of emotive response (love) and knowledge (Alison Jaggar). Likewise, Moltmann insists that "reason has to be woven into the fabric of the feelings, and consciousness has to be assimilated into the experiences of the body."[83]

In this respect, Gunton would suggest we include and explore all activities within our awareness, even prereflexive functions. If indeed humanity is fundamentally drawn to constitute authentically in relation to the Other, then moral reflection is first a matter of responding to such a call, awareness, and response antecedent to "willing" or "doing." This relocates the heart of ethics from the typical notion of the will to the person's disposition and willingness to fully enter into a responsible gaze. *Seeing* is passive; however, how passive is "passive"?

Gunton quietly, and perhaps inadvertently, informs us that "the woman" *gave* "her full attention." This giving is obviously a willful activity, at least a chosen disposition that is alterable; in other words, she could have *remained* within her shortened or overdetermining awareness. Furthermore, within the gaze, as we previously considered within our emotive states, lie all sorts of prereflexive possibilities and choices within the holistic reciprocity of *analogia spiritus*. Therefore, Gunton considers that this "passive" function is itself volitional; that moral response ultimately lies within the passive function of awareness, the *how* (awareness), rather than the conventionally understood reflexive or active responses. The conventional understanding of the will is the cognitive deliberation between competing desires, thereby choosing the correct action. We must expand our articulation of the gaze to dive deeper into these insights.

If Gunton's implications are correct, the woman has a prereflexive choice based on her current relational disposition. The ethical choice occurs in her willingness to venture all of herself into the relationship (reality). The desire for more is the result of God's nature (*perichoresis*) immanently reflecting within our relations, and her opening to it annuls her existing relational disposition with its habitual protective behaviors, beliefs, patterns, and reactions and creates a desire to perceive the relationship more clearly. To the degree she is *willing* to relate in truth, she sets herself up

---

82. Gunton, *Enlightenment*, 75.
83. Moltmann, *SL*, 173, referencing Jaggar, "Love and Knowledge."

for transcending her existing relational inhibitors and social structures. The factors previously inspiring resentment now open to reconfiguration within a more holistic gaze that allows her to become spirit (Kierkegaard's venturing all)—*analogia spiritus*—putting her in a position to *passively* experience "in spirit and in truth." There is a reason this often-appearing biblical phrase synonymously links these two concepts.

Sin is the refusal to *see* and relate as full-self to full-reality. Repeating John Milbank, "if all that 'is' is good and true, then no positive reality can be false as a 'mistake,' or as 'non-correspondence,' but only false as deficient presence, embodying the shortfall of an inadequate desire. Now desire, not Greek 'knowledge,' mediates to us reality."[84] When we refuse to *acknowledge* full reality, we bifurcate our soul to relate within a self-created "world" rather than in the full reality of the relationship—we control or deny aspects of reality unwilling to "bear all things, believe all things, hope all things, and endure all things." This bifurcation of self that weakens or distorts spirit produces competing desires, which are ultimately insatiable. Such desires are empty, demonic, and unrelenting, with the ability to become complete "personalities" and lived "worlds" within persons (the demonic). However, a still small desire perennially haunts those "worlds" of our making (Kierkegaard's despair), which constantly calls us to a sustaining gaze that offers greater fullness of life. Therefore, the moral deliberation and decision between competing desires is a misnomer; what Gunton describes as "demonic,"[85] and Milbank, a shortening of desire. True ethical action is antecedent to the creation of desire. In the battle between conflicting desires, the greater substantial desire will always win when it comes into the constellation of the gaze. In the temptation of a sexual affair, we instantly create a separate "world" non-inclusive of our spouse and children (and what they would think). Although the ethical process seems like a reflexive deliberation, human reflexion is always the result of a prereflexive ethical disposition and *how* we gaze. Again, our relational disposition is affected by one's openness to the desire for perichoretic encounter within our relations from the presence of that Power that constitutes all relations. Every person has universal access to this highest desire within them, equal responsibility, and the freedom to open, or not, to that desire.

A significant factor in our relational disposition ultimately rests upon what we believe is at the center of the universe, specifically the power that constitutes our relationships—be it by nature omnibenevolent, destructive, or indifferent. Only to the degree that we believe in an omnibenevolent

---

84. Milbank, "Postmodern," 234.
85. Gunton, *Enlightenment*, 73–74.

force, specifically, that a benevolent Power constitutes all relationships (reality) can we risk everything into the relationship. This perennial taunting call within our broken selves draws us to personhood, toward becoming spirit. Kierkegaard argues that such a state—*analogia spiritus*—is only completely attainable through the knowledge of Christ (Religiousness B). I conditionally agree, but how we identify the character of such knowledge is far more complex in our current age of suspicion that Kierkegaard helped initiate. Nevertheless, such convictions and beliefs (the *what*, conscious or subconscious) deeply affect our relational disposition to the degree they emerge in the self fully-ventured (the *how, analogia spiritus*). In one respect, we are free to love only to the degree we perceive we are loved. Nevertheless, we can reduce much of ethics to an openness, or not, to that one perennial call to perichoretic relations inherent in all relationships, the inescapable face of Lévinas.

It is worth noting that risk, not caution, was Jesus' perennial and emphatic exhortation. In the Matthean Sermon on the Mount, Jesus describes seemingly inescapable desires as immoral or destructive even before any potential conscious action or decision might be made. He is not condemning the person for having the thoughts or desires; he is simply pushing the ethical nexus from conscious reflexive deliberation (human will and thought) to an antecedent level of relational activity. He knows that such redemptive transformative ground is *unreachable* by "no flesh and blood," but only through the transformative dynamics of *analogia spiritus*, a function not yet conceptually available to his disciples during his life. Only after the formal and conceptual fullness of experiencing the Spirit at Pentecost and the Spirit's doxastic installation into the dynamics of the church, was Paul able to proffer the human condition for redemption—exposing and beholding: (1) openness to self exposure (motivated by wanting more) and (2) the beholding the grace and glory (Presence) that (a) perichoretically creates the wanting, and, once open, (b) facilitates our ongoing transformations. As Loder insists, one cannot be had without the other.

> To be convicted of sin . . . would be unbearable, totally offensive, even unrecognizable if it were not that such a realization is preceded by the grace that makes such a realization not only bearable but profoundly generative of a new being. The Creator Spirit must create *ex nihilo* in individuals as it created in the beginning of the whole of creation. Thus, mortification preceded the illumination in our accounting of it, but in the

sphere of the spirit, the illumination precedes and anticipates the mortification.[86]

Through the ongoing process of exposing our relationally destructive interactions (from innocence or denial), bringing them into the light, they transform by the perichoretic *beholding* (gazing) of Reality through *analogia spiritus*:

> When one turns to the Lord, the veil is taken away. Now the Lord is the Spirit; and where the Spirit of the Lord is, there is liberty. But we all, with unveiled face, beholding as in a mirror the glory of the Lord, are being transformed into the same image from one degree to another, from the Lord, the Spirit. (2 Cor 3:16–18, my translation; cf. Eph 5:13)

Note the active dispositional choice antecedent to the passivity of being transformed. "When one *turns* to the Lord, the Spirit," the socialized veil conditioning reality tears open, and the person encounters truth as *we* and our desires transform without will or discipline. All things the light exposes becomes light.

Ethical telos will emerge within each relationship according to what is relevant (the relative) to that relational occurrence. In the case of Abraham: (1) It may entail killing his son as directed by God, which Abraham can only perceive if he is willing to venture everything within this relationship bearing eschatological (ontic) weight—the Word of God (infinite resignation—openness). (2) It also reveals Abraham coming to his own conviction and decision that this is the appropriate action, then acting on it (faith—closure). In the case of Jacob: (1) Jacob passionately resists the potential demise of the blessing from God (Isaac, Esau, or Leban)—a blessing acquired through seemingly "unjust" methods and deception. Jacob cannot imagine this possibility of grace but *openly* keeps desiring within his pre-reflexive struggle with God. Infinite resignation into faith does not mean relinquishing all desire but coming to the relationship (and God) with *our entire self, including our desires*, yet open to transformation and/or equitable synchronization within the relationship (God). (2) This can only happen if Jacob's relational disposition is one of passion, willing to risk *everything* for more, he becomes spirit, and passionately wrestles against God's potential action otherwise within the *de-liberational process* that is *analogia spiritus*. This usually transpires in the twinkling of an eye, actively rising within an emotion-all *moment*, or he literally wrestles with Christ in Christ's Time (eschatologically). Willing to die for such attainment, Jacob receives the

---

86. Loder, *KM*, 116.

blessing and the appropriate wound (closure). "He resigned everything infinitely, and then he grasps everything again by virtue of the absurd [faith]."[87]

Genealogy of Faith: From Ethical Telos to Personal Transformation

From where and what within relational logic does the influence of the ethical telos emerge? Furthermore, what are the causal dynamics within such "passivity"? For Gunton, this influence and reconfiguration begins within the gaze and is simply the desirable response in view of the greater reality and collective possibilities. When fully open to reality (the relationship), the light of the Other improves our understanding and response, often transforming our desires. "Obedience," in this respect, is merely the enactment of transforming or expanding desire. The Sovereignty of Good that comes into focus as the light reveals reality in greater fidelity transforms us within the new event occurrence, which for Gunton, is Christ in the midst of the relationship. So, when Hodgson and the immanentalists decry imposition, Gunton might respond, "so it is." But, is it?

The problem, again, is the linear causal structuring employed by almost all above. As a result, Gunton and Barth, as well as the immanentalists, need to consider the *full nature* of *perichoresis* and the mutual co-conditioning transformative dynamic of *analogia spiritus* within human "passivity." The perichoretic dynamic within *analogia spiritus* is transtemporal including the sequential; in other words, no entity, person, God, or desire takes asymmetrical priority in the prereflexive *de-liberation*—every instrument in the orchestra christologically harmonizes within Kierkegaard's *Fullness of Time*. Each reflects the Other within this harmonizing moment, all things considered: all relevant desires, wishes, hopes, and dreams of every participant within the relationship, including God. Nevertheless, during this process, the personhood of each participant intensifies. Nothing but the nature of *perichoresis* (love) overshadows, manipulates, forces, or imposes itself on another fully ventured person. Once de-liberated, our desires will be transformed by that orchestrating Power that adjudicates all relevant desires of all relevant participants, to each person's satisfaction from perspectives

---

87. Cf. "With infinite resignation he has drained the cup of life's profound sadness, he knows the bliss of the infinite, he senses the pain of renouncing everything, the dearest things he possesses in the world, and yet finiteness tastes to him just as good as to one who never knew anything higher, for his continuance in the finite did not bear a trace of the cowed and fearful spirit produced by the process of training; and yet he has this sense of security in enjoying it, as though the finite life were the surest thing of all. And yet, and yet the whole earthly form he exhibits is a new creation by virtue of the absurd" (Johannes de Silentio [Kierkegaard], *FT*, 51).

eternal. To bemoan such personal transformations to the Other as impositional is nonsense.

A description of perichoretic marriage reveals relationship without imposition and linear causality. In broad generalities, the primary historical model of marriage has been patriarchal. The male dominates most marital decisions as the female sacrifices herself to the decisions of the male. This makes for an easy and efficient economy but compromises fullness of life for both, especially the female. In the twentieth century, egalitarian marriage arose with greater equality (a misnomer) and compromise. When compromise was unattainable, for example, person X wanting x and person Z wanting z, the unit might do x this time and z next time. This provides a challenging economy in which each person alternately sacrifices their will to the will of the other. Such a model questionably produces more fullness of life than Patriarchal marriage. In perichoretic marriage, neither person ever sacrifices their will to the other; they sacrifice it to the transforming Power within the relationship itself. When X wants x and Z wants z, and both fully express their desires, fears, and dreams for x and z respectively to the Other, the emergent result is often X gets xz, and Z gets zx. The goals and desires of each transform into a relational constellation even more satisfying than the original desires for x and z.

Again, love has never been strictly sacrificing oneself simply for the betterment of the other. To primitive ego-bound persons struggling for survival, it is the first step. Love is allowing oneself to know the Other in authentic and transformative relationship, or, as Loder claims, taking "nonpossessive delight in the particularity of the other,"[88] truly knowing the Other (Matt 12:24, 31–32 + 25:31–46 + 7:21–23 = John 17:21). To this day theological scholars and pastors continue to trumpet Jesus' limited admonition "that there is no greater love than to lay down one's life for another," the beginning of love (but a political convenience as well). Because of the linguistic limitations describing relational dynamics Jesus' one line comment plays into institutional dysfunctions (Christendom) that tend to draw those willing to sacrifice themselves in love into well-organized political agendas rather than learning to responsibly think and act for themselves (the other half of love). Often followers are full of openness with little courage for closure, and the powerful (little openness, full of closure) are ready, willing, and train to abusively unify their collectives through codified sets of doctrine, behaviors, teaching, and hierarchical leadership. Christendom, not Christianity, is enmeshment, a co-dependent community forcing difference into controllable unity rather than fostering the love that unifies difference,

---

88. Loder, *LS*, 266.

well differentiated persons, and a willingness to suffer the conflictual environment necessary for a transformational community. Paul's wider description in 1 Cor 13, in no sense complete, provides a fuller balance and deeper understanding of love.

The improper imposition of time and cause-and-effect dynamics *within* notions of Eternalized Time forces theology into the false dichotomy of immanence and/or transcendence. From such vantages, *perichoresis* and *analogia spiritus* are always enigmatic, confusing, "spiritually" ad hoc, and contradictory. From that same vantage the preeminence of Jacob becomes enigmatic. The dynamic of *analogia spiritus* within our awareness mode is intensely significant in resolving these issues. As shown, *analogia spiritus* resituates the christological activity and contingency within human relations as orchestrational rather than impositional. Because every cosmic interaction to some degree affects every other interaction throughout space and time, especially within local interactions, orchestration of freedoms is necessary, *especially across time*.

Therefore, the *formational process* toward human response becomes the site of human freedom and agency through the prereflexive interaction in *analogia spiritus*, the gaze, before reflexive response. Within the *moment* the woman was active subconsciously constructing the response similar to our emotive states that tacitly de-liberate a complex of contingencies, desires, and decisions. Nevertheless, within the analogical dynamic of spirits, the Spirit and Christ correlate and synchronize the emergent processes of all desires, motives, and relational contingencies relevant within the relationship and ultimately all history. In this way, human and divine agency co-conditionally emerge together in Time. As such humans play a vital role in defining and shaping the teleological.

The story of Joseph and his strained relationship with his brother imaginatively illustrates the potential transtemporal complexity of this divine-human interaction. Having captured Joseph, the brothers were considering his demise. In those final reflective de-liberating moments of trying to decide what to do, their internal struggle within *analogia spiritus*, widens their unconscious awareness within their conflicting de-liberations, transforming their desires and thoughts concerning Joseph. They subconsciously sensed a better alternative from this transtemporal influence for themselves and everyone concerned. The brother's truncated relational disposition in that moment (and throughout their respective lifetimes) was open enough to allow God's Spirit to recondition their immediate desire to kill Joseph *with their own deeper desires and future desires*, transforming their immediate desire to kill into the more transtemporally informed desire that they sell Joseph into slavery to a foreign traveler. They were open to the thought (influence) of selling rather than killing him but not open enough toward further reconciliation at that moment (all without God becoming impositional). We can say God, "tacitly aware" of the relational openness they would have in the future, providentially influences the greatest expression of love possible in consideration of each person's agency and existing openness. Or, more properly, we can remember that *analogia spiritus* is not sequential but instantly transtemporal, that there is no first action upon another, and that all emerge in co-conditioning response altogether separate through the *perichoresis* of Time and Eternity. Therefore, it is not so much that God influences the brothers, but that the influencing "imposition" was their own future desires and holistic prereflexive "witnessing of" and sense within the *analogia spiritus* that tacitly and dynamically frame their decision. We must at this point remember that within the prereflexion of God's Eternal awareness God is not acting in a manner to bring about specific results, but orchestrating the greatest free and equitable set of perichoretic relations (love) that facilitate the creating of relational theosis in humanity. Within a sea of freedoms, if perichoretic relations continue to increase throughout history the results will follow. In *analogia spiritus* the Spirit contextually Eternalizes the time of the brothers in a way for them to sense "a better way," a higher order of response. In times of existential crises and decision, our gaze can deepen, and our purview expand as we passionately search for higher resolution, order, and greater fullness of life. Loder tells us,

> Prigogine suggests that time is not chronological or durational but transformational moving from order-to-chaos-to-new order. The implicit connection between time and eternity lies in the unfailing emergence of new order. In the Christomorphic perspective the convergence is evident in the "fullness of time" (Karios), the point at which the new order appears and becomes definitive for the whole sequence.[89]

Though they could not articulate the future consciously, their limited openness releasing their spirits into *analogia spiritus*, thereby holistically ("emotively") readjusting their choice, led Joseph to comment later, "you meant evil against me; but God meant it for good, in order to bring it about as it is this day" (Gen 50:20). They could have still deferred and killed Joseph, but something *in them* suggested a different course, and they chose it. Is that impositional? Did God force the hand of the brothers? In the end, every brother would have said absolutely not. They were simply saved from their shortened desire. In effect, the brothers, not unlike Jacob, passionately and

89. Loder, "Place of Science," 39.

decisively entered into their struggle with God within the *analogia spiritus*, and God christomorphically integrated their freedoms and times into the transtemporal fabric of redemptive history without destroying those freedoms.

Can an ontology of *telos*, of the Eternal, emerge within the interstices of our relational dynamics that transform time, especially when God does not know the future or *telos* before it is happening? God is not an agency passing information back and forth in time before it happens. The Eternal aspect of God does not focally know as such. The prophet numinally (ontologically) experiences within the eternal gestalt process the emergence of a future occurrence (*telos*) through *analogia spiritus*. This conditions their contemporary perspective. Because of *analogia spiritus*, this experience is ontological, not merely psychological or conventionally epistemological. For Moltmann, this "creative and life-giving Spirit therefore arrives at consciousness of itself in the human consciousness"[90] (I would add through *perichoresis*), in much the same manner, the Word of God speaks into human existence.

Perichoresis in Christological Time, Theodicy, and Jacob

In sustained *analogia spiritus*, one moves in mutual co-conditioning unison with Christ in eschatological Time rather than in "worlds," fantasies, or the demonic. With the risen Christ, the Eternal moment not only breaks into time through prereflexion but moves reflexively with Time. The Trinity experiences deliberation within *analogia spiritus*, humanity in history experiences de-liberation *from* our "worlds," the demonic and the social structures of powers and principalities when in relation to Christ through *analogia spiritus*. Such movements of perichoretic faith transcend existing stage relational structuring and live in transformation, a sustained Pentecost that de-liberates and synchronizes all persons within the relational occurrence in *perichoresis* within Christ's Time.

In Religiousness A, the Eternal conditions reflexion through the prereflexive moment. In Religiousness B, the Eternal potentially breaks out of the black hole of the *moment* in temporal dialogical cycling and thrusts the person into eschatological or christological Time—what Jacob might have actually experienced in wrestling God. In Religiousness A, the *moment* progressively creates and transforms the world from within its immanent dynamics. In Religiousness B, like Pentecost, the Eternal, through and in personal unison with the Spirit and Christ, transforms all open persons into

---

90. Moltmann, *SL*, 228.

existential Time, holistically employing "immanent" and "transcendent" dynamics within the unitive action of *perichoresis*.

> For the Father judges no one, but has committed all judgment to the Son.... For as the Father has life in Himself, so He has granted the Son to have life in Himself, and has given Him authority to execute judgment also, because He is the Son of Man.... I can of Myself do nothing. As I hear, I judge; and My judgment is righteous, because I do not seek My own will but the will of the Father who sent me. (John 5:22, 26–27, 30)

When Christ rose from the dead, his time became completely Eternalized (Time). As such, he perceives ("sees" and "hears") through his relationship with the Spirit all the prereflexive states within creation, then synchronizes ("holds together") all reflexions copacetically as they emerge from their prereflexive de-liberation. This integrates all freedoms in love, giving all to all in deference to others and the world. One might think of it as Christ allowing us to create our world through him in radical freedom but respectful of billions of other freedoms. Giving himself to the world for this end, he copacedically synchronizes all freedoms toward God's singular goal—creating a humanity capable of knowing God as God. In his synchronization there are no ethics other than attaining this goal within the dynamics of love (*perichoresis*), which is God's fundamental nature. From any cosmic perspective in time, Christ's synchronizing judgments will often seem indiscernible, illogical, unethical, or destructive. The radical freedom necessary for beings to evolve as such transcends all ethical systems (Matt 10:34–39).[91] Ethics are never teleologically suspended; they transfigure dynamically, usually imperceptibly, within Time, emerging appropriately within each event occurrence. Humanity transforms throughout history much like a child's provisional system of rules relax with adolescent maturity. And it is not that ethics and telos do not exist; indeed, the tree of good and evil exists. However, like manna, God picks and supplies the fruit appropriately within each developing stage and relational occurrence (Rom 14:14–23). Not only does this mean the "teleological suspension of the ethical" in Abraham's obligation, it means that Christ ultimately is responsible for allowing the conflict and wars within humanity that provide the required freedom and space necessary for the demonic to work itself out under the noncoercive perennial call of love to perichoretic relations and personhood. It is necessary to attain filial relations. Again, if every step of our redemption (evolution) is not free to allow or choose order out of chaos, the end

---

91. Caputo, *Against Ethics*, is one text among many that caution us in our attempt at systematizing or universalizing ethics.

result of humanity is anything but theosis. We must relinquish our concerns for what is appropriate, egalitarian, loving, and ethical to that Power that sees all and orchestrates all de-liberations in synchronicity toward creating a being of relational theosis—a theodicy. Robert Penn Warren, concludes:

> The creation of man whom God in his foreknowledge knew doomed to sin was the awful index of God's omnipotence. For it would have been a thing of trifling and contemptible ease for Perfection to create mere perfection. To do so would, to speak truth, be not creation but extension. Separateness is identity and the only way for God to create, truly create, man was to make him separate from God himself, and to be separate from God is to be sinful. The creation of evil is therefore the index of God's glory and his power. But by God's help. By His help and in His wisdom. . . . But that will be a long time from now, an soon we shall . . . go into the convulsion of the world, out of history into history and the awful responsibility of Time.[92]

Christ as God's Incarnation represents God's freedom and choice, but our ultimate *knight* of faith reveals the radical nature of human freedom and its passionate inclusion into the act of creation through the immanent transcendence within the human spirit in relation to God's Spirit. Because Jacob had no knowledge or conception of a God-man, he could not pull the wrestler into the light of conscious reflexion. And yes! Whether historical or mythical, Jacob wrestles not mere man, angel, or Yahweh, but, the risen Christ himself, and therein suffers his own wound—the taking into himself "what was lacking in the affliction of Christ" (Col 1:24; cf. 2 Cor 1:5–7).

If you feel the impulse to immediately correct the term Christ with the Angel of the Lord, the Logos, or any pre-incarnational form you consider as the pre-existence of the second person of the Trinity before the birth of Jesus Christ, then remember the beginning of this chapter. The Son, Jesus Christ, is begotten and comes into existence on Christmas day. Nothing of what he is was or will become ontologically precedes Christmas day. But time is relative! Relationships do not exist in a Newton spacetime box; time is a quality *of* relationship. His immanent and transcendent presence before his resurrection primarily occur within the Jacobian night of dialogical prereflexion or in relation to Christ's Time. Any personal interactions with people before his birth were drawn into christological Time and necessarily remain incognito, in darkness. This is why Jacob could not hold Christ into the dawning daybreak of consciousness. Jacob knows he is wrestling a man and yet God; in his amazement, he asks the man his name and immediately

---

92. Warren, *All the King's Men*, 607, 609.

gets asked, "Why is it that you ask about My name?" The Incarnation and mystery of Christ within humanity (theosis) are inconceivable to Jacob, so Christ cannot answer. For Graham Ward,

> It is the explicit displacements of [Jesus Christ's] own body which interests [him], the various assumptions or trans-figurations that occur in which the divine is manifested. . . . The transfiguration does not simply portray a resurrection hope, it performs it. . . . The physical body of Jesus is displaced—for it is not the physical body as such which is the source of the attraction but the glorification of the physical body made possible by viewing him through God as God. . . . These bodies of Jesus bear analogical resemblance to each other, but they are not literally identical. The body is analogical by nature—it moves through time and constantly changes, and yet all these changes are analogically related to each other.[93]

Could Jacob have wrestled in Time with Christ outside the prereflexive moment? Yes. Because of the internal relationship of the Trinity, the risen Christ is not physically bound by sequential or paralleling times, nor a Newtonian box concept of space. During the forty days after his resurrection it is entirely possible for him to be in two different relationships (appearances) at the "same time." Unless directly related, various locations and times do not exist in parallel or in each other; "parallel" implicitly assumes a Newtonian world "out there." Just as each participant at Pentecost heard in their mother tongue regardless of the disciples' language, the bodily presence of Christ manifests appropriately (differently) for every respective relationship without contradictions or scheduling conflicts. From our illusory framework of Newtonian time, we see different Christs simultaneously, but they are the same Christ merely in *different* times and relational occurrences. Both the freedom of God and the freedom of humanity integrate into history through the *perichoresis* of time and Eternity through the mutual co-conditioning of humanity in *analogia spiritus* and the grace of Christ's call to personhood.

Being caught up into christological Time is not experiencing reality as it really is through the life of Christ (the mistake of most neo-orthodox thinking). The "I, not I, but Christ" is not experiencing the world through Christ "within" us or our thinking; it is experiencing the world in perichoretic relation to Christ as synchronized by Christ. Christ does not just end "all rule and all authority and power" but "puts all things under him," in other words, synchronizes (transforms) them into perichoretic relations. Our time reflects and becomes Christ's Time, not in him or he in us. Within

---

93. Ward, "Bodies," 165–66, 173–74.

the world of the relationship—the space that the Spirit opens up, the medium of the relationship—Christ de-liberates all desires and freedoms into a synchronous unity for those willing to pick up their cross and follow him (knowingly or unknowingly: Matt 25:31–46). In full redemption and presence, one does not experience the world through Christ but perichoretically with Christ. Yes, Christ is the one who holds all things together and adjudicates all freedoms within that "awful responsibility of Time," but all receive everything they passionately desire that can synchronize with the same in all Others.

If an immanentalist still decries imposition, they have a skewed understanding of freedom or a distorted understanding of God and love. Our freedoms and self-determinations must make room for the same in others and the world. God even provisionally and necessarily provides the grace and freedom to live and move within the demonic, fantastical, and illusory "worlds" of our own making for redemptive purposes. But if human beings with limited knowledge are to move with each other in love there must be an orchestration of our freedoms. Therefore, those who believe that an Eternal trinitarian God imposes a predestinating erasure of human freedom, haplessly imprisons themselves within a Newtonian box of absolute spacetime. This no longer squares with STR, quantum mechanics, and thermodynamics systems theory.

If the orthodox, specifically Reformed theology, decry the limiting of God's freedom, they too fail to understand that the Trinity, just like humanity, maintains their freedom according to God's nature, *perichoresis*, which is love. They, too, remain imprisoned by the same Newtonian illusions of spacetime and sequential cause and effect relations. Christ, who gives himself for the world, integrates both the freedom of God and that of creation. The Father leaves all such judgments (limitations) to the Son.

(2) Word of God and *Analogia Spiritus*

When our hearts open to God, God speaks, and we perceive thoughts, words, and meaning. Speech and its meaning, however, construct through no single loci *within the listener*. Neither the text, the prophet, the numinal experience, the person's psyche, nor the cultural-linguistic system play the total role in meaning construction. God's Word and its meaning are the product of all the above in each unique occurrence. The only *foundational* aspect of the Word of God, however, is the *way* God relates and its reflection within cosmic relations—*perichoresis* and *analogia spiritus*, the rock upon which Jacob and Peter experience God as God, face to face. God will bring forth his people and establish his church upon this cornerstone. In speaking God's Word, God harnesses all dimensions of existence.

With human communication, we do not form and speak our words that the listener must secondarily interpret within the autonomy of their own mind. But, as we considered in this study's first and second chapters, something much more complex and dynamic occurs. The moment a person intends another or a text, a unifying *trans*jective[94] field of spirit-to-spirit instantly emerges between them that holistically facilitates and supports all communitive interaction. This "groundless"[95] "superordination of the spiritual"[96] collects and de-liberates all relevant aspects in holistic animation within the encounter. Christologically, each participant within the communicational field will understand the equivalent meaning from within their personal meaning-frame and linguistic capacities. Nevertheless, much more is being expressed than the sum total of the words; in this respect, though both are needed and function in complementarity, spirit (the whole of the person) takes asymmetrical priority over word.

Paul, in Romans 8, points to the dual dialogical aspects of the divine-human encounter in which God's communication to the person transcends their existing linguistic structures. He acknowledges the Spirit's "groanings" on our behalf "which cannot be uttered" (cf. also 2 Cor 12:4) as the "Spirit . . . bears witness with our spirit." Optimally, much of the ineffable within the exchange involves transcending the individual's spatial and temporal context in the spirit-to-Spirit communitive interchange drawing all relevant concerns into co-conditioning with an Eternal God in trinitarian deliberation. In our attempts to communicate with God, something transpires prereflexively and holistically that precludes and transcends our focal conception within reflexion; those ineffable elements within the communicative exchange are indeed affective, meaningful, and upon which words ultimately find their full meaning. Therefore, meaning is never solely in the Other, the text, or the self but in the emerging field of the perichoretic relationship between them.

Therefore, the Word of God analogically, meaningfully, adn uniquely emerges within each person and event encounter appropriately. God's Word is born within the context sensitive reciprocity of *analogia spiritus*. Jean-Luc Marion suggests the person "sees from the point of view, not of the world, but of the exteriority of the world—between world and Gxd. He sees the

---

94. Dabney, "Otherwise," 160–61.
95. Smith, *Concept of the Spiritual*, 152.
96. Smith, *Concept of the Spiritual*, 154.

world not to be sure, as Gxd sees it, but as seen by Gxd."[97] In other words, all persons, God or human, constitute from out of the relationship, but, note that Marion's past tense, "as seen," acknowledges the prereflexive nature of the activity of *analogia spiritus* (gaze)—Gxd's seeing, and then Christ's reflexive gift to us in our existent "seen."

> It is not a question, for the "theologian," of reaching that which his discourse speaks (well or poorly—what does it finally matter, for what norm in this world would decide?) of Gxd, but of *abandoning* his discourse and every linguistic initiative to the Word, in order to let himself be said by the Word, as the Word lets himself be said by the Father—him, and in him, us also. In short, our language will be able to speak of Gxd only to the degree that Gxd, in his Word, will speak our language and teach us in the end to speak it as he speaks it—divinely, which means to say *in all abandon*.[98]

To the extent we wholly abandon ourselves into our prereflexive de-liberation is the degree to which the Word appropriately manifests within us, *beyond hermeneutical speculation*. We then experience the world as Christ would experience it but from our own personal and contextual framework. Once the Word of God conditions our gestalt, its authority perichoretically becomes our own through *analogia spiritus*. Commenting on the Emmaus event, Marion tells us,

> At the very moment of his recognition by the disciples, the Word in flesh disappears: "for it is to your advantage that I go away" (John 16:7). For what? So that the Word recognized in spirit, recognized by and according to the Spirit, should become the site where those might dwell who live according to this Spirit.... The Word ... does not disappear so much as the disciples ... discover themselves assimilated to the one whom they assimilate and recognize inwardly.... This place—in Christ in the Word—is opened for an absolute hermeneutic, a theology."[99]

Though God inhabits the Eucharistic site of humans who in "abandon" (144) give themselves wholly in relation to him, Christ is not satisfied until his disciples identify him, not by flesh and blood, but through the antecedent encounter of *analogia spiritus*, in other words in infinite resignation (Matt

---

97. Marion, *God without Being*, 129; Marion uses "Gxd" to refer to "the very God that no mark of knowledge can demarcate.... To cross out Gxd, in fact, indicates and recalls that Gxd crosses out our thought because he saturates it" (46).

98. Marion, *God without Being*, 114, emphasis added.

99. Marion, *God without Being*, 151.

16:13–20). The Word emerges from within the relationship, meaning-full, no noumena, no phenomena. Therefore, the Word of God is both "transcendently" God's and becomes both "transcendently" personal for us and "immanently" ours ("I, not I, but Christ"); the resulting meaning for either God or us is contingent upon the living perichoretic nature of the interaction between us—what Johannes Climacus insists must be subjective.

To the degree we wholly constitute in open perichoretic relation to God and the world, we circumvent the hermeneutical task and the question of truth-value, as evident in Abraham's unwavering response. However, we rarely achieve this because of sin (our bifurcated social selves). Nevertheless, even disfigured, the dynamic remains the same. The Ancient Hebraic egocentric "arrogance" emerges from this same dynamic, in their belief that humans were the imago Dei and their receiving the spoken *dabhar*.[100] Such was the immediate determination in Abraham's resolve to sacrifice all. All de-liberation had already occurred upon reflexive arrival, instantly imbuing God's Word with clarity, authority, and power. It is as if Abraham transports through time and ontologically witnesses his nation before him and all outstanding contingencies became superfluous. This, indeed, is an ontological aspect of what actually happens in the experience of genuine Christian faith (Heb 11:1). Sacrificing his only child now becomes relatively incidental regarding how he would father a nation.[101] Unlike Abraham's faith experience in this instant, we rarely constitute in complete wholeness; therefore, the hermeneutical task is perennially with us. Nevertheless, the point is the perfect divine communicative act, the Word and the meaning, emerge within the relationship without remainder and without speculation. As a principle, within perfect relations, the eventual meaning, truth quality, and authority of each speech act emerge together inseparable. The entire self as spirit in *analogia spiritus* holistically relates and transforms accordingly.[102] Relation to the absolute telos always results in a "transformation by which *everything* in the existence of the individual is altered, in and through his mode of existence, so as to bring it into conformity with this highest good."[103]

---

100. MacDonald, *Hebrew Philosophical Genius*, describes the irreducibility of personhood: "Our 'I think therefore I am' and the Muslim 'I will therefore I am' was for them 'I am therefore I am'—an expression of their egocentric subjectivity" (6).

101. This, however, does not minimize the personal struggle that Abraham would experience in killing someone so dear to him.

102. Kierkegaard tells us: "If in relating itself to the individual's existence the absolute telos fails to transform it absolutely; the relationship is not one of existential pathos, but aesthetic pathos" (*CUP*, 347).

103. Kierkegaard, *CUP*, 348, emphasis added.

God's Word, therefore, is not a word upon which we hermeneutically deliberate and correspondingly act. Instead, it uniquely and transformatively awakens within us, again and again. It becomes our word, it becomes us as our own transformational dynamics transform in relation to the Spirit in *analogia spiritus*. To the extent we experience the fullness of *analogia spiritus*, we experience shared meaning with no remainder, no marginal notes. Such is the Word of God.

Continuity in the Word of God through Time

The Word of God or God's self-disclosure through Christ and the Spirit is a living expression in and for each occurrence, a unique disclosure with each new reading. The Eternal dimension analogously conditions each new moment so that the Eternal Word will always become meaningful within each subsequent reading and relational occurrence while analogically maintaining continuity with its former utterance and meaning despite the evolution of contexts and meaning-frames. The original meaning may existentially expand and transform over time because of developing relational categories, contextual concerns, and linguistic capacities. The Eternal ground upon which the Word of God comes forth extends behind and yet beyond all developmental categories transforming each relative interactional context to Itself, and yet it speaks through (*katoptrizomenoi*, "beholding as in a mirror" 2 Cor 3:18) the relativities of each unique relationship.

The Word of God (and the Scriptures as such) has as many specific meanings as there are those who hear. All these meanings spring forth ultimately (and optimally) without contradiction and with unending synchronous complexity within the Eternal. We might refer to this as a *hermeneutical invariance theory*, similar to Einstein's "invariance theory" (STR), in which Christ, that Power that constitutes all relationships, becomes the absolute continuity of meaning, as light is for spacetime.[104] He is that transparent dynamic that meaningfully facilitates and sustains *continuity* within all our linguistic development in a river of relations that we never enter twice. William James, using J. Trevor, provides an example of the tacit nature and continuity of God's revelatory movement:

---

104. "To be sure, the life of the man Jesus has a beginning, and His time was once future. Yet this does not mean that it did not then exist. The life of Jesus has duration.... Yet this does not mean that it was present only in its duration.... The life of Jesus comes to an end and therefore it became past. Yet this does not mean that it then ceased to be" (Barth, *CD* III/2:463-64).

> These highest experiences that I have had of God's presence have been rare and brief—flashes of consciousness which have compelled me to exclaim with surprise—God is *here!* . . . But I find that, after every questioning and test, they stand out to-day as the most real experiences of my life, and experiences which have explained and justified and united all past experiences and all past growth. Indeed, their reality and their far-reaching significance are ever becoming more clear and evident.[105]

Our past numinal encounters are always present within *analogia spiritus*, to some degree transforming all future conceptual consciousness in relation to their Eternal dynamics. Therefore, when we genuinely remember or convey those experiences, they often freshly re-constitute alive (reoccur) within our recounting of them because of their ontic simultaneity with the original experience. Within the *perichoresis* of time and Eternity, we might consider that the transfiguration of Jesus, Moses, and Elijah happen simultaneously within three histories that are ontologically inseparable. Jesus' transfiguration, Moses' burning bush, and Elijah's still small voice experiences might have all been the same unified experience manifesting uniquely in all three historical locations simultaneously.[106] In this way, church doctrines and dogmas are free to expand and deepen with ongoing conceptual linguistic growth and in depth of experience, yet maintain continuity with previous meanings-within-their-whole. Only the Word of God, as person, and the dynamic relationality he institutes within the world are the same yesterday, today, and forever.

(3) Kingdom of God and Time

The *perichoresis* of time and Eternity also becomes apparent in the emergence of the Kingdom. The Kingdom of God is not a second "universe" or separate existence that parallels our everyday existence, which occasionally but tangentially intersects with history. Another misconception is that after death, we soul-sleep or resurrect to a parallel existence with the resurrected until the end of history. Informed by modern physics, there are likely no worlds or states of being that temporally parallel history. As Barth argues, there is only the presence of God and his Time. Within a perichoretic world, time is a product of and emerges only as a quality of relationships.

---

105. James, *Varieties*, 388–89.
106. Moltmann tells us, "Faith is the beginning of a freedom that renews the whole of life and 'overcomes the world.' . . . This faith is an experience which never again leaves the people who have once really been possessed by it" (*SL*, 114).

Those who die *throughout history* instantly enter the parousia upon death when Christ enters it. This constitutes what we could consider a time warp or the bending of time, similar to the transfiguration mentioned above. Thomas Torrance similarly suggests the ascension is the same event as the parousia.[107] The consideration of soul-sleep is only the perspective of those still in history. In a moment, one is instantly gathered into the presence of God at the end of history, into the "new heaven and earth."

Christ Ensarkos Constitutes in Perichoretic Relation to the Eternal

Karl Barth argues that Jesus Christ *ensarkos*, not *Logos asarkos* or *decretum absolutum*, was with God in the beginning and was the election of God.

> Before all created reality, before all being and becoming in time, before time itself, in the pre-temporal eternity of God, the eternal divine decision as such has as its object and content the existence of this one created being, the man Jesus of Nazareth, and the work of this man in His life and death, His humiliation and exaltation, His obedience and merit. . . . In and with the existence of this man the eternal divine decision has as its object and content the execution of the divine covenant with man, the salvation of all men. In this function this man is the object of the eternal divine decision and foreordination. Jesus Christ, then, is not merely one of the elect but *the* elect of God.[108]

Therefore, the transtemporal Jesus Christ *ensarkos* is the elected, chosen, and first (only) risen of many, upon whom all creation is ontologically contingent. In fact, this paradoxical insistence of Barth, that "the man Jesus already was even before He was,"[109] implies that somehow *Jesus* Christ, as historical person, was with God from the beginning of creation. How can we better understand this dynamic reality? Christ *ensarkos* is the first to rise bodily into the presence of the Father and the Spirit. By definition, their Time emerges perichoretically within their trinitarian relations, what we refer to as Christ's Time through which cosmic time reflectively emerges.

Although the man Jesus is with God at the beginning of history, how does Barth understand this divine relation being "*before* all created reality, . . . all being and becoming in time, . . . [and] time itself?" This is Barth struggling to express the ultimately inexpressible relation between Time

---

107. Torrance, *Resurrection*; cf. Barth *CD* III/2:464.
108. Barth, *CD* II/2:116.
109. Barth, *CD* III/2:464.

and Eternity without a clearer picture of the *perichoresis* of time and Eternity. Christ *ensarkos* does not experience life "before" *all* cosmic history in the sense that his pre-determination by the Father and his perichoretic instantiation within the Eternal happens *in totum* prior to the block of linear history (creation). Christ is pre-determined, but this occurs within the "pre-temporal eternity of God," or what we have been referring to as *Christ's* human moments of prereflexion *throughout Time*, and with him, the same of all humanity in relation to him. As the Eternal perichoretically draws into Time through Christ, this pre-determining becomes essentially active within the infinite prereflexive deliberations of the Trinity throughout Christ's Time, who is in dialogical relation with creation. Similarly, every constituting *moment* of personhood and relationship throughout history is pre-determined within each unique prereflexive *moment* throughout history. This is the meaning of Barth's comments above as Christ accomplishes this in his transtemporal activity during the forty days between his resurrection and ascension. We can describe this experiencing and consciousness as occurring within the trinitarian Eternal gestalt process through the Spirit, and therefore happening as a "predetermination from all eternity"[110] as Christ elects (adjudicates) all possibilities providentially. The *perichoresis* of time and Eternity softens what many consider impositional in Barth's description of divine predetermination. Eternity *has come into our midst*, in the *moment*, within the interstices of our dialogical alternations, and there Christ creates (predetermines) all relationships (reality), considering every passionate cry of humanity in *analogia spiritus* before constituting them.

Therefore, the concept "before" does not describes the relation of Christ *ensarkos* to the block of history itself. John Zizioulas helps articulate this:

> Our continuity, therefore, with the Christ event is not determined by sequence or response based on distance; it is rather a continuity in terms of *inclusiveness*: we are *in* Christ, and this is what makes Him be *before* us, our "first-born brother" in the Pauline sense.... In a linear type of "Heilsgeschichte" the "before" indicates *a part* of history—a period preceding another one—just as it happens with historical consciousness as it is known especially in modern times. But if the historical consciousness is decisively determined by eschatology, the "before" is *comprehensible* only in terms of the "last," the final.... It is obvious that all this makes no sense in terms of linear "Heilsgeschichte." ... He thus *in the Spirit* contains by definition the eschata, our final destiny, ourselves as we shall be.[111]

110. Barth, *CD* III/2:484.
111. Zizioulas, *Being as Communion*, 182–83, last two emphases mine.

In effect, because of an undeveloped theological anthropology, Barth places Christ *ensarkos* before all history and fails to effectively include humanity within every *analogia spiritus moment*. Though Barth correctly temporalizes God's Eternal dimension, he fails to show how humanity's agency is included in the *perichoresis* of time and Eternity. This incomplete institution of *perichoresis* into the divine-human relationship (both with the Father and Christ, and Christ and the Spirit with humanity) leads to an insufficient *inclusion* of human agency and freedom within each interaction. Note that Zizioulas qualifies our inclusion with Christ "in the Spirit," which for this thesis means inclusion via *analogia spiritus*. As with Reform faith in general, Barth never lets Jacob wrestle within the eternal *and* win. As evident in Barth's never recognizing the preeminence of Jacob, he entirely misses the more radical inclusion of human freedom through *analogia spiritus* that the Jacob narrative announces in living color. Nevertheless, what Barth ultimately seeks within his understanding of a pre-existent Christ *ensarkos* is attainable in a resurrection to the beginning of the "before" (prereflexion) within every unique *moment* of every relationship the Spirit and Christ create and constitute—the Eternal conditioning Christ's creative activity within the midst of every dialogical interaction.

The primary point for Barth is that Christ's election is *causally antecedent* to all history and *preeminent* within each relational (historical) event. Zizioulas adds that Christ is our *inclusiveness*, which also necessitates the Spirit. Furthermore, a thorough perichoretic ontology then includes each *human de-liberating* moment *of analogia spiritus* within the Eternal dynamic singularity as well.[112]

"Immanence" through Inclusiveness into the Eternal Singularity: *Analogia Spiritus*

The general and biting criticism against dogmatic theology is that it cannot satisfactorily account for an aspect of God's "immanence" within the world and therefore removes God to a wholly other status, thus diminishing the possibility of mutual relations and self-determination. However, the *perichoresis* of time and Eternity reveals how "immanent" dynamics within cosmic relations can attain reciprocity with an active "transcendent" God. In other words, what Barth considers "transcendent" necessitates the complementarity of the "immanent" in *analogia spiritus*. In this respect,

---

112. To use an electrical concept, putting each human being in parallel relation (not series) to the Spirit *and* Christ respectively before being constituted in Time accomplishes this.

Barth fails to allow Kierkegaard's Religiousness B to draw and transform Religiousness A into itself.

An understanding of Christ *ensarkos* as he socially and personally relates to the Father sequentially *before* creation is only possible if: (1) Christ is causally instrumental in creating and constituting every *moment*, in every relationship, and every human prereflexion within history. The simultaneity of Christ's Time, Easter-time, accomplishes this,[113] and (2) through him, human possibility, in like manner, prereflexively draws into it.[114]

Therefore, when Christ ascends into the presence of the Father, to the beginning and the end, the fullness of every *Eternal moment* of history goes with him. Because he arose to the Father, the Spirit of the Eternal also impregnates every moment of history. Christ is still *the elect*. Christ is still he in whom God relationally constitutes in *perichoresis*. And Christ and the Spirit are those through whom all history prereflexively is co-conditioned by the Eternal activity of the Trinity and ultimately given the possibility of "real time." This latter concept, as stated, would seem, for the most part agreeable with Barth; however, a particular understanding of the internal dynamic in which Barth configured this concept seems problematic and in need of further development or clarification. Concerning Christ, Mary Cunningham explains that,

> Barth's desire to protect the historical reality of the incarnation can . . . be seen in his insistence in *CD* IV/2 that Jesus is "not eternal as God is." He continues: "He is only the creature of God—bound to time, limited in other ways too, unable in his own strength to escape the threat of nothingness." He concludes that Jesus is "before all things, even before the dawn of his own time" because "this is what God sees and wills [*CD* IV/2:33]."[115]

Again, to some, this might suggest that the person Jesus was socially active within the Trinity before the block of history began.

---

113. Barth, *CD* III/2:464: "For as such, according to its manifestation in Easter-time, it is also the time of God; eternal time."

114. Barth, *CD* III/2:466: "Jesus Christ belongs not only to yesterday, or to-day, or an indefinite future. He belongs to all times simultaneously. He is the same Christ in all of them." "This means that every choice and decision made in human history, and indeed in the whole course of created time, is subordinated to the choice and decision made in God's eternity before all created being and its time. . . . At this last and highest stage, the pre-existence of the man Jesus coincides with His eternal predestination and election, which includes the election of Israel, of the Church, and of every individual member of His body" (484–85).

115. Cunningham, *Theological Exegesis*, 41.

In his later years, Barth obviously includes a more kenotic christology, but he incorporates it with no small amount of unnecessary paradox. Nevertheless, as Macquarrie tells us, Barth's christology is complex, and his extreme christological statements are usually balanced by others.[116] Barth only partially implements Kierkegaard's anthropological implementation of time and eternity, which he initially set out to do. He identifies the need for the "infinite qualitative" separation of the infinite and finite, but more than likely, because of his reactive response to liberal Protestantism, he did not adequately posit this christological *and pneumatological* potentiality perichoretically into his anthropology. As R. H. Roberts points out, this then becomes, for Barth, "an eschatological crisis, a confrontation of the temporal by a consuming eternity . . . an eschatological annihilation of time by eternity."[117] Therefore, he argues, Barth confuses the categories and falls back into a Hegelian synthesis, failing to maintain the existential synthesis within the christological (or relational) event. He, likewise, delimits the analogical interrelation of the human "infinite" with the divine Infinite, which takes place for Kierkegaard by virtue of the Christ event. Therefore, his most significant problem was his earlier undeveloped anthropology, which, as we have seen, he later acknowledges as an overreaction.

Barth's only argument for how Jesus Christ existed "before the dawn of his own time" is simply because this is "what God sees and wills." Again, Barth becomes partially misunderstood because of this sequentially interpreted concept of "before." I believe his formulations of God as "wholly other" and an over-generalizing "Nein" to the *vestigium Trinitatis* result from his failure to follow through and develop Kierkegaard's perichoretic understanding of human existence as a differentiated unity. A correction to such monophysite anthropological tendencies is now in order.[118]

If Christ himself, and therefore human beings, constitute as a differentiated unity of the temporal and the eternal, we can assume two things. First, Christ *ensarkos* in some way includes within himself the ability to personally incarnate in relation to those with authentic faith throughout history. His disciples witness a variety of personal incarnations of Christ after his resurrection, notwithstanding the earlier consideration that Christ might have been the person with whom Jacob wrestles, is present in Moses' "burning bush," and in Elijah's "still small voice." Graham Ward argues that

116. Macquarrie, *Modern Thought*, 288.

117. Roberts, "Karl Barth's Doctrine of Time," 96.

118. We should note, however, that Bonhoeffer's *Sanctorum Communio* was in the process of making the proper anthropological turn, and furthermore, it was Bonhoeffer from whom Barth acquired the concept of *analogia relationis*. One wonders what might have happened if Bonhoeffer had survived the war.

the resurrecting bodies of Christ are as different as the number of his incarnations, each appropriate for each relational occurrence:

> In each case, from the hiddenness comes the revelation, the realization which has the structure of an initiation—the move from what is familiar to what is strange. . . . These bodies of Jesus bear analogical resemblance to each other, but they are not literally identical. . . . With the new identifications ("It is the Lord"; "Their eyes were opened"; "Rabboni") *a new relationship and understanding are opened up*. The logic of the displacement-deferral of the Word is a pedagogical logic.[119]

This adjusts the sequential temporal interpretation of Barth's "before" into a wider frame of infinite christological (dialogical) prereflexions and corresponding reflexions. Unlike Moltmann, we can read Barth as periodically projecting sequential historical time materially (focally) *into* the complete godhead, installing an eternal quality materially into a Docetic Christ. Kierkegaard never materially (focally) temporalizes the Eternal aspect of God, as are the oft interpretations of Barth. Eternity and Time perichoretically synthesize only in the existential relationship or consciousness, which occurs only in the person of Christ. Yes, time perichoretically draws into the trinitarian relations and conditions each person of the Trinity accordingly, but Christ *ensarkos* accomplishes this only within his specific cosmic relations. However, such a rendering does not destroy the causal antecedence Barth requires for maintaining God's prevenient grace (and God's personal freedom). We only need to reconfigure and resituate prevenience into the de-liberating process that the Spirit and Christ facilitate within every prereflexive dynamic constituting all dialogical relations.

This christological perichoretic dynamic reconfigures the notion of "before." Because Christ *ensarkos* is "there" from the beginning because he perichoretically relates to the Eternal, he constitutes personally within the Trinity no less than he does in relation to all history. Barth concludes that "first He is not far from us in His eternity, but near us; not turned away from us, but turned to us; not indifferent or hostile, but gracious, the One who loves us. And second, He is not just hidden from us in His eternity, but also manifest."[120] Barth wants to express the nearness of Christ's Eternity that is open to us, this coming and call of Christ that we can now locate within the dialogical dynamics of human relations, but as stated from the outset, Barth did not have the anthropological resources available to us today. Indeed, God's Eternity is "hidden" from our abstraction in reflexive cognition;

119. Ward, "Bodies," 173, emphasis added.
120. Barth, *CD* III/2:552.

however, it lies functionally *antecedent and within* it. In relation to God, Eternity tacitly conditions our prereflexive awareness—*analogia spiritus*—producing the ontological co-conditioning experience of faith. Remember our study of Heb 11:1 and the transfiguration in their *perichoresis* of time and Eternity; we are not given information from the future but *ontologically* experience the object of faith to some degree in its fruition. We perichoretically experience something of the *reality* of what we are hoping for and a *demonstration* of what is unseen; as Paul says, the Spirit is not a trust deed but a "deposit" (2 Cor 1:22) or "down payment" (2 Cor 5:5) of that which is future. So, whether the object of faith is a nation emerging from our loins, retaining a blessing we acquire through seemingly specious means, or experiencing a living God, we *experience* something of the reality (and nature) of that future or unseen promise.

Within this perichoretic and existential synthesis of our relations, God's Eternal presence manifests for us in *this* Time and *for* this Time. Likewise, all manifestations of God's Word within history constitute Christ *personally* throughout history. This resounds in Francis Watson's insistence that "it is more appropriate to see the revelation or word of God as located *within the process of dialogue* thereby initiated than to locate it solely in the statement that opens it."[121] The Father relates only to a historically active and creating Christ, and there is no personal Christ consciousness as such outside Time.

Predetermination of Christ

Because of his *reaction* to nineteenth-century immanentalism, Barth refuses any systematic formulation of the immanent presence of God within his early christological development. He insists that all theological formulation must concern itself only with the living person of "Jesus Christ Himself as attested by Holy Scripture."[122] This "absolute singularity," Barth insists, is dependent "on its predetermination from all eternity."[123] It is this "predetermination" that is offensive to the immanentalist's sensitivities when considering moral teleological principles. However, as discussed, we can make room for the "immanent" aspect within our relations to God and still affirm God's preeminence in all things *if* a perichoretic dynamic exists within divine-human relations that prereflexively de-liberates human existential concerns (chapter 3) in relation to the Eternal dynamic of God (chapter 4).

---

121. Watson, *Text*, 116, emphasis added.
122. Barth, *CD* IV/3:173–74.
123. Barth, *CD* III/2:484.

This pre-determination happens inclusively in and through Christ and his orchestration. Yet, Christ *ensarkos* is the one taken directly into the presence of God before the eschaton and instantly becomes Eternally related to all of history because of the Spirit.

Panentheism?

Does such a reconfiguration of relationality reflect a panentheism of sorts? Not at all. Most panentheisms problematically find their home in the Cartesian metaphysics of Modernity. Either God is outside the world system, making room for creation, or bringing creation into God. However, this thesis proffers *perichoresis* as an alternative metaphysic, which inevitably renders "immanence" and "transcendence" false dichotomies or at least limiting descriptors. In this respect, the theologies of Barth, recent immanentalists, and panentheisms are incomplete because of underdeveloped anthropologies.

If we define panentheism as creation *within* God, then perichoretic theology is not panentheistic. Within perichoretic dynamics, *perichoresis* irreducibly maintains the differentiation of persons while facilitating mutual communication, interaction, and co-condition relation, within divine-human relations. Even though human beings are contingent upon such living dynamics, the dynamics of *perichoresis themselves* pertain. The dynamics within the metaphysics of *perichoresis* are impossible to articulate completely within Greek dialectical and metaphysical categories and linguistics. Neither creation nor anything of humanity is literally inside the being of God or vice versa. Perichoretic dynamics liberate and expand our articulation toward greater accuracy. The meaning of statements like "In Him we live and move and have our being" (Acts 17:28a), held in bondage by Greek metaphysics, must expand into something like, "We live and move and have our being through the very nature of the triune God reflecting within us and our relations because of God's relations to us in Christ," which substantiates the last half of this passage, "For we are also His offspring" (Acts 17:28b). We are a completely differentiated being from God, that (increasingly) share in God's relational nature. Could God create anything that is not, in some minimal way, reflecting his nature? Ultimately moot, this is a rhetorical question that makes a strong point.

Panentheism, as in Hodgson or process theology, rejects the view of God's differentiation as a person outside the world or differentiated from the world. This radically alters the classical attributes of impassability, omniscience, and eternity. To attain mutuality between God and creation, they draws God entirely into time, and omniscience is limited to past and present. In this manner, God and the world are co-emanational within history, and God becomes altogether immanent. If, however, we can describe panentheism as a co-emanation whereby "God in history" does not "know" the future *before it happens* but conceptually emerges christologically in relation to history *while* in tacit perichoretic relation (synthesis) to the dynamic singularity of Eternally conditioned Time, then the goals of God's mutuality within immanent theologies and the transcendent personal God of Barth both obtain.

On the other hand, Barth insists that Time enters the godhead through Christ, and I might add, it emerges non-intentionally as a product of the relationship itself, by the nature of *perichoresis*. Therefore, *if we posit humanity as, to some degree, mutually perichoretic in nature, and consider the Eternal mode* (seinsweise) *of God as transtemporal within its trinitarian relations, then mutual relations are possible between human and divine person within the dialogical cycling of perichoretic dynamics.* Rather than creation in God, I see no prohibition inhibiting creation or humanity analogically sharing or reflecting God's relational nature—*perichoresis*—and thus by definition of *perichoresis*, necessarily remaining not-God, yet divinized. *Perichoresis* always necessitates differentiation of being. Nevertheless, humanity retains its freedom in Kierkegaard's necessity that persons become fully spirit (a self), *or not*, when in relationship to another. Is it too difficult to imagine that humanity is contingent upon an analogical reflection of God's relational nature while in relation to God and yet, by the nature of *perichoresis* simultaneously differentiated from God? Of course, this is an oversimplification, but the question of analogy stands.

Though history christologically conditions and affect God, God never focally "knows" transtemporally any more than the dancer "knows" *within* the prereflexion process before gestalt. The dancer only focally "knows" at gestalt and only tacitly (holistically) during gestalt formation. Christ as Logos within the world never constitutes in the world outside his contextually appropriate Word in history. However, he always existentially constitutes perichoretically within his tacit trinitarian relations from which he receives his teleological character. In this way, God has always proleptically related to the world as person. Because the Father knows the Son, God filially knows humanity and the world (maybe a billion worlds, through a billion Incarnations, through a billion Trinities; who would be so arrogant to dare limit Gxd otherwise).[124]

---

124. "He was and is there first, the One whom God has elected and willed, who is there in being. And we in the world, and our being and existence before Him" (Barth, *CD* IV/2:33).

Because every *moment* of history enters the Eternal intimacy and dynamic singularity of the godhead through the abundance of the Spirit in *analogia spiritus*, and every divine or cosmic gestalt de-liberates christologically, we can consider God and creation, in a sense, "panentheistically" interactive as dipolar persons to a dipolar God to the degree person's become spirit—mutually relating co-creators. Though this thesis differs from some of the trajectories of Keith Ward, it is consonant with the relational dynamics he suggests concerning the development of value:

> The creative pursuit of values is itself the work of God, in which both the subject's apprehension and the object's presentation of material for apprehension must be taken together for the value to be realised. This is a radically different view from that of the Thomist concept of an immutable self-complete being; but it seems to be a direct implication of Christian belief in God as Spirit. . . . The historical process must thus be seen as the progressive realisation of new values, all grounded in the mysterious beyond of God, yet realised only in the interaction of subject and object. . . . Man is the vehicle for this continuing historical process, which is the action of God, in contributing to God's general purposes in specific and contingent ways.[125]

Values emerge, for Ward, within human existence through the "creative loving contemplation of objects" (Gunton's "gaze") and require a responding "obedience." Values and virtues are not simply a gift of God; they are relational qualities that perichoretically and co-conditionally emerge within genuine relationship *between* humanity (as spirit) and God. And though Ward may likewise lack complete anthropological or adequate relational expression, he attempts to place the point of divine-human contact at a more immanent and pervasive interactive level between God and humanity within human existence. For example, "prayer, too, is not the influencing of a mastermind who can fiddle with the predestined course of things. It is the openness of minds to each other at a deep and often unconscious level."[126] Therefore, through something reflecting the prereflexive *interacti*on of human persons (as spirit), God (as Spirit), the church, and all history co-condition each other in reciprocating relations and, in a sense, a co-emanation.

In conclusion, the relational configurations of panentheism do not parallel perichoretic dynamics. Such panentheistic terms as "contained within," "indwell the other," or conversely, "existence independent of" resist formal or complete fit or translation into perichoretic metaphysics. Much

---

125. Ward, *Concepts of God*, 217.
126. Ward, *Concepts of God*, 226.

the same, however, must be leveled at Classical theology. Nevertheless, because of the irreducible tripartite structuring of perichoretic dynamics, the typical subject-object distinctions that define the theologies of panentheism fail to fully satisfy.

(4) Missing Link in Barth and Hegel: *Analogia Spiritus*

Amid the construction of Barth's dogmatics, he concludes that eternity is not timeless. Eternity is "the simultaneity and coinherence of past, present, and future."[127] And again, eternity is "the immediate unity of present, past and future; of now, once and then; of the centre, beginning and end; of movement, origin and goal."[128] This transtemporal dynamic within Barth enables the personhood of God in Christ to focally constitute within existence *yet* couple tacitly within Eternity. Therefore, the primary difference between Barth and this thesis is primarily anthropological.

Barth's incomplete development of Bonhoeffer's *analogia relationis*, forwarding theology as it did, nevertheless limits the possibility of his anthropological expressions. Instead, *analogia spiritus* expands his internal logic, which some describe as perichoretic.[129] Because these dynamics never properly extend into his anthropology, they produce a rigidity within his dogmatics that renders *analogia relationis* indivisible between divine and human spirit, leaving much of its implied "immanent" dynamics inexpressible and undeveloped. This understanding of human nature (ultimately a political reaction) ultimately leads Barth into a limiting theology, which wagers a soteriological universalism in exchange for God's total freedom. It leaves us with no immanent dynamics through which *humanity*[130] can

127. Barth, *CD* III/2:526.
128. Barth, *CD* III/1:67.
129. Because something (e.g., personhood) is irreducible does not conclude our inability to understand its constitutional nature being the product of two distinct sources (Kierkegaard), nor the value of what knowing these sources might be able to teach us about God and humanity.
130. Though I acknowledge Bouillard's Bultmannian proclivities, and Bultmann's understandings of "pre-comprehension" (not to be confused with *analogia spiritus*), Bouillard makes a good point when he insists against Barth that though the objective possibility of faith resides in a unilateral divine movement, "the subjective foundation of its possibility resides necessarily in us; otherwise, it would not be our certainty" (Torrance, *Incarnation*, 39). However, I am uncomfortable with Bouillard's consideration of a subjective *foundation* placed squarely in natural theology. I prefer to install a divine preeminence in Christ's adjudicating and synchronizing all spirits in constituted relations after all intersubjective and prereflexive interactions in *analogia spiritus*. Nevertheless, I appreciate his insistence that human persons are active at this fundamental level of dialogical dynamics and interaction with God.

meaningfully, mutually, and genuinely move and interact in faith with God, or not.[131]

Analogia spiritus creates the possibility of human freedom and mutual co-conditioning relations with God that fully explains the textual preeminence given to Jacob's victory over God. Though humanity is contingent upon the nature of God analogically reflecting within its relations, it only enters into the co-creating process of the world in love through its relationship both "immanently" and "transcendently" to a trinitarian God. In *analogia spiritus*, there technically is no determined imposition of God that lies outside the pre-determinative de-liberational interplay of spirits within the Eternal, which only *then* results in a manifest Word. In agreement with Barth, however, this can be humanly suppressed (sin). As Christ's bride, the church not only follows his lead within the bridal dance but because of what she is and *how* she gives herself within the dance, she definitively conditions the shaping of his Eternally co-conditioned lead.[132] Nevertheless, we all dance to the music of *perichoresis*. Just as time is the product of relationship, so is *perichoresis* an analogical quality within all cosmic interactions.

Because humans are perichoretically spirit, they can relate to the world as a differentiated unity. They can constitute as a differentiated beings *in relation to* the world rather than merely emerge as *part* of it or in complete determinate reaction to it. There is Eternity and infinite possibility in our hearts. Optimally we are co-creators of and have dominion over creation itself and in Jacobian *moments*, even over God. How is it that humans are to have dominion (co-creation) over creation if they cannot somehow constitute in whole, as spirit, in differentiated unity to it? Therefore, for humans to merely *have* spirit rather than *be* spirit[133] compromises

---

131. "To do Barth justice," says Torrance, "it must be said that his stress upon the infinite qualitative difference between God and man was intended to throw into sharp relief the fact that while there is no way of man's own devising from man to God, there is indeed a bridge between man and God created through the invasion of God in his Godness into time and human existence and his activity within them" (*Transformation*, 286). Though I agree with Torrance's assessment here, which reflects Barth's later convictions, and though I also affirm his conviction of God's preeminence, the primary point of my thesis is that we must push the point of contact further into the heart of relational dynamics—*analogia spiritus*—where God retains Christ's preeminence, humanity retains its freedom and self-determination of personhood in relation to that preeminence, which maintains a relationality of mutual import.

132. This is why I believe (facetiously) that Tango is God's dance, the only dance I have studied in which the ladies are free to interrupt and momentarily take the lead, causing the male to adjust and alter his creation of the dance.

133. Gunton's conviction that humans *have* spirit rather than *are* spirit primarily concerns maintaining the contingency of humanity upon God's sustaining human spirit. However, I am reticent to place the sustaining contingency of human spirit upon

the notion of persons as *perichoresis* in mutual relations to God and its co-creation (dominion) potential within creation. No one has the dominion status to say to a mountain, "Into the sea," and it occurs without their attaining *complete* spirit and immersed in love—*perichoresis*. Nevertheless, an aspect of human relations to the world must frame itself from "beyond it," or more appropriately, as self in relation to the whole. The night of Jacob is not a fairytale or a divine rhetorical device. On the contrary, it is a truth so monumental it became the missing hermeneutical key to the entire story of Israel. Only upon this rock does Israel emerge within the world. Unable to find a room in the theological stable, this rock has been left in the dark, a night so saturated with light that light itself cannot escape—"the absolute to the Absolute." Silentio's Knight of Faith "resigned everything infinitely, and then he grasped [wrestled] everything again by virtue of *his faith*."[134] The Writer had his hands on the monster, at times expressing the night of faith, yet unable to tame it, or locate, or maybe he intentionally left it for us to discover indirectly. Nevertheless, the march of history is all about clarification.

In conclusion, there is no vital recovery of orthodoxy necessary. That would be tragic. As stated in the introduction, there is no going back. As Bonhoeffer would argue, orthodoxy is constantly in motion, growing in clarity and intensification. Our only interest should be maintaining continuity with orthodoxy and specifically the Scriptures while we seek greater coherence and meaning to the text, as well as greater fullness of life within the faith experience of the church. The former strictures of language and limiting forms of life must constantly give way to greater fullness of life. In the end, God knows humanity because of Christ, and humanity knows God because of the Spirit (*analogia spiritus*).[135] A God-man be known, is just a man; but in Spirit and Truth he is known as Jesus Christ, as God. The explication of *perichoresis* is paramount, not just as a theological dynamic inherent within the Trinity, but as the very nature of God analogically active in constituting human existence. We need to further explore the logic and dynamic of Kierkegaard's *moment*.

> And now the *moment*. Such a *moment* has a peculiar character.
> It is brief and temporal indeed, like every moment; it is transient

---

God's "personal" action rather than God's perichoretic nature reflecting within humanity *through simple perichoretic relations to God* in Christ and the Spirit, which sustains humanity as a relation unto itself and all cosmic relations to the Other. This is where the "personal" becomes difficult to parse in perichoretic relationality. Gunton, *One, Three, Many*, 188.

134. Kierkegaard, *FT*, 51.

135. Lossky, *Image*, 97–98, "The descent (κατάβασις) of the divine person of Christ makes human persons capable of an ascent (ἀνάβασις) in the Holy Spirit."

as all moments are; it is past, like every moment in the next moment. And yet it is decisive, and filled with the Eternal. Such a *moment* ought to have a distinctive name; let us call it the *Fullness of Time*.[136]

---

136. Kierkegaard, *PF*, 22, emphasis added on "moment."

5B

Quantum Dynamics
Relationship (Consciousness) Constitutes Reality

> In the beginning there were only probabilities. The universe could only come into existence if someone observed it. It does not matter that the observers turned up several billion years later. The universe existed because we are aware of it.
>
> MARTIN REES[1]

> Quantum Delayed Choice Eraser is not evidence for retro-causality; rather, it reveals the flexible nature of time that supports a simultaneous co-conditioning causality across time, which appears as retro-causality from within time.
>
> G. S. GORSUCH

The Trinity is born on Christmas day. Fully God, fully human; either way Christ is person in full perichoretic relations within the godhead, in whom something of God becomes human. His birth and resurrection are "causally" antecedent to his sustaining relationship with all cosmic history. He is the first human to bodily resurrect from the dead into the eschaton, the first to become "aware" in *full* relationship to the Eternal. Upon resurrection, like back-lightening, he acquires the presence, consciousness, awareness, and relationship to everything from the beginning to the end of cosmic

---

1. Rees, "Anthropic Universe," 46.

history (the alpha and the omega). This is possible only because through him, Eternity potentially conditions Time. From this grand entrance, all Jacobian wrestling, the passion (faith) of all humanity, emerges with him together in co-conditioning simultaneity.

THE QUANTUM ENIGMA AND PERICHORETIC CHRISTIANITY

Quantum theory has been extensively tested for a century, and all of its predictions have been proven correct. And yet, the quantum enigma persists: matter as we know it is somehow the effect of and ultimately dependent upon consciousness.[2] The Enlightenment notion that there is a reality "out there" that is independent of consciousness is no longer tenable.[3] No other theory in science has been so well tested, and though it leads to such seemingly counterintuitive and implausible results, it brings physics to the current edge of its discipline. Physicists have no definitive theories or understanding of consciousness, so many physicists who study this indeterminate "beyond" contend that this enigma will likely fall into an interdisciplinary dance with psychology, philosophy and theology. The number of diverse interpretations of quantum dynamics grows each decade, with no one interpretation harnessing more than 20 percent of the primary physicists seriously researching it. As is, the enigma remains a skeleton in the closet of physics; it will more than likely remain there until interdisciplinary efforts broaden the theoretical base within physics itself. Like the earlier thoughts on method, interdisciplinary interaction, analogies, and associating dynamics will begin to emerge, enriching the internal thinking of each participating discipline respectively. Already analogies and associating dynamics are beginning to appear in a few disciplines; in this chapter, we will explore some of the quantum analogies along with the dynamics of *perichoresis* and *analogia spiritus*. At various points, these analogies suggest dynamics in common. For the time being, within physics, these associations will remain only speculative, for some meaningless, for others repugnant. Within theological development, however, such associations will provide

---

2. Eugene Wigner: "The laws of quantum mechanics itself cannot be formulated without recourse to the concept of consciousness" ("Probability," 232).

3. Werner Heisenberg: "In the experiments about atomic events we have to do about things and facts, the phenomena that are just as real as any phenomena in daily life. But the atoms or elementary particles themselves are not real; they form a world of potentialities or possibilities rather than one of things or facts" (*Physics*, 160).

fertile interpretive ground for expanding Christian theology, further insight into the Scriptures, and the concept of *perichoresis*.

Not only is quantum mechanics (QM) revealing evidence that matter and consciousness are interconnected, but that human choice, from the temporal perspective of that choice, influences past events that happened "before" the choice.[4] Bell's Theorem's suggest that if we are to maintain the "metaphysical good life in quantum mechanics, keeping locality, realism, and special relativity," we must sacrifice free will. Cambridge philosopher Huw Price alternatively suggests:

> We may help ourselves to the metaphysical advantages—locality and Einsteinian realism—but save free will. Roughly speaking, the trick is to reinterpret the same formal possibility in terms of backward causation.[5]

This eventually leads to an understanding of causal holism (co-conditioning) in nonlocal relations and also between times.[6] Though many quantum theorists resist the general idea of retrocausality within quantum dynamics, it remains a viable consideration, and physics has yet to effectively argue it away from its tested phenomenon and experimental results. Physicists Daniel Rohrlich states to his fellow physicists: "You can run from it, but it's still there."[7] Price continues,

> The temporal perspective of the interpreter imposes a dominant but not a universal causal orientation. This will give us a useful characterisation of the objective core of what might more accurately be called the *advanced action interpretation*. It simply amounts to the suggestion that the correlational structure of the microworld is of the latter (non-classical) kind. . . . [Thus] the advanced action approach is not only both physically and metaphysically respectable, but seems to have a striking advantage, over and above its application to quantum mechanics.[8]

---

4. The experimental results of Kim, "Delayed," and further argued by Rohrlich in Rohrlich, "Reasonable Thing"; Rohrlich and Hetzroni "GZR States as Tripartite"; Rohrlich and Hetzroni, "GZR States and PR Boxes."

5. Price, "Route to Realism," 2.

6. Teller, "Relational Holism."

7. Rohrlich, "Retrocausality."

8. Price, "Route to Realism," 4. Price accordingly notes (n5): "This enables us to clarify the assertion above that the backward causation interpretation has the same objective core as Bell's own 'no free will' model: both amount to the suggesting that quantum mechanics shows that what is in world is simply a particular pattern of correlations (a pattern that classical physics really had no business to exclude *a priori*). Whether we choose to interpret this pattern in terms of predetermination or backward

We will close this chapter by noting an alternative dynamic to retrocausality that expresses more of a dynamic simultaneity of mutual co-conditioning rather than the temporal distinctives of causality (cause and effect) in which specific quantum interpretations echo the irreducible holistic co-conditioning we have been considering within *analogia spiritus* and Eternity.

For those readers unfamiliar with quantum thought, and before we look at this groundbreaking Delayed Choice Quantum Eraser experiment, we briefly need to look at the original double-slit experiment from decades ago. Through it, we learn that light sent through a barrier with vertical double-slits acts as wave function on the backside readings. But, if the experimenter tests (looks for) the light as particles (photons) just before entering the double-slit, then the backside readings reveal particle-like behavior. On the other hand, if we are looking for wave function, the light produces wave-like phenomenon. Light exhibits either of these properties but never both at the same time. This suggests that Einstein's "spooky action at a distance" is real.[9] In other words, something outside the normal "realm" of physics was affecting the test result. Earlier, this issue led noted physicist Eugene Wigner to state that "Solipsism may be logically consistent with present quantum mechanics, monism in the sense of materialism is not."[10] Their results were shocking to themselves, but physicists were beginning to consider that observation itself creates reality. Physicsworld.com published an article entitled "Quantum Physics Says Goodbye to Reality" (April 20, 2007). In that article, Anton Zeilinger says, "We have to give up the idea of realism to a far greater extent than most physicists believe today."[11]

Many physicists and philosophers began gravitating toward the idea of a naïve materialism in which the particles were really there when looking for wave function, but they did not notice the truth of their existence until they saw them (i.e., both are there, but only one can appear at a time). Then, in 2011, Zeilinger and his associates published an experiment that critically damaged the naïve realism theory.[12] "No naïve realistic picture is compatible with our results because whether a quantum could be seen as showing particle or wave-like behavior would depend on a causally disconnected choice. It is therefore suggestive to abandon such pictures altogether."[13] At

---

causation thus turns out to be in an important sense beside the point—the brute physical facts are the same in either case."

9. This violates Bell's inequality theorem. Einstein's "spooky action at a distance" was real. Aspect, "Bell's Inequality Test"; cf. Zeilinger et al., "Violation."

10. Wigner, "Remarks," 176.

11. Zeilinger et al., "Non-local Realism."; Similarly, Leggett, "Nonlocal."

12. Zeilinger et al., "Indivisible Quantum."

13. Zeilinger et al., "Quantum Erasure."

this point, quantum dynamics resolutely reveals that human consciousness influences reality, possibly playing a role in creating it to some degree. In this regard, Price reminds the physics world that

> as [Bell] puts it elsewhere, the view commits us to saying that "there are influences going faster than light, even if we cannot control them for practical telegraphy. Einstein local causality fails, and we must live with this." (Bell 1987, 110) As I have emphasised, the advanced action interpretation requires no such reconstruction of special relativity. . . . [The] extent to which Bell's Theorem undermines this Einsteinian view is commonly exaggerated. . . . Bell's result simply undermines *local* versions of such a view—which, given that it appears to undermine locality generally, can hardly be counted a decisive objection to Einstein. . . . Given that orthodox quantum mechanics does not embody the required "backward influence," only a model which takes the orthodox theory to be incomplete will be capable of doing so. Only some version of the Einstein view seems able to save locality in this way.[14]

In this respect, Price believes that Einstein gets his realism when we acknowledge the "spooky" as an observer "version" of the phenomenon and that realism expands to include the "spooky." In other words, the structure of the microworld contains *advanced action* (action caused by future events). Price continues,

> The processes that produce such things are simply physical processes, albeit physical processes of rather specialised kinds. . . . It seems fair to assume that backward causation is not in itself contrary to spirit of Einsteinian realism. On the contrary, a realist of Einstein's empiricist inclinations might well think that the direction of causation is a matter to be discovered by physics. But then why should the existence of backward effects of human activities be any more problematic for realism than the existence of their "forward" cousins? Provided we make it clear that in the first place the view is that certain *physical* interactions have earlier effects, and not that certain specifically *human* activities do so, the position does not seem to be one that an empiricist of Einstein's realist persuasions should object to *a priori* (17–18).

---

14. Price, "Route to Realism," 16. Price further notes (n20): "Far from being the man who proved Einstein wrong, Bell thus appears in this light to be the man who provided a new reason to think that Einstein was right."

Price concludes with a hard but unnecessary distinction between physical interactions vs. specific human action in order to shed the problematic issue of human free will. However, the *analogia spiritus*, as developed thus far, with the forthcoming theories of Kastner, resolves Price's concerns on this matter.

Returning to the Delayed Choice Quantum Eraser experiment and the issue of influencing "back history": If we do not look or test for photons the light produces wave function phenomena (readings). If we observe light as photons (matter), they "collapse" into photons and produce a differing measurable effect of photons. In the Delayed Choice Quantum Eraser experiment, a light beam is refracted and sent to station A and B. The testing apparatus is placed before the double split station B, which is much farther away from the light source than station A. From the temporal perspective of the experimenter, the choice at station B effectively determines the recorded state of the light beam at station A even though it was recorded before the choice was made.[15] Remember, this is a psychological rendering, not specifically ontological.

What seems evident as retrocausality and the demise of materialism[16] within QM is still disturbing for many physicists. Unfortunately, many physicists default to claims that such counterintuitive results will resolve with further advancement in physics or through future adjustments in our current Cartesian or Newtonian worldview. Indeed, a resolution is forthcoming, as Price suggests, through transforming worldviews but not by those disciplines isolating themselves into truncated methodologies refusing the interdisciplinary interaction it needs for comprehensively engaging *all* reality (whatever that may entail). If there is more to our world than what we currently know or what many restrictively consider within physics—materialism—then *how* we know must continue to transform. Currently, many physicists are considering the stabilizing presence of a collective consciousness or predominately eastern religious notions of Reality (the divine) similar to John Hopkins physicist Richard Conn Henry.

> Why do people cling with such ferocity to belief in a mind-independent reality? It is surely because if there is no such reality, then ultimately (as far as we can know) mind alone exists. And if mind is not a product of real matter, but rather is the creator

---

15. Henry Stapp suggests: "The solution hinges not on quantum randomness, but rather on the dynamical effects within quantum theory of the intention and attention of the observer" ("Attention," 5).

16. Materialism here refers to the idea that all reality is reducible to matter or energy, governed by Newtonian and Einsteinian laws and dynamics (e.g., it generally argues that nothing can exceed the speed of light).

of the illusion of material reality (which has, in fact, despite the materialists, been known to be the case, since the discovery of quantum mechanics in 1925), then a theistic view of our existence becomes the only rational alternative to solipsism.[17]

Henry lets the cat out of the bag by considering material reality to be an "illusion" created by the mind, a well-known doctrine of most pantheistic religions (e.g., Buddhism, Hinduism, and pantheistic forms of Christianity). However, Christianity, laden with ancient literature forwarding a tripartite ontology, notably *perichoresis*, analogically reflects the quantum enigma more thoroughly than its pantheistic cousins. One wonders why the current literature on the quantum-consciousness enigma is not brimming with Christian theological analogies, especially when the predominance of those physicists engaging this issue are from Western cultures.[18] In short, Christianity historically posits *creatio ex nihilo*, and more recently *creatio continua* by a God in whom an aspect of God is both inside and outside creation. In this respect, the earlier integration of the dynamics of special relativity and perichoretic theory, and the possibility of transtemporal co-conditioning between a transcendent God, human consciousness, and cosmic reality easily account for quantum's seemingly nonlocal and retroactive causality. In fact, such dynamics are not only possible in orthodox Christian theology but integral.

Interfacing *Perichoresis* and Quantum Dynamics

Most of those considering pantheistic notions of spirituality in factoring consciousness within quantum studies (either Eastern or Hegelian theologies) dismiss most forms of materialism and critical realism out of hand. Such dismissal produces all sorts of fantastical theories like many worlds/multiple universes, consciousness as multiple "computer" simulations, and holographic interconnectedness (though each explains only isolated aspects within quantum dynamics). On the other hand, a Christian perichoretic approach (loosely Kierkegaardian in structure) offers a complex of relational dynamics in which all persons (human or divine) constitute within (1) a complementarity of time and eternity (physicality and spirit), (2) as a relationship unto themselves, self-reflecting with differentiated self,

---

17. Henry and Palmquist, "Non-local Realism," 650.

18. In all probability, this points to current agendas that have overtaken the academy (alluded to in the Prologue). If one wishes to maintain a position at a "credible" institution of learning, there are clear distinguishable agendas and unwritten rules of adherence necessary for advancement in one's field of study.

and (3) mutual relation to the Other, all of which amazingly complement QM. Rather than observation and consciousness creating the *illusion* of a material world, *a perichoretic* ontology creates reality from probabilities at each moment within every encounter. Each prereflexive *moment* (engaging the probabilities and possibilities available—wave function) constitute by and within relationships as agents engage, choose, and act (consciousness, constituting reality—particle function). Remember, in a perichoretic ontology, consciousness is a relationship and reality emerges from relationships.

Perichoretic dynamics parallel quantum dynamics accordingly: (1) All persons at their most basic level are a dynamic synthesis of the eternal and time. The eternal dimension reflects quantum indeterminacy—the wave function state—which is also the holistic site and potential for mutual and transtemporal causality (transtemporal mutual co-conditioning of persons, locations, and times through the mediating third term of perichoretic dynamics). In persons, the eternal dimension influences and enables the fundamental level of consciousness by mediating the holistic relation between mind and brain (body). (2) At the personal level of self, the eternal interaction creates the possibility of prereflexive awareness within consciousness. This creates the capacity for narrative and kairotic experiences of time, as well as the ability to stand outside oneself in self-awareness and determination. (3) In relationship to another, the eternal dimension facilitates the prereflexive concept of *analogia spiritus* that creates mutual interanimation and shared meaning. This mediating dynamic between all persons and things facilitates the union of different worlds through the instantaneous emergence of a prereflexive field of mutuality, de-liberating *potentiae* awaiting actualization within relations. Relational potentials must remain indeterminate when two or more engage in order for free and genuine encounters to occur over determinacy. From this prereflexive, de-liberating potential comes actuality, encounter, and gestalt. As we have considered earlier, time (reality, realism) emerges from and affected by the eternal through spirit, whether human or divine.

As the Father comes to awareness of the world through Christ and the Spirit, we perichoretically experience the possibility of transcendence within time, in our midst. Christ, in this regard, becomes he in whom "all things are held together" (Col 1:17). Does the moon exist when no one is looking at it? No. But God, through God's trinitarian perichoretic relations, is always looking at it. In relation to Christ, all humanity and human consciousness perichoretically reflect the same sustaining dynamics or at least affect them in Christ and the Spirit. This presents the potential source of all cosmic and human possibilities that emerge within the Heisenbergian *potentiae* and Hilbert Space.

Again, time is a property of relationships; relationships do not happen in time; time happens *only* inside interactions. According to STR and QM, it is technically possible for Christ, resurrecting in a transcendent manner in relation to the cosmos, to engage an infinite amount of relationships throughout all of history during the forty days before his ascension (Barth, *CD III/2*). Time is scientifically relative, and a risen body and person, not just a metaphysical presence as some logos, is capable of such interactions. Linear time is a local perception within our relations and enculturation. However, Christ and the Spirit transcend this enculturation within their trinitarian relations, mediating (bringing into mutual co-conditioning) all relations both synchronically and diachronically. "For where two or three are gathered in My name [his call to the cross, "infinite resignation"], I am there in the midst of them" (Matt 18:20). What our "consciousness" pre-reflexively encounters within *analogia spiritus* dynamically presents our potentialities, possibilities, and the integrating parameters of our potential choices and freedom. Optimally, our possibilities and choices synchronize through the Spirit and Christ with billions of other freedoms and choices relevant to each event occurrence. This wave function state, therefore, presents the integrational possibilities in which persons (consciousness) copacetically choose, influence, "collapse" into particle state (reality), and co-create within each specific relational occurrence. This conditioned freedom emerges *from within* each prereflexive *moment* in time.[19] Physicist Stapp concludes,

> [This] radical shift in the physics-based conception of man from that of an isolated mechanical automaton to that of an integral participant in the a non-local holistic process that gives form and meaning to the evolving universe is a seismic event of potentially momentous proportions.[20]

He speaks of the potential for human consciousness drawing into the very act of influencing and co-creating reality—a beautiful expression of the Jacobian act of faith. Our personal local and specific position in time conditions our influence and co-conditioning relationship to that Power that constitutes all relationships. As philosopher Colledge states:

> Here is the climax of the Kierkegaardian paradigm: through faith the individual to some extent participates in the eternal, not by erotic self-ascending, but by faithfully allowing oneself to

---

19. Biophysicist David Presti thinks: "Perhaps the greatest lesson of biophysical science is the deep interconnectivity of all physical phenomena. Nothing exists except in interdependent relation with everything else" ("Mind," 22).

20. Stapp, *Mindful Universe*, 140.

> be drawn by the "impossible" action of the God who brings the infinite into the finite, the eternal into the temporal, within—and only within—the existing faithful individual.[21]

In other words, the ability to say to a mountain, "into the sea," and it happens, has everything to do with our willingness for infinite resignation to and decisive action with that Power that synchronizes all cosmic interactions and facilitates faith within us, and knows whether or not others live on that mountain. Within the quantum world, Price suggests:

> The moral is that things may *seem* more objective than they actually are, when the source of the subjectivity is not an obvious one. The main constraint turns on the fact that counterfactuals are used in *deliberation*, and that *deliberation is a temporally asymmetric process*. Considered as structures in spacetime, agents (or "deliberators") are asymmetric, and thus orientable along their temporal axis.... Although our temporal orientation is probably a contingent matter—there might be agents with the opposite temporal orientation elsewhere in the universe—it is not something that we can change.... What we have here is a *relational truth*, a truth about how things are from a perspective, rather than absolute truth about the world. The account thus provides a kind of quasi-objectivity (last two emphases mine).[22]

Price emphasizes that we have many agents in whom each one's de-liberation eventually locates and constitutes in time. If we allow humanity such pervading influence over reality, *something* must mediate humanity's temporal and limited perspective in relation to the world and others; this *something* must fully understand humanity (*ipso facto* be human) and yet transcend human limitations and de-liberations in time. And so we have come full circle back to Christmas day.

Before the daybreak of conscious reflexion (reflexion being the particle, reality, the Abrahamic "yes"), we must enter the indeterminate prereflexive world of *analogia spiritus* (wave function, the synchronizing ideality, the Jacobian "no" or passion).[23] Human response *always* constitutes in relative time. However, the Christian notion of God is also temporally sensitive. Yes, humanity constitutes within relative dynamics, which leads

---

21. Colledge, "Between," 59–60.
22. Price, "Route to Realism," 23.
23. Again, this dynamic is twofold through infinite resignation followed by self-determination and action (choice). Richard Colledge similarly identifies these creative pre-Socratic distinctions in Kierkegaard's enigmatic paradox of God-man in "Between," 58.

to subjectivity. But, in light of quantum theory, what about God? What is God's "perspective"? Price thinks:

> The contrast is a subjective one, a feature of what it *feels like* to be an agent, so that such difference would not be apparent from a genuinely external perspective. An atemporal God would just see a pattern of correlations in both temporal directions between the deliberator's internal states and various environmental conditions (and wouldn't regard the temporal ordering implied by the terms "input" and "output" as having any objective significance, or course).[24]

Price considers God's awareness as atemporal. But, is the Christian God atemporal? Atemporality (an antiquated derivative of Greek cosmology) is not a quality of the trinitarian God of transtemporality. The Incarnation perichoretically temporalizes the Eternality of the Father, creating the Father's own personhood, character, and subjectivity within the godhead. Through Christ's Time, God mutually relates to human personhood in time. Unlike Price's model, within a perichoretic ontology, it becomes possible for the de-liberation of humanity to occur in mutual co-conditioning with the deliberation of the dual aspect dynamics of God in Time (Christ). Outside of Incarnation, and human being as a complementarity of body and spirit, as in Eastern, Process, or Hegelian notions of divinity, we suffer the loss of true mutuality and, inevitably, personhood. Each person holistically *as* spirit (in *analogia spiritus*—absolutes), not *with* spirit, constitutes in time (with Christ—relativities) as a complementarity. In this respect, much of Enlightenment Christianity struggles with this concept of mutuality (the incarnational imperative of mutuality), erring in its understanding of Kierkegaard's "infinite qualitative difference" (IQD).

To this end, this thesis attempts to expand the notion of complementarity in Loder and Neidhardt (Neidhardt being a physicist). They consider quanta containing *both* wave and particle, but only one is observable at a time. In a fully perichoretic model, the collapse of wave function into particle creates that moment's reality within each specific relational transaction in dialogical alternation. In this respect, each person relating to a specific quanta will experience its *potentiae* within their personal relational reality (*analogia spiritus*) rather than as an observer of an observer-independent

---

24. Price, "Route to Realism," 23–24. Price further notes (n31) that "this phenomenological account will appeal more than the formal one to philosophers who seek to ground folk concepts in folk experiences. Do we need to adjudicate between the two? I don't think so. It seems reasonable to expect that they will turn out to be complimentary. In effect, the formal approach will simply be describing the internal structure of the pattern of correlations on which the phenomenological approach depends."

reality (*analogia entis*). This quanta as possibility then constitutes (or not) within each relative personal relational reality through Christ's mediation, without ultimate contradiction. This presents a relational ontology of difference. Christ, or God, experiences similarly but through their respective character within the godhead and as a relational whole. So, adjusting Loder and Neidhardt, outside of relationship, particle function drops back into wave function *alone*. The two quantum states never exist at the same time. Outside of Christ's Time and our time, they remain potentia gracefully present through the Spirit as we move and have our being with him. The godhead maintains the same IQD within itself. Thus, the necessity of a trinitarian dialogical God.

Nevertheless, the collapse of wave function into particle does not create a local illusion of reality; it is an existential reality that must become so again and again each moment—*creatio continua*. Overly simplified and overstated for clarity, metaphysically nothing (of being), like manna, carries forward from one moment into the next but is contingent upon the ongoing synchronization of all possibilities from within the relational cycling of the Eternal and Time in which creation continues from each moment to the next. Is there true substance or materiality? Yes, but only within the interstices of the Eternal/temporal cycles *within* each relational occurrence (gestalt). Is there flow within time? Yes, but only within the conscious tension of time *transformin*g in relation to the eternal.

Physics began by experimentally collapsing the wave function of light into a photon through observation. They are now repeating similar quantum "jumps" with atoms and, most recently, with molecules! These molecules transcend locality and jump instantaneously from one place to another (faster than c). Do such phenomena within the world of physics surprise us who believe in the resurrection of a Christ who walks through walls and disappears upon our recognition of him as God?

ANALOGIES FROM QUANTUM PHYSICS

Physicists Bruce Rosenblum and Fred Kuttner have efficiently compiled a list of analogies that quantum researchers theorize in describing the relationship between quantum dynamics and consciousness.[25] Each of them parallels aspects of perichoretic dynamics.

> a) *Duality:* We cannot deduce the existence of consciousness from properties of the material brain. Consciousness involves

---

25. Rosenblum and Kuttner, *Quantum Enigma*, 193–94.

two qualitatively different processes. Similarly, in quantum theory, the actual event comes about not by the evolving wavefunction but by the collapse of the wavefunction by observation. This too, reveals two qualitatively different processes.

In perichoretic dynamics and orthodox Christianity (and at Kierkegaard's insistence), human nature is a tensive (existential) synthesis of two qualitatively different poles that *cannot* materially or qualitatively synthesize into an eternal or temporally third term. Each of these poles (wave function and particle) correspondingly represents the infinite and finite, the eternal and temporal, possibility and necessity, ideality and reality. The emergence of consciousness happens as a result of relationship. Whenever an observer observes anything, they are coming into relationship with what they are observing. The collapse of wave function (possibility) into reality happens because of the interaction, which includes the observing.

In this regard, persons in relationship experience consciousness as a repeating dialogical cycling between prereflexive de-liberation in relation to the Eternal during awareness (possibilities and potentialities, what physicists call Hilbert space, wave function) and cognitive response into time, gestalt (the collapses into spacetime reality). Therefore, the mind and brain will never reveal direct observable "mechanisms" between the two because of the qualitative difference that exists between the infinite and finite, the eternal and temporal. Nevertheless, this tensive polarity produces life, a living being in motion—consciousness. All life springs from and is contingent upon Christ and the Spirit coming into time.

> b) *Nonphysical influences:* If there's a "mind" that's other than the physical brain, how does it communicate with the brain? This mystery recalls the connection of the two quantum-entangled objects with each other ... what Bohr called "influences."

What force is active and instantaneous between two split electrons so that when we reverse the polar spin on one electron, the other miles away instantly reverses as well? This coordination and communication come from neither a material nor an energy source that is limited to c; the nonlocal reaction is instantaneous. Whether we consider the phenomenon as altered spatial, temporal, or communicational dynamic, it is a force or dynamic that inhabits, interacts with, and influences the world we know and experience. As much as this force or dimension is undeniable, the point of contact is unknown, possibly unknowable. Again, Kierkegaard's relational ontology that humanity is a synthesis of the temporal and the eternal, the finite and the infinite, comes full force into consideration, as well as his complementarity of God-man as fully God, fully divine. Such distinctions reflect the perichoretic activity in persons and relationships. In *perichoresis*: (1) That Power that constitutes (creates) all relationships (reality) is transparent and, within its basic functioning, unknowable. (2) The Eternal and the temporal, *eo ipso* cannot be made the same or combined. We cannot synthesize them into anything other than a living consciousness in which the eternal, at best, moves with time. They can affect, influence, and condition each other but are not of the same essence. This analogy reflects not only an evolved orthodox Christianity but ancient Christianity.

This polar distinction is theologically not just within Christ and the Trinity, it also echoes within human dynamics. Because of this, human consciousness (or relationship) affects quantum collapse, is capable of faith, and parallels the notion that Jacob's passion can mutually affect God (Christ). Only by the nature of this Power (*perichoresis*) pervading the universe, pervading the relational structures of humanity and the cosmos, is it possible to bring humanity into co-conditioning relations with God without subsuming the person or all humanity into God and eventually compromising identity and personhood. This dynamic force within relationships is not so much contingent upon the person of God and God's personal intentions as such, but according to the nature of God that reflects within all cosmic relations (not by *entis*, but by a dynamic of *relationis* that creates *entis-creatio continua* within perichoretic relations).

> c) *Observer-created reality:* George Berkeley's "to be is to be perceived" is the preposterous solipsistic view of the effect of consciousness. But it is reminiscent of what happens with our object in a box pair. [Whichever of the two boxes you choose to open, there is the particle, the other is empty.]

This physics experiment leaves us with the uncomfortable result that consciousness literally influences or creates reality; this leads some physicists, like Henry, suggesting the necessity of theism or some notion of a cosmic/omniscient consciousness that maintains a minimal basic level of reality. In the theology of *perichoresis*, the prereflexive dynamic within human relations co-conditionally relates with the Trinity influencing God's creative action (affecting basic desires within everyday life to intentional prayer). Though we might also consider that God "sustains" creation, inevitably this is a misnomer. As Einstein has shown us, the past and future are no less determinately real than the present. From the Eternal perspective, God creates in one dynamic *momentary* action constituting unlimited relationships within a synchronizing singularity. From the temporal view, God is not sustaining creation as much as re-creating it each *moment*. To the extent we achieve infinite resignation (bearing our cross) and act decisively, we can influence each respective creating *moment*, or in the case of Jacobian faith, potentially hijack it (rather than remain in Skinnerian deterministic reaction to the world, or God).

In this respect, perichoretic dynamics obviate the idealism of Berkeley, includes the quantum phenomena of observer-created reality, and proffers a realism that existentially takes shape from one moment to the next, *and* with the potential of divine-human co-conditioning of each moment of creation. Because of Christ within his trinitarian relations and humanity's co-conditioning influence, solipsism is avoided. The minor "creative" action of an experimenter collapsing a wave function into a particle bespeaks of the limited but enormous potential of a person in transparent relation to that Power that constitutes all relationships (reality)—to be is to relate with the world in full relation to that Power that constitutes all relationships.

> d) *Observing thoughts:* If you think about the content of a thought (its position), you inevitably change where it is going (its direction, motion). On the other hand, if you think about where it is going, you lose the sharpness of its content. Analogously, the uncertainty principle shows that if you observed the position of an object, you change its motion. On the other hand, if you observe its motion, you lose the sharpness of its position.

The Eternal truth can indeed condition time; it is no less truth despite its relativistic nature. But it is the truth conditioning each interaction. Like manna, it must resign into the existential dusk to emerge again from the Eternal blackhole into the dawn of every new time, always slightly changing, always unique within each relative occurrence, always making things new. Though a product of the infinite, the finite conditions being. The pre-reflexive awareness of (diachronic) possibilities is a state of "infinitizing" us to the Infinite and Eternal. Our constituting reflexive gestalt into time is the state of "being" in relation to the world and all other persons in time ("being" relativized). In pulsing cycles, they never combine or overlap, not even in God, *eo ipso* God's nature, a tripartite ontology—a Trinity. Without it, creation and the divine implode into a Parmenidean pantheistic everything/nothingness. In conclusion, there are verbs and nouns, and never the two are one; yet, in the tension of sentence structuring, perichoretically, they create a world.

> e) *Parallel procession:* Neuronal action rates are billions of times slower than those of computers. Nevertheless, with complex problems, human brains can still compete with the best computers. The brain presumably achieves its power by working

on many paths simultaneously. Computer scientists attempt to achieve this same massive parallel processing with quantum computers, whose elements are simultaneously in superpositions within many states.

As we are learning from the bicameral brain functions, this phenomenon alone is evidence for the existence of spirit as a different dimension of reality[26] than soul, mind, or brain, all of which in totality are spirit, but none in themselves spirit. Spirit is that living holistic function that relates to and within the Eternal (what physicists often refer to as wave function dynamics that draw from Hilbert Space). Hibert Space may be the interactions of all "manifestations" of spirit, all cosmic, human, and divine spirits (dynamics). The dynamic of spirit interaction is much faster than the speed of light; it is the "spooky" function that instantaneously integrates, informs, influences, and enables "multiple paths" simultaneously. More likely, the dynamic of spirit, an integral aspect of human nature, transcends the brain's limiting neural "paths" and holistically and instantly integrates all relevant factors and parallel processes into a unified result (or gestalt).

The relation of *analogia spiritus* is instantaneous—Kierkegaard's *moment*, the *metabole* (*exaiphanes*), the "sudden blow." It is a dynamic synchronizing singularity to which the idea of just paralleling processes alone is offensive. Johannes Climacus argues: "It is only momentarily that the particular individual is able to realize existentially a unity of the infinite and the finite which transcends existence."[27] The processing within spirit or *analogia spiritus* is not only instantaneous, but also subconscious and inarticulable within the existing individual—the Jacobian *night* of faith. It explains where the dynamic of hypothetico-deductive thinking comes from, the activity of deriving a geometric equation as we wait in open searching expectation before all the derivations of equations burst forth in one flash into time. It is like our thoughts emerging in conversation when we begin to express them without review. The entirety of the thought comes as a "sudden blow," but the words (details) emerge in linear procession in hermeneutical delay to the listener (and speaker!), with both the listener for the first time, and the speaker redoubling a new gestalt, both experiencing a shared meaning simultaneously bursting forth together upon gestalt. Many scientific discoveries holistically explode in convictional force in the scientist long before the final articulating gestalt. It may take years before they completely articulate or validate the theory.

---

26. I am using reality here as an integral *aspect* of what is or produces reality.
27. Kierkegaard, *CUP*, 176.

RELATIONAL ONTOLOGIES IN QUANTUM INTERPRETATIONS

The Relational Quantum Mechanics (RQM) interpretation of quantum physics vividly corresponds to the dynamics of *perichoresis* developed within this thesis. In its preliminary development, RQM considers a mathematical model that refers to two quantum systems rather than one, an ontology that emerges between relating systems—through the relationship. In other words, two systems (or persons) that come into relation constitute or create reality. Similar to the dynamics in Kierkegaard, it establishes and maintains difference in differentiated unity. "Understood in this manner the quantum state is always and only a *relative state*."[28] QM displaces a strong version of realism for an ontology of difference *within* a universal relational dynamic creating integrating relations. The radical claim of RQM, therefore, is that: "different observers can give different accounts of the same set of events (Rovelli 1996: 1643) . . . and emphasises the fact that the observer itself behaves as a quantum system, when acting on other systems."[29] In other words, like *perichoresis*, the quantum dynamics that create and support the world are analogically the same dynamics active within the perichoretic nature of humanity. It creates a unique ontological connection within each respective relational occurrence that provides for real (ontological) rather than merely perspectival, solipsistic, or illusionary engagement with material reality (Henry). This is consonant, for example, with dynamics mentioned earlier in the biblical account of Pentecost, in which the listeners heard the speaker in the listener's mother tongue regardless of the speaker's language. Each could perceive and "give different accounts of the same set of events," and each could ontologically share the truth of the utterance from within their unique meaning-frame and relationship to that truth. Physicist Carlo Rovelli argues that special relativity historically warrants such quantum dynamics interpretations.[30] Likewise, W. H. Zurek thinks:

> Properties of quantum systems have no absolute meaning. Rather, they must be always characterized with respect to other physical systems . . . [and] correlations between the properties of quantum systems are more basic than the properties themselves."[31]

---

28. Laudisa and Rovelli, "Relational," 1.4.
29. Laudisa and Rovelli, "Relational," 1.1.
30. Rovelli, "Relational," 2.
31. Zurek, "Pointer," 1516.

Therefore, reality takes place within relationships rather than relationships taking place within a conscious-independent reality. This is the world of *perichoresis*, in which reality emerges within relationships. Each aspect of reality constitutes within an emerging co-conditioning mutuality of the relational unity itself, again and again, and according to the evolving scope and in-tensions of relevant persons or systems. As we have noted earlier with special relativity, time also is a property emerging from relationships.

Various interpretations of relational quantum theory have begun to effectively explain many quantum anomalies, notwithstanding the enigma of time and causality, transforming our understanding of time and causality. These interpretations express the same characteristics for time and causality as *perichoresis* and *analogia spiritus*.

Satosi Watanabe argues that information coming from forward-moving quantum evolving states is incomplete and fails to explain the entire quantum phenomenon.[32] He proposes we can only fully describe quantum states as a result of information coming from *both* forward and backward evolving quantum states. This involves vectors of information flow evolving from the initial condition toward the future and another coming from future boundary conditions backward toward the initial condition. This theory grew into the Two-State Vector Formalism (TSVF) during the 1960s and suggests that quantum dynamics contain a relational nature that emerges within the relationship of two causal vectors (systems). Under this theory, physicists no longer consider that such phenomena are due to backward causation alone—what appeared to be backward causation within the Delayed Choice Quantum Erasure experiment. Instead, it was a causal effect resulting from *both* the past (forward causation) and the future (retrocausation). In the double-slit experiment, the forward vector of causation originates with the light-emitting source, and the retrocausal vector originates from the choice of the experimenter. The final causal or influencing activity becomes a co-conditioning combination of these two informational vectors determining the state of the light as it passes the slits.

In harmony with TSVF research, physicist John G. Cramer went on to develop the Transactional Interpretation of Quantum Mechanics (TIQM, or TI), describing the quantum event as a "handshake" exchange of both forward and backward waves triggering a transaction between waves that are real within their dimension rather than mere mathematical information. The initiating quantum state creates a two-way "transaction" (*transjective*) process between the emitters and the absorbers. The beauty of this theory is that the collapse of wave function is "atemporal" and therefore

---

32. Watanabe, "Symmetry."

happens outside spacetime, which supports Kierkegaard's notion of the *moment*—the instant of eternity. Such dynamics also nicely support our earlier reflections on the dynamic interactions (de-liberations) going on within the transtemporality of perichoretic notions of faith in light of special relativity. Such dynamics within quantum relationality reinforce the plausibility and definition of faith in Hebrews 11:1—an ontological experiencing of some aspect of that which is future and unseen yet holistically perceivable within the interactional eternal *moment*. This suggests that more than just information flows from the future to the past, but the possibility of holistically experiencing an ontological aspect of that future reality in the present *moment* (via *analogia spiritus*) or the co-conditioning wave function interaction of that future state.

Ruth Kastner, a philosopher of physics, develops Cramer's work even further in her Possibilist Transactional Interpretation (PTI). She agrees with Cramer that spacetime emerges from transactions but argues that according to PTI,

> Collapse is not a process that occurs within spacetime, . . . collapse corresponds to the creation of spacetime events from a *quantum substratum*. That substratum comprises physical possibilities described by quantum states: as well as virtual processes described by time-symmetric propagators, which are the precursors to those states. Two spacetime events are created via an actualized transaction: (i) the emission and (ii) the absorption of real energy. . . . The connection between these two events is the transfer of real energy/momentum from the emitter to the receiving absorber. The transfer defines a spacetime interval and a temporal direction, the emission defining the past and the absorption defining the present for that absorber. Thus we gain deep physical meaning corresponding to the mathematical facts that energy and momentum are the generators of temporal and spatial translations, respectively.[33]

Kastner points to a dynamic transaction that occurs prereflexive to conscious reflexion, which actively presents the possibilities and potential deliberation within Hilbert Space (the universal holistic sea of wave function interactivity). Hilbert Space reflects the trinitarian activity adjudicating and synchronizing the possibilities and potentials in which humanity is potentially active in all relevant contexts. It is a product of the inter-trinitarian relationship before the creation of time *within* every *moment* in history. This represents the freedom from which humanity moves and has its being. The

---

33. Kastner, "Transactional," 10, emphasis added.

transfer of "real energy/momentum" between quantum systems (persons) outside of spacetime does not diminish the realness of the "transaction." It expands our temporally laden concept of causation with a fuller understanding of relational dynamics as *mutual co-conditioning influence*, which occurs prereflexively in human interaction). Nevertheless, as Kastner suggests, our understanding of realism must expand to incorporate dynamics below the typical iceberg level of consciousness; we must appreciate that the realist "territory must be bigger than we thought."

> In addition, many think we can only achieve a consistent realist ontology within the transactional picture if the higher-dimensional multi-particle states refer to actual entities in an extra-spatiotemporal manifold in or described by Hilbert Space.[34]

Transactional space describes the *moment* of *analogia spiritus* that occurs in relation to the Eternal in the midst of time. In this respect, the Hilbert Space of quantum physics is similar to the Eternal dimension of God in which the Trinity has its pre-creational play, and the quantum event represents the drawing of humanity into some degree of the creative process (via *analogia spiritus*). The "extra-spatiotemporal" quantum manifold parallels that same activity, where the de-liberating life of humanity prereflexively synchronizes with others and that Power that constitutes all transactions. During this deliberational process, the *instant* of Eternity, Christ adjudicates the entirety of billions of quantum systems (human persons), providing possibilities and synchronizing potentials in which humanity might move and have its being, lovingly coexisting in a freedom that is only limited by other freedoms, most notably God's. The Spirit of God mediates the quantum world drawing humanity into this sea of unlimited but appropriate possibilities and potential. "PTI treats space-time events as unidirectionally emergent from the underlying time-symmetric processes, which are seen as taking place in a pre-spatiotemporal domain of Heisenbergian *potentiae*."[35] This clearly describes aspects of our developing concept of *analogia spiritus* quite well.

How might this theologically translate into personal faith and divine action? Many theologians discount miracles, like those of Moses, because of their transcendently interventional or impositional nature. A much more complex and integrated activity occurs within a perichoretic ontology. For example, neither God (nor Moses in faith) instantly create a plague of locusts out of thin air and send them in at the appropriate time. Nor does God, in foresight, generate the locusts through his direct activity in cultivating them

---

34. Kastner, "Transactional," 11.
35. Kastner, "Retrocausation," 1.

by influencing biological factors. That would still be impositional. Remembering that well over 90 percent of human desires and decisions are unconscious, Christ, likewise, actively integrates every relevant and prereflexive *moment* throughout history. In the quantum world, this emits "offering waves" during such *moments* to which every human and cosmic cry for liberation responds as the absorber with a "confirmation wave" (both backward and forward in time), with offering and absorbing waves flowing from all directions. In other words, every relevant quantum system (Christ, Moses, the Hebrew people, the locusts, the rains that feed the grass that feed the locust, etc.), all analogically according to their nature and potential influence, take part in creating that event reality.[36] Therefore, God alone is not the sole agent; all these factors are integrally active in *influencing* (co-conditioning) the event, each at its own level of potential influence. From Moses' perspective and longings, he synchronously moves in faith with God within the "substratum reality" of the Eternal (Hilbert Space) and already prereflexively experiences this potential phenomenon (reality) within that "substratum reality" via *analogia spiritus* while constituting in relation to Christ's Time, which analogically synchronizes with his personal time. In this respect, God can say to Moses, "*Your* faith has set you free." The passionate longing of the oppressed Hebrews, along with every cry of every human heart in every generation struggling for liberation co-conditionally affect and influence this moment of creation in which the locusts came. Therefore, contra Pannenberg and Process Theology, for whom faith is an "intelligent anticipation prior to secure comprehension," a mere hypothesis, or Augustine's notion of faith as "thinking with assent (*cum assensione cogitare*),"[37] perichoretic faith involves experiencing "the *reality* of things hoped for, the *evidence* of things not seen" (Heb 11:1 NKJV, emphasis added).

Quantum reality reveals a potential substratum that explains how biblical miracles might emerge in a non-impositional manner. This transforms Christendom's "folk tales" back into the power of God and humanity within the world to which the Scriptures attest. The disciple's fear (subconscious but albeit passionate prayer) co-conditions Christ's action of ending a raging storm at sea. He constantly introduces a world to them over which they potentially have some dominion control. With the disciples, he heals,

---

36. For Moses, the experience is probably different than all the other cosmic influences in that Moses may have been experiencing closer to what Kierkegaard regards as Religiousness B; the others might have been experiencing similar to Religiousness A. Because of the personal nature of his encounters with God, Moses moves with God in Time, in which his prereflexive *moments* flow reflexively with Christ in his Time (the "substratum").

37. Pannenberg, *Systematic Theology*, 3:145n146.

commands, and recreates the world (weather, bread, fish, etc.). His resurrected body walks through walls, appears, and disappears. The quantum world of nonlocal and transtemporal interaction, and observer-dependent world, both re-legitimize such activity in a modern world and reveals how a transcendent God works co-conditionally (in immanent transcendence) with humanity and the cosmos.

Through it all, the Spirit and Christ draw the disciples to new levels of life and consciousness. He constantly challenges them to exercise their ability to do the same, and that if they believe with all their heart and have no doubt, they can say to a mountain into the sea, and it will happen. The only thing that angers and frustrates Jesus, besides social injustice, was humanity's, specifically the disciple's, inability or unwillingness to act in faith—take dominion over the world in recreating it into a world that reflects God's love. In one instance of the disciples's failure to heal, Jesus decries, "O faithless and perverse generation, how long shall I be with you? How long shall I bear with you? Bring him here to Me" (Matt 17:17). Jesus expresses genuine confusion at their inability or unwillingness to recreate the world as he did. For the sake of maintaining Christendom, we remove the expectations of Christ from Christian theology and ecclesia.

The quantum world shows us that human consciousness or relationship collapses wave function into reality (relationship), and now we are collapsing more substantial things than photons—atoms and even molecules; does this not suggest we rethink and appropriately expand our theological considerations? Perhaps QM is just beginning to reveal the power of human interaction (love) within the quantum world and its latent potential. Two impediments limit our freedom in this regard:

- Sin. The unwillingness to enter our relationships in infinite resignation, pick up our cross and offer all we are each moment into transformative relations. The other half of sin is the unwillingness to stand in faith outside (and when needed against) our social systems within the church and the world, to stand in counter-distinction as a self to the Other, often against the world (Abraham), and at times against our current understanding and still developing relationship with God (Jacob). God ultimately seeks a relationship not over us, but as Jacob reveals, with us. If we passionately enter our desires and longings, they become accessible to God's transforming action, bringing us deeper into co-conditioning relations from one degree to another, often transforming God (Christ) as well (John 14:12). Kierkegaard is screaming as much from his grave.

- Our freedom must be synchronized with eight billion potential co-creators on earth together with God, rather than billions of solipsistic worlds. There must be a deliberating consciousness that synchronizes all freedoms, all consciousnesses into a copacetic unity (e.g., within a de-liberating "substratum" that does not transcend, but trans-relates all cosmic relations). We must be willing to work with that synchronizing person (consciousness) who knows all of humanity's desires, longings, and disappointments through *analogia spiritus*. Also, this synchronization and adjudication must occur without imposition upon *the* human freedom necessary for creating a living being capable of knowing God as God.

Christ and the Spirit are that foundational synchronizing contingency within a *living* quantum substratum. He is human, feels as human, knows as human, and therefore, able to adjudicate all human freedoms and desires into a world in which love grows out of evil, order out of chaos. Christ is that person through whom billions of other *living* systems can steadily emerge into a relationship and faith through which to create a world, their world in differentiated unity.

"Even Physicists Don't Understand Quantum Mechanics," says physicist Sean Carroll.[38] Until we resolve the quantum enigma, no one will understand the quantum world

> because quantum mechanics is the most fundamental theory we have, sitting squarely at the center of every serious attempt to formulate deep laws of nature. If nobody understands quantum mechanics, nobody understands the universe. You would naturally think, then, that understanding quantum mechanics would be the absolute highest priority among physicists worldwide.[39]

But, as Carroll says, within the world of physics, the opposite is happening. Few physics departments have researchers working on this subject. Students interested in the quantum enigma are firmly—"maybe not so gently"—told, "Shut up and calculate!" A professor's interest in resolving this issue can cause them to lose their grant money. Since the 1930s, "what has mattered was using a set of *ad hoc* quantum rules to construct models of particles,"[40] rather than continue research for legitimate models and interpretations of the quantum world. Over the last few decades, Carroll thinks the tide is starting to change as new models, like Kastner's, are beginning to emerge.

38. Carroll, "Don't Understand."
39. Carroll, "Don't Understand," para. 9–10.
40. Carroll, "Don't Understand," para. 12.

These analogies between quantum dynamics, consciousness, and perichoretic dynamics reveal striking associations. As we have seen, they reflect the same ontological phenomena emerging in multiple disciplines. Within theology and philosophy of religion, the associating dynamics of a perichoretic theology and QM resonate far more than any other religious or theological associations within the literature. Pantheistic ontologies, in which materiality and realism are considered illusions, will eventually struggle against the quantum enigma and its complementarity of wave function and particle realities. It has been difficult to shake the concept of a material reality altogether, and within the trinitarian and perichoretic understanding of God, there is no need to do so. We simply need to understand it as relationally relativistic within a relational ontology. Attempting to reduce all reality into a single divine unity or Absolute Spirit is also at odds with the quantum phenomena. Likewise, Christian theologies with limited descriptive categories from antiquity or theologies conditioned by Enlightenment philosophy will struggle with QM because of their notion of personhood as substance in the classical Newtonian sense.

Kierkegaard expands these limiting views of humanity by his insistence that self is spirit (not just a soul and body), and eternity has come into time through Christ and the Spirit inviting humanity into existential relationship with an Eternal God. Ontologies that separate the notion of substance from its dynamic contingency within a relational ontology and refrain from developing a holistic concept of spirit, both human and divine, will continue to struggle with quantum reality. They also bear the weight of their scriptural incoherent and selective readings against the fuller readings of perichoretic theology. In consideration of quantum mechanics and special relativity, our traditional understanding of substance, causality, choice, and time is undergoing needed transformation within momentous paradigm shifts. These enigmatic shifts are supplying new and vital dimensions that associate perfectly with and condition our understanding of πνεῦμα (spirit) as used within the Scriptures. Therefore, we must further develop these concepts for theological use.

Though frozen for nearly a century, the established quantum phenomena and resulting enigma have yet to affect other disciplines of thought significantly. Much of this, as in all paradigm shifts, has to do with the intransigence of the academy and institutionalization of the church due to the potential diminishment of one's former life's works and unspoken agendas of the academy. To think that such findings will not affect theology, as all past scientific paradigm shifts have significantly done, would be notoriously naïve, even arrogant. Nevertheless, a growing number of physicists believe the expansion of quantum thought will come through interdisciplinary dialogue with philosophy, psychology, and even theology, just like two intensely devout Christians with strong mystical tendencies initiated a radical revolution in science by positing their outrageous concepts of electromagnetic field theory. The Christian faith experience and theology once again stand to condition the emergence of another scientific paradigm shift today. History is rife with examples of what happens to the church when it does not engage interdisciplinary development. Christianity must be free to imaginatively explore these new findings in science and their subsequent interpretations if it is to continue its transformational growth and that of the sciences as well.

6

The Perichoretic Redemptive Relation of Christ to the World

The Complementarity of Church and Culture

In the previous chapters, we explored the possibility of mutual perichoretic relations in divine-human communication, specifically the *perichoresis* of time and Eternity, and how that occurs in the dialogical dynamics of humanity and God (Trinity). Within the dynamics of relationships and personal consciousness (a relationship unto itself), Moltmann points to "a perichoretic understanding of the different modes of time, which interpenetrate one another qualitatively, and cannot simply be quantitatively separated from one another"—which produces consciousness or relationships.[1] What does all this mean for the church and its relationship to culture? How is Christ redemptively active in the world outside of the church? Christ and the Spirit are redemptively active in the church and the world in differing ways. The signs of redemptive relations are evident within the church and the world just as order continues to emerge from chaos, and as Paul says, "from one degree to another."

The Old Testament narratives reveal the progressive nature of relations evolving into ever greater intimacy with God and each other.[2] Paul reveals

---

1. Moltmann, *GC*, 125–26. The latter idea he develops within the section "The Time of Creation," 104–39.

2. This is evident in the progression of sexual practices toward higher shared intimacy toward monogamy. During the time of Abraham, Judah was in no way morally suspect for his involvement with a harlot (Gen 38). By the time of Moses, marriage became the exclusive domain of sexual relations. In the time of Abraham, a brother need

redemption as a progressive process (2 Cor 3:18). The advent of the Incarnation and subsequent Spirit of God institute powerful conceptual heuristics that began to slowly accelerate the progressive nature of Christianity culminating in the work of Augustine. This effectively brought the divine-human relationship from the toddler stage of imposed laws and social code into the greater freedom and intimacy of young adolescence. Each stage of development reveals the progressive emergence of humanity's perichoretic endowment and contingent relationship with God (*analogia spiritus*). As we have already reviewed, the writer of Hebrews clearly portends this progressive development of divine-human relations, within its immanent transcendence, transforming humanity through the grace of time in ongoing interpolation socially and with God. The initial guiding divine structural interventions (law) steadily guide transformation of human relations perichoretically, bringing the external imposition of the law into the desires of the heart (John 17:21). Moltmann is emphatic: "God unceasingly desires the freedom of his creation. God is the inexhaustible freedom of those he has created.... By virtue of friendship with God in the Spirit, we have the chance to influence God and to participate in his rule."[3] Though creation is far from such messianic goals, *analogia spiritus* perpetually calls humanity through ever-increasing perichoretic relations (empathy) while slowly transforming humanity into the image of Christ from degree to degree. The risen Christ proleptically engages the world in an ongoing sanctifying cosmic process through which he, as the first risen one, actively orchestrates, facilitates, and steadily transforms all rule, authority, and power, bringing all things into synchronicity. At this point, "then the Son Himself will also be subject to Him who put all things under Him, that God may be all in all" (1 Cor 15:28). The transforming redemptive relations of Christ are not only with the church but the entire world through his personal transcendence within the church and his immanent and sustaining cosmic relations to the world.[4]

---

only inseminate a dead brother's childless wife; after Moses, marriage was required. By the time of Jesus, the institution of marriage was becoming monogamous, and Jesus promotes this.

3. Moltmann, *TKG*, 218, 221 (203–22).

4. Cf. Col 1:20: it pleased the Father "through Him to reconcile all things to Himself"; and also 1 Cor 15:20, 22–25: "but now Christ is risen from the dead . . . even so in Christ all shall be made alive. But each one in his own order: Christ the first fruits, afterward those who are Christ's at His coming. Then comes the end, when He delivers the kingdom to God the Father, when He puts an end to all rule and all authority and power. For He must reign until He has put all enemies under His feet. The last enemy that will be destroyed is death."

At such time Bonhoeffer tells us: "*Now the objective spirit of the church really has become the Holy Spirit, the experience of the 'religious' community now really is the*

Jacob and the Night of Faith

H. Richard Niebuhr, in *Christ and Culture*, attempts to express how we might understand this enigmatic relationship between Christ, the church, and culture. Is there common ground between the church and culture? Furthermore, what effect does each have upon the other? My original claim was that the current crisis in metaphysics with culture's growing discomfort toward religious meta-narratives in a pluralistic age and the increasing irrelevance of historical structures of atonement to what Bonhoeffer refers to as humanity "come of age," creates a desperate need for identifying common ground between church and culture. Therefore, it might be helpful to reconsider Niebuhr's insights in light of perichoretic dynamics. Moreover, from this discussion, I wish to reveal the perichoretic dynamics that are in active complementarity in redeeming the church *and* evolving culture(s).

H. RICHARD NIEBUHR

In his concluding chapter, Niebuhr argues that four relative aspects affect being a Christian in any culture. "They depend on the partial, incomplete, fragmentary knowledge of the individual; they are relative to the measure of his faith and his unbelief; they are related to the historical position he occupies and to the duties of his station in society; they are concerned with the relative values of things."[5] Therefore, our acts and understanding of faith "are made, it appears, on the basis of relative insight and faith, but they are not relativistic. They are individual decisions, but not individualistic. They are made in freedom, but not in independence; they are made in the

---

experience of the church, and the collective person of the church now really is 'Christ existing as church-community.' It is beyond what we are able to conceive now as to how it will come to pass that all become one and yet each keeps their own identity. All are in God, and yet each remains distinct from God. All are united with each other, and yet distinct. Each possesses God totally and by themselves in the grace-filled dual solitude [*Zweieinsamkeit*] of seeing truth and serving in love, and yet never is solitary because they always really live only within the church-community. We walk by faith, but we shall see—not only God but also God's church-community. We shall no longer merely believe in its love and faith, but see it. At every moment we shall be aware of God's will to rule [*Herrschaftswille*] and implement it within the realm of the church-community. Here the realm of Christ has become the Realm of God. . . . No longer repentance and faith, but service and sight. Here the weeds are separated from the wheat; the age of the historical church in all its affliction has passed away. God will wipe away the tears from all eyes. The victory is won, the Realm has become God's" (*SC*, 288–89). Note that the "objective spirit of the church" does not reflect Hegelian Absolute Spirit as Bonhoeffer struggles to beautifully describe *perichoresis* as a Spirit reflectively enabling *both* shared community while maintaining personhood.

5. Niebuhr, *Christ and Culture*, 234.

moment but are not nonhistorical."[6] We cannot express our faith independent from the "nature of things and the processes of nature."[7] In this respect, Christ's relationship with his church integrates cultural relativities. As Moltmann concludes, "Culture and religion cannot be separated."[8]

Niebuhr presents various understandings of this relationship, two in particular: the paradoxical (Luther) and the transformative (Calvin). He admits we must settle with loose categorizations and acknowledges overlapping characteristics. Notably, he places Kierkegaard's thinking within both. The paradoxical relationship or "dualist" model considers human culture as godless, but the church must live within culture, and therefore God in grace sustains it. Nevertheless, "God has revealed Himself in Christ, but hidden Himself in His revelation; the believer knows the One in whom he has believed, yet walks by faith, not sight."[9] Though cultural aspects are integral, they can never be directly associated with faith, nor can any progress of culture enable any progress within the faith action of the church.[10] Likewise, a "Christian culture" is no less destitute than a pagan one, and faith does not directly affect culture. Niebuhr says this "position makes sharp distinctions between the temporal and spiritual life."[11] Such a position, therefore, tends to be non-sectarian.

Conversely, in the conversionists understanding, Niebuhr presents Christ as the transformer of culture (Calvin), although they maintain a strong distinction between church and culture. The world is considered a prologue to the attainment of Christ's work; however, unlike the earlier model in which culture was evil, here, culture is "perverted good" (Calvin). "Eternal life is a quality of existence in the here and now."[12] "Spiritual and natural events 'are interlocking and analogous.'"[13] The fall is not so much a historical event as it is our current bifurcation and "falling away from the Word."[14] In this respect, "variety brought disorder... because men mistook their partial contributions to truth for the whole truth."[15] Therefore, each culture within church life transforms into Christian life, from degree to degree. However,

6. Niebuhr, *Christ and Culture*, 234.
7. Niebuhr, *Christ and Culture*, 235.
8. Moltmann, *CPS*, 162.
9. Niebuhr, *Christ and Culture*, 157.
10. Niebuhr, *Christ and Culture*, 165.
11. Niebuhr, *Christ and Culture*, 171.
12. Niebuhr, *Christ and Culture*, 195.
13. Niebuhr, *Christ and Culture*, 197.
14. Niebuhr, *Christ and Culture*, 200.
15. Niebuhr, *Christ and Culture*, 227.

because the church is a distinct transforming culture, it tended to establish a sectarian relation with the surrounding non-Christian culture.

Either way, our expression of faith is both partial and culture-laden. But, according to Niebuhr, this does not mean we are without an absolute.

> They can accept their relativities with faith in the infinite Absolute to whom all their relative views, values and duties are subject.... They can make their confessions and decisions both with confidence and with the humility which accepts completion and correction and even conflict from and with others who stand in the same relation to the Absolute.[16]

Therefore, if God's reflecting nature sustains all humanity and calls all persons into authentic relations, our primary mission is to facilitate the constant removal of all relational distortions in our lives and social interactions.[17] The removal of distortions within our social interaction steadily moves us analogically closer to that Power that constitutes us.

> If I consider [another] in his value-relations to all his neighbors and also in his value-relation to God, then there is room not only for relative justice but for the formation and reformation of relative judgments by reference to the absolute relation. The relation to the Absolute will not come into consideration as an afterthought... but *as a forethought and a cothought* that determines how everything is done that is done to him and for him.[18]

However, Niebuhr believes that our relative values within their well-suited contexts can relate in *phronesis* to another's values within their respective context through each of our personal relations to the "absolute relation." Most significantly, he acknowledges that this "absolute relation" transpires prereflexively ("forethought") and analogically co-conditional ("co-thought") within the relationship. "In our decisions we need to go beyond what is intelligible and yet hold fast to it."[19] This is a stark acknowledgment of *analogia spiritus* within perichoretic relations. In this respect, no relative *what*, in itself, bears universal correspondence, significance, or meaning, but thrusts all potential mutuality, continuity, and truth upon the nature of the relationship, it's *how*—the quality of our "relation to the Absolute."

Luther, according to Niebuhr, is sensitive to the stark distinction between God and humanity. However, he thinks that the absolute aspect of

---

16. Niebuhr, *Christ and Culture*, 238.
17. McFadyen, *CP*, 454–55.
18. Niebuhr, *Christ and Culture*, 240, emphasis added.
19. Niebuhr, *Christ and Culture*, 243.

faith that transcends all relativities eucharistically gathers those relativities in such a way as to paradoxically express the Eternal through them in time. It paradoxically lies within our enculturated experience. To establish any connection between Christ's work and culture would be, for Luther, to destroy the one clear distinction that exists between the church and culture.

On the other hand, Calvin's emphasis was upon that aspect of faith that transforms the whole person and analogically one's actions and meanings within culture. The redemptive activity of Christ in the world and the church provides reconfiguring sanctification to what is already good within the world. In this respect, we can consider the primary distinction of the church to be its transformed life as a culture in relation to surrounding worldly cultures. To separate our cultural and spiritual lives was to deny the fullness of Christ's contrast to the world and his church.

Why these two positions emerge with such differences is more complex than this study can engage; nevertheless, each was eager to separate and distinguish one of the two *aspects* of what this thesis presents as a dual complementary dynamic that is ultimately indivisible. The appropriate metaphysics of such a dialogical relational paradigm that can appropriately synthesize both these concerns into one unitary dynamic did not yet exist for Niebuhr within theological discourse. The first aspect is the prereflexive experience in the process of awareness (the absolute relating to the Absolute). By indwelling the relationship the holistic dynamic of *analogia spiritus* produces more than we can fully articulate within our conceptual structures. This is the dynamic processing, coming together of spirits, which creates and communicates more than the relative structures and existing sum of the constituent elements can directly communicate. Here, creation *ex nihilo* occurs. Luther knows this dynamic well and marks it as the primary site of God's work in persons.

The second aspect of dialogical relationality was the reflexive constituting of the individual as a finite, whole, and temporal person-in-relation. This represents the conceptual gestalt resulting from the reconfiguring and transforming of our previous structures and forms of life for employment within the immediate relationship. Calvin emphasizes this dynamic in creation and human relations.

Luther consigns faith to a dimension in which we relate absolutely to the Absolute and relatively to the relative. In this consideration, our faith experience is equal to that of any other time or cultural context. And so it is that all persons in infinite resignation are able, within the call, to venture all within the inner infinity of the self toward a fullness of faith. Conversely, Calvin emphasizes another aspect of faith and, in so doing, provides us with a developmental process of relational sanctification within the church. This idea, likewise, parallels the social progress that is evident within the relational or social evolution throughout history. Therefore, perichoretic dynamics affirm both Calvin and Luther in their positive and seemingly conflicting assertions on these matters. If, however, our relations transformatively sanctify throughout time, are we to consider that Christian faith grows throughout history? Calvin would affirm a degree of this, but Luther would not. From the perspective of perichoretic theology, the answer is yes and no.

THE COMPLEMENTARITY OF REDEMPTION AND RELATIONAL EVOLUTION

Perichoresis presents an irreducible tripartite dynamic that creates mutuality of relations while maintaining the integrity of and intensifying the polarities within relationship. Each participant constitutes within the dynamic forming mutuality of the relational unity itself. Within this dialogical bipolarity of relations, God's trinitarian relation to humanity accents the cycling transitions, pulling Eternity into an analogical co-conditioning relation at each transitional *moment*. It is necessary and responsible for all life itself. The quality of relating absolutely to the Absolute within our dialogical movement of faith is a contingency within faith experiences equal to all. Yet, within the relative, the potential of fullness of life within our faith experiences express varying degrees of faith experiences, suggesting that our growth of expanding forms of life and cognitive capacities produce greater fullness of life and expressions of faith. Therefore, the dynamic of *analogia spiritus* within awareness and the extent to which we *fully* venture ourselves is a matter of personal possibility that we universally share.[20] For Kierkegaard, according to Timothy Jackson, this universal access, equal responsibility, and human freedom are available to every person in every *moment* remaining unaffected by contextualization.[21] As such, any primitive venture into faith may have been as complete as any today.

---

20. Philosopher Michael Gelven believes that worship and gratitude are a universal condition of human existence that is "grounded on a spectacular acknowledgement, a surrender to a truth far greater in its meaning than all possible doubt" (*Spirit and Existence*, 79).

21. "A number of themes characterize Arminianism, . . . three related ones are central to Kierkegaard's corpus: (1) a commitment to *universal access* to the highest things, over against belief in double predestination of Christ's limited atonement for the elect; (2) a commitment to *equal responsibility* before the highest things, over against strong versions of sacerdotalism or spiritual collaboration; and (3) a commitment to *human freedom*, against fatalistic doctrines of irresistible grace or an overly rationalized account of moral and religious commitment" (Jackson, "Armenian Edification," 238).

This relational disposition establishes *how* we enter and become aware of the call to relationship. Once we engage, we enter the *process* of awareness and *analogia spiritus*. From out of this active process of awareness, our personal closure takes place in which we conceptually constitute according to our developed personal and cultural contingencies, the *what* of relationship. The cultural relativities, which conceptually shape the relationship, reflect a fusion of complex forms of life that optimally evolve into ever more satisfying forms of life. Today, these forms of life are far more conceptually articulate and experientially expansive than those of, for example, Abraham's day. Abraham tacitly and analogically experiences the same holistic fullness of God's action and self-disclosure toward him, however, continuing relational development allows more developed cultures to express and experience this same faith-producing relationship with God at more articulated and intimate levels of perichoretic interaction. In this respect, our consciousness of the world and God continues to transform in clarity and intimacy from one degree to another. Within the ongoing evolution of relational development, greater conceptual articulation differentiates us from our embeddedness within the world, which enables greater interpenetration within our relationships.[22] This interdependently expands our social context, increasing the breadth of our cognitive experience, creating a greater capacity for intimacy and fullness of life. Within this increasing context, the dynamic of *perichoresis* creates greater integration while preserving the integrity of the other's distinctiveness.

The degree of personal wholeness or presence within our prereflexive awareness corresponds to our openness to the Other. As Moltmann tells us: "We are in God and God is in us whenever we are wholly there, undividedly present."[23] The degree to which we wholly enter the relationship is the degree of its sanctifying process within us and our relationships. This *how* of relationship, Luther's primary concern, transcends the relativities of culture; again, for Luther, this aspect of relational dynamics within faith presents the distinctiveness of the believer and the church, in contrast to culture. It is indeed transformative but in an intra-paradigmatic manner. Like the Blues (in music), It brings depth of experience (holistically) and sanctifies our relations within its cultural structures.

---

22. Again, Kegan reminds us: "Each new evolutionary truce further differentiates the self from its embeddedness in the world, guaranteeing, in a qualitatively new way, the world's distinct integrity, and thereby creating a more integrated relationship to the world. Each new truce accomplishes this by the evolution of a reduced subject and a greater object for the subject to take, an evolution of lesser subjectivity and greater objectivity, an evolution that is more 'truthful'" (*Evolving Self*, 294).

23. Moltmann, *SL*, 211.

The cultural relativities, however, in which we constitute within the reflexive mode of conceptualization, constantly evolve. These progressively transform through ongoing relational activity in open relation to the compelling analogical forces of perichoretic relations immanently transcendent within our relations. The Word, Christ, the transformer of culture, mediates this transformative dynamic constituting persons-in-relations from within the mutuality of the relationship. This Christomorphic dynamic creates mutual forms of meaning for those within the relationship—establishing the *what* of relationships. This dynamic action of Christ's progressive reintegration of the existing cultural structures within the transforming influence of the Spirit was, for Calvin, the distinction between the church and culture, much like Jazz is within music (the play of differentiation).

A perichoretic ontology reveals the possibility that Luther and Calvin each emphasized different polar aspects of perichoretic dynamics that were useful within their respective social paradigm and context. Perichoretic relationality, however, incorporates both these dynamics within one irreducible dialogical dynamic. Furthermore, depending on how we define the church, it is challenging to definitively separate and attribute relational sanctification to either the church or cultural relational evolution. Nevertheless, because all relations are to some degree perichoretic (ontologically interpenetrating and mutually co-conditioning), the redemptive activity of Christ in the church has a sanctifying effect upon all society (1 Cor 7:12–15). If we strictly apply the relational concept of *perichoresis*, *both* the church and culture have positive, negative, and progressive impacts on each other. The church holistically draws culture to greater fullness of life through its own process of sanctification attained by its "transcendent" and personal relationship to Christ and the Holy Spirit (priesthood/older brother), while culture, in greater freedom "immanently" and indiscriminately stumbling toward greater fullness of life through desire alone, in its successes (relational and cultural evolution) holistically calls the church out of its oft reticence and complacency into further development and growth through the emergence of love, beauty, and truth (prophetically/prodigal).

Evolving relational structures in culture and our deepening understanding and practice of love within the church constantly emerge from its Edenic innocence and shortened desires (sin). Sin, in this case, is the reluctance to move out of innocence when evolving relational contexts expose such possibilities. In this respect, new transformed forms of life emerge *ex nihilo*. Most forms of redeemed life are *not* the recovery of former ethical ideals or established morals but rather the emergence of new relational and social dynamics never before experienced in history. Both social and ecclesial structures slowly evolve, degree by degree, respectively. Though we may tacitly experience the fullness of faith and power of Christ's movements within the church, it always occurs within our relational dynamics and enculturation, even though faith transcends (Luther) and transforms (Calvin) these structures. Therefore, though Abraham may have experienced the same openness and willing response to God within his own faith action, he could not relationally experience the fullness of life that accompanies the *optimal* interaction of faith today, dynamics that reflect within the quality of all his relationships. For example, it has only been in recent history that we have begun to evolve from patriarchal forms of marriage into more perichoretic or unitive marriage relations. Though it was possible for Abraham to experience an equivalent fullness of experience in his passion and love for Sarah, it is not possible to attain the intimacy and fullness of life possible within today's marriages because of his existing enculturation. To claim otherwise would be anachronistic historicity. It is merely a stage of innocence within the developmental progression that becomes ethically culpable in our insensitivity or lack of openness to the transforming *analogia spiritus* when the appropriate social environment holistically announces the possibility for more. The complementary relational development of both church and culture fuels these possibilities.

The process of relational sanctification and relational evolution stimulate each other's progress—both our lives with God and our enculturated social lives. Each aspect of the dialogical bipolarity forms a dialogical complementarity, reflecting both the "immanence" and "transcendence" through which Christ's (and the Spirit's) redemptive work transpires. Our personal relationship with God and the church becomes fuller as the understanding and experience of our natural and social relationships develop. Jesus acknowledges this complementarity when he prays, "Help them to relate as we relate *in order that* they might relate with us" (my translation). The emergence and implementation of each transformation into Christ-likeness occurs co-conditionally in both relations, human-human, human-divine (emerging together, no horse, no cart). Amazingly, the free and adventurous explorations of culture motivate greater ecclesial sanctity. Ideally, the call to genuine relationship through the constant re-contextualizing call and love of Christ within our relations should be enough to produce the freedom and release from existing structures to facilitate increasing perichoretic relations within the church that drive development, but it is not. The church constantly struggles with its ecclesial and institutional intransigence toward change and transformation within relations, its priestly function. Therefore, the natural and social relations within our cultural institutions, which experience greater freedom from the impositions of existing "revealed" religious and accepted moral structures, are more sensitive to the "immanent" desire for and existing lack of greater perichoretic relations (and fullness of life) than what the church experiences. Though the unquenchable longings and desire for more within these non-ecclesial relations almost always result in perversion, their unfettered insistence that there is "more" ultimately becomes the prophetic and deconstructive eye that exposes the church's unwillingness to develop from degree to degree out of its Edenic relational innocence and patterning. When avoidance and dissociation result in avoidance of such sanctifying forces of development within human social dynamics, the innocence of the church becomes her sin.[24] The natural forces within culture should perichoretically stimulate the church into its ongoing Jacob-like wrestling with God for the fulfillment and transformation of all relations on earth as it is in heaven.

Together this dynamic complementarity becomes the process through which the limited capacity of divine and human laws fade away into the infinite capacity of love (*perichoresis*) in our hearts, capable in all situations. Perfect interactive order and full perichoretic relations cannot genuinely emerge without emerging in radical freedom from ongoing fluctuations and chaos. The roles of the church and culture are not entirely separate. If either fails to remain open to the process of sanctification and relational development, it will fall into obsolescence lagging behind the abundance of the Spirit within the world. In other words, if the church in fear retracts into its oft-posturing sectarianism, culture will attempt its own restructuring (e.g., the emergence of psychoanalysis). God will not be mocked or held captive within an ecclesial prison. God will holistically employ the increasing fullness of life against the other's closedness. The same dynamics are active within our relationships with each other. If the existing church fails to maintain its ongoing sanctifying and transformative relations with God

---

24. When Robert Waller's heroine in *The Bridges of Madison County* says at her death that the four days of her adulterous relations amid her otherwise morally and socially acceptable marriage were the four days in which she was most fully alive, he levels a biting critique of the church. This is not to legitimize adultery, but neither can we dismiss the totality of this woman's experiences as entirely demonic. The cry of the human heart longs for an intimacy our present relational structuring cannot provide, even within the church. It is the church's business to affirm all that is good, wherever we find it, and correspondingly help others and ourselves to wholeness, exposing the faulty relational structures *within each specific relational context*, both in the church and culture. It is to relate what Christ means and gives to each situation. The church's appropriate response should be to transform Wallace's two categorical choices within the story, (1) leaving the husband or (2) remaining with her dissatisfying (incomplete) relationship, by adding the choice of (3) remaining within the marriage and risk losing it by initiating the conflictual environment necessary for transforming it into the greater fullness of life for which she longs. In this respect, she fails to trust in the grace and Power that transforms.

and culture, a new one will emerge from the perichoretic relations between what remains within church and culture (reformation).

We cannot segregate the church and culture even in their relation to the Eternal and temporal; their relational structure and dynamics are analogically the same. Therefore, is there a fundamental (universal) human redemptive criterion by which we can distinguish between the human condition for redemptive activity (on whatever level), that transcends the often questionable lone criterion of stated "belief in Christ" (Matt 7:21–23; 12:31–32; 25:31–46)? According to Christ, there is. It is the willingness for open perichoretic relations, *the willingness to venture our whole selves into authentic relations, allowing such relations, when genuine, to affect and transform the whole of our existence (the Cross)*. As McFadyen begins, it should be the church's living relation to Christ that frees it for re-contextualization and transformation within genuine relationship—love. Therefore, to the extent Christ is truly engaged within relations, freedom and openness manifest. Redemptive activity begins with infinite resignation into the *analogia spiritus*. This is why Christ prioritizes submitting our whole selves into our relations—becoming spirit—over what or who we *think* we know and how well we *think* we know them. "Anyone who speaks a word against the Son of Man, it will be forgiven him; but whoever speaks against [resists] the Holy Spirit, it will not be forgiven him, either in this age or in the age to come" (Matt 12:32). Only by engaging the antecedent *analogia spiritus* in perichoretic relationality can we begin to understand this seemingly undecipherable and paradoxical admonition of Christ.[25] The Spirit and Word are active in one irreducible communicative dynamic. Least we come before the Other with our entire self, becoming human spirit therefore in full relation to the Spirit of God (*analogia spiritus*) antecedent to knowing Christ, we cannot know him in Truth as God.

How we know him is foundational. Without the proper how, the what becomes redundant (Matt 16:13–20). He even places the primary fundamental criterion for salvation upon *how* we believe in him before *what* or who we believe. He is simply prioritizing the necessary antecedent relational disposition that allows us to know him in his divinity. Words, propositions, actions, and relations (i.e., our epistemology), are nothing to the extent they

---

25. Hagner tells us Christ's insistence that "anyone who speaks a word against the Son of Man, it will be forgiven him," is a difficult passage that does not exactly encourage optimism in the exegete (*Matthew*, 347). Furthermore, Davies and Allison say, "Matt 12.32 has no obvious meaning.... We remained stumped" (*Matthew*, 2:348), and Luz. (*Matthew*) finds no explanation satisfactory. At the time of presenting this exegesis to professor Hagner in 1992, no commentary had given a satisfactory meaning to this enigmatic utterance by Jesus that seems contrary to the body of biblical literature inferring otherwise. Professor Hagner affirmed the veracity of this exegete.

do not holistically constitute as whole person (spirit) within the relational occurrence (Jer 29:13). If indeed *analogia spiritus*, the Jacobian night, is the preliminary site upon which all our conceptualizations take shape and acquire authentic meaning—the necessity of wholly and solitarily encountering the Other—then it would logically follow that any resistance to this condition of picking up our cross would distort all relative aspects within the knowing event.

Therefore, if we do not know Christ through the experience (encounter) of the Holy Spirit with our fullness (i.e., in spirit, in authentic relations), then he is not, in truth, known. One would do better "who lives in an idolatrous community pray[ing] with the entire passion of the infinite, although his eyes rest upon the image of an idol . . . [This] one prays in truth to God though he worships an idol."[26] Therefore, neither "acknowledging" Christ nor personal and "sacrificial" activity and "commitment" within the Christian community is redemptively fundamental (Matt 7:21–23); rather, the individual must be willing to receive and engage the truth of Christ (the Other) with their whole being. If the human spirit is open, and to this degree, the Word will appropriately manifest itself accordingly, and we will meaningfully and appropriately identify Christ (directly or indirectly) within any meaning-frame, Christian or not.

The issue of truth is a quality of relationship that depends upon the individual's willingness to remain relationally attuned. This necessitates an openness within the church to wisely engage its culture (often its prophet) and continue to wrestle from its own stages of innocence. Because of his Eternal trinitarian relations, Christ is the same yesterday, today, and tomorrow; however, our understanding and experience of him amid our relativities are not. Christ's perichoretic relation to the world respects the autonomy and dignity of each person and, in grace, provides the space and time to transform within their freedom. Should the church do any less? Moltmann tells us the church should have no

> suspicion or jealousy at the saving efficacies of the Spirit outside the church (p. 65). . . . If it is Christianity's particular vocation . . . to make ready the way for the coming redemption, then no culture must be pushed out and no religion extinguished. On the contrary, all of them can be charismatically absorbed and changed in the power of the Spirit. They will not be ecclesiasticized in the process, nor will they be Christianized either; but they will be given a messianic direction towards the kingdom.[27]

---

26. Kierkegaard, *CUP*, 180.
27. Moltmann, *CPS*, 163.

Moltmann is not discounting the uniqueness of Christ as the way of salvation for humanity or the world. Instead, he is inadvertently interpreting Christ's prioritizing the antecedent encounter of *analogia spiritus* within all relations. This is the rock of Jacob's passion and Peter's recognition. The church needs to acknowledge this prioritization in its theology and praxis while pointing to Jesus Christ, the critical distinction between the church and culture. Nevertheless, only God's relational dynamic of *perichoresis*—love—expressed to us remains changeless in our experience. Only our tacit experience of the Eternal within our hearts is changeless, and this characterizes, backgrounds, and facilitates continuity in our knowledge of God, Christ, and our relationships at all levels.

Christ *and the Spirit* are God's self-disclosure to humanity. But, if we are to relate as Christ relates to the Father, perichoretically, we must deepen our theological understanding of human beings as spirit and the intermodal (*seinsweise*) aspects of the divine-human interaction. The Persons of the godhead come to consciousness in relationship to each other, not after they are first conscious persons and then relate to each other. Consciousness is relationship. In relational dynamic, there is no horse before the cart; personhood and relationship inextricably emerge a differentiated unity. Barth's trinitarian model of the godhead set the stage for a correspondingly more profound complex social expression of personhood in Moltmann and Pannenberg as a new theological paradigm of humans as persons-in-relation began to emerge (in concert with the rest of the humanities); one in which we are beginning to understand human consciousness as emergent only within a social and indeed perichoretic relations. Even the self is a relationship unto itself. We started by revealing within human personhood and society a holistic dynamic, a mode of existence that was truly holistic and prereflexive. Multiple disciplines are now beginning to recognize it as the ground upon which all social and personal forms of life develop, maintain, and acquire meaning. Commensurate with the Scriptures, the *analogia spiritus* is a theological dynamic within dialogical relations upon which all relational discourse, interaction, and movement emerge. It must become the first philosophy of Christian theology—Jacob must return to the preeminence of which the Scriptures so boldly witness.

Both personhood and relational context condition consciousness. The dynamic of *perichoresis*, together with Kierkegaard's understanding of the self, help explain Paul's enigmatic description of the sanctification process in Romans 7.

> For what I am doing, I do not understand. For what I will to do, that I do not practice; but what I hate, that I do. If, then, I

> do what I will not to do, I agree with the law that it is good. But now, it is no longer I who do it, but sin that dwells in me.... For I delight in the law of God according to the *inward man*. But I see another law in my members, warring against the law of my mind, and bringing me into captivity to the law of sin which is in my members. (Rom 7:15–17, 22–23, emphasis added)

Kierkegaard suggests we are a relationship unto ourselves, yet we are a negative relation until the relation becomes a positive third term in relation to the Other. Within the third term is that Power that constitutes us as a relation unto ourselves or another person. When we wholly relate (become spirit), we come into relation with our "inward man," as Paul says. This is the seat of "conscience" (Rom 2:15). On the other hand, when we constitute as person-in-relation, we constitute as spirit in relation to the socialized spirit of the community, with all of its suppressive mechanisms and distorted relational choreographies. These two aspects of relations condition each other and create the struggle. Because perichoretic relations facilitate interpenetration and interanimation within the relationship and maintain the integrity and identity of the person, the relationship reflects the characteristics and enculturation of those with whom we relate. We cannot completely separate ourselves from them and doing so is unnecessary. Paul tells us that if we are genuinely aware and sincerely acknowledge these "fleshly" patterns of social behavior within our relations, we have done what is needful for the process of redemption to continue, despite our immediate undesirous behavior. Our hope lies in the transforming light of Christ. If, when the redemptive process exposes these destructive choreographies, we acknowledge them in humility and sorrow, the relationship itself will transform us over time. "All things that are exposed, are made manifest by the light, and become light" (Eph 5:13, my translation). While we bear the potential to walk eschatologically with Christ in his Time within our enculturation, our enculturation perichoretically interpenetrates our relations and, therefore, transforms from "degree to degree" (2 Cor 3:18). This warrants humility in our relation to culture.

7

Conclusion

Perichoresis All in All

Relational dynamics reflecting *perichoresis* are emerging within every aspect of human experience and many disciplines of thought. Though perichoretic dynamics as developed within this thesis are both exploratory and introductory, such recent attempts by Moltmann, Gunton, and Loder in theology and by Gergen, Shotter, Kegan, and Loder/Kierkegaard in communication theory and developmental theory have only just begun to reveal these dynamics as fundamentally inherent within all reality. Though its potential force and critical explication lie before us, I believe it will continue to emerge until, with shock of recognition, theology once again expands in newness. Bonhoeffer finds

> God ... [is] not at the boundaries but at the center, not in weakness but in strength.... God is the beyond in the midst of our life.... The church stands ... in the center of the village.
>
> The world come of age is more god-less and perhaps just because of that closer to God than the world not yet come of age.[1]

As we have seen, the role of perichoretic dynamics is vital and metaphysically important within theology, as with other discourses. Moreover, they will undoubtedly facilitate further development in all these discourses, most notably theology. If indeed a theory finds merit by the amount of data it explains and the unifying, even transformative, effect it has on formerly

---

1. Bonhoeffer, *Prison Letters*, 366-67, 482.

disparate traditions of thought, then *perichoresis* as the tripartite structure of relations (reality) and its fundamental concept of *analogia spiritus* can provide adequate ontological structuring within postmodernity.

In closing, I list some primary theological and anthropological hypotheses of a perichoretic theology noting *analogia spiritus* as the locus and initiation of divine-human reciprocity. Following this, I summarize some of the theological issues that such an ontology adjusts, corrects, and deepens within the faith.

- Kierkegaard's *infinite qualitative difference* between time and Eternity, the finite and the infinite, must be understood in conjunction with its corollary of the *incarnational imperative of mutuality*, which stipulates that if God is to have a filial relationship with humanity, something of God must become human (Christ) and something of humankind must become divine (relational *theosis*); this then necessitates that persons (God and human) constitute from dual aspects *within* themselves that then relate with the dual aspects of the Other, respectively. Kierkegaard's "absolute relating to the Absolute" theologically postulates the *analogia spiritus*, which remains in cyclical co-conditioning separateness from the christological and human reflexion into time ("the relative relating to the relative").

- All relatedness dynamically constitutes within some degree of perichoretic differentiated unity, which is irreducibly contingent upon the analogical reflection of God's tripartite nature in all relations.

- Human persons *mutually* relate with God, who as person constitutes within a temporalized Eternity in relationship to the Son. To the degree humans wholly relate with the Other (become spirit), they mutually and analogically constitute in eternalized time in relation to the Spirit (the Eternal) and Christ (the Relative) in perichoretic relations. Unwillingness to *wholly relate* and appropriately *maintain differentiation* within relations (sin) compromises the *mutual co-conditioning* and transformative nature of each interaction.

- The fundamental force, longing, and meaning constituting human nature is the *desire* to relate perichoretically.

- The perichoretic relational dynamic of differentiation and unity consists of dialogical cycles in alternation: an analogical "infinite mode" of opening awareness into relationship (the absolute relating to the Absolute—in the Eternal), which co-conditions the reciprocal closure of all participants from out of the third term of the relationship, constituting each person respectively within their finite mode and social context (the relative to the relative—in spacetime). Both polar aspects of each relational cycle irreducibly create an indivisible differentiated unity (a complementarity).

- The active divine-human co-conditioning nexus occurs within the human prereflexive process of awareness, culminating in the *moment* of transition just before reflexive response (gestalt). In dialogical terms, prereflexion is the open cycle of relationship.

- Each stage of human development conditions the previous stage, yet the ultimate meaning emerges from the futurity—the whole—of its Time that humans experience through the quality of their perichoretic relations to that Power that creates all relations. In this respect, future stages bear upon the present in a futurity that transparently transforms each transitioning *moment* between prereflexion and reflexion. The transformational dynamics within the person transforms in analogical relation to that Power that posits it.

- God's relation to humanity in the Holy Spirit and Christ opens up the immanent transcendent possibility in which the holistic prereflexive de-liberation of human beings analogically and *dynamic*ally relate with God's Eternal action through *analogia spiritus*. By drawing the human prereflexive dynamic into perichoretic correlation with God's preeminent activity of creation, God from Eternity establishes humanity in its own free and mutual relationship to a triune God.

- Within a perichoretic ontology, the mediating third term of the relationship facilitates mutual unity and relations while maintaining differentiated personhood. Furthermore, it facilitates the mutual interaction of temporal and eternal modalities between persons, which relativizes our notions of reality, causality, and simultaneity within each event occurrence. This is transparently contingent upon the nature of trinitarian *perichoresis*. This dynamic replaces the ontology of a universal frame of reference in which all things similar mutually relate (*analogia entis*) with *a universal dynamic of relationality* through which all things different mutually and meaningfully relate (*analogia spiritus*).

In conclusion, I summarize a few of the theological implications of these hypotheses.

(1) We might characterize the current issues within *hermeneutics* as the result of opposing emphases on either the immanent or transcendent characterizations in meaning construction. In Classical metaphysics, the primary locus of meaning construction becomes either the reader or the

text, respectively. A perichoretic hermeneutic rejects either emphasis. Either emphasis immediately exposes the dualistic paradigmatic structuring of subject-subject relationality. Perichoretic relationality, subject-relationship-subject, offers an alternative dynamic not possible within Classical metaphysics. In the tripartite dialogical structuring of a unitary dynamic of *perichoresis*, the third term as the relationship itself, *analogia spiritus*, mediates a co-conditioning mutual interaction between the reader and text (the subject and the Other). Meaning is *never* in, nor the sole property of the text or the reader; it lies within the dynamism of the relationship itself and then analogically extends into the temporality and unique meaning-frame of each faithfully engaged constituent, respectively. Indeed, all the sedimentation of former relations that make up the constituent members within the relationship contribute to the resultant meaning. Meaning, however, only exists within the living dynamics of each existential relational occurrence. As each relational purview extends or shifts, the *what* analogically transforms accordingly.

The creating and sustaining activity of the Spirit and Christ (the *how* and the *way*, *truth*, and *life*) make possible all emergent relationships, whether transparently active immanently in time or personally active transcendently in Time. Always a new creation, all meaning arises from the perichoretic world of each unique interaction always in new and transforming possibilities. It never allows any one constituent sole ownership of meaning. All share in a unity of meaning, each from within their personal differentiated meaning-frame. This does not denigrate the rational nature and complexity within our meaning and relations; instead, it cautions and defers our hermeneutical project to a much more complex holistic interaction and yet, in another way of thinking, a simpler function. To the degree we are holistically present and inclusive within our relations (infinite resignation) and *appropriately* differentiate ourselves in distinction to the world, we experience a degree of *fullness of life* within ourselves and between contrasting contextualizations.

On the other hand, reason is alive and well *within* perichoretic relations. However, it becomes a far more complex operation of deduction than historically acknowledged—a complexity that cautions our dogma necessitating grace and openness. Each sociology and language game is correspondingly mediated by a developed, objective, yet living spirit that is instrumental within *analogia spiritus*. Each has their own rational structure as a cosmic manifestation of spirit that play a vital role in meaning construction in the co-conditioning orchestration of the Spirit and the risen Christ within all relations. "I am the way, the truth, and the life. No one comes to the Father [or anyone] except through Me" (John 14:6; cf. Col 1:16–18).

(2) Perichoretic anthropological dynamics speak deeply to our *ethical* dilemmas. If indeed we can correlate the dialogical distinctions of awareness (openness) and conceptual constitution (closure) respective to Kierkegaard's modal distinctions of human existence as eternal and temporal, then we must continue to shift the focus of our ethical deliberations from the *what* to the systemic *how* of beliefs and relations. Moral culpability now shifts to include the disposition of openness to the Other *and* the closure and integrity of the self in differentiation. This includes an individual's or society's *willingness* to openly engage genuine transformative relations *(holistic presence) and* their appropriate closure of self in differentiation (action). The *what* of belief and social action—its accuracy and rightness— meaningfully emerges with respect to *how*.

(3) A relational ontology of *perichoresis* obviates the former metaphysical emphasis and language of *either* substance in diverse relations or the contrasting emphasis of relations creating relative substances. Instead, it presents an irreducible dynamic *complementarity of substance-in-relations* as ontologically reflective of its perichoretic and sustaining relations with the Trinity.[2] This ultimately assuages the postmodern critique of repetition, alterity, and reason, though it re-configures our current understanding of how reason, unity, and continuity function. Theologies insisting upon the priority of either of these distinctions, substance or relations, within subject-subject relations and Newtonian spacetime heuristics continue the current scriptural incoherence and imprison the greater meaning of the Scriptures and the Christian faith. Outside of perichoretic theology, Jacob's preeminence and the co-conditioning, freedom, and self-determination of humanity is compromised. For Kierkegaard, faith is our filial experiencing of God, not the doctrines we affirm, our moral discipline ("love"), or correct theology. As Kierkegaard points out in *Training in Christianity*, faith is living in expectation of miracle, experiencing the contemporaneousness of Christ, and knowing God as God—our absolute relating to the Absolute. When we step into the fullness of any relationship with our fullness (becoming spirit), the miracles of life, passion, and transformation occur.

This thesis presents a modified emergentist view in which all things constantly become new each moment in analogical perichoretic continuity with the past and future. For Kierkegaard, becoming spirit obviates the repetition of the past and the determinism of socially patterned responses by thrusting us existentially into *new* and unique relations as we transformatively move altogether separately in mutually meaningful relations. Such a dynamic necessitates a tripartite structure to relationality.

2. Cf. Gunton, *One, Three, Many*, 188–209.

This brings a new and fuller meaning to the Judeo-Christian notion of *creatio ex nihilo*, which resists the deistic and Newtonian container understanding of creation. The idea that God creates substance (being) only at the beginning of creation history, then action and relations transpire within it (form) is an imposition of Classical Greek derivatives upon the text, which diminishes the meaning and power of Christ's and the Spirit's actions to which it stands witness. By interjecting Eternity into the ever-present existential *moment*, Kierkegaard portends the coming incontrovertible discoveries of Einsteinian and quantum dynamics, the bending of time, and the emerging order out of chaos within thermodynamic theory that point to a new irreducible dynamic of reality in which time and eternity are two differing yet "related aspects of reality."[3] This seismic metaphysical shift opens new and radical notions of freedom for humanity because of *the nature of God's relation to us*, contrary to the truncated assumptions of Sartre and modern anthropology.[4] This irreversibly transfigures the theological landscape. The *perichoresis* of time and Eternity begins not only to suggest a direction for further paradigmatic re-structuring but provides the conceptual space for *creatio ex nihilo* and *creatio continua* within every *moment*.

(4) The *perichoresis* of time and Eternity within anthropological considerations begins to open the theological space for deepening our *understanding of faith and prophecy*, correcting the theological abuses of modern scientific agendas (materialism) with the advent of postmodern science (relativity and quantum physics). Every chapter within this study leads to and ultimately depends upon some aspect of the *perichoresis* of time and Eternity within personhood as social interaction for creating the dynamics necessary for human freedom, self-determination, and co-conditioning relations with an Eternal God of providence (Trinity). If indeed, actual mutual co-conditioning relations exist of a personal nature between God and humanity, such a dynamic must be active within human relations as well as the Trinity. If we view as absurd the technical possibility of a prereflexive holistic interaction analogically and dynamically drawing into dynamic relations with the Eternal activity of the Trinity, then we must likewise be willing to view as absurd the current developments of physics and thermodynamic theory. The biblical notion of faith and prophecy as an analogical proleptic *ontological, not psychological* conditioning of the future upon the present (Heb 11:1), together with the freedom of humanity in authentic personal relations with God, necessitates a co-conditioning dynamic like *analogia spiritus*. In this respect, perichoretic theology emerges in stark

---

3. Prigogine and Stengers, *Order Out of Chaos*, 310.
4. Badcock, *Light*, 259–60.

contrast to Hegel's concept of Absolute Spirit, immanental, panentheistic, and process theologies yet appropriately attains their goals and potentially well-intentioned corrections to Classical Christianity. These theologies, however, significantly diminish the personal nature of God and the ontological nature of prophecy, prayer, and faith as otherwise clearly expressed in the Scriptures.

(5) When Christ prayed that "they may all be one; even as Thou, Father, art in Me, and I in Thee, that they also may be in Us" (John 17:21), this became the ontological and dynamic reality within every *moment* of creation—*analogia spiritus*. The answer to this prayer was the proleptic transtemporal decree, "Let Us make man in Our image" (Gen 1:26). When we can begin to conceive of how Christ's petition was ontologically and relationally (causally) antecedent to the Father's decree (response) in Genesis, or possibly the *same* utterance uniquely manifesting within both times (i.e., simultaneous moments in history), then we can begin to understand the perichoretic bending of time through Eternity that occurs in Christ and the Spirit. This relativization of simultaneity creates the unique relational dynamic of co-conditioning rather than imposing unilinear causation upon every aspect of relational dynamics. With this decree, humanity's fundamental and constitutive nature and the call to personhood and fullness of life became the desire to relate perichoretically—love. Herein lies the common ground of all humanity. All people not only desire to relate, they desire to relate in a particular way, one that is still emerging and evolving in relation to that Power within our relations, one that leaks through all our attempts to deny its reality within us. It is always immanently transcendent within our relations, as evident in our constant disgust and disappointment in failing to attain. When the call of *analogia spiritus* invisibly announces *more*, a *way* beyond, only then can we realistically pick up the cross, enter the void, where new life emerges out of chaos, and meaning out of meaningless.

Because of God's love of and relation to all persons, we are perichoretically and, therefore, immanently *and* teleologically (transcendently) drawn toward ever greater expressions of love—*perichoresis*. Regardless of what we feel or believe, it is inescapable; we can only suppress and misshape the ghost of this primal desire that haunts our relations, but we cannot kill it. Such an infinite longing is longsuffering against all our efforts to bury the freedom and void through which we must pass into ongoing transformations. We retreat into predetermined patterns of "safety" and control rather than risk acknowledging the darkness and crucifixion that opens to transformation. Nevertheless, the freedom to assume a safe and controlled closed (guarded) disposition for all eternity is necessary to create a being capable of knowing God as God. Moltmann insists that the passage "You shall not make for yourself an image or any likeness," applies to images of God, our relational interactions, and our understanding of love. "Love fulfils the commandment, because it does not tie anything down to what was once reality, in the past. It throws open the new free spaces of the future."[5] This infinite longing, which only finds its ultimate rest in relationship to God, is often sold into bondage as we purchase the socially patterned idols that offer us control—persons, things, and choreographies less than perichoretic. And though our understanding of full perichoretic relationality will always lie beyond full articulation, we must acknowledge the emerging social, psychological, and scientific knowledge that increasingly reveals the shape of such a dynamic. These growing insights emerge from the complementarity that is human person (temporal and eternal) and human society (church and culture), with whom God relates through all things, general or special. The ongoing dialogical fluctuations and conflicts of active social engagement (Matt 10:34–39) will continue to expose and transform our faulty relational structures and metaphysics, gradually revealing what is more true or adequate, what is the perichoretic pattern of relationship, what is love. When faulty relational structures and choreographies are appropriately exposed, we are convicted simply because of this fundamental longing that facilitates such conviction within us, constantly drawing us toward greater fullness of life.

Though this study of a perichoretic ontology has fallen into the incapable hands of a dyslexic theologian and, therefore, difficult to access through the density and weblike treks of a nonlinear thinker, I hope the reader has encountered enough evidence to acknowledge the potential and power of perichoretic theology. Because of the relative obscurity of these concepts within current theological discourse, they are concepts the reader may greet with great skepticism. These ideas, however, are not entirely new. Their fecundity has been slowly emerging for almost two centuries. Since my encounter with God alone in a room that night as an atheist physics major during my undergraduate days, I have struggled to find a satisfying theology that appropriately reflects what happen to me in that night. After a lifetime of study, what lies within this book is what I found. The church may be ready to enter its most challenging time in history, as the social engineering of a rising technocracy intensifies. At the same time Bonhoeffer's humanity "come of age" has raised the bar as antiquated theologies struggle to keep abreast of Christ and the Spirit in the world, culture, and church. I end this exploration with its beginning:

> The transformation into the divine image will become ever more profound, and the image of Christ in us will continue to

5. Moltmann, *SL*, 263.

increase in clarity. This is a progression in us from one level of understanding to another and from one degree of clarity to another, toward an ever-increasing perfection in the form of likeness to the image of the Son of God.... And all of us, who with unveiled faces let the glory of the Lord be reflect in us, are thereby transformed into his image from glory to glory.[6]

For "the world come of age is more god-less and perhaps just because of that closer to God than the world not yet come of age."[7] Just as Marion returns us to the de-naming of Gxd, Bonhoeffer, likewise, would have us reconsider human persons without being: "*The person ever and again arises and passes away in time. The person does not exist timelessly; a person is not static, but dynamic.* . . . The person is re-created again and again in the perpetual flux of life. Subjective spirit becomes eternally significant only in relation to the absolute spirit"[8]—the *analogia spiritus*.

Faith has come into the world, and Time bends to hold all that we are in a *moment*. Our alpha and omega rush in with a fullness not our own. Christ is closer to us now than ever, invading our mind, body, and spirit with ever-increasing intimacy. Christ and the Spirit appear in the world all around us, for "God . . . [is] not at the boundaries but at the center, not in weakness but in strength; . . . God is the beyond in the midst of our life. . . . The church stands . . . in the center of the village."[9]

---

6. Bonhoeffer, *Discipleship*, 286.
7. Bonhoeffer, *Prison Letters*, 482.
8. Bonhoeffer, *Sanctorum Communio*, 48.
9. Bonhoeffer, *Prison Letters*, 366–67.

Bibliography

Agamben, Giorgio. *The Church and the Kingdom*. Translated by Leland de la Durantaye. London: Seagull, 2010.
Allen, Diogenes. *Christian Belief in a Postmodern World: The Full Wealth of Conviction*. Louisville: Westminster, 1989.
Allen, George. "The Aims of Societies and the Aims of God." In *Process Philosophy and Christian Thought*, edited by Delwin Brown et al. New York: Bobbs-Merrill, 1971.
Alston, William P. "Divine Action, Human Freedom, and the Laws of Nature." In *Quantum Cosmology and the Laws of Nature: Scientific Perspectives on Divine Action*, edited by Robert John Russell et al., 185–206. Vatican City: Vatican Observatory, 1993.
———. "Emotion and Feeling." In *The Encyclopedia of Philosophy*, edited by Paul Edwards, 2:479–86. New York: Macmillan, 1967.
———. "Emotive Meaning." In *The Encyclopedia of Philosophy*, edited by Paul Edwards, 2:486–93. New York: Macmillan, 1967.
Anderson, Ray S. *The Gospel according to Judas*. Colorado Springs, CO: Helmers, 1991.
———. *Self Care*. Wheaton, IL: BridgePoint, 1995.
Aristotle. *Politics*. Translated by H. Rackham. Cambridge: Harvard University Press, 1932.
Aspect, Alain. "Bell's Inequality Test: More Ideal Than Ever." *Nature* 398 (1999) 189–90.
Augustine. *The Confessions of St. Augustine*. Translated by Rex Warner. New York: Mentor, 1963.
Aves, John. "Persons in Relation: John Macmurray." In *Person, Divine, and Human: King's College Essays in Theological Anthropology*, edited by Christoph Schwobel and Colin E. Gunton, 120–37. Edinburgh: T. & T. Clark, 1992.
Badcock, Gary D. *Light of Truth and Fire of Love: A Theology of the Holy Spirit*. Grand Rapids: Eerdmans, 1997.
Bakhtin, M. M. *The Dialogic Imagination*. Edited by Michael Holquist. Translated by Caryl Emerson and Michael Holquist. Austin: University of Texas Press, 1981.
———. *Problems of Dostoevsky's Poetics*. Edited and translated by C. Emerson. Minneapolis: University of Minnesota Press, 1984.
———. *Speech Genres and Other Late Essays*. Edited by Caryl Emerson and Michael Holquist. Translated by Vern W. McGee. Austin: University of Texas Press, 1986.

———. *Toward a Philosophy of the Act*. Edited by Michael Holquist. Translated by Vadim Kiapunov. Austin: University of Texas Press, 1993.
Banich, M. T. "Interaction between the Hemispheres and Its Implications for the Processing Capacity of the Brain." In *The Asymmetrical Brain*, edited by K. Hugdahl et al., 261–302. Cambridge: MIT Press, 2003.
Barbour, Ian G. *Religion in an Age of Science*. San Francisco: Harper, 1990.
Barth, Karl. *Church Dogmatics*. Edited and translated by T. F. Torrance and G. W. Bromiley. Edinburgh: T. & T. Clark, 1936–69.
———. "Concluding Unscientific Postscript on Schleiermacher." In *The Theology of Schleiermacher*, edited by Dietrich Ritschl, translated by Geoffrey W. Bromiley, 261–79. Grand Rapids: Eerdmans, 1982.
———. *The Humanity of God*. Translated by J. N. Thomas et al. Atlanta: John Knox, 1974.
———. *Protestant Theology in the Nineteenth Century*. Translated by B. Cozens et al. London: SCM, 1972.
Bettenson, Henry, ed. and trans. *The Later Christian Fathers: A Selection from the Writings of the Fathers from St. Cyril of Jerusalem to St. Leo the Great*. Oxford: Oxford University Press, 1970.
Berkhof, Hendrikus. *The Doctrine of the Holy Spirit*. Atlanta: John Knox, 1982.
———. *Two Hundred Years of Theology: Report of a Personal Journey*. Translated by John Vriend. Grand Rapids: Eerdmans, 1989.
Billig, Michael. *Arguing and Thinking: A Rhetorical Approach to Social Psychology*. 2nd ed. European Monographs in Social Psychology. Cambridge: Cambridge University Press, 1996.
Bloesch, Donald B. *Theology of Word and Spirit*. Downers Grove, IL: InterVarsity, 1992.
Bonhoeffer, Dietrich. *Discipleship*. Edited by Martin Kuske et al. Translated by Barbara Green et al. Dietrich Bonhoeffer Works 4. Minneapolis: Fortress, 2003.
———. *Letters and Papers from Prison*. Edited by Wayne Whitson Floyd Jr. et al. Translated by I. Best et al. Dietrich Bonhoeffer Works 8. Minneapolis: Fortress, 2009.
———. *Sanctorum Communio: A Theological Study of the Sociology of the Church*. Edited by Wayne Whitson Floyd Jr. et al. Translated by Reinhard Krauss and Nancy Lukens. Dietrich Bonhoeffer Works 1. Minneapolis: Fortress, 1998.
Bouillard, Henri. *Knowledge of God*. Translated by S. D. Femiano. London: Burns & Oates, 1968.
Bracken, Joseph. *The Triune Symbol: Persons, Process, and Community*. Lanham, MD: University of America Press, 1985.
Braine, David. *The Human Person: Animal and Spirit*. Notre Dame: Notre Dame University Press, 1992.
Bretall, Robert, ed. *Kierkegaard Anthology*. Princeton: Princeton University Press, 1946.
Bringuer, Jean-Claude. *Conversations with Piaget*. Chicago: University of Chicago Press, 1980.
Browning, Don S. "Psychological and Ontological Perspectives on Faith and Reason." In *Process Philosophy and Christian Thought*, edited by Delwin Brown et al., 296–308. New York: Bobbs-Merrill, 1971.
Bruner, Jerome. *Acts of Meaning*. Cambridge: Harvard University Press, 1990.
———. *Studies in Cognitive Growth*. New York: Wiley and Sons, 1966.
Bultmann, Rudolf. *Theology of the New Testament*. Translated by Kendrick Grobel. New York: Scribner, 1970.

Calvin, John. *Institutes of the Christian Religion.* Translated by Henry Beveridge. Peabody, MA: Hendrickson, 2007.

Capra, Fritjof. *The Tao of Physics.* New York: Bantam, 1977.

Caputo, John D. *Against Ethics.* Bloomington: Indiana University Press, 1993.

Carroll, Sean. "Even Physicists Don't Understand Quantum Mechanics." *New York Times*, September 7, 2019.

Clayton, Philip. *Explanation from Physics to Theology: An Essay in Rationality and Religion.* New Haven: Yale University Press, 1989.

Cobb, John, Jr. "Christian Natural Theology." In *Process Philosophy and Christian Thought*, edited by Delwin Brown et al., 99–110. New York: Bobbs-Merrill, 1971.

———. "Natural Causality and Divine Action." In *God's Activity in the World: The Contemporary Problem*, edited by Owen C. Thomas, 101–16. Chico, CA.: Scholars, 1983.

———. "A Whiteheadian Christology." In *Process Philosophy and Christian Thought*, edited by Delwin Brown et al., 382–98. New York: Bobbs-Merrill, 1971.

Cobb, John, B., and David R. Griffin. *Process Theology.* Philadelphia: Westminster, 1976.

Colledge, Richard. "Between Ultra-Essentialism and Post-Essentialism: Kierkegaard as Transitional and Contemporary." *Contretemps* 3 (2002) 54–65.

Copleston, Frederick. *The History of Philosophy.* 9 vols. London: Image, 1993.

Craig, William Lane. "God and Real Time." *Religious Studies* 26 (1991) 335–47.

Cunningham, Mary K. *What Is Theological Exegesis? Interpretation and Use of Scripture in Barth's Doctrine of Election.* Valley Forge, PA: Trinity Press International, 1995.

Dabney, D. Lyle. "Otherwise Engaged in the Spirit: A First Theology for a Twenty-First Century." In *The Future of Theology*, edited by Miroslav Volf et al., 154–63. Grand Rapids: Eerdmans, 1996.

Damasio, Antonio. *Descartes' Error: Emotion, Reason, and the Human Brain.* New York: Penguin, 1994.

Davies, W. D., and Dale C. Allison. *A Critical and Exegetical Commentary on the Gospel according to Saint Matthew.* Vol. 2. Edinburgh: T. & T. Clark, 1991.

Dawkins, Richard. *The Selfish Gene.* Oxford: Oxford University Press, 1989.

Derrida, Jacques. *Margins of Philosophy.* Translated by Alan Bass. Chicago: University of Chicago Press, 1982.

De Sousa, Ronald. *The Rationality of Emotion.* Cambridge: MIT Press, 1991.

Desmet, Mattias. *The Psychology of Totalitarianism.* White River Junction, VT: Chelsea Green, 2022.

Deuser, Hermann. "Religious Dialectics and Christology." In *The Cambridge Companion to Kierkegaard*, edited by Alastair Hannay and Gordon D. Marino, 376–96. Cambridge: Cambridge University Press, 1998.

Devinsky, Orrin, and Rachel Laff. "Callosal Lesions and Behavior: History and Modern Concepts." *Epilepsy Behavior* 4 (2004) 607–17.

Drees, Willem B. "A Case against Temporal Critical Realism? Consequences of Quantum Cosmology for Theology." In *Quantum Cosmology and the Laws of Nature: Scientific Perspectives on Divine Action*, edited by Robert John Russell and Nancey Murphy, 331–65. Vatican City: Vatican Observatory, 1993.

Eco, Umberto. *The Name of the Rose.* Translated by William Weaver. London: Mandarin, 1983.

Eddington, A. S. *The Nature of the Physical World.* New York: Macmillan, 1948.

Einstein, Albert. "On the Electrodynamics of Moving Bodies." *Annalen der Physik* 17 (1905) 891–921.
Einstein, Albert, et al. *The Principle of Relativity*. Translated by W. Perrett and G. B. Jeffery. New York: Dover, 1952.
Evans, C. Stephen. "Kierkegaard's View of the Unconscious." In *Kierkegaard in Post/Modernity*, edited by Martin J. Matuštík and Merold Westphal, 76–97. Indianapolis: Indiana University Press, 1995.
Fann, K. T., ed. *Ludwig Wittgenstein: The Man and His Philosophy*. New York, Dell, 1967.
Fenton, John Young. "The Post-Liberal Theology of Christ without Myth." *Journal of Religion* 43 (1963) 93–104.
Ferreira, M. Jamie. "Faith and the Kierkegaardian Leap." In *The Cambridge Companion to Kierkegaard*, edited by Alastair Hannay and Gordon D. Marino, 207–34. Cambridge: Cambridge University Press, 1998.
Feyerabend, Paul. *Against Method*. London: New Left, 1975.
———. "Consolations for the Specialist." In *Criticism and the Growth of Knowledge*, edited by I. Lakatos et al., 197–203. Cambridge: Cambridge University Press, 1970.
Flew, Antony. *A Dictionary of Philosophy*. 2nd ed. New York: St. Martin's, 1984.
Fraisse, Paul, and Jean Piaget, eds. *Experimental Psychology: Its Scope and Method*. New York: Basic, 1968.
Furth, Hans G. *Piaget and Knowledge*. 2nd ed. Chicago: University of Chicago Press, 1981.
Gadamer, H. G. *Truth and Method*. Translated by G. Barden et al. 2nd ed. New York: Seabury, 1975.
Gangadean, Ashok. "Universal Grammar, Natural Reason, and Religious Discourse." Thirteenth Annual Philosophy of Religion Conference, Claremont Graduate School, April 3, 1992.
Gelven, Michael. *Spirit and Existence*. London: Collins, 1990.
Gendlin, Eugene, T. *Experiencing and the Creation of Meaning: A Philosophical and Psychological Approach to the Subjective*. New York: Free, 1962.
Gergen, Kenneth, J. *Realities and Relationships: Soundings in Social Construction*. Cambridge: Harvard University Press, 1994.
———. "Social Theory in Context: Relational Humanism." Unpublished manuscript, 1997.
———. "Technology and the Self: From the Essential to the Sublime." In *Constructing the Self in a Mediated World*, edited by Debra Grodin, 127–40. London: Sage, 1996.
———. "When Relationships Generate Realities." Unpublished manuscript, 1998. https://systemika.g-i.cz/record/2102/files/Gergen.pdf.
Glare, P. G. W. *Oxford Latin Dictionary*. Oxford: Clarendon, 1976.
Gorsuch, Gregory S. "*Perichoresis* and Projection: A Response to Kilby's Trinitarian Minimalism." *Perichoresis Theological Journal* 21 (2023) 21–39.
———. "*Perichoresis* as a Hermeneutical Key to Ontology: Social Constructionism, Kierkegaard, and Trinitarian Theology." *Perichoresis Theological Journal* 20 (2022) 51–101.
Griffin, David R. *A Process Christology*. Philadelphia: Westminster, 1973.
———. "Relativism, Divine Causation, and Biblical Theology." In *God's Activity in the World: The Contemporary Problem*, edited by Owen C. Thomas, 117–36. Chico, CA: Scholars, 1983.

———. "Schubert Ogden's Christology and the Possibilities of Process Philosophy." In *Process Philosophy and Christian Thought*, edited by Delwin Brown et al., 290–303. New York: Bobbs-Merrill, 1971.
Gunton, Colin E. *Becoming and Being: The Doctrine of God in Charles Hartshorne and Karl Barth*. Oxford: Oxford University Press, 1978.
———. *Enlightenment and Alienation*. Grand Rapids: Eerdmans, 1985.
———. *The One, the Three, and the Many*. Cambridge: Cambridge University Press, 1993.
———. *The Promise of Trinitarian Theology*. Edinburgh: T. & T. Clark, 1991.
———. "Trinity, Ontology, and Anthropology: Towards a Renewal of the Doctrine of the Imago Dei." In *Persons, Divine, and Human*, edited by C. Schwöbel et al., 47–64. Edinburgh: T. & T. Clark, 1991.
———. *The Triune Creator: A Historical and Systematic Study*. Edinburgh Studies in Constructive Theology. Edinburgh: Edinburgh University Press, 1998.
Hagner, Donald A. *Matthew 1–13*. WBC 33a. Dallas: Word, 1993.
Hall, Ronald L. *Word and Spirit: A Kierkegaardian Critique of the Modern Age*. Indianapolis: Indiana University Press, 1993.
Hands, John. *Cosmosapiens*. New York: Overlook, 2016.
Happel, Stephen. "Metaphors and Time Asymmetry: Cosmologies in Physics and Christian Meaning." In *Quantum Cosmology and the Laws of Nature: Scientific Perspectives on Divine Action*, edited by Robert John Russell et al., 105–35. Vatican City: Vatican Observatory, 1993.
Hart, Ray I. *Unfinished Man and the Imagination*. New York: Herder and Herder, 1968.
Hefner, Philip. "God and Chaos: The Demiurge versus the *Ungrund*." Zygon 19 (1984) 469–85.
———. *The Human Factor*. Minneapolis: Fortress, 1993.
———. "Sociobiology and Ethics." In *Religion, Science, and Public Policy*, edited by F. Birtel, 115–37. New York: Crossroad, 1987.
Heidegger, Martin. *Being and Time*. Translated by John Macquarrie et al. New York: Harper, 1962.
———. *Existence and Being*. Translated by W. Brock. Chicago: Regnery, 1967.
Heisenberg, Werner. *Physics and Philosophy*. London: Penguin, 1958.
Henry, Richard Conn, and Stephen R. Palmquist. "An Experimental Test of Non-local Realism." *Journal of Scientific Exploration* 21 (2007) 649–50.
Herbert, Nick. *Quantum Reality*. New York: Anchor, 1985.
Heron, Alastair I. C. *The Holy Spirit*. Philadelphia: Westminster, 1983.
Heschel, Abraham J. *The Prophets*. Vol. 2. New York: Holt, 1992.
Hick, John. *An Interpretation of Religion: Human Responses to the Transcendent*. New Haven: Yale University Press, 1989.
Hodgson, Peter C. *God in History: Shapes of Freedom*. Nashville: Abingdon, 1989.
———. *New Birth of Freedom: A Theology of Bondage and Liberation*. Philadelphia: Fortress, 1976.
———. *Winds of the Spirit: A Constructive Christian Theology*. London: SCM, 1994.
Hofstadter, Douglas R. *Gödel, Escher, Bach: An Eternal Golden Braid*. New York: Vintage, 1980.
Holland, Tom. *Dominion*. New York: Basic, 2019.
Huyssteen, J. Wentzel van. *Essays in Postfoundationalist Theology*. Grand Rapids: Eerdmans, 1997.

BIBLIOGRAPHY

Jackson, Timothy P. "Arminian Edification: Kierkegaard on Grace and Free Will." In *The Cambridge Companion to Kierkegaard*, edited by A. Hannay and Gordon D. Marino, 235–56. Cambridge: Cambridge University Press, 1998.

———. "Kierkegaard's Metatheology." *Faith and Philosophy* 4 (1987) 71–85.

Jaggar, M. Alison. "Love and Knowledge: Emotion in Feminist Epsitemology." In *Gender/Body/Knowledge: Feminist Reconstructions of Being and Knowing*, edited by A. Jaggar and S. Bordo, 145–71. New Brunswick, NJ: Rutgers University Press, 1989.

James, William. *The Varieties of Religious Experience: A Study in Human Nature.* New York: Modern Library, 1902.

Kaiser, Christopher, B. "Christology and Complementarity." *Religious Studies* 12 (1976) 37–48.

———. *The Logic of Complementarity in Science and Theology.* PhD diss., Edinburgh University, 1974.

Kant, Immanuel. *Critique of Pure Reason.* Translated by F. Max Müller. New York: Anchor, 1966.

Kastner, Ruth E. "Is There Really 'Retrocausation' in Time-Symmetric Approaches to Quantum Mechanics?" *AIP Conf. Proc.* 1841 (2017) 1–6. https://doi.org/10.1063/1.4982766.

———. "The Transactional Interpretation and Its Evolution into the 21st Century: An Overview." *Philosophy Compass* 11 (2016) 1–13. https://arxiv.org/abs/1608.00660.

Kegan, Robert. *The Evolving Self: Problem and Process in Human Development.* Cambridge: Harvard University Press, 1982.

Kerr, Fergus. *Theology after Wittgenstein.* Oxford: Basil Blackwell, 1986.

Kierkegaard, Søren. *Christian Discourses.* Translated by Walter Lowrie. Oxford: Oxford University Press, 1940.

———. *The Concept of Dread.* Translated by Walter Lowrie. Princeton: Princeton University Press, 1957.

———. *Concluding Unscientific Postscript.* Translated by David F. Swenson and Walter Lowrie. Princeton: Princeton University Press, 1941, 1968.

———. *Edifying Discourses.* Translated by David F. Swenson. Minneapolis: Augsburg, 1943.

———. *Either/Or.* Translated by David F. et al. 2 vols. Princeton: Princeton University Press, 1944.

———. *Fear and Trembling.* Translated by Walter Lowrie. Princeton: Princeton University Press, 1941.

———. *The Journals of Kierkegaard.* Edited and translated by Alexander Dru. New York: Harper and Row, 1959.

———. *Journals and Papers.* Edited and translated by Howard V. Hong et al. 7 vols. Bloomington: Indiana University Press, 1967–68.

———. *Philosophical Fragments.* Translated by David F. Swenson, revised by Howard V. Hong. Princeton: Princeton University Press, 1962.

———. *Philosophical Fragments.* Translated by Howard V. Hong et al. 7 vols. Princeton: Princeton University Press, 1985–.

———. *Purity of Heart Is to Will One Thing.* Translated by Douglas V. Steere. New York: Harpers, 1956.

———. *Sickness unto Death.* Translated by Walter Lowrie. Princeton: Princeton University Press, 1941.

———. *Training in Christianity*. Translated by Walter Lowrie. Princeton: Princeton University Press, 1960.

———. *Works of Love*. Translated by Howard V. Hong and Edna H. Hong. New York: Harper and Row 1962.

Kim, Yoon-Ho, et al. "A Delayed 'Choice' Quantum Eraser." *Physical Review Letters* 84 (2000) 1–5.

Kuhn, Thomas S. *The Structure of Scientific Revolutions*. 2nd ed. Chicago: Chicago University Press, 1970.

Kulka, Tomas. "Some Problems concerning Rational Reconstruction: Comments on Elkana and Lakatos." *British Journal for Philosophy of Science* 28 (1977) 325–44.

Lakatos, Imre. "Falsification and the Methodology of Scientific Research Programmes." In *Criticism and the Growth of Knowledge*, edited by Imre Lakatos and A. Musgrave, 91–196. Cambridge: Cambridge University Press, 1970.

———. "History of Science and Its Rational Reconstructions." *Boston Studies in the Philosophy of Science* 8 (1971) 91–136.

———. "Why Copernicus's Programme Superseded Ptolemy's." In *The Compernican Achievement*, edited by Robert S. Westman, 354–83. Los Angeles: University of California Press, 1975.

Landmann, Michael. *Philosophische Anthropologie*. Berlin: de Gruyter, 1976.

Laudisa, Federico, and Carlo Rovelli. "Relational Quantum Mechanics." In *The Stanford Encyclopedia of Philosophy*, edited by Edward N. Zalta. https://plato.stanford.edu/archives/win2021/entries/qm-relational/.

Lawrence, Fred, ed. *The Beginning and the Beyond*. Chico, CA: Scholars, 1984.

Leeper, Robert W. "The Motivational and Perceptual Properties of Emotions as Indicating Their Fundamental Character and Role." In *Feelings and Emotions*, edited by Magda B. Arnold, 187–203. London: Academic, 1970.

Leggett, A. J. "Nonlocal Hidden-Variable Theories and Quantum Mechanics: An Incompatibility Theorem." *Foundations of Physics* 33 (2003) 1469–93.

Lévinas, Emmanuel. *Ethics and Infinity*. Translated by Richard A. Cohen. Pittsburg: Duquesne University Press, 1985.

Lindbeck, George A. *The Nature of Doctrine: Religion and Theology in a Postliberal Age*. Philadelphia: Westminster, 1984.

Linnemann, Eta. *Historical Criticism of the Bible, Methodology, or Ideology? Reflections of a Bultmannian Turned Evangelical*. Translated by R. W. Yarbrough. Grand Rapids: Baker, 1990.

Liston, Gregory J. "Third Article Theology." In *The Anointed Church: Toward a Third Article Ecclesiology*, 7–34. Minneapolis: Fortress, 2015.

Loder, James E. *The Logic of the Spirit: Human Development in Theological Perspective*. San Francisco: Jossey-Bass, 1998.

———. "Normativity and Context in Practical Theology." In *Practical Theology: International Perspectives*, edited by Friedrich Schweitzer and Johannes A. van der Ven, 359–81. New York: Lang, 1999.

———. "The Place of Science in Practical Theology: The Human Factor." *International Journal of Practical Theology* 4 (2000) 22–41.

———. *The Transforming Moment: Understanding Convictional Experiences*. London: Harper and Row, 1981.

Loder, James E., and W. Jim Neidhardt. *The Knight's Move: The Relational Logic of the Spirit in Theology and Science*. Colorado Springs, CO: Helmers and Howard, 1992.

Lonergan, Bernard, J. F. *Divinarum Personarum Conceptionem analogicam*. 2nd ed. Rome: Pontifical Gregorian University, 1959.

Lossky, Vladimir. *In the Image and Likeness of God*. Edited by John H. Erickson and Thomas E. Bird. Crestwood, NY: St. Vladimir's Seminary Press, 1974.

Lucas, George, R. *Two Views of Freedom in Process Thought*. Missoula, MT: Scholars, 1979.

Lucas, J. R. *The Future*. Oxford: Basil Blackwell, 1989.

———. "The Temporality of God." In *Quantum Cosmology and the Laws of Nature: Scientific Perspectives on Divine Action*, edited by Robert John Russell et al., 235–46. Vatican City: Vatican Observatory, 1993.

Luz, Ulrich. *Matthew 1–7: A Commentary*. Translated by Wilhelm C. Linss. Hermeneia. Minneapolis: Augsburg, 1989.

Lyons, William. *Emotion*. Cambridge: Cambridge University Press, 1980.

MacDonald, Duncan B. *The Hebrew Philosophical Genius*. Princeton: Princeton University Press, 1936.

MacIntyre, Alasdair. *After Virtue*. Notre Dame: Notre Dame University Press, 1981.

———. "Epistemological Crises, Dramatic Narrative, and the Philosophy of Science." In *Paradigms and Revolutions*, edited by Gary Gutting, 54–74. Notre Dame: Notre Dame University Press, 1980.

———. "The Rationality of Traditions." In *Moral Disagreements: Classic and Contemporary Readings*, edited by Christopher W. Gowans, 204–16. London: Boutledge, 2000.

———. *Three Rival Versions of Moral Enquiry: Encycloaedia, Genealogy, and Tradition*. Notre Dame: Notre Dame University Press, 1989.

Macmurray, John. *The Clue to History*. London: SCM, 1938.

———. *Reason and Emotion*. London: Faber and Faber, 1935.

Macquarrie, John. *Jesus Christ in Modern Thought*. Harrisburg, PA: Trinity Press International, 1990.

Marion, Jean-Luc. *God without Being*. Translated by Thomas A. Carlson. Chicago: Chicago University Press, 1991.

Matson, Wallace I. *A New History of Philosophy*. Vol. 2. Chicago: Harcourt Brace Jovanovich, 1987.

Matthiessen, Peter. *At Play in the Fields of the Lord*. New York: Vintage, 1965.

Matuštík, Martin J., and Merold Westphal. Introduction to *Kierkegaard in Post/Modernity*, edited by Martin J. Matuštík and Merold Westphal, viii–xii. Indianapolis: Indiana University Press, 1995.

Marx, Karl, and Frederick Engels. *Collected Works*. Vol. 5. London: Lawrence and Wishart, 1920.

Maximus the Confessor. "Various Texts 2:26." *Philokalia*. Edited by G.E.H. Palmer. London: Faber and Faber, 1981.

McFadyen, Alistair, I. *The Call to Personhood*. Cambridge: Cambridge University Press, 1990.

———. "Healing the Damaged." In *Essentials of Christian Community*, edited by David Ford and Dennis L. Stamps, 91–103. Edinburgh: T. & T. Clark, 1996.

———. "Sins of Praise: The Assault of God's Freedom." In *God and Freedom*, edited by Colin Gunton, 32–56. Edinburgh: T. & T. Clark, 1995.

———. "Truth as Mission: The Christian Claim to Universal Truth in a Pluralist Public World." *Scottish Journal of Theology* 46 (1993) 437–56.

McGilchrist, Ian. *The Master and His Emissary: The Divided Brain and the Making of the Western World*. New Haven: Yale University Press, 2010.
Merleau-Ponty, Maurice. *Éloge de la Philosophie*. Paris: Gallimard, 1960.
Milbank, John. "Only Theology Overcomes Metaphysics." *New Blackfriars* 76 (1995) 325–43.
———. "'Postmodern Critical Augustinianism': A Short *Summa* in Forty Two Responses to Unasked Questions." *Modern Theology* 7 (1991) 225–37.
———. *Theology and Social Theory: Beyond Secular Reason*. Malden, MA: Blackwell, 1990.
Milner, A. David. "Vision without Knowledge." *Philosophical Transactions of the Royal Society of London* 352 (1997) 1249–56.
Moltmann, Jürgen. *The Church in the Power of the Spirit: A Contribution to Messianic Ecclesiology*. Translated by Margaret Kohl. New York: Harper and Row, 1977.
———. *The Coming of God: Christian Eschatology*. Translated by Margaret Kohl. Minneapolis: Fortress, 1996.
———. *The Crucified God: The Cross of Christ as the Foundation and Criticism of Christian Theology*. Translated by R. A. Wilson and John Bowden. New York: Harper and Row, 1974.
———. *God in Creation: An Ecological Doctrine of Creation*. Translated by Margaret Kohl. London: SCM, 1985.
———. "Reflections on Chaos and God's Interaction with the World from a Trinitarian Perspective." In *Chaos and Complexity: Scientific Perspectives on Divine Action*, edited by Robert John Russell et al., 205–10. Vatican City: Vatican Observatory, 1995.
———. *The Source of Life: The Holy Spirit and the Theology of Life*. Translated by Margaret Kohl. London: SCM, 1997.
———. *The Spirit of Life: A Universal Affirmation*. Translated by Margaret Kohl. London: SCM, 1992.
———. "Theological Proposals towards the Resolution of the Filioque Controversy." In *Spirit of God, Spirit of Christ*, edited by Lukas Vischer, 164–73. London: SPCK, 1981.
———. *The Trinity and the Kingdom of God: The Doctrine of God*. Translated by Margaret Kohl. London: SCM, 1981.
———. "The World in God or God in the World." In *God Will Be All in All*, edited by Richard Bauckham, 35–41. Edinburgh: T. & T. Clark, 1996.
Moltmann-Wendel, Elizabeth. "Does Nothing Good Dwell in My Flesh?" In *The Future of Theology: Essays in Honor of Jürgen Moltmann*, edited by Miroslav Volf et al. Translated by D. Scott, 233–40. Grand Rapids: Eerdmans, 1998.
Montmarquet, James A. *Epistemic Virtue and Doxastic Responsibility*. Lanham, MD: Rowman & Littlefield, 1993.
Mooney, Edward, F. "*Repetition*: Getting the World Back." In *The Cambridge Companion to Kierkegaard*, edited by Alastair Hannay and Gordon D. Marino, 282–307. Cambridge: Cambridge University Press, 1998.
Murdoch, Iris. *Sovereignty of the Good*. London: Routledge, 1970.
Murphy, Nancey. "Acceptability Criteria for Work in Theology and Science." *Zygon* 22 (1987) 279–98.

———. *Beyond Liberalism and Fundamentalism: How Modern and Postmodern Philosophy Set the Theological Agenda.* Valley Forge, PA: Trinity Press International, 1996.

———. "Divine Action in the Natural Order." In *Chaos and Complexity: Scientific Perspectives on Divine Action*, edited by Robert John Russell et al., 324–57. Vatican City: Vatican Observatory, 1996.

———. "From Critical Realism to a Methodological Approach: Response to Robbins, van Huyssteen, and Hefner." *Zygon* 23 (1988) 287–90.

———. "The Limits of Pragmatism and the Limits of Realism." *Zygon* 28 (1993) 351–59.

———. Review of *Theology in the Age of Scientific Reasoning*, by J. Wentzel van Huyssteen. *Religious Studies* 27 (1992) 231–34.

———. "Textual Relativism, Philosophy of Language, and the Baptist Vision." In *Theology without Foundations*, edited by Stanley Hauerwas et al., 245–70. Nashville: Abingdon, 1994.

———. *Theology in the Age of Scientific Reasoning.* Ithaca, NY: Cornell University Press, 1990.

———. "What Has Theology to Learn from Scientific Methodology?" In *Science and Theology: Questions at the Interface*, edited by Murray Rae et al., 101–27. Grand Rapids: Eerdmans, 1994.

Naess, Arne. *Life's Philosophy: Reason and Feeling in a Deeper World.* Athens, GA: University of Georgia Press, 2002.

Neisser, Ulric. *Cognitive Psychology.* New York: Appleton, 1967.

Niebuhr, H. R. *Christ and Culture.* New York: Harper and Row, 1951.

Nolfi, George, dir. *Adjustment Bureau.* Written by George Nolfi and Philip K. Dick. Universal Pictures, 2011.

O'Donoghue, Noel Dermot. *Heaven in Ordinarie.* Edinburgh: T. & T. Clark, 1979.

———. *Lovelier Than the Dawn: Meditations on the Mystical Teaching of St. John of the Cross.* Dublin: Carmelite Centre of Spirituality, 1984.

———. "The Mystical Imagination." In *Religious Imagination*, edited by James P. Mackey, 186–205. Edinburgh: Edinburgh University Press, 1986.

Oliver, Harold, H. *A Relational Metaphysic.* Studies in Philosophy and Religion 4. London: Nijhoff, 1981.

Otto, Rudolf. *The Idea of the Holy.* Translated by John W. Harvey. Oxford: Oxford University Press, 1923.

Pailin, David A. Review of *God in History*, by Peter G. Hodgson. *Perkins Journal* 43 (1990) 17–18.

Pannenberg, Wolfhart. *Anthropology in Theological Perspective.* Translated by Matthew J. O'Connell. Edinburgh: T. & T. Clark, 1985.

———. *Systematic Theology.* Vol. 3. Translated by Geoffrey W. Bromiley. Grand Rapids: Eerdmans, 1998.

———. *What Is Man?* Translated by Duane A. Priebe. Philadelphia: Fortress, 1970.

Pascal, Blaise. *The Mind on Fire: An Anthology of the Writings of Blaise Pascal.* Edited by James Houston. Portland: Multnomah, 1989.

Peacocke, Arthur. "Chance and Law in Irreversible Thermodynamics, Theoretical Biology, and Theology." In *Chaos and Complexity: Scientific Perspectives on Divine Action*, edited by Robert John Russell et al., 123–43. Vatican City: Vatican Observatory, 1996.

———. "The Disguised Friend: Biological Evolution and Belief in God." In *Religion, Science, and Public Policy*, edited by Frank T. Birtel, 30–48. New York: Crossroads, 1987.

———. "God's Interaction with the World: The Implications of Deterministic 'Chaos' and of Interconnected and Interdependent Complexity." In *Chaos and Complexity: Scientific Perspectives on Divine Action*, edited by Robert John Russell., 263–88. Vatican City: Vatican Observatory, 1996.

———. *Theology for a Scientific Age: Being and Becoming—Natural and Divine*. Oxford: Basil Blackwell, 1990.

Peters, Ted. *God as Trinity: Relationality and Temporality in Divine Life*. Louisville: Westminster John Knox, 1993.

———. "The Trinity in and Beyond Time." In *Quantum Cosmology and the Laws of Nature: Scientific Perspectives on Divine Action*, edited by Robert John Russell et al., 263–91. Vatican City: Vatican Observatory, 1993.

Peukert, Helmut. *Science, Action, and Fundamental Theology: Toward a Theology of Communicative Action*. Translated by James Bohman. Cambridge: MIT Press, 1984.

Piaget, Jean. *The Origins of Intelligence in Children*. Translated by Margaret Cook. New York: Norton, 1952.

———. *Six Psychological Studies*. Edited by David Elkind. Translated by Anita Tenzer and David Elkind. New York: Random House, 1967.

Poirer, Maben. "Michael Polanyi and the Question of 'Objective' Knowledge." *Philosophy Today* 32 (1988) 312–26.

Polanyi, Michael. *Knowing and Being: Essays by Michael Polanyi*. Edited by Marjorie Green. Chicago: University of Chicago Press, 1969.

———. *Personal Knowledge*. New York: Harper and Row, 1962.

Polkinghorne, John. "Setting the Problem." *CTNS Bulletin* 10 (1990) 8–12.

Pollard, William G. *Chance and Providence*. London: Faber, 1958.

Popper, Karl. *The Logic of Scientific Discovery*. New York: Basic, 1961.

Poteat, William H. *Polanyian Meditations: In Search of a Post-Critical Logic*. Durham, NC: Duke University Press, 1985.

Potter, Jonathan, and Margaret Wetherell. *Discourse and Social Psychology: Beyond Attitudes and Behaviour*. London: Sage, 1987.

Pound, Ezra. *Caudier Brezeska: A Memoir*. New York: Lane, 1916.

Prenter, Regin. *Spiritus Creator*. Translated by John M. Jensen. Philadelphia: Muhlenberg, 1953.

Presti, David E. "Putting Mind Back into Nature: A Tribute to Henry P. Stabb." *Activitas Nervosa Superior* 61 (2019) 18–23.

Price, Huw. "A Neglected Route to Realism about Quantum Mechanics." *Mind* 103 (1994) 1–35. https://arxiv.org/abs/gr-qc/9406028.

Prigogine, Ilya. "Unity of Physical Laws and Levels of Description.." In *Interpretations of Life and Mind: Essays Around the Problem of Reduction*, edited by Marjorie Grene, 1–13. New York: Humanities, 1971.

Prigogine, Ilya, and Isabelle Stengers. *Order Out of Chaos*. New York: Bantam, 1985.

Putnam, Hilary. "Time and Physical Geometry." *Journal of Philosophy* 64 (1967) 240–47.

Rees, Martin. "The Anthropic Universe." *New Scientist* 115 (1987) 44–47.

Ricoeur, Paul. "Fatherhood: From Phantasm to Symbol." In *Conflict of Interpretations: Essays in Hermeneutics*, edited by Don Ihde, 468–97. Evanston, IL: Northwestern University Press, 1974.

———. *Freud and Philosophy: An Essay on Interpretation*. New Haven: Yale University Press, 1970.

———. *Oneself as Another*. Translated by Kathleen Blamey. Chicago: Chicago University Press, 1992.

———. *The Symbolism of Evil*. Boston: Beacon, 1967.

Rietdijk, C. W. "A Rigorous Proof of Determinism Derived from the Special Theory of Relativity." *Philosophy of Science* 33 (1966) 341–44.

Roberts, Richard H. "Karl Barth's Doctrine of Time: Its Nature and Implications." In *Karl Barth: Studies of his Theological Method*, edited by S. W. Sykes, 88–146. Oxford: Clarendon, 1979.

Roberts, Robert C. "Existence, Emotion, and Virtue: Classical Themes in Kierkegaard." In *The Cambridge Companion to Kierkegaard*, edited by Alastair Hannay and Gordon D. Marino, 177–206. Cambridge: Cambridge University Press, 1998.

———. "What an Emotion Is: A Sketch." *Philosophical Review* 97 (1988) 186–209.

Robertson, Jenefer. "Emotion, Judgment, and Desire." *Journal of Philosophy* 80 (1983) 731–41.

Rogers, Carl R. *Client-Centered Therapy: Its Current Practice, Implications, and Theory*. Boston: Houghton Mifflin, 1951.

Rohrlich, Daniel. "A Reasonable Thing That Just Might Work." (2015) 1–14. https://arxiv.org/abs/1507.01588v1.

———. "Retrocausality as an Axiom." Lecture at Ben-Gurion University of the Negev, Hebrew University of Jerusalem, January 5–8, 2015. https://www.youtube.com/watch?v=yJ5SGdV7DMU.

Rohrlich, Daniel, and Guy Hetzroni. "GZR States and PR Boxes in the Classical Limit." *Entropy* 20 (2022) 1–12. https://arxiv.org/abs/1606.04274v1.

———. "GZR States as Tripartite PR Boxes: Classical Limit and Retrocausality." *Entropy* (2018) 1–8.

"Retrocausality as an Axiom." Lecture at Ben-Gurion University of the Negev, Hebrew University of Jerusalem, January 5–8, 2015. https://www.youtube.com/watch?v=yJ5SGdV7DMU.

Rolston, Holmes, III. *Genes, Genesis, and God: Values and Their Origins in Natural and Human History*. Cambridge: Cambridge University Press, 1999.

Rorty, Amélie O. *Explaining Emotions*. Berkeley: University of California Press, 1980.

Rosenberg Larsen, Rasmus. "The Posited Self: The Non-theistic Foundation in Kierkegaard's Writings." *Kierkegaard Studies Yearbook* 20 (2015) 31–54.

Rosenblum, Bruce, and Fred Kuttner. *Quantum Enigma: Physics Encounters Consciousness*. Oxford: Oxford University Press, 2006.

Rovelli, Carlo. "Relational Quantum Mechanics." *International Journal of Theoretical Physics* 35 (1996) 1–21.

Russell, Robert John. "Introduction." In *Quantum Cosmology and the Laws of Nature: Scientific Perspectives on Divine Action*, edited by Robert John Russell et al., 1–32. Vatican City: Vatican Observatory, 1993.

———. "Is the Triune God the Basis for Physical Time?" *CTNS Bulletin* 11 (1991) 7–19.

Schachtel, Ernest G. *Metamorphosis: On the Conflict of Human Development and the Development of Creativity*. London: Routledge, 1963.

Schleiermacher, F. D. E. *Hermeneutics: The Handwritten Manuscripts.* Edited by Heinz Kimmerle. Translated by James Duke and Jack Forstman. Atlanta: Scholars, 1977.
Shaffer, Peter. *Equus.* New York: Penguin, 1973.
Shotter, John. *Conversational Realities: Constructing Life through Language.* Inquiries in Social Construction Series. London: Sage, 1993.
———. "Life inside the Dialogically Structured Mind: Bakhtin's and Volosinov's Account of Mind as Out in the World between Us." In *The Plural Self: Multiplicity in Everyday Life*, edited by John Rowan and Mick Cooper, 71–92. London: Sage, 1999.
Sinclair, Upton. *I, Candidate for Governor.* Berkeley: University of California Press, 1994.
Sklar, Lawrence. *Space, Time, and Spacetime.* Berkeley: University of California Press, 1974.
Smith, Steven G. *The Concept of the Spiritual: An Essay in First Philosophy.* Philadelphia: Temple University Press, 1988.
Staniloae, Dumitru. "The Procession of the Holy Spirit from the Father and His Relation to the Son, as the Basis of Our Deification and Adoption." In *Spirit of God, Spirit of Christ*, edited by Lukas Vischer, 174–86. London: SPCK, 1981.
Stapp, Henry P. "Attention, Intention, and Will in Quantum Physics." https://arxiv.org/pdf/quant-ph/9905054.pdf.
———. *Mindful Universe: Quantum Mechanics and the Participating Observer.* 2nd ed. Berlin: Springer, 2011.
Steiner, George. *Real Presences.* Chicago: Chicago University Press, 1989.
Stoeger, William R. "Describing God's Action in the World in Light of Scientific Knowledge of Reality." In *Philosophy, Science, and Divine Action*, edited by F. LeRon Shults et al., 111–39. Boston: Brill, 2009.
Stokes, Michael C. "Heraclitus of Ephesus." In *The Encyclopedia of Philosophy*, edited by Paul Edwards, 3:480. New York: Macmillan, 1967.
Strasser, S. "Feeling as Basis of Knowing and Recognizing the Other as an Ego." In *Feelings and Emotions*, edited by Magda B. Arnold, 291–308. New York: Academic, 1970.
Stump, Eleonore, and Norman Kretzmann. "Eternity." *Journal of Philosophy* 78 (1981) 221–37.
Sullivan, Harry Stack. *The Interpersonal Theory of Psychiatry.* Edited by Helen Swick Perry and Mary Ladd Gawelst. New York: Norton, 1953.
Suppe, Frederick. *The Structure of Scientific Theories.* Champaign, IL: University of Illinois Press, 1977.
Taylor, Mark C. *Altarity.* New York: University of Chicago Press, 1987.
Teller, Paul. "Relational Holism and Quantum Mechanics." *British Journal for the Philosophy of Science* 37 (1986) 71–81.
Templeton, John, M. *The Humble Approach: Scientists Discover God.* London: Collins, 1981.
Teresa of Avila, St. *The Collected Works of St. Teresa of Avila.* Translated by Kieran Kavanaugh et al. Washington, DC: ICS, 1980.
Theological Dictionary of the New Testament. Edited by Gerhard Kittel and Gerhard Friedrich. Translated by Geoffrey W. Bromiley. 10 vols. Grand Rapids: Eerdmans, 1964–76.
Thiemann, Ronald F. *Revelation and Theology: The Gospel as Narrated Promise.* Notre Dame: Notre Dame University Press, 1985.

Thiselton, Anthony C. *Interpreting God and the Postmodern Self: On Meaning, Manipulation, and Promise.* Edinburgh: T. & T. Clark, 1995.

Thomas, Heywood J. "Kierkegaard's View of Time." *Journal of the British Society for Phenomenology* 4 (1973) 33–40.

Thomas, Owen C. *God's Activity in the World: The Contemporary Problem.* Chico, CA: Scholars, 1983.

Torrance, Thomas F. *Belief in Science and in Christian Life.* Edinburgh: Handsel, 1980.

———. *The Ground and Grammar of Theology: Consonance between Theology and Science.* Edinburgh: T. & T. Clark, 2001.

———. *Karl Barth, Biblical, and Evangelical Theologian.* Edinburgh: T. & T. Clark, 1990.

———. *Space, Time, and Incarnation.* London: Oxford University Press, 1969.

———. *Space, Time, and Resurrection.* Edinburgh: Handsel, 1976.

———. *Theological Science.* Oxford: Oxford University Press, 1969.

———. *Theology in Reconstruction.* Grand Rapids: Eerdmans, 1965.

———. *Transformation and Convergence in the Frame of Knowledge.* Belfast: Christian Journals, 1984.

———. *The Trinitarian Faith.* Edinburgh: T. & T. Clark, 1988.

Tracy, David. "God's Reality: The Most Important Issue." *Anglican Theological Review* 55 (1973) 218–24.

———. "Literary Theory and Return of the Forms for Naming and Thinking God in Theology." *Journal of Religion* 74 (1994) 302–19.

Underhill, Evelyn. *Mysticism.* New York: New American Library, 1974.

Vaihinger, H. *The Philosophy of "As If."* Translated by Charles Kay Ogden. 2nd ed. London: Routledge, 1935.

Vanhoozer, Kevin J. *Remythologizing Theology: Divine Action, Passion, and Authorship.* Cambridge: Cambridge University Press, 2010.

Vattimo, Gianni. *After Christianity.* Translation by Luca D'Isanto. New York: Columbia University Press, 2002.

Vogel, Arthur. *Body Theology.* New York: Harper & Row, 1973.

Volf, Mirolsav. *Exclusion and Embrace: A Theological Exploration of Identity, Otherness, and Reconciliation.* Nashville: Abingdon, 2019.

———. "Theology, Meaning, and Power." In *The Future of Theology*, edited by Miroslav Volf et al., 98–113. Grand Rapids: Eerdmans, 1996.

Volosinov, V. N. *Marxism and the Philosophy of Language.* Translated by Ladislav Matejka and I. R. Titunik. Cambridge: Harvard University Press, 1986.

Wallace, Anthony F. C. "Revitalization Movements." *American Anthropologist* 58 (2009) 264–81.

Waller, Robert James. *The Bridges of Madison County.* New York: Warner, 1992.

Watanabe, Satosi. "Symmetry of Physical Laws. Part III. Prediction and Retrodiction." *Review of Modern Physic* 27 (1955) 179–86.

Ward, Graham. "Bodies: The Displaced Body of Jesus Christ." In *Radical Orthodoxy*, edited by John Milbank et al., 163–81. London: Routledge, 1999.

Ward, Keith. *Concepts of God: Images of the Divine in the Five Religious Traditions.* Oxford: Basil Blackwell, 1974.

———. "God as a Principle of Cosmological Explanation." In *Quantum Cosmology and the Laws of Nature: Scientific Perspectives on Divine Action*, edited by Robert John Russell et al., 247–63. Vatican City: Vatican Observatory, 1993.

———. *Rational Theology and the Creativity of God.* Oxford: Basil Blackwell, 1982.

Ward, Tim. "Making Meaningful the Claim that God Speaks." Unpublished essay, 1997.
Warren, Robert Penn. *All The King's Men*. Boston: Mariner, 1946.
Watson, Francis. *Text, Church, and World*. Edinburgh: T. & T. Clark, 1994.
Webber, Otto. *Foundations of Dogmatics*. Vol. 1. Translated by Darrell L. Guder. Grand Rapids: Eerdmans, 1981.
Welker, Michael. *God the Spirit*. Translated by John F. Hoffmeyer. Minneapolis: Fortress, 1994.
Wertsch, J. V. *Vygotsky and the Social Formation of Mind*. Cambridge: Harvard University Press, 1988.
Westphal, Merold. "Kierkegaard and Hegel." In *The Cambridge Companion to Kierkegaard*, edited by Alastair Hannay and Gordon D. Marino, 101–24. Cambridge: Cambridge University Press, 1998.
Whitehead, Alfred N. *Adventures of Ideas*. London: Macmillan, 1933.
———. *Process and Reality: An Essay in Cosmology*. New York: Macmillan, 1967.
Wiles, Maurice. *God's Action in the World*. London: SCM, 1986.
Wigner, Eugene. "The Probability of the Existence of a Self-Reproducing Unit." In *The Logic of Personal Knowledge*, edited by Michael Polanyi, 231–35. Glencoe, IL: Free, 1961.
———. "Remarks on the Mind-Body Problem." In *Symmetries and Reflections*, 171–84. Bloomington: Indiana University Press, 1967.
Williams, Daniel Day. "Time, Progress, and the Kingdom of God." In *Process Philosophy and Christian Thought*, edited by Delwin Brown et al., 441–63. New York: Bobbs-Merrill, 1971.
Wittgenstein, Ludwig. *The Blue and Brown Books*. London: Harper and Row, 1960.
———. *Philosophical Investigations*. Translated by G. E. M. Anscombe. New York: Macmillan, 1953.
Wolterstorff, Nicholas. "Faith and Philosophy." In *Faith and Philosophy*, edited by Nicholas Wolterstorff and Alvin Plantiga, 3–36. Grand Rapids: Eerdmans, 1964.
Wright, John H. "Divine Knowledge and Human Freedom: The God Who Dialogues." *Theological Studies* 38 (1977) 450–77.
Zagzebski, Linda T. "The Place of *Phronesis* in the Methodology of Theology." In *Philosophy and Theological Discourse*, edited by Stephen T. Davis, 204–28. New York: Macmillan, 1997.
———. *Virtues of the Mind*. Cambridge: Cambridge University Press, 1996.
Zee, Anthony. *Fearful Symmetry: The Search for Beauty in Modern Physics*. New York: MacMillan, 1986.
Zeilinger, A., et al. "Experimental Non-classicality of an Indivisible Quantum System." *Nature* 474 (2011) 490–93.
Zeilinger, A., et al. "An Experimental Test of Non-local Realism." *Nature* 446 (2007) 871–75.
Zeilinger, A., et al. "Quantum Erasure with Causally Disconnected Choice." *PNAS* 110 (2013) 1221–26.
Zeilinger, A., et al. "Violation of Bell's Inequality under Strict Einstein Locality Condition." *Physical Review Letters* 81 (1998) 5039–43.
Zimmermann, Jens. *Dietrich Bonhoeffer's Christian Humanism*. Oxford: Oxford University Press, 2019.
Zizioulas, John D. *Being as Communion: Studies in Personhood and the Church*. Crestwood, NY: St. Vladimir's Seminary Press, 1985.

———. "Human Capacity and Human Incapacity: A Theological Exploration of Personhood." *Scottish Journal of Theology* 28 (1975) 401–47.

———. "On Being a Person: Towards an Ontology of Personhood." In *Persons, Divine, and Human*, edited by Christoph Schwöbel and Colin E. Gunton, 33–46. Edinburgh: T. & T. Clark, 1991.

Zurek, Wojciech H. "Pointer Basis of Quantum Apparatus: Into What Mixture Does the Wave Pocket Collapse?" *Physical Review* D24 (1981) 1516–25.

Name Index

Agamben, Giorgio, 221n88, 235n118, 241n135, 275–76, 284n39, 291n56, 298n66
Alston, William P., 151n5, 152n11, 153–54
Anderson, Ray S., 123n187, 151, 157
Anselm, St., 221
Aquinas, Thomas, 3, 197n3, 338
Aristotle, 22, 32n78, 54, 97, 131–33
Aspect, Alain, 346n9
Augustine, 5n9, 7, 24, 128, 145–46, 255n37, 258n49, 263–64, 287, 363, 369
Aves, John, 158n37

Badcock, Gary D., 24n61, 388n4
Bakhtin, M. M., 56, 66, 91–94, 97–100, 103, 185
Banich, M. T., 173–74
Barbour, Ian G., 76n70, 276–77, 299
Barth, Karl, xi–xii, xvii, 4, 12, 43–44, 50–51, 63n29, 67, 73–75, 117, 142, 198n7, 201n20, 207–8, 237, 240n132, 251n24, 252n30, 270, 274n25, 278, 285–87, 290, 293n58, 295n61, 301, 306, 315, 327n104, 328–40, 351, 381
Bettenson, Henry, 5n9
Berkhof, Hendrikus, 44n106
Billig, Michael, 91n106
Bloesch, Donald B., 61n19

Bonhoeffer, Dietrich, xiv, xvi, 1–2, 17n45, 20–21, 23n60, 28–29, 45n108, 46, 50n121, 87n96, 119n177, 136, 142, 157n31, 248, 280, 333n118, 339, 341, 369n4, 370, 383, 390–91
Bohr, Niels, 201–2, 205–7, 355
Bouillard, Henri, 110n157, 121n182, 339n130
Bracken, Joseph, 28–29
Braine, David, 236n122
Bretall, Robert, xiii n8
Bringuer, Jean-Claude, 209n43
Bruner, Jerome, 91n106, 209n41
Bultmann, Rudolf, 117n171, 182n26, 220, 339n130
Burke, Edmunds, 96

Calvin, John, xx, 46, 117–18, 122, 198–99, 371, 373–74, 376–77
Caputo, John D., 320n91
Carroll, Sean, 365
Catherine of Siena, St., 63–64, 112–13
Clayton, Philip, 26, 50, 57, 69, 74, 76
Cobb, John, Jr., 304
Colledge, Richard, 304n77, 351
Copleston, Frederick,, 6n10, 272n16
Craig, William Lane, 297n65
Cunningham, Mary K., 332

Dabney, D. Lyle, 11–14, 324n94

NAME INDEX

Damasio, Antonio, 109n155, 152, 157–58
David R. Griffin, see Cobb, John, J.
Davies, W. D. and Dale C. Allison, 379
Dawkins, Richard, 8–9, 204n24
Derrida, Jacques, xvi n15, 78, 191n50
De Sousa, Ronald, 150, 156
Desmet, Mattias, 66
Devinsky, Orrin, and Rachel Laff, 173
Drees, Willem B., 287n65, 297

Eco, Umberto, 245, 267n86
Eddington, A. S., 43
Einstein, Albert, 104, 142–43, 230, 220, 241n134, 269, 272, 327, 345–48, 388
Evans, C. Stephen, 17n45, 18, 21

Fann, K. T., 75n64
Faraday, Michael, xxii
Feyerabend, Paul, 68, 80
Flew, Antony, 89
Fraisse, Paul, 210n47
Piaget, Jean, 41, 66, 95–96, 146, 160, 196, 207–18, 226, 244
Furth, Hans G. 213n56

Gadamer, H. G., 62, 65, 80, 131–33, 191n50, 219–20, 279
Gangadean, Ashok, 65n36
Gelven, Michael, 125, 374n20
Gendlin, Eugene, T., 61–62
Gergen, Kenneth, J., 2n4, 56, 91–92, 96–97, 100–101, 104, 111, 139n223, 159, 189, 192, 383
Gorsuch, Gregory S., 38
Gunton, Colin E., 3–4, 24–29, 32, 39n92, 75, 104n144, 105n147, 125–26, 128, 140n224, 146, 158, 161, 191, 196, 210n17, 214–15, 236n120, 250, 253n33, 302, 310–12, 315, 338, 340n135, 383, 387n2

Hagner, Donald A., xxv, 379n25
Hall, Ronald L., 224–25
Hands, John, xxi–xxii
Hart, Ray I., 1

Hefner, Philip, 9,19, 29–31, 57–62, 68n43, 85–86, 110n156, 114, 118–19, 126, 146
Heidegger, Martin, 8, 11, 19, 61, 78, 94n121, 101n140, 103–4, 117, 123n188, 130, 137, 141, 154n24, 159n38, 186, 220, 231, 265, 269n4
Heisenberg, Werner, 344n4, 359, 362
Henry, Richard Conn and Stephen R. Palmquist, 348
Herbert, Nick, 206n30, 292n57
Heron, Alastair I. C., 146
Heschel, Abraham J., 156
Hetzroni, Guy see Rohrlich, Daniel
Hick, John, 73, 276
Hodgson, Peter C., 1, 128n202, 233, 282–83, 297, 304, 308, 315, 336
Hofstadter, Douglas R., 199–200
Holland, Tom, 87, 306n78
Husserl, Edmund, 167, 171
Huxley Darwin, Thomas, 6
Huyssteen, J. Wentzel van, 68n44, 76–77, 80–81, 90n104

Jackson, Timothy P., 76n65,301, 374
Jaggar, M. Alison, 113n164, 151n6, 153–56, 311
James, William, 156n26,327
John Damascene, 24

Kaiser, Christopher, B., 202, 205–6
Kant, Immanuel, 20, 43, 61, 96, 109n154, 200, 230–31, 249, 276, 281
Kastner, Ruth E., 348, 361–62, 365
Kegan, Robert, 197n2, 216–18, 226–27, 375,383
Kerr, Fergus, 69–75
Kierkegaard, Søren, x–xiv, xvii, xix–xx, xxiii, 6n11, 8n16, 16–19, 21–28, 34, 38n88–46, 50n121, 52, 67, 72, 76, 78–83, 87, 92–93, 101–14, 114–15, 126, 130, 132, 141–44, 146, 148, 167–69, 174, 176–77, 180, 182–83, 187–88, 191, 193–94, 196, 198, 201–5, 207, 213, 215, 218–26, 228–30,

NAME INDEX

233–4, 242, 244–45, 247, 249, 251, 253, 260n61, 262, 265, 268–71, 273–76, 278n34, 280–82, 284, 286–88, 291–92, 294, 296, 298–301, 306–7, 312–13, 315, 326, 332–34, 337, 339, 341–42, 349, 351–53, 355, 358–50, 361, 363n36, 364, 366, 371, 374, 380–84, 387–88
Kierkegaard pseudonyms: Johannes de Silentio, xi, xiv, 315n87, 341; Johannes Climacus, 18n47, 22, 27, 72n57, 109n154, 187, 193, 246n2, 306–7, 326, 358; Anti-Climacus, 17n45, 22, 45, 189, 274n23, 306–7; Frater Taciturnus, xi
Kim, Yoon-Ho, 345n4
Kuhn, Thomas S., 56–57, 67, 134
Kulka, Tomas, 80n80

Lakatos, Imre, 11, 56–61, 65, 67–68, 76, 80–84, 86, 110, 113, 115, 124–26, 142
Landmann, Michael, 116n169
Laudisa, Federico and Carlo Rovelli, 359n28
Lawrence, Fred, 220n79
Leeper, Robert W., 150–54
Leggett, A. J., 346n11
Lévinas, Emmanuel, xvii, 9n21, 13, 18n50, 124, 313
Lindbeck, George A., 67, 76–77, 79, 84, 86, 126–27, 143, 191
Linnemann, Eta, 73
Loder, James E., xxv, 4, 9, 18, 24–25, 28, 41–42, 50–52, 89, 96n125, 104n144, 139, 145, –46, 148, 160–61, 163, 184, 191, 193, 196, 198, 199–203, 205–31, 234–35, 239, 242, 244, 247, 249–50, 253, 257–58, 271n12, 276n28, 289, 301–2, 307, 309, 313–14, 316, 318, 353–54, 383
Lonergan, Bernard, J. F., 251n26
Longinus, Dionysus, 96
Lossky, Vladimir, xvi, 341n135
Lucas, George, R., 281, 307

Lucas, J. R., 90n104, 273n19, 275, 290
Luther, Martin, xx, 129n204, 142
Luz, Ulrich, 379n25

MacDonald, Duncan B., 326n100
MacIntyre, Alasdair, 11n26, 57, 58n11, 83, –85, 125, 188–92
Macmurray, John, 157–59
Macquarrie, John, 333
Marion, Jean-Luc, xviii n18, 74n62, 104n146, 125n193, 136n219, 137n220, 144n233, 191, 230n112, 236n121, 325n97
Matthiessen, Peter, 108n153
Matuštík, Martin J., 45
Marx, Karl and Frederick Engels, 72n58, 198–99, 371–77
Maximus the Confessor, 5n9
Maxwell, James Clerk, xxii, 190n48
McFadyen, Alistair, I., xxv, 38–39, 117n171, 143n231, 146, 148, 164, 176–95, 203, 207, 219, 226, 244, 247n7, 301, 372n17, 379
McGilchrist, Ian, 33, 109n155, 157n32, 162–75, 206n29, 225, 229n109, 238
Merleau-Ponty, Maurice, 151, 167, 171, 235
Milbank, John, 76, 122, 125n195, 128–31, 140, 161, 162n44, 295n62, 312
Milner, A. David, 229n199
Moltmann, Jürgen, 4–5, 25–26, 34, 36–39, 49n117, 50n121, 52–53, 62–63, 77, 80, 88, 113, 116–19, 122, 125n195, 147n6, 156, 205n27, 223, 232n116, 236n120, 238n125, 240n128, 242, 244–67, 274, 278, 285–86, 300–301, 311, 319, 328n106, 334, 368–369, 371, 375, 380–81, 383, 389–90
Moltmann-Wendel, Elizabeth, 113, Montmarquet, James A., 88n97
Murdoch, Iris, 310
Murphy, Nancey, 3, 48, 56–70. 75–90, 100, 110, 112–13, 126, 191, 243

411

NAME INDEX

Naess, Arne, 169
Neidhardt, Jim see Loder, James E.
Neisser, Ulric, 214n61–62
Niebuhr, H. R., 122, 199n9, 370–73
Nietzsche, Friedrich, xx, 6, 78, 156n26

O'Donoghue, Noel Dermot, 187n41
Oliver, Harold, H., 190n46
Otto, Rudolf, 26

Pailin, David A., 283n38
Pannenberg, Wolfhart, xix, 4, 17n43, 38n88, 49–51, 59, 85, 200, 207–12, 214–15, 227, 242, 251, 276, 363, 381
Pascal, Blaise, 124n191
Peacocke, Arthur, 127n199
Peters, Ted, 276–77
Piaget, Jean, 41, 66, 95–96, 160, 196, 207–18, 226, 244
Polanyi, Michael, 68, 104, 127n196, 158, 177n2, 199–202
Polkinghorne, John, 200, , 270241n133
Pollard, William G., 264n70
Popper, Karl, 58n11, 228
Poteat, William, 127n196
Potter, Jonathan and Margaret Wetherell, 91n106
Pound, Ezra, 229
Presti, David E., 351n19
Price, Huw., 345, 347–48, 352–53
Prigogine, Ilya, 42–43, 115n167, 196n1, 213n57, 222, 235n119, 242, 271n13, 308, 318, 388n3
Putnam, Hilary, 268n2, 273n17

Quine, W.V.O., 57, 76, 81, 113

Rees, Martin, 343n1
Ricoeur, Paul, 31n77, 44, 49n117, 63n29, 74, 86, 125n192
Rietdijk, C. W., 268n2, 273n17
Roberts, Richard H., 285–86, 306, 333
Roberts, Robert C., 151n4, 152–55, 159n39
Robertson, Jenefer, 153, 155
Rogers, Carl R., 10n25
Rohrlich, Daniel, 345

Rolston, Holmes, III, 9, 204n24, 276–77, 299
Rorty, Amélie O., 154n21
Rosenblum, Bruce and Fred Kuttner, 354
Rovelli, Carlo, 359

Schachtel, Ernest G., 214–15
Schleiermacher, F. D. E., xii n6, 12, 74n62
Shaffer, Peter, 144n235
Shotter, John, 56, 91n106, 92–102, 124n190, 139n223, 189, 192, 383
Sklar, Lawrence, 268n2, 268, 272–73
Smith, Steven G., xx, 11–14, 33, 324n95
Staniloae, Dumitru, 252n32, 253n33
Stapp, Henry P., 348n15, 351
Steiner, George, 92, 97–98, 167
Stengers, Isabelle see Prigogine, Ilya
Stoeger, William R., 48n113, 82
Strasser, S., 151–52, 160, 162
Stump, Eleonore and Norman Kretzmann, 273n19
Sullivan, Harry Stack, 9–10
Suppe, Frederick, 80n80

Taylor, Charles, xxii
Taylor, Mark C., ix–xi, xiii, xvi–xvii, xix,
Teller, Paul, 345n6
Templeton, John M., 135
Teresa of Avila, St., 63–64, 69, 112–14
Thiemann, Ronald F., 49–50, 55n2, 61, 76–77, 79, 84, 191
Thiselton, Anthony C., 86n93, 141n228
Thomas, Heywood J., 273, 274
Tillich, Paul, 201, 220
Torrance, Thomas F., 11, 44, 67n41, 90, 110n157, 111, 146, 190n48, 197n4, 198, 221, 240, 269–70, 287, 329, 339n130, 340n131
Tracy, David, 86

Underhill, Evelyn, 5n9

Vanhoozer, Kevin J., 26, 80n78
Vattimo, Gianni, 87n95

Vogel, Arthur, 177n5
Volf, Mirolsav, 8n18, 48–49, 107
Volosinov, V. N., 95

Wallace, Anthony F. C., 61n21, 105n145, 178
Waller, Robert James, 378n24
Watanabe, Satosi, 360
Ward, Graham, 322, 333–34,
Ward, Keith, 338
Ward, Tim, 68
Warren, Robert Penn, 321
Watson, Francis, 288, 335n121
Weil, Simon, 54, 310
Wertsch, J. V., 91n106
Westphal, Merold, 45

Whitehead, Alfred N., 281, 288n50
Wigner, Eugene, 344n2, 346
Wittgenstein, Ludwig, 6, 11, 23n60, 56, 58, 60, 67–76, 84, 91, 98, 125n195, 128, 166, 168
Wolterstorff, Nicholas, 68, 111

Zagzebski, Linda T., 81n83, 88, 113n164, 115n168, 136, 140n227, 156
Zee, Anthony, 272n15
Zeilinger, A., 346
Zimmermann, Jens, 8n15, 50n121
Zizioulas, John D., 350–51
Zurek, Wojciech H., 359

Subject Index

absolute, the: definition absolute (Kierkegaard), xiii; absolute, xiii–xv, x–xx, xxii, 17, 20, 40, 46, 174, 184, 187n38, 191n49, 274, 277–78, 281, 298, 326n102, 372, 391

absolute relating to Absolute (Kierkegaard), xi–xii, xv, xviii, xx, 18, 21, 27, 33, 184, 186, 190, 193, 240, 284, definition 291, 296, 298–99, 303, 309, 326, 341, 353, 372 (Niebuhr), 373–74, 384, 387

absolute spirit (Hegelian), xi, xvi–xvii, 29n71, 51, 103, 258, 281–82, 288, 306, 366, 369n4, 389

Abraham, x–x1, xiii–xv, xvii, xix, 4, 13, 69, 194, 242, 266, 274, 277–78, 287, 296, 302, 304–6, 314, 320, 326, 352, 364, 368, 375, 377

accommodation, 194, 208

adaptational equilibrium, 208

analogia spiritus: initial definition, 31–36

analogia entis, xvii, 5, 11, 44, 191, 302, 354, 385

analogia relationis, xvii, 237, 296, 333n118, 339

Anselm, 221

assimilation, 193–94, 208, 212, 215

asymmetrical priority, 9, 11–12, 21, 33, 40, 47, 51, 67, 89, 109, 111, 139, 141, 161, 166, 168, 231, 288, 306, 315, 324; asymmetry, xviii, 4, 15, 51, 90, 109, 112, 161, 164, 167, 201–2, 205–7, 246, 288, 300, 352

aufhebung, 288

authentic/genuine relationship, 9–11, 15, 20, 22, 35, 78n77, 82, 88, 90, 99, 101, 105, 114, 116, 131, 138, 162, 177, 182, 188, 207, 213, 227, 310, 338, 372, 377, 379–80

awareness (pre-cognitive modality), 32, 34, 37–38, 40, 42, 68, 74, 89, 93, 99, 103, 105, 108–9, 114, 120, 122–23, 125, 127, 138, 142–43, 146–47, 152–53, 157, 160, 166, 176–77, 183, 198, 200–201, 205, 214, 221, 231, 241, 243, 261, 265–66, 280, 287, 290, 292, 296–98, 311, 317–18, 335, 350, 353, 355, 357, 373–75, 384–85, 387

Bell's theorem, 206, 292, 345–47

blind spot, xvii–xviii, 22, 199

Cartesian (Descartes), xvii, 25, 47, 55–56, 61–62, 90, 92–93, 109, 151, 299, 336, 348

Chalcedonian christology, 202, 205

Christ *ensarkos*, 240, 329–34, 336

Christendom (Kierkegaard), xxiii, 23, 44, 87, 185, 306, 316, 363–64

SUBJECT INDEX

circuminessio, 24
co-condition(ing), xv, xvii, xix–xx,
2n5, 4, 7, 16, 21, 24–26, 33–35,
36, 44, 46–47, 49, 51, 57, 82,
99–100, 102, 104–5. 110, 122,
138–39, 144, 147–48, 159,
163–65, 167, 174, 180, 184–85,
193–94, 197, 200–204, 227,
229–31, 237, 239, 242, 244, 249,
260, 263, 265–67, 273–74, 278,
280, 284–85, 287–95, 297–300,
304–5, 307, 309, 315, 317–19,
322, 324, 332, 335–36, 338, 340,
343–46, 349–51, 353, 356–57,
360–64, 372, 374, 376–77,
384–89
coinherence, 41–42, 145, 204, 224, 234,
243, 295, 339
complementarity, 18–19, 68, 107, 112,
124, 141, 161, 167, 183, 198–99,
202–12, 218, 220, 222, 224, 235,
243, 246, 250–51, 255, 259, 267,
269, 285–86, 289, 324, 331, 349,
353, 356, 366, 368, 370, 374,
377–78, 385, 387
co-ordinate, 197, 201, 244
chronos, 297
creatio continua, 295, 313, 349, 354,
356, 388
creatio ex nihilo, 104, 145, 349, 373,
388; *ex nihilo*, 37, 164, 376

dance (of spirits), x, xiv, xvi–xx, 24, 31,
91, 135, 143, 195, 287–95, 337,
338, 340, 344
de-liberation, x, xvi, 35, 40, 144, 155,
163–64, 168, 178n8, 184, 192,
202, 234, 265–66, 287, 290–91,
293, 296–97, 299–301, 307,
314–15, 317, 319–21, 325–26,
340, 352–53, 355, 361, 385
différance (Derrida), xvi n15, 74n62
differentiated unity, xvi, xx, 3–4, 26, 31,
36, 73, 102, 104, 120, 127, 137–
38, 143, 197, 198, 200–202, 223,
235, 240, 244, 249–50, 256, 275,
290, 305–8, 333, 340, 359, 365,
381, 384–85

ἔλεγχος (proof, verification), 270n11
Eliade, 263
emotions, 33, 40, 69, 91, 146, 148–69,
183, 244, 294, 296, 311
eschatology, 235
eschatological, ix, xvi, xix, 102, 116,
125n195, 158n37, 163, 181–82,
184, 199n9, 219, 239–40,
264–65, 271n12, 284, 291n56,
296–97, 305, 314, 319, 330, 333,
336, 382
eschaton, xix–xx, 15, 343

Hellenistic derivatives, xi, xiv, 5, 7,
11–13, 20–23, 25, 27, 36–37,
47, 52, 199, 232
Heraclitus, 22, 185, 219, 255
Hilbert space, xxi, 350, 355, 358,
361–63
Høffding, 212
ὑπόστασις (reality, essence, substance),
270n11
horror religious, xiii, xix, 304

incarnational imperative of mutuality
(IIM), definition, xi; 27, 241,
255, 271, 300, 303, 305, 309,
353, 384
infinite qualitative difference (IQD), xi,
xvii, 27, 265, 278, 284, 288, 303,
307, 333, 340n131, 353, 384
Irenaeus, St. (Irenaean), 105, 250, 275

Jacob (Jacobian), ix–x, xiv–xviii, 4–6, 8,
13, 21, 24, 26n68, 30, 33–35, 69,
82, 103, 106, 114, 125, 130, 143,
147, 159–60, 162, 164, 171, 184,
193–94, 200–202, 242, 260n61,
265–67, 271, 274, 277–78, 280,
282, 284, 287, 291, 293–94,
296, 299–300, 302–4, 306–8,
314, 317–19. 321–23, 331, 333,
340–41, 344, 351, 352, 356–58,
378, 380–81, 387
kairos, 17, 197, 219, 221, 239, 264, 269,
286, 290–91, 294, 297–98, 350

416

SUBJECT INDEX

Kierkegaard pseudonyms: Johannes de Silentio, xi, xiv, 315n87, 341; Johannes Climacus, 18n47, 22, 27, 72n57, 109n154, 187, 193, 246n2, 306–7, 326, 358; Anti-Climacus, 17n45, 22, 45, 189, 274n23, 306–7; Frater Taciturnus, xi

magic mirror (κατοπτριζόμαι: 2 Cor 3:18) translucent, 37, 237–38, 327

moment (Kierkegaard), x, xiii, xv–xx, xxiii, 4, 20–24, 29–31, 33–35, 40, 42, 44, 82, 97–98, 103–6, 114, 122n184, 138, 143–44, 146–47, 166–67, 169, 183–85, 191, 193–96, 197, 199–201, 203, 205, 215, 219–222, 234, 239, 241–43, 244, 258, 261–63, 266n81, 274, 279, 284–93, 294, 298–99, 301, 303, 305, 307–8, 314–15, 317–19, 322, 325, 329–33, 338, 340–42, 350–51, 354, 356–58, 361–64, 370, 374, 385, 387–89, 391

Newtonian, xxii, 2, 25, 173, 184, 206, 212, 240, 270, 277, 299, 309, 322–23, 348, 366, 387–88
night of faith, x, 194, 321, 341
night of faith, ix, xii, 26n68, 265, 341, 358
nonlocal action, 25, 345–46, 349, 355, 364

Other, the, ix, xi, xiii, xix, 6, definition 6n11 and 18n50, 9, 18–23, 25, 29, 32–34, 36, 40, 46, 63, 78, 82n85, 88, 90, 92–93, 98–99, 102, 121–23, 132–33, 135, 139–40, 146–47, 154, 158–62, 168–69, 177–79, 183, 185, 193–95, 204, 213, 233, 239, 258, 266, 276, 282, 292, 294, 311, 315–16, 323–24, 341, 350, 364, 375, 379–80, 382, 384, 386–87

Panentheism, 257, 336–39
Parmenides, 22, 183, 219–20, 255, 357
parousia, 269, 291, 329
passion of the infinite (Kierkegaard), 109, 306, 380
perichoresis, initial definition, 22–30
Peter, x, xv–xiii, 106, 267, 274n23, 276, 280, 299, 323, 381
phronesis, 65, 68, 74, 79, 80, 88, 112–15, 127, 131–33, 137, 163, 201, 372
Possibilist Transactional Interpretation (PTI), 361–363, 365
postmodern, xvi n15, xxiii, xxv, 6, 10, 43, 46, 56, 58, 60, 77n73, 79, 80, 85, 96, 119, 188, 270, 272, 384, 387–88
poststructuralism, ix–xiv, xvi–xx, 5–6, 78–79, 135, 141, 191
predestination, 293, 301, 332, 374
prefigure, 222
prereflexion, 38, 103, 200–201, 215, 259, 284, 307, 309, 318–19, 321, 330–32, 334, 337, 385
Process theology/philosophy, 3, 38, 262, 283, 288, 290, 297, 304–5, 336, 363, 389
Prodigal, xv, 54, 267, 376–39
pure duration, 43, 285, 290

quantum theory, xxiii, 2, 5, 32–33, 37, 42–43, 46, 89, 173–75, 202–3, 205–7, 222, 240n132, 241, 246, 253, 255, 273, 292, 323, 343; quantum substratum, xx, xxi, 361, 363, 365; quantum enigma, xvii, 46, 344, 349, 365–66; relational quantum mechanics, 359–64; retro-causality (backward causation), 2, 228, 343, 345–46, 348–49, 360

reflexion, 38, 42, 105, 153, 160, 166, 215, 259, 287, 300, 307, 312, 319–21, 324, 334, 352, 361, 384–85
Relational Quantum Mechanics (RQM), 359

SUBJECT INDEX

relational sublime, 96–97, 99, 101, 106, 111
Religiousness A and B (Kierkegaard), xix, 19, 21–22, 105–6, 109–10, 146, 218, 242, 262, 284, 306, 313, 319, 332, 363
retroactive conditioning, 294, 297–98
retrospection (retro-temporal), 124, 220, 243, 290, 297

self-determination, xi, xiv, xvi, xviii, 4–5, 32, 35, 229, 278, 283, 292, 296, 299, 303–4, 307–9, 323, 331, 340n131, 387–88
Sermon on the Mount, 170, 186, 243, 280, 294, 313
simultaneity, xviii, 5, 264, 269, 273, 285n40, 293, 295, 328, 332, 339, 344, 346, 385, 389; simultaneous, 26, 249, 253, 273, 285, 288, 290, 343, 389; simultaneously, xv, 24, 91, 97, 103, 110, 139, 140, 173, 230, 234, 240–41, 250, 253, 257, 269–73, 291, 293, 322, 328, 332, 337, 358
social constructivism, 25, 56–57, 72, 90–102, 105, 217, 251
social poetics, 97–99, 101, 189
Special Theory of Relativity (STR), 2–3, 43, 46, 220, 241, 246, 264, 268, 270, 272–73, 292, 323, 327, 345, 347, 349, 351, 359–61, 366, 388
Spirit: Holy Spirit, xii n6, xvi n16, 14–15, 32, 36–37, 39, 51, 67, 69, 121, 145–46, 183–84, 198, 201, 225, 232, 234, 239, 248–50, 252–54, 257–61, 266, 278, 341, 369, 376, 379–80, 385; *Spiritus Creator*, 32, 36–37, 146–47, 162, 190, 239, 254, 258–59, 261, 307; *ruach* (*dabar, dahbar*), 147n6, 256

spirit-to-Spirit, xvi, 118, 206–7, 243, 260, 324
spirit, human, xii, xxiv, 4, 12, 16, 18–20, 25, 33, 36n86, 37, 39–40, 51–52, 82, 145–47, 150, 159, 161, 163, 167, 182–84, 187, 199, 201, 207, 212, 218, 224, 234, 236, 239, 243, 254, 256, 258–59, 261, 287, 296, 302, 307, 310, 321, 339–40, 379–80
suicide, 9, 160–61, 215
sunesis, 132–33, 136
supervenience, xxii, 19, 88–90, 119, 154n22, 174, 202, 207, 217, definition 229, 231, 236, 239, 243, 255, 259–60, 306
synchronization, xv–xvi, xviii–xix, 7, 13, 24, 98, 103–4, 120–21, 132n214, 178, 204, 247, 286, 294n59, 295–96, 298–99, 304, 314, 317, 319–23, 327, 339n130, 351–52, 354, 356, 358, 361–63, 365, 369-thermodynamics (Chaos Theory), 2, 4, 43, 46, 83, 115, 121, 124, 204, 213n57, 222, 235, 271n12, 303–4, 308, 318, 320, 323, 365, 368, 378, 388–89

third term (of the relationship), 5, 7, 16–18, 24, 28–29, 35, 92, 102, 104, 121, 123, 132–33, 135, 138–40, 159, 167, 174, 197, 201, 211, 228–30, 234, 244, 247n7, 260n61, 274n24, 302, 309, 350, 355, 382, 384–86
Tillich, 201, 220
time bending, 2, 267, 270, 329, 388–89, 391

vestigium trinitatis, 146, 255n37, 286n46, 287, 333

waste land, the, xii, xx

Scripture Index

Genesis
1:26	389
9:16–17	163
28:11–22	ix–x
32:24–28	x
38	368
50:20	318

Exodus
33:20	xvi

1 Kings
19:12	xx

Psalms
104:29–30	147, 256, 258

Proverbs
20:27	49

Ecclesiastes
12:7	147, 256

Isaiah
34:16	232

Jeremiah
29:13	

Ecclesiasticus
1:7	

Matthew
5:17–6:34	121n183
5:23	140
7:21–23	15, 219, 306, 379, 380
7:31–46	219
10:34–39	121n182, 320, 390
10:37–39	xix n20, 143
11:23–26	106n148
1:31–46	323
12:31–32	379
12:32	15, 47, 306, 379
16:13–20	325–26, 379
16:15–19	x
16:18–19	106
16:17	67
17:17	364
18:16, 20	141n229
18:20	351
19:10	6n13
25:14–30	147n7
25:31–46	15, 306, 379
25:45	140

SCRIPTURE INDEX

Mark

2:14	109
8:35	105
10:15	105
10:29–30	105, 132n214, 143

Luke

12:11–12	141n229
12:49–53	64
14:26, 27, 33	xix
23:9	105

John

1:18	xvi
5:16–30	293
5:19–30	175, 185, 294n59
5:22, 26–27, 30	320
14:6	386
14:12	364
16:7	325
17:11	120
17:21	1, 6, 24–25, 195, 316, 369, 389
19:19	105

Acts

2	232
8:28–40	xvii
17:28	236, 336

Romans

2:15	382
5–7	139
7	381
7:15–17, 22–23	382
8	324
8:16, 26	xviii
8:16	201
9:32–33	31
10:6	113
14	88
14:14–15:6	136
14:1–5:6	107
14:14–23	134–35, 320

1 Corinthians

1:28	48
2	201n18, 346
2:1	67
2:5	49
2:10	51
2:11–16	239
6:12	179
13	50n120, 114, 317
13:6–7	185
13:12	238
14	179
15:2	6
15:20–49	20
15:20–18	121
15:20–28	23
15:20, 22–25	369
15:24	134n216, 297
15:25	195
15:28	369
17:12–15	376

2 Corinthians

1:5–7	321
1:22	335
3:16–18	314
3:17–18	23, 207, 237
3:17	35
3:18	xviii, 6, 20, 25, 28, 37, 107, 121, 129n204, 163, 195, 303, 327, 369, 382
5:5	335
6:2	291
12:4	230n111, 324

Galatians

2:20	41

Ephesians

5:13	313, 382

Colossians

1:16–18	386

1:17	54, 105, 118, 132n214, 146, 230, 350	8:13	195
		10:12–14	23, 195
		10:16	122
1:20	163, 369n4	11	13
1:24–27	122n184	11:1, 13	270
1:24, 27	242	11:1	27, 270, 326, 335, 361, 363, 388
1:24	321		
1:26	xv		

1 Peter

1:2–4	35

1:16–17

2:15	247
3:16	49

2 Peter

1:4	139, 255, 303

1 Thess

5:8	219

1 John

1–5	87n96
2	67

Hebrews

1–13	195
1:3	54n1
4:12	115
5:8	136

Revelation

17:12–18	121n182

www.ingramcontent.com/pod-product-compliance
Lightning Source LLC
Chambersburg PA
CBHW052049290426
44111CB00011B/1674